0   10km

Eastern Bali p.206–259

Bungkulan Point

Penarukan Pt.
Singaraja
Jaga Raga
Sukasada
Panji
Gitgit
Waterfall
Gitgit
Lake
Buyan

Kubu
Tambahan
Memali
Sudaji
Silang Jana
Lemukih
Bantang
Daub
Catur
Belanga

Pacung

Tejakula
Les
Sembiran
Madenan
Siakin

Yeh Mempeh
Waterfall
Bantang

Tembok
Ngis Point

Belandingan
Songan
Tianyar
Sukadana
Sukadana Point

Bali Handara
Kosaido
Country Club
Botanical Garden
(Kebun Raya)
Lake
Tamblingan
Mount Mangu
2020m
Puraluhur Beratan
Bukit Mungsuindah
Mount
Batukaru
2271m
Bangli
Pura Luhur
Batukaru
Jatiluwih
Apuan
Babahan
Tengkudak
Hot Spring
Dalang
Historic
Site
Kesiut
Gadungan
Marga
Trunjuk
Penatahan
Keliki
Sembung
Marga
Memori
Tabanan
Abian Semal
Mengwi
Sibang Kaja
Beraban
Kaba-kaba
Buduk
Kerobokan Kaja
Kerobokan

Kintamani
Mount
Batur
1412m
Batur
Selatan
Mountain Batur
View Tengah
Pelaga
Bunutin
Sekaan
Abuan
Sekar
Dadi
Pengotan

Crater Lake
Trunyan
Bali Aga Village, Gede
Pancering, Jagat Temple
Hot Spring,
Volcanic Lake
Buahan
Suter

Kubu
Dukuh
Tulamben

Diving WW II
"The Liberty" Wreck
Tulamben Marine
Reserve
Batu Niti Point

Laba Sari
Culik
Bunutan

Mount Agung
2567m
Pura Pasaran
Agung

Pidpid
Tista
Pura
Lempuyang
Bukit

Persiapan
Sulangai
Taro
Petang
Penglumbaran
Kayu Buhi
Pempatan
Besakih
Historic Site
Tirta Ayu
Sebudi
Buda Keling
Subagan
Amlapura
Pura Taman Ujung
(Floating Palace)
Ujung Beach

Holy Spring
Tirta
Empul
Tampak Siring
Gunung
Kawi
Demulih
Abuan
Melinggih
Rice Terraces
Monkey Forest &
Pura Bukit Sari
Sangeh
Ubud
Peliatan
Goa
Raksasa
Pejeng
Bedulu
Cempaga
Udisan
Bangli
Pesaban
Sidemen
Rendang
Selat
Traditional
Village
Manggis
Candidasa
Gili Bia/
Kambing Island
Mulu Point

Tulikup
Gianyar
Bona
Semarapura
Kusamba
Goa Lawah (Bat Cave Temple)
Padangbai
Marine Reserve
Padangbai Harbour
Labuhanamuk
Bay

Blahkiuh
Wana Sari
Batuaji
Mas
Theng
Mebling
Tunjuk
Gadungan
Bongan
Singapadu
Batu Bulan
Libung
Ketewel
Sukawati
Guwang
Dangin Puri
Dauh Puri
DENPASAR
Historic Site
Seminyak
Legian Beach
Kuta
Kuta Beach
Ngurah Rai
International
Airport
Jimbaran
Beach
Dreamland
Bingin
Pecatu Indah
Resort
Pura Luhur
Uluwatu
Pecatu
Nyangnyang
Surfing
Ungasan
Green Bowl
Surfing Area
Jimbaran
Nusa Dua
Nusa Dua Beach
Bali Camel Safari
Tanjung Benoa
Tanjung Benoa Beach
Benoa
Sanur
Sanur Kaja
Sanur Beach
Sindhu Beach
Sanur Kauh
Sesetan
Serangan
Serangan Island

Pering
Blahbatuh
Gamelan Maker
Sukawati

Black Sand

Badung Strait

Lacerations
Surf Break
Jungutbatu
Ceningan Reef
Surf Break
Nusa
Ceningan
Batubelede Point
Banah Point

Pura Ped
Ped
Lembongan
Nusa Lembongan
Toyapakeh
Sakti
Bunga Mekar
Spring
Sebulun
Waterfall
Maling Cape
Sebulun

Batu Nunggal
Buyuk
Karang Sari
Cave
Puseh Point
Pura Batu Madan
Pura Batu Kuring
Klumbu
Suana
Nusa Penida
Tanglad
Wates
Kuning Point
Bakung Cape
Sekar Taji

Nusa Penida p.140–149

Southern Bali p.72–149

The Tuttle Story: "Books to Span the East and West"

Our core mission at Tuttle Publishing is to create books which bring people together one page at a time. Tuttle was founded in 1832 in the small New England town of Rutland, Vermont (USA). Our fundamental values remain as strong today as they were then—to publish best-in-class books informing the world about the countries and peoples of Asia. The world has become a smaller place today and Asia's economic, cultural and political influence has expanded, yet the need for meaningful dialogue and information about this diverse region has never been greater. Since 1948, Tuttle has been a leader in publishing books on the cultures, arts, cuisines, languages and literatures of Asia. Our authors and photographers have won numerous awards and Tuttle has published thousands of titles on subjects ranging from martial arts to paper crafts. We welcome you to explore the wealth of information available on Asia at **www.tuttlepublishing.com**.

Published by Tuttle Publishing, an imprint of Periplus Editions (HK) Ltd

www.tuttlepublishing.com

Copyright © 2018 by Periplus Editions (HK) Ltd

All rights reserved. No part of this publication may be reproduced or utilized in any form or by any means, electronic or mechanical, including photocopying, recording, or by any information storage and retrieval system, without prior written permission from the publisher.

LCC No. 2018939955

ISBN 978-0-8048-4640-0
(Previously published under ISBN 978-0-8048-4206-8)

Distributed by

North America, Latin America & Europe
Tuttle Publishing, 364 Innovation Drive
North Clarendon, VT 05759-9436 U.S.A.
Tel: 1 (802) 773-8930;Fax: 1 (802) 773-6993
info@tuttlepublishing.com
www.tuttlepublishing.com

Japan
Tuttle Publishing
Yaekari Building, 3rd Floor
5-4-12 Osaki, Shinagawa-ku, Tokyo 141 0032
Tel: (81) 3 5437-0171; Fax: (81) 3 5437-0755
sales@ tuttle.co.jp
www.tuttle.co.jp

Asia Pacific
Berkeley Books Pte. Ltd.
61 Tai Seng Avenue #02-12
Singapore 534167
Tel: (65) 6280-1330; Fax: (65) 6280-6290
inquiries@periplus.com.sg
www.periplus.com

Indonesia
PT Java Books Indonesia
Kawasan Industri Pulogadung, Jl. Rawa
Gelam IV No. 9, Jakarta 13930
Tel: (62) 21 4682-1088; Fax: (62) 21 461-0206
crm@periplus.co.id
www.periplus.com

21 20 19 18   10 9 8 7 6 5 4 3 2 1
Printed in China   1807RR

TUTTLE PUBLISHING® is a registered trademark of Tuttle Publishing, a division of Periplus Editions (HK) Ltd.

Bali

The Ultimate Guide to the
World's Most Spectacular Tropical Island

TIM HANNIGAN & LINDA HOFFMAN

TUTTLE Publishing

Tokyo | Rutland, Vermont | Singapore

CONTENTS

INTRODUCING BALI

A Vision of Paradise

Bali is one small island in the middle of a vast nation, but it sometimes seems as though Indonesia isn't big enough to contain it. After all, there can be few other places on earth so loaded with imaginings, projections, and fantasies. Ask any would-be globetrotter to name the ultimate tropical paradise, and chances are they'll say "Bali." It may be just a small Indonesian island, but Bali looms large in the world's imagination.

The word "Bali" prompts a rush of images: a teetering pagoda-roofed temple, framed by volcanic peaks; long lines of Indian Ocean surf unpeeling before a sunset sky; concertinaed rice terraces, fanning out over precipitous hillsides; processions of village women in vibrantly colored sarongs and *kebayas* striding in stately lines towards some religious ceremony with mountainous offerings balanced elegantly atop their heads; a blue-green netherworld of pristine coral and flickering tropical fish, opening just beyond an arc of pale sand.

The thrilling fact is that all those visual clichés really do exist in Bali, along with a great deal more besides.

Starry-eyed international travelers have been falling under Bali's spell since the early years of the 20th century, when the island was a part of the Dutch East Indies. And inevitably, for almost as long, there have been those cynics all too eager to proclaim the place "spoilt" by tourism.

It's certainly true that the heavily urbanized southern part of the island, close to the international airport and the location of the original

Pura Tanah Lot, perched on an islet on the wave-lashed west coast of Bali, is one of the holiest of the island's temples—and the setting for some of its most dramatic sunsets.

beach resorts, is a long way from the ideal of a desert island idyll. Hotels, villas and restaurants extend for miles along the seafronts in an unbroken sprawl; in the hugger-mugger of narrow streets back from the beaches the traffic has long since reached saturation point; and there are inevitable social and environmental headaches associated with rampant development. Even Ubud, Bali's artistic linchpin, has long since gone from sleepy upland village to New Age metropolis.

But anyone who takes away their only impression of Bali from these places has missed out quite spectacularly, for this island is home to myriad parallel universes. Strike out from Kuta, Sanur or any of the other southern resorts, and within an hour you can be in another world—be it high clifftops and crashing surf, misty mountaintop isolation, or rustic rice field greenery.

And remarkably, in an island that has been a travel hotspot for a century, the unbeaten track is never very far away. As often as not it only takes a few sideways steps to be on some untrammeled backroad, shaded by overarching foliage and flanked by ageless red-roofed villages where a passing foreigner is still very much a novelty.

The ultimate magic of Bali, however, comes from its culture. Unique in Indonesia, Bali is still home to a distinctive indigenous form of Hinduism that long predates the arrival of Islam or Christianity in Southeast Asia. This is a remarkably vigorous and vibrant religious tradition, and even in the heart of the most commercial quarters, it still underpins everything.

Keep your eyes open and you'll spot well-tended shrines in the gardens of five-star villa complexes, and waitresses in traditional dress laying out delicate offerings to the spirits on the thresholds of the trendiest bars and restaurants. From the art to the architecture, Bali's belief system extends to every aspect of life. At the same time, the Balinese people are gloriously open about their traditions: the island's thousands of temples welcome hordes of curious visitors, and the locals are perfectly happy for their endless round of religious festivals to double as dramatic tourist spectacles.

This beguiling warmth and openness was what captured the hearts of the first tourists a century ago, and it's still what gives Bali its magic today. Whether you're here to eat, pray or love—or to surf, party, or shop—Bali is a place that will always make the rest of the world seem a little more drab and joyless by comparison.

—*Tim Hannigan*

The Best of Bali

Almost every day there are temple anniversary celebrations somewhere in Bali.

H ere is short list of things and places you should definitely try to do and see in Bali.

Ubud
Ubud started out as a small village in the rice fields, and although it is now a sprawling New Age megalopolis, seething with visitors looking to eat, pray, and love, it still has an undeniably beguiling atmosphere. From yogic endeavors to organic indulgences, you'll find it all here in a town still underpinned by a remarkably proud sense of local community.

Undersea adventures
In Bali there's always magic beneath the surface. The warm, clear waters that lap the eastern and northern coasts make for some of the finest, most accessible diving and snorkeling on the planet. Even if you're a total newcomer to aquatic excursions, the sheltered reefs off Amed and Padangbai are the perfect places to take your first dip, while elsewhere, in the coral seas off Nusa Lembongan, in the teeming shallows near Tulamben, and in many other places besides, there are plenty of world-class dive sites.

Uluwatu
There are thousands of temples in Bali, but few can rival the magnificent Pura Luhur Uluwatu when it comes to location. Perched atop the sheerest of limestone cliffs with surf churning far below, the temple here is like a bowsprit for a vast ship, forging westwards

Sheer cliffs line Bali's southern shore around Uluwatu, site of Pura Luhur Uluwatu temple.

towards the sunset. And then, of course, there are the monkeys, both the real simians which swarm around the statuary, and the humans who form the chattering chorus line for the brilliant *kecak* "monkey dance," performed here every evening.

Sidemen
If anyone tells you that Bali is "spoilt," its natural charms swamped by a flood of commercial development, send them to Sidemen. Slotted between high green ridges and with the mighty Mt. Agung for a backdrop, this sleepy valley is like a lost world. A journey here is like stepping into a Walter Spies landscape painting, with deep ravines, dark forests, and emerald terraces all cast at improbable angles. This is also where you'll find some of Bali's most appealing rural hideaways, making it the perfect place to seek out a room with a view.

Bedugul
Back in the colonial era, when the Dutch officials had had enough of the steamy heat at sea level, they headed to the hills. There's still a lot to be said for such an approach, and a night in the cool of Bali's central mountains can be as invigorating as any spa treatment. While not the highest of Bali's uplands, the lush green area around Bedugul, with its crater lakes, waterfalls, and creeping mists, is the most charming.

Festivals
Every day is a festival in Bali, they say—and they're not exaggerating. Besides the major, island-wide annual religious celebrations such as Galungan and Kuningan, there are literally thousands of other ceremonies at places of worship all over the island, marking full moons, new moons and temple

anniversaries, all featuring fabulously colorful offerings and cheerful crowds in ceremonial dress. And then, of course, there's Bali's
enviable calendar of secular events, with
festivals of jazz, yoga, literature, kite-flying
and more.

The Arts
From cheeky carved wooden souvenirs to the
most exquisite of traditional paintings, and
from funky jazz fusion to epic traditional
dance-dramas backed by the fluid rhythms of
the gamelan, creativity in music, performance, and the visual arts is an essential part
of everyday life in Bali. Even the daily leaf-
tray offerings, laid out in their thousands all
over the island, are miniature masterpieces.

Padangbai
There's still a hint of the Hippie Trail in
sleepy Padangbai, a harbor village that would
be horizontal if it were any more laid-back. It
might be the port for the ferries to Lombok
and the hopping-off point for speedboat trips
to the Gilis, but the real attraction here is the
atmosphere. A clutch of rustic inns on an arc
of pale sand, with perfect little beaches
tucked behind sheltering headlands to the north
and the south, this is a place to slow the pace.

Bali by the backroads
If all you see of Bali is the hectic thoroughfares between the main urban centers, with
their blaring buses, swarming scooters, and
thundering trucks, then you're missing out.
Beyond the busy highways, the island is tra-
versed by hundreds of quiet country lanes,
many mirroring the general north-south
orientation of the rivers. Swing onto any of
these by car or motorbike—or bicycle if

Travelers relaxing at a beach bar in Seminyak

you're fit enough—and you'll quickly realize
that urban chaos is still the exception, not
the rule in Bali.

Seminyak
The most fashionable seaside town east of
San Tropez, Seminyak is the queen of Bali's
southern beach resorts. Brash Kuta, sleepy
Sanur, cossetted Nusa Dua—its rivals all
have their appeal, but none can possibly compete with "the Yak" when it comes to glitz,
glamor, chic shopping, and cutting-edge dining. And then there's the beach, of course, a
glorious expanse of wave-lashed sand.

West Bali National Park
Bali's final frontier, far beyond the world of
villas and luxury spas, is an expanse of jungle, mountain, and scrub at the westernmost
tip of the island. Once upon a time the forests
here were home to tigers. These days the
biggest felines you'll find are the timid leopard cats, but you'll also run into a vast array of
avian wildlife. If you're particularly blessed
you might even catch a black-and-white
glimpse of the Bali starling, one of the rarest
birds on earth. Off the coast of the park,
meanwhile, there's some of Bali's best diving.

Nusa Penida
"Like Bali thirty years ago" is not just a meaningless cliché when it comes to this rugged
outlying island. Long an impoverished backwa-
ter, Nusa Penida is the one part of Bali province
which has remained almost completely untouched by tourism. The harsh limestone landscapes are spectacular, the hard-to-find beaches
of the south coast are stunning, and the locals
couldn't be more welcoming. The first resorts
are finally appearing so things may change
quickly, but for now this is the ultimate place
for off-the-beaten-track adventures.
—*Tim Hannigan*

An amazing sunset at Pura Ulun Danu Bratan

GEOGRAPHY & ECOLOGY

An Island Built by Volcanoes

E very aspect of Bali's geography and ecology is influenced by the towering range of volcanic peaks that dominate the island. They have created its landforms, periodically regenerated its soils, and helped to produce the dramatic downpours that provide the island with life-giving water. The Balinese recognize these geophysical facts of life, and the island's many volcanoes, lakes, and springs are considered by them to be sacred.

Bali is continually being re-formed by volcanic action. The island lies over a major subduction zone, where the Indo-Australian plate collides with the rigid Sunda plate. A violent eruption of Mt. Agung (3,142 m/ 10,308 ft pre-eruption; 3,031 m/9,944 ft now) in 1963 showered the mountain's upper slopes with ash that slid off as mud-flows, killing thousands of people and laying waste to irrigation networks and rice fields that had been built up over many years; 2018 saw another major, though less cata-strophic, eruption. Mt. Batur (1,717 m/5,633 ft) to the west is also active, with greater frequency but less violence.

A mild, equatorial climate

Lying between 8 and 9 degrees south of the equator, Bali has a short, hot wet season and a longer, cooler dry season. The mountains are wet year round, averaging 2,500 to 3,000 mm (100 to 120 in) of rain annually, with warm days and cool nights. The lowlands are hotter and drier, but fresh and persistent winds make the climate less oppressive here than elsewhere in the equatorial zone.

The wet season lasts from November to March, and is also the hottest time of year (30–31° C by day, 24–25° C at night, 86-88° F, and 75-77° F respectively). The dry season is from April to October, when southeasterly winds blow up from the Australian interior (28–29° C by day, and a pleasant 23° C at night, 82-84° F, and 73° F respectively), with nearly 12 hours of sunshine daily.

By itself, the rainfall in the lowlands is not enough for wet rice cultivation. In other parts of Indonesia, particularly Java, flood waters following heavy rains can be collected behind dams, but the steep, narrow valleys of Bali offer no good dam sites. Over the centuries,

Volcanoes, such as the magnificient Mt. Agung, are considered sacred and dominate the landscape.

the Balinese have instead devised many sophisticated irrigation systems that optimize the water available from rain and rivers.

Bali's volcanic soils are, in fact, not naturally well suited to wet rice cultivation. They are deep, finely textured and well-drained, so water soaks through them rapidly. While this reduces the risk of floods, it wastes precious water. Paradoxically, the solution is vigorous and repeated plowing, which actually renders the soils less permeable. Irrigated areas also receive a supply of nutrients from river water enriched by domestic effluents.

Man has extensively modified the natural vegetation of Bali. The entire forest area now covers only 121,271 ha, or 23 percent of Bali's total area, mainly in the western mountains and along the arc of volcanic peaks from Mt. Agung to Mt. Batukaru. About a quarter of the forest is protected in four nature reserves, the largest of which is Bali Barat National Park (19,000 ha or 46,950 ac). Further reserves are planned to protect another quarter of the island's forests.

In the 21st century, attention is also being paid to coastlines. Recent studies show that Bali's shores are receding at an alarming rate, accounting for a loss of 181.7 km (113 miles) of land in the last decade, amounting to 41.5 percent of the island's total shoreline. Primarily resulting from environmental neglect, it is obvious that solutions must be found before more damage occurs.

An island of great contrasts

Bali may be small, but its physical geography is complex, creating an island of great variety. In simple outline, three major areas emerge: the mountains, the coastal lowlands and the limestone fringes. The mountains are lofty and spectacular, dominated by Mt. Agung and its neighbors, Abang and Batur. Dramatic lava flows on the northeastern flanks of Agung are Bali's newest land-forms, demonstrating what the entire island probably looked like a million years ago.

The western mountains provide the last major wildlife sanctuary. Cultivation here is limited to coastal areas that are very dry in the north, but more prosperous and fertile in the south. Coconut groves, cattle pastures and rain-fed fields line the foothills, while rice fields are found along the coast. Unique canals vanish into foothill tunnels excavated as protection from landslides. In the extreme southwest, the Palasari Dam forms the island's

Large lakes inside of Bali's volcanic craters serve as reservoirs to store water, which then seeps out from sacred springs further down the slopes.

only manmade lake. On Bali's western tip, the coral reefs and clear waters around Menjangan Island provide fantastic scuba diving.

The southern lowlands formed the cradle of Balinese civilization. Here it is possible to grow two or more irrigated rice crops per year. Based on this agricultural surplus, eight small but powerful kingdoms arose, symmetrically lining the parallel north-south river valleys that shaped their early growth.

In contrast to the south, the north coast hosted only a single kingdom, centered on the less extensive but equally productive rice lands around Singaraja. Terracing here continues well into the hills, on slopes that elsewhere would be regarded as a severe erosion hazard. On Bali, these terraces stand as firm as masonry because of peculiar clay minerals within the soil. Further east, the dry coast is relieved by several major springs that emerge from fissures in the lava flows. The spring water is used for irrigating table grapes, a crop that thrives here.

The southern limestone fringes stand in complete contrast to the rest of Bali. These are dry and difficult to cultivate. The Bukit Peninsula south of the airport has impressive cliffs and many large caves. Across the sea to the east, Nusa Ceningan, Nusa Lembongan and Nusa Penida are dry limestone islands with scrubby vegetation and shallow soils. Villagers on Penida have built ingenious catchments to collect rainwater. Springs also emerge from the base of its high southern cliffs, and locals have built precarious scaffolds to collect water. Just as water is the measure of richness in the interior, so is it the measure of survival around the periphery. In Bali, water is truly sacred.

—*Stephen Walker*

BALINESE AGRICULTURE

Nourishing Body and Soul

Wet rice cultivation is the key to the agricultural bounty in many areas of Bali. The greatest concentration of irrigated rice fields is found in southern-central Bali, where water is readily available from spring-fed streams. Here, and in other well-watered areas where wet rice culture predominates, rice is planted in rotation with *palawija* cash crops, such as soybeans, peanuts, onions, chili peppers, and other vegetables. In the drier regions corn, taro, tapioca, and beets are cultivated.

Rice is, and has always been, the essence of life for the Balinese. As in other Southeast Asian countries, rice is synonymous with food and eating. Personified as the "divine nutrition" in the form of the goddess Dewi Sri, rice is seen by the Balinese to be part of an all-compassing life force of which humans partake.

Bali's subak *irrigation system is unique.*

Rice is also an important social force. The phases of rice cultivation determine the seasonal rhythm of work as well as the division of labor between men and women within the community. Balinese respect for their native rice varieties is expressed in countless myths and in colorful rituals in which the life cycle of the female rice divinity is portrayed, from the planting of the seed to the harvesting of the grain. Rice thus represents "culture" to the Balinese in the dual sense of *cultura* and *cultus*: cultivation and worship.

Irrigation cooperatives (*subak*)

Historical evidence indicates that since the 11th century, all peasants whose fields were fed by the same water course have belonged to a single *subak*, or irrigation cooperative. This is a traditional institution that regulates the construction and maintenance of water-works, and the distribution of life-giving water that they supply. Such regulation is essential to efficient wet rice cultivation on Bali, where water travels through very deep ravines and across countless terraces in its journey from the mountains to the sea.

The *subak* is responsible for coordinating the planting of seeds and the transplanting of seedlings so as to achieve optimal growing conditions, as well as for organizing ritual offerings and festivals at the *subak* temple. All members are called upon to participate in these activities, especially at feasts honoring the rice goddess Sri.

Subak cooperatives exist entirely apart from normal Balinese village institutions, and a single village's rice fields may fall under the jurisdiction of more than one *subak*, depending on local drainage patterns. The most important technical duties under-taken by the subak are the construction and maintenance of canals, tunnels, aqueducts, dams, and waterlocks.

Other crops

Visitors often get the impression that nothing but wet rice is grown in Bali, because of the vast, unobstructed vistas of irrigated rice fields between villages in southern and central Bali, but this is not so. Out of a total of 563,286 ha or 1,391,910 ac of arable land on Bali, just 81,482 ha (about 14.47 percent) are irrigated rice fields (*sawah*). Another 136,796 ha or 338,030 ac (24.29 percent) is non-irrigated dry fields (*tegalan*), producing one rain-fed crop per year. A further 127,271 ha or 314,493 ac (23 percent) are forested lands primarily belonging to the government, and 121,797 ha or 300,967 ac (21.62 percent) are estate crops such as coffee (both arabica and robusta), cloves, coconut, and cacao; 99,151 ha or 245,007 ac are devoted to cash crop gardens (*kebun*) with tree and bush culture. From the mid-1980s through the late 1990s, vanilla experienced a boom period, with over 50 percent of Indonesia's production coming from Bali. From the turn of the 21st century production declined, because of plant disease and falling prices, though small-scale plantations remain, and local conditions are still ideal for growing vanilla. Tobacco production has also long been an important part of Bali's agricultural economy, though it has declined somewhat in recent years. In mountainous regions such as Bedugul, meanwhile, new vegetable varieties more at home in temperate regions—from mushrooms and potatoes to strawberries and apples—have been intensely cultivated.

Other export commodities include copra and related products of the coconut palm. For subsistence cultivators, the coconut palm remains, as always, a "tree of life" that can be utilized from the root up to the tip. It provides building materials (the wood, leaves, and leaf ribs), fuel (the leaves and dried husks), kitchen and household items (shells and fibers for utensils), as well as food and ritual objects (vessels, offerings, plaited objects, food, and drink).

The "green revolution"

Changes in Balinese agricultural practices have brought about fundamental alterations in the relationship of the Balinese to their staple crop. Rice production can no longer be expanded by bringing new lands under cultivation. Nor is mechanization a desirable alternative, given the current surplus of labor on the island. For these reasons, the official agricultural policy since the mid-1970s has been to improve crop yields on existing fields through biological and chemical means.

The cultivation of new, fast-growing, high-yielding rice varieties, in concert with the

Coffee is an important estate crop in Bali.

application of chemical fertilizers, herbicides and pesticides, lies at the core of the government's agricultural development programs. Further aims have been to improve methods of soil utilization and irrigation and to set up new forms of cooperatives to provide credit and market surplus harvests. Over 80 percent of Bali's wet rice fields have been subjected to these intensification processes.

Under the Suharto regime, Indonesia was able to meet most of its own rice needs, thus relieving some of the pressures that created the original "Green Revolution" of the 1960s. But as more land was gobbled up with the development of resorts and golf courses, the effort failed in the late 1990s.

In the 21st century, however, self-sufficiency has once again returned. Recent years have brought on an explosion of new agricultural techniques (such as Sustainable Rice Intensification, a kind of all-inclusive permaculture) and organic farming, while Bali's provincial government has made various efforts to address general environmental issues. Perhaps the biggest challenge to the traditional agricultural productivity of this greenest of tropical islands, however, has come from tourism.

Throughout the south of Bali, and increasingly in other areas too, land that was previously worth most for growing rice has become more valuable still as building plots for resorts and villas. General population increases in the areas around Denpasar too have seen urban sprawl creeping into former rice land, and the vastly increased demands on water supplies created by swimming pools, golf courses, and all the other facets of modern tourism have begun to interfere with centuries-old irrigation networks.

—*Urs Ramseyer & Tim Hannigan*

The Biological Fringe of Asia

When it comes to wildlife, Bali is the easternmost outpost of Asia. On a clear day you can see the hills of Lombok from Bali's eastern shores, but the stretch of water that fills the space between is one of the great frontiers of the natural world, the so-called "Wallace Line" which divides the Asian and Australasian ecological spheres.

During the last ice age, falling sea levels meant that Bali was connected to mainland Asia, and continental birds and animals moved in. The strait between Bali and Lombok, however, was so deep that it never dried out, and the fauna in points east remained more closely related to that of Australia and New Guinea.

Inevitably, the dividing line has become a little blurred over the eons: human activity has shunted primates and other Asian mammals far east of the Wallace Line, while east winds have blown cockatoos into the forests of Bali. But nonetheless, there's a curious thrill in knowing that the unmistakably Asian natural environment that surrounds you in Bali is in fact the furthest bastion of an entire continent.

Animal life in Bali

A single animal species is dramatically dominant in Bali: mankind. Looking at the intricately crafted agricultural landscapes that lap high up the slopes of the central volcanoes, and that tumble to the very edges of the glittering sea, it can be hard to imagine that any large wild animals could find space to survive here. But not so long ago swathes of Bali were still under primary jungle cover, and there were plenty of big beasts. Today, a few species still survive.

The one wild mammal that virtually all visitors to Bali will encounter is the long-tailed macaque, eponymous residents of Ubud's Monkey Forest, the Uluwatu temple complex, and many other places besides. These medium-sized, light brown primates are found throughout Southeast Asia, and have a long history of living in close proximity with humans. In Hindu Bali they are associated with the monkey god, Hanuman—as well as having a reputation for stealing jewelry, sunglasses, and cameras from unwary tourists.

Long-tailed macaques—the most easily spotted wild animal in Bali—can be found in the sacred monkey forest on the outskirts of Ubud as well as at the Uluwatu temple complex.

Large monitor lizards are still common on the island of Serangan near Sanur.

Highly endangered, Bali starlings are now being bred and released on Nusa Penida.

Far more elusive is the Javan Lutung, also known as the ebony leaf monkey. Smaller and swifter than macaques, these dark-haired monkeys are usually only found well away from human habitation.

The single best place for wild animal encounters is the rugged West Bali National Park, a large expanse of forested ridges and patchy scrubland. This last true wilderness in Bali is home to numerous rare creatures, including the *banteng*, wild cattle with dark upper bodies and white legs that are the ancestors of Bali's distinctive domestic cows. The forests here are also home to *rusa* deer and muntjac.

Remarkably, given its small size and large human population, until comparatively recently there were tigers in Bali. The island was home to the smallest tiger subspecies, but lack of habitats and pressure from human activities saw it wiped out. The last recorded Bali tiger was shot in 1937. Leopards survived a little longer, but though there are still occasional unconfirmed sightings in the West Bali National Park, they too are thought to be extinct. The only wild feline still known to exist is the leopard cat, which looks like a miniature version of its namesake.

As well as the elusive mammals, Bali is home to a wide array of reptiles and amphibians. Common house geckos—known in Indonesia by the onomatopoeic name *cicak*—are a fixture in every budget guesthouse, where they do a great service in gobbling up mosquitoes. Their larger cousins, known as *tokek*—also for their distinctive call—are also sometimes seen. Bigger still are the lumbering, dragon-like water monitor lizards. These are found all over Bali, but there are some particularly large specimens on Serangan (also known as Turtle Island) near Sanur. There are also a few reticulated pythons, but these generally stick to the deeper forests, and are rarely seen.

Balinese birdlife

Far easier to spot than the wild mammals are Bali's myriad birds. The island is home to over 280 avian species, and the chorus of birdsong that greets the dawn, even in towns and resorts, attests to that diversity. Bali is, in fact, a highly rewarding destination for birdwatchers.

Amongst the species that live throughout the lush central parts of the island are the striking black-and-mustard black-naped oriole, the delicate magpie robin (which looks very much like a miniature European magpie), and the various species of egrets and herons which can often be spotted picking their way through the flooded rice terraces.

Vividly colored Java kingfishers can be seen around Bali's many rivers, and the striking, emerald-tinted green junglefowl occasionally shows itself in the patches of forest close to villages.

Once again, however, it's in the West Bali National Park that keen birdwatchers are most likely to encounter the rarer and more elusive species, including the stately crested serpent eagle, and the comically bald-headed stork known as the lesser adjutant.

And then, of course, there's Bali's most famous avian resident, one of the rarest of all birds—Rothschild's myna, better known as the Bali starling. A critically endangered population of this beautiful black-and-white bird can be found in the West Bali National Park, and also, thanks to a successful captive breeding program, on Nusa Penida and Nusa Lembongan.

—*Tim Hannigan*

EARLY BALINESE HISTORY

Artifacts and Early Foreign Influences

The early history of Bali can be divided into a prehistoric and an early historic period. The former is marked by the arrival of Austronesian (Malayo-Polynesian) migrants, beginning perhaps 3,000–4,000 years ago. The Austronesians were hardy seafarers who spread from Taiwan through the Southeast Asian islands to the Pacific in a series of extensive migrations that spanned several millennia. The Balinese are thus closely related, culturally and linguistically, to the peoples of the Philippines and Oceania, as well as other neighboring Indonesian islands.

Stone sarcophagi, seats and altars

Though precious little is known about the long, formative stages of Bali's prehistory, artifacts discovered around the island provide intriguing clues about its early inhabitants. Prehistoric gravesites have been found in western Bali, the oldest probably dating from the first few centuries B.C. The people buried here were herders and farmers who used bronze, and in some cases iron, to make implements and jewelry. Prehistoric stone sarcophagi have also been discovered, mainly in the mountains. They often have the shape

Bali's contact with Javanese Hinduism and Buddhism dates back to the eighth century A.D.

of huge turtles carved at either end with human and animal heads with bulging eyes, big teeth, and protruding tongues.

Stone seats, altars and other large rocks dating from early times are housed in several Balinese temples. Here, as elsewhere in Indonesia, they seem to be connected with the veneration of ancestral spirits who formed (and in many ways still form) the core of Balinese religious practices.

Also apparently connected with ancestor worship is one of Southeast Asia's greatest prehistoric artifacts, the huge bronze kettle-drum known as the "Moon of Pejeng." Still considered to have significant power, it is now enshrined in a temple in Pejeng, central Bali, in the Gianyar Regency. More than 1.5 m or 4.9 ft in diameter and 1.86 m or 6.1 ft high, it is decorated with frogs and geometric motifs in a style that probably originated from near Dong Son in what is now northern Vietnam. This is the largest of many such drums discovered in Southeast Asia.

Hindu-Javanese influences

It is assumed (but without proof so far) that the Balinese were in contact with Hindu and Buddhist populations of Java from the early part of the eighth century A.D. onwards, and that Bali was even conquered by a Javanese king in A.D. 732. This contact is responsible for the advent of writing and other important Indian cultural elements that had come to Java along the major trading routes several centuries earlier. Indian writing, dance, religion and architecture were to have a decisive impact, blending with existing Balinese traditions to form a new and highly distinctive culture.

Stone and copperplate inscriptions in Old Balinese dating from around A.D. 882 onwards, coincide with finds of Hindu- and Buddhist-inspired statues, bronzes, ornamented caves, rock-cut temples, and bathing places. These are often found in areas near rivers, ravines, springs, and volcanic peaks.

At the end of the 10th and the beginning of the 11th centuries there were close, peaceful bonds with the Indianized kingdoms in east

The "Moon of Pejeng"—the largest prehistoric kettledrum in Asia

Java, in particular with the Kediri realm (11th century A.D. to 1222). Old Javanese was thereafter the language of prestige, used in all Balinese inscriptions, and evidence of a strong Javanese cultural influence. In 1284, Bali is said to have been conquered by King Kertanegara of the Javanese Singhasari dynasty (1222–1292). It is not certain whether the island was actually colonized at this time, but many new Javanese elements appear in the Balinese art of this period.

According to a Javanese court chronicle known as the *Nagarakertagama* (dated 1365), Bali was conquered and colonized in 1334 by Javanese forces under Gajah Mada, the legendary general and prime minister or *maha patih* of the powerful Majapahit kingdom, which established hegemony over East Java and all seaports bordering the Java Sea during the mid-14th century. It is said that Gajah Mada, accompanied by contingents of Javanese nobles, came to Bali to subdue a rapacious Balinese king. A Javanese vassal ruler was installed at a new capital at Samprangan, near present-day Klungkung in east Bali, and the nobles were granted lands in the surrounding areas. A Javanese court and courtly culture were thus introduced to the island. The separation of Balinese society into four caste groups is ascribed to this period, with the *satriya* warrior caste ruling from Samprangan. Those who did not wish to participate in the new system fled to remote mountain areas, where they lived apart from the mainstream. These are the so-called "original Balinese," the *Bali Aga* or *Bali Mula*.

Around 1460, the capital moved to nearby Gelgel, and the powerful "Grand Lord," Dewa Agung, presided over a flowering of Balinese arts and culture. Over time, however, the descendants of the *aryas* became increasingly independent, and from around 1700 began to form realms in other areas.

Reconstructing the past

Because ancestor veneration plays such an important role in Balinese religion, many groups possess family genealogies known as *babad*. In such texts, the *brahmana, satriya,* and *wesya* clans trace their ancestry to the Majapahit kings, while the *Bali Aga* assert descent from even earlier Javanese rulers. There are also groups that claim as their ancestors Javanese Hindus and Buddhists who are said to have taken refuge in Bali following the rise of Muslim states there.

A myth popular amongst tour guides and travel writers has it that the entire Hindu-Buddhist population of Java, most notably its artists and craftsmen, fled to Bali after the fall of the last major Hindu-Javanese kingdom, Majapahit, to the iconoclastic Muslims of Demak, in the 16th century, and that this exodus is responsible for Bali's enduring artistic tendences. This story is at best a gross exaggeration, as evidenced by the significant cultural continuity between the Hindu and Muslim eras in Java, and by the fact that the decline of the Majapahit and the concurrent rise of Muslim-Javanese powers was a prolonged process. But the final demise of Majapahit certainly did produce a certain number of priestly and aristocratic refugees to Bali.

—Hedi Hinzler & Tim Hannigan

THE TRADITIONAL BALINESE KINGDOMS

History in a Balinese Looking Glass

Most of what is known about Bali's traditional kingdoms comes from the Balinese themselves. Scores of masked dance dramas, family chronicles, and temple rituals focus on great figures and events of the Balinese past. In such accounts, the broad outline of Bali's history from the 12th to the 18th centuries is an epic tale of the coming of great men to power. These were the royal and priestly founders of glorious dynasties—some mad, some fearsome, some lazy, and some proud—who together with their retainers and family members determined the fate of Bali's kingdoms, as well as shaping the situation and status of the island's present-day inhabitants.

It is possible to see the Balinese as both indifferent to history and yet utterly obsessed by it. Indifferent because they are not very interested in the "what happened and why" of professional historians, while at the same time they are obsessed by stories concerning their own illustrious ancestors.

Balinese "history" is in fact a set of stories that explain how their extended families came to be where they are. Such stories may explain, for example, how certain ancestors moved from an ancient court center to a remote village, or how they were originally of aristocratic stock although their descendants no longer possess princely titles. In short, they provide evidence of a continuing connection between the world of the ancestors and present-day Bali.

Major events are thus invariably seen in terms of the actions of great men (and occasionally women), yet to view them as mere individuals is deceptive. They are divine ancestors, and as such their actions embody the fate of entire groups. Above all, they are responsible for having created the society found on Bali today.

Each family possesses its own genealogy that somehow fits into the overall picture. Some focus on kings, their followers or priests as key ancestors. Others see the family history in terms of village leaders, blacksmiths (powerful, as makers of weapons and tools) or villagers who resisted and escaped the advance of new rulers.

The fact that such stories sometimes agree with one another should not necessarily be taken as proof that this is what really happened. There are many gaps, loose ends and inconsistencies, often pointing to the fact that generations of priests, princes and scribes have recast these tales about the past to serve their own ends. The sagas must be retold, nevertheless, in order to know what is open to dispute.

Ancestors and origins

Bali's history begins in ancient Java, in the legendary Kediri and Majapahit kingdoms, where Javanese culture is regarded (by Javanese, Balinese, and Western scholars alike) as having reached its apex. From these rich sources flowed the great literature, art, and court rituals of Hindu Java that were later transplanted to Bali.

One of the prime reasons for holding such rituals was to elevate Hindu-Javanese leaders to the status of god-like kings who were in contact with the divine forces of the cosmos. As these Javanese kingdoms expanded to take over Bali, they brought with them their art, literature, and cosmology. At the same time, the Javanese also absorbed vital elements of Balinese culture, eventually spreading some of these throughout the archipelago and elsewhere in Southeast Asia.

The great Airlangga, descendant of Bali's illustrious King Udayana, is said to have ascended the east Javanese throne and to have founded the powerful Kediri kingdom in the 11th century. Thus it was proper that his descendants would later install priests and warriors from Java to rule over Bali. Foremost among these was the son of a priest, Kresna Kapakisan, who became the first king of Gelgel (now in Klungkung Regency) in the mid-15th century.

The transition to Gelgel from a previous court center at Samprangan (now in Gianyar Regency) was made by a cockfighting member

Striking a pose: Gusti Ketut Jelantik, Raja of the northern Balinese kingdom of Buleleng, with one of his daughters and a slave in the 1870s.

of the Kapakisan dynasty who became embroiled in a struggle for the throne and attempts to save the kingdom from the mismanagement of his elder brother, or so the account goes. There is little reason to doubt this version of events, yet there are huge gaps in the story of how power moved from Java to Gelgel in previous centuries and the relationship of the Kapakisan line to earlier kings appointed by the Javanese conquerors.

Bali's "Golden Age"

Most Balinese trace their ancestry back to a group of courtiers clustering about the great King Baturenggong, a descendant of Kapakisan, who is seen to have presided over a Balinese "Golden Age" in the 16th century. Balinese accounts describe him as "a king of great authority, a true lion of a man who was wise in protecting his subjects and attending to their needs, and an outstanding warrior of great mystical power, always victorious in war." European records do not mention him by name, but attest to the wealth and influence of a Balinese kingdom which at this time had a more centralized and unified system of government than was the case in subsequent centuries.

Of equal if not greater importance in the collective Balinese memory of this era is the super-priest Nirartha. He is remembered for his great spiritual powers: a man who could stop floods, control the energies of sexuality through meditation, and write beautiful poetry to move men's souls. In the genealogies it was he who founded the main line of Balinese high priests, those whose worship is directed to Siva, Lord of the Gods. His name is associated with many of Bali's greatest temples and a corpus of literature produced by himself and his followers.

In Balinese eyes, the descendants of King Baturenggong and Nirartha presided over a period of decline, even though Baturenggong's son, Seganing, upheld some of his father's greatness and, according to the texts, fathered the ancestors of Bali's key royal lines. Balinese sources tell of the destruction of Gelgel by a rebellious chief minister, Gusti Agung Maruti, who was distinguished by possessing a tail and an overwhelming thirst for power. After his defeat by princes who established themselves in the north and south of the island, new independent kingdoms arose from the ashes of Gelgel. The Gelgel dynasty itself survived—albeit in a much reduced state—as the kingdom of Klungkung, maintaining some of its moral and symbolic authority over the rest of the island, but having direct control of only its immediate area.

Slave trading and king-making

To the outside world, as to later Balinese writers, the period following Gelgel's "Golden Age" was one of chaos in which fractious kings ruled from courts scattered about the island. This was not necessarily so in

This vintage 1930s portrait shows all eight Balinese kings gathered in the Gianyar palace grounds.

contemporary Balinese terms, where the new states must have represented a more dynamic way of conducting the affairs of state and external trade. Bali became known on the international scene at this time as a source of slaves, savage fighters, beautiful women, and skilled craftsmen.

According to traditional accounts, the fate and status of present-day Balinese families was also largely determined at this time. Kingdoms rose and fell with alarming rapidity, clans split and were demoted or even enslaved, and aspiring princes waged war and organized lavish ceremonies. Such human dramas were punctuated by a series of natural disasters such as earthquakes, epidemics, and volcanic eruptions.

Bali's principal export throughout the 17th and 18th centuries was slaves. Warfare and a revision of Bali's Hindu law codes helped provide a steady supply of slaves to meet an ever-increasing overseas demand. War captives, criminals and debtors were sold abroad indiscriminately by Balinese rulers, who maintained a monopoly on the export trade. In northern Bali, Europeans were even invited in to oversee the trade, and the Dutch in particular purchased large numbers of Balinese to serve as laborers, artisans, and concubines in their extensive network of trading ports, especially their capital at Batavia (now Jakarta), where Balinese slaves made up a sizeable portion of the population. Balinese were even sent to South Africa, where in the early 18th century they constituted up to a quarter of the total number of slaves in that country.

Likewise, Balinese wives and concubines were very much favored by wealthy Chinese traders for their industriousness and beauty and the fact that they had no aversion to pork, unlike the Muslim Javanese. An early 19th-century trader noted that Balinese women were among the most expensive slaves, costing "30, 50 and even 70 Spanish dollars, according to her physical qualities." The same observer later commented that the Balinese "regard deportation from their island as the worst possible punishment. This attitude results from their strongly-held conviction that their gods have no influence outside Bali and that no salvation is to be expected for those who die elsewhere."

The principal kingdoms which emerged during this period were Buleleng in the north, Karangasem in the east and Mengwi in the southwest. At various times, these realms expanded to conquer parts of Bali's neighboring islands. Mengwi and Buleleng moved westward into Java, where they became embroiled in conflicts with and between rival Muslim kingdoms. The Dutch came to play an ever larger role in these conflicts, until eventually the Javanese rulers discovered that they had mortgaged their empires to the gin-drinking Europeans. The Balinese were finally pushed out of eastern Java by combined Dutch and Javanese forces.

In the east, Karangasem conquered neighboring Lombok Island, and at one point even moved into the western part of the next island, Sumbawa. It also annexed Buleleng, and knocked at the gates of Bali's august, but largely impotent central kingdom, Klungkung.

By the beginning of the 19th century, the island's changeable political landscape had stabilized to an extent, as nine separate kingdoms consolidated their positions. A massive eruption of Mt. Tambora on Sumbawa in 1815 —the largest eruption ever recorded—proved to be a catalyst. A tide of famine and disease swept Bali in the wake of the eruption, shredding the traditional fabric of Balinese society and with it many of the fragile political structures of the two previous centuries.

Paradoxically, Tambora's devastating eruption brought in its aftermath a period of unprecedented renewal and prosperity. Deep layers of nutrient-rich ash from the volcano made Bali's soils fertile beyond the wildest imaginings of earlier rulers. Rice and other agricultural products began to be exported in large quantities at a time when vociferous anti-slavery campaigns throughout Europe were bringing an end to Bali's lucrative slave trade.

Two other factors served to transform the island's political and economic landscape. The first was a dramatic decrease in warfare as ruling families focused more and more on internecine struggles and competing claims for dynastic control, and the monopolies on duties, tolls and corvee labor that came with it. The second was the changing nature of foreign trade, particularly with the founding of Singapore as a British free trade port in 1819. To Singapore went Bali's pigs, vegetable oils, and rice. Back came opium, Indian textiles, and guns. Bali was now integrated with world markets to a degree unknown in the past, a fact that did not escape the ever watchful eyes of colonial Dutch administrators in Batavia.

—*Adrian Vickers*

Conquests and Dutch Colonial Rule

In the 19th century, Europe took up the fashion of empire building with a vengeance. Tiny Holland, once Europe's most prosperous trading nation, was not to be left behind and spent much of the century subduing native rulers throughout the archipelago, a vast region that was to become the Netherlands East Indies, later Indonesia.

A steady stream of European traders, scholars, and mercenaries visited Bali in this period. The most successful of the traders was a Dane by the name of Mads Lange, one of the last of the great "country traders" whose local knowledge and contacts permitted them to operate on the interstices of the European colonial powers and the traditional kingdoms of the region.

A literary character

Lange was perhaps the prototype for Joseph Conrad's *Lord Jim*, a man who failed to pick the winning side in an internecine dynastic struggle that wracked Lombok in the first half of the 19th century, but who then settled in southern Bali and found a powerful patron in Kesiman, one of the lords of the expanding Badung kingdom. He soon combined this patronage with knowledge of overseas markets and familiarity with the largely female-run internal trading networks of Bali to become extremely rich for a brief period in the 1840s.

The Dutch, determined to establish economic and political control over Bali, became embroiled during this period in a series of wars in the north of the island. They came, as they saw it, to "teach the Balinese a lesson," whereas the words of Buleleng's chief minister best expressed the prevailing Balinese view: "Let the *keris* (dagger) decide." The first two Dutch attacks, in 1846 and 1848, were repulsed by north Balinese forces aided by allies from the Karangasem and Klungkung kingdoms, as well as by rampant dysentery among the invading forces. A third Dutch attempt in 1849 succeeded mainly because the Balinese rulers of Lombok, cousins of the Karangasem rulers, used this

as an opportunity to take over east Bali. Not wishing to push their luck, the Dutch contented themselves with control of Bali's northern coast for the next 40 years. As this was the island's main export region, they did succeed in isolating the powerful southern kingdoms and in controlling much of the export trade. Lange's fortunes soon declined as a result, and he died several years later, probably poisoned out of economic jealousy.

The end of traditional rule

Not long after the cataclysmic eruption of Krakatau in 1883, on the other side of Java, a series of momentous struggles began amongst the kingdoms of south Bali, struggles that were to result in a loss of independence for all of them over the next 25 years. These conflicts began with the collapse of Gianyar following a rebellion by a vassal lord in Negara. The rebellion ultimately failed, as Gianyar was revived by a hitherto obscure but upwardly-mobile prince in Ubud, but it in turn touched off a series of conflicts that produced a domino effect across the island.

The first kingdom to go was once mighty Mengwi, former ruler of east Java, which was destroyed by its neighbors in 1891. The Muslim Sasak inhabitants of Lombok then rebelled against their Balinese overlords, which gave the Dutch an excuse to intervene and conquer Lombok in 1896.

Greatly weakened by these events, Karangasem and Gianyar both ceded some of their rights to the Dutch, leaving only the independent kingdoms of Badung, Tabanan, Bangli and prestigious Klungkung, by the turn of the 20th century.

Shipwrecks, opium, and death

The Dutch found excuses to take on these kingdoms in a series of diplomatic incidents involving shipwrecks and the opium trade. These culminated in the infamous *puputans*, or massacres, of 1906 and 1908 that resulted in not only many deaths, but completed Dutch mastery of the island.

This contemporary illustration from the French newspaper Le Petit Journal *depicts the death of the Raja of Buleleng in the puputan of 1849.*

In the 1906 *puputan*, the Dutch landed at Sanur and marched on Denpasar, where they were greeted by over 1,000 members of the royal family and their followers, dressed in white and carrying the state regalia in a march to certain death before the superior Dutch weaponry. As later expressed by the neighboring king of Tabanan, the attitude of the unrelenting Balinese ruler of Badung, when asked to sign a treaty with the Dutch, was that "it is better that we die with the earth as our pillow than to live like corpses in shame and disgrace."

A macabre massacre

In 1908 the bloody *puputan* (meaning "ending" in Balinese) was repeated on a smaller scale in Klungkung. The ghastly scene was one in which, according to one Dutch observer, the corpse of the king, his head smashed open and brains oozing out, was surrounded by those of his wives and family in a bloody tangle of half severed limbs, corpses of mothers with babies still at their breasts and wounded children given merciful release by the daggers of their own compatriots.

Ostensibly because they felt guilty about the bloody nature of their conquest, which was widely reported and condemned in Europe, the Dutch authorities quickly established a policy designed to uphold "traditional" Bali. In fact this policy supported only what was seen to be traditional in their eyes, and only if those bits of tradition did not contradict the central aim of running a quiet and lucrative colony.

Marketing ploys

Preserving Bali largely meant three things to the Dutch: creating a colonial society that included a select group of the aristocracy, labeling and categorizing every aspect of Balinese culture with a view to keeping it pure, and idealizing this culture so as to market it for the purposes of tourism. Although these may sound contradictory, they meshed well together. There were slight hiccups: those Balinese who refused to cooperate and did their best to avoid the demands of the Dutch-run state. Some were killed, while others were forced to work on road construction projects or to pay harsh new taxes on everything from pigs to the rice harvest.

Indirect rule through royalty

Another aspect of "preserving" Bali was that the traditional rulers were maintained. As on Java, the Dutch adopted a policy of ruling the villages indirectly through them, while running their own parallel civil service to administer the towns. At least this was the general idea, although here, too, there were some hitches. It took decades before a cooperative branch of the old Buleleng royal family was in place, and many members of the other royal families had to be exiled. In the case of the Klungkung royalty, the exile lasted for some 19 years after the *puputan*.

The Gianyar and Karangasem royal families adapted best to the new conditions. Gusti Bagus Jelantik, the ruler of Karangasem, embarked on an active campaign to strengthen and redefine traditional Balinese religion. In large part, he did this to head off the sort of split that had earlier occurred in the north between modernist commoners or *sudras*, who argued for a social status based on achievement, and members of the three higher castes, or *triwangsa*, who were given hereditary privileges. Ironically this split came about because of a new emphasis on rigidly-defined caste groups under Dutch rule.

The Dutch had to intervene and exile some *sudra* leaders, but modernizing moderates such as the Karangasem ruler realized the need to shape and control the changes taking place in Balinese religion and society. In this, they found ready allies among intellectuals in the Dutch civil service with a passion for Balinese culture and an international influx of artists, travelers, and dilettantes who poured into Bali during the 1920s and 1930s.

Hints of sex and magic

Some, like Barbara Hutton and Charlie Chaplin, were rich and famous and stayed only for a short time. Others, like painter Walter Spies, cartoonist Miguel Covarrubias and composer Colin McPhee, are now famous principally because of their long association with Bali.

The attraction for these well-heeled, well-connected, or simply talented Westerners was the developing image of Bali as a tropical paradise where art exists in overabundance and people live in perfect harmony with nature, an image tinged with hints of sex and magic that was officially sponsored by Dutch tourism officials. And it was certainly promoted by genuinely enthusiastic reports from those who visited and witnessed the island's intricate life, art, and rituals.

The positive contributions of these foreign scholars and artists, working in conjunction with enlightened Balinese and Dutch civil servants, included such institutions as the Bali Museum and the Kirtya Liefrinck-van der Tuuk (now the Bali Documentation Center).

But there was a negative side as well. Although the Bali lovers claimed to be the complete opposite of colonial authorities, they in fact represented the other side of the coin of Western rule. With the fan dance performances for tourists came forced labor, and in their writings, Bali-struck foreigners always conveniently ignored the poverty, disease, and injustice that made the colonial era a time of continuous hardship and fear for many Balinese.

—Adrian Vickers

The streets of Denpasar, as depicted in an oil canvas by Balinese artist Mangu Putra in 2005.

MODERN BALI

From Chaos to Tourism Development

The Dutch, complacent in their cocoon of colonial supremacy, were shocked when the Japanese invaded the Indies in 1941 — so shocked that they gave up with hardly a fight. More shocking still to the colonialists was the fact that after the war, the majority of Indonesians failed to welcome their former rulers back with open arms. *Revolution!* and *Freedom!* had instead become rallying cries around the archipelago, and these were taken up with fierce determination by the Balinese.

Those who had come to believe in colonial "peace and order" and in "Bali the Paradise" were appalled by the intensity of violence and social divisions that wracked the island in subsequent decades, from the beginning of World War II until the middle of the 1960s. In many ways the violence was worse here than in any other part of Indonesia, a situation which had its roots in the way that the Dutch had ruled Bali and the fierce pride and independence of the Balinese people themselves.

Japanese rule, brief as it was, was a period of increasing hardship, punctuated by torture and killings and the conscription of men for forced labor and women as sex slaves of the Japanese military. Although the Japanese had initially been welcomed as liberators, members of the Balinese upper class soon found themselves bearing the brunt of a campaign of terror designed to beat them into submission. Military requirements for rice and other products also dictated that the niceties of wooing the Balinese masses into devotion to the Japanese cause eventually gave way to harsher measures.

As the war dragged on and Japan's position became precarious, most Balinese suffered from serious shortages of all basic necessities. At the same time, Balinese youths were radicalized by being made to join paramilitary organizations with strong nationalistic overtones. When the Japanese surrendered, a few Balinese did welcome the Dutch back, but many others acted swiftly to seize the Japanese weapons and take up the struggle for independence. As the Dutch readied themselves to return with the triumphant Allied forces, preparations were made on Bali for a violent "welcome for the uninvited guests."

Bali's foremost revolutionary was Gusti Ngurah Rai, who led a brave but badly out-numbered and outgunned guerilla group before being defeated and killed. Bali then became the headquarters of the new State of Eastern Indonesia, which the Dutch hoped to later merge into a pro-Dutch federation. Even this state, under the leadership of the Gianyar ruler, Anak Agung Gede Agung (later Foreign Minister of the Republic), turned against the Dutch when they broke their treaty with the fledgling Republic, and so contributed to the achievement of independence, which the Indonesians declared in 1945 but which was not recognized by the Netherlands until 1949.

Mayhem and mass murder

Throughout the 1950s and early 1960s, social divisions that had crystallized during the Revolution continued to widen. Political conflicts and assassinations were rife, the key

Sukarno reads the proclamation of independence (Proklamasi Kemerdekaan) on 17 August 1945.

The 2002 terrorist bombings in Kuta killed over 200 people, most of them foreigners.

takeover of the government by pro-Western military leaders under General Suharto. In the wake of the events of September 30, a tidal wave of killings swept Java and Bali, as the military sought to dismantle the extensive structure of the PKI while rightist supporters turned this campaign into one of wholesale slaughter. An estimated 500,000 Indonesians died, and up to a fifth of them—five percent of the island's population at the time—may have been Balinese. Most Balinese have family or friends who were involved in the conflict in one way or another, but even now few will talk about it.

Bitter memories

Suharto emerged from the political storm as President of Indonesia. His "New Order" government first stabilized the country then ushered in a long period of relative peace and development, in sharp contrast to the chaotic Sukarno years that preceded it, providing basic health care, food, housing, and education to a rapidly growing population.

Over the past four decades Bali has played a key role in Indonesia's development. The tourist "paradise" begun by the Dutch has been updated and given modern form, providing a lucrative income for tens of thousands of Balinese and foreigner investors, and significant amounts of foreign exchange

split being between those who favored the old caste system and traditional values and those who rejected caste as a form of aristocratic "feudalism" designed to oppress the majority. By the mid-1960s the conflict had taken political form as a contest between the Indonesian Nationalist Party (PNI) and the Indonesian Communist Party (PKI). Attempts by the latter to organize a program of land reform exacerbated the already high level of rhetoric and bad feelings, and both sides organized rallies and pressed the Balinese to choose one side or the other.

On September 30, 1965, an unsuccessful leftist military putsch in Jakarta prompted a

Decades of tourism development have helped fuel the urbanization of southern Bali. Ubud—once a sleepy village—now has busy streets and traffic jams.

The advent of high-end resorts has brought previously unimaginable luxury to Bali.

for the nation. By the beginning of the 1990s, deregulation of the economy created uncontrollable growth in luxury hotels and other types of tourist developments. Local politicians continued to struggle with the national government, even after the fall of Suharto brought about greater local autonomy.

The downfall of the Suharto regime in 1998 inaugurated Indonesia's return to democracy. The Balinese had great hopes when Megawati, daughter of the first president and of Balinese heritage, became president in 2001, though for many her one-term presidency proved lackluster.

The first few years of this period of "Reformation" brought upheaval and opened the way for violent confrontation. On the night of October 12, 2002, two bombs exploded in the heart of Kuta's nightclub district, Bali's most popular tourist area. The effect of the blasts—the work of Islamist terrorists from outside Bali—was devastating, resulting in an appalling loss of life and a disastrous downturn in the economy. Three years later, in 2005, further terrorist attacks were staged in Jimbaran and Kuta, again bringing death and economic hardship. By the second decade of the 21st century, however, tourism had recovered and visitor numbers were higher than ever.

In 2004 Megawati was succeeded as Indonesian president by a Javanese ex-military officer, Susilo Bambang Yudhoyono (popularly known as SBY), subsequently reelected with a landslide majority in 2009. SBY oversaw impressive economic advances, and Indonesia weathered the storm of the 2008 global financial crisis with few problems. Also on SBY's watch the worst ethnic violence in outlying regions of Indonesia came to an end, and the terror groups behind the bombs in Bali were broken up.

Many difficulties still remain, of course, and SBY's successor—the former furniture salesman and sometime governor of Jakarta Joko Widodo, known as Jokowi, who was elected in 2014—inherited a raft of challenges, from entrenched corruption, parliamentary inefficiency, and a vocal extremist minority, to large-scale environmental degradation and the beginnings of an economic slow-down. Nevertheless, Bali continues to prosper as part of the world's third largest democracy. The importance of this mainly-Hindu island in such a complex, Muslim-majority state demonstrates Indonesia's ability to survive as a nation while successfully managing plurality.

—*Adrian Vickers & Tim Hannigan*

A Place of Communal Order

The Balinese village is a closely knit network of social, religious, and economic institutions to which every Balinese belongs. Most Balinese live in villages, yet even those who now reside and work in cities like Denpasar still identify with, and actively participate in, organizations and rituals in the village of their birth.

Spatial layout of the village

Spatial orientation plays an eminent role in all things Balinese. The most important points of reference are *kaja* ("upstream" or "toward the mountain") and *kelod* ("downstream" or "seawards"), although *kangin* (east), *kauh* (west) and the intermediary compass points are of almost equal importance. Note that *kaja* in south Bali lies to the north, whereas in north Bali, on the other side of the mountains, it refers to a southerly direction.

At the heart of every traditional Balinese village (*desa adat*) is the *kahyangan tiga*, the three core village temples that are physically located in close accordance with this system of orientation. Thus the *pura puseh* ("temple of origin") lies nearest the mountains, the *pura bale agung* ("temple of the great meeting hall") lies in the center of the village, and the *pura dalem* (temple of the not-yet-purified deceased and of magically charged and potentially dangerous forces) lies to the seaward side of the village.

Clustered around the *pura desa* ("village temple")—generally between the *pura puseh* and the *pura dalem*—lie the residential quarters of the village, known as *banjar*, sometimes translated as "hamlets" but actually comprising distinctive neighborhoods within the village. These are usually referred to as "eastern," "western," and "central," but are often named according to the dominant profession or caste of their residents. Thus, there are *banjar pande*, where smiths live, and *banjar brahmana*, where members of the *brahmana* caste predominate.

Each *banjar* has its own meeting hall (*bale banjar*), which is the secular counterpart of the *bale agung* temple. These *bale banjar* are the social centers of the community, today often equipped with ping pong tables and televisions and surrounded by small, portable food stalls in the late afternoon.

Each *banjar* is surrounded by rice fields and gardens. The outer boundaries of the village are usually clearly marked by hedges, valleys, streams, forests, and other natural features. There are many local and regional variations in village layout, often determined by topography and population density, but there is a common pattern for all.

The family compound

In stark contrast to the open social and religious spaces of the village, the family living quarters are enclosed and private. House compounds are surrounded by a wall and from the outside nothing much can be seen.

A family compound consists of several buildings whose location and function are strictly defined and spatially determined.

Typical Village Layout

Kaja ↑
'To the mountains'

Rice fields and gardens

↟
Pura Puseh

Bale Banjar ■

Pura Agung/
Pura Desa ↟

■ Bale Banjar

Rice fields and gardens

Kelod
'To the sea' ↓

↟ Pura Dalem

☐ Cemetery

Most Balinese still return to their home villages several times each year for communal ceremonies.

In the mountain-ward eastern corner of the compound lies the family temple. Also toward the mountains is the *bale gunung rata* or *meten bandung*, in which the parents and grandparents usually live.

The *bale dangin* or *bale gede* (the "east" or "great" pavilion) is where family ceremonies such as tooth filings and weddings are held, but the grandparents may also sleep here. Guests are normally received in the eastern pavilion. The western pavilion (*bale dauh*) is where children normally sleep. In the seaward or downhill section of the compound are the more mundane and functional structures: the kitchen (*paon*), rice granary (*lumbung*), pigsty, and the bathroom (if there is one).

It is within the house compound that a child is reared and integrated into the ways of village life with the help and care of parents, aunts and uncles, siblings and, most especially, the grandparents. Male children continue to live here; a girl moves to the compound of her in-laws when she marries.

Social and religious organization

The Balinese village may be said to be "semi-autonomous" in the sense that it is largely responsible for its own socio-religious affairs and yet still forms part of wider governmental and religious networks. The *desa adat* is the lowest administrative level of the state. A number of *desa adat* form a "sub-district" (*desa* or *perbekelan*), several of which form a district (*kecamatan*), which in turn make up the regency (*kabupaten*). The boundaries of the latter are for the most part identical with those of the former Balinese kingdoms.

The semi-autonomous status of the village creates the need for a dual village administration, a *kliang adat* or chief responsible for internal village affairs and a *kliang dinas* who is responsible to the regional government. Below these are several *banjar* chiefs.

The village is further characterized by the existence of numerous groupings, membership in which is only partially voluntary. Before marriage, a person is a member of the boys' or girls' club. These have specific duties in the context of village rituals and may be regarded as a "training ground" for the person's later participation in village affairs as a married adult. Upon marriage, a Balinese becomes a member of the neighborhood association (*banjar*), the village association, the irrigation society (*subak*), and several other groups, such as the local music club and the rice harvest association.

Every Balinese person thus lives within a complex matrix of interconnecting and overlapping associations. He or she has multiple duties to fulfill as members of these various institutions, as well as in the complex rounds of regional, village, and family-based ceremonies. It is due to the great complexity of these groups and their attendant support of the individual's personal identity that the village has retained its vital role as the focal point of Balinese life, even in the face of rapid modernization and change.

—*Danker Schaareman*

THE TEMPLE

A Sacred Space for God and Man

Above all, the Balinese temple is a sacred space in which the deities are honored with rituals and offerings. Whether a simple enclosure with only one or two tiny shrines or an elaborate complex with scores of sacred structures, the basic function of each temple is the same: to serve as a site where the Balinese pay reverence to the spiritual powers that play such a large role in their lives.

Temple types

There are literally tens of thousands of temples in Bali, and new ones are being constructed all the time. Throughout much of the year they lie eerily deserted, but on the date of their anniversary festival (*odalan*) they come to life in a brief but glorious burst of activity as the congregation adorns the temple with beautiful ornaments and arrives dressed in their finest apparel bearing elaborate gifts.

The English language has only one word for temple, but the Balinese distinguish two important types. A *sanggah* (*merajan* in the refined language) refers to private or family temples, generally translated as "house temples." Each family compound has one, containing shrines to the family's deified ancestors (*sanggah kamulan*). Thus there are several hundred thousand house temples in Bali. The other word for temple in Balinese is *pura*, originally a Sanskrit term referring to a town or palace.

On Bali, the word *pura* has come to refer to a temple in the public domain, generally located on public land. These cannot always be neatly classified, but there are generally three types associated with the three most important foci of social organization on Bali: locale, irrigation cooperative (*subak*) and descent group.

Within the group based on locality are temples of the local village, as well as temples with greater regional and island-wide significance. Irrigation cooperative temples can belong to a single *subak* or to a whole group of *subaks*. And within the group of temples based on descent are temples supported by "clans" of greater or lesser degrees of ancestral depth, variously known as *pura dadia*, *pura kawitan*, and *pura padharman*. Altogether there are at least 10,000 temples on Bali belonging to these various types.

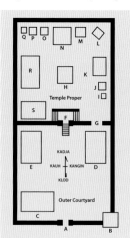

Ground plan of typical Balinese temple

A – Split gate, *candi bentar*
B – *Kulkul* tower
C – Kitchen, *paon*
D – *Balé gong*
E – *Balé* for pilgrims
F – Ceremonial gate, *padú raksa*
G – Side gate
H – *Paruman* or *pepelik*
I – *Ngrurah alit*
J – *Ngrurah gedé*

K – *Gedong pesimpangan*
L – *Padmasana*
M – *Gunung Agung*
N – *Meru*
O – *Gunung Batur*
P – *Maospahit* (*menjangan seluwang*)
Q – *Taksú*
R – *Balé piasan*
S – *Balé*

Offerings and prayers are made at many thousands of temples throughout Bali.

Three village temples of special significance are the *kahyangan tiga* ("three sanctuaries"): the *pura puseh* ("temple of origin"), at the upper end of the village, the *pura desa* ("village temple") or *pura bale agung* ("great meeting hall temple") in the village center, and the *pura dalem* (death temple or "temple of the mighty one") lying near the cemetery and cremation grounds at the lower or seaward end of the village. These temples are linked with the gods of the Hindu trinity: the *pura puseh* with Brahma the Creator, the *pura desa* with Wisnu (or Vishnu) the Preserver, and the *pura dalem* with Siva the Destroyer.

The famous temple sites that tourists visit are regional or island-wide temples. These include Besakih, the "Mother Temple" high up on the slopes of Mt. Agung, as well as the major temples Ulun Danu (Mt. Batur), Lempuyang, Goa Lawah, Uluwatu, Batukaru, Pusering Jagat (Pejeng), Andakasa, and Pucak Mangu. These are nearly all mountain or sea temples, marking the primary poles of the sacred landscape in Bali.

Lesser regional temples, numbering in the hundreds, are sometimes called *pura dang kahyangan*, or "temples of the Sacred Ones," because they are associated with legendary priests who brought Hinduism to Bali from Java. Their supporting congregations are drawn from a wide area, and in the past such temples were often supported by local princely houses. Nowadays, regional governments have taken on the same role. Important regional temples include Pura Sakenan, Pura Tanah Lot, Pura Kehen, Pura Taman Ayun and many others.

Shrines and pavilions

A temple may contain just one or two shrines within a small courtyard, or it may contain dozens of shrines and other structures within two, or often three, courtyards. The innermost courtyard is the most sacred. Shrines are usually located here in two rows, one lining the mountain (*kaja*) side and the other lining the eastern (*kangin*) side. Toward the center of the courtyard is a large structure where the gods gather during rituals. A variety of open pavilions complete the arrangement.

Among the shrines lining the mountainward side there is often a pair of small, closed shrines (*gedong*), one with an earthenware dish on its roof, the other with a pointed roof. These honor protective deities of the greatest importance: Dewi Sri, goddess of rice and prosperity, and her consort Rambut Sedana, god of wealth. A small shrine with a deer's head is called *menjangan saluwang* and honors the legendary priest Mpu Kuturan or a deity called Bhatara Maospahit.

A particularly striking structure is the *meru* or Balinese pagoda, which has an odd number of roofs, up to a maximum of 11. A *meru* honors a god or a deified ancestor, depending on what kind of temple it is. It was probably introduced from Java during the 14th century.

In the mountain-ward eastward corner, between the rows of shrines, there is often an open seat-type shrine. In its fully developed form, adorned with cosmic turtle and serpents, this is called a *padmasana* ("lotus throne") and honors the high god Sanghyang Widhi in his manifestation as Siva Raditya, the sun god. Modern Balinese Hinduism stresses its monotheistic aspect, and the *padmasana* has recently become more prominent.

Temple festivals are held according to one of two calendrical systems. When it appears on the 210-day *wuku* (Balinese) calendar, a festival is called an *odalan*; when it follows the lunar calendar, it is often referred to as an *usaba*. Various factors, such as local tradition and the size of the ritual, determine whether a festival is officiated by the temple's own priest (*pemangku*) or by a *brahmana* high priest (*pedanda*).

— David Stuart-Fox

BALINESE RELIGION

A Life of Ritual and Devotion

The majority of Balinese practice a form of the Hindu religion which they call *Agama Hindu Dharma* ("Religion of the Hindu doctrine"). Also called *Agama Tirtha* ("Religion of the Holy Waters"), it represents a unique amalgamation of foreign Hindu and Buddhist elements that were grafted onto a base of preexisting, indigenous religious customs. After Indonesia declared independence in 1945, the Balinese became more self-conscious of their religion and strengthened their religious organization. This resulted in the establishment of the Satya Hindu Dharma in 1956 and the Parisada Hindu Dharma Bali in 1959. The state philosophy, Pancasila, also had an impact on Balinese Hinduism as well.

Hinduism and Buddhism arrived in Bali partly via Java and partly direct from India between the 8th and 16th centuries. Elements

Villagers are blessed with sprinkled holy water during a temple anniversary celebration

of the two religions have developed further and merged here. The Indian division into four castes was adopted, and religious practices are closely connected with social hierarchy. Balinese society is separated into four main groups: *brahmana, satriya, wesya* and *anak jaba* or *sudra,* which are in turn subdivided into many more.

Basic principles

Balinese Hinduism encompasses a vast range of practices and doctrines, dominated by Siva-type characteristics. Siva is the main god, manifesting himself as Surya, the Sun. Buddhistic elements in the Balinese *Hindu Dharma* derive from a Tantric form of Mahayana Buddhism (the main branch of Buddhism, practiced in China, Tibet, Korea, and Japan). Only small groups of Balinese Buddhists exist today, mainly Brahmans living in Budakling village in Karangasem Regency. However in Banjar, in northwest Bali, a Buddhist monastery is strongly influenced by Theravada Buddhism (practiced today in Sri Lanka, Burma and Thailand).

The three basic principles of the Hindu religion are knowledge of the epics (the *Mahabharata, Ramayana* and commentaries), knowledge of philosophy and theology, and ritual worship (*puja*) connected with devotion (*bakti*) and offerings (*banten*). The central questions in Balinese Hindu philosophy are: where from and where to? Where does humanity come from, how can we attain release? In which offspring will he or she reincarnate? What is the origin of the cosmos, and how should one behave to guarantee the continuation of cosmic processes? These questions and their answers can be expressed in visual symbols, such as a mountain with a tree of life, a lotus pond, or a heavenly nymph.

The stability of the cosmos is expressed by emphasizing the quadrants of the compass and their colors, and the gods with their mounts and attributes. Oppositions like creation-annihilation, good-bad, heaven-earth, and fire-water are visualized in the nadir and the zenith. The swastika, wheel of the sun, is the symbol for the Hindu religion in general and shows the perpetual cycle of life.

The five ritual categories

The purpose of every ritual is to cleanse objects and people. Holy water, fire, and ash can all be used. This can also be done by rubbing or touching with objects symbolizing purity—for instance eggs, geese, ducks, and leaves of the *dapdap* tree. It is believed that one's soul may have accumulated impurities through evil deeds during one's life or previous lives, resulting in punishment in hell followed by rebirth as a miserable creature. In order to avoid this, the deceased and his or her soul must be purified by means of fire (the cremation) and holy water. A soul that has been released becomes a god (*bhatara*).

All Balinese rituals—tooth-filings, cock-fights, cremations, and others—can be held only on specific occasions according to the Balinese calendar. In all, there are literally hundreds of rites and festivals that each person participates in during his lifetime, and a great deal of time and expense is devoted to them.

Yadnya is a term of Sanskrit derivation meaning "worship" or "sacrificial rite" that is collectively applied to all Balinese ceremonies. Each rite may have any number of meanings ascribed to it, but all serve to create a sense of wellbeing and of community, both of which are important concepts to the Balinese. They are also a means of maintaining a delicate balance among the various forces in the Balinese cosmos. The Balinese themselves distinguish five ritual categories, the *panca yadnya*.

Ritual exorcisms

The first of these, the *bhuta yadnya*, are rites carried out to appease the spirits of chaos, personified in the form of ogres, witches, and demons, and to cleanse humanity and their surroundings from those influences. Ritual offerings known as *pacaruan* are set out by the women of the household every 15 days to appease and banish these baleful influences from the house compound.

An annual *pacaruan* offering ritual on a much larger scale, the Tawur Agung, is carried out on the day before Nyepi, the Balinese "New Year." Its aim is the purification of an area from the bad influences that have

A high priest performs a tooth filing ritual

accumulated during the previous year. The rite is usually carried out at a crossroads, supervised by a *pedanda* high priest. Five sorts of fluids are used: water, *arak* (palm liquor), palm wine, rice wine, and blood. Blood is thought to be one of the most purifying ingredients and in most cases has been taken from a cock which has been killed during a ritual cockfight. Afterwards, men carry torches through the village and make a huge commotion beating gongs and bamboo tubes to expel the demonic forces. Simultaneously young men carry ornate papier-mâché *ogoh-ogoh* or demon images through the streets, which are subsequently burned at the night's end, symbolically extinguishing their negative energies. The same is done in every house compound, without the *ogoh-ogoh*.

More elaborate exorcisms are undertaken once in five, ten, 25, and 100 years. The elaborate Panca Wali Krama rites at Besakih temple. The greatest ritual exorcism of them all—the Eka Dasa Rudra purification of the universe, which is held only once every century—was most recently celebrated in Bali's "Mother Temple" in 1979 to mark the transition to the Saka year 1900.

Rites of passage

The *manusa yadnya*, or life cycle rites, are designed to ensure a person's spiritual and material wellbeing. From conception until after death a person is believed to be in the company of the "four companions" (*kanda empat*). After birth these are expressed as personifications of the amniotic fluid, the blood, the *vernix caseosa*, and the afterbirth. The latter is buried by the entrance of the sleeping house and covered with a river stone. The umbilical cord is often kept in a little silver box hung around the baby's neck.

Entire villages regularly stage elaborate offerings, processions and performances.

The companions will protect if treated well; if not, they may create problems.

Twelve days after birth the ceremonial cutting of the navel string occurs. At this time the child is given a temporary "baby-sitter," a deity called Dewa Kumara. This deity is instructed by his father, Siva, to protect the baby until its first tooth appears. A small shrine next to the child's bed is hung with flowers and bananas as an offering for the protecting spirit.

Forty-two days after birth, a ceremony is held to cleanse the mother, who is thought to be impure after birth. On this day also the natural force of a "brother/sister," which has accompanied the baby since birth departs, and the child is now considered to be fully human. Another ceremony is held three months after birth to consolidate the baby's body and soul. At this time, the child's official name is announced, and he or she may touch the earth for the first time.

After 210 days, the baby's first "birthday" or *otonan* is celebrated. The hair is cut for the first time and the mother makes an offering in the village temple to announce that her child has arrived in the village.

In some communities, the onset of puberty is celebrated by a ritual held in the house, followed by the young person involved being paraded around the streets to announce their new status. This is held for girls on the occasion of her first menstruation; for boys when his voice changes. The next major ceremony occurs as the child reaches the end of puberty. This is the well known "tooth filing" ceremony whose aim is to symbolically eradicate the animal or "wild" nature in a person symbolized by the six enemies: greed, lust, drunkenness, anger, envy, and confusion. During the ceremony, the six central upper canine teeth are filed down slightly. A

communal responsibility, taking place during temple anniversaries either once every 210 days of the *wuku* year, or once in a lunar-solar year of 360 days. The gods or divine ancestors are then invited to come down to earth and reside in their temples. For at least three days they are feasted and regaled with offerings, music, dance, and hymns. Priests perform the rituals to summon the gods; those who support the temple pay their homage.

Apart from these anniversaries, major temple festivals are held on Galungan and Kuningan, two holy days according to the Balinese calendar. Another important festival is Tumpek Uduh — held every 210 days — when useful trees and garden plants are honored with offerings. On this day no tree may be cut or fruits taken. In a similar way, rituals are performed for household and agricultural tools and other objects made out of metal on Tumpek Landep, for domesticated animals on Tumpek Kandang, and for puppets and performing arts objects on Tumpek Wayang.

Ritual worship is supervised by specialists: the priests. Their main task is to prepare holy water for the believers. People of higher castes cannot receive holy water from priests belonging to a lower caste. The highest and most distinguished priests are the Brahman *pedanda*, who can offer holy water to any person, because they occupy the highest rung in the social hierarchy. Members of the *satriya dalem* and *wesya* castes may use priests from their own class, the *resi*, but they prefer a *pedanda*. The Pasek, Sengguhu, Pande and Bali Aga groups all have their own priests as well, but being so low in the hierarchy, they can only offer holy water to members of their own group.

The *resi yadnya* are rituals to ordain priests. To be ordained as a *pedanda*, a Brahman must study with a high priest for many years. A ritual ordination, or *padiksan*, is then organized for him by the family with the help of other villagers. During the ritual, the candidate undergoes a symbolic death and cremation. Thereafter, he is "reborn" as a pure man. After his ordination, his guru continues to act as his advisor, and it is only after another year of study that he is able to perform rituals on his own. Male priests are consecrated along with their wives, meaning the wife may take over the priesthood after the death of her husband.

— *Hedi Hinzler & Ida Ayu Agung Mas*

person should now behave as an adult, able to control his or her emotions.

Full adulthood begins after marriage, and the person is then treated as a full-fledged member of the community. If the child is the eldest or youngest son, he will replace his father in carrying out certain village duties.

Completing the cycle and returning the soul safely to the other world are the *pitra yadnya* or ceremonies for the dead (see "The Ceremony Cremation"). After death, the soul of the deceased joins the ancestors and is worshipped with the gods in special shrines within the house compound. The hope is to regularly communicate with one's ancestors, and every Balinese has a sense of wellbeing, knowing he or she is protected by them.

Rites for gods and priests

Dewa yadnya ceremonies are performed to honor the divinities. Such ceremonies are a

THE CREMATION CEREMONY

The Pitra Yadnya Rites for Ancestors

L ife, death, rebirth. This cyclical conception of existence lies at the very heart of Balinese Hinduism. During each life on earth the eternal soul occupies a temporary vessel—the physical body—which at death must be returned to the *pancamahabhuta*, the five elemental substances: solid, liquid, radiance, energy, and ether. Only then can the soul be released and reincarnated. Of all Balinese rituals, the cremation (*pangabenen, palebon*) is the most complex, lasting for many days and culminating with the spectacular burning of not only the corpse, but of vast quantities of valuable ritual objects especially created for the occasion.

Calling the soul

Due to the huge amount of time and expense involved, a cremation is usually postponed for months or even years. In the meantime the body of the deceased is temporarily buried. Family members first wash and groom the corpse, then wrap it in cloths and mats. A raw egg is rolled across it and smashed to the ground, removing all impurities. The body is then transported to the cemetery on a simple bier and buried without a casket.

Once a favorable day has been set, an army of ritual specialists, artists, priests, family members, friends, and neighbors of all ages and sexes is mobilized, calling upon an encyclopedia of communal knowledge in the creation of offerings of every imaginable shape, color, and ingredient and the performance of a series of elaborate rites.

Before cremation a "soul calling" ritual must be held at the grave. Offerings are made, and as the corpse cannot be returned to the house once it has been buried, the soul is taken home in a *sangah urip* effigy containing soil from the grave. Outside the house a paper and coconut shell lamp—a *damar kurung*—is hung to guide the soul home.

The washing of the corpse is symbolically repeated on an *adegan*, a small board with a human figure drawn on it. The day before the cremation, a priest prays for favorable treatment of the soul in the afterlife. Various types

Cremations are expensive affairs: bodies may be buried for years until families can afford one.

of holy water are made and offerings are purified. The *angenan*, an eggshell lamp mounted on a decorated coconut, serves as a memorial.

The procession

On the day of the cremation, once the sun has passed the zenith, loud gong music is played and a lively procession starts the journey to the cemetery. Dozens of offerings and ritual objects lead the way, and the body is carried in a colorful tower (*wadah, bade*) fashioned of wood, bamboo, and paper, shouldered by scores of shouting men. Platforms at the base represent the earth, sometimes resting on the cosmic turtle and serpents of the underworld. On the back of the tower may be a winged and fanged face of the son of the earth, and higher up a goose symbolizing purity.

Above these platforms is an open space for the body, and crowning the tower is an odd number of roofs representing the heavens. The caste and clan of the deceased determine the number: 11 for royalty, less for persons of more humble birth. Attached to the front of the tower is a long, white cloth (*lantaran*) held by family members to represent their ties to the deceased. The tower is rotated at each crossroads to disorient and prevent the soul from returning to disturb the living.

Release through fire and water

Arriving at the cemetery, the body is taken down and a pair of birds set free, symbolic of the soul's release. On a bamboo platform under a high roof stands a wooden sarcophagus (called a *patulangan* or *palinggihan*) decorated with cloth and paper, sometimes carried in procession ahead of the tower. The sarcophagus is generally in the shape of a mythical animal such as a bull or winged lion.

The sarcophagus is opened and the body or newly exhumed remains (sometimes simply an effigy) are carried around it and placed inside. The shroud is opened; jars of holy water are poured over the body and shattered. Cloths, letters of introduction to the gods, and effigies are piled inside, and the sarcophagus is closed. Offerings are placed below to start the fire, and the sarcophagus and corpse are consumed by flames. The tower is burned separately.

Death brings with it the opportunity to fulfill all duties toward the deceased, and there is no public display of mourning if the deceased has lived a long and full life. Weeping near a corpse disturbs the soul, making it unwilling to leave. Grief is

A cremation tower holds the body of the deceased so that its soul may ascend to heaven.

expressed in private, however, especially if a young person has died prematurely as the result of serious illness or a tragic accident.

Purification and deification

When the corpse has finally been reduced to ashes, the flames are doused and the family hunts for bone fragments, forming them into a small human shape. The bones are pulverized and placed in an effigy made from a coconut, which is taken on a bier to the sea or river and cast into the waters. Three days later another ceremony removes the ritual pollution brought by death upon the living.

Twelve days after the cremation, the soul of the deceased is purified in a *ngrorasin* rite, often accompanied by rituals (*mukur, nyekah, ngasti, maligia*) designed to deify the ancestor. A *sekah* effigy is made for the soul and placed in a high pavilion. In the evening, family members pray and offer their respects. Early the next morning, the image is broken and burned, and the ashes placed in a decorated coconut. A tower (*bukur, madhya*) then transports them to the sea for disposal.

Finally, in the *nyagara-gunung* ceremony, the family expresses thanks to the gods of the oceans and the mountains. Offerings are brought to important sea and mountain temples, often including Besakih, after which the deified soul is enshrined in a clan or family temple as a protective ancestral spirit.

—*Garrett Kam*

THE TRADITIONAL BALINESE CALENDAR

A Cycle of Holy Days and Anniversaries

Except in a number of once-isolated mountain villages and ancient court centers, most of Bali follows both a 12-month lunar calendar and a 210-day ritual cycle. Together these two parallel calendrical systems determine the incredibly complex and busy schedule of holy days and anniversaries observed throughout the island, with many important festivals being determined by the conjunction of particular dates in the two systems. Every day also has associated with it numerous auspicious and malevolent forces that must be considered when selecting dates for everything from construction to cremation.

Two parallel systems

The lunar calendar, similar to that used in parts of India, is based upon phases of the moon. Each 29- to 30-day lunar month (*sasih*) begins on the day after a new moon (*tilem*), with the full moon (*purnama*) occurring in the middle.

Twelve lunar *sasih* months comprise a normal year, with an intercalary 13th month added every two or three years to keep it synchronized with the longer solar year. The years are numbered from the founding of the Indian Saka Dynasty in A.D. 78, so that the year 1900 in Bali began in 1979.

The 210-day *pawukon* cycle, on the other hand, is indigenously Balinese, and its repetitions are not numbered or recorded as years. It may have had its roots in the growing period for rice, but the following Oedipal myth is associated with it as well. A woman discovers that her husband is in fact her own son, who ran away as a child. Vain with power, he challenges the gods but is defeated; 27 children by his mother and aunt are sacrificed. The 30 weeks (*wuku*) of the calendar are named after these characters.

The 210 days of the *pawukon* "year" are divided into many shorter cycles, which run concurrently. The most important of these are the three- (Pasah, Beteng/Tegeh, Kajeng), five- (Umanis, Paing, Pon, Wage, Kliwon) and seven-day "weeks," whose conjunctions

determine most holy days. Each day has its own deity, constellation and omen that indicate good or bad times for a variety of activities.

The *pawukon* year is also subdivided into 35-day "months" (*bulan*) determined by a complete cycle of five- and seven-day weeks. Each date in the *pawukon* calendar is referred to according to the combination of days in the various weeks, for example: Kajeng Kliwon Menail, Anggarkasih Dukut, Buda Cemeng Ukir. The passage of six *bulan*, a full *pawukon* year, marks a birthday (*otonan*) or anniversary (*rahinan, odalan*).

Sasih holy days

Purnama and *tilem* in the *sasih* calendar are for praying and making offerings, a time when rituals and sacred dances are held in many temples. Temple anniversaries (*odalan*) often take place on the full moon. Siwalatri, the "Night of Siva," falls on the eve of the new moon of the seventh *sasih*, in January. On this night many Balinese meditate, sing classical poetry and keep all-night vigils in temples of the dead.

The days immediately before the start of the lunar new year are especially full of activity. Processions of offerings and loud gong music accompany the icons of every temple to the coast for a ritual cleansing (*malasti, makiis, malis*). On the eve of the new year, demon-appeasing sacrifices are held everywhere. That night, a great commotion is made to chase demons away, sometimes accompanied by torch processions of huge bamboo and paper monsters (*ogoh-ogoh*).

The next day is Nyepi, literally "the day of silence," when Bali appears completely deserted. No fires are lit or electricity used, visiting and entertainment are not permitted, and people stay at home to meditate. This continues until the following morning, when normal activity resumes.

Pawukon holy days

Kajeng Kliwon is the only significant conjunction of the three- and five-day weeks. Offerings are placed at house entrances to bar demonic forces. Ceremonies and sacred dances are held at temples, many of which celebrate an *odalan* anniversary. On Anggarkasih, when Tuesday coincides with Kliwon, household offerings are made to safeguard its members, and many temple *odalans* take place.

The influence of Buddhism can be seen in the holy days falling on Buda or Wednesday. Buda Umanis is a very auspicious day for ceremonies. Buda Cemeng is a day for praying and meditating. Buda Kliwon is often a particularly holy day, when prayers and offerings are made to ensure the blessings of the gods.

Pagerwesi falls on Wednesday of the week Sinta and means "Iron Fence," a time when humanity must stand firm to protect the world and its creatures. Rituals begin two days before and prayers are said for the continued wellbeing of the universe.

Galungan and Kuningan

The days between Galungan (Wednesday of the week Dunggulan) and Kuningan (Saturday of the week Kuningan) are full of celebrations. Kuningan marks the end of a series of festivals. This 42-day holy period is based on an ancient harvest festival, and it is still forbidden to begin planting at this time.

Each day before Galungan is marked by a special activity: ripening fruits, making offerings and slaughtering animals. Temples are cleaned and decorated for the upcoming visit of the ancestral spirits. On Galungan eve, *penjor* bamboo poles are set up in front of every house and temple, arcing over roads with flowers, fruits and palm leaf ornaments hanging from them, symbols of fertility.

Nearby altars for offerings are decorated with *lamak* scrolls of delicate palm-leaf cutouts as welcome mats for the ancestors. On Galungan day, prayers are intoned, people visit and feasts are held. *Barongs* dance from house to house and receive donations in return for their blessings. On Kuningan day, new offerings and decorations are put out and tools are honored. — *Garrett Kam*

A pelelintingan, *or traditional astrological chart*

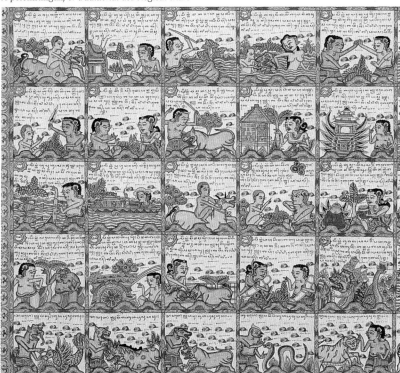

A Rich Literary Heritage

Three languages are spoken on Bali: Balinese and its dialects, Indonesian, and a kind of Old Javanese called Kawi. Contacts with Hindu-Buddhist Java between the 9th and 16th centuries exerted a strong influence on the language and literature of Bali. Later contacts with Muslim Java, Blambangan and Lombok between the 17th and 19th centuries also left their traces. The Indonesian language, which derives from Malay, is used in schools, in the mass media, and as the *lingua franca* of commerce and government, has also had a great impact on the Balinese language.

Standard Balinese uses different levels, each with its own set of parallel vocabulary, to indicate the caste or status of the speaker vis-à-vis the person spoken to. There are three main levels: *alus* (high), *kasar* (low) and *mider* (middle). This means that a low caste person uses formal high Balinese words in speaking to a person of higher status, while the latter will reply using the low vocabulary. Only several hundred words are covered by these parallel vocabularies, but they tend to be the most commonly used ones.

Indonesian is spoken and taught at school, and children from six years onwards are thus brought up bilingually with a stress on Indonesian. Additionally, intellectuals and many Balinese parents in towns like Denpasar and Tabanan consider it more fashionable to speak only Indonesian. As a result, knowledge of formal or "high" Balinese among the younger generation is declining.

Kawi is now mainly a literary language, surviving in spoken form only in the theater. Heroes representing high caste characters from the classical literature express themselves in Kawi, but it is only understood by a few specialists, by *dalangs* (puppet masters) and by some of the older people in the audience.

Courtly literary genres

Much of the diversity displayed by Balinese literature today has historical roots. Written sources can be found in the following languages on Bali: Sanskrit, Old Balinese, Old Javanese, Middle Javanese, Balinese, Sasak (from Lombok), Malay, and Indonesian.

Sanskrit was used in royal edicts dating from the ninth to the 11th centuries and still today in hymns (*stuti, stawa*) recited by priests. There are many Sanskrit loanwords in Old Javanese, Balinese, and Indonesian. Old Balinese was used in edicts issued between A.D. 882 and the early 10th century.

A sample of traditional Balinese Kawi writing, based on the Pallava script from southern India

Makasami manusane kaembasin mahardika lan pateh. sajeroning kahanan lan kuasa. ipun kanugrahin wiweka lan budi. pantaraning manusa mangdane paras-paros masemetonan.

By the end of the 10th century, when close links were established with east Java, Old Javanese was used in the inscriptions, and it is likely that Javanese literature came to Bali at this time also. Ironically, while Old Javanese is still known and used in Bali, it has all but disappeared on Java. Poems and prose works on religion, grammar, metrics, magic, medicine, history, and genealogy are still being produced there in Old Javanese.

During the culturally rich Gelgel period (1550–1600), the kings of Bali kept Balinese or Javanese scribes in their service who wrote in Middle Javanese and introduced a whole new genre of laudatory poems on the beauty of women (the queen in particular) or the death of a beloved. They also produced works on politics and ancient history to legitimize the position of the king.

Later east Javanese literature, including stories of Muslim knights such as the Menak and Kidung Juarsa tales, became known in Bali in the 17th century. When Karangasem took control of western Lombok at the end of the 18th century, Sasak literature was brought to eastern Bali as well. Many Sasak words occur in poems in Karangasem.

As Balinese nobles formed their own independent courts and became more powerful around 1700, they began to sponsor works of court literature. Brahman authors were very popular, probably because they knew Old Javanese and were well-versed in religion, politics, and the classical literature. The language of these new *kidung* poems was Old Javanese with many Balinese elements added.

A new genre of poetry (Geguritan or Parikan)—epic histories and love stories about Balinese kings, princes, and heroes written in Balinese—developed at the end of the 18th century. Folktales, riddles and rhymes were also noted in Balinese from the end of the 19th century onwards.

When the Dutch began their conquest of Bali early in the 20th century, at a time when the Balinese themselves were constantly at war, a new genre came into being: poetry about the devastation (*rusak* or *uug*) of a realm.

Most works of Old Javanese and Balinese literature are anonymous. The manuscripts consist of *lontar* palm leaves, prepared and cut to size (usually 3.5–4.5 cm high and 35–50 cm long), and then bound together by means of a string run through perforations in the center or the left hand side of the leaves.

The Balinese language has different vocabularies that are used in more or less formal situations.

An iron stylus is used to inscribe them and the lines are then blackened with soot. Other illustrated manuscripts also date from the late 19th and beginning of the 20th centuries.

For the most part, Balinese literature is not meant to be read silently but should be sung and recited, for example during rituals and in theater performances. Certain passages are sung or adapted for the *wayang* (shadow puppet play) or the stage. There are also special clubs (*seka bebasan*) devoted to the singing and recitation of poems.

New ideas, new language

With the increase of Western influence during the 1920s and 1930s, many Balinese, especially the Brahmans, came to feel that the local population was becoming alienated from their religion and culture. To counter this, they composed religious treatises in Balinese. Dissertations on Balinese script, grammar, and language were also produced under the influence of Dutch scholarship.

After the Indonesian Revolution against the Dutch, Balinese authors began to write novels in Indonesian, and later also poetry, and a Balinese literary movement came into being. The Balai Penelitian Bahasa library, now based in Denpasar, began a Balinese folktale series in 1978.

In the 21st century, the local newspaper, *The Bali Post*, its broadcast counterpart, *Bali TV*, and other competitors such as *Dewata TV* all have sections and programs made completely in Balinese. Even though Indonesian is spoken by nearly all segments of the population, Balinese is still the main language heard on the streets. —*Hedi Hinzler*

BALINESE FOOD

Everyday Fare and Ritual Feasts

N *gajeng! or Makan!* (meaning "Eat!" in Balinese and Indonesian respectively) are expressions often heard when passing people in Bali who are enjoying their food. In fact, this is not an invitation to join the meal, but rather an apology for eating when the passerby is not. It is a reflection of a strong sense of community found on Bali and of the great cultural importance attached to food and eating.

Basic ingredients

The staple food of Bali is white, polished rice. Nowadays cooked rice (*nasi*) is of the fast-growing "Green Revolution" variety found everywhere in Asia. The traditional Balinese rice (*beras Bali*) tastes better and is more aromatic, but is restricted to a few areas and is now mainly used as a ritual food. Other, less frequently grown varieties are red rice (*beras barak*), black rice (*ketan injin*), sticky rice (*ketan*) and a variety (*padi gaga*) grown in non-irrigated fields in the mountains. Rice consumption averages 0.5 kg or 1.1 lb per day.

Many local vegetables grow in a semi-wild state. These include the leaves of several trees and shrubs, varieties of beans (including soybeans), water spinach (*kangkung*), the bulbs and leaves of the cassava plant, sweet potatoes and maize. The flower and trunk of the banana tree, young jackfruits (*nangka*), breadfruits (*sukun* and *timbul*) and papayas may also be cooked as vegetables. Foreign vegetables such as cabbage and tomatoes are now also commonly found.

Though they form a major part of the diet, vegetables are considered low-status; high status foods are rice and meat. Because it is expensive, however, meat is reserved for ritual occasions. Like their Hindu counterparts in India, many Balinese do not eat beef. Surprisingly, fish plays a relatively minor role as a source of protein; though the seas surrounding Bali are rich, the Balinese are not avid fishermen.

The distinctive flavor of Balinese cuisine derives from a *sambal* condiment and spice mixtures. A standard mixture will include shallots, garlic, ginger, turmeric, galangal, and red chilli peppers ground together in varying proportions depending on the recipe.

*Satay (*sate*) is ubiquitous throughout Indonesia, and the Balinese have their own versions.*

A distinctive flavor is also imparted by strong-smelling shrimp paste (*terasi*) and chopped *cekuh* root.

The usual drink served with Balinese food is water or tea. Apart from this, there are three traditional alcoholic drinks, drops of which are sprinkled onto the earth during rituals to appease the *bhuta* or negative forces. *Tuak* (or *sajeng*) is a mild beer made from the juice of palm sap. Before the flowers bloom, the sap is tapped in the afternoon, the juice gathered overnight in a suspended container, and the next morning it is collected and the fresh juice is ready to drink. To ferment it, it is either left to set a bit longer or other ingredients, such as the bark of certain trees, are added.

Arak or *sajeng rateng* ("straight *sajeng*") is a 60–100 proof liquor distilled from palm or rice wine. It is basically colorless, but may have a slight tint from the addition of ginger, ginseng, turmeric, or cloves. Visitors should be aware that "fire *arak*" or *arak api*, which is sold locally is sometimes mixed with dubious ingredients (notably, and most dangerously, methanol) to make it more potent, which has resulted in a number of deaths.

Brem is a sweet, mildly fermented wine made from red or white sticky rice. Yeast is added to the cooked rice, which is wrapped, and after about a week liquid squeezed from it is ready to drink.

Everyday fare

Upon waking around 5 or 6 am each morning, the typical Balinese woman goes to the kitchen to boil water for the morning coffee and cook rice and other dishes for the day. Cooking is done only once and the food is then eaten cold throughout the day. Breakfast in most cases consists only of coffee and fried bananas or rice cookies. Some Balinese eat small portions of rice with vegetables, often bought in a nearby *warung* (kiosk).

When the woman has finished cooking, she will prepare a number of small banana leaf mats on which she places rice and other foods. These are then offered to the gods, placed in the house shrines, on the ground by the entrance gateway, and in front of all buildings in the compound. Only after this has been done can the main meal of the day commence, usually at about 11 am. A smaller evening meal is had between 5 and 7 pm, just before or after dark.

It is quite unusual for a family to sit and eat together, in sharp contrast to ritual meals,

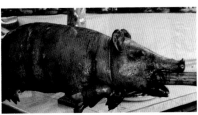

Babi guling *(spit-roast pig) is a Balinese specialty.*

which stress togetherness. Everyday meals are taken in private; one goes into the kitchen, takes what is there and retreats to a quiet place to eat alone, more or less in a hurry, with the right hand. Nothing is drunk with meals; afterward there is lukewarm tea or plain water to rinse the mouth and hand.

Everyday meals consist of rice, one or two vegetable dishes, *sambal*, peanuts, grated coconut with turmeric and spices, and perhaps a small piece of fried fish bought in a nearby *warung*. Usually, the same meal is eaten several times, and in general there is not much variation from day to day.

Vegetables are cooked with coconut milk and spices and served dry or with plenty of broth. Cooked maize with grated coconut and sugar, boiled sweet potatoes, fried bananas, and rice cookies are popular snacks. *Rujak*, a plate of raw fruits mixed with lots of chillies, shrimp paste and/or palm sugar, is also popular.

Ritual feasts

Special ritual foods are prepared for each ceremony by the family or community involved. Villagers contribute materials and labor, and the dishes are prepared in the temple's own kitchen. Usually there is a strict division of labor. Men slaughter and butcher the pigs, mix the spices, grate the coconuts, and prepare the *sate* (meat skewers) and other dishes such as blood soup and pork tartar, usually very early in the morning (between 3 and 5 am). Women cook the rice and prepare vegetable offerings, which may be consumed after their consecration.

Each village or area has its own ritual cooking specialists who direct the work. There is a great deal of local variation in dishes, and people from different regions can spend hours discussing differences in traditional foods. For instance, the ritual meat dishes from Gianyar are said to be "sweet" while those from Karangasem are "hard" or "biting."
—*Danker Schaareman*

Cloths of Great Power and Artistry

Indonesia enjoys an enviable reputation as a veritable paradise for textile connoisseurs. On Bali, as elsewhere in the archipelago, traditional textiles are much more than simply decorative pieces of cloth. To the Balinese they represent a mark of cultural identity and religious exclusivity, while the use of certain cloths also convey subtle differences of birth, age, sex, title and caste. Traditional fabrics also serve many sacred and ritual functions, distinguishing the holy from the profane and the good from the evil.

Humans are not the only ones who wear clothes; the Balinese cover with fabric almost everything which possesses a head, a body and feet. Buildings, shrines, altars, ancestor stones, and statues are all wrapped in costly

A Balinese bride is dressed like royalty.

or magically permeated apparel during rituals. The cotton yarns are said to bring strength to both men and objects, protecting them and warding off harmful influences. Red, white and black threads when braided together are called *tridatu* and when these colors are combined, the wearer is protected from the spirits of chaos, particularly those that visit Bali during the sixth month of the Balinese calendar, when disease is more rampant due to the rains.

The ritual wardrobe

The ritual or *adat* wardrobe of the Balinese consists of several lengths of cloth of various sizes. These are not tailored, but are used in the form in which they are woven, and then draped artfully around the body. Boys and men wrap a large skirt (*kamben* or *wastra*) around themselves and tie it in such a way that a long fold hangs down in front between the legs, nearly touching the ground. Girls and women wrap their bodies below the waist clockwise as tightly as possible.

In some rituals, an inner cloth is wound around the body as an undergarment (*tapih* or *sinjang*). A *kamben* or *wastra*, which can extend down to the ankles, is then wrapped over the undergarment. The end is tucked in at the waist near the left hip, and the *kamben* is generally secured by a narrow sash wound around the body several times.

Tube skirts (*sarung*) do not belong to the traditional wardrobe, though imported Javanese cloths with batik patterns are commonly used as *kamben*. During the past few years, Balinese woven *ikat* cloth from Gianyar, Sidemen, Singaraja, and Bayan (East Lombok) have increasingly come into use.

A smaller sash, known as *saput* or *kampuh*, is wound round the hips or the chest by boys and men, falling approximately to the knees. The belt (*umpal*) attached to the end of this cloth is wrapped around the body and knotted below the upper edge of the *saput*. Another type of sash, known as *sabuk*, is generally so long that it is wrapped once around the body and then knotted. Men also wear a graceful head cloth, sometimes in the form of a little boat-shaped hat (*destar* or *udeng*).

Women's outer garments consist of a long band similiar to a belt (*sabuk, setagen*) holding the skirt together and a breast-cloth (*anteng*) wrapped tightly around the upper part of the body. Sometimes a part of the *anteng* will be draped over one shoulder. In former times, women also wore loose shoulder sashes (*selendang*).

Until the 1930s, Balinese women were usually naked above the waist in everyday situations, but they always covered the upper parts of their bodies when bringing offerings to the temple or taking part in festive court events. Even though traditional bare-shouldered dresses are still seen at temple feasts and family rituals, this has now been replaced in many parts of Bali by long-sleeved, lacy *kebayas* from Java, which are now considered part of the national dress. In the 21st century, most women wear a tube top of similar color to their *kebaya* underneath, providing a modicum of modesty under these often transparent blouses.

Traditional textile forms

The art of Balinese textile decoration is best expressed in men's skirt, chest, and head cloths, and women's chest and skirt cloths. There are three distinguishable categories, the first comprising cloths decorated with gold leaf, called *prada*, traditionally produced for royalty and still used by girls and boys during tooth-filing and marriage ceremonies. The outlines of the design are first drawn on the cloth and coated with glue before applying the gold leaf. Stylized blossoms, plants, and birds are the most common motifs, and the edges of the cloth are often decorated with intertwined swastikas, the symbol of Balinese Hinduism. Other pieces show a distinct Chinese influence.

A second group just as brilliant and expensive as the *prada* cloths are the Balinese *songket* brocades. Supplemental gold- and silver-colored weft threads are added for decoration when these cloths are on the loom. The range of patterns extends from simple crosses and stars to elaborate compositions with trees, vines, flowers, and snakes as well as stories from the *Ramayana* and *Mahabarata* epics.

Gold painted prada *cloth is used for important ritual occasions.*

From a historical point of view, the production of brocaded fabrics with ornamental wefts of gold and silver was for centuries the exclusive preserve of the higher castes. Today, Brahman women, along with wives and daughters in the princely *satriya dalem* and *satriya jaba* families, continue to show considerable skill in this art. Centers of *songket* production are still found in the aristocratic and brahmanical neighborhoods Karangasem (Amlapura and Sidemen), Buleleng (Bubunan and Bratan), Klungkung (Gelgel) and Jembrana (Negara).

In 1980, the then-governor of Bali, Professor Ida Bagus Mantra, appealed to his fellow citizens to employ Balinese textiles in their ceremonial dress. Apart from promoting village crafts and encouraging the development of the Balinese economy, it had the effect of reducing the role of these textiles as aristocratic symbols. Thereafter, anyone of a certain position or wealth was able to flaunt their *songket* publicly at religious and social events. As a result, the demand for *songket* cloth increased dramatically.

The third major type of Balinese textile is weft *ikat* or *endek*, the weft threads of which are dyed prior to weaving. Areas to remain uncolored are bound tightly together to resist the dyes. Different color combinations may be achieved by repeating the binding and dyeing process several times. Dye is also sometimes applied by hand to the unwoven weft.

Endek is by far the most popular Balinese textile form, and its designs are consequently more reliant on fashion and current trends. The demon heads and *wayang* figures of the older cloths have nearly all been replaced by finer geometric motifs. The popularity of *endek* has spread beyond Bali to the rest of Indonesia and abroad as enticing new designs are created.

In recent years, natural dyes have become much more popular, in part thanks to the efforts of the Ubud based foundation, Yayasan Pecinta Budaya Bebali (www.threadsoflife.com), which encourages the planting of natural dye plants and community weaving cooperatives. Natural dye textiles with intricate designs are unique and appeal to a more elite Balinese market that takes pride in wearing such works of art.

Magical textiles from Tenganan

The famous double *ikat* cloths from Tenganan Pegringsingan, eastern Bali, rank among the masterworks of Southeast Asian textile art. In double *ikat*, the weft and the warp threads are both patterned using the *ikat* tie and dye method. This is an immensely difficult process, requiring great precision not only in

Geringsing, double ikat ceremonial textiles, in Tenganan village (photo by Jonathan Copeland)

dyeing but also in maintaining the proper tension in the threads on the loom so that the patterns will align properly.

The showpieces of Tenganan are called *geringsing*, instantly recognizable by their muted colors—red and reddish brown, eggshell, and blue-black—achieved by dyeing or over-dyeing with red *sunti* root bark and *taum* or indigo dyes. It is often claimed that the traditional production of the fabric required blood from human sacrifices. These wild rumors have been refuted many times over but persist in the tourist literature, despite the protests of scholars and the people of Tenganan.

All *geringsing* are made of cotton yarn decorated with geometrical or floral motifs, lozenges, stars, or small crosses. The *geringsing wayang* is best known: large four-pointed stars (*lubeng*) surrounded by four scorpions divide the main field into semi-circular segments, while inside each section are buildings, animals, and *wayang* figures in the style of ancient east Javanese bas-reliefs ranging across the cloth in groups of twos and threes.

Geringsing cloths are said to possess the power to protect against malevolent earthly and supernatural enemies. Produced only in two other small villages in the world—in Japan and India—the fame of the cloths' power has spread throughout Bali, making it conceivable that the independence and wealth of the Tenganan community might be due in part to a monopoly in the creation of these magically potent fabrics.

Geringsing are of importance to all Balinese, irrespective of whether they are used as protective or destructive agents. It is still the custom in quite a few villages to wind the *geringsing* cloths around the seats and sedan chairs in which the gods are carried to the sea or the river to be bathed. Outside of Tenganan, the *geringsing cemplong* textile is also used in tooth-filing ceremonies, and for cremation purposes the *wayang kebo* is used.

Narrow cloths called *geringsing sanan empeg* ("broken yoke") are worn by men or women when a younger or older sibling has died, leaving them as the remaining middle child. During their ritually impure period of bereavement and its associated rites, the cloths are thought to be instrumental in protecting the wearer. It is noteworthy that the people of Tenganan do not use *geringsing* to heal disease in people and animals as is done

Black and white poleng *cloths represent the Balinese philosophy of duality.*

on other parts of the island. Instead, they used fragments of Indian double *ikat,* which are reputedly just as magical as *geringsing.* These cloths, called *pitola sutra* (also *patola*) are woven of silk and were imported to Indonesia for many centuries during the spice trade era. However, since most of these *patola* cloths have been sold to collectors, the *geringsing* cloth is used for this purpose.

Holy stripes and squares

The red weft *ikat cepuk* cloth has the same structure of the *pitola sutra* or *patola* textiles but has its own specific function in Balinese ceremonial life. *Cepuk* is used for all types of ceremonies: Pitra Yadnya, Manusa Yadnya, and Dewa Yadnya as well as for animal sacrifices (*mepada*) and at cremations. They are also worn by Rangda dancers as a protective cloth. The centers for weaving the *cepuk* cloth were formerly Kerambitan (Singaraja) and Nusa Penida Island. Today, Tanglad village on Nusa Penida is the main production center for these cloths, which can be found in larger markets throughout Bali, sold together with other sacred textiles.

Sacred hip and breast cloths with simple checkered patterns (*poleng*) or small, circular fabrics (*wangsul, gedogan*) are usually worn during rites of passage (especially the three-month birthday, the 210-day birthday, and for tooth-filing ceremonies). The *gedogan* is referred to as *kadang kuda* or "that which can harness what is difficult to control," such as human appetites. This cloth is used for the inauguration ceremonies for high priests or priestesses.

The *poleng*, or black-and-white checked cloth, relates to the philosophy of duality (*Rwa Bhinneda*) and teaches believers to maintain a balance between the polarities of dark and light.

    —Urs Ramseyer, revised by I Made Raiartha

BALINESE ART

A Fusion of Traditional and Modern

Modern Balinese "export" art has been charming visitors and collectors around the world for many decades and is generally far more popular than the traditional, sacred, and ritual pieces that the Balinese originally produced for themselves. It is notable that while displaying many Western and other influences, modern Balinese art has important traditional roots.

Art of the tradition

In the past, Balinese artists were patronized by kings, princes, and temple councils. The majority of their works served ritual and magical functions, emphasizing the symbolism of a temple ceremony or domestic sanctuary, or supporting claims of divine authority by the ruler. Traditional calendars, with their attendant astrological symbols, also formed an important category of works.

A major center of traditional painting was and still is located at Kamasan, near Gelgel in Klungkung Regency. Village craftsmen here once served rulers who reigned over the whole of Bali. Other centers were located in Gianyar, Bangli, Karangasem, Tabanan, Sanur, and Singaraja, where local rulers resided or were influential. After the Dutch conquered Bali in the 19th and early 20th centuries, the authority of the rulers waned and new patrons had to be found. As a result, modern influences soon manifested themselves.

Traditional drawings for magical purposes (*rerajahan*) were inscribed with a stylus on palm leaves, pot shards, and metal, then blackened with soot. Others on cloth or paper were executed in black ink. The ink formerly made of soot, and paints handmade from natural dyes have been replaced with Chinese ink and imported acrylics. Cloth

A traditional-style painting from the village of Kamasan depicting an episode from the Mahabharata, "The Temptation of Arjuna" (by an unknown artist)

paintings were only displayed during religious ceremonies; the subject matter being chosen to harmonize with the intent of the ritual.

Artistic conventions were passed down from father to son, and there are fixed elements of style, ornamentation, and overall composition. Human figures are represented in the *wayang* style, a reference to the leather figures in *wayang kulit* puppet plays. The figures have characteristic clothes, jewelry, coiffures, and headdresses, and their facial features and figures indicate their class, age, and character. Sky, rocks, and ground are indicated by specific shorthand ornaments. There is no perspective.

Stories are often depicted, the scenes being divided by rock ornaments that act as frames. A back-to-back arrangement of the figures is another way of indicating different scenes. Important scenes are placed in the center and those containing gods are at the top, with demons or animals at the bottom.

The subject matter of traditional paintings derives from religious texts, in particular Old Javanese and Balinese versions of the *Mahabharata* and *Ramayana* epics, the Pancatantra fables, Javanese tales about the wandering Prince Panji, and Balinese folk-tales, such as the story about Pan and Men Brayut, who were blessed with many children.

The oldest extant Balinese paintings are on two wooden planks in the Pura Panataran and Pura Batu Madeg temples in Besakih. They date from 1444 and 1458 and depict a small lotus flower and the elephant-headed deity, Ganesha. The next oldest work is the wooden cover of a *Ramayana* manuscript dating from 1826, containing painted scenes from the epic at the top and sides.

Cloth paintings dating from the 1840s are in museums in Denmark and Germany, de-picting among other things scenes from the *Ramayana*.

Traditional Balinese art should not be thought of as static. Important innovations occurred at the end of the 19th century. In drawings from Sanur and Singaraja of this period some perspective was used, and figures and scenery were given naturalistic features. More important innovations date from the end of the 1920s, when a naive, naturalistic style incorporating *wayang* elements developed in the Gianyar area. Apart from traditional subjects, scenes from daily life were also depicted on paper in crayon or gouache.

The influence of Western artists

German artist Walter Spies (1895–1942) settled in Campuan, near Ubud, in 1927 and was the first and most influential of a number of Europeans who made Bali their homes around this time. Dutchman Rudolf Bonnet (1895–1978) visited Bali in 1929 and settled in Ubud in 1931. The paintings of these two exerted a great influence on local artists. Spies' dense landscapes are characterized by trees with bright leaves, stylized animal and human figures, and double or triple horizons. Bonnet painted naturalistic, romantic portraits. The Mexican painter Miguel Covarrubias, who spent the early 1930s in the Sanur area, was another important figure.

Three modern art centers developed in the 1930s, each with its own characteristic style and subject matter. The first of these was in Ubud, where the style was characterized by refined, polychrome *wayang*-type figures surrounded by Spies-like scenery or Bonnet-like men and women, naked to the waist amidst plants and trees. The figures are harvesting, planting, making offerings, and dancing. Witches and scenes from the Old Javanese and Balinese epics were also popular. Illustrious artists from the Ubud area are: Ida Bagus Kembeng (1897–1952),

A work by Dutch artist Rudolf Bonnet entitled "Two Balinese Girls" (1955)

Ida Bagus Made Poleng (1915–1999), Anak Agung Gede Sobrat (1917–1992), his cousin Anak Agung Gede Meregeg (1902–2001), and Wayan Tohjiwa (1916–2001).

A second center developed around Sanur, where the style is characterized by softly-colored or black-and-white ink drawings with half-*wayang*, half-naturalistic animals in human dance poses, huge insects, and birds (for example, by I Sukaria, Gusi Made Rundu, I Regig); or naive village scenes and landscapes with trees bearing huge leaves (by Ida Bagus Made Pugug, Ida Bagus Rai).

The third center was Batuan, characterized by its stylized half-*wayang*, half-naturalistic figures with pronounced, heavily-shadowed vertebra, leafy Spies-like trees, and a very distinctive use of perspective. Originally only black ink and crayon were used on paper. The idea of coloring with crayon came from the Neuhaus brothers, who began selling Balinese drawings from their art shop in Sanur in 1935. Today, watercolors, gouache and canvas are used as well.

Typical early representatives of this style are Ida Bagus Made Djata (*sura*) (1910–1946) and Ida Bagus Made Togog (1916–1989). Some Balinese painters refused to imitate Spies or Bonnet. I Gusti Nyoman Lempad (b. 1862 or 1875, d. 1978) made naturalistic but highly stylized flat human figures with almost no scenery. I Gusti Made Deblog (1906–1987) placed figures clad in *wayang* gear in romantic landscapes.

In the 1930s, many paintings were already being sold to tourists in art shops in Ubud, Denpasar, and Sanur. At this time, Spies, Bonnet, and the Dutch archeologist W. F. Stutterheim feared that tourism was having a negative impact on the quality of paintings and drawings being produced, and so with the help of Cokorda Gede Raka Sukawati, they formed the Pita Maha artists' association in Ubud on January 19, 1936.

About 150 painters, sculptors, and silversmiths became members, with Lempad playing an important role. The main aim was to organize sales exhibitions in Java and abroad, and to make the artists aware of the importance of quality standards. In this way modern Balinese art began to be purchased by collectors and museums abroad. The Pita Maha ceased operation in 1942 following the Japanese occupation. Spies died as a prisoner aboard an Allied troops ship; but Bonnet returned to Bali from a Japanese

"The Bumblebee Dance" by Anak Agung Gede Sobrat of Ubud, one of the original Pita Maha artists

Sobrat's The Vain Monkey *was declared by the Dutch artist Rudolf Bonnet to be the first painting in the new Balinese style, showing a departure from tradition in its narrative, secular elements.*

prison camp in 1947 and tried to reorganize the artists. Combining again with Cokorda Gede Raka Sukawati, he formed the Ubud Painters' Club (Ratna Warta), and painters from Batuan and Sanur began to work as well as before.

A new style of painting was introduced by Dutch painter Arie Smit (1916–2016), who came to Bali in 1956 and became an Indonesian citizen. In Penestanan near Ubud he taught groups of young boys. Their naive style, characterized by strong colors and primitive, naturalistic human figures soon became well known; their subjects of daily life, festivals, animals and birds are now widely imitated. The group was dubbed the "Young Artists," from which a third generation has emerged today.

Balinese painting today

As Bali opened up to tourists after 1965, young Balinese painters and sculptors as well as many Javanese, Sumatran, and Western artists settled in the area between Mas and Ubud. Almost every year a new art style (Pop Art, Macro Art, Magic Realism) emerges and new materials and techniques (batik, silk-screen) have become highly fashionable.

Only a small number of Balinese painters receive formal art training either abroad or at the Indonesian art academies in Yogyakarta (operating since 1950) and Denpasar (founded in 1965). Formally trained artists work in styles and with subjects that differ completely from those of other Balinese painters.

The work of the non-academic painters is still heavily influenced by stories from the epics and folktales, to the extent that many cannot be understood without knowledge of Balinese literature. All painters, however, are fond of depicting daily Balinese life, with its rituals and dramatic performances. Most non-academic painters produce primarily for the tourist market. Many less talented ones, often children, engage in mass production of imitations of works by their more talented colleagues for sale in "art markets" and shops.

Balinese art is now displayed in many galleries and several museums in Bali. Through Bonnet's efforts, a museum for modern Balinese art, the Puri Lukisan, was built between 1954 and 1956 in Ubud. In 1979, an Arts Center, also designed for tourists, was opened in Denpasar. Expositions of paintings and sculptures are now held there, especially in conjunction with the yearly Bali Arts Festival from July to August. The galleries that host the most contemporary local artists of today include Komaneka and Gaya in Ubud, Tony Raka in Mas, Griya Santrian in Sanur, and Ganesha at the Four Seasons in Jimbaran.

—*Hedi Hinzler*

A dancer in elaborate costume performs the Baris Tunggal, *celebrating the prowess of a Balinese warrior.*

BALINESE DANCE & DRAMA

A Vibrant World of Movement and Sound

Dances and dramatic performances form an important part of nearly every ritual on Bali. They are seen as an integral part of Balinese religion and culture and are employed as an expression of devotion to the gods (*ngayah*) as well as a means of instilling centuries-old values in each new generation of Balinese through the medium of movement, music, and words.

Training and *taksu*
Balinese children are exposed to dance at a very early age. They are taken to performances long before they can walk, and begin to take dance lessons soon after. Most take great pleasure in this, whether or not they perform, as they are just as interested in the learning experience as in the final product.

There are no warm-ups before a lesson begins, and the teacher plunges right into the dance. The movements are not taught individually; the child stands behind the teacher and follows her movements. When the teacher feels that the pupil understands the basic sequence, she will move behind the student, take her wrists or fingers and move them through the desired positions. The student's body must be both full of energy and relaxed, "listening" to the teacher's fingers as much as to her words, which are soft syllables imitating the music.

After many hours of such manipulations, the movements are said to have "entered" the student. He or she then dances alone, with the teacher correcting from behind as needed. Only after completely memorizing a dance will the student practice with a full *gamelan* orchestra.

Balance is essential in Balinese dance, as in everything the Balinese do; rarely do they trip or fall. Control is also important; the dances demand domination of every limb, muscle, and emotion. The dancer must learn how to express the character of his or her role as opposed to expressing one's "true self" (a very un-Balinese concept). It could be said that dance involves a displacement of the ego.

The most important aspect of Balinese dance is that of *taksu* or "divine inspiration," the electrifying presence that mesmerizes audiences and transports performer and viewer to another time and place. *Taksu* can transform a plain-looking dancer into a great beauty and a technically deficient one into a stellar artist. A dancer studying Topeng (masked dance) will often sleep with a mask above his bed so he can absorb its character. Masks have their own special *taksu*. One who lacks *taksu* is likened to a "weak flame," and dancers pray to the god of *taksu* before each performance. It doesn't always come though; even the Balinese have off nights.

Sacred versus secular dances
There are literally hundreds of dance forms on Bali, from the starkly simple Rejang to the highly intricate Legong. Concerns about the impact of tourism caused a team of scholars to convene in 1971 to determine which dances were to be deemed sacred and which secular, to keep the sacred ones from becoming secularized. The result was that all dances were placed into three categories depending on the area of the temple in which they are performed, and this has now become the standard classification system used for Balinese dance forms.

Wali dances are those performed or originating in the *jeroan*, or innermost courtyard of the temple, where the sacred icons are kept and worshipped. These dance forms are often performed in groups with no dramatic elements. They are considered indigenously Balinese, and as with all Balinese dances, are performed to propitiate the ancestral spirits. Rejang, Baris, and Sanghyang trance dances all fall into this category.

Bebali dances are ceremonial, performed in the *jaba tengah* or middle courtyard of the temple, the meeting point of the divine and the worldly. These are primarily dance dramas whose stories derive from the Hindu-Javanese epics, including Gambuh and Wayang Wong.

/

Balih-balihan dances are secular and are performed in the *jaba* or outer courtyard, usually beyond the prescribed sacred space itself (although often this space will be consecrated by a priest before the performance). Into this category fall a number of classical and modern forms, like Legong, Baris, Arja, Kebyar, Sendratari and others.

As with most things Balinese, these categories are not rigidly adhered to. Dance dramas may be performed in the *jeroan* and magically-charged sacred dances may be held in the *jaba*. As the Balinese are fond of saying, everything has a place, a time, and a circumstance (*desa, kala, patra*), and things vary greatly from district to district, from village to village, and even from time to time. The performing arts are no exception, which is why the *barongs* in different villages are unique. This variety is one of the delights of Bali.

Rejang, Baris, and Mendet

The most truly indigenous dances of Bali are the sacred Rejang, Baris Gede, and Mendet, which are considered temple "offerings" in and of themselves. These are usually performed in stately lines by groups of men or women, with an occasional priest or priestess leading, in the *jeroan* of the temple. The dancers often bear holy water and offerings which they present to the gods.

Balinese dance traditions feature precision of movement and graceful comportment.

On the first days of an *odalan* or temple festival, the Rejang and Baris Gede are usually performed in the early morning or late afternoon, sometimes in tandem. The **Rejang** dance consists of a procession of females ranging in age from two up to 80. They move in a slow and stately fashion toward the altar, twirling fans or lifting their hip sashes. Costumes range from simple temple attire (Batuan) to elaborate gold headdresses and richly-woven cloths (Asak and Tenganan).

Baris dances are rooted in courtly rituals of war; the term *baris* refers to a formation of warriors. In the Baris Gede or Baris Upacara, a weapon of some sort is used, while in the Baris Pendet an offering is carried. Various Baris dances are named after the particular weapon involved, and a mock battle between two warriors is often re-enacted. Trance sometimes occurs, and the main function of this dance is devotional; it matters not if the dancers are in unison with one another or with the music. Baris Upacara is performed in mountain villages near Lake Batur, in the Sanur area, in Tabanan, and now in Ubud.

Late at night at the end of a temple festival a **Mendet** dance is performed by the married women of the village, although in some cases young women and girls join in as well. The women carry woven offering baskets, holy water, or libations of distilled liquor to offer up to the gods on their divine journey home. A procession is formed and they weave around the temple grounds, stopping before each shrine to offer up their gifts. Mendet, like Rejang and Baris Upacara, is not taught but learned through performance.

The divine descent

The word *sanghyang* means "deity" and performers of the sacred Sanghyang dances are said to be possessed by specific deities who enable them to perform supernatural feats. Their role is an overtly exorcistic one; they assist in warding off pestilence and ridding the village of black magic.

Trance is induced through incense smoke and chanting by two groups of villagers: women who sing the praises of the gods and ask them to descend, and a chorus of men who imitate the *gamelan*, using the word *cak* and other sounds.

There are many kinds of Sanghyang. In **Sanghyang Dedari**, two pre-pubescent girls (chosen through a "trance test") are gradually put into trance, dressed in costumes very

Traditionally, the Sanghyang Jaran *is performed by men put into a trance ahead of the dance.*

similiar to the Legong. In fact, many scholars feel that the Legong developed from this form. They are then carried on palanquins or shoulders around the village, stopping at magically-charged spots such as crossroads, bridges, and in front of the homes of people who can transform themselves into *leyak* or witches. After this, the *sanghyangs* lead the villagers back to a dancing arena at the temple or *bale banjar*, where, with eyes closed, they dance for up to four hours. Stories from the Legong repertoire or dramatic forms based on the Calonarang and Cupak are re-enacted. In some villages, the *sanghyang dedari* execute the entire dance mounted on the shoulders of men, performing astounding acrobatic feats. This part of the ritual is accompanied by a complete *gamelan* group who have been thoroughly trained and rehearsed.

In **Sanghyang Jaran**, a small number of men are put into trance, but their transition is much more violent: they fall, convulsed, to the ground and rush to grab hobby horses. During the pre-trance chanting, coconut shells are lit, leaving red hot coals. The trancers are said to be attracted by all forms of fire and onlookers are required not to smoke. The entranced dancers leap into the coals, prancing on top of them, picking up the hot pieces and bathing themselves in fire. The *sanghyangs* are accompanied only by a *kecak* chorus of chanting men.

Both types of Sanghyang are performed several times a week in Ubud, where the trance state is better left to the viewer's imagination.

Dramatic courtly forms

In the 14th century, Bali was conquered by East Java's great Majapahit kingdom. As a result, a number of Javanese nobles and courtiers settled in Bali, bringing with them their dances, their caste system, and a variety of ceremonies which quickly became interwoven with the rich tapestry of indigenous beliefs and rituals.

The stories of the **Gambuh** dance drama are principally based on the Malat tales concerning the adventures of a Javanese prince, Panji Inu Kertapati, and his quest for the beautiful princess Candra Kirana. However, the dramatic action centers around the courts and the pomp that infuses royal battles. The ideals and manners of 14th century Java and Bali are thus preserved in this form.

The language of Gambuh is Kawi or Old Javanese, which very few Balinese understand. There is little clowning, as more attention is paid to the choreography than to the story. Perhaps because of this, there are very few active village troupes left on the island, most of them in Batuan.

Gambuh is definitely worth seeing, as all Balinese dance and musical forms may be said to stem from it. Gambuh is accompanied by a small ensemble in which four to eight men play meter-long flutes. These, along with a two-stringed *rebab*, provide hauntingly beautiful melodies.

Topeng mask dramas

Topeng literally means "pressed against the face" or mask. All actors in Topeng dramas are masked. Refined characters wear full masks, and clowns and servants sport a half-mask, which facilitates speaking. Topeng is a tremendously popular form in Bali, as it relates local lore and historical tales concerning the royal lineages in scenes of everyday life. Topeng is also immensely entertaining, as the use of humor and clowns is extensive.Topeng, along with the *wayang kulit* shadow play, is the primary medium through which Balinese history, values, and even knowledge of current events are transmitted. In the end, the two factions contend, and the "bad guys" admit defeat.

Topeng *mask dramas convey historical tales and local lore in a humorous and entertaining way.*

Prembon

The Balinese love to create new genres by melding together different forms. In the 1940s the king of Gianyar, I Dewa Manggis VIII, summoned his royal dancers and asked them to create a new dance called **Prembon**, taking elements from the Gambuh, Arja (a kind of operatta), Topeng, Parwa (a non-masked form based on the Mahabharata), and Baris.

A night of Prembon often begins with a solo Baris and some other *tari lepas* (non-dramatic dance). A story of Balinese kings with characters from all these forms is then presented, although it most resembles a Topeng performance. Watching Prembon gives the uninitiated an excellent glimpse of all of these genres in a way that is easier to follow than other forms, Gambuh or Arja, for example. And often it is the best dancers of each tradition that perform these pieces.

Calongarang: battling the dark side

Every 15 days, on Kajeng Kliwon, the dark forces of Bali gather to frolic and inflict illness on unsuspecting souls. These witches or *leyaks* are humans who, through the study of black magic, are able to transform themselves into grotesque animals, demons, even flying cars. They haunt crossroads, graveyards, or bridges, and this particular day, due to its inauspiciousness for *dharma*, or the correct path, is auspicious for Rangda, queen of the *leyaks*. A performance of the **Calonarang** dance is then often held.

There are many variations on the Calonarang dance, but all involve the Barong, a mythological beast with an immense coat of fur and gilded leather

vestments. The most common and sacred is the Barong Ket, a cross between a lion and a bear, although the Barong Macan (tiger), Barong Bangkal (wild boar), Barong Celeng (pig), and Barong Gajah (elephant) also exist.

The Barong is considered a protector of the village. Of demonic origin, the people have made a beast in his image and transformed him into a playful, benevolent creature. Upon entering, he prances about the stage, shaking his great girth and clacking his jaws. He is often followed by the *telek* and *jauk*, two masked groups of men depicting deities and demons, respectively. They fight, but no one wins, a common theme in Balinese performances. Their role is simply to help restore and maintain balance.

The exquisite Legong

Perhaps the most famous of Bali's dances, the **Legong** is also by far the most exquisite. Performed by three highly-trained young girls, it is said to have been the created by the king of Sukawati, I Dewa Agung Made Karna (1775–1825), who meditated for 40 days and 40 nights in the Yogan Agung temple in Ketewel and saw two celestial angels, resplendent in glittering gold costumes. When he finished his meditations, he summoned the court musicians and dancers and taught them what he had seen, calling it the Sanghyang Legong. This was first performed in the temple with nine masks, and is still performed there every seven months.

Most scholars agree that the Legong grew out of the Sanghyang Dedari. All Legong pieces are for two young girls. Some are totally abstract with no narrative; others tell a story and the *legongs* act out different roles.

In 1932, Ida Bagus Boda, a celebrated Legong teacher, created the *condong* or female attendant role, which serves as an introduction to the piece. In shimmering costume, her body wrapped like a gilded cocoon, the *condong* makes her entrance. After a solo of about ten minutes, she spies two fans on the ground, scoops them up and turns around to face the two *legongs*. Dancing in complete unison, they take the fans from the *condong*, perform a short piece called *bapang*, and the *condong* exits. It is here that the narrative begins.

The most commonly performed tale is that of a princess lost in the woods of the wicked king of Lasem. He kidnaps her and tries to seduce her, but she spurns his advances. Upon hearing of her fate, her brother, the king of Daha, declares war on the king of Lasem. As they go forth into battle, the *condong* reappears wearing gilded wings, a *guak* (crow) or bird of ill omen. The two kings fight, with evil Lasem invariably meeting death at the hands of King Daha.

Other stories portrayed include **Jobog**, where the two monkey kings, Subali and Sugriwa, fight over the love of a woman, Kuntir; **Kuntul**, a dance of white herons; and **Semaradhana**, where the god of love Semara takes leave of his wife Ratih and goes to awaken the god Siva (represented by a Rangda mask) out of meditation. The traditional centers for Legong are Saba, Peliatan, and Kelandis, but today it is also performed in Teges, Ubud, and many other villages.

New forms: the Kecak

In the 1930s when tourism to Bali was just beginning, two Western residents, painter Walter Spies and author Katharine Mershon, felt that the *cak* chorus of the Sanghyang dances, taken out of its ritual context with an added storyline, would be a hit among their friends and other visitors. Working with Limbak and his troupe in Bedulu village, they incorporated Baris movements into the role of the *cak* leader. Eventually the story of the *Ramayana* was added, though it wasn't until the 1960s that elaborate costumes were used.

The **Kecak** dance, as it is now called, involves a chorus of at least 50 men. They sit in concentric circles around an oil lamp and begin to slowly chant: *cak-cak-cak-cak*. Up to seven different rhythms are interwoven, creating a tapestry of sound similar to the *gamelan*. One man is the *kempli*, or time beater, and his "pong" cuts through the chorus. A *juru tandak* sings the tale of the *Ramayana* as the drama progresses. Tourists call this the "Monkey Dance," because at the end of the play the men become the monkey army sent to rescue the heroine, Sita. The *cak* sound also resembles the chattering of monkeys. Kecak is performed solely for tourists; never in temple ceremonies. Even though it has its roots in the Sanghyang trance dances, the Kecak dancers themselves do not go into trance.

The Legong, *performed exclusively by young girls, is perhaps the most celebrated of all Bali's dances.*

The exhilarating Kecak is perhaps Bali's best known dance drama spectacle.

Kebyar: lighting strikes

At the turn of the last century, north Bali was the scene of great artistic ferment, as *gamelan* competitions were common and each club vied to outdo the other. In 1914, **Kebyar Legong** was born, a new dance for two young women who portray an adolescent youth, the prototype for the dynamic Taruna Jaya, choreographed by I Gede Manik in the early 1950s. There was no story, the emphasis being instead on interpretation of the music, which was a new phenomenon. This form swept the island like lightning, which is what *kebyar* literally means. The music is equally electrifying, full of sudden stops, starts, and complex rhythms.

Four years later, the king of Tabanan commissioned a *gamelan kebyar* to perform at an important cremation. One member of the audience was so taken with the music that he began to compose and choreograph his own pieces in this style. This was I Ketut Maria (also known as "Mario"), the most illustrious Balinese dancer of the 20th century.

In 1925 Mario debuted his **Kebyar Duduk**, a dance performed entirely while seated on the ground. With no narrative to tell, the Kebyar dancer presents a range of moods, from coquettishness to bashfulness, and from sweetly imploring to anger. Mario himself performed this while playing the *trompong* (a long instrument with 14 inverted kettle gongs), using theatrics and flashy moves to coax sound from the instrument.

In 1951, Mario was approached by British enterpreneur John Coast and Anak Agung Gede Mantera of Peliatan to create a new piece. They wanted a boy-meets-girl theme for their world tour in 1952. Tambulilingan Ngisap Madu ("a bumblebee sips honey"), now known as **Oleg Tambililingan**, was the result, created for Ni Gusti Raka, one of the tiny Peliatan *legong* dancers, and Gusti Ngurah Raka, Mario's prize Kebyar student. It is a story mimed in abstract terms of a female bumblebee sipping honey and frolicking in a garden. A male bumblebee sees her, encircles her in a dance of courtship, and they finally mate.

Into the spotlight: Sendratari

During the political upheavals of the 1960s, many new ideas in dance and music were ushered in. A team of Balinese artists at KOKAR (now SMK, the High School for Performing Arts) in 1962 created a new form called **Sendratari**, from *seni* ("art") and *tari* ("dance"). Instead of having dancers speak their lines, as in Gambuh, Topeng and Arja, a *juru tandak* sits in the *gamelan* and speaks to them in Kawi and Balinese. The dancers pantomime the action on stage. Since then, KOKAR and SMK artistes have created new Sendratari every year for the **Bali Arts Festival**, filling to capacity the open-air theater at the Art Center, which seats 5,000. These are lavish spectacles with casts of hundreds. The stories are usually taken from the *Ramayana* and the *Mahabharata*.

The Arts Festival showcases some of the best dance and music on the island. It begins in mid-June and runs through mid-July. Schedules are available from the Regional Tourism Office in Denpasar.

Birds and other beasts

The 1980s ushered in new forms which added to the classical repertoire of Balinese dance. These Kebyar style forms may be popular for a year, a decade, or a century, and most of them are created by teachers and students at SMKI in Batubulan and ISI (Indonesia Institute of Art) in Denpasar. In 1982 these teachers inserted a bird scene into one of the Mahabharata Sendratari episodes. This team effort was then refined into Tari Manuk Rawa ("long-legged bird dance") by I Wayan Dibia, one of Bali's most prolific modern choreographers.

Such was the popularity of Manuk Rawa that other bird forms sprung up, notably Tari Kedis Perit ("sparrow dance") by Ni Ketut Arini Alit, and Tari Belibis (a story of a mother swan and her young) and Tari Cendrawasih ("bird of paradise dance") both by Ni Luh Suasthi Bandem, also a lecturer at STSI.

Two dances that can be seen everywhere are **Kijang Kencana** (by I Gusti Ngurah Supartha), a "golden deer dance" performed by tiny girls with abundant energy, and **Jaran Teji** by I Wayan Dibia, a humorous dance of horseback riders that has become a real hit.

New creations

The *kreasi baru* or "new creations" once referred to the colossal Sendratari productions of the dance schools. Today, however, this term encompasses what in the West would be called "performance art," which means in Bali, anything quite out of the ordinary. Most of these *kreasi* come out of the academies, SMKI, and ISI. There are national festivals every year of new music and modern dance that encourage these forms. Some of the young composers and choreographers are fusing elements of East and West into spectacular and original forms; others are wallowing in mediocre attempts at self-expression and self-indulgence.

Many Japanese and Western composers and choreographers are coming to Bali to collaborate with Balinese performance artists and create innovative works. Some of the groups to see are: **Bona Alit** (*gamelan* fusion), **Balawan Ethnic Fusion** (guitar and *gamelan* fusion), **Wayang Listrik** by I Made Sidia of Bona, contemporary dance by **I Nyoman Sura**, and *gamelan* fusion by **I Nyoman Windha**.

The tradition of dance in Bali is a strong and a rich one. Even with the influx of modern, Western culture the classical Balinese forms are still the most popular and will undoubtedly remain so for a very long time to come.

—*Rucina Ballinger*

The Calonarong, *featuring the beloved Barong, tells the story of a triumph of good over evil forces.*

BALINESE MUSIC

The Deep Resonances of the Gamelan

Few places in the world have as concentrated a musical tradition as Bali. The sheer quantity of ensembles and musical forms is impressive enough: there are thousands of active *gamelan* ensembles composed of more than 20 distinct types on an island barely 140 km (87 miles) across. Almost all are intertwined with dance, recitation, theater, puppetry, or other artistic traditions. But Bali's musical achievements go far beyond mere quantity. Considering the sophistication and stylistic breadth of its orchestral compositions, the famed ensemble skills of its musicians, and the fact that its performing arts traditions are still evolving, it becomes clear what an unusual living musical tradition this tiny island has nurtured.

Music in Balinese culture

Part of the vitality of Balinese music rests in its cultural resonance. Fundamental aspects

Frames for gamelan *instruments are carved of jackfruit wood by skilled artisans.*

of Bali-Hindu cosmology—the way people perceive the universe and humankind within it—are reflected. Ideas of interdependence, balance, and unity are manifest in the very fabric of the music, the tuning of the instruments and in the ways musicians interact as an ensemble. Dazzling interlocking melodies composed of two complementary parts reflect *rwa bhineda*, the Balinese belief in dualism and interdependence. The same idea is expressed in paired tuning systems, in which partner tones separated by small frequencies "beat" together in a vibrating, co-dependent relationship. The deep resonances of the large suspended gong—the heart of most bronze *gamelan* orchestras, born of the fires of ancient bronzesmithing traditions—bring unity to musical, spiritual, and sonic realms.

Music and dance are practiced and performed intensively in Bali. This may arise partly from the sheer love of theatrical display, of which the Balinese are justly famous. Or perhaps it is an outgrowth of the communal nature of Balinese society, since playing *gamelan* is one of the most sublime expressions of shared, coordinated effort. Regardless of the underlying impulse, it is evident that the performing arts are highly valued and integrated into daily social and religious life. This integration has helped to maintain the vitality of the arts in the midst of a century of social change, strife, rapid modernization and mass tourism. Ceremonies in the temple or home are considered incomplete without music and dance. They are essential not only in the creation of the right atmosphere but to the enactment of many core rituals. Performances are felt to entertain gods and humans alike, an attitude that largely helps bypass the divide between "secular" and "sacred" or between "classical" and "popular," familiar in other traditions. An offering dance in the inner temple, a performance for tourists and a *gamelan* competition before thousands of screaming fans have far more in common than is apparent at first glance.

Balinese musicians not only maintain but actively develop their musical traditions. New works are composed and premiered alongside established repertoire, which is also continually developed. In fact, there is often no clear distinction between new and traditional, since Balinese musicians borrow, rework, and rearrange existing material and forms with great freedom. Theirs is still a collectively shared musical language; musical evolution arises more from collaborative endeavor than individual genius.

As a result, music seems ubiquitous even in the modern, bustling Bali of tourist buses and instant messaging. From a quiet vantage point—now rare—the ringing tones of metallophones, gongs, and drums drift across the rice fields from a nearby village temple ceremony as they have for centuries. From a more typical present-day perspective, senses are assailed by the crash of cymbals competing with the din of motorcycles and trucks as a local *baleganjur* (marching *gamelan*) group rehearses in their *bale banjar*. Surroundings may change, but the excitement derived from making music has not faded.

What is a *gamelan*? Who plays it?

Technically the term *gamelan* refers to a set of instruments: bronze, iron, or bamboo percussion instruments that are created and tuned together to form an indivisible whole.

But in common usage *gamelan* also refers to the group of musicians who play them. They come together in the spirit of a club (*seka*), with a strong collective identity and organizational structure that often outlives its original membership. Players, *seka gong*, come from all layers of Balinese society, from farmers and laborers to civil servants to well-to-do descendants of the princely castes. In this sense it is a true popular art. The cooperative atmosphere of a *gamelan* club is a reflection of the *banjar*, the fundamental unit of village or neighborhood community that hosts most groups. This is evident not only in the team spirit and de-emphasis of individual virtuosity but in the ensemble interaction itself. Unity and precise synchronization of the various parts are essential to the musical flow. It is no surprise that solo performance is nonexistent in Bali.

Although ISI Denpasar (Indonesia Institute of the Arts Denpasar) has helped elevate *gamelan* performance to a professional level for many of its graduates, most musicians are amateurs. Aside from the rare commissioned performance or international tour, there is little money to be made from playing *gamelan*. The lure to play still comes primarily from the prestige of performance in community and religious contexts: village celebrations (both religious and secular), festivals and the ever-popular "battle of the

A four-piece ensemble consisting of an ugal, *a* kempli, *and two* kendang *drums*

Every banjar *has its own* gamelan *troupe that performs at rituals and temple ceremonies.*

bands"-style *gamelan* competitions. Any income generated is typically used for instrument upkeep, costumes, refreshments during rehearsals, and an occasional feast for the players. However, there is a rise of private music and dance centers, *sanggar*, which seek some income to complement the great fun of playing *gamelan* and dancing.

Styles, instruments, and tuning

The diversity of musical ensembles on Bali and styles is striking. More than 20 forms of *gamelan* have been documented, with numerous sub-varieties depending on dramatic function. And the number is increasing as a younger generation experiments with new ideas of instrumental combination. Ensembles range in size from the small *gender wayang*, a quartet of musicians that accompanies the *wayang kulit* (shadow puppet play), to the massive *gamelan gong gede* ensemble of 35–40 musicians who perform a repertoire of ancient and stately ceremonial pieces in the temple.

A variety of materials are used in the production of instruments. The most common types of *gamelan* instruments have bronze keys suspended over bamboo resonators in carved wooden frames. These are combined with a variety of tuned gongs, drums,

cymbals, and flutes to make a complete orchestra. With the exception of the largest gongs made on Java, the bronze instruments are all hand-forged by Balinese smiths using techniques essentially unchanged over the last few centuries. Each set of instruments is laboriously tuned by filing and hammering the metal keys and gongs to match a pentatonic (five-tone) or heptatonic (seven-tone) scale that is unique to that particular set of instruments. While *gamelans* of a particular type—for example, the *gamelan angklung*—are tuned to approximately the same interval structure, there is no uniform standard of reference for *gamelan* tuning. This is another indication of the unique identity of each orchestra. However, two large families of tunings, in scales known as *pelog* and *slendro*, are known and easily distinguished by their intervals.

The *gamelan gong kebyar*, which appeared about a century ago, remains the most common type of *gamelan* on Bali. As described by writer Miguel Covarrubias as early as the 1930s, it is the "modern orchestra par excellence." Like most *gamelan* (and not dissimilar to a Western orchestra), the *gamelan gong kebyar* is composed of instrumental families that are subdivided according to the instrument's range, function, timbre, and performance technique. The eight or ten *gangsa* or highest-pitched, ten-keyed metallophones play the main melodic material. The *calung* or *jublag*, five-keyed midrange metallophones, play the *pokok* or core melody lines. The lowest *jegogan*, also five-keyed, reinforce the *pokok* by regularly stressing certain tones (for example, every fourth *jublag* note). The *reong*, a row of tuned gong chimes played by four musicians, plays another layer of figuration or melodic doubling, parallel to the *gangsa*; at other moments it joins the drums in non-pitched rhythmic patterns. Various small gongs are struck to punctuate the phrases in regular fashion. The *kajar*, for example, keeps the beat, a difficult task in this syncopated and rhythmically complex music. The medium-sized gongs, called *kempur, kemong,* and *kempli,* punctuate the phrases at important junctures, while the largest gong is reserved to mark the phrase endings: periods at the end of sentences.

Leading the entire group is a pair of drummers (*kendang*), accompanied by the cymbal or *cengceng* player, that cue accents, dynamics and changes in tempo. In dance performances, drummers are the vital link between the dancers and other musicians. The lead drummer provides signals to other musicians that translate the detailed cues of the dancer's movements into musical gestures.

Many other types of *gamelan* survive, and occasionally new ones are created. Some are used only in the context of religious ritual. One of the rarest is the *gamelan selunding*, a sacred ensemble with instruments of iron keys suspended over simple trough resonators. Special ceremonies and offerings must accompany it, as the iron keys are thought to be charged with great spiritual energy. Some *selunding* melodies are themselves sacred, not to be played or even hummed except during ceremonies.

Most bamboo *gamelan* ensembles, in contrast, evolved as vehicles for popular village entertainment. The most widely known is the *gamelan joged* which accompanies the flirtatious *joged* dance. As with bronze orchestras, bamboo ensembles are found in various sizes, styles and specific instrumentations. Some are composed exclusively of bamboo marimbas; others include non-pitched percussion instruments, such as cymbals and drums. Of all bamboo orchestras the most impressive is the *gamelan jegog*, which

evolved in Jembrana, western Bali. It is named after the enormous bass instruments, *jegogan*, which use bamboo tubes up to 30 cm or 12 in in diameter and 3 m or 10 ft in length. Struck with large, padded mallets, they produce bass tones of awesome power.

Sonority, structure, and dance

The music of the Balinese *gamelan* is, at its most characteristic moments, a densely patterned, contrapuntal web of sound, based in duple meters. The texture is made more complex by the "paired tuning" system, in which each tuned key and gong is paired with another, tuned slightly higher or lower. When struck simultaneously, the two tones produce a rapid beating as a result of the difference in frequency that creates the shimmering sound quality characteristic of the Balinese *gamelan*. Some observers have compared the sound to the nightly choruses of crickets and frogs in the rice fields.

Though some music experts use a written notation, which supplies a skeletal outline of the trunk melody and punctuating gong tones, its function is only for documentation or study. In day-to-day performance practice no notation is used; everything is learned by imitation from a teacher's model. A teacher repeats each musical fragment until the players master it, a time-intensive but satisfying rehearsal process. Once mastered, a piece is further honed and shaped according to the group's individual character and skills, making it their own. This is brought about through subtle shadings of dynamics and tempo, as well as stylistic variations characteristic of that group or region.

This direct and interactive approach is also important in learning the complex interlocking parts (*kotekan* or *kilitan*) for which Balinese music is renowned. Two complementary parts are woven together to form a complete melody; they fit together in perfect rhythmic tandem as two pieces of a puzzle. Aside from the pure fun of fitting the parts together, the technique of *kotekan* enables musicians to play at dazzling speeds, much faster than could be done alone. The collective Balinese spirit and finely tuned sense of musical interaction enable *gamelan* musicians to scale heights usually reserved for the most accomplished of virtuosi in other musical cultures.

—Wayne Vitale

THE WAYANG KULIT SHADOW PLAY

A Unique Vision of the World

Wayang kulit, the shadow theater of Bali, is one of the longest running theatrical spectacles the world has known. For centuries it has survived changes in politics, ideology, and fashion, continually renewing itself and providing the Balinese with a unique vision of the world and of themselves.

The elements of the performance are simplicity itself: a white screen, a flame, music, and flat puppets that move and tell a story. Balinese audiences delight in seeing their favorite characters in familiar predicaments. There is the braggart caught in his own lies, the old fool who isn't so foolish, the invincible hero who needs to be rescued, the gods needing help from humans, and of course the beautiful princess, abducted, rescued, and stolen back again.

The shadow puppets are made of rawhide, carved and perforated to create lacy patterns of light and dark. The puppets and screen are flat, but when all elements of a performance are in place—flickering firelight, *gamelan* music, voice, and movement—they take on an unearthly dimension.

A new type of puppetry has come to the forefront this century called *wayang listrik* or electrified *wayang*, named for the use of electrical light bulbs and projected Power Point images on the screen replacing the traditional oil lamp. This is coupled with live dancers performing on both sides of the screen and makes for quite an innovative and entertaining show. New puppets are being made out of mirrored glass, paper, and plastic.

The characters are all recognizable at a glance by their headdresses, costumes, and facial characteristics. There are two main types: *alus* and *kasar*. *Alus* means refined and controlled. *Kasar* is vulgar and quick to

Flickering shadow puppets transport the audience to an ancient world of heroes and villains, where good ultimately triumphs over evil.

anger. *Alus* is not necessarily good nor *kasar* bad; what is admired is the right combination of attributes at the right place and time.

A performance is usually a kind of offering that marks the completion of a ceremony. The occasion could be a wedding, a funeral, or any other major event in the life of the individual or community. In urban areas, a performance may be two hours long. In rural areas, expectations are greater and work schedules more flexible, so a performance is likely to begin after 10 pm and last three to five hours. Farmers often go directly from the performance to the fields.

Most puppeteers, or *dalangs*, in Bali specialize in *wayang parwa* stories from the *Mahabharata* myth cycle about two families in conflict over succession to the throne. Although each side has valid claims, one operates from greed and self-interest, while the other is more altruistic. The five Pandawa brothers struggle to assert their best quali- ties, pitted against the 100 Korawas, who lust for power.

An apprentice *dalang* will spend years following his father or teacher from one performance to another. Gradually his understanding of composition, rhetoric, and humor become instinctive. He is expected to improvise in several languages, to give convincing and inventive explanations of local customs and events, and to be adept in the use of proverbs and slapstick comedy.

The performance

The shadow play group usually arrives sev- eral hours before the performance. As they chat with their host and exchange gossip, the *dalang* will listen for ways to adapt the story for his audience. He never announces which story he is going to perform, reserving the right to change his mind.

In a given performance, 30 to 60 puppets are used. While the musicians play the overture, the *dalang* makes his selection. Antagonists are placed to his left, protago- nists to his right. Major characters are placed closest to the *kayon*, the "tree of life" puppet that marks the beginning and end of major scenes. The shadows are purposely indistinct at this point, symbolizing that the creation of the story has begun, but that like a child in the womb, no one knows what it is going to develop.

There is singing as each character is presented. The first scene is the meeting scene, where problems central to the night's episode are introduced. It is entirely in Kawi, the ancient language of poetry, religion, and theater. Then there is a sound like someone clearing his throat, followed by a slow, deliberate laugh. A hush settles over the audience as a large figure moves ponderously across the screen and bows. This is Tualen, and for the first time, Balinese is spoken.

Tualen is one of four *punakawan*, advisors and servants to the king, and interpreters for the audience. They are the only puppets with lips; when the *dalang* pulls a string attached to their jaws, it looks as if they are talking.

During the initial scene it might be re- vealed that an army is gathering to attack; that someone is missing, kidnapped, or stuck in a dream; that a rare object is needed to complete a ceremony, or that everyone is invited to a marriage contest. There are hundreds of possible openings. They all end with a decision to solve the problem.

In pursuit of their goal, they might journey through a forest filled with dangerous animals, visit a hermit in his cave, enlist the help of an ally, climb mountains, or cross an ocean. There will be a meeting between the two sides, ending with sharp words and a battle. There might be a romantic interlude as one of the Pandawas and a beautiful enemy princess fall in love.

Ultimately, fighting ensues and magical weapons fill the air. Eagles fight snakes. Fire fights rain. Ogres change shapes, fly, and become invisible. The *penasars* are every- where, fighting, arguing, joking, dodging weapons and providing a commentary which gives the musicians a chance to rest.

The *dalang* works furiously. His assistants try to second guess him and hand him the right puppet when he needs it. The musicians pay close attention, emphasizing each arrow shot with a resounding chord. The audience cheers, laughs, and groans, gripping each other in anticipation of what is to follow.

When the *dalang* feels the audience is satisfied, he will play a rousing battle scene ending in victory for the right side. This is not so much the ultimate triumph of good over evil as the re-establishment of a balance between the two. The clowns have a last word, then the *kayon* appears at the center of the screen, and the *dalang* utters the words: "Though the fighting is over, the stories go on forever. We apologize for stopping so soon."

—*Larry Reed*

TOURISM IN BALI

Creating a New Version of Paradise

Bali has long been characterized in the West as the last "paradise" on earth, a traditional society insulated from the modern world, whose inhabitants are endowed with exceptional artistic talents and concentrate a considerable amount of time and wealth staging sumptuous ceremonies for their own pleasure and for that of their gods, and now also for the delectation of foreign visitors.

This image is due in large part, of course, to the positive effect Bali's manifold charms have on visitors, but it is also the result of certain romantic Western notions about what constitutes a "tropical island paradise" in the first place. Additionally, it should be understood that Bali's development into a popular tourist destination has been the result of specific actions and decisions on the part of governing authorities for more than a century.

Colonial beginnings

To become a prime tourist destination, Bali had to fulfil two conditions. First, an island which had previously been known mainly for the "plunderous salvage" of shipwrecks and "barbarous sacrifice" of widows on the funeral pyre had to become an object of curiosity for Westerners in search of the exotic. Secondly, the island had to be made accessible. Barely a decade after the Dutch conquest of Bali, both conditions were met.

It was in 1908, just after the fall of Bali's last raja, that tourism in the Indonesian archipelago had its beginnings. In this year, an official tourist bureau was opened in the colonial capital, Batavia (now Jakarta), with the aim of promoting the Netherlands Indies as a tourist destination. Initially focusing on Java, the bureau soon extended its scope to

Titled "President Reagan Visits Bali," this painting by I Made Budi shows a Balinese view of foreigners.

include Bali, then described in its brochures as the "Gem of the Lesser Sunda Isles."

In 1924, the Royal Packet Navigation Company (KPM) inaugurated a weekly steamship service connecting Bali's north coast Buleleng (Singaraja) port with Batavia and Surabaya on Java and Makassar on Sulawesi. Shortly thereafter, the KPM agent in Buleleng was appointed as the tourist bureau's representative on Bali, and the government began allowing visitors to use the rest houses or *pasanggrahan* originally designed to accommodate Dutch functionaries on their periodic rounds of the island.

In 1928, the KPM erected the Bali Hotel in Denpasar—the island's first real tourist hostelry—on the very site of the *puputan* massacre and mass suicide of 1906. Following this, the KPM also upgraded the *pasanggrahan* at Kintamani, which from then on hosted tourists who came to enjoy the spectacular panoramas around Lake Batur.

Early visitors to Bali sometimes arrived aboard a cruiser that berthed at Padangbai for one or two days, but more often aboard the weekly KPM steamship via Buleleng. Passengers on this ship usually disembarked on Friday morning and departed aboard the same boat on Sunday evening, giving them just enough time to make a quick round of the island by motorcar. The number of people visiting Bali in this way each year increased steadily from several hundred in the late 1920s to several thousand during the 1930s.

The Master Plan

With the landing of Japanese troops at Sanur in 1942, tourism on Bali came to an abrupt halt, and recovery after the war was slow. In fact, until the late 1960s, Balinese tourism was severely hampered by the rudimentary state of the island's infrastructure and by unsettling political events in the country. Yet President Sukarno adopted Bali as his favorite retreat (his mother was Balinese) and made it a showplace for state guests. Eager to use the island's fame to attract foreign tourists, he undertook construction of a new international airport in Tuban and the prestigious Bali Beach Hotel in Sanur, the latter financed with Japanese war reparation funds. Opened in 1966, rebuilt in 1994, and now called the Inna Grand Bali Beach Hotel it remains a major landmark and the only real high-rise building on Bali.

When General Suharto became President of the Republic in 1967 his New Order government rapidly moved to reopen Indonesia to the outside world. This move coincided with a period of high growth in international tourism, and from this time onward tourism expanded rapidly on Bali.

This development was the direct result of a decision made by the government in their first Five-Year Development Plan (1969–74), primarily in order to address a pressing national balance of payment deficits. Bali's prestigious image, formed during the pre-war years, meant that the island naturally became the focus of tourism development in Indonesia.

Accordingly, the government heeded the advice of the World Bank and commissioned a team of French experts to draw up a Master Plan for the Development of Tourism on Bali. Their report, published in 1971 and revised in 1974 by the World Bank, proposed construction of a new 425 ha (1,050 ac) tourist resort at Nusa Dua and a network of roads linking major attractions on the island.

With the Master Plan's official promulgation in 1972, tourism was ranked second only to agriculture in economic priority in the province. The Master Plan was designed to attract tourists in the upper-income range who were expected to stay at luxury hotels. But it turned out that a considerable proportion of visitors were not of the target group but comprised young, low-cost travelers staying in small homestays and budget accommodations. As the Balinese were quick to adapt to this unexpected clientele—for years derogatorily described as "hippies"— new resorts sprang up in places like Kuta, Ubud, Lovina, and Candidasa.

Further developments

In the late 1980s, tourism development on Bali shifted into high gear with a sharp upsurge in visitors arrivals followed by an even more rapid rise in hotel investment and other tourism related facilities. In 1988, alleging the pressure of demand, the governor designated 15 tourist areas around the island, thus in effect lifting the regional restrictions imposed by the Master Plan which had prohibited the building of large hotels outside of Nusa Dua, Sanur, and Kuta. From then on, there has been a frenzy of investment and development by leading international hotel chains, enticed by the deregulation of the banking system and solicited by Asian investors, most of them backed by Jakarta-based conglomerates.

In 1993, the tourist areas were increased to 21, covering roughly one quarter of the total surface of the island. Tourism development continued apace, proving remarkably resilient to world events. But when in October 2002 bomb blasts killed over 200 people—foreign tourists for the most part—visitor arrivals dropped sharply. Tourism had begun to recover in earnest when Bali was hit for the second time by a terrorist bombing in October 2005. The death toll was far lower than the first time, and unlike in 2002, there was no mass exodus of tourists. Nonetheless, arrivals went down markedly for the next couple of years, only starting to rise anew in 2007 and increasing ever since.

The pace of development in the last decade is nothing short of amazing, not only in traditional tourist areas but also in regions previously almost totally unaffected by tourism, with sometime off-the-beaten-track hideaways such as Amed and Sidemen swiftly becoming major accommodation centers. From fewer than 30,000 in the late 1960s, foreign and domestic arrivals were heading towards six million by the start of the second decade of the 21st century. During the same period, hotel capacity increased from less than 500 rooms to over 78,000.

Tourism: bane or boon?

One significant result of this development has been spectacular economic growth on Bali, so that the province now has one of the highest average income levels in all of Indonesia, with more automobiles per capita in Denpasar than in the nation's capital, Jakarta. Another highly visible result has been the ever-accelerating physical transformation of the island as more and more hotels, villas, restaurants, and souvenir shops dot the landscape.

While tourism has boosted the economic growth of Bali, the uneven distribution of economic benefits within the population and throughout the island, as well as the growing encroachment of foreign interests, have become matters of serious concern. While the resorts employ local staff, they are mostly low-skilled, and many of the tourist dollars end up with the owners in Jakarta or overseas. Land prices have soared in many areas, and rural Balinese, unable to pay the increasing land taxes, have sold their lands to investors below market values. Agricultural output is falling, as more and more farm land is given over to tourism developments.

Additionally, as a result of inadequate planning and lack of control, the environment on Bali has come under pressure, to the point that the island is now rife with air and water pollution, beach erosion and reef destruction, water and electricity shortages, saturation of solid waste disposal; not to mention traffic congestion, urban sprawl, overpopulation, crime, and social tensions. Worse in the eyes of the Balinese is the transformation of land into a marketable commodity and its massive conversion, which has caused family as well as communal feuds and has uprooted the local population, alienated from land ownership. This shift in the function of rice fields has important implications for food production and the livelihood of farmers, and it poses serious threats to the perpetuation of traditional Balinese culture, which grew out of a communal-agrarian society.

More difficult to assess, however, are the implications of tourism on Balinese society and culture, and opinions on this subject are as contradictory as they are passionate. Many foreign visitors, after only a day or two on the island, are quick to say that Bali is finished —almost. The Balinese, so the story goes, have been thoroughly corrupted by tourist dollars and the entire island is up for sale. Authentic traditions are being packaged to conform to tourist expectations, legendary Balinese artistry is being harnessed to create souvenir trinkets, and age-old religious ceremonies are being turned into hotel floor shows. In short, tourism is engulfing Bali, and the island's culture cannot survive much longer. So hurry up and see what you can; next year may be too late.

Other observers who deem themselves better informed will counter that this kind of apocalyptic attitude is neither very accurate nor even very new. Travel narratives penned during the 1930s tell a similar tale, these authors having already persuaded themselves that they were witnessing the swan-song of Bali's traditional culture, while in fact that culture is as vibrant as ever, with tourism now sparking a cultural renaissance of sorts by providing the Balinese with much-needed economic outlets for their artistic talents.

This view is reinforced, in turn, by deeply-rooted assumptions about the resilience of Balinese culture. Indeed, the Balinese have been universally praised for their ability to borrow foreign influences that suit them while maintaining their own unique identity. Witness, for example, the blend of Hindu-Javanese and indigenous ideas that inspire current Balinese religious practices. Today, so the argument goes, the Balinese are coping with the tourist invasion of their island by taking advantage of their culture's appeal without sacrificing their basic values on the altar of monetary profit.

What the Balinese think

Faced with such contradictory statements by foreigners, it is interesting to examine how the Balinese themselves feel about the tourist "invasion." To tell the truth, the Balinese did not really have a say in the decision of the central government to trade on their island's charms in order to refill the coffers of the state, and they were never consulted about the Master Plan. Presented with a *fait accompli*, they attempted to appropriate tourism in order to reap its economic benefits. In 1971, Balinese authorities proclaimed their own conception of the kind of tourism they deemed suitable to their island, namely a "Cultural Tourism" (*Pariwisata Budaya*) that is respectful of the values and artistic traditions that brought fame to the island in the first place.

From the start, the Balinese have evinced an ambivalent attitude towards tourism, which they perceived as being at once filled with the promise of prosperity and yet fraught with danger. The foreign invasion was seen to contain the threat of "cultural pollution," which might destroy those very traditions that provided Bali's main attraction for tourists.

By official accounts, "Cultural Tourism" has achieved its mission, reviving Balinese interest in their traditions while reinforcing a sense of cultural identity. In actual fact, tourism has neither "polluted" Balinese culture nor entailed its "renaissance," much less simply contributed to "preserving" it, to quote the terms which have tended to monopolize the debate. This is because tourism should not been seen as an external force striking Bali from the outside, as over the years it has instead become an integral part of Balinese society. In addition, tourism is only one of many factors bringing about rapid change on the island, which is enmeshed in both national Indonesian policy and globalization.

Still, it could be said that the interest shown by foreign tourists has made the Balinese aware of the fact that they are the lucky owners of something precious and perishable, their "culture," which they perceive at once as a capital to be exploited and as a heritage to be protected. And so it is that their culture became reified and externalized in the eyes of the Balinese, turning into an object that could be detached from themselves in order to be displayed and marketed for others, but also, consequently, of which they risked becoming dispossessed.

—*Michael Picard*

Culture shock—a group of Italian tourists turns a cremation ceremony into a photo op.

EXPLORING BALI

On the Road in Paradise

From misty mountain tops to baking beaches, and from boutique-lined thoroughfares to beetling backroads through the rice fields, the full gamut of Bali's landscapes and experiences is laid out before every new visitor.

One of the greatest attractions of this island-like-no-other is in how very easy it is to explore. It's possible to drive the entire perimeter of Bali in one long day, and wherever you are based, virtually every corner of the island is accessible as a day trip. You can breakfast with your toes in the Indian Ocean, take lunch at 2,000 m (6,500 ft) on the rim of a volcanic caldera, stop off for afternoon tea surrounded by emerald rice terraces and timeless temple complexes—and still be back to base in time for a gourmet beachfront dinner with a sunset view.

Ultimately, Bali's most impressive feature is its sheer diversity, and whatever your first impressions, you can be sure that the island has an infinity of alternative faces, all within easy reach. The place is as colorful and compact as the leaf-tray offerings, laid out on the thresholds of every home and business each morning.

Selecting a base of operations

A trip to Bali is whatever you make of it, but even if you arrive with just one thing in mind—be that seaside fun, spiritual replenishment, or aquatic adventures—you should make the effort to strike out to another corner of the island at least once.

Bali's small size means that it is perfectly possible to choose a single base of operations for the entire duration of your stay, and still manage to see all the major attractions—north, south, east, and west—on day trips. Of the resort areas in Southern Bali, **Sanur** is probably the most convenient for a single-base visit with multiple excursions, lying as it does just off the main road giving access to

Bali's compact size makes hiking around the Batur crater possible on a day trip from the coast.

the north and east, but **Kuta** and **Seminyak** also make perfectly practical bases, as does **Nusa Dua** since the opening of the convenient toll road linking it with Sanur.

Ubud is a particularly good base for excursions: many key attractions are nearby, and it stands at a relatively central point. The accommodation centers of Eastern Bali— **Padangbai**, **Candidasa**, and **Amed**—are a long way from the key sights in the south and the west, but they are very well placed for those in the central mountains, and are brilliant destinations in their own right.

If you are planning to see as much of Bali as possible without having to sleep in a different bed every night, a particular good approach can be to divide your time between two bases: begin in the south, either in Ubud or at one of the beach resorts, and then shift to another center in the east, north or west for the second part of your trip.

Of course, Bali has such a wide array of landscapes, and such a brilliant array of places to stay outside of the major accommodation centers, that you could easily spend a month on the road, never staying more than a couple of nights in each place, and tracing a route from laid-back beach towns to mountain hideaways, and from frenetic resorts to rice field hideaways. The relatively small distances that need to be covered mean that if you do embark on such an odyssey you'll rarely need to be on the road for more than a couple of hours a day.

Getting around

Whether you plan to explore from a single base, or on a multi-stop journey, you'll need to consider transport options.

One thing that Bali does lack is decent, practical public transport. Comfortable, air-conditioned coaches hurtle between Denpasar and the cities of neighboring Java, but within Bali there are only a few battered local buses and *bemo* (minibuses), rattling between the main towns.

It is almost always impossible to travel directly between major tourist destinations such as Kuta and Ubud by public transport, and while bemo and public buses can be a viable means of making short trips in the east, for example between Klungkung, Padangbai and Amlapura, even the most diehard budget back-packers will likely end up hot, frustrated—and quite possibly out of pocket—if they attempt to journey extensively by this means.

Exploring more remote corners of the island is not without its challenges, but having your own transport opens up endless possibilities.

Happily, however, there are some excellent alternatives. Tourist shuttles—usually modern minibuses—run between all the main accommodation centers, and increasingly to second-string places such as **Sidemen** and **Munduk**. These can be booked through any hotel or travel agent, and most will pick you up at your accommodation.

However, if you want to get off the beaten track and to explore the spaces between the accommodation centers, you'll need to find some kind of private transport. Cars with drivers are easily arranged, and this is certainly the most relaxed way to explore. Most accommodations should be able to arrange a car and driver on short notice.

For even more freedom, you might want to consider driving yourself. Self-drive car rental is available in most of the main resorts, and motor scooters can be rented virtually everywhere.

The traffic in the busy urban areas of the south is thoroughly intimidating, of course, and Bali is probably not the place to hit the road on a motorbike unless you're already an experienced rider. But scooters can also be rented in places such as **Amed** and **Candidasa** where the roads are much less hectic (if you do choose this option you must ensure that you have a valid international driving license and an insurance policy that covers you for motorbike travel). The risks and challenges should always be carefully considered, but having your own wheels— whether four or two—will certainly give you ready access to a whole lot more of Bali.

—*Tim Hannigan*

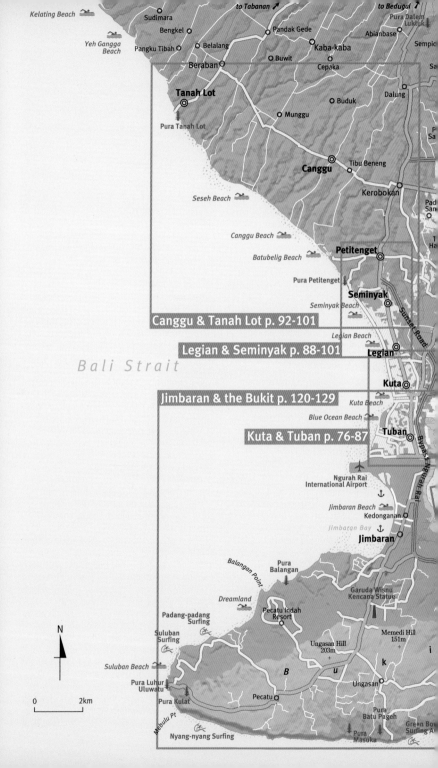

Kelating Beach

to Tabanan ↗

to Bedugul ↗

Pura Dalem
Lukluk

Sudimara

Bengkel

Pandak Gede

Abianbase

Sempic

Yeh Gangga
Beach

Pangku Tibah

Belalang

Kaba-kaba

Beraban

Buwit

Cepaka

Sa

Dalung

P
Sa

Tanah Lot

Buduk

Munggu

Pura Tanah Lot

Canggu

Tibu Beneng

Kerobokan

Pad
San

Seseh Beach

Canggu Beach

T
Ha

Batubelig Beach

Petitenget

Pura Petitenget

Seminyak

Canggu & Tanah Lot p. 92-101

Seminyak Beach

Legian Beach

Legian & Seminyak p. 88-101

Legian

Kuta

Bali Strait

Jimbaran & the Bukit p. 120-129

Kuta Beach

Blue Ocean Beach

Kuta & Tuban p. 76-87

Tuban

Ngurah Rai
International Airport

Jimbaran Beach

Kedonganan

Jimbaran Bay

Jimbaran

Balangan Point

Pura
Balangan

Dreamland

Garuda Wisnu
Kencana Statue

Padang-padang
Surfing

Pecatu Indah
Resort

Memedi Hill
151m

Suluban
Surfing

Ungasan Hill
203m

k

i

Suluban Beach

B

u

Pura Luhur
Uluwatu

Ungasan

Pura Kulat

Pecatu

Pura
Batu Pageh

N

Mebulu Pt

Nyang-nyang Surfing

Pura
Masuka

Green Bo
Surfing A

0   2km

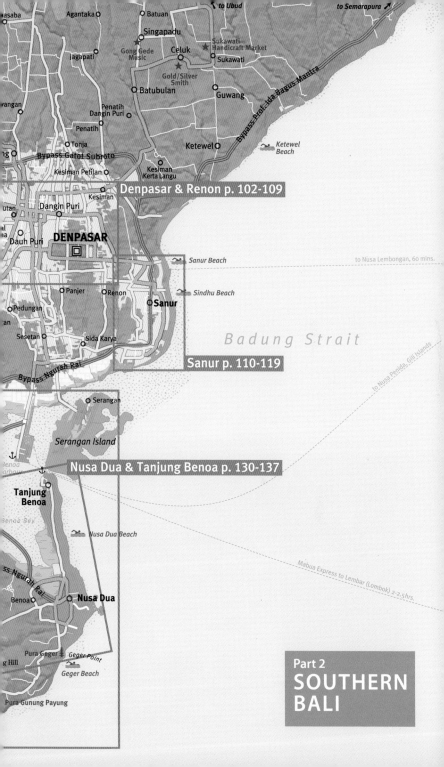

to Ubud

to Semarapura ↗

asaba

Agantaka ○

Batuan ○

Singapadu

Jagapati ○

Gong Gede Music

Celuk ○

Sukawati Handicraft Market ★

Sukawati ○

Gold/Silver Smith ★

Batubulan ○

Guwang ○

wangan

Penatih Dangin Puri ○

Penatih ○

Tonja ○

Bypass Gatot Subroto

Ketewel ○

Ketewel Beach

Kesiman Petilan ○

Kesiman Kerta Langu ○

Denpasar & Renon p. 102-109

Kesiman ○

utan

Dangin Puri ○

a

Dauh Puri ○

DENPASAR

Sanur Beach

to Nusa Lembongan, 60 mins.

Panjer ○

Renon ○

Sindhu Beach

Pedungan ○

○ **Sanur**

an

Badung Strait

Sesetan ○

Sida Karya ○

Bypass Ngurah Rai

Sanur p. 110-119

to Nusa Penida, Gili Islands

Serangan ○

Serangan Island

Benoa arbour

Nusa Dua & Tanjung Benoa p. 130-137

Tanjung Benoa

Benoa Bay

Nusa Dua Beach

ss Ngurah Rai

Benoa ○

Nusa Dua

Mabua Express to Lembar (Lombok) 2-2.5hrs.

Pura Geger

Geger Point

g Hill

Geger Beach

Pura Gunung Payung

Part 2
SOUTHERN BALI

INTRODUCTION

Visiting Southern Bali

Southern Bali is where it all began. It was here, back in the final decades of Dutch rule, that the first low-key tourist hotels began to appear; it was here that penurious hippies on pan-Asian odysseys and pioneering Australian surfers in search on empty waves fueled the beginnings of a budget travel scene in the early 1970s; it was here that mass resort-based tourism took off in the final quarter of the 20th century. And southern Bali is still the area where the vast majority of the island's visitors base themselves. Ngurah Rai International Airport—point of entry for almost all tourists—is here, but it's not just convenience that makes this part of Bali so appealing. Urban sprawl and seething traffic may have swamped most of the former rice fields and palm groves, but the surf, the broad beaches, and the magnificent sunsets are as good as they ever were. And if action is high on your agenda, be it in the form of pulsing nightlife, pounding surf, gastronomic indulgence, or retail extravagance, then there is no better place to be.

Choosing a base of operations

Today urban development stretches across much of southern Bali, but there is a huge variety in terms of atmosphere between the different places that make up this busy region. Each of the key tourist areas here has its own distinctive vibe—and its own distinctive budget designation, from low-cost to ultra-lux.

Kuta Beach, on the west coast, is the island's most famous stretch of sand, and was the original focus of mass tourism development. This boisterous district still has the largest concentration of budget accommodations, as well as an ever-increasing selection of more expensive options. It's also home to the most raucous nightlife and the cheapest shopping. The southern extension of Kuta is **Tuban**, a somewhat quieter and more upscale quarter, which is also where the airport is located.

To the north Kuta merges seamlessly into **Legian**, a marginally more sedate and up-market area, which in turn gives way to

Kuta Beach has been a haven for surfers and beach bums since the 1960s.

Seminyak and **Petitenget**. This is by far the most fashionable part of Bali, playground of the beautiful people and packed with exclusive boutiques, stylish eateries, and luxurious villas.

On the northern fringes of Seminyak, **Kerobokan** and **Canggu** were until recently predominantly rural areas, favored by those looking for exclusive villas amidst the rice fields. These days the development has surged northwards, and they have become increasingly built-up. But this is still the quietest section of the west coast, and a good place to go if you want to get away from it all.

On the opposite coast, **Sanur** is a long-standing resort area, far less inclined to constant redevelopment than its western counterparts. It has a reputation as a haunt of middle-aged, well-heeled tourists, but it also has plenty of good budget accommodations, popular with backpackers keen to escape the maelstrom of Kuta.

Heading south past the narrow isthmus where the airport is located, the southernmost part of Bali differs from the rest of the island in geography, climate, and atmosphere. Tourism development began in this area in the 1970s with the establishment of an exclusive resort enclave on the east coast at **Nusa Dua**, which remains an upmarket, secured, isolated community today. On the opposite side of the peninsula is **Jimbaran**, featuring luxury resorts behind a sheltered beach and perched atop cliffs overlooking crashing surf.

South of Jimbaran is **Bukit Badung** — generally known as "the Bukit" — a high limestone plateau. Until comparatively recently this was an overwhelmingly rural area, visited mainly by surfers and dotted with just a handful of opulent, secluded resorts. In the past few years, however, the Bukit has seen intense resort and villa development. It's by no means as quiet as it once was, but it still has spectacular views, and some magnificent beaches.

Denpasar, the provincial capital and Bali's major city, is mainly a working local community which sees few foreign tourists, but it has some interesting cultural attractions.

Finally, southern Bali also includes a pair of radically contrasting offshore islands, **Nusa Penida** and **Nusa Lembongan**, both accessible by boat from Sanur, or from **Benoa**, Bali's main port. Tiny Nusa Lembongan is crowded with accommodations, and is very popular with both day-trippers and

The famous rock islet of Tanah Lot is one of Bali's holiest sites and most popular tourist attractions.

overnighters who come for the excellent snorkeling and diving, and the good surf in the dry season. Its much bigger neighbor, Nusa Penida, is worlds apart. One of the last parts of Bali to remain almost completely untouched by tourism, it is a fascinating and beautiful place for those seeking to get totally off the beaten track before the inevitable future development arrives.

Southern Bali excursions

There are several half- or full-day trips, easily available from any of the southern Bali bases.

Reconstructed in the 16th century and renovated in the late 19th century, **Pura Luhur Uluwatu** is the Bukit's most sacred temple. Perched at the top of one of Bali's most perilous cliffs, it is a pilgrimage site for many Balinese.

Pura Tanah Lot is another of southern Bali's sacred temples and is particularly beautiful at sunset, when it can be very crowded. For a more peaceful viewing, go during the day and combine the visit with a drive through the countryside at Canggu.

Denpasar has many interesting cultural and historic sites — museums, **Puputan Square** and several old temples — not to mention the bustling traditional marketplaces **Pasar Kumbasari** and **Pasar Badung**. Also check schedules locally to see what cultural events are being held at the expansive **Werdhi Budaya Art Center**. Several boat companies offer day trips: cruises to Nusa Lembongan for lunch and snorkeling are the most popular.

Seminyak's street-long "boutique row," meanwhile, is the place to shop for designer goods, and also one of the best places to hunt out high-quality restaurants and coffee shops.

KUTA & TUBAN

Kuta Beach: Bali's Tourist Epicenter

For many years, **Kuta Beach** was Bali's best-known tourist destination. Bounded on the north by Legian and on the south by Tuban (where the airport is actually located), Kuta is living proof that one man's hell is another man's paradise. This bustling beach resort spontaneously burst onto center stage of the international tourist scene in the 1970s, after first being discovered by European backpackers traveling to the East in the 1960s. It is here that many visitors form their first (if not only) impressions of what Bali is all about. Many are shocked and immediately flee in search of the "real Bali" elsewhere on the island.

The truth is, however, that certain souls positively thrive in this labyrinth of boogie bars, beach bungalows, DVD shops, and honkytonks, all part of the Kuta lifestyle. What, then, is the magic that has transformed this sleepy fishing village overnight into an overcrowded tourist haven with no end in sight to its haphazard expansion?

Before tourism came to the area, Kuta was one of the poorest places on Bali, plagued by poor soils, endemic malaria and a surf-wracked beach that provided little protection for shipping. In the early days, it nevertheless served as a port for the powerful southern Balinese Badung kingdom, whose capital lay in what is now Denpasar.

Rice, slaves, and booty

Though Bali was never very trade-oriented, it did supply neighboring islands with several commodities, mainly rice, and notably slaves. Also, the booty salvaged from shipwrecks provided an occasional bonanza for the hardy inhabitants of this coastal outpost.

After an earlier Dutch trading post had been abandoned as commercially unviable (even the illegal trade in slaves proved disappointing), there arrived in Kuta a remarkable Dane mounted on a proud stallion, the likes of which the Balinese had never seen. Mads Lange, as he was called,

Kuta Beach was the original attraction that prompted the development of mass tourism in Bali, and it's still one of the island's finest seaside resorts.

had the audacity to march straight to the palace of the *raja* of Badung and demand an audience. Despite his bravado, Lange had in fact recently been a victim of his own intrigues on the neighboring island Lombok, where he had aided the wrong *raja* in a war and lost all. As fate would have it, Lange not only survived his move to Bali, but prospered, building here an extensive new trading post, coconut oil factory and luxurious residence stocked with wines and other delicacies.

Within the walls of his fabled Kuta residence, Lange wined and dined a succession of visiting scholars, adventurers, princes, and colonial officials. During the tumultuous 1840s, he repeatedly played a critical role in mediating between the Balinese rulers and the Dutch. Today, his grave can be seen in a Chinese cemetery at the center of Kuta, not far from a Buddhist temple and the crumbling remains of his once-regal house.

The annual Kuta Carnival is a celebration of this original resort town's vibrancy and resilience.

A tourist caravanserai

It took a young Californian surfer and his wife to first notice Kuta's tourism potential. The year was 1936. Robert and Louise Koke decided to leave Hollywood and start a small hotel on Bali. In Louise Koke's book, *Our Hotel in Bali*, she describes their discovery of Kuta as follows: "The next day we cycled…to the South Seas picture beach we had been hoping to find. It was Kuta…the broad, white sand beach curved away for miles, huge breakers spreading on clean sand."

The hotel they founded was called the Kuta Beach Hotel, naturally. It was a modest establishment, but things went reasonably well in spite of an occasional malaria attack and a run-in with a young and fiery American of British birth who went by the name of K'tut Tantri, and who managed to stir up controversy wherever she went during her 20-odd years in Indonesia.

After World War II, tourism in Bali all but disappeared. And when the first tourists began to trickle back during the 1960s, Kuta was all but forgotten. Suddenly and without warning, however, a new kind of visitor began to frequent the island during the 1970s, and their preferred abode on Bali was Kuta beach.

Nobody quite knew what to make of the first long-haired, bare-footed travelers who stopped here on their way from India to Australia, nobody, that is, except for the enterprising few in Kuta who quickly threw up rooms behind their houses and began cooking banana pancakes for this nomadic tribe.

The main attraction here was and still is one of the best beaches in Asia, and the trickle of cosmic surfers and space age crusaders in search of paradise, mystical union, and good times soon turned into a torrent, as tales of Bali spread like wildfire on the travelers' grapevine. Stories of a place where travelers could live out extravagant dreams on one of the world's most exotic tropical islands—for just a few dollars a day—seemed too good to be true.

Within the space of a few years, Kuta's empty beaches and back lanes began to fill up with homestays, restaurants, and shops. Most visitors stayed on as long as the money lasted, and many concocted elaborate business schemes that would enable them to come back, investing their last dollars in handicrafts and antiques before leaving.

In Kuta, the clothing or "rag trade" developed rapidly. Fortunes have been made and a handful of young entrepreneurs who began by selling batiks out of their backpacks have made it big. With the new affluence came a lifestyle of flashy villas and sultry tropical evenings beneath moonlit palms.

By the end of the 1970s, nobody knew quite what was going on. Upscale tourists were mixing in increasing numbers among the "hippie travelers," and deluxe bungalow hotels were popping up between $2-a-night homestays. With them came the uncontrolled proliferation of shops and bars and tourist touts lurking on every street corner. By the 1980s, Kuta was no longer a secret.

The Bali Bombing memorial is a rare place of reflection in the heart of the Kuta action.

Kuta's reincarnation

Many changes, good and bad, have come to Kuta over the years. The good includes excellent food, great shopping, and a vibrant nightlife; the bad includes mundane problems such as traffic jams, pollution, and dirty beaches and escalates to the devastating terrorist bombings of 2002. Along with the Balinese who lived and worked in the affected areas, Australian tourists—who once dominated the Kuta scene—made up the largest number of casualties. For several years thereafter, many Australians avoided Bali altogether, further damaging Kuta's tourism-based economy. By the end of the first decade of the 21st century, however, Kuta had made a remarkable recovery—perhaps due to the speedy arrests and trials of the perpetrators and the world's view that terrorism occurs not only in isolated spots, but across the globe. Today it is truly international, the spectrum of visitors ranging from macho Brazilian surfers to prim Japanese secretaries. There is a memorial to the bombing victims on Jl. Legian at the former site of Paddy's Bar and opposite the Sari Club site where the 2002 explosion took place. Each year on the anniversary—October 12—there is a ceremony attended by Balinese and international visitors to mourn the lives lost as well as those changed forever.

After the bombings, an equally rapid rise in domestic tourism began, with the Jakarta central government's appeals to Indonesia's wealthier citizens to holiday at home rather than abroad, and in particular to support Bali and to show international travelers that it was safe to return. Large numbers of out-islanders have also settled here, opening businesses or simply hanging out in this Indonesian version of a gold-rush boom town. The impression visitors may get is that the local Balinese have become a minority in their own community.

For many, this litany of change reads as an indictment of yet another paradise lost.

Kuta's accommodation ranges from budget to mid-range and is generally quite comfortable.

Kuta sunsets provide the impetus for daily communal gatherings of visitors from all over the world.

Certainly for those who knew Kuta in an earlier, more innocent state, the new Kuta is often difficult to accept. But what of the local Balinese; what do they think of all this? The most common answer is that despite the changes, the Balinese community remains strong, if wary. The traditional ceremonies are still being held, so there is as yet no need to worry, they feel. One need only witness the powerful *calonarang* dance in Kuta beneath a full moon to understand this. In fact, goods and services have improved, and Kuta enjoys a standard of living higher than almost anywhere else in Indonesia.

Above all, though, Kuta beach has become a major cross-cultural international meeting spot with few peers. Love it or leave it, only one thing is definite: the old Kuta has passed away, and nobody knows what the future may bring.

Kuta sights

The biggest tourist attraction at Kuta is, of course, its beach, which first attracted back-packers and surfers five decades ago. With no dangerous rocks or corals, it remains a good place for beginners to try their luck. There are several surfing schools that will happily teach novices the ropes. Boards are also available for rent on the beach, with local dudes standing by offering basic lessons. As there are some very strong currents here, stay between the flags when swimming. There are trained lifeguards on duty to keep the oblivious in safe areas and to assist those in trouble.

The major drawback to Kuta beach are the tradespeople who annoy sunbathers into submission to have their nails manicured or hair braided, get a massage, or buy a souvenir.Ifuninterruptedsolitude—orpristinesands—are desired, skip this beach. However, these irritants don't deter the young and young-at-heart.

Shopping opportunities are perhaps Kuta's second biggest draw, its streets and alleys lined with kiosks and stores selling T-shirts, sarongs, cheap jewelry, sandals, and souvenirs. On the north end of Jl. Kartika

Kuta has gone upmarket of late with the arrival of flashy hotels and shopping malls.

Souvenir shops abound on every street corner.

Plaza, **Kuta Square** is only the beginning of a long line of more upscale shops selling surfwear and fashions.

At the end of each day, twilight is celebrated with beachside **sundowners** to watch fabulous sunsets. Following darkness, the **partying** begins and progresses from one watering hole to the next until the wee hours of the following day.

Kuta's southern neighbor

Considered by most outsiders to be part of Kuta, Tuban is actually a separate community with its own characteristics.

Tuban begins at its north where Jl. Bakung Sari, heading west toward the sea,

turns south and then becomes Jl. Kartika Plaza (also called Jl. Kartika). Markedly quieter than its northern neighbor, Tuban is a good place to stay for those who want to play in Kuta, just a short walk away, but don't want to sleep there. The beach is not as crowded here, and the street traffic is not quite as congested.

Most of the accommodation in Tuban is in the midrange and luxury categories. Whereas in Kuta, the "beachfront" properties are actually on busy Jl. Raya Kuta, in Tuban, most hotels literally open up onto the sand. The other notable thing about Tuban is that it is peppered with independent restaurants serving a variety of cuisines.

Tuban's most prominent landmark is **Ngurah Rai International Airport**, coded DPS, for Denpasar, in the airline world. A lot more fun than the airport is the wild and wet **Waterbom** on Jl. Kartika Plaza, a longstanding waterpark with an array of slides, rides and pools, a fine place to cool down on a sizzling day.

Across the street from Waterbom is the huge **Discovery Shopping Mall**, sprawling along prime beachfront property. Along with upmarket department stores **Centro** and **Sogo**, the basement houses stalls and kiosks selling low-quality handicrafts and souvenirs, and several DVD shops. On the top floor is a food court with inexpensive Asian food.

The Kuta-Legian-Seminyak beach strip is still party central, with a wide spectrum of nightlife.

ACCOMMODATION PRICE CATEGORIES Prices are for a double room, including breakfast $ = under $30; $$ = $30–$70; $$$ = $70–$130; $$$$ = over $130. DINING PRICE CATEGORIES Prices are for based on a meal for one, without drinks $ = under $5; $$ = $5–$10; $$$ = over $10.

VISITING KUTA See map, page 81.

The 3-miles-long (5-km) arc of white sand stretching north of the airport is still arguably the best beachfront on Bali. The villages along the coast are far from being the fishing communities they once were: the area is now a booming resort and its streets are clogged with tourists and traffic.

Kuta Beach is practically a household name around the globe, but it's not for the fainthearted. It's a rabbit's warren of accommodations and eateries, bars, and souvenir kiosks, jam-packed with people from every corner of the world. But there's no denying that sunset at Kuta is fabulous. Those who love it often return many times and wouldn't think of going anywhere else.

ORIENTATION
The area often referred to collectively as "Kuta" is actually three separate beaches and communities, each with its own personality and attracting a certain type of clientele. They are:

TUBAN Often referred to as "South Kuta," Tuban begins at Bali's Ngurah Rai International Airport, with its northern boundary at the top of Jl. Kartika Plaza, now also called Jl. Dewi Sartika. There are some major resorts here, as well as a plethora of smaller midrange accomodations.

KUTA's southern boundary begins north of Jl. Kartika Plaza (Jl. Dewi Sartika) and stretches to Jl. Melasti in the north. It includes Jl. Legian and Jl. Pantai Kuta (the beachfront drive) and the little lanes in between, extending east past Jl. Imam Bonjol out to Jl. Sunset Road. Jl. Legian is the commercial artery of Kuta and the location of many of its restaurants, shops and nightspots. Another line-up of seaside resorts starts at the corner of Jl. Pantai Kuta with the Hard Rock Hotel all the way to Alam Kul Kul with the Harris Resort Kuta Beach in between.

LEGIAN Legian is the northern extension of Kuta proper, stretching from Jl. Melasti to Jl. Arjuna (formerly called Jl. Double Six) in the north. This is a more upscale area, home to a number of expats and long-stay tourists, and acting as a buffer zone between brash Kuta and classy Seminyak. Note that even though it's a bit further, it's usually faster to travel from Kuta and Legian to Seminyak by using Jl. Sunset Road instead of the traffic-packed Jl. Raya Seminyak/Legian.

GETTING THERE & GETTING AROUND
Kuta is just a short ride from the airport, where you'll find prepaid taxis for the trip. **Taxis** ply the streets of the resorts, hunting passengers. Bluebird and Bali Taxi are reliable companies. Cars and minibuses are available for charter, and ojek (motorbike taxis) will take you on short rides for negotiable fares.

Kuta is a major hub on the tourist shuttle bus **network**, with minibuses departing every morning for all the main tourist accommodation centers in Bali, from Ubud to Amed. These are the easiest way to get out of town. Any accommodation or travel agent will book seats for you, and many operators will pick you up wherever you are staying. **Perama** (Jl. Legian 39, www.peramatour.com), with its convenient location and fast and efficient service, is Kuta's most active travel agent, with its own daily shuttle buses.

Both **motorbikes and cars** are available to rent in Kuta, and you'll get cheaper daily prices here than anywhere else in Bali—as little as $4/day for a long-term scooter rental—so it's a good place to get set up if you're planning to explore the island for several weeks under your own steam. But be warned: the traffic in both Kuta itself, and on the surrounding highways, is the most hectic in Bali.

ACCOMMODATIONS
Kuta has thousands of rooms, ranging from tiny $10 a night concrete boxes to upscale resorts. There are literally hundreds of **losmen** or homestay "inns" scattered throughout Kuta. The rooms are basic (though many have shifted slightly upmarket in recent years), but a breakfast of fruit salad or toast and tea or coffee is almost always included. There are also now lots of modern midrange "city hotel" type properties away from the beach and catering to Indonesian business travelers needing to be near the airport, as much as to tourists. They don't have much atmosphere, but they can be excellent value.

The best way to find a room that suits you is to shop around. There are several online booking services. Try www.agoda.com for good prices. Otherwise, grab almost any old place the first night, then hit the ground the next morning and upgrade yourself. If you're in a hurry, you can book through the hotel association counter at the airport. The recommendations here are intended to give some points of reference.

Hotels are often fully booked during the peak seasons (Christmas–New Year, July–August, and during Ramadan), so make a reservation for a day or two and look around if the hotel is not to your liking. In the low season most hotels offer discounts of up to 40 or even 50 percent.

100 Sunset Boutique Hotel, Jl. Sunset Rd No 100 tel: 847-7360, www.100sunsetboutiquehotel.com. A modern minimalist boutique hotel with 28 rooms and 17 short-term and long-term apartments. All rooms here have kitchenette, air-con, Wi-Fi, and sound system. There's a spa onsite. **$$-$$$**

Alam KulKul Boutique Resort, Jl. Raya Pantai Kuta tel: 752-520, www.alamkulkul.com. A four-star newly refurbished boutique resort across the road from Kuta Beach. Tropical gardens and cascading pools surround thatched villas and spacious rooms, with antique furniture and local handicrafts in contemporary facilities. **$$$$**

Fat Yogi's, Gang Poppies I, tel: 751665. Set back down an alleyway 300m from the beach is this laid-back and very central place with pool. Originally a cheap surfers' hangout, it has shifted towards midrange, with well-kept rooms, with air-con and hot water and nice balconies. This lane, Poppies I, is a bit more tranquil and family-friendly than the rowdier Poppies II further north. **$$**

HARRIS Resort Kuta Beach, Jl. Pantai Kuta www.harris-kuta-bali.com. Located around a free-form swimming pool overlooking gardens, this large resort has 191 guestrooms and suites in simple modern style. It's very close to the beach, and surrounded by recent midrange retail and lifestyle developments, and is a good option for families wanting to be in a more salubrious quarter of Kuta. **$$$**

Kedin's II, Gang Sorga (north of Gang Poppies I) www.kedins-inn.com. A long-standing budget favorite on a quiet backstreet, Kedin's has simple, clean rooms around a swimming pool. There's an attached café for breakfast, and the location is peaceful by Kuta standards. There's another property, Kedin's I, nearby on Poppies I. Booking is advisable if you want to be sure of a room at either. **$-$$**

Komala Indah II Sunset, Jl. Pantai, tel: 751-670. Unpretentious, clean, fan or air-con rooms with hot water in a quiet area under palms, a skip away from the beach. The sister property, Komala Indah I, is on Jl. Benasari. **$-$$**

Poppies Cottages, Gang Poppies 1, www.poppies-bali.com. A long-time Kuta favorite, the complex here includes 20 quaint cottages in secluded tropical gardens in the heart of Kuta. Natural swimming pool and Jacuzzi; five-minute walk to Kuta Beach. Open-air restaurant serves good international food. **$$$**

Ramayana Resort & Spa, Jl. Bakung Sari www.ramayanahotel.com. With a good location on the border of Kuta and Tuban, this large, modern resort is just a short walk to the beach and Kuta Square. There are full resort facilities onsite. **$$$**

Villa De Daun, Jl. Raya Legian, www.villadedaun.com. Amidst the Kuta mass-market mayhem, this is a seriously exclusive little secret. The 12 villas are designed to mimic a traditional village, with rustic stylings. Each comes with its own garden compound, pool, outdoor leisure space, and kitchenette. Butler service is available and there's an award-winning spa. **$$$$**

Yulia Beach Inn, Jl. Pantai Kuta 43, www.yuliabeachinns.com. One of the original Kuta places, and still going strong, Yulia is a solid midrange choice, only five minutes from the beach. Service is excellent and welcoming, and the bungalows, set in a nice garden, are clean and comfortable, and good value. **$$**

DINING

The entire beach area from Tuban all the way north has become a culinary paradise. New places open frequently and competition is fierce, but those that stay the course offer great food at unbeatable prices. You'll find the world on a plate here, with cuisines from the four corners, Mexican, Indian, Japanese, Mediterranean, Moroccan, and more.

The Balcony, Un's Hotel, Jl. Benasari 16, tel: 750-655. This stylish restaurant has long been a standout for its excellent European-style food and service. It is best known for its variety of brochettes, juicy meat, and seafood skewers. Special offers available every day of the week. Un's Hotel also offers rooms. Breakfast, lunch, and dinner. **$$**

Kori Restaurant & Bar, Gang Poppies II, www.korirestaurant.com. With a fantastic interior and idyllic garden setting, this is a long-running favorite in Kuta. The extensive international menu has western favorites, such as bangers and mash and roast beef with Yorkshire pudding. Also try the giant seafood kebab for two and reasonably priced imported and local wine, cocktails, or ice cold beer to wash it all down. Lively poolside bar with regular cocktail promotions. Always busy. Lunch and dinner. **$$-$$$**

Made's Warung, Jl. Pantai Kuta 16A, www. madeswarung.com. A reliable old-time favorite and popular hangout for people-watching and great food (Indo-International). Specialties include Thai and Vietnamese salads, prawns in chili sauce, squid fillet, black rice ice cream, and cappuccino. Has a breakfast special that includes fruit juice, eggs, bacon, toast, fresh fruit yoghurt, and frothy cappuccino. There's another branch in Seminyak. Breakfast, lunch, and dinner. **$$**

Mama's German Restaurant, La Walon Shopping Center, Jl. Legian, www.bali-mamas.com. Since 1985, the place for homemade sausages from their own butchery (the owner is from Hamburg) and yummy German dishes. Breakfast, lunch, and dinner. **$$**

Kopi Pot, Jl. Legian, Tel 752-614. A range of dishes, outrageous homemade cakes, fine coffees from around the world, plus tasty shakes are on offer in this multi-level eatery, set back from the main drag. The stylish Lone Palm Bar serves the coldest beers on Jl. Legian. Breakfast, lunch, and dinner. **$$-$$$**

Nero Bali Mediterranean Restaurant & Lounge
Jl. Legian Keloid No 384, www.nerobali.com. A high-class restaurant and bar serving excellent Greek and Italian food in a stunning interior. From outside it looks expensive but it's actually very reasonably priced; modern, simple, exquisite, delicious. Breakfast, lunch, and dinner. **$$-$$$**

Papa's Café, Jl. Pantai Kuta, tel: 755-055. Facing the beach, this alfresco-style restaurant is among the island's very best for Mediterranean cuisine. Known for its inspired fresh seafood dishes, superb coffee drinks, and good service. **$$**

Poppies Restaurant, Gang Poppies I, www. poppiesbali.com. One of the original restaurants in town. The lane on which it is located is named after it, not the other way around, and Kuta has grown from a simple fishing village to a tourist megalopolis around it, but Poppies is still going strong, with an upmarket atmosphere and menu. Fresh seafood, steaks, shish kebabs, as well as salads, a selection of Indonesian dishes and an extensive wine list are served up in a romantic garden setting. Advance bookings are a must during the high season. Breakfast, lunch, and dinner. **$$-$$$**

TJ's, Gang Poppies I, tel: 751-093. Authentic and delicious enchiladas and margaritas are on offer here in a walled garden setting. The nachos and salsa are perfect with a cold beer. Try a frozen strawberry margarita. Breakfast, lunch, and dinner. **$$**

Warung 96, Jl. Benesari, Gang Poppies II, tel: 750-597. An old surfers' favorite, Warung 96 has seen similar places around it come and go over the years, but it's still doing great, cheap crispy wood-fired pizzas, burgers, fresh salads and Indonesian classics. Breakfast, lunch, and dinner. **$-$$**

NIGHTLIFE

Bali's nightlife is legendary and these days there are two very different "scenes": the young boisterous crowd that dominates the Kuta circuit and a cooler, slightly older expat Euro and Jakartan crowd that frequents the beach cafes and chic restaurants of northern Legian and Seminyak.

When the sun begins to set, the whole southern Bali coastal strip from Tuban to Canggu comes to life. There's no dress code in Kuta. Get down in board shorts and T-shirts or get all gussied up.

From 9 pm–11:30 pm, on the **Hard Rock's Centerstage**, local and international bands play in an unplugged format each night of the week—and no cover charge! Look out for big national and international acts from 11 pm–2 am.

As the night wears on, those looking for a little more class generally head north to Legian and Seminyak, but there's plenty of rowdy action in the heart of Kuta along Jl. Legian. Be prepared for heavy security, ID checks, traffic jams, and parking problems. Also be wary of cheap liquor sold on the streets. Several locals and tourists have died recently from drinking contaminated homebrewed *arak*.

Some of the current ear-splitting rowdy faves are **Apache**, a thoroughly rowdy spot with live reggae music. The **Bounty** is the grand-daddy on this strip, a raucous complex centered on a life-size pirate ship (honestly). **Embargo** sends gangsta rap into the air, and there's also **Brandy's HipHop Club**, **Sky Garden Lounge**, **Red Room Discotheque**, **Eikon**… the list goes on.

Away from Jl. Legian, try **Twice Bar** on Gang Poppies II for punk (it's owned by Indonesia's biggest punk band, Superman is Dead, and they sometimes play here). For something more soothing, **Gabah Terrace Lounge** in the Ramayana Resort & Spa on Jl. Bakungsari has jazz.

SHOPPING

Kuta is a shopper's dream. This is partly because it's an important manufacturing center of summer wear, jewelry, decorative handicrafts, and homewares, which are exported all over the world. Most of the goods are designed by expatriates from Europe, the US, and Japan.

The best areas for shopping are Jl. Legian, Jl. Bakungsari, Jl. Melasti, and nearby back lanes such as Poppies I and II. Some bargains, though, can still be struck as far away as Seminyak and Kerobokan. Before buying, check wares carefully because goods are not returnable.

Bali Galleria Shopping World is a large mall on Jl. Bypass Ngurah Rai with a huge duty free shop in front favored by busloads of Asian tourists. The best for one-stop-shopping are the **Matahari** stores, with their huge selection of goods from clothing to homewares. There is a branch in Kuta Square. Their supermarket is a good source of snacks, dry goods, and processed foods.

Clothing & fabrics

A whole range of clothing prices and styles can be found in Kuta, from gaudy T-shirts to exclusive designer labels. Always check the quality of costly items to ensure you don't get export remnants. Counterfeit branded goods are abundant. In small shops, bargain hard. The established manufacturers generally have more than one outlet in Kuta and Legian. Various shops can also make almost anything to order for both men and women, from suits to shoes, from bathing suits to neckties. Tailors often have a large stock of different fabrics to choose from and offer speedy service.

Body & Soul, Kuta Square 32D, Jl. Pantai Kuta, tel: 755-227; Discovery Shopping Mall; and Bali Galleria Shopping World, 1st floor Unit 1A-39, Jl. Bypass Ngurah Rai, www.bodyandsoulclothing.com. Trendy fashion lycra pants, shirts and bright prints aimed at the younger market. Other outlets in Seminyak, Legian, Nusa Dua. Factory outlets in Legian and Seminyak.

By the Sea, Jl. Legian 186, tel: 757-775. A striking range of cool leisurewear for the whole family.

Milo's, Kuta Square, www.milos-bali.com. One of the original overseas designers to discover the artistry of Balinese batik workers and translate it into Western styling, this three-story boutique stocks a wonderful and tactile range of expensive silks. Also has outlets in Seminyak.

Children & teens

Colorful children's wear is popular throughout Kuta. Quality fabrics and trendy styling means that when you get back home, the gear will hold up. Stock up on basic playwear such as jeans and T-shirts at a quarter of the prices abroad.

Indigo Kids. Six stores in Kuta, Legian, Seminyak, and Nusa Dua selling a great collection of children's wear for kids aged three months to 12 years. Established in 1983, also sells wholesale. Australian designs manufactured throughout Indonesia. Reliable quality, affordable prices. Specializes in fine handicrafted details. Also sells children's accessories.

Kahuna Surf Kids, Jl. Legian Kaja 476, tel: 755-927. Kid's colorful surf wear.

Rascals. Two stores located on Kuta Square Block D-6, Jl. Pantai Kuta, and Jl. Legian 86, tel: 461-357. Cute range of kids' swimwear and accessories styled in traditional batik that look good on and off the beach.

Furniture, antiques & reproductions

There's a plethora of "antique" stores in southern Bali. Be wary: many objects aren't genuine. Most authentic pieces were bought up years ago, but with luck it's still possible to buy the genuine article between 25 and 40 years old from Bali, Java, Kalimantan, and Nusa Tenggara. Make sure any furniture bought here has been kiln dried so that the wood won't crack in drier climates when you get it home.

Hishem Furniture, Jl. Sunset Road 86C, www.hishem.com. Manufacturer of rattan furniture.

Homewares & interiors

House of Yanie, Kuta Square, www.houseofyanie.com. Over three floors brimming with a selection of fine gifts and homewares, both domestic and international, selected by Yanie during her travels in Indonesia, Asia, and abroad. From traditional to contemporary fashion, souvenirs, toys, and ornaments—retail or wholesale—can be found in this eclectic treasure trove.

Jewelry

Many large hotels have upmarket jewelry shops. Attractive accessories such as bracelets, earrings, and brooches can be found in many of these shops.

Mayang Bali Fine Jewelry, Kuta Square A 12, Jl. Pantai Kuta, www.mayangbalijewelry.com. Sterling silver jewelry set with many beautiful and unusual gemstones: diamonds, lapis lazuli, garnets, moonstones, labradorites, sapphires, and rubies set in over 500 different designs manufactured by their own craftsmen. Open 9 am–9 pm daily.

Suarti Design Collection. Factory and showroom are in Celuk (central Bali)—Bali's silver center—but Ibu Suarti's fashion jewelry is found in a large number of jewelry outlets in the major shopping centers in southern and central Bali. Offers unique designs executed by experienced craftsmen reflecting the culture and tradition of Indonesia.

Surfwear & Sporting Goods

Surfwear is ubiquitous in southern Bali, with hundreds of surf shops, selling the latest boardies, bikinis, skirts, and tops of the surfing world.

Rip Curl, Kuta Square, Jl. Pantai Kuta, tel: 865-035. and 10 other outlets. One of the biggest surf gear shops on Bali. Stocks a full range of surf labels, both beachwear and gear. Open Monday–Saturday, 10 am–11 pm.

Surfer Girl, Jl. Legian 138, next door to Quiksilver surf shop. Bali's best all-girls surf shop and largest in the world. Complete collection of beach and resort wear.

Volcom, Kuta Square, Blok AII, www.volcomind.com. Excellent selection of surf and skate gear and accessories. Open 9:30 am–11 pm.

MONEY

ATMs are abundant and found throughout Kuta. Those attached to banks usually allow for larger withdrawals than standalone ones in kiosks, or inside convenience stores.

Kuta has a great number of **moneychangers**, with every other shop on the main streets displaying an exchange rate board. They do, however, have a terrible reputation for dodgy dealing and sleight of hand chicanery, so be very careful when trading your cash. The large, thoroughly professional **Central Kuta Money Exchange** on Jl. Raya Kuta (tel: 762-970) is the best bet for fair dealing.

COMMUNICATIONS
Internet

Virtually every restaurant and accommodation in Kuta, and even some of the convenience stores, offer **free Wi-Fi** connections, so **cyber cafés** are rapidly becoming a thing of the past. There are a few still scattered around Kuta, however, generally charging around Rp500/minute. Many travel agencies also maintain a few computers for public Internet access, which can be useful if you need to print out airline tickets.

Post

The **Kuta Post Office** is located on Jl. Slamet, a small lane off Jl. Raya Kuta, open 7 am–2 pm Monday–Thursday, 7–11 am Friday, 7 am–1 pm Saturday. Many shops double as postal agents (look for the orange sign "approved by the post office") sell stamps, handle parcel shipments, and offer courier services.

DOUBLE TROUBLE

Getting your bearings in the small but traffic-congested and crowded beach areas is difficult enough without the additional challenge of streets bearing more than one name. Several street names have been changed, some of them more than one time. The problem is that not all of the ads in tourist magazines—or the shops and restaurants themselves—have conformed to the new monikers.

Below are the confusing names most commonly encountered:

New name	Former name(s)
Kuta:	
Jl. Singosari	Jl. Bakung Sari
Legian:	
Jl. Blue Ocean	Jl. Pantai Legian
Jl. Werkudara	Jl. Pura Bagus Taruna; Jl. Rum Jungle
Jl. Yudistira	Jl. Padma
Seminyak:	
Jl. Arjuna	Jl. Double Six
Jl. Abimanyu	Jl. Dhyanapura; Jl. Camplung Tanduk; Jl. Gado-Gado
Jl. Kayu Aya	Jl. Laksmana; Jl. Oberoi
Jl. Raya Basangkasa	The northern stretch of Jl. Raya Seminyak
Tuban:	
Jl. Dewi Sartika	Jl. Kartika Plaza

VISITING TUBAN See map, page 81.

Tuban is the southernmost beach and is sometimes called "South Kuta." It stretches south to the airport. Most of the accommodation here is in the midrange band, interspersed with large, family-friendly resorts.

ACCOMMODATIONS

HARRIS Hotel Tuban, Jl. Dewi Sartika (Jl. Kartika Plaza) www.tuban-bali.harrishotels.com.
A friendly and efficient boutique business hotel, five minutes from Bali's airport, and a short walk to the beach. There are 66 rooms and suites, and a swimming pool, and the place is quiet in spite of its busy location. $$-$$$

Bali Garden Beach Resort, Jl. Dewi Sartika (Jl. Kartika Plaza), www.baligardenbeach resort.com. A four-star hotel set amidst tropical gardens directly across from Waterbom Park, this place has a huge range of facilities onsite, and the beach is right on the doorstep. Rooms and suites come at a wide range of prices and good Internet discounts are often available. $$$
Bali Dynasty Resort, Jl. Kartika Plaza, www. balidynasty.com. A huge resort with upgraded rooms, everything here comes with fresh modern design, and the rooms come with the latest technology along with the usual creature comforts. There

are three swimming pools and multiple restaurants. The focus is on families here, and there are lots of good activities onsite. **$$$$**

Discovery Kartika Plaza, Jl. Kartika Plaza, www.discoverykartikaplaza.com. A state-of-the-art modern hotel with ocean views and award-winning environmental standards, this is an excellent place to stay if you're looking for luxury. The gardens surround a pool and stretch right down to the seashore, and the hustle and bustle of Tuban and Kuta seems a world away. Rooms, suites and villas are sleek and modern, but with little dashes of Balinese color, and there are some excellent restaurants onsite. **$$$$**

Holiday Inn Resort Baruna Bali, Jl. Wana Segara 33, www.bali.holidayinn.com. Guest rooms here match the usual Holiday Inn international standards, and there are several restaurants onsite and a good spa. **$$$$**

Risata Bali Resort & Spa, Jl. Wana Segara, www.risatabali.com. Rooms, suites and villas at this popular resort feature modern home comforts and private balconies. There's a large swimming pool, kids' playground, pool table, and gym. There's also a good pizza restaurant, and a spa. **$$$**

The Vira Bali Hotel, Jl. Kartika Plaza No. 127, www.thevirabali.com. A chic four-story, four-star hotel with 56 rooms and suites, contemporary minimalist design, and Balinese hospitality. Central and cozy, there's a swimming pool with waterfall and fountains, enhancing the hotel's tranquil atmosphere. **$$$**

DINING

Golden Lotus, Bali Dynasty Resort, Jl. Kartika Plaza, tel: 752-403, Specializing in Cantonese and Sichuan cuisines, in particular Peking duck, this is one of the best Chinese restaurants in Bali, with ornate décor reminiscent of a stylish Hong Kong eatery. There are private rooms for exclusive dim sum lunches. Everything on the menu is delicious. Lunch and dinner. **$$$**

Gracie Kelly's Irish Pub, Bali Dynasty Resort, Jl. Kartika Plaza, tel: 752-403. With friendly staff, warm atmosphere, an open brick fireplace, this is the archetypal brand-Ireland international pub-restaurant. Typical home-cooked pub favorites are on offer,

including freshly baked bread, Irish stew, and a classic fish and chips. There are pool tables, darts, and a live band every night. Breakfast, lunch, and dinner. **$$**

Kin Khao, Jl. Kartika Plaza 170, tel: 753-806. This popular restaurant has been serving up authentic Thai food since 1994, ranging from tom yum soup to *khao neow mannuang* (sticky rice with mango). The cooking is thoroughly flavorsome, and the curry pastes, tea, and coffee are imported from Thailand. Breakfast, lunch, and dinner. **$$**

MaJoly, Kupu Kupu Barong Beach Hotel, Jl. Wana Segara, www.ma-joly.com. A stunning spot for sunset, this stylish restaurant offers french and international fine dining with great wines and excellent service in a smart-casual beachside setting. Also serves fresh fish from Jimbaran, fresh fruit juices, cocktails, and fine coffees. Lunch and dinner. **$$$**

Stadium Café, Jl. Kartika Plaza, Complex Kuta Sidewalk 5–8, tel: 764-100. Inexpensive food favored by—as the name suggests—the sports crowd, who flock here for live telecasts of international events. In addition to cold beer, recommended are nachos, pasta, and pub fare. Breakfast, lunch, and dinner. **$$**

SHOPPING

Discovery Mall, Jl. Kartika Plaza, www.discoveryshoppingmall.com. This massive shopping mall is right on the beach—for better or for worse—squeezed in between five-star resorts. Includes two large department stores (Centro and Sogo) and 98 shops, from Crocs to Nike. In the basement is a large handicrafts market; 19 food outlets.

Talimas, Jl. Raya 83 E, tel: 763-863. A textile wholesale and retail gallery offering a wide variety of woven, knitted, printed and dyed fabrics. A computer is available if you want to create your own designs.

ACTIVITIES

Waterbom, Jl. Kartika, www.waterbom-bali.com. Great for the whole family—17 exhilarating slides, Pleasure Pool for swimming and volleyball, Jungle River relaxing float. Supervised kids' area, Splash Bar, food court, massage. They're always adding something new to this ever-popular park, keeping the wet and wild endlessly entertained for decades. Open daily 9 am–6 pm.

LEGIAN, SEMINYAK, PETITENGET & KEROBOKAN

Trendy Beach Areas North of Kuta

Visitors will be forgiven if they are unable to determine where one neighborhood stops and another begins along the 5 km (3 miles) stretch of beach that is often erroneously called "Kuta." There are no markers differentiating one from another, yet each has its own distinguishing characteristics; and less obvious is that each is governed by a different set of village leaders who attend to rituals, festivals, ceremonies, and tourism.

North of Kuta, Legian is slightly quieter than the central beach at Kuta. It is difficult to tell where Kuta ends and Legian begins. However, north of Legian, Seminyak, Petitenget, and Kerobokan have decidedly different auras. Developing later than Kuta and Legian, these communities opted to appeal to higher-end travelers and those seeking a bit more peace and quiet.

Legian
As with Tuban, south of Kuta, Legian blossomed into action to cash in on Kuta's fame in the 1970s. At its southern boundary it begins

Full gallop on a stretch of Legian beach

Seminyak's bars and cafés tend to be less rough and ready than those further south.

just north of Jl. Melasti and in the north merges into Seminyak at Jl. Arjuna. Legian has historically attracted a slightly older crowd than Kuta's and for many years, expatriates on a budget who weren't into the beach scene at Kuta lived and gathered here. Many of those resident foreigners have now moved their homes and social lives elsewhere, but Legian remains a good location for family-friendly, midrange accommodations, nightlife a little less frenzied than that of Kuta, and, of course, glorious beach life. The exception to this more sedate reputation is a gaggle of bars off Jl. Arjuna (formerly called Jl. Double-Six) on the beach, where the partying goes hard until the wee hours.

Life in Legian revolves around the beach, and there's not a lot else to see here. **Surfing lessons** can be arranged from one of the reputable schools, and **surfboards** and **boogie boards** can be rented on the beach. On the northern stretch of sand south of Jl. Arjuna there are friendly **football games** every late afternoon, with both locals and visitors joining in the mayhem. On Saturday and Sunday evenings crowds gather here for jam sessions and everyone is invited to exhibit their talents. Some folks prefer to take the sidelines and enjoy both happenings at one of the beachfront cafés with a yummy fruit juice, cocktail, or an ice cold beer and a snack.

The only other pastime in Legian is **shopping**. From Jl. Arjuna in the north to Jl. Melasti at the southern boundary, all the side streets running perpendicular to the sea are filled with kiosks selling items Bali has always been known for: souvenirs, handicrafts, sarongs, and sportswear. An **art market** on Jl. Melasti near the beach will happily take any leftover shopping money.

A bit more exciting, however, is Jl. Legian from Jl. Padma as far north as weary feet can take shoppers. It has already happened in Ubud, and now it's happening here: shops filled with cheap trinkets and poor quality T-shirts are gradually being replaced by classier boutiques offering quality items. As with accommodations and restaurants, further north toward Seminyak is where the more exclusive shops are. Look for **jewelry stores** showcasing gemstones, intricate designs, and the superb craftsmanship that Bali has become known for internationally. Many of the garment businesses that formerly made clothing here for export have now set up boutiques in Bali, eliminating the markup that customers would pay in stores abroad. **Interiors shops** have also sprung up along Jl. Legian featuring tableware, lamps, and other top-end accessories at much more afford-0able prices than in Western countries. The bonus is that these boutiques are air-conditioned.

Bali can be a great place to take surfing lessons.

Seminyak

Expensive boutiques, spas, villas, restaurants, and nightspots proliferate in Seminyak. Home to a large community of well-heeled expatriates — many running their own tourism or export businesses, others simply enjoying the high life — Seminyak and points north are the high end of the beach strip. Seminyak's southern boundary is Jl. Arjuna (formerly called Jl. Double Six), which becomes Jl. Nakula east off Jl. Raya Seminyak. Jl. Arjuna also divides some of the beaches' hippest nightspots, leaving **Bacio** on the Seminyak side of the border and its sister and brother party hubs, **De Ja Vu** and **Zanzibar**, on the northern end of Legian.

The exclusive Seminyak beach's northern boundary can be confusing. Technically, at Jl. Kayu Jati and eastward in a zigzag fashion

Tourists enjoy a sunset drink with a few friends at a beach bar on Seminyak beach.

Visiting international DJs are on tap nightly in some of Seminyak's trendy nightspots.

toward Jl. Raya Kerobokan (north of Jl. Laksmana), it becomes Petitenget and Kerobokan. Until fairly recently, few people knew or cared where the dividing lines were; however, now that Petitenget and Kerobokan are developing at lightning pace, the new establishments to the north are using the correct district names, while the old ones elsewhere still call the entire area "Seminyak."

Serious shopping is the name of the game in Seminyak when the sun gets too hot beachside. The day can be broken up with stops for a cappuccino, lunch, and high tea at any of a number of fancy cafés and restaurants, or a spa treatment or two before heading back toward the sea for a sundowner at the end of the day. When the sun has disappeared behind the horizon, then it's time to go back to the villa or five-star resort—there is almost no budget accommodation here—to freshen up for the evening.

Nighttime activities in Seminyak run the gamut from romantic dinners in some of Southeast Asia's most exclusive eateries, to nights on the tiles in some of its most fashionable bars and nightclubs—where rubbing shoulders with a celebrity or two is always a possibility.

Petitenget

An extension of the Seminyak beachside lifestyle, Petitenget used to be happy to be known as nothing more than a suburb of its glitzy southern neighbor, until village chiefs wisely decided that the community could establish a unique reputation of its own. With the dividing line between Seminyak and Petitenget being a major street filled with all sorts of tourist temptations—Jl. Laksmana—addresses are often listed in Seminyak when they are actually located in Petitenget. Which community is which actually makes no difference to visitors: just be aware that there might be confusion locating addresses close to the boundary.

The only cultural landmark in Petitenget is **Pura Petitenget**. Built in the 16th century, this temple was completed when the area was covered by dense jungle of a different type than the urban one of today, in honor of the Javanese priest Danghyang Nirartha, who constructed Tanah Lot further up the coast. There is a large parking lot where the trees once stood, serviced by men of the local community. It's wise to park here and walk down—or up—the beach to avoid Seminyak's horrendous traffic congestion.

Kerobokan

Without the Indian Ocean at its borders to lure visitors, inland Kerobokan has developed based on rice field views and serenity away from the noise and hubbub of the southern beaches—though much of the original farmland has disappeared beneath tourism developments and villa complexes. It is near enough to get to the shopping and nightlife, but the setting is still rather more sedate. As with Petitenget and Seminyak, it is difficult for casual visitors to discern where one area ends and the other begins.

There are too many private villas in Kerobokan to count. Some are for rent, and most come with a cook and gardener and car and driver. Online research or word of mouth recommendations are the best way of finding the perfect slice of heaven.

Romantic Double Six beach in Seminyak

CANGGU & TANAH LOT

Gorgeous Beaches and a Famous Temple

Northwest of Petitenget and Kerobokan is a handful of villages collectively called **Canggu** by some, at least for now. As development continues everywhere in southern Bali, the trend is that new establishments are using the correct area names to distinguish themselves. However, more mature settlers still use the old names. In the not-too-distant future, the areas with hitherto unknown labels will be as familiar to travelers as Kuta and Legian are now, as the area continues to evolve. Get there by going north on Jl. Kerobokan (the road to Tanah Lot, which should definitely be avoided at rush hour times) until it becomes Jl. Raya Canggu. Then follow any of the real estate sales signs down little lanes west toward the sea.

The pounding waves along this coast originally attracted surfers and there are a few homestays, *warungs*, and board repair kiosks still here. The big shock, though, is the amount of construction equipment traveling up and down along the narrow country roads. Hotels and villas—some of which can best be described as mansions—are popping up everywhere on beaches named **Berawa**, **Canggu (Batu Bolong)**, **Echo (Batu Mejan)**, **Pererenan** and **Selasih**, stretching all the way from Kerobokan and Petitenget to the Tabanan Regency border northwest of Tanah Lot. Where there are tourists, there will soon be eateries, bars, and shopping, but for now rice fields still dominate much of the land.

Off the main road, small lanes lead to the various beaches. **Jl. Pantai Berawa** (also spelled Brawa), the road to Berawa Beach, is lined with rice fields—with enormous villas on the horizon—and is the location of the **Canggu Club**, a cricket club of sorts with swimming pool and spa. Day passes are available. Foreigners riding bicycles and motorbikes equipped with surfboard racks abound, as do construction sites. At the end of the road there is a *warung* offering surfing lessons, gear, board repair, and pizza in its

The beaches along the Canggu coast have good spots for both intermediate and beginning surfers.

Surrounded by the churning waters of the Indian Ocean, Tanah Lot—like so many of Bali's important temples—is dramatically located on a jagged rock that becomes an island during high tide.

garden café near **Legong Keraton Beach Hotel**—right on the beach—which undoubtedly attracts the new generation of more affluent surfers than those who stayed in cheap *losmen* (hostels or inns) in the past. Berawa Beach vendors gather here to sell sarongs and souvenirs to tourists.

There are not many villas yet along Jl. Pantai Batu Bolong (also called Jl. Canggu Beach) but there is a large parking area, as this beach has long attracted intermediate and experienced surfers. Nearby is the long-established **Hotel Tugu Bali**. Filled with antiques and art, it is part museum, part art gallery, all packaged under the humble title "hotel."

Returning to the main street, Jl. Raya Canggu, the next small road to the sea leads to Echo Beach, also known as Pantai Batu Mejan. It is possibly the fastest growing development, with wall-to-wall private villas. Echo Beach has already earned a reputation for being a "happening" place. On Sunday afternoons the beach turns into a mini-Woodstock with music and frivolity.

Down another small road to the sea—Jl. Melayan—is **Canggu Tua** (Old Canggu), which still has a few glimpses of what the region must have been like before the foreigners with money started moving in, despite the villas which are already proliferating.

A temple in the sea

All old Balinese realms have a mountain-to-the-sea axis, an ordering of the physical landscape that mirrors the ordering of the cosmos, with major points marked by temples. Each former Balinese kingdom thus has six major temples, the *sad kahyangan*, consecrated to the six most significant features of the landscape: the forest, the mountains, the sea, the lakes, the earth, and the rice fields. Similarly, there are six cardinal temples for the whole of Bali. **Pura Tanah Lot** seaside sanctuary is one of them.

Continuing northwest on the crowded road leading to the Canggu beaches, at Baraban village there are good signs indicating the turnoff to majestic Pura Tanah Lot. Tanah means earth and lot means south or sea (written *lod*), or "Temple of the Earth in the Sea." It is actually constructed atop a large, jagged outcropping of rock just off the coast and is accessible by footpath only during low tide. The temple itself is quite modest, consisting of two shrines with tiered roofs (seven and three), a few small buildings, and two pavilions.

Like so many other temples on Bali, Tanah Lot is connected with the Brahman priest, Danghyang Nirartha, who fled from Java to Bali in the 16th century after the fall of the Majapahit kingdom to the new Muslim state of Demak. On one of his journeys he decided to sleep in this beautiful spot, and then afterwards advised the Balinese to erect a temple here, which they did, making it one of the (*sad kahyangan*), or six most holy temples for all of Bali.

Folklore has it that the poisonous, black-and-white sea snakes that live between the rocks surrounding the temple were originally Niratha's sashes that fell into the sea and became transformed. The snakes are said to guard the temple and keep evil away.

The *sad kahyangan* were meant to be in sight of one another, uniting all of Bali, and on a very clear day Pura Uluwatu is just visible to the south. Many Balinese—and tourists—enjoy sitting on the beach or on a bluff overlooking the temple in the late afternoon, watching the tides change and enjoying the silhouettes of the temple *meru* (pagodas) against the brilliant setting sun. Foreigners are forbidden to enter the temple itself, but still they come by the busloads, especially at sunset. Visit at any other time and the place will be empty, except for the vendors and warungs.

A quiet sunset walk with the kids at Canggu

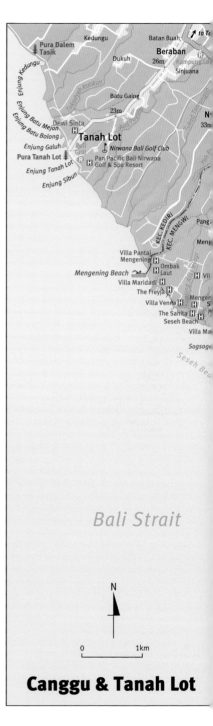

Bali Strait

N

0   1km

Canggu & Tanah Lot

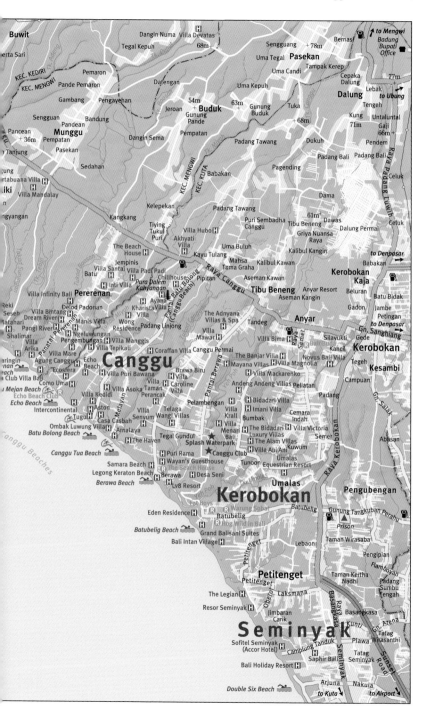

ACCOMMODATION PRICE CATEGORIES Prices are for a double room, including breakfast $ = under $30; $$ = $30–$70; $$$ = $70–$130; $$$$ = over $130. DINING PRICE CATEGORIES Prices are for based on a meal for one, without drinks $ = under $5; $$ = $5–$10; $$$ = over $10.

VISITING LEGIAN See map, page 91.

Legian looks very different, depending on where you are coming from. Come from the south, from Kuta, and it's a definite shift upscale—the hotels, shops, restaurants and tourists displaying a distinct dash of class, the Bintang singlets giving way to flowing cotton and ethnic jewelry. Head south from Seminyak, however, and there's a clear sense of standards sliding. In short, it's a buffer zone between these two wildly contrasting areas on Bali's west coast, and the perfect place to stay if you want the best of both worlds—or if you find both scenes equally unbearable.

ACCOMMODATIONS

FuramaXclusive Ocean Beach, Jl. Arjuna No. 88X www.furamaxclusive.com. A striking exterior of contemporary glass and metal seems odd in Bali but it certainly stands out from the crowd. There are five levels of AC rooms and suites —some with kitchenettes—and villas. The interiors continue the starkly modernist theme, but they are very comfortable. There's a beachfront fine dining restaurant, seafood bistro, and tapas bar. **$$$$**

Hotel Kumala Pantai, Jl. Werkudara, www.kumalapantai.com. The rooms here are arrayed in three-stories around a garden filled with old trees and Balinese, which brings a little atmosphere. The rooms themselves are well-kept and functional, though not particularly stylish, but the beach is very close, which is a bonus. There are occasionally dance and music performances in the attached bar. **$$$**

Legian Beach Hotel, Jl. Melasti, www.legianbeachbali.com. A complex of tropical thatched bungalows facing the beach, this large resort is good value. The palm-shaded grounds extend right to the edge of the sand, and there are rooms with disabled access (a rarity in Bali). The Ole Ocean View Patio beside the pool has great views and upbeat music. **$$$$**

Legian Paradiso Hotel, Jl. Raya Legian No. 118 www.legianparadisto.com. There's a hint of the Mediterranean in this good-value hotel, with rooms arranged around a central pool and gardens. The rooms themselves are bright, clean, and businesslike, and the staff are extremely friendly. **$$$**

Sari Bunga Hotel, Jl. Arjuna, www.balivillagehotel.com. The well-kept rooms here come with queen-sized beds and balconies, and are arrayed around a palm-shaded swimming pool. The beach is a short stroll away, and there's a generous buffet breakfast included in the price, all of which makes for excellent value. **$$**

Three Brothers Bungalows, Off Jl. Raya Legian Tengah, www.threebrothersbungalows.com. Bohemian-style bungalows surrounded by tropical gardens. The bungalows have living rooms and semi-open baths on the ground floor and air-con bedrooms on top floor, all with TV and hot water. There's a large swimming pool and kids' pool, restaurant and bar. **$$**

DINING

Indo-National, Jl. Padma 17, www.indo-national restaurant.com. The busy, Australian-owned restaurant is still going strong under new managers, offering good Western and Indonesian food and ice cold beers in a clean setting. Breakfast, lunch, and dinner. **$$**

Yut'z Place, Jl. Werkudara 521, www.yutzplace.com. Open all day, beginning with hearty breakfasts and serving generous portions of an unusual selection of European dishes, cold plates, appetizers, and Indonesian food, all at reasonable prices. Breakfast, lunch, and dinner. **$$-$$$**

NIGHTLIFE

Legian flows into Seminyak at Jl. Arjuna (Jl. Double Six), with some of the hottest nightspots on the beach on both sides of the road. The Legian and Seminyak crowd tend to start the ball rolling with sundowners on the beach at **Blue Ocean,** or **Zanzibar** at the bottom of Jl. Arjuna (Jl. Double Six), followed by dinner and further frivolity at nightspots on lively Jl. Abimanyu (Jl. Dhyanapura) in Seminyak.

Blue Ocean Bali, Jl. Pantai Arjuna, www.blueoceanbali.com. Opened in 1969, a favorite haunt for travelers from all over the world; specializes in fresh seafood at reasonable prices. Terrace has ocean views for spectacular sunsets while enjoying coolers and cocktails. There's excellent live music at the weekends, and a solid sunset crowd every night of the week.

DeJaVu, Jl. Blue Ocean Beach/Arjuna 7 X, tel: 732-777. A relaxing lounge bar with comfy sofas and stools, impromptu parties, and some of the best cocktails and DJs on Bali every day of the week. Popular from about midnight until 3 am, when the all-nighters move on.

Zanzibar, Jl. Arjuna, www.zanzibarbali.com. On Double Six Beach, this glitzy bar-restaurant serves Mediterranean dishes and seafood as well as breakfast, lunch, daily finger food buffet and special drinks. It's a lively spot at night when dinner morphs seamlessly into a party scene.

VISITING SEMINYAK, PETITENGET & KEROBOKAN   See map, page 91.

Seminyak is five-star luxury, nothing less will do, and is also home of some of the most vibrant, glittery nightlife in southern Bali. To the north, Seminyak gives way to Petitenget and Kerobokan, which are in many ways more laid-back versions of their neighbors to the south: less crowded and more suitable for longer stays. Get ready to shop to the point of exhaustion here, for Seminyak is home to some of the most sophisticated retail in Southeast Asia.

ACCOMMODATIONS
Although the resorts and villas in this area range from expensive to mega-expensive, off-season Internet rates often make them more affordable. Also look for packages that include spa treatments for better rates.

Anantara Seminyak Resort & Spa, Jl. Abimanyu, www.bali.anantara.com. Sleek suites with plasma screen TVs, contemporary Asian-inspired furniture, and spacious balconies are the name of the game at this, one of the finest Seminyak resorts. There are excellent in-house restaurants, a spa, and glorious, edge-of-the-ocean infinity pools. $$$$
Oberoi, Jl. Kayu Aya, www.oberoihotels.com. The original upscale hotel in Seminyak has changed with the times, but kept its unique tropical style a constant. There are dozens of cottages and villas, tucked away in a vast expanse of tropical gardens and the sea at the northern end of Seminyak beach. Traditional Balinese thatched-roof style villas have private pools, garden bathrooms. $$$$
The Elysian Boutique Villa, Jl. Sari Dewi 18, Seminyak, www.theelysian.com. A super-cool villa hotel, the private villas each come with a pool, super-sized bed, sunken bath, and a full suite of Apple technology products. The design is a cunning blend of Scandinavian-style minimalism with tropical touches, and there's excellent dining in the attached restaurant. $$$$
The Legian, Jl. Kayu Aya, www.ghmhotels.com. Confusingly located in Seminyak rather than Legian itself, this all-suite hotel has seaview units on a private, quiet stretch of beach. This is hi-tech accommodation, with lots of state-of-the-art devices in the rooms. Service is exceptional. $$$$
Island Villas & Spa Bali, Jl. Raya Petitenget No. 469, www.islandvillasbali.com. Each of the villas here is individually decorated and comes with its own gourmet kitchen, dining and lounge area, sunken tub for two, private pool and sundeck. Butler service is available; there's a spa, and an excellent restaurant. $$$$

Kanishka Villas, Jl. Kunti 8Y, www.kanishkavillas. com. The luxury pool villas here are tucked away down a quiet lane. Each has an extravagant bathroom and fine fittings, including Jim Thompson fabrics, and a sense of the tropical running throughout. $$$$
Uma Sapna, Jl. Drupadi No. 20XX, www.umasapna. com. A complex of secluded private villas, each with plunge or swimming pool, and a sense of cool seclusion. The in-house chef can prepare high quality food for guests and their parties. Massage and meditation are on offer. $$$$
Villa Bali Asri, Jl. Sari Dewi No. 29, www.villabaliasri. com. With a small array of private vacation villas on a quiet back road in the heart of Seminyak, this is a fine place to escape the crowds. The villas stand in a wooded space surrounded by trees, the sharp lines of the modernist architecture cleverly contrasting with the verdant nature. $$$$
Villa Coco, Jl. Arjuna, www.villacoco.com. The villas here all have private entrance and garden, and a kitchenette. In-house catering is available. There's a pool with pool bar. $$$$

DINING
Jl. Laksmana, informally known as **Jl. Oberoi**, is arguably Bali's trendiest restaurant strip, or "eat street," hosting a mind-boggling array of dining venues. Many of them experience a metamorphosis after dinner and transform into nightspots, where the beautiful people come to see and be seen. No singlets and board-shorts here, please.
Bali Buda, Jl. Banjar Anyar 24, www.balibuda.com. Vegan, raw food, vegetarian dishes, salads, soups, pasta, chicken or fish burgers, super health drinks, healthy breakfasts, and yummy baked goods—what more could you ask for? Breakfast, lunch, and dinner. $-$$
Biku, Jl. Raya Petitenget No 888, www.bikubali.com. An absolute Seminyak institution, beloved of resident expats and artistically-minded locals, this glorious tropical teahouse is set in a 150-year-old teakwood joglo from East Java. There's always a buzz here, and the effortless ambiance is as delicious as the dishes, a range of "tropical comfort food." The highlight is the classic high tea, served up each afternoon with scones, jam, fresh whipped cream, finger sandwiches and homemade cakes. There's a carefully curated selection of handicrafts and books on sale, and live music and literary events are also on the menu. Lunch and dinner. $$
Café Jemme, Jl. Raya Petitenget 28, www. jemmebali.com. A place to wine, dine, and shop for exquisite jewelry, at reasonably affordable prices.

Dishes are prepared with fresh seasonal vegetables from the Jemme's own farm near Negara, western Bali. Lunch and dinner. $$

Chandi Restaurant, Jl. Laksmana No. 72, www.chandibali.com. Pan-Asian fine dining is the name of the game in this renowned Seminyak eatery. Chefs use organic greens and spices from local farmers, imported meats, and soy products made in Bali. The two bars offer some of Bali's wildest cocktails. Lunch and dinner. $$$

Earth Café, Jl. Laksmana No. 99, www.dtebali.com. From the Down to Earth Organic Vegetarian Foods kitchen, Earth Café focuses on working with the universe for healthier life. Supports local farmers and educating the community about the importance of kitchen hygiene and the use of unprocessed products. Gourmet vegetarian cooking classes. Breakfast, lunch, and dinner. $$

Khaima, Jl. Laksmana, www.khaimabali.com. Originally a specifically Moroccan restaurant, Khaima has burst out of its geographical bounds and now serves up a menu of mixed North African and general modern European cuisine, beautifully presented, in a striking setting. Lunch and dinner. $$

Ku De Ta, Jl. Kayu Aya No. 9, www.kudeta.net. One of the hippest spots on the Seminyak seafront for years, Ku De Ta is still at the leading edge of the scene. This is a favored hang-out for the "beautiful people," famed for not only its Australian-style cuisine but also for its cocktails. It's the in-place for after dinner drinks. You may feel out of place if you don't dress smartly. Dinner reservations are essential. Lunch specials change daily and are easier on the pocketbook. Lunch and dinner. $$$

Kuni's, Jl. Laksmana, www.kunisbali.com. A favorite among Japanese travelers, which testifies to its authenticity. Fresh food in subtly lighted, elegant surroundings here. Lunch and dinner. $$-$$$

Mannekepis Jazz & Blues Bistro, Jl. Raya Seminyak No. 2, www.mannekepis-bistro.com. A Belgian bar and bistro serving Belgium beer and other drinks, with a side order of jazz and soulful blues. Belgian specialties and international dishes make up the menu. Lunch and dinner. $$

Metis, Jl. Petitenget No. 6, www.metisbali.com. Spirited haute cuisine Chef Nicolas "Doudou" Tourneville, formerly of all-time favorite Kafe Warisan, presents French-Mediterranean cuisine, personal attention, and flawless service in his acclaimed Seminyak restaurant. There's an attached gallery and boutique with contemporary fashions, hand-crafted jewelry, and unusual *objets d'art*. Also open for lunch with a lighter menu. Lunch and dinner. $$$

Mykonos Taverna, Jl. Laksmana No. 52, www.mykonos-bali.com. A high quality restaurant that serves traditional authentic Greek cuisine.

Renowned for its hearty home-cooked food at reasonable prices, including tangy dips, Greek salad, gyros pitas and tender shish kebabs. Lunch and dinner. $$-$$$

La Lucciola, Jl. Kayu Aya. With its beach lounges and great service, this is a favorite spot for sunset cocktails. Indoor-outdoor seating right on the beach, delicious Italian and contemporary food. Friendly staff. Scrumptious Sunday brunch. Reservations recommended. Breakfast, lunch, dinner. $$$

Queen's Tandoor, Jl. Raya Seminyak No. 73, www.queenstandoor.com. A two-story building with a large outdoor patio, scents of Indian spice waft out onto the tropical air here. Classic dishes from all corners of India make up the menu. Try their chicken tikka, naan (butter, herb, or cheese) or 20 different curries. Deliveries are available. $$-$$$

Sarong Restaurant, Jl. Petitenget No. 19X, www.sarongbali.com. The Australian chef-patron dishes up super-stylish Asian-influenced cuisine in this intimate restaurant that's been riding high on the Seminyak wave for several years. Starters include salmon, chicken, or raw tuna with betel leaf and local spices, scallops, oysters, and Wagyu beef. Dinner. $$$

Zula Vegetarian Paradise, Jl. Dhyanapura No. 5, www.dtebali.com. Owned by the same folks who run Earth Café and billed as totally vegan, this café features the highest quality ingredients, fresh organic produce, nutritional principles, and genuine enthusiasm from the staff. Breakfast, lunch, and dinner. $-$$

NIGHTLIFE

Much of the Seminyak action happens in and around **Jl. Abimanyu,** Bali's party street. With its scores of cocktail bars and cafés, at night it's the busiest street in Seminyak and attracts droves of people until around 2:30 am. Since Seminyak spills over into Legian at Jl. Arjuna (Jl. Double Six), also check Legian "Practicalities" for more of the hottest nightspots on the beach.

Gado-Gado, Jl. Camplung Tanduk No. 99, www.gadogadorestaurant.com. In business since the 1980s, this club's revamped beach lounge features the latest international music, fine dining, respectable wine list, flavorful coffee, inventive cocktails, great atmosphere, and an unbeatable view. Open for lunch and dinner seven days a week, with the party kicking off after dark.

Hu'u, Jl. Petitenget, www.huubali.com. A Bali beach institution and a popular hangout for expats and tourists, who chill out in comfortable lounges or dance to the DJ beats. The lychee martinis here have been voted the best on the island. The party goes on very, very late here.

Jaya Pub Bali, Jl. Raya Seminyak No. 2, tel: 735-310. An old-timer on the Seminyak night scene, this place has a cozy dining area serving Western and Indonesian food, separated from a huge bar and lounge-loft overlooking the stage. Live bands play every night and things keep going until around 2 am.

Red Carpet Champagne Bar, Jl. Laksmana 42, tel: 737-889. A great little bit of chic in the middle of Seminyak, this over-the-top glam bar is the closest most people will come to posing for the paparazzi. Guests are escorted to their table, while champagne is the order of the day. It's open to the street, so a great place for people watching.

Santa Fe Bar & Grill, Jl. Abimanyu No. 11A. In business since 1993 and open 24 hours/day, with a wide selection of food and beverages, specializing in Mexican cuisine and pizza. Live bands play every night and there are generous happy hour drinks specials.

SHOPPING

If you thought Jl. Laksmana was only for eating, watch out shopaholics as you may not be able to restrain yourselves. There are more shopping options here than we could ever list, with new places popping up every month.

Fashion

Animale, Jl. Raya Seminyak 31. A stylish ladies clothing store occupying three floors, with sizeable collections of bright day, night and beach wear, for the most part coordinating printed separates that appeal to a more mature clientele. Also a range of French imports and plus sizes. Factory outlet at Jl. Raya Kuta No. 82.

Biasa, Jl. Raya Seminyak No. 34 & 36, www.biasagroup.com. Displays an excellent range of women's clothes with an emphasis on cool comfort in a variety of whites, pastels, and bright colors using Indian-style cottons and silks. Also men's and children's wear, shoes, bathing suits, and an innovative selection of homewares.

Dinda Rella Fashion Boutique, Jl. Laksmana No. 45, www.dindarella.com. Also in Legian. Fashions created for women who love quality and glamorous dresses. Also exotic accessories.

Jemme Jewelry & Café Jemme, Jl. Raya Petitenget No. 28, www.jemmebali.com. Exporting to Europe and Australia for 25 years. Silver, 18K gold and white gold jewelry with semi-precious stones for men and women. Excellently designed and handcrafted in Bali and Java workshops.

Milo's, Jl. Laksmana No. 992, www.milos-bali.com. One of the original overseas designers to discover the artistry of Balinese batik workers and translate it into Western styling, this boutique stocks a wonderful and tactile range of expensive silks. There are several other branches.

Paul Ropp, Jl. Raya Seminyak 39, tel: 734-208, www.paulropp.com. Ethnic fashions using hand-woven materials. Other outlets in Jimbaran, Kerobokan, and Ubud.

Homewares, interiors & ceramics

DeLighting, Art of Illumination Gallery, Jl. Laksmana 20/14C, www.de-lighting.com. Designers and manufacturers of innovative quality lighting, furniture, and accessories. Also has office, showroom, and factory in Kerobokan.

Haveli, Jl. Basangkasa No. 15 & 38, www.havelishop.com. Art de la table, art de vivre, home decoration.

Piment Rouge, Jl. Sunset 60X, www.pimentrouge-lighting.com. Lights and lamps using a myriad of materials as a basis for innovative designs. Other stores in Ubud, Legian, and Kerobokan.

Vinoti Living, Seminyak Square, www.vinotiliving.com. Furniture, accessories, and artwork designed for great living.

Souvenirs

Geneva, Jl. Raya Kerobokan No. 100, Banjar Taman, Petitenget. Three floors of handicrafts from across the island selling in quantity for lower prices. Rattan tableware, ceramics, incense, wood carvings, local textiles, pillows, stone carvings, furniture.

MARKETS

Bintang Supermarket, Jl. Raya Seminyak, tel: 730-552. Shop in air-conditioned comfort. Wide choice of food, household items, art supplies, even children's toys (upstairs). On the outside is a newsstand and mobile phone vendors.

Earth Café and Market, Jl. Laksmana No. 99, Seminyak, www.dtebali.com. And organic supermarket and café which every two weeks hosts a market with other producers, suppliers, not-profit organizations, organic growers, healers, and new age crafts.

SPAS, MASSAGE, YOGA & BEAUTY

There are several options in this category. Most of the larger hotels have their own spas, the majority of which also have a complete salon for hair treatments, facials, waxing, pedicures, and manicures.

AMO Beauty & Spa, Jl. Petitenget 100X, www.amospa.com. A full-service beauty spa on two levels. Upstairs are wet rooms, facial and waxing rooms, singles' and couples' massage rooms. Hair salon, manicures, reflexology. Walk-ins welcome.

Body Works, Jl. Kayu Jati. A very popular and sumptuous spa. Try the various treatments including body scrubs, massages, and cream baths, and a divine hair treatment that includes head, neck, and shoulder massage.

Disini Spa, Jl. Mertasari No. 28. www.disinivillas.com. Located within Disini Luxury Spa Villas. Morning, evening, and all-day spa sessions using organic ingredients.

Jari Menari, Jl. Raya Basangkasa #47, www.jarimenari.com. Massage menu includes Jari Menari Favorite Massage, Gentle Soul, Tibetan Singing Bowl, Gourmet Massage. Learn Massage every Tuesday. Also in Nusa Dua.

Prima Spa at The Villas, Jl. Kunti 118 X, www.thevillas.net. For something different try the luxurious Moroccan-style spa.

ACTIVITIES

Cocoon Beach Club & Restaurant, Jl. Arjuna, www.cocoon-beach.com. In the style of Mediterranean beach clubs, this is a place to hang out all day and play all night. Changing rooms for swimming in pool or sea, fine dining, great chill-out music on the terrace, a grass terrace for kids to play on, boutique carrying resort wear and gifts, amphitheater for events, luggage storage for airport delays, and shuttle to airport.

ART GALLERIES

Biasa ArtSpace, Jl. Raya Seminyak No 34, www.biasaart.com. Fosters some of the most significant new developments in contemporary Indonesian art, working closely with prominent emerging artists and curators.

Kendra Gallery of Contemporary Art, Jl. Drupadi No. 888, Seminyak, www.kendragallery.com. Highlights both established and young artists from Indonesia, Europe, Asia, and the United States. Lectures, films, workshops, and performances.

VISITING CANGGU See map, page 94-95.

The area called Canggu (pronounced *chang-gu*) is actually several small rural villages and six beaches which, until recently, had not seen many tourists. The area begins at Jl. Petitenget to the north of Petitenget and Kerobokan and extends to Tanah Lot.

Not long ago this was all rice fields, and there is still a fair amount of green space along the potholed lanes. Enjoy it while you can, though: tourism development in Canggu is spreading like wildfire. There are still a few homestays and *warungs* here catering to surfers, but there are also a burgeoning crop of resorts and more villas than anyone could count.

ACCOMMODATIONS

Canggu Club Bali, Jl. Pantai Berawa, Banjar Tegal Gundul, www.cangguclub.com. This ultimate expat hangout can look a little like a weird throwback to the colonial era, with wealthy resident westerners at play. As well as all the activities on offer here there are luxury villas set in the manicured grounds so you can be right at the heart of the scene. **$$$$**

Chillhouse, Jl. Kubu Manyar No.22, Banjar Pipitan, www.thechillhouse.com. A funky resort with an outdoorsy theme, this place has bungalows with bright, breezy castaway stylings, and a happy, laid-back atmosphere. Many people stay here on packages, combining accommodation with surfing or biking tours, or yoga. **$$$-$$$$**

Desa Seni, Jl. Kayu Putih No. 13, Berawa, www.desaseni.com. Set in the middle of a rice field, an unusual collection of antique wooden Indonesian homes that have been restored and formed into a "village." The focus is an authentic Indonesian experience through exploring culture, religion, food, and complete wellness. It is a ten-minute walk to Canggu Beach. **$$$$**

Hotel Tugu Bali, Jl. Pantai Batu Bolong, Canggu Beach, www.tuguhotels.com. Part museum, part boutique hotel, this is one of the most distinctive accommodations in Bali. The rooms are set amongst lotus ponds, and the whole property showcases a rare collection of over 1,000 pieces of Indonesian statuary, artworks, and unique Balinese and Javanese architecture. Each room is individually designed, all with oversized beds and private plunge pools. **$$$$**

Legong Keraton Beach Hotel, Jl. Pantai Berawa, Canggu, www.legongkeratonhotel.com. Right on the beach, this sleek resort has several room categories and beachfront cottages. There's a swimming pool, meeting room, spa, and wedding facilities. **$$$-$$$$**

Wayan's Guesthouse, Jl. Pantai Berawa, Berawa Beach, www.balitransport.com. This place started out as a bare-bones backpacker hangout, many moons ago. These days it's gone decidedly upscale, with new air-con rooms with flat-screen TVs and hot water. It's still set in a family compound, however, with a homely atmosphere and a warm welcome, and the beach is just a few steps away. **$$**

DINING

Bali Puputan, Tugu Bali Hotel, Jl. Pantai Batu Bolong, Canggu Beach, www.tuguhotels.com. This dining venue, full of museum quality artifacts, serves a *rijstaffel* dinner in grand colonial-style on a giant marble-top table used in the Dutch governor's residence in Surabaya 150 years ago. Also in the same hotel is Waroeng Tugu, serving delicious traditional and authentic Javanese *warung* food (but not at *warung* prices). Lunch and dinner. $$$

Hog Wild in Bali, Jl. Batubelig 41, www.hogwildinbali.com. Ubud's favorite hangout, Naughty Nuri's, has a second location in Canggu. The name might be different, but you'll still find Nuri's famous ribs, salads, curries, and fabulous martinis, plus margaritas and bloody Marys without having to go up the hill! Lunch and dinner. $$-$$$

The Beach House Restaurant, Jl. Pura Batu Mejan, Echo Beach, www.echobeachhouse.com. Popular with surfers, this place offers a seafood BBQ and organic salads every night, live DJ music every Sunday night, and home deliveries. Breakfast, lunch, and dinner. $$-$$$

Warung Sobat
Jl. Batu Belig No. 11A, tel: 4738-922. Owned by a Balinese family who has farmed this land for generations, owner Made and his wife began selling food to construction workers, then later enlarged their dining area to cater to the new villa tourists. $$

ACTIVITIES

Canggu Club Bali, Jl. Pantai Berawa, Banjar Tegal Gundul, www.cangguclub.com. A members-only club with lavishly manicured grounds, a swimming pool, gym, and some of the best sporting facilities on Bali. Tennis, soccer, gymnastic, and swimming academies, squash courts, Wellness center, restaurant, pub. Emphasis is on wholesome family life for the well-heeled. Day passes available for around $30.

VISITING TANAH LOT   See map, page 94–95.

Shortly before Tabanan on the main highway west from Denpasar a signboard indicates the southwest turnoff to Tanah Lot. Alternative access is north of Legian, turning west toward Canggu, and then following the signs from there. There are a great number of shops and restaurants nearby. Tourists congregate at this Balinese landmark by the busloads at sunset.

ACCOMMODATIONS & DINING
Inexpensive *warungs* are around the parking lot, and both sides of the coastal path to the east and above the temple are lined with restaurants. Recommended is the open-air Dewi Sinta Restaurant inside the hotel by the same name. Several upscale dining outlets are found in the Pan Pacific Bali Nirwana Resort.

Dewi Sinta Hotel, Spa & Restaurant, Taman Wisata Tanah Lot, www.dewisinta.com. Spacious deluxe rooms at the back of the complex here look out on rice fields. All rooms come with air-con and hot water, and the place is clean, well-run, and friendly. The pleasant restaurant serving Indonesian, Chinese, seafood, and European cuisine is a bonus. $$

Pan Pacific Bali Nirwana Resort, Jl. Raya Tanah Lot www.panpacific.com. A luxury hotel with an 18-hole world-class Greg Norman golf course, the deluxe rooms, executive suites, presidential suite and villas are set on 103 ha of manicured grounds. $$$-$$$$

SHOPPING
Numerous kiosks surround the entrance to the temple in organized market fashion. Aside from Balinese souvenirs, clothing, and novelties, there are plentiful counterfeit branded goods. Also money changers.

Market stalls with colorful clothes and accessories at the Tanah Lot Art Market

DENPASAR & RENON

A Tour of Bali's "Big City"

Denpasar is a "village-city" with an aristocratic past. Born from the ashes of the defeated Pemecutan court following the *puputan* massacre of 1906, Denpasar became a sleepy administrative outpost during Dutch times. Since independence, and especially after it was made the capital of Bali in 1958, it has been transformed into a bustling city of around 900,000 souls that provides administrative, commercial, and educational services not only to booming Bali, but to much of eastern Indonesia as well. Denpasar is Bali's largest city and the most dynamic urban center east of Surabaya in Java.

Although not a tourist destination in its own right, it attracts visitors because—as the provincial capital—it has a large financial district (including many banks), airline offices, bus terminals, and all the other services normally found in large cities. The surrounding streets are filled with small shops, homestays, hotels, and eating establishments frequented by both foreign and domestic travelers. Traffic here is chronic during business hours, so be forewarned.

New city, old villages

Originally a market town—its name literally means "east of the market"—Denpasar has far outgrown its former boundaries, once defined by the Pemecutan, Jero Kuta, and Satriya palaces and the Tegal, Tampakwangsul, and Gemeh brahmanical houses. Spurred in all directions by population pressures and motorized transport, urban growth has enveloped the neighboring villages and obliterated huge amounts of the surrounding rice fields, leaving a new metropolitan landscape in its wake.

To the east, urbanization spills across the Ayung River into the village of Batubulan, known for its *barong* dances. To the south, it reaches to Sanur and Kuta, while the Bukit further south has become a haven for

Denpasar, a busy city, still has to make space for Balinese ritual life—without the attendant tourists.

foreign-owned villas and five-star resorts. To the west, it sprawls as far as Kapal, whose beautiful temple now has to be seen above the din and dust of suburban traffic.

This unchecked growth has swallowed up many old villages of the plain, yet in many ways they remain as they were, their architecture focused around open courtyards, their intricate temples and collective *banjars*. The power structure itself, although adapted to new urban tasks and occupations, has also not changed much. Local *satrias* (the warrior caste), be they hotel managers or civil servants, remain princes, still have control of land and territorial temples, and may mobilize their "subjects" for ceremonies. Local Brahmans are even more powerful, continuing to provide ritual services for their followers and occupying some of the best positions in the new Bali. Thus Denpasar is a showcase of Balinese social resilience: still "Bali" and worth a visit for its gates, its shrines, and its royal mansions.

But Denpasar is nevertheless a modern city. Shops, roads, and markets have conquered the wet rice field areas leased and sold by village communities. Here, urbanization has taken on the same features found elsewhere in Indonesia: rows of gaudily-painted shops in the business districts; pretty villas along the *protokol* streets; narrow

The striking Tugu Bajra Sandhi is one of Denpasar's recently-installed public monuments.

alleys, small compounds, and tiny houses in the residential areas.

Experiment in integration

This new urban space continues to welcome waves of new immigrants, Balinese as well as non-Balinese. As such, it represents an experiment in national integration. Inland Balinese indeed make up the majority of the population. The northerners, southern princes, and Brahmans were here first. Beneficiaries of a colonial education, they took over the professions and the main administrative positions and constitute, together with the local nobility, the core of the local middle

Roadside stalls in Denpasar tend to offer snacks and everyday items rather than tourist trinkets.

Local banjar residents preparing for a dance performance on the outskirts of Denpasar

class. Their villas—with their roof temples, neo-classical columns, and Spanish balconies—are the modern "palaces" of Bali.

More recently, a new Balinese population settled here, attracted by jobs as teachers, students, nurses, and traders. Strangers among the local "villagers," these Balinese are also the creators of a new city landscape and architecture. Instead of setting up traditional compounds with their numerous buildings and shrines, they build detached houses with a single multi-purpose shrine. In religious matters, they are transients retaining ritual membership in their village of origin, praying to gods and ancestors from a distance through the medium of the new shrine. They return home for major ceremonies to renew themselves at the magical and social sources of their original villages.

There are also several non-indigenous minorities in Denpasar, comprising perhaps a quarter of the total population. Muslim Bugis came to Bali from Makassar as mercenaries as early as the 18th century. They have their own *banjar* in Kepaon village, where they live alongside the Balinese, speaking their language and intermarrying with them. Old men of Pemecutan can take visitors to a "Bugis" shrine in a small temple near the family cremation site.

The Chinese came early as traders for the local princes. They integrated easily, blending their Chinese and Balinese ancestry. They also have a shrine, the Ratu Subandar or "merchant king's" shrine up in Batur, next to the shrines of Balinese ancestral gods. Later, new Chinese, often Christians, arrived, attracted by Bali's booming economy.

There are also Arabs and Indian Muslims who came in the 1930s as textile traders and

have since become one of the most prosperous minority communities. They live in the heart of the city, in the Kampung Arab area, where they have a mosque.

Most migrants, however, are Javanese and Madurese, known collectively as *Jawa*. They fill the ranks of the civil service and the military (Sanglah and Kayumas areas) as well as the working classes, skilled, and unskilled (Pekambingan, Kayumas, and Kampung Jawa areas). Relatively new actors on the Balinese social stage, they introduced new habits, such as food-selling and peddling. They are also builders of new housing: shacks and tiny houses that bring Denpasar into line with other cityscapes of modern Indonesia.

Thus Denpasar is very much a place where the theme of nation-building is played out. It brings together within earshot of one another the high priest's mantra, the muezzin's call, and the parson's prayer. *Eka Wakya, Bhinna Srutti*—"The Verbs are one, the scriptures are many"—so goes the local saying. Balinese tolerance within a national tolerance.

Balinese city, Indonesian nation

Nation-building is also very much a Balinese concern. Denpasar is the center from which the national language, Bahasa Indonesia, is spread to other parts of the island, and people here speak Indonesian interspersed with Balinese words.

Denpasar is also the breeding ground for a revamped traditional culture. It is here that the concepts of Balinese Hinduism are being re-Indianized by the Parisada Hindu Dharma (Hinduism Religious Council), beyond the maze of Bali's old *lontar* manuscripts and oral traditions. The supreme god, Sanghyang Widhi Wasa ("All-in-One God"), assumes precedence here, relegating the ancestors to minor functions. New prayers are taught (*Tri Sandhya*) and new government priests officiate, called from Denpasar to the villages for the rites of officialdom and for inter-caste rituals. Reversing the old village-based trend, Denpasar is also home to the new arts. Modern dances and music are created and taught, spreading into the villages from the city.

Last, but not least, Denpasar is the home of a new breed of Balinese, born to the sounds of contemporary music, raised in a world of new wishes and desires, taught in the words of a national language and culture. Their thoughts take form in a world of Kuta discos and lavish Sanur villas. They are the avant-garde of the new, Westernized Indonesia. Resilience, renewal and decadence: Denpasar is the stage for modern Bali.

Modern city with a traditional touch

As a microcosm both of modern Bali and of present-day Indonesia, Denpasar is easier to understand than to see. Nevertheless, it awaits the intelligent traveler who wants to learn about Bali's future as well as the past, and who wishes to take home more than just a few images. So forget taking photos for a while. Forget the traditional village Bali; and have a look at the new urban Bali.

Motorbike traffic in a leafy suburb of the city

To begin an exploration of contemporary Bali, go first to **Puputan Square** in the center of the city, a large park commemorating the suicidal battle of the Badung kingdom against the Dutch in 1906. Bounded on the north by the main west-east artery, Jl. Gajah Mada, which changes its name to Jl. Surapati east of the roundabout, this is a good orientation point as well as a nice spot, surrounded by gardens, to rest weary feet. On its northwestern corner is another landmark: the **Catur Mukha** ("God of the Four Directions") statue gazes impassively through one of its faces at the monument to the fallen of the *puputan*. Across the street to the northeast corner of the park on Jl. Surapati is the Tourist Information Office (closed weekends and public holidays). On the east side of the Square is Pura Jaganatha, Bali Museum, and the massive military headquarters.

The **Bali Museum** (closed weekends and public holidays) was established by the Dutch in 1932 and displays archeological finds, masks, weapons, dance costumes, handicrafts, paintings, and Ming ceramics. The main building represents the Karangasem palace (east Bali) architectural style featuring a wide veranda. The Tabanan palace style (west Bali) is represented by the windowless building on the right, and the brick building on the left resembles the Singaraja (north Bali) palace. On the north side of the museum is the Javanese-*pendopo*-styled governor's residence, **Jaya Sabha**. The Bali Arts Festival procession held every June or July begins in front of this building.

Denpasar's temples and palaces

In the very heart of Denpasar, just behind Jl. Gajah Mada are many traditional compounds, their gates, shrines, and pavilions in among the multistory Chinese shop-fronts.

For a look at Denpasar's more typical villages, travel the streets of Kedaton, Sumerta, and particularly Kesiman villages, east of the city center. **Kesiman** has some of the best examples of the simple, yet attractive Badung brick-style, a dying witness to a passing grandeur that is being replaced by the new baroque of the Gianyar style and the ugliness of reinforced concrete.

Of the temples, the most ancient is **Pura Moaspahit**, in the middle of the city on the road west to Tabanan (Jl. Sutomo). It dates back to the early Javanization of Bali in the 14th century. Every 15 days, at the full moon and the dark moon, Moaspahit is filled with young Balinese who come to pray, with *wayang kulit* (shadow puppet) performances often following. No less interesting, although more recent, are the temples of the royal families: **Pura Kesiman**, with its beautiful split gate, **Pura Satria** and the lively **Pasar Burung (Bird Market)** next door (north on Jl. Veteran), and **Pura Nambangan Badung** near the Pemecutan and Pemedilan princely compounds.

A "modern" temple also worth a visit is **Pura Jagatnatha**, the temple of the "Lord of the World," in Puputan Square. Its tallest building is a big *padmasana* lotus-throne shrine and has a gilded statue of the supreme god, Sanghyang Widhi Wasa.

Among the palaces, the most typical is **Jero Kuta**, north on Jl. Setiabudi, which still has all the functional structures of a traditional princely compound. The **Pemecutan Palace** on Jl. Imam Bonjol has been transformed into a hotel. The **Kesiman Palace**, a private mansion, houses an elaborate family temple. Now consisting of two buildings on Jl. Supratman northeast of the city center, one of them is open to tourists.

Denpasar's two main markets, Pasar Kumbasari and Pasar Badung, are separated by a canal.

Other sites

The vast **Werdhi Budaya Art Center** on Jl. Nusa Indah in the Sumerta area east of the city center is not only a cultural venue dedicated to visual and performing arts, it is a monument to Balinese temple and palace architecture. Its large grounds house three art galleries, exhibition space, and several performance venues, including the grand **Arda Candra Amphitheater**. Check schedules on arrival for exhibitions and performances. There is always something—painting, photography, or textile exhibitions, or performances—going on here. Next to the Art Center is **Indonesia Institute of the Arts Denpasar** (ISI Denpasar), an accredited state university offering Bachelor and Master of Arts degrees in both traditional and contemporary arts.

A visit to Denpasar would not be complete without some shopping, and the best places to do that are where the locals go. **Pasar Kumbasari** on Jl. Gajah Mada is a beehive of activity that is a combination of traditional morning market on the first floor, selling everything from farm-fresh vegetables to live chickens, spices and offering flowers, and an open-air "shopping mall" the rest of the day. The second level sells handicrafts, clothing, and art, and on the third floor are traditional cooking utensils and ceremonial temple accouterments. Across the river to the south is **Pasar Badung**, which is similar to Kumbasari, minus the handicrafts and art shops. Don't forget to bargain. Both are open until 10 pm. South of the markets is a nice shop-lined street with wide sidewalks and potted plants.

Amidst large bank buildings on Jl. Gajah Mada and on Jl. Thamrin are a myriad small stores selling many different items, such as textiles. **Jl. Hasanudin** is locally known as the "gold street," where 18-22K gold jewelry is bought and sold at current market prices, which are posted and updated each day. Nearby **Jl. Sulawesi** is a haven for fabric lovers. **Pasar Satria**, north of Jl. Gajah Mada on the corner of Jl. Veteran and Jl. Nakula, is smaller than Pasar Badung, but also sells handicrafts on the second level with a traditional market on the ground floor.

Renon

Travelers in need of consular services must make their way south of Denpasar city and then east to **Renon**, a "new" suburb built to house governmental offices and the main financial district, passing the impressive **University Udayana** on a modern four-lane boulevard en route. Tribute must be paid to the Balinese architects who designed this part of town.

Foreign consulates dominate the main west–east street, **Jl. Puputan**, passing Renon's own version of Puputan Square. Side streets to the north are lined with large, shady trees that look anything but new, and the offices here are stately and handsome, unlike the stark, unimaginative government buildings found elsewhere in Indonesia. The area is surrounded by department stores, doctors' offices, mobile phone shops, and fast-food outlets, making Bali Province's civic center an oasis at the outskirts of a bustling city.

ACCOMMODATION PRICE CATEGORIES Prices are for a double room, including breakfast **$** = under $30; **$$** = $30–$70; **$$$** = $70–$130; **$$$$** = over $130. **DINING PRICE CATEGORIES** Prices are for based on a meal for one, without drinks **$** = under $5; =**$$** = $5–$10; **$$$** = over $10.

VISITING DENPASAR See map, page 106–107.

Denpasar is the bustling commercial heart of Bali. At its center is a grassy town common, Puputan Square. Jl. Gajah Mada is the main street, running east–west. Its name changes to Jl. Dr. Wahidin to the west and Jl. Surapati to the east. The center of commercial activity is Jl. Diponegoro and the streets around Puputan Square. The government administrative district and many consulates are in Renon to the southeast.

ACCOMMODATIONS

Denpasar has two hotels of historical and cultural note—**Inna Bali Hotel** and the **Pemecutan Palace Hotel**. Sanur is part of Denpasar officially, and it's just ten minutes' drive from the center of town.
Nakula Familiar Inn, Jl. Nakula 4, www.nakulafamiliarinn.com. This place has been welcoming budget travelers for decades, and a great choice to see a slice of life away from the beach. The eight large, modern rooms each have a balcony and shower, and a choice of fan or air-con. **$**
Inna Bali, Jl. Veteran 3, www.innabali.com. This hotel is Bali's first, built by the Dutch in 1927. Authors Miguel Covarrubias, Colin McPhee, and others stayed here when they first arrived on Bali. These days it's a government-owned business hotel with conference facilities, a good central location, and a swimming pool. There is still a decidedly nostalgic atmosphere, and the restaurant serves old-fashioned *rijsttafel*. **$$**

DINING

Denpasar is a great place for all styles of Indonesian and Chinese food and prices for upscale eateries are much better value than in the nearby resorts. Check out the **night markets (*pasar malam*)**, usually from sunset until around 11 pm, where you sit under the stars and eat at small open-air food stalls. The biggest is at Kereneng terminal, another is outside the Kumbasari Shopping Center, Jl. Hayam Wuruk/Jl. Kamboja. The food is mostly Javanese and Balinese, but there's also Chinese, fiery Padang, and Madurese goat and chicken satay with sauces, and plentiful sweets like fried bananas (*pisang goreng*) and *kue putu* (green *pandan* cakes) smothered in coconut shavings.
For the whole range of local food in a cleaner environment try the food centers in the city's big shopping centers, where a vast array of Indonesian, Chinese, and ethnic cuisines are sold at unbeatable prices in cool and clean surroundings. A bonus is watching the spectacle of mall life.

There are dozens of upscale eateries in the central area, and in Renon. The best bet is to look for places with the most shiny SUVs pulled up outside—a sure sign that the place has the locals' approval!
Bhineka Jaya Kopi Bali, Jl. Gajah Mada 80, Tel: 222-053. This is the biggest producer and distributor of coffee on Bali. You can order your favorite brew here and also buy beans from Sumatra, Sulawesi, Java, and of course Bali. Balinese coffee make great souvenirs too. **$**
Dapur Bebek, Jl. Teuku Umar, tel: 784-2525. Delicious Balinese duck (*bebek*) crispy fried or grilled with rice and spicy *sambal*. **$**
Hongkong Restaurant, Jl. Gajah Mada 99 (near Badung Market), Tel: 233-296. A local favorite for Chinese food with small, medium, and large sized portions. Karaoke in the evenings. **$$**
Samudra Seafood Restaurant, Jl. Teuku Umar 69, Tel: 221-758. Good quality food at very reasonable prices in an air-conditioned setting. Get the chili crabs; choose live seafood from their aquariums. Condiments are free. **$$**

SHOPPING

Denpasar is a great place to shop. Store hours generally follow the 9–5 Western format, but some still close at 1pm for lunch. In addition to the treasures to be found at the **traditional markets**, also try the **arts and craft shops** on Jl. Sulawesi and Jl. Gajah Mada. The handmade wooden furniture center is along Jl. Bypass Ngurah Rai, particularly around the Sanur Bypass area, as well as in Batubulan.

Jl. Hasanuddin, near the city's massive traditional market, is lined with **gold shops**; a few others are found on Jl. Sulawesi. There are several large stores selling fixed-price handicrafts, sarongs, T-shirts, and trinkets. Two good options are **Krisna**, on Jl. Nusa Kambangan 160A, and the very similar **Erlangga**, also on Jl. Nusa Kambangan. These are great places to get a great deal for the same stuff on the streets near the resorts.

Jl. Sulawesi, beside Pasar Badung, known locally as "Kampung Arab," is the street for contemporary and traditional **textiles**, especially Indian or Muslim-style fabrics. A number of shops also carry batik, ikat, and traditional songket cloth (woven with silver strands). A good tip is to buy cloth by the meter and have dresses and shirts made by local tailors, leaving a perfectly fitting garment to copy. **Kencana** at Jl. Imam Bonjol 169 is Denpasar's premier fabric vendor.

The Bali Beach Hotel, originally opened in the early 1960s, was Bali's first high-rise luxury hotel.

SANUR

Bali's First Beach Resort

The black and white checkered cloth—standard of Bali's netherworld—is nowhere more aptly hung than on the ancient coral statues and shrines of Bali's largest traditional village, Sanur. This was Bali's first beach resort, a place of remarkable contrasts.

Sanur is a golden mile of "Baliesque" hotels that has attracted millions of paradise-seeking globetrotters. And yet, within the very grounds of the ten-story **Inna Grand Bali Beach Hotel**—originally funded by war-reparations from the Japanese—is the sacred and spiky **Ratu Ayu** temple of Singgi, the much feared spirit consort of Sanur's fabled Black Barong. The district is legendary throughout Bali for its sorcery. Black and white magic pervades the coconut groves of the resort's hotels like an invisible chess game. At the same time—and seemingly in contradiction—the local community is modern, prosperous, and at ease with its long-established tourist economy.

Sanur is one of the few remaining Brahman *kuasa* villages (controlled by members of the priestly caste) on Bali and has among its charms some of the handsomest processions on the island, Bali's only all-female *keris* dance and the island's oldest stone inscription. Even the souvenirs sold on the beach—beautifully crafted kites and toy outriggers—are a cut above those found on the rest of the island.

Traditional Sanur
Just a stone's throw from any of Sanur's beachside hotels lies one of a string of very ancient temples. Characterized by low coral-walled enclosures sheltering platform altars, this style of temple is peculiar to the white sand stretch of Sanur coast from its harbor in the north to **Mertasari Beach** in the south. Inside, the altars are decorated with fanciful fans of coral and rough-hewn statuary, often ghoulishly painted but always wrapped in a *poleng* checkered sarong.

The rites performed at the anniversary celebrations of these temples are both weird and wonderful, the celebrants often dancing with effigies strapped to their hips, while the priests are prone to wild outbursts, launching themselves spread-eagled onto a platform of offerings and racing entranced pell-mell into the sea.

The area, with traditional Intaran village at its heart, has evidently been settled since ancient times. The Prasasti Belanjong, an inscribed pillar placed here in A.D. 913, is Bali's earliest dated artifact, and is now kept in **Pura Belanjong** temple in south Sanur. It tells of King Sri Kesari Warmadewa of the Sailendra Dynasty in Java, who came to Bali to teach Mahayana Buddhism and then founded a monastery here. It may be presumed that a fairly civilized community existed then, as the Sailendra kings built Borobudur in Central Java at about the same time.

It is interesting that the Intaran village square is almost identical to that of Songan

Ogoh-ogoh, huge papier-mâché or styrofoam demons, are prepared for community parades ahead of Nyepi, the Balinese New Year.

Sanur's sheltered beach is still home to a fleet of traditional outrigger fishing boats or jukung.

village on Mt. Batur's crater lake, particularly the location and size of the *bale agung* (great meeting hall), the *wantilan* community hall and associated buildings. The priests of Sanur-Intaran are often mentioned in historical chronicles dating from Bali's "Golden Age," the 13th to the 16th centuries. However, it was not until the early 19th century that the king of the Pemecutan court in Denpasar saw fit to place his *satria* princelings outside the village's medieval core.

Before that, Sanur consisted of Brahman *griya* (priestly mansions) in Intaran and several attendant communities, among them the Brahman **Anggarkasih** *banjar*, **Belong** fishing village (which still holds a yearly *baris gede* warrior dance at the **Pura Dalem Kedewatan** temple near the Inna Grand Bali Beach Hotel), and **Taman** village, whose Brahmans have traditionally served as the region's chief administrator, or *perbekel*. Taman is also home to an electric *barong* troupe with an impish *telek* escort, a *pas de deux* by the freaky *jauk* brothers and a spine-tingling last act featuring the evil witch Rangda, all amidst fluttering *poleng* checkered banners.

Westerners in Sanur

In the mid-19th century Sanur was first recorded by Europeans as more than just a dot on the map. Mads Lange, a Kuta-based Danish trader of the time, mentioned the special relationship that the Sanur *perbekel* enjoyed with his great friend the king of

Kesiman, Cokorda Sakti. In a less flattering light, it was also a Sanur *perbekel* who turned a blind eye to the landing in 1906 of Dutch troops on their way to the massacre of the Pemecutan royal house, one of the most ignoble days in Dutch colonial history. The full story was immortalized by 1930s Sanur resident Vicki Baum in her book, *A Tale of Bali*.

In another international nod to Sanur, the BBC produced a film of a local trance medium "possessed" by the spirit of a beer-swilling English sea captain to whose semi-divine memory a trance *baris* dance, called Ratu Tuan, is performed by Banjar Semawang. The costume consists of Chinese kung-fu pajamas of black-and-white checkered cloth.

The first half of the 20th century also saw Sanur's emergence as prime real estate for the Bali-besotted. Beach bungalows in what Miguel Covarrubias referred to as "the malarial swamps of Sanur" were built by, among others, Dr. Jack Mershon and his choreographer wife Katharine (inventor, with Walter Spies, of the *kecak* dance), writer Vicki Baum, anthropologist Jane Belo (author of *Trance in Bali*) and art-collector Neuhaus, who was killed by a stray bullet during a skirmish between local guerillas and Japanese occupation forces in 1943 while playing bridge on the verandah of his home.

Belgian impressionist Adrian-Jean Le Mayeur arrived on Bali in 1932 and at the age of 55 married a 15-year old Balinese *Legong* dancer, Ni Polok. His former studio-home is now **Le Mayeur Museum** on Jl. Hang Tuah (tel: 286-201), beachside north of the Inna Grand Bali Beach Hotel. Le Mayeur's heavenly courtyard was the inspiration for his breasty, nymph-filled paintings, mostly featuring his wife. The house remains much as it was before his death in 1958, its gardens filled with statues and carvings, a living memorial to days gone by.

These early "Baliphiles" hosted a steady stream of celebrity visitors during the 1930s, including Charlie Chaplin, Barbara Hutton, Doris Duke, and Harold Nicholson. It was probably more from the travel reports of these sophisticates than from the movie with a sarong-draped Dorothy Lamour that Bali's fame spread abroad.

Bali's most famous expatriate of the era, artist-writer-musician Walter Spies, was a frequent visitor to Sanur's shores, but his aversion for coastal Bali can be traced to one particular visit. It was the day of a lunar eclipse and the birthday of Spies' young nephew, who was visiting him in Bali. A soothsayer warned the boy not to go near the water that day, but he defied the warning and swam at Sanur, where he was supposedly taken by a shark (despite shark attacks being virtually unknown in Indonesian waters). A weird coincidence: the Balinese symbol for an eclipse is the giant-toothed mouth of the demon spirit Kala Rauh devouring the moon goddess.

Tourism isn't as all-consuming in Sanur as on the Kuta side, and local rituals get plenty of space.

Australian artists Ian Fairweather and Donald Friend also chose picturesque Sanur for their Bali retreats. Donald Friend lived here in imperial splendor with an in-house *gamelan* and Bali's finest art collection within the grounds of his home, north of the Bali Hyatt.

Modern Sanur

At about the same time, two Sanur Brahmans were leaving their mark on the community. The first, high priest Pedanda Gede Sidemen, was entering the twilight of a prolific career that spanned 70 years as south Bali's most significant temple architect, healer and classical scholar. His life and the pride he brought to his native home inspired a

July and August see the skies above Sanur filled with huge kites, as part of an annual kite festival.

generation of local Brahmans, who may otherwise have contemplated abandoning their Vedic scriptures for a different life.

The second, Ida Bagus Berata—nephew of Pedanda Sidemen—insisted during his tenure as mayor of Sanur from 1968 to 1986 that the area should be economically as well as culturally autonomous. To that end Ratu Perbekel, as he was affectionately known, established a village-run cooperative that to this day operates several businesses and owns land in Kuta and Denpasar. This strident new economic approach provided a friendly environment for the establishment of many other Sanur-based tourist businesses.

By the 1980s the writing was on the wall. Sanur's bread and butter (but not its lifeblood, its culture) was mass tourism. The Intaran Brahmans are now hotel owners, their "serfs" are building contractors and room boys, and the farmers of the area have become taxi drivers and art shop owners. Beachside there is no land left, and the ribbon of "Bali Baroque" mansions is thick along the highway. Sanur's Brahman priests are met at dawn by convoys of limousines, their schedules of incantations and blessings as busy as those of any senior statesman or tycoon. The proud heritage of yesterday is gone and forgotten, and the new generation of rich and famous are obsessed more with diet and commerce than with intrigue and traditions. But late at night, when the cash registers are asleep under their batik cozies and the mobile phones are turned off, Ratu Ayu steals from her throne into the night to a temple near you. Sanur's checkeredness is not a thing of the past.

Exploring Sanur

Today, Sanur's glory as the island's most upscale resorts has been replaced by even more luxurious properties throughout the island, yet it remains the favorite of many returning guests who appreciate its mature, upmarket ambience, wide selection of restaurants and accommodations, and its reef-protected beach that is safe for swimming, thus attractive to families.

While the cheaper lodgings in Kuta attract the often-noisy younger set and expensive Seminyak is home to many affluent foreigners, Sanur remains stable and relaxed, with a slower pace of both life, and of change.

Water sports are a key activity in Sanur, from parasailing to kite surfing and from kayaking to waterskiing. Sanur is not at the top of Bali's roster of prime surfing locations, and for much of the year the seas here are particularly tranquil. However, during the rainy season, from October to March, there are often decent waves at several points along the offshore reef. Boards can be rented on the beach—though this is not really a place suitable for beginners. A **beachfront walk**

Sanur women in ceremonial dress take part in a Melasti or annual purification ritual on the beach.

runs for 4 km (2.5 miles), and is ideal for jogging or simply strolling. Between June and August, look for the giant kites—some up to 10 m (32 ft) long and taking five or six men to launch—that are flown here, especially during a huge **International Kite Festival** in August, part of the month-long **Sanur Village Festival**.

Serangan's Turtle Temple

Serangan (locally known as "Turtle Island") is a classic example of tourism development gone *amok*. A small island lying just off Bali's southern coast near Sanur, it has an area of only 72.8 ha (180 ac) and once had a population of about 2,500. Being too dry for wet rice farming, its residents grew corn, maize, peanuts, and beans and made shell trinkets to sell to the tourists. However, their main source of income was the trade in endangered sea turtles, as many Balinese are fond of turtle meat, which is also eaten at certain ceremonial occasions.

The most popular edible species is the Green Turtle *(Chelonia mydas)*, and in addition to buying them from fishermen, Serangan residents caught the cumbersome reptiles when they swam ashore to lay eggs in a shallow pit in the sand before returning to the sea. The eggs are also considered a great delicacy, and were dug up immediately and sold in local markets.

During the mid-1990s the entire island was flattened as part of a scheme to create a huge tourist resort. "Reclaimed" land was added, and a causeway was built connecting Serangan to the mainland, forcing the fisher families who lived there to leave. However, long before the first hotel buildings were constructed the project failed due to the Asian economic crisis of 1997, leaving the former rural island a stark wasteland of scrubby vegetation and crushed limestone—redeemed only by a couple of pleasant, east-facing beaches and good, reliable surfing conditions during the rainy season.

Although not a tourist destination today by any stretch of the imagination there are two things of interest on Serangan. One is the **Turtle Conservation and Education Center** (tel: 857-7881), which has a hatchery and also cares for injured adults until they can be returned to the sea. Its biggest tasks, though, are reeducating many Balinese that the consumption of turtle meat is not a good practice, and protecting an historic hatching site from

The Turtle Conservation Center on Serangan is working to save these endangered marine reptiles.

settlers, who are now returning to live on stretches of abandoned land along the coasts.

Manis Kuningan festival

The other reason to visit Serangan is that annually on the holy day Manis Kuningan in the 210-day Balinese calendar thousands of worshippers wearing their colorful finery flock to **Pura Sakenan** temple for the anniversary of its founding by Mpu Kuturan, which, according to the Prasasti Belanjong inscription, occurred during the 10th century. The Sakenan complex consists of two *pura* on the north coast of the island just west of Dukuh, a small fishing village that survived the destruction. The festival lasts for two days, beginning on the last day of *Kuningan wuku* (week) and ending on the first day of *Langkir wuku*.

Inside the first *pura* there is only a single shrine in the form of a *tugu* or obelisk. This is the seat of Dewi Sri, the goddess of prosperity and welfare. In the second and larger part of Pura Sakenan there are typical Balinese-style shrines for the *prasanak*, relatives of Sri who come to visit the temple on its anniversary day. On arrival, worshippers pray at the shrine of Dewi Sri to ask her for a prosperous year in the fields or in business.

Mangrove restoration

Thanks to funding by the Japanese government, 600 ha (1,483 ac) southwest of Sanur were set aside for mangrove restoration to protect part of the eastern coastline from erosion and pollution. At the **Mangrove Information Center** (Jl. Bypass Ngurah Rai, Km 21, tel: 726-969), educating school kids and visitors about the environmental dangers of losing mangrove forests is a top priority. The first stop is the visitors' center to learn about mangrove inhabitants, followed by a stroll on one of two boardwalks through the forest.

ACCOMMODATION PRICE CATEGORIES Prices are for a double room, including breakfast **$** = under $30; **$$** = $30–$70; **$$$** = $70–$130; **$$$$** = over $130. **DINING PRICE CATEGORIES** Prices are for based on a meal for one, without drinks **$** = under $5; **$$** = $5–$10; **$$$** = over $10.

VISITING SANUR See map, page 117.

Sanur is where Bali's first luxury beach hotel was built 50 years ago and subsequently it became the prime spot for five-star seaside accommodations. Although there are now even more elegant accommodations in other areas, Sanur's 5 km (3 mile) stretch of beach remains a favorite of many due to its location and relaxed pace.

The main attraction here is the white sand beach bordering a reef-sheltered lagoon. The beach stretches south from the Inna Grand Bali Beach Hotel and ends up in the mangrove marshes opposite Serangan Island. Due to the protection of the lagoon, it is one of the safest beaches on the island, and thus ideal for families. Swimming isn't possible at low tide, but at other times this is the best place in Bali for windsurfing and sailing.

Money

A word of caution: moneychangers in Sanur are notoriously shifty. Use only "licensed" outlets, take your own calculator, ask for a receipt and count your money carefully before leaving. There are ATM machines everywhere.

GETTING THERE & GETTING AROUND

Sanur lies just off the main Jl. Ngurah Rai Bypass, and just north of the end of the toll road that connects to the airport and Nusa Dua, making it the most conveniently located of all the southern resorts. Getting out of Sanur is far easier than getting out of Kuta or Seminyak, and once you do hit the road you'll be on your way to Ubud or points east in no time. Sanur is well served by **tourist shuttle buses** from various companies, including Perama, which run direct to all major tourist destinations around Bali. You'll also find **fast boats** departing from the beach to Nusa Penida and Lembongan, as well as to the Gilis.

Sanur stretches over a large area, so having your own transport will be helpful. Along Jl. Danau Tamblingan—Sanur's main street —are many **car**, **motorbike**, and **bicycle rental** outlets.

ACCOMMODATIONS

The choice of accommodations in Sanur ranges between the larger luxury establishments to the intimacy and personal attention of smaller bungalow hotels and guesthouses.

Although it has a reputation as a midrange paradise, Sanur has plenty of budget accommodations, making it a great choice for backpackers wanting to avoid Kuta. The budget end of town is along Jl. Hang Tuah in northern Sanur (Sanur Kaja)—handy for restaurants and other services and only a short walk to the beach and the brilliant promenade. There's a whole cluster of cheapies opposite the entrance to the Inna Grand Bali Beach Hotel.

For those with deep pockets, an alternative to hotels is to rent luxury bungalows owned by foreign residents. These can work out relatively reasonably if accommodations are needed for a large number of people and if food and drink are bought at supermarket prices. Prices range from $250/day for a villa for two to $1,500/day for a two-hectare beachfront estate with 14 staff, an archery range, and use of a game fishing boat.

Flashbacks, Jl. Danau Tamblingan 110, www.flashbacks-chb.com. With an array of bungalows, rooms, suites, and a small saltwater swimming pool, this is a welcoming little oasis. The cheapest rooms are fan-cooled; the more expensive ones have some quirky furnishings and funky tiled bathrooms, and the attached Porch café does excellent food. $-$$

Hotel La Taverna, Jl. Danau Tamblingan 29, Tel: 288-497, www.latavernahotel.com. With a blend of Mediterranean stucco and Balinese thatched roofs, this is a place that has stood the test of time. Rooms are furnished with antiques, and the whole place has an appealing aura of simple creativity. The attached Isola beachside restaurant serves Italian dishes, pizzas, and Indonesian favorites. $$$

Kesumasari Beach Hotel, Jl. Pantai Kesumasari, www.kesumarihotel.com. Right on the beach near shops and market, restaurants and bars, the redbrick cottages here come with plenty of quirky style. Each has a little shaded terrace, with lavishly decorated doors opening into clean, comfortable rooms. There is a small restaurant and a friendly, family atmosphere. $$

Laghawa Beach Inn, Jl. Danau Tamblingan 51 Batujimbar, www.laghawabeach.com. A small hotel on the beachfront with hand-carved doors, windows and sculptures, Balinese antique furniture and beautifully landscaped grounds. There are modern facilities and courteous and efficient staff. The Laghawa Grill specializes in steaks and seafood. $$-$$$

Palm Garden Hotel, Jl. Kesumasari 3, Semawang, www.palmgarden-bali.com. Including a first-class continental breakfast, this is one of the best deals in

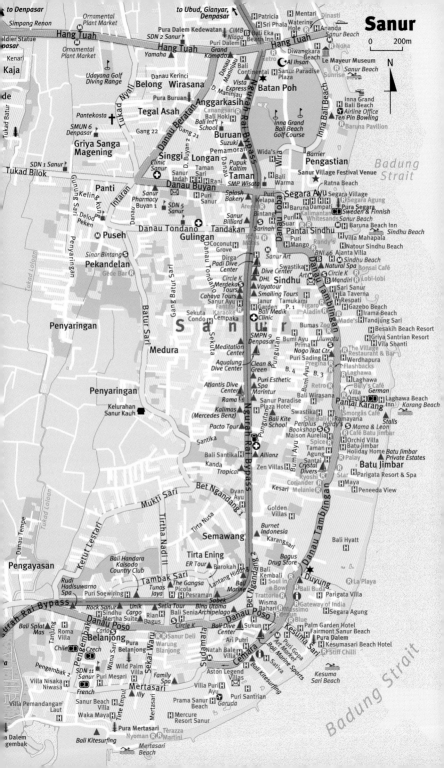

Sanur. Only 16 rooms, very personal, friendly staff; comfortable, peaceful and just a two-minute stroll to the beach and its outstanding seafood restaurants. All rooms come with bathroom and adjoining living room. **$$-$$$**

Peneeda View Beach Hotel, Jl. Danau Tamblingan 89, www.peneedaviewbeachhotel.com. Set on the beachside with expansive gardens and open-air facilities, including an attractive beachside restaurant and bar, and three swimming pools, this is a good value option. **$$**

Natah Bale Villas, Jl. Cemara 32, www. natahbalevillas.com. A small complex of attractive villas, each with private entrance, open living room, dining room, fully-equipped kitchen, outside-inside bathtub, and shower, this is a very peaceful place. The beach is only a few meters away, and there's a restaurant and swimming pool. **$$$**

Sanur Paradise Plaza Hotel, Jl. Bypass Ngurah Rai 83 www.spph.pphotels.com. Some way from the beach, the rooms in this low-rise complex are set around a serpentine landscaped swimming pool and lush gardens. There are plenty of onsite facilities, including activities for children and several restaurants. Request a room away from noisy Jl. Bypass. **$$$**

Sativa Sanur Cottages, Jl. Danau Tamblingan, www. sativahotels.com. With ten two-story cottages on the beach with Balinese atmosphere, handcrafted wood furniture and local art, this is an atmospheric place to stay. There is a good restaurant, and a swimming pool. **$$**

Segara Village Hotel, Jl. Segara Ayu, www. segaravillage.com. The 120 rooms in this large beachfront property are arranged in five distinct "village" areas which creates an intimate and welcoming atmosphere despite the scale of the place. There are several swimming pools. The Beach Restaurant and Bar has Indonesian and international menu. Jacuzzi Bar serves cocktails while being soothed by water jets with ocean views. **$$$-$$$$**

Tandjung Sari Hotel, Jl. Danau Tamblingan 41, www. tandjungsari.com. The 26 beachfront bungalows here were built in 1967, and they are still leading the way when it comes to boutique hotel style, with charming décor and tranquil, elegant atmosphere. The bungalows are reminiscent of those found in the pleasure gardens of the Balinese rajas, and the staff will treat you like royalty. **$$$$**

DINING & DRINKING

Sanur's fine dining international and specialty restaurants run the gamut from affordable classic French and Indian to nouveau cuisine and Italian. Many offer free pickup and drop off in the Sanur area.

The hotels have a wide variety of restaurants, buffets, and coffee shops. Restaurants outside the hotels offer a greater variety of food in a broad price range. Most close at 10 pm. Jl. Danau Tamblingan has many bars serving cocktails and cold beer. The cheapest and most colorful food spot at night is the **Sanur Night Market**, located in the Art Market at the north end of Jl. Danau Tamblingan. The food is spicy, but nothing is cheaper.

The majority of fine dining restaurants offer similar fare and prices; menus generally feature grilled seafood. Many also stage dance performances and offer pick-up services. Some of the best places for those who want to dine in luxury are found in hotels, such as La Taverna (good seafood, brick-oven pizza) and Tandjung Sari, known for its Indonesian rijsttafel and its Balinese palace atmosphere.

Café Batu Jimbar, Jl. Danau Tamblingan 152, www. cafebatujimbar.com. The hanging vines, open-air seating and sturdy furniture gives this trendy eatery the look of a Riviera café, a favored haunt of the local expat community. The café offers light, healthy mixed cuisine, organic food, great salads, and daily specials. Coffee and baked goods are their specialties, and there are newspapers and magazines to encourage lingering. Breakfast, lunch, and dinner. **$-$$$**

Kalimantan Bar & Restaurant, Jl. Pantai Sindhu 11 Tel: 289-291. Those looking for breakfasts, sandwiches and burgers should try this cozy restaurant among the trees down beside the Segara Village Hotel. It has a loyal following among local expats. Bob, the owner, is an old-time Bali resident with a voluminous store of knowledge about the island. Lunch and dinner. **$$**

Kayu Manis, Jl. Tandakan 6. Delicious international food comes at great prices at this welcoming restaurant, popular with expats. The cuisine features European-style presentation with pan-Asian accents. Lunch and dinner. **$$**

Massimo Il Ristorante, Jl. Danau Tamblingan 206, tel: 288-942. Using only the finest imported ingredients, the menu blends the taste of good old-fashioned Italian home cooking with a warm and friendly atmosphere. Excellent wine cellar. Also delivers to homes and villas. Lunch and dinner. **$$-$$$**

Ryoshi, Jl. Danau Tamblingan 150, tel 288-473.

An island-wide favorite for dependable authentic fresh sushi and typical Japanese fare. Good value. Lunch and dinner. $$

The Village Restaurant & Bar, Jl. Danau Tamblingan 66, Tel: 285-035. Innovative cuisine that ranges from New Orleans Creole to Italian, seafood, and vegetarian dishes. Breakfast, lunch, and dinner. $$

Warung Blanjong, Jl. Danau Poso 78, tel: 285-613. This open-air Indonesian-style restaurant serves a classic Balinese nasi campur, a complete meal of rice accompanied by meat and a vegetables for just a couple of dollars. Or try their *ayam betutu*, roast chicken, tender and succulent, with a delicious stuffing. Also a full selection of dishes from other islands, all cooked with great attention to the authentic flavors. Because of their low prices and free home delivery, the place is very popular with local expat community, who know where all the bargains are. Breakfast, lunch, and dinner. $

SHOPPING

At the end of Jl. Danau Toba in north Sanur, the Sanur Beach Market has a wide range of stalls selling inexpensive gift items. Jl. Danau Tamblingan has scores of shops selling local handicrafts, homewares, textiles, carvings, paintings, leather, and silver goods. Also check out Pasar Sindhu at the north end of Jalan Pungutan and the Art Market at the end of Jl. Hang Tuah.

Otherwise, go to the arcades in the main hotels for high quality goods and no bargaining or to the many designer boutiques opposite the souvenir kiosks. Some other interesting shops are:

Clothing & textiles

Mama & Leon, Jl. Danau Tamblingan 99A, tel: 288-044. A long-established designer very popular with fashion hounds who want something out of the ordinary.

Nogo Bali Ikat Center, Jl. Danau Tamblingan 100, www.nogobali.com. Traditional hand-woven textiles from throughout Indonesia made into modern clothing. They also take special orders.

Uluwatu, Jl. Danau Tamblingan, www.uluwatu.co.id. A beautiful collection of clothing and sleepwear in crisp cotton and silky rayon finished with handmade Balinese lace. Also has attractive homewares.

Food

There are mini-markets throughout Sanur selling snacks, beer, cold drinks, toiletries, and the like. For something more substantial, try **Hardy's**

Supermarket at Jl. Danau Tamblingan 193, which has everything anyone could ever need, including wine and spirits.

ACTIVITIES

Golf & art

Inna Grand Bali Beach, Jl. Hang Tuah 58, www.grand-balibeach.com, has a well-maintained nine-hole course for those interested in a quick round. It is also home to **Maha Art Gallery**, in the Club House (www.mahaartgallery.com), an art space in an unusual location, with goals including creating an interaction between artists, collectors, and art lovers while improving general education about the arts.

WATER SPORTS

Almost every water sport imaginable is available in Sanur. Most of the facilities are right on the beach around the Art Market and in front of the big hotels. Sanur's diving and snorkeling is not the best on the island, but there are several agents that organize trips to better underwater sites. The surfing is not great at Sanur, either, but there is one spot with good waves during the rainy season; boards are available for rent on the beach, though this is not really a good place for beginners.

Blue Oasis Beach Club, Sanur Beach Hotel, Jl. Danau Tamblingan, www.blueoasis.com. Excellent and professional, has a good dive site in front of a protected reef, kitesurfing in the nearby lagoon, as well as windsurfing, sailing, kayaking, waterskiing, and wakeboarding. Also offers PADI certification and dive tours. Pro shop with new and second-hand equipment.

Bali Kitesurfing, Jl. Cemara No. 72,www.bali-kitesurfing.org. Established in 1999, specializes in board- and kitesurfing (also called kiteboarding), combining the speed of windsurfing, the tricks of wakeboarding and the jumps of surfing. Rental equipment and lessons. Website has good information on Bali and other Indonesian islands, including wind and wave forecasts.

Crystal Divers Scuba Centre, Crystal Santai Hotel, Jl. Danau Tamblingan 168, www.crystal-divers.com. Owned by a PADI Course Director, and in business since 1997, this is a very professional operation, running dive safaris and day trips on their own boats. PADI courses and non-certification courses. "Explore Dive" program lets divers who have discovered a new spot name the site.

JIMBARAN & THE BUKIT

Bali's Cliff-faced Southern Shores

At Bali Island's southernmost point is a shoe-shaped peninsula, Bukit Badung ("Badung Hill"), and the "ankle," or isthmus that connects it to the mainland, is Jimbaran.

Since in the past, visitors only went to the peninsula for Nusa Dua stays, traveling along the eastern mudflats and mangrove swamps, the west coast went unnoticed by everyone except extreme surfers until the 1980s. Before that, there were no hotels or home-stays, no tourist restaurants, no shops, few artists, and not many English speakers. All that has changed, though, and the fine beaches at Jimbaran and the Bukit, as it is familiarly called, are now backed by one of the largest concentrations of luxury hotels and villas anywhere else on the island.

Despite the proliferation of infinity pools and bone-white masonry where once there was little but maize fields and forest, the Bukit is still one of the most striking parts of Bali, defined by huge limestone cliffs, fiery sunsets, and fearsome waves, unfurling in ceaseless procession over the offshore reefs. This region also has places of cultural significance, the most renowned being Uluwatu Temple (Pura Luhur Uluwatu).

Bali's fishing center

Jimbaran encompasses the area on the isthmus just south of Bali's international airport. Most of its 12,000 or so inhabitants live in a cluster of traditional *banjar* neighborhoods at the narrowest part of the isthmus, but the Jimbaran area also includes the sparsely populated northwestern corner of the Bukit plateau.

Jimbaran village is unique in that it borders two separate coasts lying less than 2 km (1.2 miles) apart, each of which has a markedly different geography. To the west is the broad expanse of Jimbaran Bay and the Indian Ocean. To the east is a tidal mudflat enclosing the shallow and sheltered Benoa

Towering cliffs and churning surf at Uluwatu, Bali's iconic southwestern temple.

Jimbaran is famed for its beachfront restaurants serving up seafood on the sand with sunset views.

Harbor. The ecosystems of the two strands, and the occupations of villagers who live on them, differ dramatically.

Salt-making and lime production are the principal livelihoods on the eastern side, while fishing is the main industry on the west. The salt is made by sloshing seawater onto the flats, to be dried by the sun.

Jimbaran's lovely western beach is protected from larger waves by a fragmented reef behind which lies shallow water, an ideal anchorage for large fishing boats. However idyllic it may appear during the dry season, the beach is often rather unpleasant from about November through March, when high waves assault the shore, and the sand becomes littered with flotsam of every description.

Fishing is the principal activity all along the bay, not only in Jimbaran itself but also in Kedonganan and Kelan villages to the north. Kedonganan's catch always surpasses that of Jimbaran. The fishermen—who are mostly Javanese—use large, motorized *prahu* made in Madura to catch enormous quantities of fish with huge purse-shaped seines. They depart in the late afternoon and return just after dawn to sell their catch to wholesalers at the Jimbaran **fish market** (*pasar ikan*).

In contrast to those in Kedonganan, almost all fishermen in Jimbaran are local Balinese who use *jukung* (small outrigger boats) and fish with gill or large, round cast nets. The gill nets are set out in the bay in the late afternoon and the catch is collected early the next morning. During the fishing season there is a lot of interesting activity just after sunrise when the boats go to the market from both areas to sell their catch. A dawn trip to Jimbaran's *pasar ikan* is certainly well worth the early start, to see fish being unloaded and iced down, ready to make their way to smaller markets and restaurants throughout southern Bali. Also, Jimbaran's **produce market** is located on the northeast corner of the main crossroads in the village, just across the street from Pura Ulun Siwi. There are no handicrafts sold specifically for tourists, but there is a considerable variety of local products, including baskets and mats produced by the weavers of nearby villages such as Ungasan and Pecatu. Look for the chefs of Bali's best restaurants doing their daily shopping. The market is open daily, and activity is greatest early in the morning, almost ceasing by noon.

Today, Jimbaran is best known to travelers as the home of magnificent **seafood dinners**, thanks to three clusters of about 50 restaurants right on the sand that draw those who love great food and eye-popping sunsets. The first group is just south of the *pasar ikan*, the second is near Jimbaran's main intersection, and the third is just before reaching Four Seasons Resort Jimbaran. The setting sun, the lights of fishing platforms twinkling across the horizon, the

Jimbaran & the Bukit

0   1km

N

Bali Strait

Jimbaran B...

Muaya

PI's

Rock Bar
Daya

Four Seas
Resort

Pura Tegal Wangi

Gending Kedi

Batu Layah Beach

Ayana Resort & Spa

Pat-Mase Villas

Balangan Point

Springhill Villas
Rimba Jimbaran

Bu
Jimb
Villa Jimba
High L

Balangan Beach

Kesambi Kembar

Bukit Hijau

The Rich Prada

Puri Gading
Raya Gading 1

Jumeirah Bali

Dreamland Beach

Klapa Club & Resort

New Kuta

Adaya

Frangipani Villa

Pecatu Indah Resort

Wyndham Dreamland

Bingin Beach

The Sterling

Le Grande

Cengiling

138m

Impossibles Beach

Grand Summit

Tundun Penyu

Anantara Uluwatu
Resort & Spa

C151 Luxury Villas

Blok Natural Residential

Swiss-Belresort

163m

Griya Permata

The
Pondok

Padang Padang Beach

Suarga

Radisson Blu

+76m

Suluban Surfing

Blue Point Bay
Villas & Spa

Labuan Sait

Bangket

+156m

Dreamland Luxury
Villas & Spa

Ung
Simp

Suluban Beach

The Dreamland
Luxury Villas

Bingin

Blok
Natural
Residential

Bakung Sari

Uluwatu
Surf Villas

Les

Ashana

Umpeng

Indah Manis
Villa Bali

Blok Nuri

152m

Wana Giri

The Ritual

+61m

133m

166m

Blok Sahadewa

164m

Tregge Surf
Camp

62m

14?m

198m

Suluban

Kulat

Sarikaya

Uluwatu

60m
64m

Song Bintang

Dauh Puseh

Temu Dewi

Kertha Lestari

Pura Luhur
Uluwatu

109m

Pecatu

Raya Uluwatu

+210m

+144m

★ **Kecak Dances**

107m

Bustegeh

115m

Karang Bromo

173m

Giri Sari Selonding

Aisis Luxury
Villas Bali

153m

140m

Mebulu Point

Puri Bali
Nyang Nyang

The Sanctus
Villa

145m

Raya Uluwatu

164m

Pulukpuluk
Villa

Bangbang Kembar

Majestic Water
Village

Wijaya Kusumah

Nyangnyang Surfing

Solymar

Khayangan
Estate

Bulgari
Resort

213m

155m

Tembiyak

Karma
Kandara

Ocean
Wedding
Chapel

160m

The Edge

165m

Six
Sense

Alila Villas
Uluwatu Bali

Pura Masuka

Waiting for the perfect wave: surfers checking out the conditions at Nusa Dua.

candlelit tables overlooking the beach, and the barbecue racks billowing smoke all make for an enchanting atmosphere. Be advised to arrive early—around 5 pm—to select a restaurant and grab a ringside seat.

The **swimming** is also good in Jimbaran Bay, which is protected by a reef system, whereas further south crashing waves and strong undertows make it too dangerous to swim. However, the primary pastime in Jimbaran is relaxing and luxuriating in one of the area's divine resorts.

Pura Ulun Siwi

Pura Ulun Siwi (or Ulun Swi) is Jimbaran's best-known "sight" for the Balinese as well as for tourists. This large temple lies at the north-western corner of the principal crossroads, across the street from the market. It is unusual for several reasons. First, it faces east, rather than south. During prayers, the worshippers face west, rather than to the north to Gunung Agung, as is the usual practice. This is attributed to the fact that the temple, once a primitive shrine, was "converted" to Balinese Hinduism fairly early, in the 11th century. At this time, the Javanese holy man who founded the temple, Mpu Kuturan, still followed the custom of his homeland in orienting his temples toward holy Mt. Semeru, in East Java. It was only much later that Gunung Agung became the focus of Balinese Hinduism.

The temple has only two courtyards, instead of the usual three. The spacious interior courtyard measures 66x30 m (210x100 ft) and is dominated by an enormous 11-tiered *meru* tower that is more massive than artistic. The temple has been periodically renovated but remains simple and rustic, lacking the ornate *paras* stone carvings that characterize Gianyar's temples to the north.

The principal gate, a *kori agung* with wings, is very similar in construction to that of Pura Uluwatu on the Bukit, except that it is made of brick instead of coral stone. There is a close connection between these two temples, and it is said that one should pray at Pura Ulun Siwi before proceeding to Pura Uluwatu.

Ulun Siwi is unusual in yet another way. It is the principal temple in Bali dedicated to the welfare of both wet and dry rice fields, and the spirits which live in the temple are thought to control the mice and insects that periodically infest the fields. Farmers regularly come to Pura Siwi to get water, which they then take back home and sprinkle on their fields, either to protect them from these pests or to rid them of those already present.

Lesser-known temples

Jimbaran also has the usual three village temples, the Pura Dalem (called Pura Kahyangan locally), Pura Puseh and Pura Desa. The latter two are combined into one enclosure, as occurs in many villages. These tend to be overlooked in favor of the more spectacular and better-known Pura Ulun Siwi, but each is interesting in its own right.

Pura Kahyangan lies just to the west of the cemetery. **Pura Puseh** and **Pura Desa** are about 50 m (160 ft) northeast of the market. It is interesting to note that the *odalan* or anniversary ceremonies of these three temples, and of Pura Ulun Siwi, all occur within four days of each other, commencing on the third day after Galungan, which is the biggest holy day in the traditional Balinese calendar. Jimbaran becomes a beehive of ritual activity at this time of year.

One of the most important ceremonies in Jimbaran is the Barong procession. The Barong is a mythical beast that acts as protector of the village and its people, represented by a huge masked effigy that is paraded through the area during ceremonial occasions. Jimbaran's inhabitants spare no expense to support the Barong, making offerings to it, praying, and performing the ritual. Appearances of the Barong on Jimbaran's main street between Pura Ulun Siwi and the market are always accompanied by the evil witch Rangda and her two cohorts, and by a retinue of about a dozen other dancers.

Trance plays an important part in a Barong performance, and the actions of the trance dancers who try to stab Rangda are bizarre and unforgettable to any foreign visitor.

Luxury villas, and a surfer's paradise

South of Jimbaran, the road climbs steeply up several switchbacks onto Bukit Badung plateau, offering dramatic panoramas back up the beach to the ricelands and the volcanoes on a clear day and of the pounding surf far below.

The first noticeable thing about **Bukit Badung**—commonly known as the Bukit—is that the landscape is totally different from most of the rest of the island. A large part of Bali is volcanic, rich soils watered year-round by runoff from mountain lakes and streams that support dense, tropical vegetation. In contrast, the Bukit is a non-volcanic limestone plateau which has its own unique ecology.

The Bukit has an ecosystem characterized by its lack of surface water. The soil lies on a base of cracked, porous limestone, and any rainfall quickly seeps through fissures into a very low water table. The area is thus ill-suited to agriculture during the dry season, when the scrubby vegetation looks more Mediterranean than tropical. During the rainy season, however, the region becomes quite lush, and crops of soybeans, sorghum, cashew nuts, manioc, beans of various sorts, and corn, flourish.

The plateau, which constitutes most of the peninsula, rises abruptly to about 200m (650 ft) above sea level, and is ringed on all sides by steep cliffs. Many lovely beaches line the shores of the peninsula and the isthmus, although access is often difficult. The biggest beach is at Jimbaran Bay, on the western coastline south of the airport, but more secluded and equally beautiful sands are found further to the south along the south-western shores of the Bukit plateau.

The whole area has a host of natural attractions for those willing to invest the time to explore. Grand, gray-white cliffs overlook long, white rollers that are world famous among surfers. Graceful fishing boats sway at anchor in tranquil Jimbaran Bay. The quiet, empty bush areas of the elevated plateau are ideal for experienced hikers, though few good maps of the area are available.

All around the western and southern edges of the plateau, limestone cliffs tower above the pounding surf 70 m (230 ft) below, where some of Bali's best surfing is found. Heading south from Jimbaran, **Balangan** is the first of a string of rare white sand beaches on the west coast favored by surfers during the dry season (April–October). Skipping the fabled, once-beautiful **Dreamland**, which has now been decimated by a resort development dubbed "New Kuta

The waves at Padang-Padang are unpredictable, but on a good day they are some of the best on Bali.

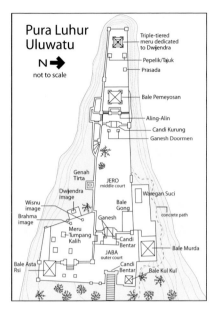

Pura Luhur Uluwatu

N ➡

not to scale

- Triple-tiered meru dedicated to Dwijendra
- Pepelik/Tajuk
- Prasada
- Bale Pemeyosan
- Aling-Alin
- Candi Kurung
- Ganesh Doormen
- Genah Tirta
- JERO middle court
- Dwijendra image
- Wisnu image
- Brahma image
- Bale Gong
- Waregan Suci
- concrete path
- Meru Tumpang Kalih
- Ganesh
- Candi Bentar
- Bale Murda
- JABA outer court
- Bale Asta Rsi
- Candi Bentar
- Bale Kul Kul

peaks strung along a stretch of sharp coral reef. This is the most consistent dry season surfing venue in Bali, and there will be decent waves here even on days when Kuta Beach is as calm as a swimming pool. It is categorically not a spot for beginners, however, with fearsome rip currents and a tricky paddle-out from a cave, but the clifftop cafés all offer grandstand views for spectators, and at low tide there's a small but beautiful stretch of beach and some sheltered pools for swimming.

A glimpse of the past

The Bukit bears witness to a long history. There are limestone caves throughout the area, and evidence of prehistoric human occupation has been found in a cave called Gua Selonding. Before Uluwatu became a Hindu temple, it was the site of worship for more ancient cults. The foundation of the temple itself is dated by Balinese tradition to the 11th century.

The poverty of the soil and its geographical isolation have shaped the social landscape of Bukit Badung. There was never any wet-rice farming here, and other crops and cattle breeding did not feed the population. So those who could not subsist in traditional ways looked to the sea for salt, lime, and fish, while others migrated to rice-growing areas. Old men of Sukawati once talked of Bukit peddlers exchanging betel lime and salt for gleaning and accommodation rights in other

Beach," the next idyllic spot is **Bingin**, followed by **Padang Padang**. Furthest south is **Suluban**, generally known to surfers as "Uluwatu," which sometimes leads to confusion as Uluwatu itself, a dramatic clifftop temple, lies some way further along the cliffs.

The Suluban/Uluwatu surf spot is the most prized in Bali, with several left-handed

The nightly Kecak dance performance at Uluwatu is one of the highlights of a visit to Bali.

The soft local limestone used at the Uluwatu temple allow it to be elaborately carved.

parts of the island.

Bukit Badung is also known as a region where the overlords of the Mengwi and Badung kingdoms banished malcontents and defaulting debtors. Nowadays the population is growing, the region having become a major focal point of Bali's relentless tourism boom.

Uluwatu

The Bukit's most famous landmark is **Pura Luhur Uluwatu**, an exquisite monument situated on a headland at the westernmost tip of the peninsula. The carvings which decorate the temple are very well preserved in comparison to many of Bali's temples, due to the extremely hard, dark gray coral stone used in its construction.

Uluwatu was reputedly built by the priest Mpu Kuturan in the 11th century as one of the six major *sad kahyangan* territorial temples of the island. The reformer priest, Pedanda Wawu Rauh, rebuilt it in its present state in the 16th century. He is said to have attained his *moksa* (release from earthly desires) here. The temple is home to a large colony of monkeys who have caused some damage to the temple over the years, but still retain their protected status as sacred

creatures. It is advised to remove all eyeglasses and jewelry before entering the temple and to hold tightly to purses and bags. They can expertly swoop down, grab anything that attracts them quickly and be out of sight before you can say "naughty monkey."

The temple's structure follows the tripartite pattern of godly, human, and demonic courtyards. The outermost entrance is a *candi bentar* split gate shaped as a set of carved Garuda wings—an unusual feature as they are usually left smooth. Inside the temple, a second gate is capped by a monstrous Kala head guardian figure. At the foot of the gate are two Ganesha "elephant god" statues. The temple underwent renovations in the late 19th century, again in 1949, and more recently in the 1980s, and some parts are actually as new as they look. Despite its mixture of old and contemporary, it is a breathtakingly beautiful spot, especially when the sun begins to set.

The island's south coast

Continuing east from Uluwatu, the towering cliffs of the Bukit's southern shoreline are topped by some of Bali's most opulent and secluded resorts, including **The Bulgari Resort Bali**. There are several stunning beaches on this coastline, including Nyang-Nyang and Green Bowl, both reached via steep flights of steps from clifftop access points.

The craggy cliffs of the Bukit are now dotted by dozens of upscale luxury resorts.

ACCOMMODATION PRICE CATEGORIES Prices are for a double room, including breakfast $ = under $30; $$ = $30–$70; $$$ = $70–$130; $$$$ = over $130. DINING PRICE CATEGORIES Prices are for based on a meal for one, without drinks $ = under $5; $$ = $5–$10; $$$ = over $10.

VISITING JIMBARAN AND THE BUKIT See map, page 122-123.

Jimbaran Bay is located on the isthmus 2 km (1.2 miles) south of Ngurah Rai International Airport and a continuation of the soft white sands of Kuta Beach. Tranquil compared to Kuta, popular with the Balinese, family-friendly with its shallow water and lack of sharp corals, Jimbaran also still retains much of its fishing village charm and remains free of aggressive vendors.

The peninsula at Bali's southernmost tip is Bukit Badung, locally referred to as "the Bukit" (meaning "the Hill"). This area has now, together with Jimbaran, mushroomed into Bali's largest concentration of high-end resorts and luxury villas, with accommodations scattered across the peninsula.

GETTING THERE & GETTING AROUND
Jimbaran is a short taxi ride from the airport, and a few tourist shuttle operators run minibuses here from other major tourist areas. Generally you'll need private transport for getting around the far south of Bali. Ojek motorcycle taxis can be found around the Jimbaran market for short hops.

ACCOMMODATIONS
Most visitors heading for this part of Bali stay in exclusive resorts and villas, of which most offer free shuttles to Kuta. There is a dizzying array of private rental villas in this area—search online for details.

JIMBARAN
Ayana Resort & Spa Bali Jl. Karang Mas Sejahtera www.ayanaresort.com. With rooms and villas overlooking a rugged bluff and the sea, this place has beautiful, secluded surroundings with two-tiered swimming pool, 18-hole golf putting course, tennis courts, kids, programs and a wide array of restaurants. The resort is also home to The Rock Bar, 14 m (45 ft) above the Indian Ocean, and is one of the most glamorous night spots in Jimbaran. **$$$–$$$$**
Balquisse Heritage Hotel, Jl. Uluwatu No. 18X, Jimbaran, www.balquisse.com. A boutique hotel 300 m (330 yds) from the beach with superior and deluxe rooms and a family bungalow. There is plenty of distressed wood, and masses of vintage furnishings and shabby-chic style of the sort beloved by fashionistas. The rooms make a delightful change from the of generic Bali style or international luxury found in other resorts. **$$$–$$$$**
Four Seasons Resort at Jimbaran Bay, Jl. Bukit Permai, www.fourseasons.com. The elegant villas and private residence rentals here comprise three

Balinese-style pavilions for sleeping, bathing, and living, a courtyard, and a plunge pool. Individual villas are arranged in "villages," each with its own staff and service center. The Indonesian spa offers massages, body, facial, and Avuryeda-inspired treatments and salon services, and there's dramatic hilltop and seaside dining and stunning sunset views. **$$$$**
Gending Kedis Luxury Villas & Spa Estate, Jl. Karang Mas Sejahtera 100Y, Jimbaran Bay, www. gendingkedis.com. Each of the luxury villas has a private pool, kitchen and spacious living areas. There's a clubhouse with gym, a spa, salon, gym, Alcedo Restaurant, and cocktail lounge, and a lagoon swimming pool. **$$$$**
Kayumanis Jimbaran, Jl. Yoga Perkanti, www. kayumanis.com. Spacious villas here are hidden among swaying coconut palms, and come with immaculate service, including 24-hour on-call butler. Tapis Restaurant serves Indonesian cuisine, and there is an excellent spa. **$$$$**
Puri Bambu, Jl. Pengeracikan, Kedonganan, www. puribambu.com. Set in Kedonganan village 180 m (591ft) from the beach, the air-conditioned rooms and villas here are each furnished with modern ethnic furniture. There's an attractive pool with sunken bar. The management offer free airport and Kuta transfers. **$$$**
Udayana Eco Lodge, Jimbaran Heights, www. udayanaecolodge.com. Set in a conservation area for birds and butterflies on 30 ha (74ac) of bush land overlooking Mt. Agung, Jimbaran, and Benoa Bay, and frequented by visitors to Udayana University and people working in Bali, all rooms have air-con and garden showers. The resort is home to the Udayana Cricket Club. Free Wi-Fi. Inquire about packages to other Eco Lodges in some of Indonesia's remote national parks. **$$$**

THE BUKIT (CLIFFSIDE HOTELS)
Alila Villas Uluwatu, Jl. Belimbing Sari, Banjar Tambiyak, Pecatu, www.alilahotels.com. The villas here are designed and constructed to be environmentally sustainable, each with private pool and cabana overlooking the Indian Ocean. You get your own personal butler, and there are several fine dining and traditional warung-style restaurants, a cliff top pool and bar, spa, gallery, library. **$$$$**
Banyan Tree, Jl. Melasti, Banjar Kelod, Ugasan, www. banyantree.com. Clifftop living with magnificent views, privacy, and comfort. All villas have infinity

pools, living and dining areas, and private gardens, and the resort has a private beach (though it is not safe for swimming). Bambu restaurant has indoor/outdoor cooking stations, sushi counters, grill, and barbecue. $$$$

The Bulgari Resort Bali, Jl. Goa Lempeh, Banjar Dinas Kangin, Uluwatu, www.bulgarihotels.com. One of the most prestigious resorts in Bali, the villas here, 150 m (500 ft) above the sea with a 1.5 km (1 mile) beach, are accessible only through the resort's inclined elevator. The luxurious interiors and amenities are the finest available. Balinese antiques and exotic art pieces feature amongst the décor. Restaurants and spa treatments are available onsite, and day trips to neighboring islands and volcano visits by helicopter are available. $$$$

DINING

Stretching all along the beach from the Jimbaran *pasar ikan* (fish market) south is an ever-burgeoning and very affordable selection of 50 or so seafood beach restaurants that come alive after sunset (Arrive by late afternoon to get the best ringside seats.) These smoky, palm-thatched, open-air establishments grill the choicest prawns, squid, snapper, and lobster over coconut husk fires. Choose your fish from big ice boxes, pick a table and enjoy with an array of special spices, *sambal* (a spicy mixture of chilies, onions, and garlic) and a tomato and cucumber salad.

There are three main concentrations, all with good parking: one small strip close to the road on the way to PJs at the Four Seasons, another longer row if you turn west towards the sea at Jimbaran's main intersection, and yet another cluster up north on the way to Jimbaran's fish market. It is currently generally considered that the best group lies between the Bali InterContinental and PJs. Other than the fish restaurants, the best cuisine in Jimbaran is prepared in resort kitchens.

Gorgonzola Restaurant, Jl. Uluwatu No 55x, www.gorgonzolarestaurant.com. Just off the busy main road that leads south, up onto the high ground of the Bukit towards Uluwatu, this unobtrusive restaurant is a favorite with the area's resident expats. There are some excellent, authentic pasta dishes on the menu, including delicious gnocchi and pizzas. The staff are very welcoming, and the casual ambiance encourages diners to linger over coffee and dessert. $$

Ko Japanese Restaurant, InterContinental Bali, Jl. Uluwatu 45, www.bali.intercontinental.com. Authentic Japanese cuisine in a variety of settings: the Sushi Lounge & Bar serves drinks and light snacks, sushi, sashimi, yakitori, robotayaki skewers, tempura, noodle and rice dishes and teppanyaki. Lunch and dinner. $$$

PJ's at Four Seasons Resort at Jimbaran Bay, Jl. Bukit Permai, tel: 701-010. This outstanding seafood restaurant on the bay also serves superb pizzas, foie gras, green tea soba sushi rolls, and Australian sirloin, to name a few. The romantic setting includes 25 canopied dining-beds on the beach. The delicious food and casual seaside atmosphere makes it worth the drive out there. Lunch and dinner. $$$

Padi, Ayana Resort & Spa Bali, Jl. Karang Mas Sejahtera, tel: 702-222. An open-air Asian restaurant surrounded by terraced lotus ponds, the chefs from Thailand, Indonesia, and India create favorite dishes from their home countries with flair and fast-paced action. Breakfast and dinner. $$$

SHOPPING

Jenggala, Jl. Uluwatu 2, www.jenggala-bali.com. A state-of-the-art manufacturing facility producing a stunning range of simple, elegant ceramics with fine finishings, glassware and homeware. Individual pieces are designed in-house. There is a café which serves light meals, freshly brewed coffee and tea.

Jimbaran Gallery, Jl. Bypass Nusa Dua 99 X (if coming from the west, beside Bali Taxi on the left side of the road), Tel: 774-957. Extensive and eclectic range of paintings, statues, lighting, furniture, handicrafts, antiques, and interiors. A treasure trove for the bargain hunter.

Lotus Gourmet Garage, Jl. Bypass Ngurah Rai, Jimbaran, www.lotusfood.com. Wide selection of local as well as imported food, including an excellent selection of fresh fruit, vegetables, cheese, meats, and deli items. Cookbooks, kitchenware, and spa products. Also has a café.

ACTIVITIES

Cultural performances. Many of the resorts have cultural performances. Inquire upon arrival about times and locations. Pura Uluwatu presents *Kecak* ("monkey") dances every evening 6–7 pm.

Surfing. The far south of Bali is where you'll find the very best of the dry season waves at spots which are household names amongst the international surfing fraternity. There is a decent reef break at the northern end of Jimbaran Bay, close to the end of the airport runway, known as Airport Rights (it's a right-handed wave). You'll need to charter a boat from Jimbaran to get here.

Further south, you'll reach Balangan, Bingin, Dreamland, Impossibles, Padang Padang, and Suluban (usually known simply as "Uluwatu" to surfers). There are also a couple of remote spots at the bottom of the cliffs on the southernmost coastline. None of these places are at all suitable for beginners—head to Kuta Beach if you're just starting out.

NUSA DUA & TANJUNG BENOA

A Well-Manicured and Gated Resort

Although some people call the Bukit's east coast and the stretch of land that juts out into the sea above it "Nusa Dua," the two regions—Nusa Dua and Tanjung Benoa—each have their own attractions.

Geologically, the area is quite different from the rest of Bali, and even from the rest of the Bukit peninsula of which they are a part. Instead of rice fields or limestone cliffs, the soil reaches down to a long, picture postcard sandy beach protected by a reef. Coconut palms are everywhere, as Nusa Dua was once a huge coconut plantation. The climate here is also drier than the rest of Bali, freshened by mild ocean breezes.

The genesis of a beach resort

Once upon a time, so the story goes, the Balinese giant and master builder Kebo Iwa decided that the Tanjung Benoa marshes should be transformed into rice fields, so he went to the Bukit and picked up two scoops of earth. While shouldering them along the coast, his pole broke, dropping the earth into the sea. Two islets appeared in front of where the Bali Collection shopping complex is now: the **"Nusa Dua"** ("Two Islands").

The marshes were never to become rice fields; the bay remained a bay with a long cape, Tanjung Benoa jutting into it. Nevertheless, the mythical Kebo Iwa, who created the area, became engaged in another venture: luxury hotel development.

Making Nusa Dua into a tourist paradise was a consciously implemented government effort designed with the help of the World Bank in the early 1970s. Two main concepts underlay the project: to develop as a revenue-earning industry an up-market tourist resort, beautiful, secure, with ease of access, and with the most modern facilities, while keeping the disruptive impact on the natural and social environment as low as possible. Also unique for its time was the collaboration between Suharto's government and the private sector. It was hoped that this isolation

Nusa Dua is all about cocooned luxury, with the noise and chaos of nearby parts of Bali held at bay.

Nusa Dua's hotels are luxurious and self-contained.

of tourism into one area of formerly unproductive land would shield the rest of Bali from the impact of the anticipated onslaught of visitors and serve as an example for tourism development while retaining the cultural aspects of other Indonesian islands.

Bualu, an excruciatingly poor area whose residents subsisted on copra, fishing, and coral collection, was chosen for this ambitious project, both for its scenic location and for its relative isolation from densely populated areas. By 1971, a master plan designed by a French consulting firm was ready. Infrastructure construction began in 1973. With many challenges to overcome, it was projected to take 20 years to complete: a water supply system, electricity, sewage treatment, and waste disposal plants, storm water drainage and irrigation systems, telecommunications and roads. And a highway connecting Denpasar and the airport with Nusa Dua had to be built. The first order of business was to get the Hotel and Tourism Management Training Center (BPLP) up and running, which opened in 1978. It was a 50-room training hotel that gave priority to people from Bualu and Benoa villages. Eventually it expanded to include language labs and Bachelor and Master of Arts degree programs, and has since been relocated and accepts students from throughout the nation. The first hotel, Garuda Indonesia airline's 450-room Nusa Dua Beach Hotel, was inaugurated in 1983.

The early days

The project did have its teething pains. Farmers and fishermen had to be relocated and trained for other jobs, investors were reluctant to spend their hard-earned cash on such a pie-in-the-sky scheme, and then there were all the temples. These obstacles were all eventually settled: tenants got land, fishermen started taking tourists sailing for a fee, the investors eventually came through, and the temple festivals continued.

The entrance to the complex consists of a tall *candi bentar* split gate. Facing it 200 m (650 ft) away is a modern-style *candi dwara pala pada* fountain-gate surmounted by a monstrous *kala* head. The outer split gate separates while the inner gate unites; the cosmic complementarity of Bali and tourism in a nutshell.

The hotels are landmarks of the new Balinese architecture. The design committee specified that buildings be no higher than the coconut trees and that their layouts be based on Balinese macro- and micro-cosmic models. Thus, the Club Med was constructed with its head in a Padmasana shrine to the northeast and its genitals and bowels in the discotheque (naturally!), with the kitchen to the southwest. Open modular architecture was required and the use of indigenous building materials was encouraged. Roofs had to be made of terracotta. Land use had to be low-density (limited to 50 rooms per hectare or 2.5 ac), and buildings had to be set back from the beach by 25 m (80 ft), and could only cover 30 percent of each lot.

Nusa Dua today

Today's Nusa Dua is exactly what its designers, planners, and instigators dreamed it would

Beachfront properties line the coast all the way up to Tanjung Benoa.

Nusa Dua is a fantastic place to chill out, read a book and snooze the afternoon away.

be: an exquisite self-contained resort, perfect in almost every way, housing some of the world's finest resorts, and attracting travelers who want to escape from reality, if only just for a little while.

The area had, and keeps, very special features. Its best known ritual is an appeasement of the sea to protect the land from any incursion by the fanged monster lurking beyond the waves—Jero Gede Mecaling—harbinger of death and illness. People present him with offerings in his many shrines along the coast. The area sea temples are still tended by villagers, with the nearby resorts assisting in whatever way they can, and *pengelem* duck sacrifices to the sea are offered under the eyes of passing tourists. **Pura Bias Tugel** on the southern of the "two islands" is the site where the 16th-century Javanese sage Pedanda Sakti Bawu Rau composed poetry.

The outstanding **Bali National Golf Club** has done more than its share to attract the type of tourists that Nusa Dua was created for. Its championship 18-hole course hosts international tournaments and professional golfers. In front of the Westin, the Bali International Convention Center is a venue used for a variety of events, bringing large groups to the area.

The impressive **Museum Pasifika** is a collaboration between a foreigner and an Indonesian, both art collectors, and focuses on Indonesian, European, Asian, and Polynesian artists with both permanent and rotating exhibits. A sprawling shopping and entertainment complex called **the Bali Collection** houses a department store, designer boutiques, cafés, restaurants, and bookshops without the traffic and touts of the Seminyak area.

In addition to practically every imaginable water sport being available within walking distance of luxury suites and villas, there are other more relaxed opportunities to enjoy nature. The water management system north of Nusa Dua where it connects with Tanjung Benoa was lovingly designed to be camouflaged from the public and to be environmentally sound. Its carefully planned greenery is now a wonderful spot for birdwatching, attracting both local and migratory birds. There is a 7 km (4.3 mile) long **walking path** that stretches from the Ayodya Resort at Nusa Dua to the Grand Mirage on Benoa that is pleasant for strollers, particularly early mornings and late afternoons.

Tanjung Benoa: a revamped port

For centuries, and particularly after Bali's major harbor was moved from Singaraja to **Tanjung Benoa** in 1953, the natural means of communication between this area and the rest of Bali was by boat from the northern tip of the peninsula, as this was easier than the

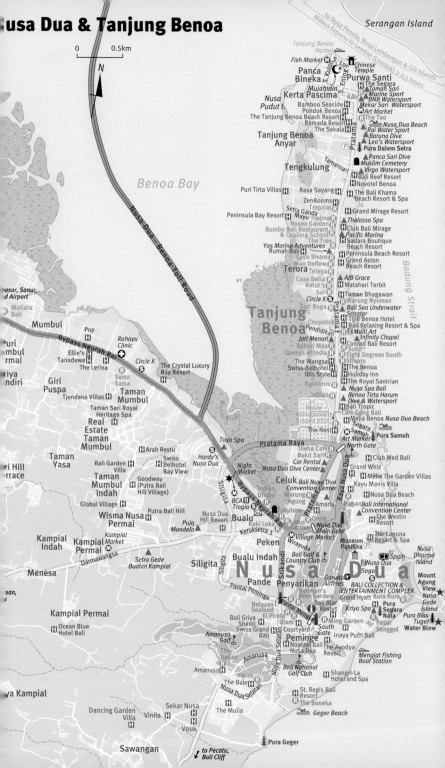

overland route via Jimbaran. Tanjung Benoa was in fact a trading port for Badung and eastern Bukit, with a world outlook extending across the archipelago. Its population bears traces of this mercantile past. Chinese have lived here for centuries: a **Ratu Cina shrine** in the local temple bears witness to their long presence. Although most families have moved to Denpasar, there is still a Buddhist *klenteng* temple here, where local fishermen now inquire about the secrets of the stars with a Chinese abbot. There is also a **Chinese cemetery** about mid-way up the peninsula. Benoa village also has a Bugis quarter with a small **mosque**, and there's a **Muslim cemetery** across from the Tanjung Mekar Hotel and a Christian cemetery further south.

A Chinese temple dedicated to Mazu, the patron goddess of sailors, is a reminder of Benoa's heritage as a multicultural port.

The **harbor** itself is worth seeing. On a given day there may be Navy vessels, local fishing boats, cargo vessels, oil tankers, public ferries and private yachts at anchor. Many leisure expedition and liveaboards are berthed here, offering dive trips and excursions to Nusa Penida and Lembongan, day trips, dinner cruises, and extended trips to other Indonesian islands. There are also high-speed boats to the Nusas and to Lombok here. Many have comfortable departure lounges, where guests can sip cocktails or cold fruit juices while waiting to board.

The main reason travelers choose to stay on Tanjung Benoa is for the total beach experience. Although it is also almost exclusively populated by luxury resorts and villas, it has a much more laid-back ambience than its sister to the south. Every **water sport** in the world is available here: ocean kayaks, windsurfers, paddle boats, boogie boards, Hobi cats, banana boats, jet skis, parasailing, water skiing, glass bottom boat excursions, diving and snorkeling, as well as offshore fishing trips, to name a few. Even though the same activities are available at Nusa Dua, the bonus is that Tanjung Benoa's multicultural village life—absent in Nusa Dua—reminds visitors that they're having a holiday on Bali.

Tanjung Benoa is the water sports capital of Bali—with jet skis, boat-powered parasailing, and much more.

ACCOMMODATION PRICE CATEGORIES Prices are for a double room, including breakfast
$ = under $30; **$$** = $30–$70; **$$$** = $70–$130; **$$$$** = over $130. DINING PRICE CATEGORIES
Prices are for based on a meal for one, without drinks **$** = under $5; **$$** = $5–$10; **$$$** = over $10.

VISITING NUSA DUA & TANJUNG BENOA See map, page 136.

Nusa Dua is a world apart: a pristine complex of resorts where congestion, crowds, chaos—and, it has to be said, much of the appealing Balinese color—are all kept at bay. If you want a serene, resort-based holiday, or a tranquil and safe cocoon into which you can retreat after a day's sightseeing, then Nusa Dua will definitely appeal.

There is also a series of gorgeous beaches here, and some excellent organized watersports, especially in Tanjung Benoa, the narrow spit of land which extends northwards from Nusa Dua.

NUSA DUA

Nusa Dua's beach resorts front a shoreline of sugary white sand with gentle waves. Boats are only allowed to pick up passengers at designated jetties, and an offshore reef protects swimmers, moving the surf quite a distance from shore.

The beach in southern Nusa Dua, in front of the Ayodya, is superior to that in the north. It's clean, free of stones, and the lagoon is wider (the reef starts further out). As you walk north and hit the Grand Hyatt, there are more rocks and coral in the water.

There's a lovely seaside park south of the Westin, with a picnic rest area and nearby rocky outcroppings with spectacular blowholes created when waves blow up through fissures in the coral. This is also a great birdwatching area.

A beachside footpath connects Nusa Dua to Tanjung Benoa, beginning at the Ayodya and ending at the Mirage in Benoa.

ACCOMMODATIONS

Amanusa, Jl. Amanusa, www.amanresorts.com. Thatched-roof suites here offer the highest standards of luxury. Every suite has a queen-size four poster bed, patio, and garden shower, and many have commanding views of the golf course and ocean. All resort facilities are available onsite, from spas to restaurants. **$$$$**
Ayodya Resort Bali, Jl. Pantai Mengiat, www.ayodyaresortbali.com. Formerly the Bali Hilton, there are several hundred rooms here, each with private balcony, as well as a selection of cottages and luxury suites built around 11.5 ha or 28 ac of quiet gardens. There is a free-form swimming pool that stretches all the way to a luscious 300-m (100-ft) long beach, all-weather tennis courts, squash courts, health club, gym, and spa, and an 18-hole golf course next door. **$$$$**

Bale, Jl. Raya Nusa Dua Selatan, www.thebale.com. Rather more personal in atmosphere than the vast resorts nearby, this small complex has a range of deluxe and double private "pavilions," each with their own pool, within sight of the sea. Wellbeing, sophisticated spa treatments, and organic food are all part of the mix here. **$$$$**
St. Regis Bali Resort, www.stregisbali.com. Adjacent to the Bali National Golf Club, the rooms and sites here feature handcrafted Balinese art, balconies, and butler service. There is a full range of onsite spa and leisure facilities, and the sports center can arrange snorkeling, kayaking, windsurfing, canoeing, and kite surfing. **$$$$**
Westin Resort Nusa Dua, www.westinnusaduabali.com. There are several hundred stylish and comfortable rooms at this slickly run resort. The hotel's lagoon meanders through 7 ha (17 ac) of landscaped grounds, and regular refurbs keep the rooms and public areas spick and span. **$$$$**

DINING

Nusa Dua's five-star resorts contain a great number of high-end restaurants (with matching prices) serving European, Chinese, Balinese, and Indonesian cuisine.

Worthy of note is the **Grand Hyatt's Pasar Senggol**, a brightly-lit and sprawling affair that recreates a local "night market" where guests wander among open-air artisans' and food stalls with the deep notes of a monstrous bamboo tube *jegog gamelan* orchestra resonating in the air. **The Boneka** at The St. Regis has a marvelous Sunday brunch. **Faces** in **The Bale** has raw and vegan dishes.

Cheaper eateries are found on Jl. Bypass Ngurah Rai beyond the Nusa Dua main gate, where **Lotus Garden, Indian Dhaba,** and **Fukutaro** are located. All offer free transport to and from area hotels. Along **Jl. Pantai Mengiat** just outside Nusa Dua's south gate, is another string of restaurants.

The **Bali Collection** shopping center has numerous eateries covering a wide range of styles, from Asian and Italian to grills and bars.

NIGHTLIFE

Nusa Dua is not for party animals, and things get very quiet here after dark; the rowdiest it gets is live music in a café or a jazz trio by the pool. In Nusa Dua, this is deliberate: people come here to get away from all that. If you want to go clubbing, head over to Jimbaran or the Kuta-Legian-Seminyak area.

SHOPPING

Bali Collection, www.bali-collection.com. A shopping, entertainment, and dining complex containing the island's most up-market shops, away from the traffic and hassles. Top-end designer shops such as Body & Soul, Indigo Kids, and Coco appear here, as do restaurants, lounges, brasseries, and cafés, health and beauty spas, children's playground, and entertainment. There are also handicraft and art shops, an excellent bookstore, a supermarket, a pharmacy and a Garuda airlines service center.

Also within the same complex is **Museum Pasifika** (www.museum-pasifika.com), a world class institution featuring Indonesian, Asian, European, and Polynesian artists, with permanent collections and revolving exhibitions. Open daily 10–6.

ACTIVITIES

Bali Golf & Country Club, www.baligolfand countryclub.com. Designed by Robin Nelson and Rodney Wright, a championship 18-hole course that has hosted international golfing events. Club facilities include a driving range, putting and chipping greens, pro shop, restaurant, bar, clubhouse and pool. Club and shoe rentals. Pick-up and drop-off from surrounding hotels. Also has three- and four-bedroom villas nestled around the ninth hole with kitchen, chef, staff, and personal butler. Villa guests have priority tee-off times.

Water sports

Most resorts offer water sports, or you can find them along the beach. There is also good surfing offshore, especially during the rainy season. Enquire at your accommodation or book directly on the beach. Prices are fairly consistent (about $25–30 for most activities). **Nusa Dua Dive Center** (www.nusaduad-ive.com) is a well-established PADI International Resort Association member offering PADI courses and dive safaris to other parts of Bali. It also does reef dives just a few minutes by boat from Nusa Dua.

TANJUNG BENOA

North of Nusa Dua, the narrow peninsula of Tanjung Benoa is outside of the gated resort and therefore more chaotic (some would say, reflecting the "real" Bali). There's a local fishing community here, with narrow lanes featuring Chinese, Hindu, and Muslim places of worship.

There are still lots of resorts here, but they are smaller and more moderately priced than those in Nusa Dua. Tanjung Benoa's main significance to visitors is as the watersports capital of Bali. If you want to get wet, this is the place.

ACCOMMODATIONS

Conrad Bali Resort & Spa, Jl. Pratama No. 168 www.conradbali.com. The chill-out atmosphere with its clean, contemporary design caused a lot of buzz when the property first opened, and it's still impressive today. 360 rooms and suites with private patio or balcony featuring tribal Indonesian art. Suite guests receive exclusive access to the Conrad Suites Lounge, Beach Club and a pool that wraps around the hotel among other top-notch amenities. **$$$$**

Ellie's at Bali Sari, Jl. Tanan Lawangan 1, Banjar Mumbul, www.ellies-bali.com. A real treasure, with charming rooms decorated in contemporary, chic style, facing the sea, the hills, or the pool. There is a small outdoor restaurant and bar, rooftop terrace, DVD library, and reading spaces. Management can arrange car and motorbike hire, guided tours, diving, and whitewater rafting. **$-$$**

Rasa Sayang Beach Inn, Jl. Pratama 88 X, tel: 771-268. The best value accommodation on the peninsula, this old-style two-story hotel has very simple rooms with terraces. It's a comfortable spot for those on a budget, though it can be a bit noisy. **$**

Royal Santrian, Jl. Pratama, Tanjung Benoa, www.theroyalsantrian.com. A collection of 20 villas designed for seclusion and comfort on 2.5 ha (6 ac) of gardens sloping to a sparkling white sand beach; private pools, open-air gazebos with dining and living areas, and some excellent eateries onsite. **$$$$**

DINING

A great variety of good restaurants (many of which offer free pick-up for Tanjung Benoa and Nusa Dua areas) are found on both sides of Jl. Pratama, the main road, all the way from the turnoff to Nusa Dua to Benoa village.

Each of the premier hotels have beachfront restaurants with romantic ambience and clear views of the white cliffs of Nusa Penida, and they present seafood barbecues several times weekly. Menus are a mixture of European, Indonesian, and Asian-fusion. Theme night entertainment such as South Seas, Barong, or Monkey Dance usually takes place 7 pm–10 pm. Check upon arrival for current schedules.

Bumbu Bali, Jl. Pratama, www.balifoods.com. Rated amongst the best restaurants in Indonesia, this fabulous eatery is set in the open-air courtyard of a Balinese home. It offers Balinese home-cooking combined with five-star finesse, generous portions, and reasonable prices. The service by waiters dressed in Balinese attire is impeccable. The sumptuous *rijstaffel* is exceptional value. Cooking classes are also available. Lunch and dinner. **$$-$$$**

Eight Degrees South, The Conrad Bali Resort & Spa, Jl. Pratama No. 168, tel: 778-788. A first-rate beachfront restaurant with gourmet pizzas, pasta, lobster, and seafood. You can also create your own organic salad. Low-key DJ sets accompany dinner service some evenings. Dinner. **$$$**

The Tree, Jl. Pratama in front of Peninsula Beach Resort, tel: 773-488. A sister restaurant to the popular Nyoman's Beer Garden in Nusa Dua, this place does a reliable array of Balinese and European food, seafood, pizza, vegetarian, plus cocktails and a wide wine selection. There is daily entertainment, free Wi-Fi, and free transport in the Nusa Dua/Benoa area. **$$$**

ACTIVITIES

Cooking School

Bumbu Bali Cooking School, Jl. Pratama, Tanjung Benoa, www.balifoods.com. Bumbu Bali restaurant has an enormous following, even among affluent Balinese, who know what authentic Balinese cuisine should taste like. Run by flamboyant chef Heinz von Holzen, the cooking school begins early with a trip to the morning market to select the day's catch and the freshest vegetables. After creating the day's masterpiece, you get to eat it for lunch. A delightful way to spend a day. Classes are held Monday, Wednesday, and Friday 6 am–3 pm. Reservations recommended.

WATER SPORTS

The mantra for Tanjung Benoa is marine sports. Water sport company offices and dive shops line the entire strip, facing a gentle and shallow shoreline on the peninsula's eastern side. Some people complain about the noisy jet-skis, water scooters, motorboats, and banana boat rides, but eco-friendly recreation is also available, all at generally less expensive prices than Nusa Dua. Enthusiasts may enjoy parasailing, scuba diving, snorkeling, water-skiing, wakeboarding, glass-bottom boats, speedboats, reef fishing, and trawling expeditions. The intensive training for parasailing takes all of 120 seconds.

Tirta Harum Dive & Water Sport, Jl. Pratama No. 36X, www.tirtaharum.com. With long experience in the marine sport business, this operator is a member of PADI and of the Indonesia Marine Tourist Association. In addition to diving and snorkeling, they offer jet skiing, parasailing, banana boats, wake boards, knee boards, waterskiing. Their Dive Walker is a walk among the fish on the sea floor wearing a helmet connected to air by a hose and accompanied by a professional diver. They also have Flying Fish, the newest water sports "toy" on the market.

Yos Marine Adventures, Jl. Pintas Tanung Benoa No. 3, www.yosdive.com. Highly respected marine operator with two decades' experience and a PADI International Resort Association active member, Yos Marine has been appointed by many leading hotels and resorts in Bali to teach introductory Discover Scuba Diving at their pools to augment and enhance their existing in-house recreational programs. PADI dive courses, daily dive trips, dive safaris. Also offers boat charter, snorkeling, dolphin tours, water sports, and fishing. Dive trips to Komodo and Lembeh (north tip of Sulawesi). Branches in Candidasa, east Bali and Pemuteran, north Bali.

SAILING EXCURSIONS

At the northernmost tip of the peninsula is a busy working harbor servicing all sorts of vessels from fishing boats to Navy ships. It is also the home of the Royal Bali Yacht Club as well as many cruise companies that offer diving and sailing excursions to nearby Nusa Penida and Lembongan, up the east coast of Bali, and further east to remote Indonesian islands. Below are some of the other boats that berth there.

Adelaar, www.adelaar-cruises.com. Owned by a German doctor and his American wife, this wonderful boat has been completely refurbished to provide en suite bathrooms in private cabins as a liveaboard. Sailing and diving charters to Nusa Penida and Nusa Lembongan, as well as along the east Bali coastline and to Menjangan Island in the West Bali National Park. Also to Lombok and to Komodo Island.

Bali Hai Cruises, www.balihaicruises.com. This outfit puts together a variety of fun, family-oriented, and romantic sailing excursions and packages that deliver an unforgettable experience.

Bounty Cruises, www.balibountycruises.com. Three-deck catamaran with cruising speed of up to 30 knots and state of the art equipment. Offers Nusa Lembongan transfers, day cruises, dinner cruises, offshore night cruises, and party charters.

Sea Safari Cruises, www.seasafaricruises.com. Specializes in leisure expeditions on custom-built *phinisis* (traditional Sulawesi sailing rigs). Destinations include Lembongan, Komodo, Labuanbajo (Flores), and Sumbawa. Also does private dinner cruises and liveaboard dive trips to Raja Ampat (Papua).

Seatrek Sailing Adventures, www.seatrekbali.com. Includes a fleet of 3 schooners—*Ombak Putih*, *Katharina*, and *Atasita*—and a 23 m (75 ft) yacht, the *Merrymakin*. The *Katharina* and *Ombak Putih* have scheduled "leisure expeditions" departures to the islands east of Bali and to Papua, Ambon, and the fabled Spice Islands. The liveaboard Atasita specializes in diving cruises, and the *Merrymakin* is available for private charters.

Waka Dinner Cruise, www.wakaexperience.com. Relax under the stars on a harbor dinner cruise aboard Waka Experience's luxury catamaran. Excellent cuisine in an intimate setting.

NUSA PENIDA, NUSA LEMBONGAN & NUSA CENINGAN

A World Apart: Bali's "Nusa Islands"

From the high ground of the Bukit, or all the way along the coast to Candidasa, a tantalizing prospect presents itself on the eastern horizon. Rising from the bright, breeze-cut waters is a hulk of rugged land, looking decidedly different from mainland Bali. There is none of mainland Bali's overwhelming greenness, and none of its symmetrical volcanic peaks. Instead there is a sun-scorched color scheme and a slab of rising ground, scored with deep stream-cuts.

Though it looks like a single landmass, this offshore vision actually consists of three islands: Nusa Lembongan closest to shore, large Nusa Penida rising beyond, and tiny Nusa Ceningan hidden between them. Nusa Lembongan is a major tourist destination, a playground for surfers, snorkelers and divers, thickly studded with accommodations. Nusa Penida, however, couldn't be more different. Almost completely untouched by mass tourism, a trip here is like stepping back some three decades into Bali's past, a chance

Nusa Lembongan is a prime surfing and diving destination away from the noise and bustle of Bali.

to explore rugged backroads, remote communities, and hidden beaches almost completely untrammeled by other visitors—for now.

Nusa Lembongan

Nusa Lembongan is a small island covered with with coconut trees, mangrove forests, and smallholdings, and surrounded by coral reefs. The island's population is split between two villages, Jungutbatu and Lembongan. Traditionally, fishing and seaweed farming were the only sources of employment here, and both are still important industries, though tourism is now the real mainstay of the island.

What began as a well-kept secret, one of several on Indonesia's south coast circuit, is now a full-blown tourist destination catering to beach and water sports lovers. Many visitors opt to take **day cruises** from the mainland, departing Sanur, Benoa, or Nusa Dua for Nusa Lembongan in the morning and returning around sunset. Others choose to revel in the laid-back atmosphere and make longer stays in one of Lembongan's many accommodations, which cater to all budgetary requirements.

The main focus of tourism development is on the west coast, which has fantastic sunset views back towards Bali. From the northwest tip of the island an almost unbroken string of guesthouses, villas and midrange resorts stretches south to the point where the coast turns westwards. More upscale accommodations are tucked away around the sheltered coves further south. The main stretch of beach doesn't offer the best swimming, with many moored boats and seaweed farms offshore, though you can get into the water at high tide.

Surfers looking to escape the crowds at Kuta and on the Bukit were amongst the first outsiders to visit Lembongan in significant numbers, back in the late 1980s, and during the dry months, from April to September, there are still excellent waves to be had here at the **Shipwreck**, **Lacerations**, and **Playground** breaks, strung along the western shoreline.

Mushroom Bay, towards the south of Lembongan, is one of several pretty coves along the island's coast.

In the deeper waters divers can explore flat reefs and walls populated seasonally with giant sunfish (mola-mola) and manta rays year round at **Blue Corner**, **Jackfish Point**, and **Ceningan Point**. The currents here can be tricky, making it imperative to be accompanied by a reputable dive operator who knows these waters intimately. Snorkelers can paddle happily at **Mushroom Bay** or hire a *jungkung* to take them to several other sites. For everyone else there is parasailing, wakeboarding, jet skiing, banana boat rides, and sea kayaking, or exploring the mangrove forests on the northern shore by outrigger boat.

Nusa Lembongan also offers excellent **walking** opportunities. Its many footpaths invite the intrepid to stroll around coastlines or over **Devil's Tear** on the southwestern coast. Next to Devil's Tear is **Sunset Beach**, with a cave carved out of the adjacent limestone cliff. Near **Lembongan village**, see the seaweed farmers at work planting, harvesting, drying, and replanting the crop that sustains them. Of course no Bali visit is complete without visiting at least one temple, and **Pura Puncak Sari** north of Lembongan village awaits.

Nusa Ceningan

Wedged in between its two sister islands, tiny **Nusa Ceningan** is relatively undeveloped, but for bicyclers and trekkers there are some scenic roads and rough paths. The simplest access is via a narrow, creaky 1km (1,100 yd) suspension bridge connecting the island to neighboring Nusa Lembongan.

The first thing to notice is the bamboo frameworks for seaweed farming in the lagoon below the suspension bridge. At 65 m (210 ft), the island's highest hill holds some stunning views. There's a surf break at Ceningan reef.

Community empowerment and conservation activist group **JED (Jaringan Ekowisata Desa) Village Ecotourism Network**, based in Seminyak, offers a tour to Nusa Ceningan using grassroots techniques and local guides. Planned and managed by the community in each village, JED tours are designed to raise funds for cultural and conservation activities and to instill pride amongst villagers. For other information, visit www.jed.or.id.

Nusa Penida

Nusa Penida is an island apart. "Like Bali thirty years ago" is an overused cliché in Indonesian travel circles, but in the case of this remarkable place it may actually be apt. More specifically, Nusa Penida is decidedly reminiscent of the similarly high, dry limestone landscapes of Bukit Badung in the decades before decent roads, mass tourism and villa developers descended. Outside of a couple of small, ramshackle townships on the accessible northern coast, the narrow, potholed roads are almost completely free from traffic; villagers go about their traditional activities undisturbed; temples built of pale limestone stand on lonely promontories; and come evening the great cone of Gunung Agung on Bali looms to the west against a fiery sky.

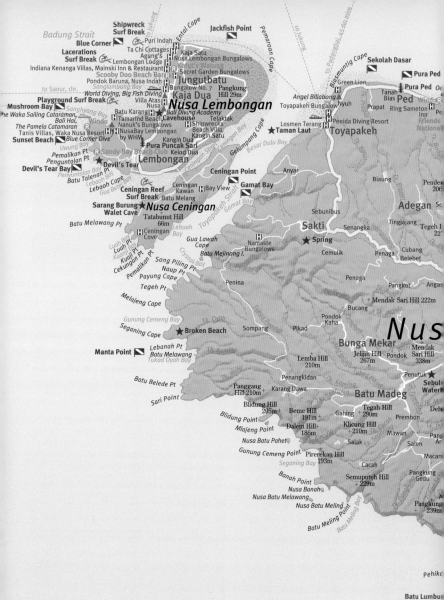

Badung Strait

Shipwreck Surf Break
Blue Corner
Lacerations Surf Break
Indiana Kenanga Villas, Mainski Inn & Restaurant
Pondok Baruna, Nusa Indah
Scooby Doo Beach Bay
World Diving, Big Fish Diving
to Sanur, 1hr.
Mushroom Bay
Sanghyang Bay
The Waka Sailing Catamaran, Bali Hai,
The Pamela Catamaran
Tanis Villas, Waka Nusa Resort
Sunset Beach
Blue Corner Dive
Uwung Bay
Pemalikan Pt
Pengulanj
Pemalikan Pt
Penguntolan Pt
Devil's Tear Bay
Batu Talenan
Lebaoh Cape
Gua Belanda
Sarang Burung
Walet Cave

Puri Indah
Ta Chi Cottages
Agung's
Kaja Satu
Nusa Lembongan Bungalows
Lembongan Lodge
Secret Garden Bungalows
Jungutbatu
Kaja Dua
Nusa
Batu Karang
Bali Diving Academy
Tamarind Beach
Nanuk's Bungalows
NusaBay Lembongan
by WHM
Telaktak
Shipwrecks Beach Villa
Kangin Satu
Kangin Dua
Pura Puncak Sari
Kelod Dua
Lembongan
Villa Atas
Nusa Lembongan

Entai Cape
Jackfish Point
pemaroan Cape

Pangkung Hill 29m

Nature's Warung
Pangkung Hill 29m

Bungalow No. 7

Ceningan Point
Ceningan Kawan
Batu Melang
Ceningan Reef Surf Break
Tatabunut Hill 66m
Ceningan Cove
Lebuah Bay
Nusa Ceningan
Batu Melawang Pt
Luah Bay
Luah Pt
Kuali Pt
Cekungan Pt
Pemalikan Pt
Song Piling Pt
Naup Cape
Payung Cape
Tegeh Pt
Melajeng Cape
Gunung Cemeng Bay
Seganing Cape
Manta Point
Lebanah Pt
Batu Melawang
Tukad Oyah Bay
Batu Belede Pt
Sari Point

Bay View
Gamat Bay
Gamat Bay
Gua Lawah Cape
Batu Mejinong I.
Crystal Bay
Penina
Broken Beach
Sompang
Penangkidan
Panggang Hill 210m
Karang Dawa
Blidung Hill 205m
Blidung Point
Mlajeng Point
Nusa Batu Pahet
Gunung Cemeng Point
Banah Point
Nusa Banah
Nusa Batu Melawang
Nusa Batu Meling
Batu Meling Point

Anyar
Sebunibus
Sakti
★ **Spring**
Cemulik
Namaste Bungalows
Penaga
Penina
Bucang
Pondok Kaha
Pikad
Lemba Hill 210m
Beme Hill 191m
Dalem Hill 186m
Pirerekan Hill 193m
Cacah
Semuputeh Hill 229m
Batu Meling Bay

Biaung
Senangka
Tingjajang
Cubang
Belebet
Pangkot
Mendak Sari Hill 222m
Bunga Mekar
Jelijih Hill 267m
Pondok
Batu Madeg
Gahing
Tegah Hill 290m
Klicung Hill 210m
Salak
Mawan
Salen
Mendak Sari Hill 338m
Penutuk
Prembon
Deh
Macan
Pangkung Gedu
Pangkung 239m

Nus

Toyapakeh Strait
Ceningan Strait
Gamat Bay
Besar Dulu Bay
Gelumpang Cape
Toyopakeh Strait
Tk. Oyah
Tk. Kenten
Tk. Mada
Tk. Ayas
Teluk Penida
Tk. Oyah
Tk. Kaming
Tukad Oyah Bay

Sekolah Dasar
to Pegadebal 45-60 mins.
to Jukung
to Jukung
Bias-muntig Cape
Green Lion
Pura Ped
Pura Ped
Tanah Bias
Nyuh
Ring Sameton
Penida Diving Resort
Ped
Prapat
Wiadra
Inn
Flylends
National
Angel Billabong
Toyapakeh Bungalow
Losmen Terang
★ **Taman Laut**
Toyapakeh

Pender
206
Adegan
Se
**Sebulu
Water**

Batu Lumbu

pehika

INDIAN OCEAN

The Nusa Islands

0   2km

N

to Padangbai

Nusa Penida Harbor

Buyuk   Edy Guesthouse
Telaga   Kutampi   **Sampalan**   **Batu Nunggal**
Buyuk   Mentigi   **Sampalan**
Nusa Garden Bungalow   Ketapang   ★ **Losmen**

Krambitan Cape

Cemara Cape

Batu Mulapan
Jepun
Malu

Tegeh Kuri Hill
288m   Minggir   Pengaud
Maos
Jurang Pahit

Lombok Strait

Telaga Sakti Hill 263m   **Kutampi**
Gelagah   Maos Hill +263m
Bila
Sebonipil   Bayuh   Pidada
Bukit   Karang Sari   ★ **Giri Putri Cave**
Pupuan

Puseh Point

ibu   Waru   Ponjok
Iseh   **Pura Puncak Mundi**
Majong Hill +363m   Angkal
Jurang Aya Hill 513m   Jurang Aya   Celagi Landan
Emas Hill 521m   Pulangan Baru   ⚑ **Malibu Point**

Suana

enida
Tulad   Gunung Sari Hill 338m
Calik   ⚑ **Samaya**
Salang   Tulad Hill 488m
Padang Sei Hill +248m   ♠ **Pura Batu Madan**
Semaya   ♠ **Pura Batu Kuring**

ill   Batu Guling
Jungkulan Hill 451m
Gejuh   Panda Hill 299m
Tukad Saang   **Pejukutan**
Gembrong Hill 228m

Gepuh Hill 458m   Caruban Hill 453m
atu Kandik   Maung Hill 451m   Ambengan
Tanjung   Duren   Paku   Caruban
Ringin Hill 441m   Ambengan Hill 363m   Ampei   Bulung Ladeh Hill 104m
Bangun Urip   Karang Gede   Karang Bilis
Bingin   Melangit Hill 451m   Putri Hill 338m   Pendem

Tegoh Sebun Bay

antang Hill 271m
Dungkap Satu   Gede Hill 438m   Pendem Hill 252m   Menasah Hill 227m
Belalu   Penyancangan   Silah Hill 427m   Juntil Hill 142m
Merenggeng   Dungkap Dua   Langki   **Tanglad**   Cemlagi

Juntil Point

Jarak   Dundungan   Tektekan   Tektekan Hill 231m   ⚑ **Pantai Atuh**
Awan   Glogor Hill 288m   Soyar   Nyahing Hill 428m   Pelilit Kubu   **Pantai Atuh** *Nusa Batu Padasan*
Buluh   Anta   Julingan   Tunjuk Pusuh Hill 452m   Pelilit Asah   *Nusa Batu Mategan*   *Nusa Batu Abah*
Bungkil   Blubuh Hill 388m   Tebe   ⚑ **Batu Abah**
Huhug Hill 273m   Tebe Hill 200m

Cleng Hill 213m
Tabuanan   Dere Hill 439m
Katekate Hill 186m   Ramuan   Penyaban   Wates

Maling Hill 196m
Tabuanan Hill 190m   **Sekar Taji**
Sedihing Dua   Sedihing Satu

Point   *atu*   *Cleng Point*
Sedihing Hill 177m
Bakung Hill 163m   Pupuan Hill 186m

Atuhlili Point

Suwehan Point

Kuring Point

Bakung Cape

The going is somewhat rough on Nusa Penida: accommodation is limited, the roads are bumpy, dining options are far from sophisticated, and getting thoroughly lost the moment you leave the main northern coast road is a near certainty. But local people are tremendously hospitable, and for hardy travelers this is the ideal place to stray far from the beaten track—and all just a short hop from the busy resorts of southern Bali.

Things are, however, beginning to change. After years of unfulfilled predictions that Penida was set to become "the next big thing" in Bali, plots of land have finally started opening up for tourism development, and the first low-key resorts have started to appear—each standing in splendid isolation for the time being. Transport links have also greatly improved, with a daily vehicle ferry from Pandangbai, and regular fast boats from Sanur bringing otherworldly Nusa Penida within two hours of Bali's international airport. Nonetheless, Nusa Penida still offers a remarkable opportunity to explore a wild, starkly beautiful, warmly welcoming, and entirely authentic island, far from the madding crowd.

The magic of seaweed
All along the gently sloping northern shores of Nusa Penida, low tides reveal a mesh of ropes and stakes, strung across the shallow reefs that lie just beyond the sands. These are seaweed farms, mainstay of the island economy. In the past, highland farmers on Nusa

Penida worked in terraced dry fields and bred cattle, which were taken to market in Denpasar aboard *jukung* (outrigger boats). However, the success of early seaweed farmers on the coast lured many away from the hills, as one *are* (10x10 m or 32x32 ft) of seaweed generated six to eight times more income than the same amount of farmland did in twice the amount of time. The seaweed—the large, green *Kotoni* sp. and the smaller, red *Spinosum* sp.—is exported to other Asian countries for use in the cosmetics industry.

Women who formerly helped their husbands in the fields now have more time for weaving *ikat* textiles, called *cepuk*. While in the past produced exclusively with hand-spun cotton and natural dyes on back-strap looms, many weavers today use foot-treadle looms and chemical dyes. They also produce *endek*, a non-ceremonial cloth.

The relative wealth brought to the island by seaweed farming has improved life for many. Electricity is now available in most areas, and in the north there is mains water. In the south, however, rainwater is collected in huge tanks for supply during the dry season, and on Penida's southern cliffs a spectacular bamboo stairway has been constructed to gather water from natural springs just above the sea. Education, job, and entertainment opportunities are scarce.

All connections with the Bali mainland are by boat. Among Nusa Penida's exports are

Many villagers on Nusa Penida and Nusa Lembongan earn a living by farming seaweed.

Crystal Bay, at the western end of Nusa Penida, has excellent snorkeling right offshore.

cattle, free-range chickens, seaweed—which is the main income for most families—and some traditional ikat textiles. Unlike the rest of Bali, fish are available year-round. Water is scarce here, so imports include vegetables and rice—which are rarely grown—as well as other items, such as cooking oil, that are not produced on the island. The advent of regular vehicle ferry service has also facilitated the arrival of other interesting items. At times of traditional or temple festivals, it is common to see expensive cars on the roads, brought over by the more affluent "natives" who now live off the island.

The cursed islands

All kinds of appalling myths have always been attached to Nusa Penida due to its former gloomy atmosphere and unrewarding conditions. Black magic is said to flourish here, and all evil affecting Bali—especially floods and diseases during the dry season—is said to come from Penida, brought by the giant demon king Jero Gede Mecaling and his army of 500 *wong samar*, invisible spirits who inhabit only dark places.

The story goes that the *wong samar* were created by the venerable Danghyang Nirartha, who came to Bali from East Java to spread the Hindu religion. It is said that Nirartha's daughter—Dewi Melanting—was cursed by Naga Basuki, king of the serpents, who made her physical body disappear. In order to keep her from being lonely, the loving father Nirartha transformed some of his followers into invisible spirits to keep her company. Throughout Bali, Dewi Melanting is revered as the protector of the economy,

and every traditional market has a shrine dedicated to her.

Jero Gede Mecaling was a very powerful magician and talented shape-shifter; he is still today thought by Balinese outside of Nusa Penida to spread disease and evil. In order to avoid sickness—which frequently occurs during the transition between wet and dry seasons—ceremonies are performed in many mainland areas. In Badung and Gianyar regencies the giant and his troops are particularly feared and are said to cross the straits and land at Lebih, where they are met and expelled by way of the *sanghyang dedari* trance dances.

Nusa Penida was once part of the Klungkung kingdom, and was used by its rajas as a place of banishment. Any aristocratic exiles shipped across the strait for displeasing the king were stripped of their noble titles, Dewi or Sri. Even today, very few Nusa Penida locals bear those titles.

Explorations off the Beaten Track

On Nusa Penida, there is almost no mass tourism yet; only a few foreigners venture this far off the beaten track, though numbers are slowly increasing, especially since the opening of a few decent accommodation options and the improvement of transport links to the mainland. However, the largest number of visitors are still Balinese who come here on ceremonial occasions to make pilgrimages. It is wonderful to walk, ride on *ojek* motorcycle taxis, or drive through the villages in the highlands and along the shore to experience the island's rough beauty. Any passing outsider will likely be met with a chorus of startled but delighted greetings from locals,

The Goa Giri Putri cave temple is a Nusa Penida highlight, visited by pilgrims from all over Bali.

children and adults alike, as yet totally unused to meeting tourists.

The main town is **Sampalan**, where the government offices are located and the island's biggest market is. This is also where the daily vehicle ferry from Padangbai docks. It's a decidedly rough and ready place, but there are a few decent budget accommodation options—most of which can help organize a rental motor scooter for further explorations.

Further west, **Ped** is still little more than a seaweed farming hamlet, but it is also where the fast passenger boats from Sanur usually land, and as a consequence it has hints of an embryonic tourist trade, with one very decent hotel and a selection of cheaper homestays, plus magnificent sunset views back towards Bali.

Nearby is the interesting **Pura Penataran Agung Ped** (also called Pura Ped). This large temple consists of four sections: Pura Dalem Segara for cleansing and for blessing the ocean, Pura Beji also for cleansing and for prosperity, Pura Ratu Gede in honor of the ruler, and the female Penataran Agung, which is visited by those who can see the invisible world. In the smaller sanctuary here, a strange tree composed of three entangled ones grows, and from the trunk a stone mouth protrudes, believed to be that of Jero Gede Mecaling's minister. The temple *odalan* (anniversary) falls on Buda Cemeng Kelawu. Every three years on the fourth full moon (Purnama Kapat), a great festival (*usaba*) is held, during which pilgrims from throughout Bali come to pray at Pura Ped.

The sacred Gandrung dance, performed by two pre-pubescent boys clad in women's attire, is still practiced on Kajeng Kliwon, Purnama, and Tilem according to the Balinese calendar. In the past this dance was traditional in other parts of Bali, but it was performed by girls and women.

Toyapakeh, Nusa Penida's second most important town because of its harbor and the closest point to neighboring Nusa Lembongan, is dominated by a mosque and is home to a large Muslim community. Many of the residents of this "Kampung Muslim," or Muslim Village, are descended from settlers from elsewhere in Indonesia, particularly Sasak from Lombok and Bugis from Sulawesi. Other local Muslims, however, identify as ethnic Balinese—unusual in a place where identity is so closely tied up with the Hindu religion. Here, as elsewhere on Nusa Penida, the inhabitants speak a distinctive Balinese dialect peppered with archaic vocabulary no longer used on the Balinese mainland. Some also understand the Lombok language, Bahasa Sasak, because of family ties to that island. There are several simple but pleasant cafés lining the beach here, and boat transport is available to Lembongan and the mainland.

Most of Nusa Penida's major sights are some distance from the accommodations. **Gua Karang Sari** (also called Goa Giri Putri) near Suana on the windswept northeast coast is one of the most spectacular sacred sites anywhere in Bali. At the top of a flight of concrete steps from the coast road, a tiny opening leads into a narrow limestone tunnel. Before going inside a purification ritual must be performed by the attendant priests. Beyond the cramped and claustrophobic entrance, a vast cavern opens, filled with softly lit shrines and thick with fragrant incense smoke. Locals say that villagers hid here from the Japanese when they arrived during World War II. The cave itself is considered to be female (*putri*) and to house a manifestation of Siva. Its many Hindu and Buddhist shrines are visited by Balinese seeking prosperity. At the furthest end of the cave daylight reappears, along with an incongruous Chinese altar, visited by ethnic Chinese pilgrims from all over Indonesia, and a second entrance gives access to a beautiful hidden valley.

On the other side of the island's central limestone ridge, **Sebuluh Waterfall** near Batu Madeg (300+ m or 980 ft), is surrounded by forest with a natural pond, Pasiraman Dedari, where only men can swim. For women there is a second spring-fed pond nearby.

There are stupendous views from the high **cliffs** all along the south coast, with awe-inspiring drops into the sea far below and several other waterfalls. Similarly stirring views can be found at **Puncak Mundi** (549 m or 1,720 ft), Nusa Penida's highest point, where a wind farm generates electricity, and an important temple, Pura Puncak Mundi, looks out over the rugged central uplands.

Nusa Penida is also home to some fabulous beaches. Those along the north coast are pretty, with good views and soft sand, but strong currents and offshore seaweed farms make them largely unsuitable for swimming. A better option is the picture-perfect **Crystal Bay** near Sakti village at the southwest tip of the island. Backed by palm trees and steep hillsides, it is a perfect arc of golden sand, sheltered by a craggy offshore islet. There are a couple of very basic *warung* offering snacks and cold drinks, and renting snorkeling gear to those wanting to explore the crystalline waters just beyond the shore. Crystal Bay is frequently visited by boats bringing tour groups from both Nusa Lembongan and the mainland, but it is far from crowded. Local fishermen offer boat trips to the various world-class snorkeling and diving sites around the coast, including **Gamat Bay**, **Manta Point** and **Batu Abah**.

There are numerous other beaches on the southern and eastern coasts, many of them rather difficult to reach. One of the finest—and one of the most remote—is the rarely visited **Pantai Atuh**, a pocket of blindingly white sand shielded by towering cliffs and reached by a very steep set of steps. Atuh is in the far southeast of the island, and getting there is an adventure in itself.

In the northwest of the island, another emerging Penida icon is Pasih Uug, popularly

Broken Beach, on the wild northwest coast of Penida, is one of the island's natural wonders.

known as **Broken Beach**, a cliff-ringed inlet fronted by a dramatic natural arch. A short way along the coast is **Angel's Billabong**, a stunning natural swimming pool set in deep cliffs.

The endangered Bali Starling

Bird and nature lovers will want to stop by the **Friends of the National Parks** (FNPF) office in Ped to hear about their remarkable conservation work. Together with The Begawan Giri Foundation they are breeding and releasing the critically endangered Bali Starling (Leucopsar Rothschild) at their Nusa Penida sanctuary. Highly prized by bird collectors, almost all of the world's surviving Bali Starlings—which are unrelated to their drab European namesakes in either taxonomy or appearance—are in captivity, and poaching for the illegal bird trade remains a major threat. By 2005, there were fewer than 10 individual birds in West Bali National Park, the only place where they still survived in the wild, and a long-running captive breeding and release program at the park had proved unsuccessful, in part due to the continued depredations of poachers.

In 1999, FNPF founder, a Balinese veterinarian named Bayu Wirayudha, realized that isolated, sparsely populated Nusa Penida might make a better location for reestablishing the bird. Enlisting the help of the leaders of the 41 traditional villages on Nusa Penida to implement ancient customary laws protecting the natural world, Wirayudha was able to get the entire island community onside. Beginning with just two captive pairs, the project quickly proved successful, hatching almost one hundred starling chicks within five years. In 2006 FNPF began releasing the birds on Nusa Penida, and small wild breeding populations are now established there, and on Nusa Lembongan and Nusa Ceningan.

FNPF—which regularly hosts international volunteers at its Penida center—continues to work on the Bali Starling breeding program, and continues to monitor the established wild birds, but it has also greatly expanded the scope of its work on the island. There are reforestation, education, and community development programs, creating jobs for the local people and habitats for the birds, as well as nurturing children to become the future caretakers of their own environment. FNPF also provides scholarships for local students. For more information about FNPF's work, visit www.fnpf.org.

ACCOMMODATION PRICE CATEGORIES Prices are for a double room, including breakfast. $ = under $30; $$ = $30–$70; $$$ = $70–$130; $$$$ = over $130. DINING PRICE CATEGORIES Prices are for based on a meal for one, without drinks $ = under $5; $$ = $5–$10; $$$ = over $10.

VISITING THE NUSAS: PENIDA, LEMBONGAN & CENINGAN
See map, page140–141.

Of Bali's trio of offshore islands—Penida, Lembongan, and Ceningan—only Nusa Lembongan has been fully developed for tourism. Penida and Ceningan remain off-the-beaten-track destinations, offering a unique serenity and beauty. Nusa Penida in particular represents the final frontier for travelers in Bali, a place until very recently completely untouched by tourism, and only now slowly starting to open up.

Boats of all sizes, shapes, and speeds ply the routes to the islands from Sanur, Benoa and Padangbai. Schedules frequently change, so the best way to find out current timetables and rates is to ask at your accommodation. If they don't have the information, they can find out quickly or can point you to an agent.

At certain times of year the sea can be treacherous, full of strong currents and even whirlpools. Ask about current conditions. During these periods, the voyage is not advisable in small boats; it's safer to take one of the large boats. You will have to wade through the water to get on and off smaller boats, and you may get splashed during the crossing, so pack everything in plastic bags.

When the sea is treacherous, water activities can be affected. Mushroom Bay on Lembongan is sheltered and safe for swimming; however, swimmers should avoid Dream Bay and Sunset Beach. Surfing at Lembongan is not advisable for beginners. On Nusa Penida, tidal rips can affect the beaches along the north coast, which also house seaweed farms in the shallows.

There are only a couple of ATMs on Nusa Penida, accepting few international cards, while the moneychangers on Nusa Lembongan, charge unfavorable rates, so bring enough cash in rupiah to last throughout your stay.

NUSA LEMBONGAN
Promoted as Bali's local weekend getaway, Nusa Lembongan has become an aquatic playground, attracting day-trippers as well as longer-stay folks with its stunning coral reefs, sandy beaches, and lively surf breaks. **Jungutbatu** was the original budget surfers' hangout. There are still cheap accommodations here, but there is also an increasing array of upscale places. The upmarket hotels and resorts are found around **Mushroom Bay** (Tanjung Sanghyang) southwest of Jungutbatu, with other accommodations stretching the length of the beach in between. Incoming boats stop either at Jungutbatu or Mushroom Bay, and some stop at both.

Nusa Lembongan is small—only 4x1.6 km (3x1 miles)—so distances aren't great. From Jungutbatu it is 5–7 mins to Mushroom Bay and 10–15 mins to Sunset Beach on the southwest tip of the island.

GETTING THERE
Sanur is the main point of departure for Nusa Lembongan, though there are also sporadic speedboat services from Padangbai. Open **public boats** depart from Sanur beach at the end of Jl. Hang Tuah. Departure times are generally around 8 am, sometimes with extra boats at 10:30 am and in the afternoon 2–3 pm. The journey usually takes about an hour. A confusing array of operators also offer **speedboat services**, crossing to Lembongan in about 30 minutes. Some make hotel pick-ups, so be sure to inquire on booking.

Perama has its own boat, which departs Sanur at 10:30 am. Amongst the other private operators **Scoot** and **Rocky Fast Cruises** have good reputations.

GETTING AROUND
Bicycles and motorbikes are available through accommodations. Alternatively, hop on the back of an *ojek* (motorbike taxi) or take a one-way or round-trip around the island via a local boat for a small fee. Large self-drive golf buggies are a recent addition to the island, available for rent from upscale accommodations.

ACCOMMODATIONS

JUNGUTBATU
Bungalo No. 7, www.bungalo-no7.com. Family owned since 1982, and named after the patriarch's boat, this place has simple but clean rooms, right on the beach. Bapak and Ibu (pop and mom) take care of guests and tend the gardens. $-$$
Indiana Kenanga Villas, www.indiana-kenanga-villas.com. French-owned and designed, this is the most upscale place in Jungutbatu, with a couple of villas and 16 suites arrayed around a pool. Excellent restaurant attached. $$$$
Pondok Baruna Guesthouse, www.pondokbaruna.com. Clean fan rooms with bamboo furnishings and

balconies facing the beach are good value here. There are also new air-con garden bungalows next to the swimming pool. Friendly staff, restaurant, and also the office of World Diving Lembongan. $-$$
Secret Garden Bungalows, www.bigfishdiving.com. Nine clean rooms with fan and semi-outdoor bathrooms. Double and twin rooms each have verandahs. Shaded by palms, frangipani, and mango trees, only 50 m (160 ft) from the beach. Good tourist information from friendly staff. Big Fish Diving Center is based here. $$
Shipwrecks Beach Villa, www.nusalembongan.com.au. A villa a few meters from the beach with three rooms, each with king-sized four-poster beds. The shared main pavilion has living and dining rooms and kitchen. Bookings are taken for minimum stays of two nights. $$

MUSHROOM BAY & TAMARIND BEACH

Nanuk's Bungalows, www.nanukbungalows.com. About 180 m (200 yds) from Mushroom Bay and Secret Bay, this pleasant, family-owned bungalow complex has clean fan rooms in thatched rice barn-style buildings, a swimming pool, restaurant, and bar. $$-$$$
Tanis Villas, ww.tanisvillas.com. A growing resort with a wide array of suites and bungalows at Mushroom Bay, this place is good value. Beds come with fancy mosquito nets, and there are attractive sunken baths in the bathrooms. Some rooms have nice sea views, and there's a decent restaurant onsite. $$$
Villa Atas Nusa Lembongan, www.nusalembongan-travel.com. Overlooking Playgrounds and Lacerations surf breaks with views as far as Shipwrecks, this villa has a plunge pool, indoor/outdoor living and dining and fabulous views. $$$
Batu Karang, www.batukaranglembongan.com. Perched on a terraced hillside looking out to sea, the 23 luxury rooms here all come with king-sized beds and outdoor bathrooms. There's a sophisticated day spa onsite, and a tempting infinity pool. $$$$
NusaBay Lembongan by WHM, www.nusabaylembongan-bali.com. Funky castaway atmosphere blends with creature comforts, making this low-key resort a great place for a romantic retreat. Activities include sailing on a traditional *perahu* (fishing boat), glass-bottom boat rides, snorkeling, and canoeing. $$$$

DINING & NIGHTLIFE

Almost all accommodations have their own eateries, primarily serving seafood, so just wander around until you see one you like and give it a try. Almost all serve beer and the larger places have cocktails.

Ketut's Warung, Jungutbatu, tel: 0821-4635-8325. A simple, family-owned restaurant serving Indonesian and Thai food, and fresh fish from the local boats. Breakfast, lunch, and dinner. $$
Sandy Bay Beach Club, Sunset Beach, www.sandybaylembongan.com. Indonesian and European food with wine cellar, great cocktails, icy beers. Freshwater pool for long, lazy lunches and free pick-up around the island. Breakfast, lunch, and dinner. $$$
Scooby Doo Beach Bar & Cafe, Jungutbatu, tel: 0812-3622-9776. A beachside bar that was formerly a ramshackle surfers' hangout, but which has tidied itself up in recent years. It's still got great views and decent, good-value meals, though, perfect for an energy boost after a session in the waves. Serves burgers and pasta. Breakfast, lunch, and dinner. $-$$

WATER ACTIVITIES

Most people visit these islands to surf, scuba dive, or snorkel. The snorkeling here is excellent. Diving and snorkeling equipment can be rented from your hotel: snorkeling trips (around $15), scuba diving ($40 per dive). For experienced divers, there are exciting drift dives at Nusa Penida. There are three main surf spots, all just offshore from Jungutbatu: Playground, Lacerations, and Shipwrecks. Not recommended for beginners; bring your own surfboard.

CRUISES

Various companies based at Benoa on the Bali mainland run day trips to Lembongan aboard luxury catamarans and cruisers, with various water sports and activities, plus dining thrown in.
Bali Hai, www.balihaicruises.com. "Island Beach Club Cruise" is a full day of marine activity at Nusa Lembongan, including ocean kayaking or rafting, snorkeling, reef pontoon, sailing, banana boating, PADI certified diving. Also village tours, swimming pools, massages, dolphin sightseeing, and beach club. Departure 9:15 am, returning 4:15 pm. Around $100 for an adult; includes snorkel equipment, hotel transfers, continental breakfast, BBQ lunch.
The Pamela Catamaran, www.sailboatbali.com. Deep sea fishing (trolling and bottom) with heavy and light fishing tackle in the crystal waters between Bali and Nusa Penida on a 9-m (30-ft) catamaran powered by two eco-friendly engines. Full day cruise includes snorkeling, sundeck, Italian and Mediterranean cuisine lunch and snack. Two cabins for resting and transport to and from hotel.
The Waka Sailing Catamaran, www.wakahotel sandresorts.com. "The Waka Sailing Cruise" aboard a 16-m (50-foot) catamaran is available every Wednesday and Saturday from Benoa, arriving at Waka Nusa Resort on Nusa Lembongan. Program

includes lunch at the resort, seaweed farm tour, snorkeling, glass bottom boat, volleyball, chess or backgammon, before returning to Benoa in the afternoon. The catamaran is also available for private charters: fun fishing, cocktails, dinners, or sightseeing. $94/person.

DIVING

Fed by deep ocean waters, the waters around the "Sister Islands"—Nusa Penida, Nusa Lembongan, and Nusa Ceningan—are excellent for snorkeling and diving. Numerous dive sites have been recorded in this area, including Lembongan Bay, Blue Corner, Mangrove Point, Ceningan Wall, Gamat Bay, Crystal Bay, Toyapakeh, Pura Ped, Sental Point, Buyuk Point, and Manta Point.

Bali Diving Academy, Bungalo No. 7, Jungutbatu; head office: Jl. Danau Tamblingan 51, Sanur, www. scubabali.com. In business since 1991, offers day trips for divers and non-diving companions. Visits over 15 dive sites.

Big Fish Diving, Secret Garden Bungalows, Jungutbatu, www.bigfishdiving.com. Uses Seaquest Wave BCDs with Aqualung Calypso regulators, 5mm full length wetsuits, a variety of masks available, all equipment in prime condition. Rents boats from local families to support the community. Emergency oxygen, life jackets, and fully stocked first aid kit accompany every boat.

World Diving, Jungutbatu, www.world-diving. com. A UK-managed 5-Star PADI international resort opened in 1998, visits 18 different dive sites with more opening in the future. Professional staff, offers first class diving in spectacular and exciting environments.

NUSA PENIDA

Nusa Penida feels more like some wildly remote islet in the far east of Indonesia than a near appendage of Bali, within two hours' journey time of the international airport. There is almost no tourism infrastructure here; the roads are rough, and traditional village lifestyles dominate—all of which makes it a magical destination for those looking to get far from the beaten track without straying too far from Bali. The first signs of change are coming, however. For the moment that's a good thing: Penida now has much better transport links with the mainland, and a wider and more attractive range of accommodations, while still retaining its beguiling air of isolation. Travel soon though: it's something of a miracle that this place has remained so undeveloped for so long while all around it tourism reigns supreme, and it can't last forever!

Sampalan is the main town on Nusa Penida. There are several guesthouses here, a market, a small hospital, and banks. There's another small town at the northwest corner of the island, at Toyapakeh. Halfway between these two settlements is Ped. Speedboats from Sanur dock near here, and there's a decent array of accommodation nearby. Inland a network of potholed roads lead between remote hamlets, high hilltops, and dramatic cliffs.

GETTING THERE

A public vehicle ferry makes the journey between Padangbai and Nusa Penida every day, usually departing from Sampalan at around 9 am for the one-hour crossing, then returning at around midday. The schedule changes regularly, however, depending on tides and weather, so ask at the harbors at either end the day before you travel.

A few speedboats also depart Padangbai daily, usually in the morning. There is also an increasing array of speedboats from Sanur, which land near Ped, with one-way tickets costing around $20. Maruti Express and Semaya One are amongst the operators. You can also charter boats for the crossing. Toyapakeh is usually the best place to do this.

Small public ferries run between Nusa Lembongan and Toyapakeh, if you want to hop between the islands.

GETTING AROUND

Public transport is very limited on Nusa Penida. A few very battered *bemos* run between Sampalan and Toyapakeh for around $1 (a useful route for getting to your accommodation when you first arrive, as it passes the cluster of homestays at Ped). Beyond that there are no regular routes, so you'll need to arrange private transport. *Bemos* can be chartered in Toyapakeh or Sampalan, and there are a few *ojeks* (motorbike taxis). You'll have far more freedom to explore if you rent a motorbike. Most accommodations should be able to arrange this, though with the limited demand rental prices are higher than on mainland Bali. Expect to pay around $8–12/day. Traffic is very, very light on Nusa Penida, even on the main north coast road, but there are lots of potholes to watch out for.

ACCOMMODATIONS AND DINING

Until very recently there was only the most basic accommodation in Nusa Penida. That's all started to change, however. There are several very pleasant budget guesthouses, and a couple of midrange options, including a wonderfully located resort in the hills of the island's southwest. Other upscale accommodations have been planned, including several rather inappropriate villa complexes, though whether these will actually come to fruition remains to be seen.

The main places to seek out accommodation are in Sampalan where there are several guesthouses, and a bustling local community, or in Banjar Bodong at Ped, further west, where a small clutch of tourism businesses form the kernel of coming development. Elsewhere it's still possible to travel as the pioneering backpackers did in Indonesia a generation ago—impromptu homestays in remote villages can often be arranged simply by asking the local *kepala desa*, or village head, though you'll need at least some spoken Indonesian to make this a practical possibility.

Dining options are generally limited to local *warungs*, of which there are a few in both Sampalan and Toyapakeh, with a few very basic places, usually serving little more than noodle soup, in hamlets elsewhere. Bodong in Ped, however, has the beginnings of a slightly more sophisticated dining scene.

Edy Guesthouse, Sampalan, tel: 0878-6233-6452. On a quiet lane a few hundred yards west of the ferry terminal in Sampalan, this pretty little guesthouse has cool rooms with lavishly carved temple-style doors and terraces in a small, verdant family compound. There are a couple of other accommodations on the same lane, and a café with sunset views. One day this may be a bustling backpacker quarter. $

Namaste Bungalows, www.namaste-bungalows. com. Perched on a breezy hilltop, miles from anywhere on the way to Crystal Bay, this beautiful little resort has a clutch of rustic, thatched-roof bungalows, and some smaller rooms stepped down the hillside with views towards Mt. Agung on Bali. There's a pool and a lovely little café. You'll definitely need your own transport, but the location is fantastic. $$-$$$

Nusa Garden Bungalow, Sampalan, tel: 0813-3812-0660. East of the market in Sampalan, look out for the sign pointing up a narrow lane inland. The rooms here are plain but tidy, with clean bathrooms, fan, and nice terraces looking out onto a garden with frangipani trees. There is also a small dormitory. $-$$

Ring Sameton Inn, Br. Bodong, Ped, www.ringsameton-nusapenida.com. For the moment this is Penida's premier tourist accommodation. Set in a peaceful location amidst the trees, back from the road in Ped, it has a nice restaurant, a large swimming pool, and pleasant public areas. The rooms are comfortable and well kept, with air-con, hot water and flat-screen TVs, though they do look a little like transplants from a city business hotel. $$

Gallery, Br. Bodong, Ped, tel: 0819-9988-7205. With art-covered walls, excellent coffee, and a small but appealing menu of classic travelers' fare, this charming café-gallery in Ped is blazing a trail for Nusa Penida tourism. $-$$

Penida Colada, tel: 0821-4532-9004, Br. Bodong, Ped. With an inspired name and a location to die for, this

is the funkiest spot on Nusa Penida. Run by an Australian woman and her local husband, it's a stylishly rustic café perched above the sand across the road from the Ring Sameton Inn. The sunset views across the water to Bali are spectacular; there's a small but appealing menu, and some seriously good cocktails. The place has a welcoming vibe, with locals and travelers alike gathering here in the evenings, and the owners are a great source of information about the island. $$

ACTIVITIES

Friends of the National Parks (FNPF), Ped, www. fnpf.org. Runs a very important Bali Starling breeding and release program on Nusa Penida, which could very well save the species from extinction in the wild. Drop by their office and inquire about treks around the island, birdwatching, their bird sanctuary, reforestation project, and *ikat* weaving in Tanglad village. They also have guest facilities, which may be available if not in use by researchers or volunteers.

Green Lion Bali, Toyapakeh, www.greenlionbali. com. Furthering Penida's reputation as a place for volunteering, this center on the north coast does sterling work breeding turtles and helping with local education projects. They take volunteering seriously here: you need to sign up for at least two weeks.

DIVING AND SNORKELING

Many dive operators in Bali offer trips to Nusa Penida, where the main attractions include seasonal oceanic sunfish (*mola mola*) and manta rays year round. Because of the swift currents, drift dives for the more experienced are favored. Most divers come direct from Nusa Lembongan or Padangbai and never actually step ashore on Penida, but there are a couple of local operators, and more are sure to pop up in the coming years as the island develops. There is brilliant **snorkeling** just offshore at Crystal Bay, and the local warungs have some equipment for rent at very reasonable prices. Local fisherman based at the beach here also offer trips to Gamat, Manta Point, and other nearby spots.

Penida Diving Resort, Toyapakeh, tel 0813-3958-6849. A well-run diving center offering not only snorkeling and dive trips to areas with ocean sunfish, manta rays, stingrays, sharks, and well preserved coral reef, but also motorcycle trips, hiking excursions, and accommodations.

Octopus Dive, Bodong, Ped, www.octopusdive-pelabuhanratu.com. In the embryonic tourist hub of Bodong near Ped, this small local dive shop has got in ahead of the field. It offers trips to all the major dive sites around the island.

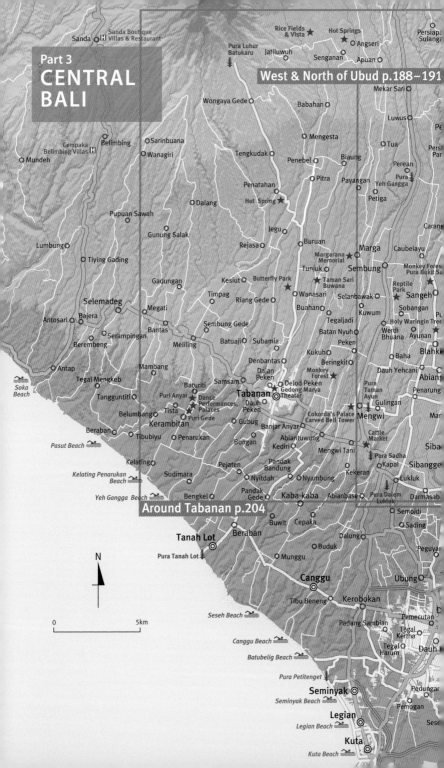

Sanda
Sanda Boutique Villas & Restaurant

Rice Fields & Vista
Hot Springs
Angseri
Persiapan Sulanga

Pura Luhur Batukaru
Jatiluwih
Senganan
Apuan

Mekar Sari

Wongaya Gede
Babahan
Luwus
Pe

Cempaka Belimbing Villas
Belimbing
Sarinbuana
Mengesta
Tua
Persi

Mundeh
Wanagiri
Tengkudak
Penebel
Biaung
Perean
Pura
Yeh Gangga

Pitra
Payangan
Petiga

Penatahan
Hot Spring

Dalang
Jegu
Buruan
Caran

Pupuan Sawah
Rejasa
Marga
Caubelayu

Lumbung
Gunung Salak
Margarana Memorial
Sembung
Monkey Fores
Pura Bukit Sa

Tiying Gading
Gadungan
Kesiut
Butterfly Park
Tunjuk
Taman Sari Buwana

Selemadeg
Megati
Timpag
Riang Gede
Wanasari
Selanbawak
Reptile Park
Sangeh

Antosari
Bajera
Bantas
Sembung Gede
Buahan
Kuwum
Sobangan
Holy Waringin Tree

Serampingan
Meliling
Batuaji
Subamia
Tegaljadi
Werdi Bhuana
Ayunan

Berembeng
Denbantas
Batan Nyuh
Peken
Baha
Blahk

Antap
Mambang
Dajan Peken
Kukuh
Beringkit
Dauh Yehcani
Abian

Tegal Mengkeb
Baturiti
Samsam
Monkey Forest
Penarung

Soka Beach
Tangguntiti
Puri Anyar
Dance Performances, Palaces
Tabanan
Gedong Marya Theater
Pura Taman Ayun
Gulingan

Belumbang
Tista
Dauh Peken
Mengwi
Ma

Beraban
Kerambitan
Puri Gede
Gubug
Banjar Anyar
Cokorda's Palace Carved Bell Tower
Cattle Market
Siba

Pasut Beach
Tibubiyu
Penarukan
Bongan
Abiantuwung
Kediri
Mengwi Tani
Pura Sadha
Kapal
Sibangge

Kelating
Pejaten
Pandak Bandung
Nyitdah
Nyambung
Kekeran
Lukluk
Darmasab

Kelating Penarukan Beach
Sudimara
Bengkel
Pandak Gede
Kaba-kaba
Abianbase
Pura Dalem Lukluk

Yeh Gangga Beach
Sempidi
Sading

Buwit
Cepaka
Dalung
Peguyar

Tanah Lot
Beraban
Buduk
Pura Tanah Lot
Munggu
Ubung

N

Canggu
Kerobokan
Pemecutan

Tibu Beneng
Padang Sambian
Tegal Kertha

0   5km
Seseh Beach
Tegal Harum
Dauh

Canggu Beach

Batubelig Beach

Pura Petitenget
Pedungan

Seminyak
Pemogan

Seminyak Beach

Legian
Sese
Legian Beach

Kuta

Kuta Beach

Pura Pusering gat

Bagus Jati Resort H

Sobek Batur Cycling

Penglumbaran
Buana Amertha Sari Coffee Farm

Pupuan

Pura Pedarman

Pura Besakih

● Besakih

Taro

Puhu

Elephant Safari Park

Antiquities of Central Bali p.192–197

Pujung
Sebatu
Holy Spring
Manukaya
Pura Sakenan

Kayu Bihi

Pempatan

Yangapi

Menanga

Paninjoan

Padangaji

Muncan
Peringsari

Bukian

Kedisah

Tirta Empul

Gunung Kawi

Sulahan

Traditional Village

Kubu

Rendang

Ngoek Hill
512m

Tampaksiring

Susut

Cempaga

Jehem

Tembuku

gih

an

Pura Kehen

Bangbang

Undisan

Nongan

alking Tours Around Ubud p.174–187

Demulih

● Bangli

Tegallalang
Keliki

Kenderan
Topeng Dance
Sanding

Abuan

Bebalang

Nyanglan

Tohpati

Pesaban

Sidemen

Tabda

linggih
Kelod

Kedewatan

Pura Telaga Waja

Petak

Bungbungan

Krama
Desa Adat
Junjungan

Suwat
Pura Kerobokan

Apuan

Timuhun

ite
er
ing

Tegallantang

Pejeng
Petulu

Tegallanting

Tamanbali

Selisihan

Tegak

Tangkup

ayan
idge

Puri
Lukisan
Museum

Pura
Puseh
Taman

Pura
Penataran
Sasih

Goa Garba

Bunutin

Nyalian

Manduang

Selat

Talibeng

estanan
yan

Bentuyung
Monkey
Forest

Pura Kebo
Edan

Siangan

Bakbakan

Aan

Akah

● Ubud

Peliatan

Pejeng
Moon of Pejeng

Bakas

Getakan

Semarapura
(Klungkung)

Besan

Pengosekan

Nyuh Kuning

Legong

Goa
Gajah

Bedulu

Tihingan

Kerta
Gosa

Paksebali

Dawan

akerta
Setia Darma House of
Masks and Puppets

Yeh Pulu

Pura
Beng

Pura Dalem

Sidan

Gamelan
Smiths

Sulang

Gunaksa

Pikat

Raksasa

Mas

Pura
Dalem
Temples, Durga
Statue

Bitera

State
Temple

Tusan

Painting, Gold &
Silver Smiths

Pesinggahan

Singapadu
Kaler

Kemenuh

Pura
Taman Pule
Buruan

Abian Base

● Gianyar

Samplangan

Temesi

Takmung

Satra

Gelgel

Jukung

Basket Weaving

Belege

Bona

Tulikup

Tojan

Kusamba

Fishing
Village

Lodtunduh

Pura Penataran
Topeng Gajahmada

Blahbatuh

Gamelan Maker

Lebih

Negari

Jumpai

Salt Pans

Sedang
Wooden
Masks

Hyang Tiba

Batuan Kaler
Pura
Desa Batuan

Wood Carving

Waterfall

Keramas

Medahan

Bypass Prof. Ida Bagus Mantra

Sea Temple

Agantaka

Batuan

Saba

Bali
Zoo

Pering

Bali Safari &
Marine Park

Purnama
Beach

Masceti
Beach

Keramas
Beach

ng Gede
Music

Bali Fun
World

Pura
Kawitan Dalem

Pura
Segara

Singapadu

Celuk

Sukawati

Sukawati
Handicraft Market

pati

Gold/Silver Smith

Barong Dance
Troupes

Guwang

ura Puseh
Batubulan

Pura Payogan
Agung

bulan

Penatih
Dangin Puri

Ketewel

Ketewel Beach

Badung Strait

Ent-al Cape

han Petilan

Kesiman
Kerta Langu

Shipwreck Surf Break

Kesiman

Pura Gede
Mecaling

Lacerations Surf Break

Jungutbatu

Karya

PASAR

Sanur Beach

Playground Surf Break

Cavehouse

Nusa
Lembongan

Renon

Sindhu Beach

Lembongan

Sanur

Nusa
Ceningan

Ceningan Reef Surf Break

Tojapakih Strait

The Road to Ubud p.154–156

INTRODUCTION

Visiting Central Bali

Central Bali's Ubud is Bali's second largest tourist destination, with many holiday-makers electing to divide their time between the southern beaches and this beautiful hillside community. A prime destination for backpackers in the 1960s and 1970s, over the years it has evolved into a high-end resort area, its streets lined with designer boutiques, upscale restaurants, and a plethora of spas, wellness centers, and yoga studios. The original art galleries, handicrafts shops, and a good number of budget and midrange accommodations and cafés remain in "downtown" Ubud, but surrounding villages have also undergone development. Standalone villas, upscale homestays, and luxurious resorts are now scattered across a wide area of countryside, and with most offering shuttle services to and from the main Ubud town, visitors have a vast array of options when it comes to choosing a place to stay.

The Ubud area is an ideal base for excursions into the countryside to other cultural and historic sites and activities, passing through scenic plantations, farmland, and rural communities en route. The only drawback is traffic, as roads are narrow and serpentine. Although distances from one

Some of Bali's most spectacular rice field views can be found in the hills around Ubud.

Young dancers performing at a full moon ceremony in Bedulu village, near Ubud

point to another may not be great, don't expect to travel at high speeds. Allow more time than you think is actually needed and be prepared for inevitable delays.

The road to Ubud

The Central Bali experience usually begins with a drive north into the hills from the airport or beaches in Southern Bali, along the way pausing for shopping and sightseeing. However, if in a rush to get up the mountain, allow plenty of time on the way back down to see some of Bali's most skilled handicraft makers and performers at work. **Batubulan** is home to the island's stone carvers, their work most often seen in statues and elaborate temple entrances. The small village is also the base for five of Bali's best Barong Dance troupes. **Celuk** is a center for silver and gold-smithing, with shops selling fine jewelry and other handicrafts. At **Singapadu**, stop by GEOKS performing arts venue, showcasing contemporary music, dance, and puppetry and the shops of excellent wood carvers.

Continuing north on the road to Ubud is **Sukawati**, an ancient court center with magnificent temple complexes. Its shadow-puppet masters (*dalang*) are known throughout the island. Bali's only zoo is also located here. Further up the road, **Batuan** was a 19th century court center. Today it maintains its regal status through dance performances. In the art world, the "Batuan style" of painting is well known and can be seen in the town's many galleries. The last stop before Ubud is the woodcarvers' center at **Mas**, where the shops feature statues, furniture, carved doors, and bric-a-brac. Also drop by the House of Masks and Puppets to see a private collection of over six thousand pieces from throughout the world.

Ubud town itself deserves at least one day of strolling in and out of shops —and eating in its fine restaurants —with avid art aficionados, wellness seekers, and certainly shoppers needing more time to pursue their passions. There are also a number of walking tours into rural central Bali that begin from Ubud and don't forget to allocate some evening hours for dance performances either in Ubud proper or in neighboring villages.

Sites north of Ubud

There are many sites that can be easily visited in a day from the Ubud area. Distances are short, the only hindrance being traffic and the amount of time spent at each stop.

Northwest of Ubud there are historic sites at **Mengwi**, and nearby are **Sangeh monkey forest** and the **Butterfly Park** in Wanasari, south of Marga. At Marga is the **Margarana Memorial**, commemorating the final battle of Lieutenant Colonel I Gusti Ngurah Rai and his men, who in 1946 fought Dutch colonial forces to their deaths rather than surrender. There is a particularly scenic drive from Marga to **Tabanan** town, an artistic center.

For a closer look at Bali life, spend a half-day in a family compound west of Marga. At **Taman Sari Buwana**, visitors can try their hands at plowing a field or planting rice,

The long carved ear lobes at the entrance give Goa Gajah its nickname: "the Elephant Cave."

Be chauffeured on an elephant from room to restaurant, watch their performances and help bathe them, all at the Elephant Safari Park (now known as the Mason Elephant Park & Lodge).

making offerings, cooking, or simply strolling around soaking in the culture, followed by lunch. Several **outdoor adventure** outfitters offer a variety of activities nearby, including all-terrain vehicle or cycling treks through fields and villages, tubing and white-water rafting. Round off the day with a healing dip in the hot water springs at **Yeh Gangga** ("Waters of the Ganges").

Northeast of Ubud, the **Elephant Safari Park** at Taro could easily consume a whole day, as could any of the rafting, kayaking, and trekking tours offered by the park's owners. For more animal adventures, the **Bali Bird Park** is a lovely way to spend a few hours. A great way to start the morning is by strolling through the park early, before the heat sets in, and finishing the tour with breakfast at its café alongside a flamingo pond.

Alternative journeys

Heading southeast from the Ubud area, visiting the antiquities in **Gianyar** regency could take an entire day, beginning with a stop at **Goa Gajah**, the ancient Hindu-Buddhist "Elephant Cave" excavated in 1923. From there stop to see the 14th century stone reliefs at **Yeh Pulu** before continuing on to **Pejeng**'s large bronze kettledrum, 11th century statues, and several temples. In the same area are a collection of 17th century *topeng* masks housed at **Pura Penataran Topeng** in Blahbatuh and the carved **Pura Dalem** at Sidan. North of Sidan is Bangli and one of Bali's most beautiful temples, **Pura Kehen**.

Near Bali's southeast coast, adventure awaits at **Bali Safari & Marine Park**, with animal shows, cultural performances, a waterpark, and eateries.

THE ROAD TO UBUD

Batubulan, Celuk, and Singapadu: Surprising Art and Craft Villages

Neighboring Batubulan, Celuk, and Singapadu villages are the first in a series of impressive art and craft centers that are encountered going north along the main road from Denpasar toward Ubud. These villages have garnered fame for a variety of skills: Batubulan for its *barong* dance and stone carving, Singapadu for its *gong saron* and *gong gede* music, and Celuk for its silver- and goldsmithing.

Batubulan: home of the Barong

Ten kilometers (6 miles) north of Denpasar, **Batubulan** is known throughout Bali for its ornate door-guardian statues, carved out of soft *paras* volcanic tuff. Until these became popular for secular use earlier in the 20th century, the carvings were only used in temples or palaces, but this art form has spread widely in recent years and is today found in many homes and public buildings. The

families of Made Leceg and Made Sura, two of the most famous carvers of the area, continue the legacy of their mentor, the late Made Loji. Both have shops on the main road, where carvings can be purchased and packed and shipped home. Roti Adhe is another well-known carver and his shops are on the Batubulan and Singapadu main road.

Batubulan is also home to five famous **Barong dance troupes** which perform five times a week at 9:30 am on their own stages before busloads of enthralled tourists. The development of these groups parallels that of tourism in Bali, but even so the Batubulan *barong* troupes are relatively young. The first, the Den Jalan Barong Group, was established in 1970, while the Tegaltamu, Puri Agung, Sila Budaya, and Jambe Budaya groups were formed later. These troupes perform on stages that were constructed for this purpose.

Bali's best Barong dance troupe perform daily at the village of Batubulan, between Denpasar and Ubud.

A vividly-colored Eclectus parrot at Bali Bird Park

While in the neighborhood, **Pura Puseh Batubulan** is well worth visiting. Four statues of Wisnu poised on carved pedestals embellished with *Tantri* tales guard the temple. If you care to shop, Galuh Art Shop offers an extensive range of Balinese batik and weavings, and Kadek Nadhi's Antique Store has many antiques, from *krises* (ceremonial daggers) and masks to carved doors. Both shops are on the main road, Jl. Raya Batubulan.

Just north of Batubulan on the way to Singapadu is the wonderful **Bali Bird Park (Taman Burung Bali)** where over a thousand birds of 250 species are housed amidst two thousand types of tropical plants. See the rare Bali Starling (*Leucopsar Rothschildi*), walk through the free-fly aviary, and have photos taken with a Brazilian Macaw. A café serving excellent food overlooks a pond of flamingos.

Next door, the **Rimba Reptile Park (Rimba Reptil)** houses 20 different species, including Komodo dragons, a 8 m (26 ft) reticulated python, water monitors, and crocodiles. An open-air area houses some of thetamer species, while the Serpent Cave holds deadlier creatures such as king cobras, mambas, and vipers.

Celuk: silver and jewelry

Although many arts and crafts have prospered in **Celuk**, the village has evolved into a center for silver and goldsmithing. Almost every home in the village contains small-scale production facilities, filling orders placed by large shops and exporters. Bracelets, rings, earrings, and brooches, to name a few of a wide range of products fashioned here, are made by special order for the export market.

Browsing the dizzying array of locally-created jewelry on sale around Batubulan and Celuk.

The silver and gold craft trade was pioneered by the Beratan clan of smiths (*pande*). Nowadays most Celuk residents, whether or not they are members of the Pande clan, have become gold- and silversmiths. Wayan Kawi and Wayan Kardana are among the better craftsmen.

Along the main road between Batubulan and Celuk are over 50 shops, most of which sell **gold and silver jewelry**. Other shops sell masks, statues, old basketry, and textiles, among other things.

Singapadu: village of famous dancers

The history of small **Singapadu** village, just up the road from Batubulan, goes back to the reign of I Dewa Kaleran, a king of Kalianget who assisted the ruler of Sukawati, I Dewa Agung Anom, in defeating the Mengwi king with the aid of two powerful *krises*.

Some believe that Dewa Kaleran's sacred *kris*, Sekar Sandat, possesses creative powers and has therefore helped dance, music, and carving to flourish in the area.

Many well-known dancers have come from Singapadu: Wayan Griya, Ketut Rujag, Wayan Kengguh, Made Kerdek, and Ni Ketut Senun. Today, there are many good ones left, such as Nyoman Cerita, Ketut Kodi, Ni Nyoman Candri, and Ketut Rumita. Made Raos, another prominent dancer, is one of Singapadu's best *barong* (*bapang*) dancers. Two other prominent figures in the field of dance, Dr. I Made Bandem and Dr. I Wayan Dibia, both deans at ISI (Indonesia Institute of the Arts) in Denpasar, are also natives of Singapadu. Dibia founded a performing arts venue called GEOKS in his home village, which showcases contemporary music, dance, and puppetry.

The late Cokorda Oka's mastery of *topeng* and *barong* mask-making has now been handed down to his pupils, I Wayan Tangguh, Cokorda Raka Tisnu, and Nyoman Juala. Wayan Pugeg and Ketut Muja also exhibit great talent in carving wood statues.

The cottage-industry style of jewelry-making in the Celuk area means you can watch artisans at work.

SUKAWATI VILLAGE

An Ancient Court and Bali's Best Dalangs

Located midway between mountain slopes and the sea on the main road north of Denpasar to Ubud, **Sukawati** is a modest town yet it has a lot to offer in rich cultural traditions. At one time, Sukawati stood with Klungkung as one of the two great *negara* or kingdoms of Bali. From Tegallalang to Ubud to Singapadu, *topeng* mask dancers still interpret the history of the old Sukawati realm in front of audiences. The arts have remained vital here thanks to royal patronage and commissions from other parts of the island.

"My heart's delight"

Early in the 18th century the Sukawati region, formerly known as Timbul, came under the influence of an evil sorcerer, Ki Balian Batur. His enemies all became violently ill due to his powerful black magic. Seeking to pacify Timbul, the raja of Mengwi, Angelurah Agung, sought help from I Dewa Agung Anom, son of the raja of Klungkung. Together they defeated the sorcerer with magic weapons brought from the Klungkung court. Ki Balian Batur is still remembered today in the name of the nearby Rangkan village, which means "place of the evil man." As a token of his gratitude, the raja invited I Dewa Agung Anom to build a palace and live there.

I Dewa Agung Anom dreamed of creating an ideal kingdom based on the example of Majapahit in East Java. From Klungkung he brought attractive men and women who were talented in the arts and were representative of the important lineages. Once in Timbul, they built the Pura Penataran Agung as a central shrine and the Puri Goro Gak as a residence for I Dewa Agung Anom and his family.

Lavishly embellished with carvings, the beauty of the great *pura* was enhanced through adding fabulous gardens and pools. Every night, the sensuous sounds of the *gamelan* were heard wafting from an enormous *bale* pavilion covered with gold leaf. The marvels of Timbul invariably caused visitors to exclaim "*sukahati-né*," which means "my heart's delight," and gradually the town became known as Sukawati.

Bali's finest *dalangs*

Sukawati residents are proud that their town has a complex of temples unrivaled outside of Besakih. Represented here is the complete *sad kayangan* group of six temples—Pura Desa, Pura Puseh, Pura Dalem, Pura Melanting, Pura Ulun Siwi, and Pura Sakti—symbolizing Bali's sacred mountains.

Pura Penataran Agung, at the center of Sukawati, is a pilgrimage site for all members of the surrounding area's royal houses: Tegallalang, Ubud, Peliatan, Batuan, Mas, Negara, and Singapadu. Destroyed in an earthquake in 1917, the temple was rebuilt on a smaller scale, which has in no way affected its importance. Next door to the temple is the **Pura Kawitan Dalem Sukawati**, which has panel-carvings of *Tantri* tales and several unusual statues in the outer courtyard. Further to the south in Ketewel village is **Pura Payogan Agung**, where it is said that the original Legong dance originated.

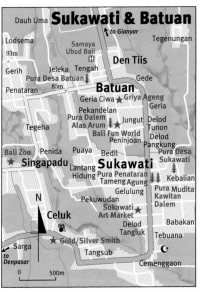

Sukawati & Batuan

The area around Sukawati is famed for its highly skilled wayang kulit puppet masters.

The **Pura Desa**'s massive *candi bentar* gate on the northeastern corner of the town is a tribute to the continuing excellence of local craftsmen. Also known throughout Bali are the *tukang wadah*, craftsmen of the great cremation towers required for royal funeral ceremonies, and the *tukang prada*, makers of gold-painted costumes and umbrellas.

Sukawati is best known, however, for its many shadow-puppet masters, or *dalang*. As many as 20 of these artists and their troupes are available for hire for ceremonial occasions, and they travel throughout Bali to perform. The Balinese say that Sukawati's *dalangs* are the best on the island because of many generations of experience.

Two renowned *dalangs* originated in Banjar Babakan: I Wayan Wija (who currently lives in Banjar Kalah, Peliatan), known for his unusual *wayang tantri* and innovative glass puppets, and I Wayan Nartha. Both can be contacted to commission a shadow play or a special set of puppets. Their nephew, I Wayan Mardika, who works in the Department of Culture and Tourism, can also be commissioned to perform a *wayang* in English. Anyone in the *banjar* can direct you to their houses.

A scholar and member of the *sangging* caste of artisans, I Nyoman Sadia turned from his family tradition of stone carving to making fine jewelry. His house and shop are just off the main road at Jl. Sersan Wayan Pugig No. 5.

The commercial center of the town is the *Pasar Seni* or **Art Market**. With patience and a sense of humor you can find bargains here on everything from woodcarvings to paintings. Just west of this market is the **wood-carving market**, which is only open from 7–10 am, and there are some choice bargains there. Along the main road, shops cater to local needs, such as baskets and ceremonial umbrellas. Directly across the road is an open-air produce market.

Wildlife conservatory

On Jl. Raya Singapadu in Sukawati is the **Bali Zoo** (**Kebun Binatang Bali**), which is privately owned and is Bali's only zoo. Set in 4.86 ha of lush tropical gardens, it includes an animal petting area, walk-through bird aviaries, Komodo dragons, and African lions in an open-range den. The purpose of the zoo is to preserve Indonesian and other wild animals and to encourage an educational experience.

Sukawati Art Market is a colorful hodgepodge of hole-in-the-wall market stalls and a great place for browsing, with some fine pieces available amongst the cheaper tourist souvenirs.

A Village of Famous Painters

For over 1,000 years **Batuan** has been a village of artists and craftsmen, old legends and mysterious tales. Batuan's recorded history begins in A.D. 1022 with an inscription that is housed in the main village temple, **Pura Desa Batuan**.

The name "Batuan" or "Baturan" mentioned here prompts villagers to joke about being "tough as stone" or "eating rocks," as *batu* means "stone" in Indonesian. But it likely refers to an ancient megalithic tradition in which standing stones served as meeting places and ceremonial sites for the worship of ancestral spirits.

Famous families

Batuan's central location in south Bali is the primary reason for its historical importance. Besides the ancient village temple, **Pura Gede Mecaling** is also here, which is said to be on the site of the old palace of the demon king Jero Gede Mecaling, whose name the Balinese are afraid to even utter. He is supposed to have moved from here to Nusa Penida Island, where his spirit still resides. In the 1600s, Gusti Ngurah Batulepang's family dominated south Bali, living as prime ministers based in Batuan. They remained prime ministers until the early 1700s, when a branch of the Klungkung royal family was established at nearby Sukawati. At that time the chief centers of the kingdom were Sukawati, Batuan, and Ketewel village nearby. Batuan still has ritual links with Ketewel that commemorate that era.

The Batulepang family scattered to the far corners of Bali in subsequent centuries as the result of a priestly curse, but a small temple for Gusti Batulepang remains on the site of his palace. The Buddhist priests, or *pedanda boda,* who later made Batuan a great spiritual center built a house, the **Griya Ageng**, on that part of Batulepang's temple where death rituals were once held. They then marshaled powerful Tantric forces here.

Brahman majority

Because Batuan became a center from which Buddhist priests and Brahmans spread to the south Bali main court centers, the village has an unusual preponderance of Brahmans living here. DeZoete and Spies, in their book *Dance and Drama in Bali*, describe it as almost entirely a Brahman village. This is not really true, but much of the village near the main Denpasar to Ubud road is inhabited by the extended family of the Buddhist Griya Ageng and of a smaller number of Siva-worshipping Brahmans who came later to Batuan. The other main high caste family are the Dewas, related to the Batuan *puri,* or extended palace family, who are in turn closely related to the Gianyar royal family. Batuan is unusual in that commoners actually form a minority in the center of the village.

Dancers perform during the temple anniversary celebration for Pura Dalem Alas Arum in Batuan.

The western area of Batuan, known as Negara, was a separate village and court center in the 19th century. It grew so powerful that it revolted against the main house of Gianyar in 1884, destroying the kingdom and setting south Bali on a path of internal conflict which opened it up to Dutch conquest. In 1900, when the Dutch took over Gianyar, Negara was incorporated within Batuan. Similarly, the adjacent area, Puaya, an important center for dance and theater ornaments, puppets, and other objects made from hide, is regarded as being quite separate.

Dancing ancient tales

The Batuan Buddhist Brahmans, in concert with the former king of the village, Anak Agung Gede Oka (1860–1947), were responsible for making Batuan the island's center for the most courtly and elegant of all Balinese dance forms, the *gambuh*. In all of Bali, it is only the troupes from Batuan that continue to preserve this tradition and still perform this theatrical presentation of tales of ancient princes and princesses on a regular basis. Performances are held on the 1st and 15th of every month.

One of these troupes is led by I Made Jimat, one of Bali's most celebrated dancers of modern times, whose genius never fails to leave his audiences breathless. His son, Nyoman Budiawan, has formed a group, Yayasan Tri Pusaka Sakti, which puts on performances featuring multiple generations: Jimat, his son, his grandchildren, and his mother, Men Cenik, who, until she passed away in 2010 at the age of nearly 90, could still command an audience.

Another troupe consists of the extended family of the greatest dancer of the generation preceding Jimat—the late I Nyoman Kakul—who passed on the skills and techniques of *gambuh* and of the other important dance forms, such as the masked *topeng* plays and the operatic *arja* theater. Ketut Kantor, Kakul's late son, led the troupe until his death in 2008. Today, Ketut Wirtawan, Kantor's son, carries on the tradition.

A third troupe, formed with assistance from the Ford Foundation, was founded in 1993 and is a community-based group comprising of dancers from all *banjars*. They train young dancers weekly and perform at the Pura Desa on the 1st and 15th of every month.

In his day, Kakul was able to call on the mask making skills of Dewa Putu Kebes, whose *topeng* masks were charged with the spiritual forces of kings and heroes from the Balinese past. Since his death, his son Dewa

Batuan's important Pura Puseh temple has elaborate carvings and a fine array of statuary.

A painting in the intricate Batuan style by I Made Budi, well known for his non-traditional subjects.

Cita and grandson Dewa Mandra have maintained the combination of immaculate skill and divine inspiration which made his work so powerful. Two of the family's pupils, Made Regug of Negara and Nyoman Medor, also uphold the fine carving tradition.

In addition to the dances, performed in the central part of the village, Batuan is also respected for its *wayang wong*, masked performances of stories from the *Ramayana*. This is exclusively performed in **Banjar Den Tiis**.

The "Batuan style" of painting

From Den Tiis also came the inspiration for the modern Batuan style of painting. In the 1930s, two brothers, I Ngendon and I Patera, began experimenting painting with ink on paper. The result was powerful black-and-white images of magic and of Balinese life. The families of these two artists are still influential in the village, and now own the **Artshop Dewata** on the main road leading to Ubud.

Ngendon and Patra originally studied under a painter living to the east of the palace, but from them the painting tradition spread back to the main part of the village, where it was enthusiastically embraced by a number of their fellow villagers. The present-day generation of artists includes Made Tubuh, Wayan Rajin, Ida Bagus Putu Gede, Made Budi, and Made Bendi, and the latter two have become loved through their humorous and insightful depictions of tourists in Bali.

Aside from painters, Batuan has also given birth to one of Bali's most easily recognizable contemporary musicians, I Wayan Balawan, who is known for his "tapping" technique on his double fretted guitar. Along with his group, **Batuan Ethnic Fusion**, he performs not only throughout Bali, but around the world.

Bali Fun World

On the lighter side, there is an indoor playground for kids in Batuan, **Bali Fun World,** which makes for a wonderful half-day outing for young ones. Open daily from 9.30 am–8 pm, this arena provides an area for toddlers, another one for under-12s and plenty of games for teens and adults, including Sumo wrestling in big plastic suits. Everything here is made from rubber and plastic, including the rock climbing wall. It's best to go in the mornings when it's cooler as it is not air-conditioned.

MAS VILLAGE

A Brahmanical Woodcarving Center

M as village lies on the main road 20 km (13 miles) north of Denpasar and 6 km (3.7 miles) before Ubud, in a hilly countryside covered with rice fields irrigated year-round by the Batuan and Sakah rivers.

Today, the village appears as a succession of palatial art shops, as **Mas** is a flourishing center for the woodcarving craft. It is difficult to imagine what it was like before dozens of tourist buses started to drop in every day, yet Mas (which means "gold") actually played an important role in Balinese history. During the 16th century, it was the place where the great Javanese priest Danghyang Dwijendra (also called Nirartha), had his hermitage (*griya*).

Descendants of holy priest

The holy man, known locally as Pedanda Sakti Wau Rauh (literally "The Newly Arrived High Priest"), came to Bali from Kediri in east Java after the fall of the powerful Majapahit kingdom, and was invited to Mas by prince Mas Wilis (Tan Kober). Here the *pedanda* acquired great fame through his teaching and gathered many disciples. His son by Mas Wilis' daughter is the forebear of one of Bali's four important *brahmana* clans, which to the present day traces its roots back to the village.

The priest's fame reached the Dalem Waturenggong court in Gelgel, who, impressed by Danghyang Dwijendra's superior wisdom, appointed him the king's counselor and court priest in 1489.

Based upon his instructions, many temples were built, especially after his *moksa* (holy death). His belongings—*bajra* (holy bell), black shirt, mattress, and staff—are now kept in the Mas *griya*, and the Pura Taman Pule temple was built on that site.

Realm of blessed craftsmen

The gods are also said to have bestowed talents on two of Mas' houses: the skill of the shadow-puppet master to Griya Dauh, and the skill of woodcarving to Griya Danginan. At first, the woodcarvers (*sangging*) were all

brahmanas who worked only on ritual or courtly projects. Their disciples (*sisya*) learned the craft from them, and woodcarving skills were transmitted from father to son. The traditional *wayang* style prevailed, featuring religious scenes and characters from the *Ramayana* and *Mahabharata* epics.

During the 1930s, under the influence of Walter Spies and Pita Maha, a new style of woodcarving developed here. The motifs were more realistic, and inspired by everyday scenes featuring humans and animals. Several of these early works are on display in Ubud's Puri Lukisan museum. During this period, woodcarvings began to be appreciated and purchased by foreigners, but only after 1970 did the real boom take place. The first art shops in Mas were those of Ketut Roja (**Siadja & Son**), followed by Ida Bagus Nyana and his son Ida Bagus Tilem, and Ida Bagus Taman (**Adil Artshop**). At first, they all produced works of quality in limited quantities, mainly working with locally-available woods. A more abstract style was later developed by Purna and Nyana,

The galleries of expert woodcarvers line the roads in Mas, where you can see the carvers at work.

featuring elongated, curved lines and woods such as ebony and sandalwood. One of Tilem's best students is I Wayan Darlun, whose work is shown at **Baris Gallery** on Jl. Raya Mas. Later on, in Pujung and Tegallalang, Cokot began to carve roots into demonic figures.

In the 1980s, many realistic, brightly painted animals and fruit trees (known here as *pulasan*), based on European designs, appeared on the market. First created by Togog in Pujung, much of the production is now of questionable quality, but the prices are very low.

Later, brightly painted and "batiked" masks were created by the now late Ida Bagus Ambara and family. **Wayan Muka**, Banjar Batan Ancak, Mas and **I. B. Anom**, whose shop flanks the northern border of the football field in Mas, carve excellent *topeng* masks.

Woodcarving shops

Bidadari Art Shop on the main road features very fine modern woodcarvings. There are also a few shops that prepare huge slabs of wood to be used for exquisite tables and doors. One of them is **Bidadari Workshop** on the small road that goes east just 100 m (320 ft) south of their shop.

To see craftsmen at work, stop by any of the galleries where there are workshops. The system is paternalistic; the shop owner gives work to his craftsmen according to their skills, the price being settled after the fact based on the final result. They work on the spot or at home. Skill is learned at an early age inside the family; tools used are still quite traditional: various types of axes, chisels, and drills made by local blacksmiths. Prices are very high, and are often in U.S. dollars. They can sometimes handle special orders. Nyoman Tekek Manis carved a giant Christ that was placed on the altar of a Catholic church in Jakarta, and inaugurated by Pope John Paul II.

Mas is also home to large numbers of furniture shops. Showrooms display all types of settees, chairs, and carved doors. Before purchasing, make sure the wood has been properly dried, and the only way to ensure this is to bring your own gauge.

Located 100 m (320 ft) from the road on the east side, **Pura Taman Pule** does not take its name from the holy *pule* trees growing behind it, but means "Beautiful

The intricate and detailed Mas carvings are made from exotic Indonesian hardwoods.

Garden." Danghyang Nirartha is said to have planted a purple flowered *tangi* tree there— still growing behind an altar in the *jaba tengah* (middle court)—from which a golden bud sprouted, giving Mas its name. At the back of the main temple, a *padmasana* surrounded by a pond is said to have been the place of Nirartha's hermitage. People from throughout Bali come here to pray, not only *brahmanas* but also commoners of the Pasek Bendesa Mas clan, especially on its five-day *odalan*, falling on Kuningan Day (Saturday).

The **Wayang Wong Ramayana troupe** is still very much alive in Mas. It was revived by artist Walter Spies, and its 22 sacred masks are now kept in the temple. A performance is held on Kuningan eve, and three more on Kuningan day, as ritual contributions (*ayahan*).

Talented *dalangs* such as I. B. Geriya and I. B. Anom usually perform ritual *wayang lemah* on Kuningan night in the Taman Pule area.

Setia Darma House of Masks and Puppets

The **Setia Darma House of Masks and Puppets,** Jl. Tegal Bingin, Banjar Tengkulak Tengah, Kemenuh was initiated by Hadi Sunyoto, a businessman and cultural enthusiast who has collected masks and puppets from different regions in Indonesia since 2003. This space, completed in 2006, is dedicated to collecting, preserving, and disseminating knowledge of these two art forms. The collection of over 6,000 pieces—and still growing—including a *wayang golek* (wooden puppet) of Barack Obama, are housed in four old Javanese *joglo* (traditional wooden houses). There are masks and puppets from all over the world, but the main emphasis is on Indonesian forms. Exhibitions, seminars, and performances are held here on a regular basis.

PELIATAN VILLAGE

Home of the Legendary Legong Dance

Peliatan, a small village of 8,000, is often overlooked, though it lies just 2 km (1.2 miles) south of Ubud on the main road. Rich in the arts, and not as packed with tourists as Ubud, it is definitely worth a visit, particularly for those who are interested in dance and music.

"That which is seen"

The Peliatan court actually preceded the one in Ubud. Although the dates are unclear, the 17th century *Babad Dalem Sukawati* (a chronicle of the Sukawati court) recounts an argument between two princes—I Dewa Agung Gede and I Dewa Agung Made—that resulted in two separate dynasties.

The former ran off to Blahbatuh and the latter to Tegallalang, taking with him a sacred heirloom, the Segara Ngelayang spear, which is now kept in the Peliatan palace. I Dewa Agung Made later moved to Peliatan to be closer to his ancestral home in Sukawati.

His children then set up palaces in Ubud, and to this day Ubud royalty still pay homage to their cousins in Peliatan.

Peliatan literally means "that which is seen," and according to some accounts this refers to the fact that Sukawati is within view down the road. Others claim that a former king of Peliatan was given religious instruction here by a priest and was therefore able to "see" **Pura Gunung Sari** before it was built. Today, this temple is a favorite with dancers and musicians who come here in search of *taksu* (inspiration).

Bali's most notable Legong

Peliatan is best known for its Legong, a graceful dance traditionally performed by two pre-pubescent girls in glittering costumes (see "Balinese Dance and Drama," page 52). In fact, the first Balinese dance troupe to travel abroad was a *legong* group from Peliatan that performed at the Paris

Peliatan village is known as a leading center for training young legong *dancers.*

exhibition in 1931 under the leadership of Anak Agung Gede Mandera (affectionately known as "Gung Kak"), a man who excelled in both music and dance. The group's performances created a sensation, and it was then that French actor Antonin Artaud first witnessed the Balinese *barong.* In 1952, the renowned Sampih and Gusti Raka performed on the American Ed Sullivan TV show. Gung Kak's descendants and students still carry on the tradition; a 1989 tour to the United States included many of his family members, who continue to dance around the globe.

Traditions of dance and music in Bali are passed from teacher to pupil and parent to child. Some teachers become very well known, such as the late Gusti Biang Sengog from Peliatan, who, in her prime, was recorded for posterity in the film *Miracle of Bali: Midday Sun* teaching young women who themselves went on to become prominent dancers and teachers. Sang Ayu Ketut Muklin, from nearby Pejeng village, was another renowned local teacher.

To see Peliatan's young *legongs* in action, travel east from Peliatan to Teges Kanginan, one of the few places on Bali where the dancers are still trained in the traditional manner.

Even though the standard of music here is quite good, with a proliferation of *gamelan* groups, there really are no individuals that match the skill of the musicians from the 1930s, such as I Made Lebah, his son I Wayan Gandera, and I Made Grindem, all long gone.

Peliatan today is home to 15 *gamelan* groups, including *gong kebyar, gong semar pegulingan, gong angklung,* and *joged bumbung.* Almost every *banjar* owns at least one set of instruments and the haunting sounds of the *gamelan* can be heard in the Peliatan area nearly every night, whether in rehearsal or performance.

Peliatan is also home to **Mekar Sari**, an all-woman gamelan troupe which was begun under the tutelage of Gung Kak, and performs weekly in Banjar Teruna. The dancers are all under 12 years old. The **Gong Kebyar Gunung Sari** also puts on a dazzling show at Puri Agung. The more lyrical sounds of **Tirta Sari Semar Pegulingan** (with two different *legongs*) can be heard on Friday night at Balerung Stage, with a younger group, Genta Bhuana Sari, performing every Tuesday night. One of the better commercial *kecak* troupes, **Semara Madya**,

Balinese children learn to play the gamelan *from a very young age as part of a village group.*

performs at Puri Agung every Thursday night. **ARMA Museum** has numerous performances, including the rarely seen Wayang Wong on Saturdays and Cak Rina every new and full moon. Check the Ubud performance schedule for complete details.

The traditional and the modern continue to flourish side-by-side here. Anak Agung Oka Dalem, one of Gung Kak's children, excels in the *kebyar* styles that Peliatan put on the map in the mid-20th century. He founded Padma Nara Suara (PANAS for short), a dance group that fuses modern choreography and costuming with traditional Balinese dance movements.

Carving and painting

Peliatan is also the home of many carvers and painters. Orchids, fruits, frogs, ducks, and birds—all favored by tourists—are fashioned out of wood throughout the village. Two of the more exceptional carvers are I Wayan Pasti—whose life-size horses and dogs inspire double-takes—and I Nyoman Togog (the original "fruit man"), a Presidential awardee.

I Ketut Madra of Banjar Kalah is an excellent painter in the traditional *wayang* style. He is not a businessman by nature and does not have a gallery, but likes to show his work to visitors and accepts special commissions.

To see the classical painting style of the 1930s, visit I Gusti Made Kuanji in Banjar Teruna and I Nyoman Kuta in Banjar Tengah. For an overview of Balinese painting, pop into the **Agung Rai Gallery** on the main road, one of the best collections on the island, as well as his museum, ARMA, on Jl. Made Lebah, where you can also relax in the garden or the **ARMA Café** after seeing the exhibition.

INTRODUCTION TO UBUD

A Village Haven for the Arts

Ubud was once known as a "quiet" haven for the arts. Set amidst emerald green rice paddies and steep ravines in the stunning central Balinese foothills some 25 km (15.5 miles) north of Denpasar, the village was originally an important source of medicinal herbs and plants. "Ubud" in fact derives from the Balinese word for medicine, *ubad.* However, since the 1990s massive changes, including an influx of foreign investors, expats looking for peace and yoga, and the inevitable traffic jams that large buses bring, have made Ubud a tourist mecca, albeit with a much larger concentration of artists than perhaps anywhere else in the world.

It was here that foreign artists such as German painter Walter Spies settled during the 1920s and '30s, transforming the village into a flourishing center for the arts. Artists from all parts of Bali were invited by the local prince, Cokorda Raka Gede Sukawati, to stay here, and Ubud's palaces and temples are adorned by the work of Bali's master artisans as a result.

According to an eighth-century legend, a Javanese priest named Rsi Markendya came to Bali from Java and meditated in Campuan (*Sangam* in Sanskrit) at the confluence of two streams, an auspicious site for Hindus. He founded **Pura Gunung Lebah** here on a narrow platform above the valley floor, where pilgrims seeking peace came to be healed from their worldly cares. To get there, follow a small road to the Warwick Ibah Luxury Villas & Spa on the western outskirts of Ubud, then take the path down toward the river.

An important 19th-century court
In the late 19th century, Ubud became the seat of *punggawa* or feudal lords owing their allegiance to the Gianyar rajas. All were members of the *satria* family of Sukawati and contributed greatly to the village's fame for performing and other arts. The Gianyar kingdom was established in the late 18th century and later became the most powerful of Bali's southern states. And while elsewhere the Dutch conquest had such disastrous

consequences for the Balinese royal houses, in Gianyar, for the most part, the raja and his subjects benefitted from a Dutch administration (between 1908 and 1930) that brought significant changes such as improved roads, irrigation networks, healthcare, and schools. Toward the end of the 1930s Ubud was prospering as a budding tourist resort due to the flowering of the arts in the area.

In the late 19th century, Cokorda Gede Raka Sukawati established himself in Ubud and was instrumental in laying the foundations for the village's fame. The area was at this time bereft of remarkable cultural features. It was in the interest of Cokorda that various artists and literati sought refuge here from other kingdoms. Ubud slowly accumulated specialists and evolved into a cultural center, with resident artists and *lontar* (palm leaf book) experts.

A prime example is the case of the young I Gusti Nyoman Lempad who, with his father, a noted writer, sought and found refuge in Ubud from the king of Bedulu. In gratitude, the young apprentice sculptor helped to decorate the **Puri Saren Agung** palace in Ubud and carved statues and ornaments on the main temple—**Pura Puseh**—of the noble family, north of the palace. He also carved the temple of learning, **Pura Taman Saraswati**. His work can still be seen on location, and some of his statues can be admired in Ubud's museum. At an advanced age he turned to pen and ink, working consistently until his death in 1978 at the age of 116.

A flowering of the arts
Between the World wars, Ubud's *punggawa*, Cokorda Gede Raka Sukawati, was a member of the Dutch colonial government's *Volksraad* (People's Council) in Batavia and was already interested in the "arts and crafts movement" spreading from Europe to Asia and Japan. He

German artist Walter Spies was instrumental in forging Ubud's reputation amongst world travelers in the 1930s. A View from the Heights, *shown here, captures the atmospheric landscapes of central Bali.*

Western artists such as Miguel Covarrubias, helped create a new style of secular painting in Bali.

encouraged the German artist Walter Spies to settle in Ubud, thus provoking a growing tide of visitors to this enchanting village.

At the turn of the century, painting in Bali was integrated into customary, or *adat*, ceremonies with the themes being taken from classical Balinese tales that were well known from *wayang* performances. Inspired by the foreign artists who settled in Ubud, Cokorda Gede Raka Sukawati gradually developed this tradition. This unique mélange of traditional Balinese and modern Western art forms came to be associated with Ubud.

In the late 1920s and early 1930s Ubud became the focal point for foreign artists and other creative people gathering around Spies, a highly gifted and versatile painter and general artistic impresario.

An artist and a musician by training, Spies heard of Bali on reading Jaap Kunst's *Music of Bali*, published in 1925, in which the Dutch musicologist highly praised the village of Peliatan for its *gamelan* orchestra. His anecdotes about Bali fascinated Spies, who was then director of the sultan of Yogyakarta's European orchestra.

Many other talented foreigners were also attracted to Ubud at this time. Among others, Miguel and Rosa Covarrubias discovered the hitherto unknown beauty of Bali upon seeing Gregor Krause's magnificent photo album, published in 1925. Krause had worked as a doctor in Bali around 1912. After living in Ubud and Sanur, Covarrubias wrote his *Island of Bali*, one of the classics on Bali to this day.

Rudolf Bonnet, the Dutch painter, was told of Bali's breathtaking beauty by etcher and ethnographer W. O. J. Nieuwenkamp in Florence and went there to seek inspiration in the late 1920s. Colin McPhee arrived to join Spies' experiments in musical traditions, which were at this time very dynamic, with new creations springing up overnight. They worked together with the legendary Anak Agung Gede Mandera of Peliatan, and McPhee later published a book on Bali's musical traditions as well as an account of his experiences here, *A House in Bali.*

Ubud rapidly became the village *en vogue* for many of these visitors, based on insider tips from the musicians, painters, authors, anthropologists, and avant-garde world travelers who passed this way, especially after Spies settled in **Campuan** next to Ubud, on what is now the site of the Hotel Tjampuhan Spa.

Spies and Bonnet both encouraged local Balinese artists, each in his own fashion. In 1936 they founded the Pita Maha, an artists' organization, together with Lempad, Sobrat, and I Tegalan, among many other excellent Balinese artists. This association was to guarantee and promote high artistic standards among its more than 100 members.

Ubud since independence

The Pita Maha movement did survive the vagaries of the Japanese occupation and the Indonesian struggle for independence. However, Cokorda Gede Agung Sukawati, assisted by Bonnet, later founded the Palace of Arts Museum (Puri Lukisan Museum) in 1953 to provide a retrospective of local achievements. Balinese artists thus continued to work together, sparking a renewal of artistic activity in the 1950s.

The Puri Lukisan Museum entrance

Ubud has become a center for meditation and yoga.

In the early 1950s, Dutch painter Arie Smit founded the Young Painters School of naive painting in Penestanan with Cakra. This style, free of any philosophical or abstract influence, led to uninhibited young school children using bright chemical colors to produce two-dimensional landscapes depicting daily life. Their work reflects the changing vision and lifestyle of young Balinese during the post-war period.

Han Snel was a young Dutch soldier who left the Dutch Colonial Army and "vanished" into Bali after his military service, finding his way to the hills around Ubud. His work captured the imagination of both foreigners and Balinese alike with its invigorating synthesis of both cultures. Following his marriage to a Balinese girl, Siti, he built a studio in a secluded spot in Central Ubud. Antonio Blanco, another Western painter, settled with his Balinese wife and five children on the Campuan heights bordering Penestanan. This eccentric even had one of Ubud's first telephones, a link between paradise and the madding crowds abroad.

The tourist boom

In the 1970s and 1980s the hotel and catering industry implanted itself in Ubud — modestly enough compared to how it had taken firm control of Kuta–Legian — but this idyllic village did nevertheless witness an ever-accelerating flow of visitors, who came to indulge in the arts and to escape from the daily grind. In short, tourism knocked gently but insistently on Ubud's door. The advent of mass tourism in the 1980s provided many young inhabitants of the area with stable employment rather than farming the fertile rice fields in the surrounding hills. Land reform and hereditary laws, in any case, had led to a scarcity of arable land.

In the 21st century the tourism boom in Ubud has continued apace, boosted by the runaway success of Elizabeth Gilbert's memoir *Eat, Pray, Love*, and a surge in villa developments in the surrounding countryside. With traffic in the center of town now frequently resembling the gridlock of the less refined resorts further south, some long-time visitors are quick to proclaim the place "spoiled." Nonetheless, Ubud still retains its unmistakably captivating atmosphere of mellow creativity, and local Balinese families remain more obviously in direct control of much of the economic activity here than in some other parts of the island. Indeed, many visitors comment on how "business-like" the Ubudians are. The unruffled calmness of Ubud continues to soothe many a visitor, while the extraordinary beauty of the surroundings still inspires the creative to work.

Nowadays, the fruits of that extraordinarily prolific period of pre-World War II Ubud are still on display through dance, music, painting, and sculpture. Dance performances are given daily in at least three places, including the main palace. Ceremonies still abound where various dance or shadow puppet performances and excellent *gamelan* music are practiced. And painters, sculptors, writers, and creative designers continue to seek inspiration in the special atmosphere of Ubud, Campuan, and nearby Sayan.

The late Ketut Liyer, famous painter and medicine man, was featured in the book Eat, Pray, Love.

A TOUR OF UBUD

On the Gallery and Temple Circuit

It is dawn and Ubud is awakening. The air is fresh, mixed with the heady scent of flowers and the incense of offerings. There are so many ways to spend a day here: visiting galleries and artists' studios, sipping drinks in garden cafes, and enjoying long strolls through the countryside. Below are a few of the "must sees."

Ubud highlights

No visit to Ubud is complete without seeing the **Puri Saren Agung** palace at the main crossroads, with its maze of family compounds and doorways richly carved by I Gusti Nyoman Lempad. The royal family temple, **Pura Pamerajaan Sari Cokorda Agung**—a storage place for the family *pusaka* (regalia)—is next door.

To the west behind a lotus pond by the **Puri Saraswati** palace (now a hotel), lies the

Pura Taman Saraswati, Ubud's temple of learning, is surrounded by a lotus pond at the center of town.

superbly chiseled **Pura Taman Saraswati** temple of learning, a *clin d'oeil* dedicated to Ubud's artistic past. From the crossroads here, walk north to Ubud's "navel" temple, **Pura Puseh**, with its delightful sculptures.

Next stop is the **Puri Lukisan Museum** to relish the paintings and sculptures and the peaceful garden. The museum was founded in 1953 by surviving members of Ubud's famed Pita Maha movement. Painted panels that Lempad executed more than half a century ago depict the Balinese agrarian cycle.

There are numerous studios and shops in the center of town. Look for Starbucks competing with the traditional market, on the corner of Jl. Ubud Raya and Jl. Monkey Forest, and tiny souvenir shops selling everything from the ubiquitous T-shirt to hand-carved coconut spoons. Opposite the *wantilan* or community hall, check in with the **Bina Wisata Tourist Office** for local performances and festival schedules.

Ubud's best commercial galleries are scattered throughout the town. Suteja Neka, whose father was a painter, is the foremost dealer and collector on Bali, and is also the founder of the **Neka Art Museum**, a bit away from the town center to the west, on Jl. Raya Ubud. Ubud's most famous artist was Lempad, and the best places to see his delicate erotic pen and ink drawings are in the Puri Lukisan, Neka, and ARMA museums.

Contemporary art can be found at the **Komaneka Gallery**, established by Neka's son, on Jl. Monkey Forest, and there are numerous artists' studios all vying for attention throughout the town. East of the Post Office is **Pranoto's Art Gallery**, showing charcoals, water colors, and nudes. Traveling west along the main road across the bridge to Campuan is the museum of the late eccentric Filipino-American painter **Antonio Blanco**, with his extravagant nudes, now run by his son Mario.

Every handicraft imaginable is available in the **traditional market**—watch out for

Macaques rule the roost at Ubud's Monkey Forest.

pickpockets and don't forget to bargain—or in many shops. Some of the more upscale (but not hard on that wallet) are Bojog on Jl. Monkey Forest, Murni's west of the market, Alam Asia Crafts, Kuluk, and Celeng in Lungsiakan. Threads of Life on Jl. Kajeng No. 24 (tel: 0361 972-187, www.threadsoflife.com) features exquisite hand-woven textiles from throughout Indonesia; profits are plowed back into community projects.

Mischievous monkeys

Another of the major "sights" of Ubud is the **Monkey Forest Temple**, actually Padangtegal village's Pura Dalem Agung, 2 km (1.2 miles) to the south of the central intersection. If for no other reason, stroll down Jl. Monkey Forest to have a look at all the shops and restaurants. Before entering the forest (there is a small admission fee) itself, however, put away all edibles, eyeglasses, or any shiny jewelry, and hold on tight to your bags. These daring rascals are rapacious thieves and can be dangerous if provoked.

For those interested in a unique collection of books, **Ganesha Bookshop** on the main road (Jl. Ubud Raya) next to the Post Office is worthwhile. With both new and used books, music, knickknacks, and daily newspapers, this is a bookshop you won't want to miss. **Periplus** has two shops in Ubud, featuring magazines, books on Bali, a travel and cooking section, and novels. Ubud's only **library** at Pondok Pekak on the football

green has a decent collection of all types of books, including a separate children's library. It also offers lessons in mask making, *gamelan,* and Indonesian language. Courses in all forms of Balinese arts, including offering making, are held at Puri Lukisan Museum and the ARMA Museum.

For **silver jewelry making**, try Studio Perak. Budding chefs will revel in the number of **cooking schools** here: Casa Luna on Jl. Ubud Raya, Laka Leke in Nyuh Kuning village behind the Monkey Forest, Taman Rahasia in Penestanan village, and Mozaic on Jl. Raya Sanggingan.

Other highlights on the must-do list are **nightly performances** at the palace and at other venues around Ubud; artists studios, boutiques, and eateries; or venture into the side alleyways, where the "old Ubud" still exists.

Aside from the arts—and the fantastic shopping—be sure to visit the **Ubud Botanic Gardens**, tap into your inner self at **The Yoga Barn**, or rejuvenate with a massage in one of the area's many **day spas**. However, be forewarned that because of the traffic, it's best to travel around Ubud by motorbike, bicycle, or on foot.

Ubud's central market offers a lively mish-mash of everyday goods and souvenirs, and is particularly interesting early in the morning.

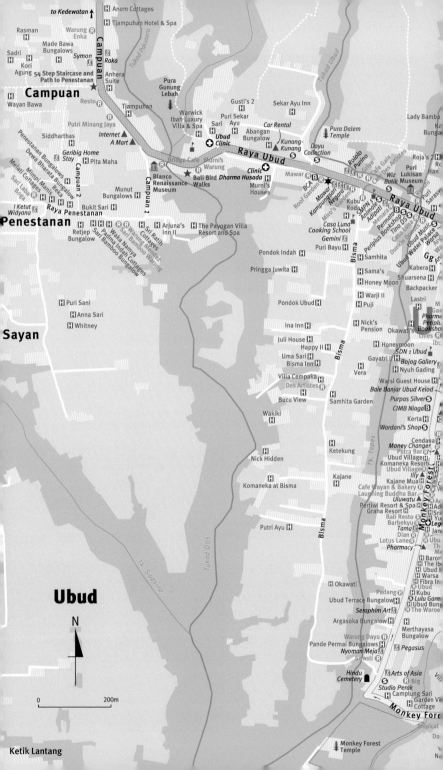

WALKING TOURS AROUND UBUD

Breathtaking Glimpses of Rural Bali

Ubud's surroundings offer many rewarding walks and excursions up hill and over dale, with breathtaking vistas and many surprising glimpses of rural, unspoiled Bali. To get a glimpse of what Ubud used to be like at the turn of the last century, hire a car, scooter, or bicycle or go by foot and visit some of the surrounding villages. Each one has its own charm. Don't hesitate to wander off the main roads and explore.

What follows is but a short list of suggested itineraries. Many more could easily be added.

Hike 1: The "high road" to Kedewatan

This is an easy, half-day hike west of Ubud up along the road through Campuan and over to Kedewetan. Get an early start at the Campuan Bridge and stop in to see the **Pura Gunung Lebah** temple that nestles in the gorge. Rsi Markendrya founded it at the confluence of these rivers in the eighth century. Follow the main road up a steep hill past the **Neka Art Museum**. Along the way are delightful views and a chance to stop in at the studios of famous artists like **Antonio Blanco** and **K.K. Ngurah**, to name a few. Be sure to stop in at Neka Museum, too, to see the works of a veritable who's who of Balinese painters, past and present.

After Neka's, the road takes a sharp turn to the left with **Ulun Ubud Resort & Spa** on the right. Inside, there is a small gallery belonging to Ida Bagus Tilem, Bali's best-known woodcarver. Continuing up the main road, you'll eventually reach the Payangan–Kedewatan T-junction. Turn right, and after a few hundred meters is **Kedewatan** village, with its extraordinary rice terraces stepping down to the Ayung River below. Look for Pura Telaga Waja, a temple with multi-tiered *merus*. Afterwards, travel by *bemo* back to Ubud.

Spectacular green rice terraces surround Ubud in almost every direction.

The Campuan ridge walk is one of the most popular day hikes from Ubud and along the way you may encounter other visitors who have stopped for a quiet meditation session.

Hike 2: To Petulu, where egrets nest

A fairly easy, half-day hike north and east of Ubud, start around lunchtime at the main Ubud crossroads in front of the Puri Saren palace, and go north along Jl. Suweta. The road is paved all the way past **Pura Puseh** (Ubud's temple of origin, with carvings by Lempad), about half a mile from the crossroads. Continuing straight ahead, you emerge in open rice fields with spectacular views of Mt. Agung on a clear day. After about an hour, you reach **Bentuyung** village. From here, either take the road back south to **Tegallanting** and **Taman** *banjars*, their temples tucked in the midst of family compounds at the crossroads.

Alternatively, turn to the right (east) through **Junjungan** to **Petulu** to see white egrets hovering over the village as they alight in lofty trees at sunset. Every evening around 6 pm hundreds of graceful egrets and a few herons make their way back to nest in the trees lining the streets, making them look like cotton-studded greenery. Local folklore has it that these birds only started coming to Petulu post-1965, and that the birds are the souls of the unpurified dead who were killed during the anti-Communist pogroms in 1965 and placed in a mass grave here. Mention any of the above places, and locals will point the way. From Petulu, take a *bemo* or walk back

to Ubud. However, be aware that *bemos* do not run after dark.

Hike 3: To Penestanan

Penestanan is just west of Ubud. To get there, go past the Campuan Bridge and take the staircase with 54 steps on the left side. At the top, continue straight along a path through the rice fields. When you come to the paved road, turn right and follow it into Penestanan, where there are lots of small shops selling beadwork. Have a drink and a massage at Taman Rahasia or spa treatment at The Mansion before heading back into town.

The following hikes will be a stretch for all but the hardiest trekkers because of their distance but can also be done by car.

Hike 4: To Nyuh Kuning

To get to **Nyuh Kuning** village—known for its wood carvers—from the center of Ubud go south on Jl. Monkey Forest, cutting through the forest to the opposite side. (Note that they charge a small entrance fee. Alternatively, you can go through the parking lot and follow the one-lane paved path on the east side of the forest entrance at no charge.) Nyuh Kuning, where the path ends, is a tiny two-street village that houses an Ayurvedic healing center, two yoga studios and an alternative healing center, a gallery selling hand-woven textiles from throughout Southeast Asia, Linda Garland's Bamboo Foundation, a locally-run orphanage, and Bumi Sehat Birthing Clinic.

Many expats have made this village their home. After a cooking class or a divine lunch at Laka Leke Restaurant, indulge in rejuvenating bodily delights or pick up a souvenir.

Afterwards, continue to the main road and turn right. Go over the bridge, and at the next major road turn left to get to **Singakerta** village to see the daily life of local farmers. Coming back, go due east toward Pengosekan, and turn left onto Jl. Hanoman and back into Ubud. This expedition will take at least half a day—without stopping for lunch and spa treatments—and is not on the *bemo* routes.

In the network of villages around Ubud, it's not unusual to stumble across a temple procession.

Hike 5: To Pengosekan

Colorful fish and birds are what makes the **Pengosekan** (pronounced: *pengo-se-kan*) painting style distinctive. The aristocrats of neighboring Mas were somewhat put out when Queen Elizabeth insisted on being taken to low-caste Pengosekan in search of a painting in 1974; and the villagers themselves were disappointed that she had forgotten to wear her crown.

In 1979 they established the island's first artists' cooperative, exhibiting and selling together and supporting each other with raw materials (in the days when the cost of a tube of imported acrylic paint would feed a large

family for three weeks). Incorporating elements of traditional Balinese communalism, they called themselves the **Pengosekan Community of Farmers and Artists**, led by *mandala* painter **Dewa Nyoman Batuan**. Painters to look for: Batuan himself, his brother Mokoh, Putralaya, Kobot, Barat, and Sena.

This village is also home to jewelry designers, *gamelan* musicians, and dancers, as well as incense and basket makers. The **Cudamani Summer Institute of Gamelan and Dance** is here as well, as is the former home of the late **Ketut Liyer**, the toothless healer from the book and movie, *Eat, Pray, Love.*

On clear days, Bali's iconic Mount Agung can be seen from the rice fields around Ubud.

ACCOMMODATION PRICE CATEGORIES Prices are for a double room, including breakfast **$** = under $30; **$$** = $30–$70; **$$$** = $70–$130; **$$$$** = over $130. **DINING PRICE CATEGORIES** Prices are for based on a meal for one, without drinks **$** = under $5; **$$** = $5–$10; **$$$** = over $10.

VISITING UBUD See map, page 172–173.

While it's possible to visit Ubud in just one day, such a short trip would barely touch the surface of this extraordinary overgrown village, which in the span of just a few decades has become renowned for its art and culture. An interesting mélange of rural Balinese life and modern services co-exist here. Only 60 minutes from Ngurah Rai airport (on a good traffic day), Ubud is close to many of Central Bali's major historic and cultural sights.

Visitors usually outnumber residents during peak periods in July and August, and tour buses jam the narrow streets. However, Ubud still retains the atmosphere of a small country town and the pace can be very relaxed. It's a great place to tour on foot or by bicycle, and there's a wide range of facilities for tourists of all budgets. For those who enjoy being in the epicenter of Balinese arts and culture, yet within easy reach of creature comforts and natural surroundings, Ubud is ideal.

ORIENTATION

The crossroads in front of Puri Saren palace is the "navel" of Ubud—its cultural, historical and commercial focal point. The main street, Jl. Raya Ubud, is lined with restaurants, mini-markets, shops, and galleries, stretching all the way from the T-junction at the eastern end of Ubud to the Campuan Bridge in the west. Small lanes with homestays, hotels, *warungs*, souvenir shops, and Balinese compounds extend north and south from the main road.

Jl. Monkey Forest, branching south from "downtown" Ubud is lined with hotels, restaurants, cafes, artists' studios, and boutiques for a distance of some 2 km (1.2 miles). A parallel road south, Jl. Hanoman, just to the east of Padangtegal is similar, though less congested. Away from these main streets, Ubud is still relatively quiet.

Roads radiate west out of the main town to Campuan (also spelled Campuhan and Tjampuhan), Payangan, Kedewatan, Penestanan, and Sayan. To the south is Batuan, Nyuh Kuning and Pengosekan. To the east is Peliatan, Tegas, and Bedulu, where Goa Gajah cave is located. To the north is Sanggingan and Petulu.

Bemos can be flagged down in the daytime on the main road and charged according to the distance traveled. Ubud to Campuan, for example, costs Rp 4,000.

TOURIST INFORMATION

For information on nightly performances, transport schedules, temple festivals, and special activities, inquire at the **Ubud Tourist Information Center**, Bina Wisata, Jl. Raya Ubud, tel: 973-285, on the southwest corner of the main intersection, across the street from the Ubud traditional market.

GETTING THERE

Ubud is 60 minutes by car from the airport and southern beach resort areas and 40 minutes from Sanur on good traffic days. Note that the roads to Ubud are narrow and winding and if an accident should occur or a ceremonial procession is in progress, travel times can be delayed. Be sure to allow plenty of travel time, particularly if airline departure times are an issue.

Taxis from the airport cost around $25. The taxi windows at both the domestic and international terminals are to the left after emerging from the baggage claim area. From Denpasar, take a bemo from Kereneng Terminal to Batubulan Terminal, then transfer to Ubud (around Rp 15,000).

Ubud is a major hub for the tourist shuttle bus network, with pre-booked minibuses departing for destinations around Bali every morning. Arrivals from elsewhere usually start to turn up in late morning. Many operators will, up to a point, drop you wherever you want to go. If in doubt, the top of Monkey Forest Road is as central as it gets. Large numbers of shuttle buses travel between Ubud and Kuta, Sanur, Padangbai, Amed, Candidasa, Lovina, and the airport. You'll also find a few running to lesser destinations including Sidemen and Munduk. Shuttle buses can be booked in advance from most accommodations and all travel agents. **Perama** has an office on Jl. Pengosekan, Ubud, tel: 973-316, with reliable departures to various destinations.

GETTING AROUND

Although it's easy to walk around Ubud, renting a bicycle can save time and effort. Bikes can be rented everywhere for around Rp 20,000–30,000 per day; motor scooters cost Rp 50,000–80,000 per day. Both are also easily arranged through most accommodations, or from travel agents and homestays.

Metered **taxis** are rare in Ubud, but—as you'll soon find out, walking the main streets—there are plenty of private cars which you can "charter."

Look for the circular yellow "E" logo on the windshield certifying them as Ubud Transport Association members.

Ask at your accommodation the current rate for the distance you're going and settle on a price before getting in. The drivers will, of course, attempt to secure longer trips by asking what your "program for tomorrow" is, and many of them actually make good guides. You can also hail transport via apps such as GO-JEK, though demand is high and supply can be low around Ubud.

ACCOMMODATIONS

Though you'll find the full gamut from ultra-basic homestays to exquisite villas, on the whole Ubud's accommodations have gone dramatically upmarket in the past several years.

Many of the cheapest accommodations are still genuine homestays, with guestrooms in family compounds down quiet alleys. You'll find places of this type all over Ubud, but Jl. Goutama or the alleys off Monkey Forest Road are good places to start looking if you want something central. In recent years many of these homestays have gone decidedly upscale, building new blocks of modern, air-con rooms to replace the simple bamboo cottages of old. Hot water is now the norm—a blessing on surprisingly cool Ubud mornings—and virtually everywhere has free Wi-Fi. Prices have climbed along with the standards, of course, and the average price of the cheapest budget rooms is now between $20 and $30. Breakfast is always included.

Travel out of Ubud in almost any direction and you'll find more homestays and bungalows tucked away among the rice fields, some with dramatic vistas. If you stay out in the paddies, it's handy to take along an electric anti-mosquito device (buy one in any local mini-market), as well as a flashlight.

Pengosekan, just south of Ubud, is cheaper and quieter. **Penestanan** and **Campuan** to the west are lovely villages where farmers still work the fields. The area is lusciously green, with bungalow complexes, private villas, shops and bamboo restaurants everywhere.

Further west, the more upmarket hotels in **Sayan** and **Kedewatan** offer luxury rooms, suites, and villas overlooking a spectacular river gorge with great views up to the volcanoes and down to the coast.

For those wanting to drop out of the rat race for a while and soak in the Ubud scene, private villas are the preferred option. There are literally hundreds of these, studding the rice fields around Ubud in all directions. Many are available for weekly or monthly rentals, and they range from fairly spartan places at very reasonable prices, to lavish luxury palaces,

complete with armies of staff and all mod cons. There are several agencies in Ubud that specialize in villa sales and rentals, and a vast amount of information online. If you're looking to stay long term it is advisable to arrive first and look around at various options before committing.

Central Ubud

Anom Cottages, Jl. Raya Sanggingan, tel: 852-8521. Fabulous ridge view in six spacious bungalow-style rooms. Breakfast is served on the terraces. **$$**

Jati Home Stay, Jl. Hanoman, www.jatihs.com. A compound belonging to a family of artists, the rooms here are all made from wood and bamboo, with nice views from the upper balconies, and a good breakfast thrown in. **$**

Ketut's Place, Jl. Suweta 40, tel: 975-304. Stay with a delightful Balinese family. Great dinner and cooking classes. **$**

Komaneka Resort, Jl. Monkey Forest, www.komaneka.com. In the heart of Ubud, and one of the finest top-end properties in the center; the perfect base from which to explore the town's shops and markets. The exquisite bungalows are set in rambling gardens with a beautiful swimming pool. **$$$$**

Murni's Houses, Jl Raya Campuan, www.murnis.com. A select set of delightful units, a five-minute walk from the center, peaceful, traditional, clean, and very reasonably priced. Beautifully furnished by Murni in Balinese style. Well-kept gardens and the excellent Tamarind Spa in the grounds. Pick up, drop, activities, tours, and classes can all be arranged. **$$$**

Nick's Pension, Jl. Bisma, www.nickshotels-ubud.com. Away from the hustle of the center, there are 24 quiet cottages on a terraced hill, bridging a stream. **$$**

Okawati's, Jl. Monkey Forest, tel: 975-063. A complex of 19 rooms with attached baths and fans around a pool. A nostalgic favorite. Ibu Okawati opened the first restaurant in Ubud. **$$**

Rumah Roda, Jl. Kajeng 24, www.rumahroda.com. With an excellent location, the newly built block stands behind the home of a Balinese family that has been welcoming travelers into their fold for many decades. You won't find a more accommodating place than this. **$**

Shana Homestay, Jl. Goutama, tel: 970-481. Off around a dozen homestays in family compounds on Jl. Goutama, an atmospheric little street off Jl. Raya Ubud, this is one of the best. There's one old bungalow and a two-story block of bright, clean rooms with terraces and tidy hot-water bathrooms. The breakfasts are very tasty, and the owners very welcoming. **$**

South of Central Ubud

Alam Indah, Nyuh Kuning, www.alamindahbali.com. Owned by the Café Wayan family, this small, exquisite hotel is a gem. Rooms are large and airy, and most have rice field views. Superb, pampering service. Free transport to and from Ubud center. Pool. Across the road are **Alam Shanti** and **Alam Jiwa**, owned by the same family, as is Laka Leke Restaurant nearby. All are highly recommended and enjoy many repeat guests. **$$$**

Bali Breeze Bungalows, Jl. Pengosekan, tel: 975-410. This friendly place has well-designed *lumbung*-style bungalows. Bedroom upstairs, toilet and sitting room downstairs. **$$**

Guci Guest Houses, Jl. Pengosekan, www.guci-bali.com. Tucked away off the road, the charming bungalows here offer plenty of peace and quiet; good breakfasts. **$**

Kebun Indah, Jl. Pengosekan, www.alamindahbali.com. Owned by the Café Wayan-Alam Indah family, this was their first guesthouse. Set back down a path about 130 m (140 yds) from the road, a peaceful oasis attracting many repeat and long-term guests. Delicious breakfasts from Café Wayan. Alam Asia Crafts shop roadside supports artisans in Southeast Asia; little Kebun Indah Spa. **$$-$$$**

East of Central Ubud

Maya Resort, Jl. Gunung Sari Peliatan, www.mayaubud.com. A luxurious five-star property on the Petanu River with a mix of modern materials and charming antiques. Three different classes of rooms from urban-style to villa and deluxe villas. Take the lift down to the spectacularly situated spa and relaxing River Café. **$$$$**

The Chedi Club, Jl. Raya Goa Gajah, Tengkulak Kaja, www.ghmhotels.com. Luxuriously appointed suites set in the middle of five ha (12ac) of paddy fields just outside of Ubud, near Goa Gajah. Offers serenity surrounded by Javanese antiques. Spa, fitness, tennis. **$$$$**

Tepi Sawah Villas, Jl. Raya Goa Gajah, Banjar Teges, Peliatan, www.tepisawahvillas.com. Owned by a Balinese art collector, this property began as a gallery, a restaurant was added, then 12 modern thatched-roof villas. Fabulous rice field views in the gorge below, excellent restaurant is a good lunch stop serving fresh food. Swimming pool, spa, art gallery. **$$$-$$$$**

West of Central Ubud

Amandari, Kedewatan, www.aman.com. In a stunning setting with ethereal valley views, the private pavilions here were designed by Australian architect Peter Muller; one of Bali's most exquisite hotels. Each villa is nestled in its own private walled compound, and several have private swimming pools. Service is exemplary. Jaw-dropping view over the Ayung River Gorge. **$$$$**

Bambu Indah, Banjar Baung, Sayan, www.bambuindah.com. Around 15 minutes southwest of central Ubud, a compound of historic Javanese teak cottages that have been lovingly restored, with public buildings created from bamboo based on traditional Sumatran architecture. Each house is unique and is decorated with collections from the global travels of famed jewelry designer John Hardy and his wife Cynthia, who live next door. Modern amenities have been cleverly camouflaged to blend in with the eco-friendly concept. **$$$$**

Four Seasons Bali, Jl. Raya Sayan, www.fourseasons.com. Rooms and villas in a labyrinth of extraordinary architectural innovations of a giant lily pond topping the restaurant, stairways, interior rivers, and waterfalls. Superb food and guest service, as is always expected of Four Seasons Resorts. **$$$$**

Tjampuhan Hotel & Spa, Jl. Raya Campuan, www.indo.com. Rooms set on terraced gardens overlooking the Campuan River and temple. Spring-fed swimming pool and tennis court. Built on the site of Walter Spies' compound of the 1930s. Many steps! **$$$**

Warwick Ibah Luxury Villas & Spa, Jl. Raya Campuan, www.warwickibah.com. Managed by Paris-based Warwick Group, 17 uniquely designed villas offering every amenity in luxurious and stylish surroundings. Saltwater swimming pool, plunge pools, restaurant, spa, library, only a five-minute walk from Ubud center. "Treetops" features suites in a single structure, with jungle canopy views and sounds from the river far below. **$$$$**

North of Central Ubud

Murni's Villas, Ponggang, Payanagan, www.murnis.com. Luxury villas, stunning infinity pool, amazing, picture-perfect views of rice terraces, hills, and forests. Beautifully furnished by Murni. Lovely staff. Ideal for weddings and honeymoons. All meals can be provided by an excellent cook. Good discounts for longer stays. Pick up, drop, activities, tours, and classes can all be arranged. **$$$**

Bagus Jati Resort, Banjar Jati, Desa Sebatu, Tegallalang, www.bagusjati.com. After about 3 km (2 miles) of country road passing through villages and forests, arrive at this serene, isolated residential health and well-being center, organic gardens, and gourmet restaurant. Deluxe and superior villas with private spa facilities set on 5 ha of hillside gardens. Offers a global palate of world-class health and well-being programs: nutrition, detox, yoga, meditation, stress relief, anti-aging, nature trekking, fitness center, cooking workshops. **$$$$**

Wapa di Ume Resort & Spa, Jl. Sueta, Banjar Sambahan, www.wapadiume.com. Award-winning bungalows, suites and villas, one with a private pool, overlooking rice fields. Architecture is in *lumbung* style to blend in with surroundings. The floor above the spa is perhaps the most ethereal meditation room in Bali. Terraced swimming pool; regular shuttle buses to Ubud. **$$$$**

DINING

Ubud has an incredible variety of places to eat. The simple *warungs* serving *nasi campur* and satay are still around, but now there is also everything else. Today, Ubud offers a choice ranging from American burgers and steaks, to country-style Japanese, sophisticated Italian pastas, and globally-acclaimed haute cuisine. A few restaurants stand head and shoulders above the crowd for the quality and originality of their food. The following is just a sampling of the area's better restaurants.

Central Ubud

Ary's Warung, Jl. Raya Ubud, www.dekco.com. Located in the heart of Ubud, Ary's is known for its friendly service and great food. Inspired by the Slow Food movement, contemporary Balinese-Asian cuisine; tasting menu offering several courses. Wine cellar, cigars and freshly brewed *kopi luwak* coffee are features. Breakfast, lunch, and dinner. **$$-$$$**

Batan Waru, Jl. Dewi Sita, www.batanwaru.com. One of the best places in town for breakfast; check out the ginger pancakes and the Florida lime pie. Chili crab on Tuesday nights. Extensive Indonesian menu without the fire. If you want it spicy hot, request it. Breakfast, lunch, and dinner. **$$-$$$**

Bebek Bengil, Padangtegal, www.bebekbengil.com. One of the most beautiful restaurant environments on Bali, offering a highly creative, cheeky menu. The specialty of the house is Balinese crispy fried duck. Low tables with cushions create a cozy atmosphere, and the food is wholesome. Local expats swear by the salads, pastas, and vegetarian dishes. Daily specials and a great selection of desserts. Lunch and dinner. **$$-$$$**

Café Wayan, Jl. Monkey Forest, tel: 975-447. One of the best places to eat in town, Ibu Wayan has cooked in California and Thailand and loves to travel; the menu reflects her diverse culinary background. On Sunday nights they put on an extravagant Balinese buffet. The Death by Chocolate Cake is legendary. Packed at dinner; not so crowded at lunch. Breakfast, lunch, and dinner. **$$**

Casa Luna, Jl. Raya Ubud, www.casalunabali.com. In the center of town, this is the centerpiece of the suite of properties run by Janet de Neefe, Ubud's literary and culinary grande dame. The restaurant offers spacious dining with an eclectic menu ranging from Western standards to Indonesian favorites, all delivered with a dash of extra flair in a fabulous atmosphere. Just inside the entrance is an excellent bakery with fresh baked breads and cakes. There are some fabulous cocktails. The highly regarded associated **cooking school** offers workshops. Breakfast, lunch, and dinner. **$$-$$$**

Ibu Oka's Babi Guling, Jl. Suweta. Ibu Oka's is an Ubud institution. People come from miles away to eat her succulent roast pig. Lunch, and dinner. **$**

Juice Ja, Jl. Dewi Sita, tel: 971-056. In the heart of Ubud, a comfortable, unpretentious café on two floors serving wholesome and delicious meals. Emphasis is on using organic and local ingredients to produce salubrious meals and baked goods for the café and for the local farmers' market. Breakfast, lunch, and dinner. **$$**

Lamak, Jl. Monkey Forest, www.lamakbali.com. A back-to-the-future restaurant with a physical space beyond compare. Dishes range from melt-in-your-mouth scallops to sumptuous risotto. Upbeat, elegant atmosphere, good music, trippy toilets, and a great wine list. Lunch and dinner. **$$$**

West of Central Ubud

Murni's Warung, Jl. Raya Campuan, www.murnis.com. An old favorite, on the Ubud side of the Campuan bridge overlooking the stunning rainforest and Wos River. This multi-storied restaurant, decorated with Asian antiques from Murni's collection, is where the eclectic menu mix of Western, Indonesian, and Balinese favorites got its start in 1974. Murni's menu and dishes have stood the test of time and the satay, *gado-gado,* and grilled fish are delectable. The Lounge Bar, loved by expats, plays soft jazz. The lower dining areas offer tranquility, with only the sound of the river accompanying the peace. Outstanding desserts and freshly-squeezed fruit juices. Breakfast, lunch, and dinner. **$$-$$$**

Naughty Nuri's, Jl. Raya Lunsgsiakan, Kedewatan tel: 977-547. An Ubud institution, this is where you come to get ribs and other grilled delights, down some great margaritas, and rub elbows with the local expat crowd, who quaff the excellent martinis by the gallons. Thursday night specials. Lunch and dinner. **$$-$$$**

South of Central Ubud

Pak Sedan's Warung, Jl. Bima, Pengosekan. Next door to the petrol station, this small *warung* is always packed with locals and in-the-know tourists, who come for the dirt-cheap but always delicious Indonesian dishes. Lunch and dinner. **$**

Pizza Bagus, Jl. Pengosekan, www.pizzabagus.com. A long-standing favorite in the south of town, this place does excellent Italian delicacies and pizzas. There's indoor and outdoor seating, and it's a fine spot for a laid-back morning coffee. Breakfast, lunch, and dinner. **$$**

East of Central Ubud

Warung Teges, Jl. Raya Peliatan. Look for this simple *warung* as the road from Peliatan to Mas opens onto fields. One of the best *nasi campur* (pork or chicken with rice and a vegetable) in Bali, served with a wonderful *sambal matah* (fresh hot chili sauce) in an attractive garden courtyard. The place hasn't changed in over three generations. Lunch and dinner. **$**

North of Central Ubud

Kampung Café & Cottages, Tegallalang, tel: 901-201. The latest in nouveau Indonesian cuisine, this gem overlooks the incredible sculptured rice fields and tropical forests of Ceking. The pastas and salads are divine, and the daily specials will impress with their innovativeness and freshness of ingredients. The chocolate brownies will keep you going all day. Service is slow, but the price is right. Breakfast, lunch, and dinner. **$$$**

Mozaic, Jl. Raya Sanggingan, www.mozaic-bali.com. Award-winning French-American chef Chris Salens' masterpiece, set in lush gardens. Food, presentation and service here are flawless. Try the 6-course Tasting Menu. The cuisine is Modern European with multiple Pacific Rim accents and Indonesian flavors, all exquisitely presented. Attached is a **kitchenware shop** selling everything from cutlery and other tableware, ceramic vases and matching glasses, to picnic baskets, linens and napkins. Also has a **cooking school**. Dinner. **$$$**

NIGHTLIFE

Ubud has never been known for its nightlife, but a few places have started opening beyond the usual 11 pm shut-down in recent years. For the most part the drinking and dining scenes intersect in Ubud, and most of the popular after-hours hangouts are restaurants first and foremost.

Start the evening at **Naughty Nuri's**, out of the center on Jl. Raya Campuan. This original expat favorite is a Balinese warung with a touch of New York, and justly famous martinis. For a laidback drinking atmosphere, try the downstairs cocktail bar at **Ary's Warung** on Jl. Raya Ubud. **The Jazz Café** (www.jazzcafebali.com) on Jl. Sukma in the eastern part of town is one of the livelier spots. It offers live jazz nightly, Tuesday–Saturday from 7 pm, plus food, fine wines, and creative stiff drinks.

Casa Luna on Jl. Raya Ubud is a fine restaurant with some excellent cocktails. It often hosts

high-caliber evening entertainment, from unusual live music to performance poetry.

Other nightspots include **Laughing Buddha** and **Lebong Café**, both on Jl. Monkey Forest Road. The latter is usually the last place in town to shut down, and is about as rowdy as Ubud gets—that is, not very!

ACTIVITIES

Courses

Casa Luna Cooking School, Jl. Bisma, www.casa-luna.com. Regular introductions to the subtle arts of Balinese cuisine are run at the Honeymoon Guesthouse. There is a weekly schedule, with different dishes and cultural elements covered each morning (sessions usually run from 8 am or 9 am to 1 pm), and some sessions include a trip to the local market for hands-on experience with fresh ingredients.

Green Camp, www.greencampbali.com. Geared for 5–14-year-olds, kids may sign up for any number of days Monday-Friday and stay in eco-yurts on overnight programs. Activities begin at 9 am and end at 6:30 pm and include fun and educational themes such as Eco-living (e.g. All Natural Wearable Arts), Teambuilding and Leadership, Environmental Education, Sustainable Agriculture (plant your own rice and learn about Bali's unique communal subak irrigation system), and Art and Culture (e.g. Mask Making). The kids would probably be much happier here than tagging along on shopping forays, and they might even learn something really cool.

Pondok Pekak Library & Learning Center, Jl. Monkey Forest Road, tel: 976-194, maintains a lending library full of holiday reading in various languages, and literature on Indonesian and Balinese culture. There's also a huge children's library upstairs with books in English and Indonesian. The house is full of kids, students, and adults of various nationalities. They also offer courses Indonesian language course, and course in music, arts and crafts. An excellent place for families to hang out.

Studio Perak, Jl. Hanoman, www.studioperak.com. Learn the basics of Balinese silversmithing and take home a ring of your own design. They also offer two- and five-day courses teaching more advanced techniques such as transferring designs onto silver and setting stones. Reservations recommended.

Cycling

Bali Eco Cycling, Jl. Raya Pengosekan, www.baliecocycling.com. Cycle downhill and see the real Bali on an eco-educational guided cycling tour from mountainous Penelokan down into the Batur caldera, then roll through the agricultural heartland of Bali via secret back roads to Ubud, with stops at cultural sites along the way. Prices start at $40, all inclusive.

Sobek Batur Cycling, www.balisobek.com. Using new mountain bikes and safety equipment, take a downhill trail from Mt. Batur through sleepy villages along little-used roads and tracks, stopping frequently to see aged temple compounds, shady plantations, and the daily lives of local people. Pick-ups from Ubud are at 8 am for the half-day trip. $79/adults, includes lunch, hotel pickup, insurance, English-speaking guides. (Some guides speak other Asian languages.)

Walking tours

Bali Bird Walks, www.balibirdwalk.com. Three-hour guided tours for bird lovers and anyone who appreciates the outdoors: butterflies, trees, and brilliant scenery. Combines exercise, nature, and cultural observations. Tours generally run on Tuesday, Friday, Saturday and Sunday, starting at 9 am from Murni's Warung by the Campuan Bridge, but call first to check the schedule. After a coffee or tea, the group sets out, getting back at around 1 pm for lunch. Of the 100 species of native birds found around Ubud, expect to see 30 or so, as well as some quite brilliant alterations of habitat. $37; includes guided bird walk, binocular use, lunch, bottled water, coffee/tea.

Bali Nature Herbal Walk, www.baliherbalwalk.com. Owners are a young couple who grew up in healer families. Their love of plants and what plants can do for good health inspired them to lead visitors on three-hour daily herb walks through the rice fields and plantations around Ubud. Tours include the chance to learn about the healing properties of local plants. They also offer classes on making *jamu*, traditional herbal medicinal and skin care ointments and tonics.

Keep Walking Tours, Jl. Hanoman 44, www.balispirit. com, offers above-average guided cultural and ecological walks (minimum two persons, around $25/pp) as well as sunrise climbs up Mt. Batur.

White water rafting

Bali Adventure Tours, www.baliadventuretours.com. This long-running operator offers rafting on the Ayung River, as well as mountain-biking and trekking.

Sobek Rafting, www.sobek.com. Ayung River white water rafting through an amazing gorge. Half day trip, Class 2 river, 25 rapids, all safe and fun for ages seven to 65. See animals and birds living along the river and pass 10 spectacular waterfalls falling into the river, which runs past steep stone cliffs and tropical rainforest. $79 includes lunch, hotel pick-up, insurance, and highly trained English speaking guides (some guides speak other Asian languages). Ask about children's rates. Many steps.

SHOPPING

There's a sophisticated range of shopping in Ubud, and though the focus is still on the arts and handicrafts that made Ubud famous, there is an increasing array of fashion boutiques that wouldn't look out of place in Seminyak. Shops are generally open 9 am–9 pm.

The more adventurous can find a cornucopia of handicrafts in many of the less-visited villages surrounding Ubud. Check out Mas village, south of Ubud, for masks, arts and crafts, and furniture.

Antiques, Arts & Crafts, Gifts

Murni's Warung, Jl Raya Campuan, www.murnis. com. Traditional arts and crafts from all over the archipelago, as well as overseas, assiduously collected by Murni who has formidable fine arts credentials and seasoned, sophisticated taste. If she's around, Murni will sign the best-selling *Secrets of Bali, Fresh Light on the Morning of the World* by Jonathan Copeland and Ni Wayan Murni.

Bojog Gallery, across from the football field on Jl. Monkey Forest, tel: 971-001. Two stories of antique furniture, textiles, puppets, masks, wood carvings, and more from Sulawesi, Sumatra, Java, Bali, and the rest of Indonesia.

Celeng Gallery, Jl. Raya Lungsiakan, Kedewatan, tel: 898-9488, mobile: 0811-396-860. Specializes in antique furniture, stone carvings, and ritual artifacts from throughout Indonesia. Ask to visit the warehouse for wholesale prices on old furniture and custom orders made from recycled teak.

Kuluk Gallery, Jl. Raya Lungsiakan, Kedewatan, tel: 975-833. Indonesian art and antiques, specializing in museum-quality ritual artifacts and antique textiles and jewelry. Also has an extensive library for research and authentication.

Tegun Folk Art Gallery, Jl. Hanoman 44, Padangtegal, www.tegungaleri.com. An Aladdin's Cave of lovely, unique, and very well-selected gifts, keepsakes, and other paraphernalia gathered from all over the archipelago. One-stop shopping for fantastic gifts, handmade and antique flutes, some jewelry, in every price range. Run by American Meghan Peppenheim and her Balinese husband Kadek Gunarta.

Books

Ganesha Bookshop, Jl. Raya Ubud, www. ganeshabooksbali.com. A book-lovers' treasure-trove, this Ubud institution packs a lot into its small space. There's an unrivalled array of books on Bali and Indonesia, from expat memoirs to obscure academic titles, plus a good stock of quality second-hand paperbacks and some attractive handicrafts. There's also a tantalizing cabinet full of antiquarian books on Indonesia, which makes for fascinating

Handwoven wickerwork is amongst the many traditional crafts available in Ubud.

browsing. The staff are very knowledgeable. There's a second branch in Sanur.

Periplus, Jl. Monkey Forest, www.periplus.com. A glossy book-filled boutique with a wide and varied selection of travel guides, coffee table books, novels, cookbooks, nonfiction, and books on Bali and Indonesia, plus lots of imported magazines. There's another branch on Jl. Raya Ubud.

Fashion, Jewelry & Textiles

Goddess on the Go!, Jl. Raya Pengosekan, www.goddessonthego.net. Brightly dyed beech cloth, perfect for traveling. Eco-friendly travel & leisure clothing in 16 colors to reflect individual personalities. Silky smooth, lightweight, wash and wear. Versatile pieces for every occasion from bed to ballroom.

Uluwatu, Jl. Monkey Forest, tel: 977-557. This boutique showcases beautifully handcrafted Balinese crisp cotton and silky rayon lace clothing and sleepwear. Also bed linens and tableware, plus a superb collection of Balinese *ikat*.

Threads of Life, Jl. Kajeng 24, www.threadsoflife.com. A truly amazing collection of museum-quality *ikat* textiles. Group strives to preserve Indonesia's many traditional hand-woven cloth cultures. Promotes use of natural dyes only if sustainably harvested. Organizes educational exhibits, courses, cultural events, and supports traditional weavers on many Indonesian islands, especially the more endangered textile traditions.

Treasures, Jl. Raya Ubud, tel: 976-697. Attached to Ary's Warung, this shop features the innovative work of a number of exclusive designers based in Bali. Precious metals (gold, white gold, silver) and precious stones are a specialty. With its works of art displayed behind glass, Treasures looks like the kind of place that needs armed guards in front of it.

Wood & Stone Carvings

For lower prices on wooden handicrafts in all imaginable sizes, shapes, and colors, head up the hill to **Tegallalang**, **Pujung**, and **Sebatu**, all northeast of Ubud. In these crafts villages are a bewildering number of shops, mostly for export purposes. Bali's modern-day center for stone carving is **Batubulan village**, halfway between Ubud and Denpasar.

For high-quality **dance masks**, the most accomplished carvers are **Ida Bagus Anom** in Mas (next to the football field), whose innovative designs are everywhere in Bali, and **Ida Bagus Alit** in Lod Tunduh, just south of the junction at Mas and Lod

The "Art Market" (Pasar Seni) in Sukawati is famous as a place to buy textiles and souvenirs.

Tunduh. Other preeminent mask makers in the area are **I Wayan Tangguh**, **Cokorda Raka Tisnu**, and **I Wayan Tedun** of Singapadu, and **Ida Bagus Oka** and **I Wayan Muka** of Mas.

The wood carvers in **Nyuh Kuning**, south of Ubud's Monkey Forest, are known for their lifelike animals carved out of *waru* wood.

Markets

Pasar Ubud (Ubud traditional market), Jl. Raya Ubud, central Ubud. This market is both a reassuring bastion of traditional life with no reference to tourism, and a must for eager handicraft hunters. Come at first light, before the tour buses turn up, and you'll find dozens of women hawking fresh fruit and veggies, fried snacks, woven leaf trays for offerings, and more, especially down in the basement level. On the upper levels, meanwhile, you'll find a mass of cheap souvenirs. Bargaining hard is essential here.

Pasar Seni Sukawati (Sukawati Art Market), Sukawati. Down the road about 5 km (3 miles) from Ubud, this maze-like two-story building and its surrounds are a hive of activity for shoppers: masks, statuary, clothes, local traditional and modern textiles, basketry and ceremonial accoutrements, such as umbrellas. Bargain hard for everything at stalls stacked nearly to the ceiling. Also check out the street beside and in back of the market where even better bargains can be found. Take note of the long line of tour buses from Java. Sukawati is where Indonesian tourists shop.

Ubud Organic Farmer's Market, www. ubudorganicmarket.com, at Pizza Bagus, Jl. Pengosekan, Saturdays 9 am–2 pm; at Warung Sopa, Jl. Nyuh Kuning, Wednesdays 9 am–1 pm. Support local farmers by buying organic produce and rice, condiments, jams and more, and feel healthier in the process.

SPAS, MASSAGE & YOGA

Most—if not all—of the upmarket resorts have their own spas with the full range of amenities, but there are also many independent ones in the Ubud area, some better than others, plus a vast array of places offering yoga.

Bali Botanica Day Spa, Jl. Raya Sangginan, www. balibotanica.com. Therapy rooms here overlook the rice paddies. There's a range of treatments and methodologies, and the management offer free transport within the Ubud area.

Fivelements Puri Ahimsa, Banjar Baturning, Mambal village, www.fivelements.com. This is a healing center in an exquisite atmosphere located along the Ayung River whose specialties are Balinese healing, living foods, and sacred arts. The bamboo hall is worth visiting on its own. Spa has Watsu and many other types of massage, and their dining room serves vegan raw foods.

Tamarind Spa at Murni's Houses, Jl Raya, Ubud, www.murnis.com. Murni's extremely popular spa gets rave reviews. Many repeat guests, including masseurs, say it's the best they've ever experienced. Well-kept gardens, fountains, sounds of running water, soothing music, healthy lunches. Reasonably priced.

The Yoga Barn, Jl. Pengosekan, www.yogabarn.com. Set in wonderfully serene surroundings, packages include group and private yoga classes, organic food and detox, spa therapies, and eco-tours. Workshops in dance, meditation, yoga, and Pilates. Open 7 am–8 pm.

POST

The Main Post Office is on Jl. Jembawan, up the small road opposite Neka Gallery. Open Monday–Saturday 8 am–2 pm, Friday 8–11 am, Sunday 8 am–noon. Regular, airmail, and express service. If you've overdone it buying heavyweight arts and crafts, **packing and shipping agents** are abundant in Ubud. One of the best is **Bisama Group**, Jl. Raya Ubud 33X, tel: 975-520. Provides full documentation and also serves as a purchasing agent for handicrafts, furniture, and garments.

MEDICAL SERVICES

Ubud Clinic, Jl. Raya Campuan 36, www.ubudclinic.baliklik.com, offers 24-hour services, and is experienced in dealing with both common travelers' complaints, and with international travel insurance providers. Serious cases are generally transferred to Denpasar.

MUSEUMS & GALLERIES AROUND UBUD See maps, page 172–173, 177.

There is often a fine line separating museums and fine art galleries which sell paintings. Many museums also call themselves galleries and almost always have a commercial showroom on the premises. Most museums and galleries open at 8 am and many remain open on demand through the early evening.

There are hundreds of "art shops" selling paintings in the Ubud area and dozens of so-called galleries selling similar types of paintings of dubious quality. However, there are also a number of commercial art galleries that showcase the best of Balinese, Indonesian, and expat artists.

ART MUSEUMS

Agung Rai Museum of Art, Jl. Raya Pengosekan, tel: 976-659, www.armamuseum.com.This monumental structure houses the private collection of the highly-regarded collector, Agung Rai, who had his humble beginnings flogging paintings on the hot sands of Kuta Beach four decades ago. See originals by famous painters such as Spies, Bonnet, Hofker, Affandi, and many others. Rotating exhibits. Bookshop, nice gardens, and shop. Offers **cultural workshops:** *gamelan*, dance, architecture, traditional healing, and offering making. Open 9 am–6 pm. Entrance Rp 80,000.

Blanco Renaissance Museum, Jl. Raya Campuan, www.blancomuseum.com. World-renowned gallery set in tropical gardens featuring Antonio Blanco's risqué paintings (none of which are for sale) with their elaborate frames, and paintings by his son Mario Blanco (very much for sale). Open 9 am–5 pm. Entrance Rp 80,000.

Museum Puri Lukisan, Jl. Raya Ubud, www.museumpurilukisan.com. Founded under the auspices of the royal family in 1953, five separate pavilions represent the whole evolution of modern Balinese painting from its inception in the 1930s until the present. Originally catalogued by Rudolf Bonnet, the current trustees continue to maintain the same standard through a continuous program of acquisitions. Tranquil setting in lovely gardens. Also offers painting, dance, and carving workshops. 9 am–5 pm. Admission fee Rp75,000.

Neka Art Museum, Jl. Raya Sanggingan, Campuan, www.museumneka.com. Five traditional buildings house Neka's private collection of work by Bali's most revered artists: Lempad, Spies, Covarrubias, I Bagus Made, and Made Wianta. Great areas for just sitting and passing the time. Open 9 am–5 pm, Sundays noon–5 pm. Closed on public holidays. Entrance: Rp 50,000.

Museum Rudana, Jl. Cok Rai Pudak 44, www.museumrudana.com. Important permanent collection of contemporary Indonesian art and commercial fine art housed in a monumental marble building. Open 9 am–5 pm. Admission: Rp 100,000.

Setia Darma House of Masks and Puppets, Jl. Tegal Bingin, Sukawati, tel: 8987-493. Thousands of puppets and masks from all over Indonesia fill four traditional Javanese houses. Even Barack Obama is made into a wooden puppet here. **Performances and events** are held in the large wantilan (pavilion) on the landscaped grounds. Open daily 9 am–5 pm.

ART GALLERIES

Adi's Art Gallery, Jl. Bisma 102, tel: 977-104. Features upcoming artists; changes shows frequently so there is always something new to see. Open daily 10 am–5 pm.

Bidadari Art, Jl. Raya Mas, Mas village, www.bidadariart.com. For one-of-a-kind woodcarvings that are well-displayed, this is the place to come. Open Monday–Saturday 8:30 am–5 pm.

Gaya Fusion Art Space, Jl. Raya Sayan, Sayan, www.gayafusion.com. Features avant garde and contemporary art. Real Italian gelato on the grounds. Open daily 9 am–9 pm.

Komaneka Fine Art Gallery, Jl. Monkey Forest, tel: 401-2217. Managed by Koman Neka, the son of Pande Suteja Neka, this gallery has revolving exhibitions of contemporary artists.

Neka Gallery, Jl. Raya Ubud, tel: 975-034.The Neka Art Museum put Balinese art on the map. This is its gallery outlet. Open daily 9 am–5 pm.

Pranoto's Art Gallery, Jl. Raya Goa Gajah, Tengkulak Kaja, tel: 970-827. A lively, active gallery in the heart of Ubud hosting life-drawing model sessions, exhibitions, and a large fine art collection of paintings by Indonesian and international artists. Open daily 9 am–5 pm.

Rio Helmi Gallery & Café, Jl. Suweta 06b, www.riohelmi.com. Acclaimed photographer Rio Helmi has been capturing images of his homeland for decades. His gallery features both his photographs and prints, and the café serves great coffee. Open 7 am–7 pm.

Tony Raka Gallery, Jl. Raya Mas No. 86, Mas village, www.tonyrakaartgallery.com. Probably the most innovative art gallery around, the exhibits here feature fresh and often wacky art.

Suteja Neka, founder of the Neka Art Museum, shows off a rare keris dagger in his collection.

UBUD DANCE PERFORMANCES: A WEEKLY SCHEDULE

There are around half a dozen individual performances of traditional dance and music around Ubud each evening. Performances usually start around 7:30 pm, and typically last around 1.5 hours. There are occasional one-off events, including performances associated with religious festivals. Ask at the Ubud Tourist Information Center for details of any upcoming special performances.

Other performances run to a weekly schedule, which is generally very reliable—some of the troupes listed below have been performing the same dance to the same timetable for years—but check at the Tourist Information Center for the latest details. The Tourist Information Center is also the best place to buy tickets. They generally cost around Rp80,0000, and transport to those in outlying areas is usually included.

Inevitably, some troupes are better than others. Amongst those listed below, Semara Ratih, Gunung Sari, and Tirta Sari all have particularly good reputations.

MONDAY
Sadha Budaya, Ubud Palace: Legong Dance, 7:30 pm.
Krama Desa Adat Junjungan, Junjungan Village: Kecak Fire (Monkey Chant Dance), 7:00 pm (*transfer to venue 6:30 pm*).
Sandhi Suara, Wantilan, Wantilan: Barong and Kris Dance, 7:00 pm.
Krama Desa Ubud Kaja Pura Dalem Ubud: Kecak Ramayana and Fire Dance, 7:30 pm.
Luh Luwih, Bale Banjar Ubud Kelod: Women's Performance, 7:30 pm.

TUESDAY 7:30 pm
Bina Remaja, Ubud Palace: Ramayana Ballet.
Semara Ratih Jaba Pura Desa Kutuh: Spirit of Bali.
Sandhi Suara, Pura Taman Sari, Jl. Hanoman: Kecak Fire and Trance Dance.
Genta Bhuana Sari, Balerung Mandera, Peliatan: Legong Dance (*transfer to venue 6:45 pm*).
Sekaa Gong Karyasa, Pura Dalem Ubud: Legong Dance.
Chandra Wati, Ubud Water Palace, Kajeng: Women's *Gamelan* with Children Dance.
Nrita Dewi, Bale Banjar Ubud Kelod: Legong Dance.
Semara Kanti, Padangtegal Kaja, Jl. Hanoman: Barong and Keris Dance.

WEDNESDAY 7:30 pm
Panca Arta, Ubud Palace: Legong and Barong Dance.
Trene Jenggala, Padangtegal Kaja: Kecak Fire and Trance Dance.
Yowana Swara, Pura Dalem Ubud: *Jegog* (Bamboo *gamelan*).

Krama Desa Adat Taman Kaja, Pura Dalem Taman Kaja: Kecak Fire and Trance Dance.
Suara Guna Kanti Abangan, Bale Banjar Ubud Kelod: Legong and Barong Waksirsa Dance.

THURSDAY 7:30 pm
Panca Arta, Ubud Palace: Legong Trance and Paradise Dance.
Semara Madya, Puri Agung Peliatan: Kecak (Monkey Chant Dance) (*transfer to venue 6:45 pm*).
Raja Peni, Pura Dalem Ubud: Barong and Keris Dance.
Cenik Wayah, Ubud Water Palace: Spirit of *Gamelan* (Barong and Child Dance).
Sandhi Suara, Pura Taman Sari: Kecak Fire and Trance Dance.
Krama Desa Sambahan, Batukaru Temple: Kecak Fire and Trance Dance.
Puspa Kirana, Bale Banjar Ubud Kelod: Legong Dance.

FRIDAY
Sadha Budaya, Ubud Palace: Legong and Barong Dance, 7:30 pm.
Tirta Sari, Balerung Mandera, Peliatan: Legong Dance, 7:30 pm (*transfer to venue 6:45 pm*).
Padang Subadra, Pura Padang Kerta: Kecak Fire and Trance Dance, 7:00 pm.
Suara Sakti, Bentuyung Village: *Jegog* (bamboo *gamelan*): 7:00 pm (*transfer to venue 6:45 pm*).
Krama Desa Ubud Kaja, Pura Dale Ubud: Kecak Ramayana and Fire Dance, 7:30 pm.
Kiduling Suwari, Bale Banjar Ubud Kelod: Legong Dance, 7:30 pm.

SATURDAY
Bina Remaja, Ubud Palace: Legong Dance, 7:30 pm.
Gunung Sari, Puri Agung Peliatan: Legong Dance, 7:30 pm (*transfer to venue 6:45 pm*).
Trene Jenggala, Padangtegal Kaja: Kecak Fire and Trance Dance, 7:00 pm.
Chandra Wirabhuana, Ubud Water Palace: Legong Dance, 7:30 pm.
Krama Desa Adat Taman Kaja, Pura Dalem Taman Kaja: Kecak Fire and Trance Dance.

SUNDAY
Jaya Swara, Ubud Palace: Legong of Mahabrata, 7:30 pm.
Trene Jengala, Padangtegal Kaja: Kecak Fire and Trance Dance, 7:00 pm.
Suara Sakti, Bentuyung Village: *Jegog* (bamboo *gamelan*), 7:00 pm (transfer to venue 6:45 pm).
Krama Desa Sambahan, Batukaru Temple: Kecak Fire and Trance Dance, 7:30 pm.
Pondok Pekak, Bale Banjar Ubud Kelod: Legong Dance, 7:30 pm.

DRIVES WEST & NORTH OF UBUD

Scenic Drives Around Ubud Provide a Bit of History and Lots of Fun!

If based in Ubud, there is a wide array of activities to choose from when you're ready to venture out and have a nice drive into the countryside, soak up a little more history or culture, or have a full day dedicated to simply having fun.

The "Baliwood Hills"

Sayan, **Kedewatan**, and **Payangan** villages constitute what expats call "Baliwood Hills." Many four- and five-star resorts are on this stunning ridge overlooking the Ayung River. *Bemos* are available on market days (*pasah*), but otherwise you'll need your own transport. From the furthest south lies the Kayumanis Private Villa & Spa, followed by Four Seasons Resort—an excellent lunch at its PJ's Restaurant—and then the **Amandari**, the first luxury hotel in the Ubud area, with a superb chef.

In between is the Gaya Art Space Gallery, which has periodic films, seminars, and exhibits and some of the best homemade gelato on the island. Continuing further north on the main road is Kupu-Kupu Barong, the Royal Pita Maha, and finally the Alila Ubud. Take the left turn at Payangan near Pura Air Jeruk to see the super-lux **Ubud Hanging Gardens**. All have stupendous views.

White water rafting

Several reliable outfitters offer white water rafting tours on the breathtakingly scenic Ayung River north of Ubud. The adventure takes novices and experienced oarsmen of all ages, led by trained guides, over Class II and III rapids through gorges flanked by magnificent waterfalls and paddy fields. Rafting expeditions with Bali Adventure Tours (www.baliadventuretours.com),

The area around Ubud is home to some of Bali's most exclusive resorts, like the Amandari pictured here.

The fast-flowing Ayung River is the main venue for white water rafting in Bali. Conditions are usually best in the rainy season (November–March).

Sangeh's Monkey Forest is an atmospheric spot.

manager of the Elephant Safari Park, can also be packaged with Park entrance and mountain cycling. Sobek (www.balisobek. com) has an almost identical white water rafting tour, an equally impressive safety record, and also offers mountain cycling.

Folktales in stone
South and west of Ubud there is a quiet, beautiful road that passes through **Mambal**, **Abiansemal**, and **Blahkiuh** villages, renowned for their stone sculptors. All of the temples, *kulkul* (bell) towers, and palaces along this road—beginning further south at **Sibanggede**—have beautiful sculptures, reliefs, and stone ornaments.

Many temples in this area were restored or refreshed after the 1917 earthquake, followed by another restoration boom during the 1930s. Reliefs with scenes from the Tantri stories, of Indian origin, were favorite subjects. In these legends, animals teach people how to live and about the good and evil they can expect from life, depending on their behavior.

One of them tells of the lion-king of the forest and the bull, the ruler-to-be, who must either have a peaceful conversation, face-to-face, or fight to the death. Another tells of two thoughtful geese holding a pole with a tortoise atop while flying away to a safe place and two greedy jackals devouring the absent-minded tortoise, who fell off the pole.

Then there is the story of the wicked heron Baka, surrounded by the bones of a fish he promised to take to a better lake, but then ate it instead. Baka wanted to take a crab also, but the clever crustacean discovered the heron's dishonorable intentions and pinched its head off.

Yet another saga is of a grateful crab and the Brahman who rescued it. Later, the crab rescued the Brahman from an evil bird and snake in gratitude.

A few kilometers before Sangeh at Blahkiuh is a huge, holy **waringin** (banyan) **tree** on the eastern side of the crossroads. In 1989 the temporary market stalls at the foot of this tree were replaced by a concrete structure. In order to do this, part of the aerial roots had to be cut, which could only be done by a specialist with enough magic power to protect himself.

Sangeh's Monkey Forest Temple
In **Sangeh**, 15 km (9 miles) beyond Mengwi, is the fabled **Monkey Forest** (not to be confused with Ubud's own Monkey Forest) and **Pura Bukit Sari** temple. This small temple may date from the founding of Mengwi, although it is also said that it existed in the 17th century. There is an old statue here of Garuda, the mount of Wisnu, who is also associated with the search for the magic elixir (*amerta*) to release his parents from their torments in hell.

The temple is surrounded by tall nutmeg trees with grayish-white trunks, which are very rare on Bali, so they must have been planted deliberately. Many monkeys roam about in the forest. Although sacred to Hindus, they are quite a nuisance, so be sure to remove eyeglasses, jewelry, and watches and hold on tightly to handbags before entering the forest. It is said that some of the monkey-general Hanoman's primate troops fell on Sangeh with the top of Mt. Mahameru when he tried to crush the evil demon king Rawana with it, and that their descendants remain in the forest to this day.

The dramatic terraced rice fields at Tegallalang are one of Bali's most photographed sights.

Sebatu's sculpted terraces

Northeast of Ubud is **Sebatu**, which can be visited all or in parts by car or bemo. From the traffic light with the archer statue at the eastern end of Ubud, head north past the police station and the Delta supermarket along a crowded, paved road that passes through **Petulu** and **Tegallalang** villages toward **Pujung**, a distance of some 16 km

A close encounter with a friendly pachyderm is the main attraction at the Elephant Safari Park.

(10 miles). The road rises gradually, reaching cooler air, and passes through verdant rice fields and coconut groves. Notice the many assembly-line woodcarvings being produced in small workshops along this road: all sorts of colorful fruit trees and animals. At Pujung, turn right to reach a holy spring at Sebatu, about 800 m (875 ft) to the east, where you can cool off in deliciously fresh pools. From Pujung, a small road continues north to Kintamani past some of Bali's most dramatic rice terraces.

Elephants, trekking, cycling & rafting

North of Ubud on 3.5 ha (8.6 ac) of land near **Taro** village, west of the road to Mt. Batur via Tegallalang, there are elephants. Established in 1996 to give "jobs" to Sumatra's vanishing pachyderms, the **Elephant Safari Park** has been rescuing and protecting elephants ever since, with a successful breeding program begun in 2006. Managed by an Australian and his Balinese wife, Bali Adventure Tours invites guests to interact with these mammoth creatures— ride, play with, and feed them—as a means to developing an understanding about one of the world's most endangered species. A member of the World Zoo Association, the Park meets international standards for animal care. Programs also include a Night Safari and an elephant talent show.

A Tour of Antiquities Found in the Ancient "Land Between the Rivers"

The narrow strip of territory lying between the Petanu and Pakrisan rivers—extending from Mount Batur in the north to the sea in the south—forms a natural replica of the Hindu-Balinese cosmos. It is no wonder, therefore, that the steep ravines, rock river-beds, and cascading streams of this area were the sites of some of the earliest king-doms and religious settlements on Bali, as evidenced by the great wealth of antiquities found here. The major ones lie along the "Kintamani Tour" route and can be seen in a day, but many more days may easily be devoted to an exploration of the other interesting sites.

Inscriptions from this area date from the end of the 10th century. In the beginning it was ruled by Hindus and Buddhists, religions probably introduced directly from India. After the end of the 10th century, as the result of a marriage between Balinese Prince Udayana and a Javanese princess, East Javanese cultural influences appeared in Bali, and the language of the inscriptions changed from Old Balinese to Old Javanese. Kings are mentioned in many of these, and there seems to have been a court center located some-where in the vicinity of Bedulu or Pejeng.

Myths and legends

Numerous myths are connected with this region, many of which concern demonic kings who lost their realms as the result of bad marriages or wicked behavior. Their palaces, battlefields, and sacred landscapes are often connected with archaeological sites. Such a king was Maya Danawa. His story is told in the 16th century *Kakawin Usana Bali*, a poem about Bali's ancient history. The center of his realm was Balingkang, close to modern-day Teges or Bedulu.

Maya Danawa was in fact the son of god-dess Dewi Danu of Lake Batur. He defeated many kings in order to extend his realm, and the god of the lake, Batara Danu, granted him

a boon: he was allowed to take a Chinese Buddhist wife. She did not feel at home in Bali, however, and soon fell ill. Maya Danawa went to the sanctuary at Tolangkir to ask for assistance, but the god did not favor someone with a false religion. Maya Danawa was so angry that he forbade the Hindu gods to be venerated, and dictated that he should be worshipped instead.

After some time his Chinese wife died, and Maya Danawa remained alone in his palace, enriching himself at the expense of his people. Twelve years later he was defeated by the god Indra, who tapped the ground at Manuk Aya (near Tampaksiring) whereupon a magical spring appeared. His warriors drank from it and received great strength. When they killed Maya Danawa, blood spouted from his mouth like a stream of gold, becoming the accursed river Petanu. Those who bathed or drank here encountered misery. The gods then bathed in a spring called Air Empul (now Tirta Empul), and from that time onward, the Hindu religion was restored and good kings reigned over Bali.

One of these kings was the Bedulu ruler, who was endowed with great magical powers. He would sit and meditate, legend has it, removing his head to reach the beyond. On one such occasion, an unnatural disturbance occurred and the king was forced to get a new head quickly. A pig happened by, and its head was taken and placed on the neck of the king. Therefore the king's name became Beda-Hulu ("he whose head is severed"). Some versions state that the king's real head fell to earth where Goa Gajah is now.

The king and his courtiers were ashamed of the pig's head, so they constructed a tower for him to live in, and his subjects were not allowed to look up, but had to kneel so they would not see the king's head. Somehow this became known in Java and the ruler of Majapahit sent his prime minister, Gajah Mada, to Bali to determine if it was true.

By means of a ruse (drinking water from a pitcher with a long spout), the visitor managed to discover the king's secret and caused his downfall.

Another story is that of Kebo Iwa, which literally means "bull" but was also the title of a court functionary in ancient Bali. Kebo Iwa was a princely giant in some versions, King Bedahulu's minister in others. He scratched rocks with his fingernails, creating many of the rock-cut monuments and reliefs found here today, for example Goa Garba and Yeh Pulu (see below). In some versions, he was killed when invited to the Majapahit court in East Java.

Goa Gajah

The first major site encountered coming from the south or from Ubud, just 2 km (1.2 miles) east of the Teges intersection, is the complex known as **Goa Gajah**, the "Elephant Cave." It overlooks the Petanu River and consists of a Siwaitic cave carved out of the rock, a bathing place, monk's chamber, a number of Buddhist stupas and statues, and several foundations. It received its name from the archeologists who discovered it in 1923 because of the giant head with floppy ears above the entrance, which was at first glance thought to represent an elephant.

The entrance to the cave itself is 2 m (6.5 ft) high and 1 m (3 ft) across, with a head sculpted above it that in fact resembles a man with bulging eyes, hairy eyebrows, protruding teeth, and a long moustache. He is surrounded by sculpted ornaments in which little creatures—men, animals, and gruesome heads—are depicted. It is as if they refer to a story, but it is not known which tale this could be, although some say they are running from an earthquake.

The grotto inside is T-shaped, containing 15 niches hewn out of the cave walls, which may have served as benches to sleep or meditate on. For this reason, it is thought that the cave once served as a hermitage. A four-armed Ganesha (the elephant-headed son of Siva) and a set of three *lingga,* each surrounded by eight smaller ones representing eight points of the compass and the center, were found at the ends. The cave may date from the second half of the 11th century. There are pavilions to both sides of the entrance, in which ancient statues have been placed. One is Hariti, the Buddhist goddess of fertility and protector of children.

The bathing spot behind the cave consists of three compartments which were discovered and excavated only in 1954. The central one is small and holy, the left one is for women, and the right one is for men. They are all sunken, flush against a wall, the top of which is level with the courtyard in front of the cave. Each side basin has three

The cave temple at Goa Gajah houses statues and scriptures of both Hindu and Buddhist origin.

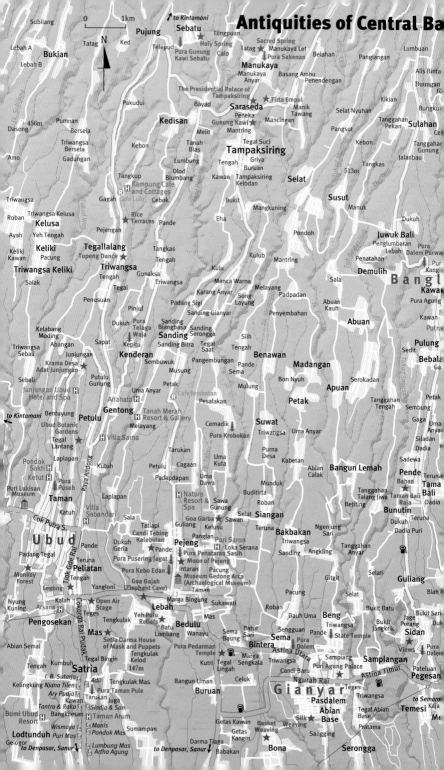

Antiquities of Central Ba

Subilang   **Tatag**   **Ked**   **Pujung**   **Sebatu**   *to Kintamani*   **Tlingpuan**

Lebah A   **Lebah B**   **Bukian**   **Telepud**   Holy Spring   Pura Gunung Kawi Sebatu   Calo   Sacred Spring   **Tatag** ★ **Manukaya Let**   **Belahan**   **Pangiangan**   **Lumbuan**

Manukaya   Anyar   Basang Ambu   Penendengan   **Alis Binta**   Buungan   6

The Presidential Palace of Tampaksiring   Bayad   ★ **Tirta Empul**   Manik Tawang   Selat Nyuhan   **Bungkua**

Pakudui   **Saraseda**   Peneka   Pangsut   Tanggahan Pekan   **Sulahan**   Ce

Kedisan   Melit   Gunung Kawi ★ Mancingan   Kebon   Tanggahan Gunung   Jalanbau

Triwangsa   + 456m   Pumnan   Bersela   Tanah Bias   Mantring   Tegal Suci   Tangkas   **Susut**   Dukuh

Dasong   Triwangsa Bersela   Gadungan   Lumbung   **Tampaksiring**   Griya   Tengah   Buruan   513m   **Juwuk Bali**

Amo   Dlod Blumbang   Tampaksiring Kelodan   **Selat**   Penglumbaran   Lebah   Pura Dalem Purwa

Triwangsa   **Roban**   **Kelusa**   Tangkup   Kampung Cafe and Cottages   Cebok   Bukit   Mangkuning   Manuk   **Demulih**   **Bang**

Ayah   Yeh Tengah   Gagah   Cafe Lulu   Eha   Pondoh   Penatahan   **Kawa**

Keliki Kawan   **Keliki**   Pacung   Rice Terraces   Pande   Kulub   Mantring   Sala   **Pulung**   Pura Agung

Triwangsa Keliki   **Tegallalang**   Topeng Dance ★   Tangkas   Kulu   Melayang   **Abuan**   Abuan Kauh   Kawan   **Putra**

Triwangsa   Tengah   Gunaksa   Manca Warna   Padpadan   Penyembahan   Sedit   **Bebala**

Salak   Tegal   Triwangsa   Karang Anyar   Song Layung   **Ga**

Penusuan   Pinjul   Padang Sigi   Sanding Gianyar   Siih   **Benawan**   **Madangan**   **Apuan**   Serokadan   Tanggahan Tengah   Sembung

Kelabang Moding   Dukuh   Pura Telaga Waja   Sanding Biangbasa   Sanding Serongga   Tegal Saat   Tengah   Gaga

Triwangsa Sebali   Abangan   Sapat   Kepitu   **Sanding**   Sanding Bitra   Pangembungan   Pande   Bon Nyuh   **Petak**   Siladan   Dadia

Sebali   Junjungan   **Kenderan**   Sembuwuk   Sema   Mulung   **Petak**   Sadewa

Krama Desa Adat Junjungan   Putulu Gunung   Musung   Petak   **Suwat**   **Bangun Lemah**   **Pende**

Junjungan Ubud Hotel and Spa   Uma Anyar   Cafe lembatan   Pesalakan   Triwangsa   Uma Anyar   Abian Calak   Baban   **Tama Bali**

Bentuyung   Anahata ★   **Gentong**   Tanah Merah Resort & Gallery   Cemadik   Purna Desa   Kabetan   Tanggahan Talang Jiwa   Taman Bali Raja   Teruna

to Kintamani   Ubud Botanic Gardens   **Petulu**   Melayang   Pura Krobokan   Munduk   Betiting   **Bunutin**   Teruna

Tegal Lantang   ★ Villa Satria   Tarukan   Uma Kuta   Buditirta   Dukuh   Dadia Puri

Pondok Sakti   Kutuh   Petulu   Cagaan   Uma Dawa   Roban   **Bakbakan**   Ngenjung Sari   **Guliang**

Ketut   Pura Puseh   Padapdapan   Natura Resort & Spa   Sawa Gunung   Selat   **Siangan**   Triwangsa   Tanggahan Anyar   Selati

Puri Lukisan Museum   **Taman**   Villa Sabandari   Sala   Goa Garba ★ Sawan   Teruna   Sanding   Angkling   Gitgit   Selat

Katuh   Tatiapi   Candi Tebing Kalebutan   Guliang   Kelusu   Loka Serana   **Guliang**

Cok Putra S.   **Ubud**   Pande   Dukuh Geria   **Pejeng**   Panglan   Puri Saron   Blah

Padang Tegal   Teruna   Pura Pusering Jagat   Pura Penataran Sasih   Pacung

Peliatan   Tengah   Goa Kebo Edan   Moon of Pejeng   Intaran   Pacung   Museum Gedong Arca (Archaeological Museum)   **Beng**   Bukit Batu   Jage Perang   Bukit Kuak

Monkey Forest   Legong   Yangloni   Goa Gajah (Elephant Cave)   Dauh Uma   Triwangsa   Bukit Jangkrik   **Sidan**   Duk

Nyung Kuning   Kalah   Arsana   Open Air Stage   Marga Bingung   Sukawati   Roban   **Teges**   Pura Dalem

Pengosekan   Teges   **Mas**   Tengkulak   **Bedulu**   Mas   Batur Sari   **Sema**   Sengguan   Pande   State Temple   Views   Pura Dalem

Abian Semal   Yeh Pulu Reliefs   Batu Lumbang   Wanayu   Sema Baung   **Bintara**   Marga Sengkala   Pura Dalem   **Samplangan**   Patele

Tengah   Kumbuh   Setia Darma House of Mask and Puppets   Tengkulak Kelod 147m   Kutri   Tegal Lingah   Candi Baru   **Ngurah Rai**   Astina Timur   **Pegesan**

Satria   I. B. Sutarja   Pura Pedarman Temple ★   Puri Agung Palace   Teges   *to Semara*   Kaja

Kelingkung Njana Tilem   Adil   Tengkulak Mas   Bangun Liman   Celuk   **Triwangsa**   **Pasdalem**   Tegal Abian Base   **Temesi**   Me

Ary Pudja   Pura Taman Pule   **Gianyar**   **Abian Base**   Pratama

Tantra & Raka I   Tarukan Juga   Siadja & Son   **Buruan**   Getas Kawan   **Bangklesan**   Taman Arum

Bumi Ubud Resort   Wismaya   Puri Mas   Manis Pondok Mas   Sumampan   Getas Kangin   Basket Weaving   Silk   **Sidan**

Lodtunduh   Gelogor   *to Denpasar, Sanur*   Lumbung Mas   Artha Agung   *to Denpasar, Sanur*   Darma Tiaga   Babakan   **Bona**   Sangging   **Serongga**

0   **1km**   **N**

Yeh Pulu is the site of many mysterious carved stone reliefs dating from the 14th century.

statues of women holding urns, from which water pours into them. There may have been a statue in the central basin as well, but it has disappeared.

Behind the complex are three remarkable carved stupas: a large one in the center and two smaller ones that look like branches coming together in one main trunk. Two sitting, meditating Buddhas, probably from the eighth century, have been found here as well. To the right of the entrance, further down, are the remains of a hermit's cave with a small pond in front.

Yeh Pulu

A couple of kilometers to the east in the direction of Bedulu just off the main road are the **Yeh Pulu** antiquities dating from the late 14th century. These consist of reliefs cut out of the rock and a sacred well. The reliefs are in a naturalistic style; horsemen, men carrying animals hanging from a pole, a sitting Brahman who holds an offering spoon, sitting women, an ascetic, a man carrying two large pots on a pole over his shoulder, the entrance of a cave or a hut, are among the figures which are depicted. So far, however, nobody knows which story is represented and what is meant by it. About 200 m (219 yd) north of Yeh Pulu is another, small bathing place consisting of two basins with naturalistic reliefs of men cut in niches in the rock at the back.

Southeast of Bedulu, in Kutri village, lies the **Pura Pedarman** temple with its 2.2 m

(7 ft) high stone statue of the six-armed goddess Durga, the spouse of Siva. She has the outward appearance of a demoness and is killing an ogre cursed to take the appearance of a bull. It is said that the statue represents Prince Udayana's Javanese wife, the mother of Airlangga. An oral tale says that Udayana was allowed to marry her provided he did not take other wives; however, he did not keep his promise. The princess became very angry and turned to black magic.

The Moon of Pejeng drum

The area north of Bedulu, around **Pejeng** and Intaran, contains many antiquities. The most important is **Pura Penataran Sasih**, which forms part of a group of three temples. *Sasih* means "moon" and refers to the "Moon of Pejeng" (see page 15), a giant bronze kettledrum decorated with geometric patterns, ogres' heads, and stars kept high up in a shrine in the temple. According to some stories, it is the ear jewel of Kebo Iwa; others say that it is the chariot wheel of the Moon God which fell in a tree in Pejeng and has been kept in the temple ever since. At first it was bright and shiny; however, a thief tried to steal it and was disturbed by the radiance of the "wheel," so he urinated on the object. As a result, it lost its luster and turned green. The thief was punished for this deed and died immediately.

Bronze kettledrums have been found throughout eastern Indonesia, and on Bali

The rock-cut Hindu temples at Gunung Kawi, the "mountain of the poet"

other, smaller drums have been found as well. Even a mould has been excavated, which proves that such drums were manufactured here. Kettledrums date from the Bronze Age, but it is difficult to determine how old the Pejeng Moon is. They were symbols of prosperity and fertility, and in eastern Indonesia form part of the dowry. Apart from the drum, the temple possesses a number of 11th-century stone statues, among them a Siva and *lingga.*

The "Navel of the World"
This area of Bali was also once considered the "navel of the world" and there is a temple bearing this name, **Pura Pusering Jagat** in Pejeng. It contains several interesting Hindu antiquities, probably dating from the 14th century, which are now placed in shrines.

Two statues, 1 m (3.2 ft) and 0.52 m (1.7 ft) high, in naturalistic style, are particularly attractive. They each contain four figures. In the taller statue there are dancing demons with bulging eyes, huge teeth, and moustaches grouped around a *lingga* in the center. The smaller one represents four gods, each with four arms holding various attributes, corresponding with the four quarters of the compass. Their heads are surrounded by a nimbus. There is also a shrine with a large *lingga.*

In a special pavilion, a 0.75 m (2.5 ft) high stone vessel is venerated. It has reliefs in a naturalistic style representing a group of gods and demons holding two snakes wound round a cylindrical mountain with trees. Animals and birds fly around it. This represents a story from the *Mahabharata* called the "churning of the ocean" in which gods and demons search for the elixir of life. They do so with a tip of a mountain (Mt. Mandara, sometimes also Mt. Meru); a snake (on Bali, two snakes) is used as a rope. In the beginning nothing happens. Then a magic horse with seven heads, an elephant with two pairs of tusks, a beautiful lady and a jewel emerge and, finally, a vessel with the elixir. This story fits well with the usage of the vessel as a container of holy water. It is dated with a chronogram corresponding with A.D. 1329.

Another temple in Pejeng, **Pura Kebo Edan**, includes the statue of a standing giant 3.60 m (11.8 ft) tall. He is called Kebo Edan, "the Mad One." The figure has a huge penis with four "penis pins" pierced through it right under the glands. The use of such pins to increase a woman's sexual pleasure is an old custom known throughout Southeast Asia. The giant stands in a dancing position and tramples a human figure, its face covered with something which may be a mask, as it is tied with ribbons at the back. The figure might represent a demonic manifestation of Siva as a dancer. There is another statue representing a fat, crouching demon holding a big skull upside down in front of his chest. The demon is wearing a diadem decorated with small skulls on his curly hair. The style of these statues points to the 13th-14th centuries.

While in the Pejeng area, stop in also at the **Museum Gedong Arca**, located just 2 km (1.2 miles) north of Bedulu on the main road. Displayed are quite a number of stone sarcophagi, Neolithic axe heads, bronze jewelry and figurines, and Chinese ceramics.

Coffee break
On the road from Pejeng to Tampaksiring, in Banjar Seributu, is **Buana Amertha Sari Coffee Farm**, where there are free samples of plain tea, lemon tea and ginger tea, as well as coffee and hot chocolate (cocoa), all grown on the property. Guided strolls through the landscaped gardens also make a nice road-trip break. Also available is *kopi luwak,* coffee made from coffee berries eaten by the Asian palm civet (*Paradoxurus hermaphroditus*), then passed through its digestive tract. It is said that the digestive juices in the cat's stomach renders the beans "special."

Rock-cut caves

From Pejeng the road begins a slow but steady ascent toward Mt. Batur. Northeast of Pejeng, **Goa Garba** lies on the western side of the Pakrisan River. The complex can be entered via steep steps through a gateway at the back of the Pengukurukuran temple in Sawah Gunung village. There is a hermitage here consisting of three caves with slanting roofs, and there is an inscription in Kadiri square script in one of these saying *"sri,"* a lucky sign. On the basis of the script, the complex may be dated to the late 11th century. Water basins with spouts are hewn in front of the niches. There are several pedestals with fragments of stone statues and a *lingga*. In the temple above, there are two stone Ganeshas, a *lingga*, and a winged stone snake with an inscription dated A.D. 1194.

Mountain of the poet

About halfway to the top, just near the source of the Pakrisan River, are two sites of great antiquity. The first, near Tampaksiring, is a complex of rock-cut monuments dating from the late 11th century and known as **Gunung Kawi**, the "mountain of the poet." The poet in this case is none other than the god Siva. In the ravines, on both sides of the river, royal tombs, a hermitage, and monks' caves have been cut out of solid rock. The main entrance to the site can be reached via a steep footpath that begins by a large parking lot lined with souvenir stalls on the east side of the road.

Upon entering the site, to the left is a rock-cut monument consisting of four facades suggesting the shape of temples. Each is surrounded by an oval-shaped niche about 7 m (23 ft) high; the reliefs are covered with a kind of plaster. On the other side of the ravine are five niches with similar facades carved in the rock. In the bases of all these, holes have been made that once contained stone boxes divided into nine squares, corresponding to the eight quarters of the compass and the center. The monuments are connected with the youngest son of the powerful East Javanese King Airlangga, who lived in the 11th century and was of Balinese descent via his father, Udayana. It is known that he issued edicts between A.D. 1050 and 1078. The central monument of the five may be devoted to him because there is an inscription in Kadiri square script at the top reading: "The king monumentalized in Jalu," which may refer to the name of the site.

Next to the monuments is a rock-cut monastery complex consisting of several caves with a free-standing building hewn out of the rock in the center. Characteristic are the large, rectangular apertures and oval-shaped entrances, with overhanging roofs, now overgrown with grass.

The sacred spring at Tirta Empul

In an inscription dated A.D. 960 discovered in **Pura Sakenan** temple in Manukaya village, mention is made of a double pool dug around a well near the source of the Pakrisan River. The king transformed this into a holy bathing place. This is the present-day **Tirta Empul**, one of Bali's most sacred spots. It lies just north of Tampaksiring along a well-marked road.

The sanctuary consists of an outer courtyard with a basin for public use and a central courtyard with two adjacent, rectangular pools (for those who fought Maya Danawa and were cleansed by the god Indra) containing clear, transparent water, all surrounded by a low wall of recent construction. There are 15 spouts in these pools. The inner court has two pavilions, one of which is for the god Indra (Maya Danawa's adversary), and more than 20 small shrines with newly-carved and wooden doors decorated with reliefs. Among these is one devoted to the rice goddess Dewi Sri, one to the Lord of Majapahit, and one to Mt. Batur.

Devotees purify themselves at Tirta Empul spring.

Sights of the Old Kingdom of Mengwi

The Mengwi rulers were well known for their temples. The oldest of these is **Pura Sadha**, a few hundred meters south of the main road in **Kapal**, about 16 km (10 miles) northwest of Denpasar. The name *sada* may derive from the Old Javanese and Sanskrit term *prasada*, meaning "a tower temple." There is indeed a huge shrine in the shape of a tiered tower in the inner court. The local inhabitants call this temple a *candi*, a funerary monument for a deceased king.

According to the chronicles of the Mengwi rulers, the son of the first Cokorda or Lord of Mengwi, I Gusti Agung Panji, received a shrine in this temple after his death around 1710. The divinity of the temple is Bhatara Jayengrat, the Divine World Conqueror.

Kapal

At present the complex is venerated and maintained by the people of Kapal, irrespective of their caste or kin group. It was severely damaged during the earthquake of 1917 and was restored in 1950. The leader of the team of Balinese craftsmen was I Made Nama, and it is said that the construction of the tall tower was quite a challenge for him and his men.

The forecourt of the temple is large and spacious; a big tree grows at the center. The temple complex is surrounded by a wall of red brick constructed in the traditional way, without mortar. By rubbing one stone against the other, a fine powder crumbles from the surface layers. When water is added to it, the stones can be simply stuck together.

A split gateway on the west side leads to the central courtyard. A second, closed gateway with a three-tiered roof on the west side gives way to the inner court, where there are 16 shrines. Right in front of the gateway is the *prasada* and behind it a square pedestal with 54 little stone seats. These are shrines for the *satya*, the servants, and facing them in one shrine in the south are the three *mekel satya*, their leaders.

The following story is connected with these shrines. A long time ago, when a king of Majapahit in East Java died, he was cremated and his ashes were carried by 54 men towards the sea in a bamboo tower (*bukur*) with a tiered roof. The tower was placed on a little boat (*kapal*), on which were seated the 54 followers (*patih*) of the deceased and three leaders (*mekel*). The boat, however, was stranded at sea.

This episode has been transposed to the temple and is symbolized in the stone tower at the center and in the pedestals with the 54 and three stone seats the tower being a replica of the bamboo cremation structure. Close to it, to the south, is a shrine with an 11-tiered roof, called "little garden with a pond" (*taman*). During the temple festival on Tumpek Kuningan, its "water" is used to bathe the god of the tower. This is in fact very convenient, because then a long tour outside the temple to a bathing place is not necessary.

Replicas of mountains that are important for south Bali (Mts. Agung, Batur, Sekanana, and Batukaru) are found in shrines in the north and the east of the inner court, which has a tiered roof in the *meru* (pagoda) style. The number of tiers is always odd, the highest being 11, which is only suitable for the most important peak. In this case it represents Mt. Agung.

There are more shrines in the north and the east devoted to various divine kings, including a *padmasana* seat in which the god Siva in his manifestation as Surya is venerated, and a little building in which a *barong* mask is kept.

Kapal to Mengwi

Along the north side of the main road in Kapal, a grand *pura puseh* temple includes relief panels on its outer wall depicting scenes from the *Ramayana*. The long *bale gede* pavilion is clearly visible from the road.

In **Mengwi** town, once the political center of the region, is the stately **Pura Taman Ayun** surrounded by tall walls with a bell tower bearing lovely carvings in the northern corner. "Taman Ayun" refers to a huge open space

Pura Taman Ayun, built in 1634, dominates Mengwi, with its multiple pagoda roofs.

(*ayun*) representing a garden (*taman*). It was constructed under the first raja of Mengwi, I Gusti Agung Putu, in 1634 as a royal family temple in which to worship ancestors, and was damaged by a violent earthquake in 1917. Repairs were done in stages to return the temple to its original condition.

Surrounded by a moat filled with lotuses — a concept duplicated from Kertha Gosa in the mighty Klungkung kingdom — it seems to "float," representing the heavens, where divine nymphs and ancestors relax in similar pavilions, enjoying themselves.

The temple complex consists of a forecourt, a central court, and a spacious inner court. A tall stone gateway with wooden doors leads into it. The inner court has rows of shrines on the north and east sides, and carved stone pedestals with wooden pavilions to the west. The total number of structures is 27. Apart from the divine ancestor of the dynasty, the mountains so important to Mengwi (Agung, Batur, Batukaru, Pengelengan, and Mangu) are represented here by shrines with slender tiered roofs in the north and the east. Replicas of temples founded by the Mengwi rulers atop these mountains (Pura Pucak) and bordering the sea (Pura Ulun Siwi), and of state temples built by former Mengwi rulers (Pura Sada, Pura Bekak) are also here. The basement of a pavilion in which the Brahman priest prepares holy water during temple festivals (*bale pawedan*) is decorated with a relief series focusing on Arjuna, who meditated to receive a grant from the gods, who sent nymphs to seduce him as a test. On the wooden wall of the *bale murda* pavilion is a colorful painting.

Today the family of Puri Gede Mengwi still maintains the temple, assisted by a committee of local traditional leaders. In 2010, vehicle traffic in front of the temple was redirected to a new parking area and the former road made into a pedestrian walkway to accommodate the large number of people who visit Pura Taman Ayun each day.

Held every Wednesday and Sunday at the **cattle market** in **Beringkit**, northwest of Kapal, herds of buffaloes and cows crowd the road and often block traffic along the Denpasar highway. Also traded are goats, chickens, and ducks, with a vibrant traditional market selling everything from clothes to flowers and agricultural equipment.

Tabanan town and the arts

Tabanan Regency is Bali's verdant "rice bowl." Medium sized and bustling, **Tabanan town** is the administrative center of the regency. Although it appears rather nondescript and has not much of a reputation among tourists, the arts are actually well represented here. At the end of the 19th century, Tabanan already had skilled woodcarvers, and there were (and still are) many good *juru basa*, or bards, who recited fragments of classic poems (*kakawin*) at festive occasions and during *Bebasan* recital club contests. Also, among the regency's citizens are award-winning artists in literature, painting, traditional Balinese architecture, dance, and puppetry.

Bali's best known dancer, the late I Ketut Maria (also spelled "Marya"), commonly known as "Mario" is associated with Tabanan. He was born at the end of the 19th century and died in 1968. Although he was actually born in Denpasar, he was raised in Tabanan under the guardianship of Anak Agung Ngurah Made Kaleran of the Puri Kaleran palace.

Mario performed as one of the dancers representing the female pupils of the witch Calonarang with the Gong Pangkung music club, founded in 1900. The Gong Pangkung, named after a village quarter in Tabanan, also possessed a set of *tingklik* instruments, bamboo replicas of a *gamelan* orchestra. Together with three fellow dancers, Mario experimented widely with this orchestra and traveled throughout Bali, giving *gandrung* (transvestite) performances. Mario's troupe also refined the lively *kebyar* musical style that had been invented in north Bali around 1900, and he developed a number of new dances for the ensemble. The most popular is the Trompong dance, in which the performer dances in a squatting position and plays the *trompong* (a row of ten bronze kettledrums).

Mario also created the Kebyar Duduk (sitting *kebyar*), in which he crouches while dancing and sensuously flirts with one of the musicians. In the late 1920s and 1930s, these dances were already well known to tourists, and painter Walter Spies made superb photos of them for the book *Dance and Drama in Bali*, which he produced with Beryl de Zoete in 1935–36.

Mario was also a teacher of many dancers who would later rise to fame, in particular I Gusti Ngurah Raka from Batuan. He was a very strict mentor and only accepted the very best pupils. Although he taught them the same dances, he assigned each pupil slightly different movements, to enable him or her to have something characteristic. To remember this dancer and teacher who put Tabanan on the map among the Balinese, a statue was erected in 1974 of the two dancers in front of the **Gedong Marya Theater**. A plaque on its base honors the beloved "Mario." Although the memorial is beautiful, the building—now covered with graffiti—is nothing special to see and serves as a community recreational hall and gathering spot instead of a proper theater. However, dance and other cultural performances are still held here. Check schedules locally upon arrival, if interested.

Just outside of town to the southeast is the **Subak Museum**, containing tools and implements connected with irrigation and agriculture. In the same complex is **Uman Bali**, a replica of a traditional thatched-roofed Balinese farmhouse.

Rich artistic traditions

Several villages southwest of Tabanan town are especially rich in dance and art traditions. **Kerambitan** (meaning "beautiful place") in particular, is noted for its *tektekan* performance, a procession of men wearing giant wooden cow bells with huge clappers around their necks and carrying bamboo split drums. They traditionally marched around the village during an epidemic or great drought to chase away the evil spirits and bring fertility to the area.

There are two palaces here, belonging to branches of the Tabanan royal family. **Puri Gede**, built in 1650, is home of the descendants of the first generation. **Puri Anyar** was erected in 1750 for second generation families and can arrange events for visitors upon prior request. "Puri Night Dinner" includes a candlelit evening meal at the palace with a *tektekan* performance. There's also a guest house here open to tourists.

In nearby **Tista** village, just 0.8 km (0.5 mile) west of Kerambitan, special versions of the *legong kraton* dance, called *leko* or *adar*, are performed. This is a dramatized adaptation of a classic tale (the *Ramayana*)

A photo by Walter Spies records the famous Mario (I Ketut Maria) from Tabanan performing the electrifying Kebyar Duduk "seated Kebyar" which he invented and popularized.

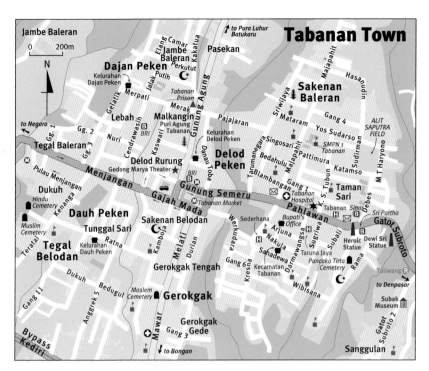

danced by three young girls: a *condong* (female attendant) and two *legong* (princesses). They change roles during the performance, but wear the same costumes.

Just over 1.6 km (1 mile) south of Kerambitan, **Penarukan** village has many good sculptors —both Brahmans and *jaba* (*sudras*)— working in wood as well as in soft volcanic *paras* stone. The village is also known for its *tektekan*, and for the painter Ida Bagus Nyoman Cekug from the Griya Gede Brahmans, who was a pioneer in the use of modern elements in his works.

Butterflies galore

Under 5 km north of Tabanan town on the scenic road to Mt. Batukaru is the **Bali Butterfly Park (Taman Kupu-kupu Lestari)** in **Wanasari**. A center for breeding, research, and education, it is home to rare and endemic species, including spectacular Birdwings (*Ornithoptera, Trogonoptera,* and *Troides*) and Swallowtails (*Papilionidae*). See a magnificent display of nature at its best when hundreds of colorful butterflies are released to fly each day. It's best to visit on sunny days, when they are most active.

A famous native son

West of Sangeh near Marga is the modern temple-like **Margarana Memorial** that's

Rare and beautiful species at the Bali Butterfly Park.

somewhat of a national shrine. About 15 km (9 miles) northeast of the town is the spot where Lieutenant Colonel I Gusti Ngurah Rai, commander of the Balinese nationalist forces fighting the Dutch, was killed, along with his 94 freedom fighters, on November 20, 1946. Greatly outnumbered by Dutch forces and under attack by land and by air, they fought to the death rather than surrender, reminiscent of the *puputan* of the Badung ruler and his family in 1906. The heroic death of Ngurah Rai is commemorated not only in this temple, but also in a poem, *Geguritan Margarana*, written a short time afterwards by a fellow nationalist fighter. His name has also been given to Bali's international airport. The memorial itself contains a stone tower, or *candi*, in which a replica of the famous letter containing his refusal to surrender is carved. Placed in rows outside are 94 pointed stone pedestals representing his fellow martyrs, bearing the names and villages of each.

Spend the day as a villager

Nearby, 15 families from one ancestor in Banjar Beng Utara, Desa Tunjuk, have cleverly developed an opportunity for travelers to spend some time with them to see how rural Balinese actually live. They call themselves **Taman Sari Buwana**, and everyone is involved, from the smallest child—who demonstrates his growing prowess at cock fighting (just for fun, of course)—to his grandpa, who chuckles with delight. Walk around the compound and identify the buildings housing the various family groups, see where the pigs and chickens are kept, and stroll through the vegetable and flower gardens. Learn to make offerings and decorations out of palm leaves (grandma and the aunties will demonstrate) and be refreshed with *kelapa mudah*, young coconut picked fresh from the tree while you watch (or participate). Mama cooks lunch, and accepts any help offered, serving it on banana leaf-lined rattan plates. This can be followed with a trip to the rice paddy to try your skills at plowing and planting, assisted by papa and the uncles.

Visitors also drop by the village school, where part of the proceeds of this excellent sustainable tourism program go to teaching the younger generation computer, English, math, and positive thinking skills. A day in the village can also include a two to three hour trek through the rice fields to a *subak*

temple and to see how Balinese ingenuity manages life-giving waters.

More adventures

East of Penatahan, Payangan village is the base of two other adventure travel groups, **Bali Quad Discovery** and its sister company, **Bali Canyon Tubing**. Traveling over small paths used by villagers via customized ATVs (semi-automatic all-terrain vehicles) or four-wheel motorcycle buggies—either solo or in tandem—tours stop at a traditional house to taste Balinese coffee, pass forests, and climb hills. White-water rafting trips conquer the Siap River, watching monkeys play and rare birds flying in surrounding forests.

Tabanan antiquities

Only a few antiquities have been discovered in Tabanan Regency. One lies in **Perean**, west of the main road to Bedugul. This stone shrine, discovered here in 1920, consists of a square basement with panels and a temple body with niches on three sides, an entrance on the fourth and a mock door with a kind of lock carved in stone. Porcelain plates of various sizes are mounted in the temple body on both sides of these niches and the entrance. The temple now has a thatched roof with seven tiers.

There are also remains here of three small, ancient buildings. The complex is surrounded by a wall with a split gateway. Inscribed stones discovered nearby bear the dates A.D. 1339 and 1429.

East of Perean, on the other side of the road, is **Pura Yeh Gangga** ("Waters of the Ganges") hot water springs.

Hot springs and ATV adventures

Further north, the **Penatahan** hot springs near **Penebel** and the rice terraces at **Jatiluwih** make the slopes of Mt. Batukaru well worth visiting. These areas can be easily reached by *bemo* on the road directly north out of Tabanan town.

Northwest of Penebel, **Tengkudak** village is the home of **See Bali Adventures** and their innovative way to visit small communities and enjoy the scenery while simultaneously getting an adrenalin rush. Exploring by ATVs, guests travel to surrounding villages and interact with local people, passing through rice fields and cacao plantations. The group also offers eco-mountain cycling trips and an Outbound Fun Learning Program.

A temple on high

The highway that passes through Wanasari ends at **Pura Luhur Batukaru** about half-way up the slopes of towering **Mt. Batukaru** (2,276 m or 7,467 ft), nominated as a UNESCO world heritage site in 2007. An unusual complex of shrines and a pool are set amidst dense tropical forests. The main enclosure lies at the northern end of the complex with two smaller temples, Pura Dalem and Pura Panyaum, to the south. A manmade lake to the east completes the "cosmic" design.

This was the state ancestral temple of the Tabanan court, and each of the shrines represents a different dynastic ancestor. Di Made, ruler of Gelgel between about 1665 and 1686, is represented by a shrine with a seven-tiered roof, and Cokorda Tabanan by one with a three-tiered roof. All of the shrines are very modest, without much ornamentation, which gives a great feeling of unity to the complex.

The nearby pond is fed by the river Aa (pronounced "ehe"). In the center are two pavilions on a little isle, one for the goddess of Lake Tamblingan and one for the Lord of Mt. Batukaru. The sacred peak thus surrounded by waters can be compared with the mythical Mt. Meru where the gods reside, enjoying themselves in floating pavilions.

East of here from Wongaya Gede, a small, rural road leads through some of the most spectacular rice field panoramas anywhere via Jatiluwuh, **Senganan**, and **Angseri**, where there are well-signposted hot springs. If continuing north to Bangli or the Bedugul Highlands (refer to p. 260 for more information about the Bedugul highlands), or back to Ubud, the country road continues until it meets the main north-south, Denpasar to Singaraja highway.

Climbing Mt. Batukaru

Only doable in the dry season (April–October), climbing Mt. Batukaru is a treacherous undertaking requiring an experienced guide, which can be arranged through most accommodations or at Pura Luhur Batukaru. It is partly covered by dense forest, and the trails can be extremely dangerous when it rains. Three trails start from Wongayagede, Sarinbuana, and Sanda and connect at Munduk Nyanggang. From there it is two or three hours of arduous climbing. The route from Sanda is the most difficult (seven hours to the summit) and from Sarinbuana is the easiest. Camping is allowed, except near the temple. Local guides can also lead nature lovers on less strenuous treks.

Sunrise at Jatiluwih, with rice terraces and volcanoes—the defining features of the Balinese landscape.

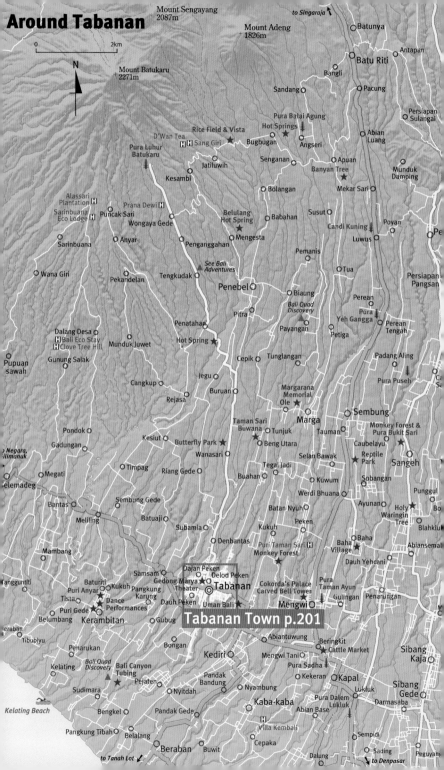

ACCOMMODATION PRICE CATEGORIES Prices are for a double room, including breakfast
$ = under $30; $$ = $30–$70; $$$ = $70–$130; $$$$ = over $130. DINING PRICE CATEGORIES Prices are
for based on a meal for one, without drinks $ = under $5; $$ = $5–$10; $$$ = over $10.

VISITING TABANAN See map, page 201, 204.

Tabanan town itself is equipped with banks, ATMs, a post office, a large Hardy's supermarket and a guest-house at the Puri Anyar palace.

ATTRACTIONS
Puri Anyar, tel: 0857-3968-5344 can arrange a "Puri Night Dinner" at the palace with candlelight and a cultural performance. Prior reservations are required. **Subak Museum**, Jl. Raya Kediri, tel: 810-375, contains agricultural tools and implements used in Bali's unique irrigation system (subak) and **Uman Bali**, a traditional thatch-roofed Balinese farmhouse replica.

TABANAN REGENCY
Tabanan Regency is Bali's agricultural heartland. The fabled rice terraces, so often photographed, are just the start: at their edges are plantations bearing many types of fruits—*salak*, durian, and mango-steen, spices such as cloves and nutmegs, and cacao and coffee plantations with small shops offering tastes of their harvests.

There are also adventure activities among the villages and a butterfly park, and some fine accom-modations, out in the countryside, including some high on the slopes of Mt. Batukaru.

ACCOMMODATIONS
Cempaka Belimbing Villas, Banjar Suradadi, Belimbing, www.cempakabelimbing.com. On the slope of Mt. Batukaru, the hotel here features 16 villas with garden, rice field or valley views. Winner of the Tri Hita Karana Emerald award for incorporat-ing the Balinese philosophy of balancing humanity and God, environment and other humans. $$$
Prana Dewi, 6 km beyond Penatahan in Wongayagede village, www.balipranaresort.com. Peaceful mountain bungalows deep in the Tabanan countryside amidst organic rice fields, water and fern gardens. The 13 rooms each come with a ter-race or deck and bale (pavilion) while the restaurant serves organic vegetarian and foods. $$$
Puri Taman Sari, Dusun Umabian, Desa Peken, Marga, www.puritamansari.com. Stay in a traditional Balinese compound owned by a member of the Mengwi royal family, surrounded by rice fields and coconut groves with three rivers running through. Participate in local life from the time *nenek* (grand-ma) wakes you with morning tea, through offerings, prayers, and mealtimes. Dance and *gamelan* lessons available. $$$-$$$$

Sanda Boutique Villas & Restaurant, Sanda village, on the western slopes of Mt. Batukaru, www.sandavillas.com. Set in an old coffee plantation, this place has spacious, luxuriously appointed rooms with air-con and large private balconies with breath-taking views. $$$
Sarinbuana Eco Lodge, www.baliecolodge.com. Four hand-crafted bungalows located at 700 m (2,300 ft) on the slopes of Mt. Batukaru 10 minutes from protected rainforest, with organic gardens that supply vegetables to the kitchen. Activities include nature walks, edible garden tour, trekking, massage, yoga, and simply relaxing. Holds cultural and eco workshops; contributes to local projects. Owners also do eco-tour consulting. $$$$
Villa Kembali, Cepaka, Tabanan, www.bali-villakembali.com. Located northeast of Tanah Lot, a private residence set among ancient trees and tower-ing palms and overlooking a graceful river. 4- or 5-bedroom villa with Bulgari bathroom accessories, full kitchen, and East meets West menu in dining pavilion. Private yoga, riverside spa treatments. $$$$

ACTIVITIES
Bali Butterfly Park, Jl. Batukaru, Banjar Sandan Lebah, Wanasari, tel: 814-282. Encounter rare butter-fly species from throughout the world released to free-fly each day, best on sunny mornings when they are most active. Among them are spectacular birdwings and Swallowtails. Open daily 8 am–5 pm, last entry at 4 pm.
Climbing Mt. Batukaru. Only the physically fit should attempt to summit in the dry season as the trails are unclear in some area, and they pass through dense forests and are usually wet in the humid mountain atmosphere. Locate an experi-enced guide ($80–100 there and back) through most accommodations or at Pura Luhur Batukaru. Camping is permitted. Take plenty of food and water, as none are available on the mountain.
Taman Sari Buwana, Banjar Beng Utara, Desa Tunjuk, www.balivillagelife.com. Highly recommended program designed by a very welcoming and large extended Balinese family. Spend the day in a tradi-tional housing compound walking through rice fields, learning to make palm leaf decorations, cooking cassava, scaling a coconut palm, or learning to plant rice or plow the field. Part of the proceeds go to village kids to learn computer, English, math, and positive thinking skills.

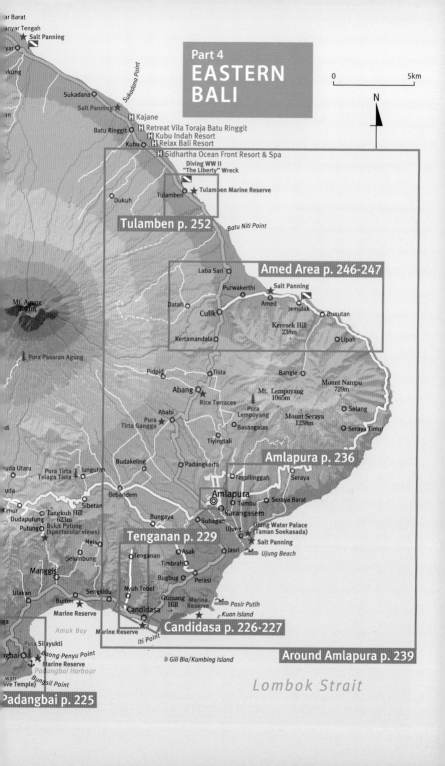

Part 4
EASTERN BALI

0   5km

N

Salt Panning

Sukadana

Salt Panning

Sukadana Point

Kajane

Batu Ringgit   H Retreat Vila Toraja Batu Ringgit
                 H Kubu Indah Resort
         Kubu H Relax Bali Resort
                 H Sidhartha Ocean Front Resort & Spa

Diving WW II
"The Liberty" Wreck

Dukuh   Tulamben ★ Tulamben Marine Reserve

Tulamben p. 252

Batu Niti Point

Laba Sari   ## Amed Area p. 246-247
       Purwakerthi
                    ★ Salt Panning
Datah   Amed   Jemulak
       Culik   Bunutan

Keresek Hill
238m

Kertamandala   Lipah

Pura Pasaran Agung

Mt. Agung
3031m

Pidpid   Tista   Bangle
                                        Mount Nampu
Abang   729m
       Rice Terraces   Mt. Lempuyang
Ababi   1065m   Selang
Pura   Pura
Tirta Gangga   Lempuyang   Mount Seraya
                       Basangalas 1238m   Seraya Timur
               Tiyingtali

Budakeling   Padangkerta   ## Amlapura p. 236

uda Utara Pura Tirta   Jungutan   Tegallinggah Seraya
           Telaga Tista
uda   Amlapura ◎
           Bebandem   Tumbu Seraya Barat
uda Sibetan   Bungaya   Karangasem
     Tangkuh Hill   Subagan Ujung   Ujung Water Palace
Dudaputung 623m   ★   (Taman Soekasada)
Putung Bukit Putung   ★ Salt Panning
        (spectacular views)   ## Tenganan p. 229
Ngis   Asak   Jasri
Selumbung   Tenganan   ≋ Ujung Beach
                           Timbrah
Manggis   Bugbug Perasi
                     Nyuh Tebel
Ulakan   Sengkidu   Gumang Marine   ≋ Pasir Putih
       Buiton ★   Hill   Reserve
       Marine Reserve Candidasa ★ Kuan Island
ga   ## Candidasa p. 226-227
                  Marine Reserve
       Amuk Bay   Iti Point   ## Around Amlapura p. 239
   Pura Silayukti
gbai ★ Baong Penyu Point   ⬠ Gili Bia/Kambing Island
      Marine Reserve
wah ↓ Padangbai Harbour   *Lombok Strait*
ave Temple) Bungsil Point
Padangbai p. 225

INTRODUCTION

Visiting Eastern Bali

In Eastern Bali all memories of hectic traffic and seething southern resorts quickly fade. Rampant greenery takes over from tarmac and concrete; the lazy rhythm of village life returns; and the vast sacred volcano at the island's heart is suddenly almost close enough to touch. For many visitors this is the best place to seek out "the real Bali," whether on a day trip from the resorts further south, or based locally in one of the area's charming, low-key accommodation centers. Eastern Bali is also prime territory for outdoors action, home to some of the island's finest diving, snorkeling, and trekking, as well as many quiet beaches.

Choosing a base camp

There are three main accommodation centers in Eastern Bali, each with its own distinctive character and appeal. Scattered through the countryside and strung along the coastline, meanwhile, there are other individual accommodations for those seeking to absorb the Balinese atmosphere in splendid isolation.

Padangbai is the closest hub to Ngurah Rai Airport and the southern resorts. This is the main port for public ferries to Lombok, as well as speedy tourist boats to the Gili Islands, but it feels more like a blissed-out throwback to the days of the Hippie Trail than a bustling harbor town. Characterful budget inns, and a smattering of midrange guesthouses, line an arc of pale sand; seafood is cheap and tasty; and there are pretty little beaches just beyond the headlands that flank the bay. Back from the waterfront, meanwhile, the sleepy backstreets still retain the feel of a village. Padangbai is also a major hub for diving and snorkeling, with an array of long-established dive shops and some very fine dive sites a short ride offshore. Many travelers stop by en route for Lombok or the Gilis, and find themselves lingering. The small town's only cultural attractions are three temples, one dating to the 11th century, which attract multitudes of devotees during ceremonial occasions. Padangbai's unique feature is ferry and chartered boat services to Lombok and to Nusa Penida, both of which lure snorkelers and divers.

Further up the coast, **Candidasa** is the gentlest, most grown-up of all Bali's coastal resorts, a string of peaceful midrange and

Eastern Bali has gorgeous rice terrace vistas, without the crowds of sightseers common around Ubud.

luxury accommodations slotted onto the narrow strip between the steep green hills and the ocean. There are a good number of dive centers here too, and a mellow, unhurried pace, favored by the many long-stay visitors.

To the north, beyond Bali's easternmost promontory, is the area known as **Amed**. Until recently this corner of Bali was miles off the beaten track, but these days there's a definite buzz about the place. "Amed" is actually a catch-all name for seven individual villages strung along several kilometers of rugged coastline, each with its own selection of accommodations. The big draw here is the diving and snorkeling, which is some of Bali's very best, but the magnificent views of Gunung Agung and the sense that the rest of the world is a very long way away are also a big part of the appeal.

Beyond the three main accommodation centers there are other appealing options for overnight stays. Around the old water palace at **Tirta Gangga**, a clutch of budget inns provide a fine opportunity for a night amidst the rice fields. The glorious **Sidemen Valley**, meanwhile, is home to a handful of wonderfully tranquil midrange hideaways.

Area sightseeing

Klungkung town, also known as Semarapura, was once the most powerful kingdom in Bali. It is close to Padangbai but is also easily reached from Candidasa. Overnighters heading for Amed can stop by to see the interesting Kertha Gosa Hall of Justice, Bale Kambang floating pavilion, and a small museum en route. Close to Klungkung is Kamasan village, an ancient artistic center known for its distinctive painting style and silversmiths. Visitors are welcome to stroll through workshops to see the artists at work, and one even offers courses.

Tenganan is one of the few remaining Bali Aga villages, home to the island's original, pre-Hindu inhabitants. It is nearest to Candidasa, but also makes an easy day-trip from Padangbai or can be visited on a stopover to Amed. Like Klungkung, an hour or two is sufficient to stroll through the historic village to observe a way of life that is completely different to that of its neighbors. However, textile and handicrafts lovers may want to allocate more time to watch the artisans at work and to shop.

Amlapura and **Tirta Gangga** can both be visited in a single day. The Karangasem

Pura Goa Lawah, on the coast road between Klungkung and Candidasa, is a busy pilgrimage center, always bustling with devotees.

palace at Amlapura affords an interesting glimpse into the lives of Balinese royalty, with its eclectic blend of European, Chinese, and Balinese architecture. Also in this area is Taman Sukasada Ujung, a bathing pool complex constructed by the last Karangasem raja. It is a tranquil place, evocative of courtly life in times past, and well worth a visit.

The bathing pools at Tirta Gangga, 15 km (9 miles) north of Amlapura on the way to Amed, are a totally different experience. The lush gardens are the result of the constant care over the decades by descendants of the Karangasem royal family. The waters here are believed to be holy, and devout Balinese Hindus are often seen bathing or circumnavigating the rock paths through the ponds. On a cliff above is a fine restaurant serving international and Indonesian food, making it a good lunch stop. Several treks can be done from here—some easy and others more strenuous—and guides can be hired on-the-spot.

An alternate route from Amlapura to **Pura Besakih**, Bali's "Mother Temple," is particularly scenic, passing through plantations, over mountains, and into valleys studded with verdant green rice fields. The multitude of steps reaching the upper levels of Besakih are steep and the compound can be crowded if rituals are taking place, warranting extra time for a careful inspection of its many shrines and vistas.

From Besakih, the road leads north to the **Kintamani highlands**: Mt. Batur, its crater lake, and Trunyan village, a Bali Aga settlement with a mysterious tomb.

GIANYAR TOWN

A Palace and a Sacred Banyan Tree

The *bemo* men on the roads from the south yell "*nyar, nyar, nyar*" in loud nasal tones, delighting in stretching the syllable as long as they can. *Nyar* is short for Gianyar, once a center of royal power, priestly learning, and the arts. Today this political and administrative capital has been passed over by the tourist boom, but in one area of creative endeavor it still reigns supreme: **Gianyar** has Bali's best **roast pig**, or *babi guling*. This most exquisite and festive of Balinese dishes can be had in a number of stalls in the market or near the main square, though everyone you ask has their own favorite and will argue its merits against all comers.

Despite the absence of tourists, the town and its surrounding districts are full of places of interest. This can be a good place to get a feel for Balinese history and culture in a non-touristed atmosphere. The heart of Gianyar is the **Puri Agung Palace**, one of the best preserved of all Bali's royal houses, and home of Anak Agung Gede Agung, heir to the throne of Gianyar, former Foreign Minister, ambassador, and a prominent political leader in the 1940s and '50s.

Unfortunately, the splendors of the palace are not open to casual visitors. But from outside the walls, the majesty of an ornamented observation pavilion overlooking the garden near Gianyar's main crossroads are visible. *Tantri* animal fables are depicted in carvings on the lower part of the outside wall at the crossroads. This palace is also one of the few in Bali to maintain the *waringin*, or **sacred banyan tree**, which was the symbol of Balinese and Javanese courts. Gianyar's still stands in the open town square across from the palace, preserving somewhat the feel of a 19th-century royal town.

The Gianyar palace was founded in the 18th century, but rebuilt in a more splendid style when the Gianyar dynasty was restored at the end of the 19th. The original palace was said to have been constructed on the site of a priest's house or *griya*. The name "Gianyar" is

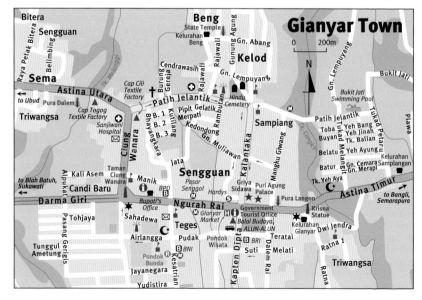

in fact an abbreviated form of *griya anyar* or "new priest's house."

Just next to the palace is **Pura Langon**, the "Temple of Beauty," which is the major temple for the extended royal family and one of Gianyar's state temples. Further to the west is the **Griya Sidawa**, home of the area's major priestly family and one of Bali's important centers of learning and priestly tradition.

Other state temples are nearby at Beng to the north, and to the south on the coast at Lebih. The temple at **Beng** is for the descendents of Dewa Manggis, who founded the royal line. At **Lebih**, a few miles to the south of Gianyar town, is the **Pura Segara** or "Sea Temple," which is visited in the course of many different festivals that occur throughout Gianyar Regency. The temple is situated where the land meets the sea in sight of the "demon's island," Nusa Penida, and is regarded as a "hot spot," a place where magical forces can be harnessed.

On the road going south from the Gianyar town square to Lebih stands a **Chinese temple**, one of only a handful found on Bali. There is another, smaller temple on the road to the west of Gianyar, just past **Kemenuh** village, hidden below the road in a ravine. 19th-century visitors remarked on the strong Chinese presence here, stating that it was once one of the wealthiest states on Bali and a center for trade. The temples recall the strong links that once existed between the trading community and the Gianyar royal family, who were their patrons. When the palace was rebuilt at the end of the 19th century, the Chinese community contributed to the work, and many of the buildings show a Chinese roofing style.

To the west of the town is the adjoining **Bitera** village where, on the southern side of the main road, is the **Pura Dalem** or "death temple" beside a river and beneath a spreading banyan tree. Also on the western side of the town are the main cotton and silk *ikat*-weaving centers. Their workshops are open to visitors. The fine cotton *ikat* produced here is used not only for the traditional *kain sarung* but for interior decoration as well.

Southwest of Gianyar lies the former **Keramas** court center, now known for its dancers, particularly of the operetta *arja*. Keramas is one of Gianyar's many theater and music centers, lesser known only because it is off the tourist path. Keramas was a major power in the area before Gianyar, and its

Bali Safari and Marine Park is home to Komodo dragons and various other creatures.

princes are supposedly descended from the great rebel Gusti Agung Maruti, who in the 17th century brought down the Gelgel kingdom. Oddly enough, today Keramas is better known for its world-class surfing beach than for its history.

Keramas is also near another old mini-kingdom, **Blahbatuh**. The rulers of Blahbatuh were descendants of Gusti Ngurah Jelantik, Gelgel's prime minister, known for a military campaign he led against Java in the early 17th century. One of the souvenirs of that expedition was a set of masks which are said to be the prototypes for all Balinese *topeng* dance-drama masks. These are still kept in a temple near the Blahbatuh palace, **Pura Penataran Topeng**. In the 19th and early 20th centuries Blahbatuh was home to some of the greatest court dancing in Bali. **Bona**, between Blahbatuh and Gianyar city, is now known for two of Bali's younger innovative artists, puppeteer I Made Sidia (son of I Made Sija) and musician Gung Alit, as well as its bamboo and rattan industries.

On the eastern side of Gianyar is **Sidan** village, just north of the Bangli intersection. Sidan has an interesting **Pura Dalem** that can be viewed from the road, featuring a series of carvings on the outer tower showing the semi-divine hero Bima fighting with the God of Death.

Near the east coast is the **Bali Safari and Marine Park**, a sister to Taman Safari Indonesia parks on Java. Fun for the whole family includes camel, elephant, and pony rides, themed exhibits for Komodo dragons and white tigers, cultural performances, and animal shows featuring birds, elephants, and orangutans. There's also an amusement park with kids' rides and a water park and an indoor theater featuring a contemporary theatrical and musical performance.

A Sleepy District Capital

Bangli is a small, sleepy town lying on the border between central and eastern Bali. It seems at first to contain nothing but concrete buildings and empty streets, which only become crowded on market and festival days. But **Bangli** is an old city, which may have been founded as early as A.D. 1204, judging from a stele in important Pura Kehen temple.

The market lies at the center of the town, surrounded by shops. On market days, the stalls spill into the street and customers flock here from the surrounding area to buy produce and manufactured goods. Opposite is the bus station, flanked by a row of shops owned by Chinese and Balinese merchants.

For most Balinese, Bangli is in fact the object of some ridicule; when someone says "I come from Bangli," everyone immediately bursts into laughter. The reason is that there is a psychiatric hospital here, a pleasantly-situated institution with beautiful grounds that was established by the Dutch.

Physically and socially, the town is dominated by the *puri*, **palaces** of the royal family. The Bangli courts established their independence from Klungkung in the 19th century and played an influential role in Balinese politics through to the post-independence era. Eight royal households are spread around the main crossroads. The most prominent is the Puri Denpasar, the palace of Bangli's last raja. Much of the palace has been restored by his descendants. The royal ancestral temple lies just to the north of the crossroads, on the western side. Huge ceremonies are held here, attended by all descendants of the royal house, including many who live in other parts of Indonesia.

Temple of the hearth

One of Bali's most beautiful temples, **Pura Kehen**, stands at the northeastern boundary of the town, seemingly erected in the midst of the forest long before the town itself. Three copper steles testify to its antiquity and importance. The earliest one, with Sanskrit writing, is dated from the ninth century and mentions the deity Hyang Api (the "God of Fire"). The second is in old Balinese, and the third is in old Javanese, the latter already mentioning Hyang Kehen and indicating eight villages around Bangli that worshipped the deity. The name Kehen is actually a variant of *kuren*, which means "household" or "hearth." The reference to Hyang Api as a symbol of Brahma may mean that there once existed a cult to the god that worshipped him with a rite called *homa*, in which offerings were burned on a small hearth. At some point, it seems that Hyang Api became Hyang Kehen, the "God of the Hearth."

Pura Kehen is the state temple of the old kingdom. It is constructed on a number of levels, after the manner of ancient animistic sanctuaries that are built into the southern slope of a hill, much like Besakih. There are

Map: Bangli Town

Steep-sided valleys and rice terraces just beyond the outskirts of Bangli town

eight terraces: the first five are *jabaan* or outer courtyards, the sixth and seventh ones are lower and upper middle courts or *jaba tengah*, and the eighth one is the sacred, inner *jeroan*. A flight of 38 stairs adorned with *wayang* statues on either side leads to the main entrance, and a frightening *kala makara* demon guardian is carved on the gateway.

In the outer courtyard stand a huge old banyan tree and a three-tiered pagoda with two *kulkuls* drums inside, as well as a flat stone for offerings. The *kulkuls* represent male and female and were used to signal war in the past. Today, their role is to announce ritual ceremonies. The walls are inlaid with Chinese porcelain, a common feature of ancient temples and palaces. The temple has 43 altars, including one 11-roofed *meru* (pagoda) to Hyang Api. Several are dedicated to the ancestors of *sudra* commoner clans, such as the Ratu Pasek and Pande, which means that worshippers from all over Bali come to pray here, especially on its *odalan*, or anniversary. The huge three-compartment *padmasana* throne in the northeastern corner has beautiful carvings at the back.

Warriors of the mountain

In the Bangli area, various types of ritual *baris* dances have developed that are typical of mountain regions, such as the *baris jojor* (eight men in a line with spears), *baris presi* or *tamiang* (eight men in a circle with leather shields), and *baris dadap* (men in pairs with bat-shaped, curled shields made from holy *dadap* wood). They are performed especially at *odalan*. One of the biggest *gamelan* orchestras in Bali can also be found in the Bangli region. It was captured from the Klungkung dynasty by the Dutch, who gave it to Bangli.

The natural scenery around Bangli is impressive. Cool air and quiet paths lead to breathtaking panoramas. About half a mile west of the town on the road toward Tampaksiring, northwest of Bangli, is a huge ravine with springs and a number of bathing pools and irrigation works sponsored by the former mayor of Bangli. Bathers and visitors must descend a long flight of steps to reach the springs, but the beauty of the spot warrants the effort. This is a favorite meeting spot for flirtatious young locals.

Bukit Demulih, literally the "hill of no return," is located farther west, about an hour's walk from Bangli on the southern side of the road. A small temple stands atop the hill, offering a magnificent vista to the west. On the way, in a landscape of bamboo clusters and farmland, there is a holy waterfall.

To the east of Bangli, there is another lovely road meandering through spectacular rice terraces and across deep ravines. It emerges finally on the main road to Besakih, just near Rendang. This road runs just south of the transitional zone between wet-rice and dry-rice cultivation, which form the two main ecological specializations in Bangli.

SIGHTS OF SEMARAPURA (KLUNGKUNG)

The Palace of Bali's Most Illustrious Kings

Semarapura (formerly called Klungkung and still often known by that name) centers around **Puri Semarapura** or "Palace of the God of Love," former home of Bali's most illustrious line of kings. So great was their power that the Klungkung kings ruled all of Bali, with lesser rajas serving as their advisers. Unfortunately, all that remains now are the great gate and garden, and two pavilions with magnificently painted ceilings overlooking the town's main intersection, one of which is the **Kertha Gosa Hall of Justice** and the larger Bale Kambang (Floating Pavilion) just behind it.

The rest of this splendid complex was razed to the ground in 1908 during the royal mass suicide or *puputan* against the Dutch, which removed the last obstacle to European domination of the island. A **monument** commemorating the *puputan* now stands across the road.

Inside Puri Semarapura, Kertha Gosa was a place for the monthly administration of traditional justice in pre-colonial times by a

council consisting of the great Klungkung king and his priests, and was also used as a reception hall for visiting dignitaries. Every year on the full moon of the fourth month of the Balinese calendar, regional kings from throughout Bali came here to discuss the needs of the "confederation" of the Kingdom of Bali. After the Dutch defeated Klungkung, Kertha Gosa retained its status as a court of justice. One table and six chairs remain. The king's chair is adorned with a lion symbolizing his position as chief of the court. The chair with the cow image was used by a priest, who served as both lawyer and adviser to the king. A third chair, bearing a dragon, was for the secretary. A Dutch controller (high official) would sometimes attend trials.

The Kamasan *wayang*-style paintings on the ceiling tell of the punishments awaiting evil-doers in hell, and of the delights of the gods in heaven. Different levels and stations in heaven and hell are described through the story of the hero Bima, who journeys to the underworld to save the souls of his parents. These scenes

The elegant Bale Kambang (Floating Pavilion) of Semarapura

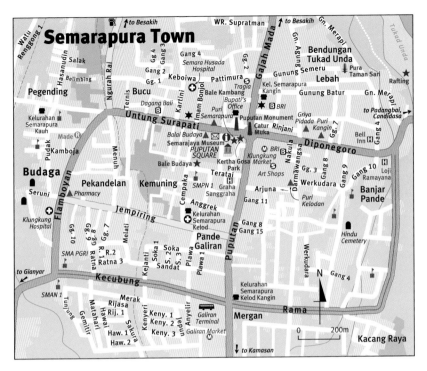

were used to alternately threaten and cajole anyone who appeared before the court. Interestingly, one section describes earthquakes and how they can foretell the future.

Like the Sistine Chapel, the Kertha Gosa presents a whole complex of ideas on the workings of fate and the role of the divine in human affairs. The ceilings themselves have been repainted three times in recent memory. The last complete refurbishment occurred in 1960 under the talented artist Pan Seken, although in 1984, weather damage meant a number of panels had to be repaired.

The **Bale Kambang**, behind Kertha Gosa in the middle of Taman Gili ("garden in a pond"), was originally a smaller, lower structure with fewer pillars, and was the headquarters of the king's guards. The Dutch restored the building, remodeling it into its present form in 1942. The ceiling was painted by Wayan Kayun, and depicts episodes from the story written in 1365 of the Buddhist king Sutasoma, who defeated his enemies through passive resistance. Also portrayed is the story of the commoner Pan Berayut, a coarse man who received great spiritual blessings. Horoscopes are the theme of another section.

Palaces and priestly estates

Members of the royal family who survived the massacre of 1908 were exiled to Lombok. They returned in 1929 and settled in Puri Kaleran to the northwest of the old site on the other side of the street. Originally built 1715–1720, only one part of the old palace remains: when the family returned from Lombok in 1929, the king enclosed it in a new compound, **Puri Agung**. Notable among the last king's heirs was Dalem Pamayun, who became a priest.

Another son, Tjokorda Gde Agung, still lives in Puri Agung and was formerly Klungkung Regency's *bupati* (regent). On October 10, 2010 in an elaborate ceremony attended by royal families from throughout Indonesia, Tjokorda Gde Agung was crowned the new king of Klungkung and was given the title "Ida Dalem Semarputra." A higher rank than "Cokorda" (Tjokorda) or "Anak Agung," "Dalem" can only be used by kings of Klungkung, as they are direct descendants of the Javanese ruler installed as Bali's king by Majapahit's illustrious Prime Minister Gajah Mada when he conquered Bali in the 14th century. When Indonesia became a republic in 1945, the reigning sultans and rajas gave

Colorful cloths on sale in Klungkung's market

up their titles and no new kings have been crowned until recently. The reactivation of royal titles on Bali is seen by some scholars as a strengthening of ethnic identity. Well-traveled, with an excellent command of English, the current king welcomes visitors any time (except at midnight, he quips). Meetings can be arranged through the **Tourist Information Office**, which is located inside the Puri Semarapura compound. Beside the Tourist Information Office is the small **Semarajaya Museum**.

There is a small entrance fee to Puri Semarapura, and visitors are asked to don a sarong, which is provided. Next door is the large, impressive-looking **Bale Budaya**, where cultural and other performances are held. Check schedules on arrival.

To the north of the main crossroads, on the right side, is a set of beautiful and important royal temples, with an ancestral shrine dedicated to the great king of Gelgel, Dalem Seganing. Just next to it is the **Pura Taman Sari**, or Flower Garden Temple, with a moat surrounding a main pagoda. Until today, it remains a sacred place for praying and meditation. In the 19th century, a famous Klungkung warrior queen meditated and wrote poetry here. There are many priestly estates (*griya*) in Klungkung with long histories connected with the royal house. The best-known is **Griya Pidada Klungkung**, once home to the chief priests of the court.

To the east of the city is **Banjar Pande**, the blacksmiths' ward, and the long-established Muslim quarter.

The best time to visit Semarapura is every third day on the Balinese day known as

pasah, when the **market** is in full swing. Tucked behind a row of shops to the east of Puri Semarapura, although it has lost some of its old atmosphere as a result of being re-housed in a new, multi-storied concrete structure, it offers a full range of local delights, including handmade homewares, baskets, flowers, vegetables, and the like.

For those interested in souvenirs, the row of **art shops** on the main road in front of the market is well-known to antique collectors. The astute old women who own them have been in business for decades, although age is now thinning their ranks. They all complain, however, that nowadays they can only occasionally find the sort of valuable items which used to routinely fill their shops.

West of the town

To the west of Semarapura bordering Gianyar Regency is the fertile district known as **Banjar Angkan**, separated from Semarapura by a spectacular ravine. This once served as a buffer zone between the two frequently warring kingdoms, and changed hands many times during the 18th and 19th centuries. Partly as a result, Banjar Angkan has developed its own unique identity quite apart from the rest of the region.

One of the objects of these frequent wars was the important **Pura Kentel Gumi** temple, "the Temple of the Congealing Earth," located on a bend in the main road west of Semarapura. The name of this temple indicates that it was a focal point around which the mystical and political forces of the former kingdoms moved.

Also to the west of Semarapura are the Tihingan and Aan villages. **Tihingan** is best known for its *gamelan* smiths or *pande gong*, who have been famous throughout Bali for centuries. **Aan** is known as the home of a learned high priest, Pedanda Aan, who advises people on the proper procedures for Bali's most important rituals. Between Banjar Angkan and Semarapura lies **Takmung** village, which also has many interesting temples, and is known as a center for the Resi Bhujangga sect, who are priestly worshippers of Wisnu.

Bali's original capital

The old court center **Gelgel** is situated 4 km (2.5 miles) south of Semarapura and actually comprises a number of distinct villages, notably Tojan and Kamasan. The entire area is filled with ancient and legendary sites from Bali's "Golden Age"—the 16th and 17th centuries—and this is the area to which all Balinese nobility and just about everyone else on the island trace their ancestry. The most important site lies at the very heart of Gelgel: the sacred **Pura Jero Agung** or "Great Palace Temple," which stands on the site of the former Gelgel palace. The temple is the ancestral shrine of the old palace, which was abandoned in the 17th century following a rebellion. Adjacent to it is the **Pura Jero Kapal**, all that remains of the second largest palace in Gelgel, that of the Lord of Kapal.

To the east of the Pura Jero Agung is an ancient temple, the **Pura Dasar** or "base temple," the lowland counterpart of Besakih providing a direct connection with the sacred "mother temple" up on Mt Agung.

The festivals held at Pura Dasar are spectacular, as all members of the royal family join in. It is here that the deified ancestors are worshipped. Inside are a number of stones set on a throne carved from rock, archaic symbols of ancestral worship. Nearby is the **Gelgel Mosque**, the oldest on Bali, which was established to serve the spiritual needs of Muslims who came from Java to serve the king in ancient times.

Further to the east of Gelgel is a large complex of graveyards and temples that are cited in the genealogies of many families from throughout Bali. Just north of this is a set of two unusual shrines, the **Pura Dalem Gandamayu**, which was the dwelling of Danghyang Nirartha, Bali's greatest priest and the ancestor of all Siva Brahmans on the island. He established this as a branch of the legendary graveyard of the same name on Java. One of the shrines at Gandamayu is dedicated to the descendants of Nirartha, while the other belongs to the *pande* or blacksmith clan.

The present Gandamayu temple was restored in the 1970s after being partially destroyed by the 1963 eruption of Mt. Agung, which devastated the whole area. The adjoining **Tangkas** village was partially wiped out and many lives were lost, but it still maintains some of its famous musical traditions, particularly the ancient and rare ensemble called *gong luang*.

To the south of Tangkas, near the coast, is **Jumpai** village, which is a reputed powerful center for magic. The benevolent *barong* of Jumpai is famous all over Bali, and there are stories of a powerful magician in the village who meditated and turned aside a lava flow that would have destroyed the village in 1963.

To the south of Gelgel is pleasant **Klotok beach**, an area of great importance in Balinese rituals. Processions to Bali's

A painting in the traditional Kamasan style

Besakih mother temple all pay a visit to Klotok to ritually bless their offerings.

Home of traditional Balinese painting

The adjoining village of **Kamasan** is a major artistic center, home of silversmiths and traditional Balinese painting. The many forms of painting found today in Bali all derive from the Kamasan or *wayang* style characteristic of this village, in which the figures depicted resemble two-dimensional shadow puppets. The style itself traces back to ancient Java, where similar figures are found on temple reliefs. The amazing thing is that this survives as a living art up until the present day on Bali.

Painters from Kamasan were once sent all over the island in the service of their royal patrons. The painters' ward is Banjar Sangging, but other parts of the village are known for their crafts as well. Nearby is Banjar Pande Mas, where gold and silversmiths work. The village also once provided dancers, musicians, and puppeteers to the court. Most of these activities have declined in recent years, but in the past they contributed to a lively creative atmosphere, providing inspiration for local painters.

The presence of *dalang*, or puppeteers, in the village was particularly important. The iconography of the two art forms is the same, as are the stories depicted, great epics like the *Ramayana* and the *Mahabharata*. Scenes portrayed in the flickering shadows of the *wayang* are rendered in red, indigo, and ocher, arranged to show the workings of natural and supernatural forces.

Kamasan's foremost artist today is the Nyoman Mandra (b. 1946), whose work best captures the refinement of the tradition. Mandra heads up a government-sponsored school devoted to ensuring that village children will continue their 500-year-old traditions. Visitors to the school can see how beginners are trained.

In addition to Nyoman Mandra there are many other practicing artists here, such as Ibu Suciarmi, who continues the tradition of female painters in what was previously an all-male profession. Artists at Nyoman Mandra's studio and workshop, where there is a small exhibit of the materials and tools used for Kamasan paintings—surprisingly captioned in English as well as Indonesian—are happy to let visitors watch them work.

Since Kamasan is off the tourist track it is refreshingly free of art shops. Visitors can visit the homes and studios of the artists, where their crafts are also sold. Don't be put off by the initial hustle of sellers on the street;

The beaches that line the coast around Kusamba feature distinctive black volcanic sand.

The "Perang Dewa" or War of the Gods ceremony at Paksabali, where participants go into a trance

Sea salt is still harvested in traditional fashion through evaporation on the coast around Kusamba.

it is difficult for these artists to make a living. One compensation for the buyer is that any money spent goes directly to the artists and is not lost on middlemen.

To the magical east

From Kamasan, there is a good road to the east coast highway. Turn east to go to Klotok beach, Goa Lawah bat cave temple (10 km or 6 miles), and to Candidasa and Padangbai. West will take you back to Denpasar (39 km or 24 miles) on a modern highway. Alternatively, go north through Semarapura to reach Besakih temple (22 km or 13 miles) and the hinterland of eastern Bali.

Moving southeast from Semarapura along the main road toward the east coast highway, on the other side of the Unda River are a number of interesting villages, including Paksabali, Satria, and Sampalan.

Paksabali is renowned for its Dewa Mapalu or Pasraman Dewa festival, the dramatic "clashing" or "meeting of the gods." This is held during the annual Kuningan festival, when idols are borne from the temple aboard palanquins down a steep ravine to the Unda River to be ritually bathed and given offerings. As the palanquin bearers proceed back up to the temple gates, they are possessed by the gods they are carrying and race madly in circles, colliding against each other in an effort to get back into the temple compound.

The adjoining village of **Sampalan** is the home of one of Bali's foremost traditional architects, Mangku Putu Cedet, who is a builder of fabulous cremation towers and traditional houses. He is thoroughly steeped in the arts of healing and white magic as well. When the Klungkung royal family holds major ceremonies, it is he who is asked to

perform a ritual to prevent it from raining.

An important village further to the east is **Dawan**, home of one of Bali's most famous high priests, Pedanda Gede Keniten. He is directly descended from the Gelgel court priest and is in great demand for major rituals. Adjoining Dawan is Besang village, known for its main temple, which has an ancient inscription under a giant pagoda. The Dawan area, situated among small hills, is another "hot spot" or center of natural and mystical power on Bali.

The main road meets the east coast highway at **Kusamba**, a fishing village with a dramatic black sand beach. For several decades in the late 18th century, the Klungkung palace was inhabited by a mad king, Dewa Agung Sakti, and Kusamba was the headquarters of his son and rival. At this time Kusamba was an important port; like Kamasan and Klungkung it was a center for blacksmith clans, whose skill in the manufacture of weapons was of crucial importance to any ruler. In 1849, when the Dutch conquered northern and eastern Bali, Kusamba was the site of a major battle in which a Dutch general was killed by order of the "virgin queen," Dewa Agung Isteri Kanya.

Not far beyond Kusamba is the unusual **Goa Lawah** bat cave temple, one of the state temples of Klungkung Regency. Legend has it that when Klungkung was ruled from Kusamba, a Mengwi prince sought protection here and entered the bat cave. He was not seen again until he emerged nearly 20 km (12 miles) to the north at Pura Besakih. It is rumored that no one has since tried to prove whether the cave really extends that far; the strong odor of bat droppings is no doubt a major deterrent.

Bali's Lofty "Mother Temple"

Driving up to Besakih from Menanga, Mt. Agung's silver-gray cone looms above, its summit still bare from the ravages of the 2017/2018 eruption. At 3,031 m (9,944 ft), this is the highest peak on Bali, and a major focus of divine power in the Balinese cosmos. The huge temple located here, **Pura Besakih**, is the greatest of all Balinese sanctuaries, the most sacred and powerful of the island's innumerable temples. For this reason, it has always been associated with state power. It lies at an altitude of 900 m (2,950 ft) on the southwestern slope of the mountain, offering spectacular views over the whole of southern Bali.

Pura Besakih is not a single temple but a sprawling complex consisting of many separate shrines and compounds, united through ritual and history into a single sanctuary. There are 22 temples in all, spread along parallel ridges over a distance of almost 1.6 km (1 mile). The highest of these, Pura Pengubengan, lies amidst beautiful groves in a state pine forest. Most of the temples, however, cluster around the main enclosure, Pura Penataran Agung.

In this same area there are many ancestral temples (*pura padharman*) supported by individual clans. Four public temples also form a distinct sub-group (*catur lawa* or *catur warga*) and are associated with certain kin groups. Local Besakih village extended families also have temples here.

Besakih is busy almost every day. Balinese often come in order to obtain holy water for ceremonies back in their home villages as a symbol of the presence of the god of Gunung Agung/Pura Besakih, which is required for most major rituals. They also come to Besakih at the end of the long series of funeral rites, after the post-cremation purification of the soul has taken place, to ready the soul for enshrinement in the family house temple. In all cases, the worshipper is sure to pay reverence at the triple lotus shrine of the Pura Penataran Agung.

Pura Besakih, with sacred Mt. Agung behind

The symbolic center

Pura Penataran Agung, the "Great State Temple," is the symbolic center of the Besakih complex. Originating probably as a single prehistoric shrine, its six terraces suggest a history of successive enlargements, the latest being in 1962. In all, there are 57 structures in the temple, about half of which are devoted to various deities. A study of these provides a glimpse of important developments in the temple's history.

The *meru* or pagodas were probably introduced no earlier than the 14th century, whereas the lotus throne (*padmasana*) dates from about the 17th or even 18th century. With the introduction of the *padmasana*, the ritual focus of the temple seems to have shifted from the upper terraces to the second lower terrace. The *padmasana* is now the ritual center of Pura Penataran Agung and of the Besakih complex as a whole.

The three seats in the lotus throne are dedicated to the godhead in his tripartite form as Siva, Sadasiwa, and Paramasiwa or, more commonly in the popular tradition, to Brahma (right), Siva (center), and Wisnu (left). These deities are associated with the colors red, white and black respectively. Behind the *padmasana* lies the Bale Pasamuhan Agung, where the gods of the Besakih temples take residence during major rituals.

Of all the present structures in the temple, only one or two predate the great earthquake of 1917. Although visitors are normally not allowed inside the main courtyard, there are several vantage points from where they can get good views of the shrines.

Temple categories

A dual structure underlies the Besakih sanctuary as a whole, through a division of the sacred areas into two parts. Pura Penataran Agung is the main temple "above the steps." Its counterpart "below the steps" is Pura Dalem Puri, the "Temple of Palace Ancestors." This small but very important temple, associated with an early dynasty of the 12th century, is dedicated to the goddess identified as Batari Durga, goddess of death and of the graveyard, as well as of magic power.

The Brahma, Wisnu, and Siva holy trinity is the basis of a three-part grouping that links the three largest temples. Pura Penataran Agung, the central temple, honors Siva; **Pura Kiduling Kreteg** ("Temple South of the Bridge") honors Brahma, and **Pura Batu Madeg** ("Temple of the Standing Stone") honors Wisnu. On festival days, banners and hangings in their colors represent these deities. Pura Batu Madeg in particular has a fine row of *meru*.

A five-way grouping links these three temples with two others, each being associated with a cardinal direction and a color. Pura Penataran Agung is at the center. Surrounding it are Pura Gelap (east/white), Pura Kiduling Kreteg (south/red), Pura Ulun Kulkul (west/yellow) and Pura Batu Madeg (north/black). This five-way classification, the *panca dewata*, is extremely important in Balinese Hinduism. At Besakih, however, it seems to have been a relatively late development, as it is not mentioned in Besakih's sacred charter, the *Raja Purana*, which probably dates from the 18th century.

The gods descend

The unity of the complex's 22 public temples becomes manifest, above all, in Besakih's great annual festival, the Bhatara Turun Kabeh or "Gods Descend Together" rite, which falls on the full moon of the tenth lunar month (*purnama kadasa*). During this month-long festival, the gods of all temples on Bali take up residence in the main shrine at Besakih. Tens of thousands of people from all over the island come to worship at the triple lotus throne, and solemn rituals are conducted by *brahmana* high priests.

In terms of numbers of worshippers, the annual ritual at Pura Dalem Puri is also quite remarkable. Within the 24-hour period of this festival, soon after the new moon of the seventh lunar month, vast crowds pay homage here, presenting special offerings with which to insure the wellbeing of family members whose death rites were completed the previous year.

But these great rituals are only the most important out of a total of more than 70 held regularly at the different temples and shrines at Besakih. Nearly every shrine in Pura Penataran Agung, for instance, has its own anniversary, almost all of which are fixed according to the indigenous Balinese *wuku*

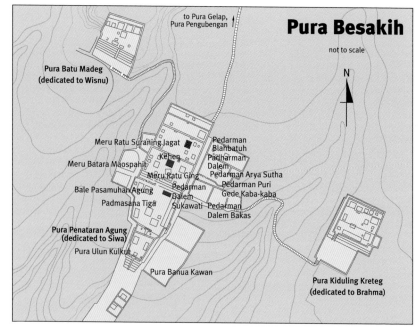

Pura Besakih

not to scale

to Pura Gelap, Pura Pengubengan

N

Pura Batu Madeg (dedicated to Wisnu)

Meru Ratu Suraning Jagat
Kehen
Meru Batara Maospahit
Meru Ratu Ging
Bale Pasamuhan Agung
Padmasana Tiga
Pedarman Dalem Sukawati

Pedarman Blahbatuh
Padharman Dalem
Pedarman Arya Sutha
Pedarman Puri
Gede Kaba-kaba
Pedarman Dalem Bakas

Pura Penataran Agung (dedicated to Siwa)
Pura Ulun Kulkul

Pura Banua Kawan

Pura Kiduling Kreteg (dedicated to Brahma)

calendar. The most important festivals, however, follow the lunar calendar. These include rituals conducted by *brahmana* priests at four of the five main temples, and also a series of agricultural rites culminating in two of Besakih's most interesting ceremonies—the Usaba Buluh and Usaba Ngeed—which center around the **Pura Banua** dedicated to Bhatari Sri, goddess of rice and prosperity. With the exception of these *brahmana* rituals, most ceremonies at Besakih are conducted by Besakih's own *pemangku* (priests).

State and temple

The performance of rituals and the physical maintenance of the temples demand considerable resources, and throughout the temple's history these have been at least partly provided by the state. During pre-colonial times, the relationship between state and temple was expressed in a largely Hindu idiom of religion and statecraft, but in the course of the 20th century this changed to one couched in legal and constitutional terms.

Besakih's earliest history consists of legendary accounts that associate the temple with the great priests of the Hindu traditions on Bali, beginning with Rsi Markandeya. In the 15th century two ancient edicts inscribed on wood, now regarded as god-symbols of one of Pura Penataran Agung's important deities, indicate heavy state involvement.

The Gelgel and Klungkung dynasties (15th to early 20th centuries) regarded Pura Besakih as the chief temple of the realm, and deified Gelgel rulers are enshrined in a separate temple here, called **Padharman Dalem**.

Through the turmoil and shifting politics of the 19th century, which saw the rise of Dutch power on the island, the temple was seriously neglected. The great earthquake of 1917 completed its destruction, but at the same time galvanized the Balinese, who then rebuilt it with Dutch assistance. Control was maintained by the princely houses, which were responsible for rituals and maintenance. After independence, Bali's regional government took over responsibility. Only in recent years has the Hindu community itself taken on a greater share of the burden involved in the temple's upkeep.

Cosmic rites of purification

The involvement of the Balinese with Pura Besakih is at no time more in evidence than

Besakih's forest of pagoda roofs is one of Bali's most iconic images.

during the great purificatory rites known as Panca Walikrama and Eka Dasa Rudra. Ideally, these are held every 10 and 100 years respectively, but in practice they have been irregular. The Panca Walikrama was held in 1933, 1960, 1978, 1989, and most recently in 2009, with the next event expected in 2019

The Eka Dasa Rudra, greatest of all rituals known in Balinese Hinduism, is an enormous purification rite directed to the entire cosmos, represented by the 11 (*eka dasa*) directions. Rudra is a wrathful form of Siva, who is to be propitiated. It has been held twice in the past century: once in 1963, and again in 1979. The Eka Dasa Rudra of 1963, held at a time of great political tensions, was an extraordinary catastrophe, for right in the midst of the month-long festival Mt. Agung erupted with violent destructive force for the first time in living memory. Such a strange coincidence prompted various interpretations, the most common being that the mountain's deity was angry, perhaps over the ritual's timing.

According to certain sacred texts, the rite should be held when the Saka year ends in two zeros. Such was the case in 1979 (Saka 1900), and it was decided to hold the Eka Dasa Rudra once again. The mountain remained calm and hundreds of thousands attended the main day of celebration, including then-President Suharto. This marked Besakih's new-found status as the paramount Hindu sanctuary not only for Bali, but for all of Indonesia.

Bali's Eastern Beach Resorts

Heading east from Semparapura, the highway crosses the border into Karangasem Regency shortly after Kusamba village, and a little further north it passes the Goa Lawah bat cave temple. Ahead lie the two main accommodation centers of Eastern Bali, low-key places that make for far quieter bases than the busier areas back to the south.

Padangbai

A right turn off the main road leads to **Padangbai** (or Padang Bay), the harbor for ferries to Lombok. The first international travelers simply stopped off here en route for points east, but they quickly discovered that Padangbai was a gem of a place in its own right. The main village lies to the east of the harbor, a network of sleepy lanes, quaint inns, and pleasant restaurants at the head of a crescent of pale sand, all ringed by steep, palm-clad hills.

The fishing boats moored on the main beach mean that it's not ideal for swimming, but a short walk over either of the headlands that flank the bay will lead you to unspoiled stretches of sand. To the south **Bias Tugel** is one of the prettiest beaches in Bali; to the north, meanwhile, **Blue Lagoon** has good snorkeling just offshore. Atop the eastern headland is the **Pura Silayukti** temple, where the Buddhist sage Mpu Kuturan is said to have lived in the 11th century. It is one of the oldest temples on Bali, and the location for a major ceremony every six months.

A few years ago Padangbai seemed to be rapidly rising as Bali's premier backpacker destination, with trendy bars opening, and a real buzz developing. A couple of abortive resort developments behind Bias Tugel made a mess of the once pristine hillside. These days, however, the majority of young travelers take direct transfers from Kuta or Ubud to the Gili Islands, and all they see of Padangbai is the car park beside the jetty, from where the fast boats across the Lombok Strait depart. As

The idyllic village of Padangbai is a great base for snorkeling and diving, away from the crowds.

Padangbai

a consequence Padangbai has slipped back into the tropical torpor that was key to its original appeal. Even the abandoned resort developments are slowly vanishing behind new greenery.

Padangbai is a major base for diving, and there are some long-established dive shops in the village.

Back on the main road, continue to **Manggis** village a few kilometers to the east. There is a lovely path from here leading up to nearby **Putung**. The path runs through woods and gardens and reaches Putung after a distance of some 5 km (3 miles), where there is a splendid view across the sea to the nearby islands. Another possible side trip is from Manggis east along a small road through isolated Ngis and Selumbung villages. The road finally rejoins the main highway in **Sengkidu** shortly before Candidasa. It is also possible to continue from Ngis on to Tenganan.

Candidasa

Continuing east another 7 km (4.3 miles) past Ulakan and Sengkidu villages, the main road enters **Candidasa** just after the Tenganan turn-off. The name was originally applied just to two small temples, one for Siva and the other for Hariti, which overlook a beautiful palm-fringed lagoon by the beach. Hariti is mainly worshipped by childless parents who pray for fertility.

A resort first grew up here in the early 1980s, but while tourism centers elsewhere in Bali have continued to forge ahead with unrestrained development, in Candidasa the pace slowed after the initial rush, and today it has a mature, easy-going aspect. At first glance the town seems like little more than a

Candidasa's low-key resort occupies into a narrow strip of land between the sea and the hills.

string of restaurants lining the main road, but lanes on the seaward side lead to tranquil luxury and midrange accommodations, particularly popular with European retirees.

There's not much of a beach at Candidasa—the original resort development destabilized the shoreline and most of the sand washed away–but it's a good base for explorations in Eastern Bali, and a much more relaxing alternative to Kuta, Seminyak, or Sanur.

Bugbug, Pasir Putih and Jasri

Four kilometers (2.4 miles) to the east of Candidasa lies **Bugbug**, a sizeable rice-growing and fishing village. Along the way, the road climbs through a series of switchbacks to the unexpectedly steep **Gumang Hill**. There is a beautiful panorama from the top, out over the Buhu River and the rice fields towards the sea, with the twin Lempuyang and Seraya mountains in the distance. On a very clear day Mt. Rinjani on Lombok is visible from here.

Bugbug and the surrounding villages are quite old-fashioned. Apart from the official village head, there is a council of elders responsible for all religious affairs. The elders are not elected, but enter the council on the basis of seniority. Another atypical feature of these villages is communal land tenure, and the presence of associations for unmarried boys and girls, which must fulfill duties in the context of village rituals.

Two rituals are especially important. The first takes place around the full moon of the first Balinese month. This ritual worship of the village gods is carried out in the central temple (*pura desa*), and lasts for several days. Most spectacular are the dances by unmarried boys (*abuang taruna*) clad in costumes of white and gold-threaded cloth, with headdresses and keris.

A second major ritual occurs in Bugbug every two years on the full moon of the fourth month. Four villages (Bugbug, Jasri–also spelled Jasi–Bebandem and Ngis) participate in a ritual "war of the gods," which is in fact the enactment of an old legend. The god of Bugbug had three daughters and one son. One of the daughters was to marry the god of Bebandem but she eloped with the god of Jasri. To appease the former, the god of Bugbug gave his second daughter and son to him, and the third daughter was married off to the god of Ngis. The war is to resolve the dispute, and the ritual battle takes place near the temple on top of Gumang Hill.

Shortly after Bugbug, close to the village of Perasi, roads to the right lead to **Pasir Putih**, also known as "Virgin Beach." This stretch of soft sand is still sometimes proclaimed a "secret" beach. It's a wonderful spot, backed by ranks of palms, and the swimming is usually safe, but the rows of sun loungers and the warungs offering food and beer make it clear that this is Bali's worst-kept secret.

A little further east at **Jasri** there's another unspoiled beach that has become the focus of low-key development in recent years. There are a number of accommodations in the area, and some eateries at the top of the beach itself. The swimming is less safe here, but it's a popular spot for surfers during the rainy season.

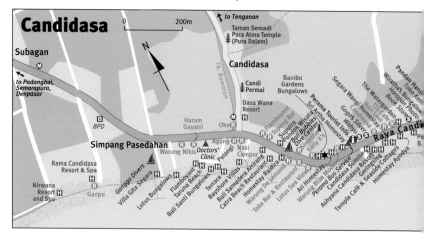

Eastern Bali offers some fantastic conditions for paragliding in the dry season (May to September).

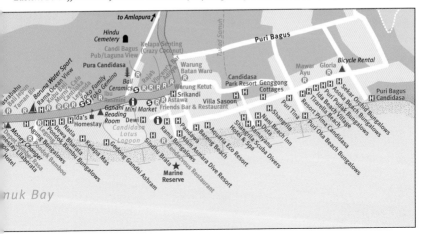

TENGANAN VILLAGE

An Ancient Village and Exclusive Community of God's Chosen Ones

Time is reckoned differently in **Tenganan Pegringsingan**. Here, each new day begins with 21 deep, throbbing drumbeats and lasts until the same pulsating tones are struck the next morning. Tourists arrive when the sun is at its zenith and the valley is glowing with light. They leave towards evening, when the all-important religious ceremonies commence. A month in Tenganan lasts exactly 30 days. Modifications to the calendar are needed to adjust to the lunar-solar year; altogether 15 days are added every three years.

The ancient, ritualistic Bali Aga (original, pre-Hindu Balinese) society of Tenganan opened up a few decades ago and became accessible to non-Tengananese. Its festivals have been publicized, and the village itself has become known as a result of its proximity to the Candidasa beach resort. Gone are the days when it was isolated and difficult to access.

It is said that all footprints of visitors to Tenganan were once literally wiped out once they left. In the 21st century, the village faces new and different problems. More parking space for the cars, minibuses and limousines that tourism brings have had to be added, and the art shops, which distort the community's divine plan, have been added.

Tenganan is frequently visited as part of organized tours of Eastern Bali, but it is also easy to visit independently if you are based in Candidasa, or are passing through with your own transport. The village is around 3 km (1.9 miles) up a well signposted lane that leads inland from the main road, just west of Candidasa. Bemo (public minibuses) traveling between Klungkung and Amlapura pass

Amongst Tenganan's many unique customs is the Perang Pandan, a ritual battle usually staged in June and fought by young men wielding bunches of thorny pandanus leaves.

the junction, where there are usually ojek (motorcycle taxis) waiting to ferry visitors up to the village. If the weather is not too hot, the walk back down to the main road is pleasant. There's a modest entry fee charged at the entrance to the village, where locals wait to guide tourists around the streets, temples and houses.

Microcosm of the universe

The *desa adat* (traditional village) Tenganan Pegringsingan is a microcosmic reflection of the macrocosm, an *imago mundi*. According to this divine plan, it is arranged systematically both in its delimitation from the outside world, as well as in its separation into distinct private and public areas within the village precincts itself.

The village is laid out in a large rectangle measuring some 250x500 m (820x1,440 ft) (about 6 ha or 15 ac), encircled by natural boundaries and walls. Three public corridors rise in terrace-like fashion, allowing the rain to flow down, running along a north-south axis from the sea toward the sacred volcano Mt. Agung. There are six lengthwise rows of compounds; the pairs located in the center and west are striking because of their closed fronts, which resemble palm leaf-covered longhouses.

The buildings and areas for public use are situated on the axes of the main central and western streets. There are a number of walled temple areas, longhouses, smaller pavilions, rice granaries and shrines, all of which suggest a strong communal life with pronounced ritual ties. This is where the 300 inhabitants of Tenganan live.

In the eastern compounds of the *banjar pandé* (community) live those who have been banished from the village, together with those whose customs are more like the majority of Hindu Balinese. Labor in the surrounding gardens and communal rice fields behind the hills is largely performed by tenant farmers from neighboring villages who receive half of the crop yield, leaving the Tengananese free to pursue their arts and rituals. Owning approximately 1,000 ha (2,471 ac) of arable land, Tenganan is one of the richest land-owning communities in all of Bali.

Divine origins

Unlike other Balinese villages, Tenganan traces its origins and its social institutions back to a written source, a holy book known as the *Usana Bali* ("Chronicle of Bali"). According to this text, the Tengananese have been chosen by their creator, Batara Indra, to honor his royal descendants through communal offerings and sacrifices. It states, furthermore, that descendants of the original villagers have been chosen to administer the surrounding lands, a consecrated place of devotion and ritual, and must use all available means to keep them pure.

The concept of territorial and bodily purity and integrity plays an exceedingly important role in the village culture. It is reflected not only in many important rituals (purifications and exorcisms), but also in the idea that only if a person is healthy, physically as well as mentally, may he or she take part in rituals. No one with a disability and no outsider can be admitted to the *adat* organizations of the village.

As a result of this divinely ordained scheme, the original layout and social organization of the village may not be changed. Houses, compounds, gardens, village council and youth groups are to be left as the gods have created them. Should anything be changed or taken away, the curse of the gods will fall upon the village, and its people will perish. Anyone guilty of not respecting the inherited order is banned from participating in village rites, and thus from sharing in communal property. In the gravest of cases, they are even banished from the village altogether. The *desa adat* is itself regarded as divine and almighty within the traditional social order.

Exclusive membership

It is not surprising that a community regarding itself as divinely blessed would strictly define its own members and place restrictions on outsiders. This exclusivity is expressed very clearly in the qualifications needed to enter the all-village council or *krama desa*. Only men and women without mental or physical defects who were born and live in Tenganan, having duly passed all ritual stages of initiation by the time they marry, are eligible to join the council. Although now more lenient, the practice of village endogamy (marrying within the village) also has had a restrictive effect until fairly recently. Women are now allowed to marry outsiders as long as they are from the upper castes, Brahma, Ksatrya, and Vaisya.

Newlyweds take their place at the lowest end of a hierarchical seating in the huge *bale agung*, the forum and sacred meeting pavilion of the village council. With the entrance of a new couple, the parents retire and everyone moves up a step, receiving new ritual responsibilities. The layout of the 50 m (160 ft) long hall is eminently suited to the numerous rites that bring together the gods, ancestors, and villagers. Here, members of the *krama desa* meet, dressed in ritual clothing, for communal meals with deities and ancestors whom they worship with prayers, offerings, dances, and music. In many cases, youths will take part in the performance of these rituals, either because the girls have been formally invited by the married women to dance before the *bale agung,* or because the village council requires one of the sacred iron *gamelan* orchestras (*selunding*) maintained by the boys' organizations to be played.

For such a society to work, a long initiation period is needed, allowing its members to prepare for their complex ritual duties and activities within the village council. When children enter a youth club between the ages of six and eight, they go through a "school of life" in which the behavior required for participation in the *krama desa* is learned, and where the manual skills and esoteric formulas needed for rituals can be practiced.

The three boys' associations of the village are named after the location of their assembly houses, located on three consecutive terraces along the western street. There are also three girls' clubs, that adhere to strict and formal relationships concerning mutual help, exchange of gifts, offerings, meals, as well as entire rituals. A girl must be at least seven years old to join a *sekaha daha* or girls' club, the meetings of which are held in the compounds of retired village elders.

The sacred *geringsing* cloths

Ritual clothing is an indispensable part of the sacred order of Tenganan. The double *ikat* cloths known as *geringsing* produced here rank among the masterworks of traditional textile art, providing a further sign of the divinely-ordained exclusivity of the society. The cloths are said to have been directly inspired by Batara Indra, the Creator, who was once sitting in a tree enjoying the beauty of the moon and stars. While contemplating the heavens, he decided to teach the women of Tenganan the art of *ikat* patterning. Since then, the community has obeyed a divine commandment to wear *kamben geringsing* or double *ikat* cloths. In this way, the villagers evince purity and the ability to perform rituals, qualities which these cloths protect from harmful outside influences.

Festival of the swings

Among the most important religious duties of Tenganan villagers is the festive reception of gods and ancestors, who from time to time descend to their megalithic thrones and altars in and around the inner village precincts. The presence of deities and ancestors is of great significance, above all during the fifth month of the Tenganan year, Sasih Sambah, for it is then that the universe, the village, and the religious community are renewed and given strength through the performance of extensive and solemn rites.

The ceremonies that take place then are reminiscent of old Vedic swinging rites performed during the *mahavrata* winter solstice celebration, which focuses on the god Indra. The swinging unites sun and earth, and together with textile techniques and recent genetic research, suggests that Tenganan may be connected with immigration from east or southeast India during Vedic times.

In a legendary account, the people of Tenganan are said to have arrived here while searching for the king of Bedahulu's favorite horse. Although it was dead when found, the king showed his gratitude by promising to give the searchers all land in the area where the horse's decomposed body could be smelled. A representative of the court, accompanied by the village head, walked around the huge area that today forms Tenganan, finding that in fact the horse's flesh could still be smelled for quite a distance. After the court officer had departed, the cunning village chief pulled a piece of bad-smelling horse meat from under his waistband. The remnants of the horse are believed to be scattered around the village as megalithic monuments.

There are other indications, too, that the Tenganan people have not always lived here. A copper inscription dated A.D. 1040 speaks of a relationship between the powerful governor from Java, a certain Buddhist reformer Mpu Kuturan in Silayukti (near Padangbai), and a nearby village named "Tranganan" that was then on the coast at Candidasa and later moved to the interior.

Proof that the Tenganan villagers moved from the seaside to their present location is provided in the design and placement of the original altars (*sanggah kamulan*) in the house compounds. In other parts of Bali this altar is always built in the corner facing east and toward the mountains. In Tenganan it is placed towards the sea.

When a member of the Tenganan community dies, his or her body is not cremated. Once the sun is past the zenith, the corpse is carried from the compound to the cemetery. At the grave the body is undressed, then it is returned to Mother Earth (Pertiwi), head seaward and face down.

Shopping in Tenganan

In addition to having an opportunity to see an ancient culture co-existing with the modern world, the other reason tourists flock to Tenganan is for their **handicrafts**, which are as unique as their culture. The Tengananese, particularly the younger generation, have adapted very well to tourism, and they are shrewd negotiators. There are no bargains here. The front of practically every house is a handicrafts "showroom," their open doors inviting visitors to step in.

The greatest treasures, of course, are the *geringsing* **weavings**. Produced in small villages in only two other countries—Japan and India—and nowhere else in Indonesia, double *ikat* involves the painstaking process of tying and dying both warp and weft threads to form a motif before the cloth is woven. Red, dark brown, blue-black, and tan are the predominant traditional colors here, and it has been said a drop of the dyer's blood is added to the colors to protect the wearer. Taking up to three years to complete one cloth, they are reserved for ceremonial occasions and are, needless to say, expensive, exacting anywhere from several hundred dollars to several thousand, depending on the size, motif and quality.

In ancient times throughout Bali, written records were inscribed on dried *lontar* (*Palmyra*) leaves. Tengananese men have revived this art, creating and selling *lontar* **leaf "books"** depicting stories, primarily from Hindu legends. Using sharp knives, a lot of patience and extremely good eyesight, they etch illustrations onto the dried leaves, then rub candlenut over the surface to make them last. The leaves are bound between two pieces of split bamboo for easy carrying and storage. A superb five-page book takes about one month to complete and fetches a higher price than lower quality works.

In the early 1990s, Tenganan's especially fine **basketry** made from the *ada* vine which grows only in this area and which is much stronger than the more common rattan. As well as large baskets, villagers also prepare place mats, urns, bowls, tissue holders, and boxes for the souvenir market.

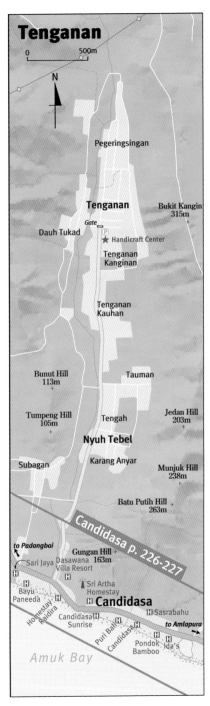

ACCOMMODATION PRICE CATEGORIES Prices are for a double room, including breakfast **$** = under $30; **$$** = $30–$70; **$$$** = $70–$130; **$$$$** = over $130. **DINING PRICE CATEGORIES** Prices are for based on a meal for one, without drinks **$** = under $5; **$$** = $5–$10; **$$$** = over $10.

VISITING PADANGBAI, CANDIDASA & SURROUNDS See maps, pages 225–227.

PADANGBAI

The bulk of the accommodations and restaurants at Padangbai are along the seafront to the east of the harbor, where you'll find the speedboat jetty for the Gilis. Bias Tugel beach lies behind a small hill to the south, with a few small *warungs* serving basic meals and drinks, while Blue Lagoon lies to the north. Rows of colorful outriggers are lined up on the sandy beach, east of the pier.

GETTING THERE & GETTING AROUND
Padangbai is about 31 km (19 miles) from Denpasar. It is well served by tourist shuttles from Ubud and the southern resorts. Perama, one of the best shuttle bus operators, has an office close to the harbor, where you can organize onwards transport. It is the main departure point for **Lombok**, **Senggigi**, the **Gilis** and **Nusa Penida**.

Large public ferries depart approximately every 1.5 hours, round the clock, for a 4 hour journey to Lembar, the main vehicle port on Lombok. Facilities on board are basic. The crossing can be very rough during the rainy season.

Several operators, with daily departures, will bring you to the Gili Islands. Tickets can be booked from accommodations and travel agents in Padangbai and all over Bali. Tickets booked in Ubud or the southern resorts usually include a transfer to the Padangbai jetty. Of the various companies plying the route, **Gili Cat** (ww.gilicat.com) has two Australian-built boats, with accredited captains and engineers. They depart Padangbai daily between 8 am and 9 am, with additional lunchtime sailings in high season.

A daily public ferry sails to Sampalan on **Nusa Penida**, usually in late morning, though the schedule is changeable. The trip takes about an hour.

The best way to explore the area's back roads is by car, motorbike (about $10 for a day; bargain for a better rate), or bicycle, all of which can arranged through your accommodation. For short local sightseeing trips, public transport is a viable option here. Bemo run to Klungkung, and to Amlapura via Candidasa and the Tenganan turn-off.

ACCOMMODATIONS
Accommodation in Padangbai is mainly in the budget and lower midrange categories, but many are very comfortable and atmospheric nonetheless. A luxury resort is perched on the hilltop north of the village.

Bamboo Paradise, www.bambooparadisebali.com. Away from the rest of the Padangbai action, this peaceful hostel has several private rooms, all spotless, and with reliable hot water, plus a tidy dorm, and pleasant communal areas for lounging around. **$**
Bloo Lagoon Ecotourism Villas, www.bloolagoon. com. Padangbai's upmarket interloper perches atop the ridge north of town, with 25 beautiful thatched villas looking out across the great sweep of Amuk Bay towards the mountains beyond. Environmental awareness and sustainability have been kept in mind here. It is, however, rather isolated from the Padangbai village scene, which is a big part of the attraction here. **$$$$**
Kembar Inn, Tel: 41364. Although it lacks the seafront location and the cheaper rooms don't offer a great deal of privacy, opening right into the communal areas, it's still good value, welcoming, and spotlessly clean, with a decent breakfast served on the breezy upstairs terrace. **$**
Padangbai Beach Resort, www.padang-bai-beachresort.com. A very pleasant option attached to a dive school, this complex of bungalows and balcony rooms is set on the main village beachfront, with a pool and a good restaurant. All rooms come with air-con and hot water, and the bungalows each have their own little pocket of private garden. **$$$**
Zen Inn, www.zeninn.com. The location isn't the most attractive, just around the corner from the port, but Zen Inn makes up for it with its assuredly funky style. The rooms come with open-air showers and tiny private gardens. **$-$$**

DINING
There are restaurants all along the main beachfront strip in the north of the village—most of them attached to accommodations—between the Gili speedboat jetty and the main harbor, and also some cheap warungs for authentic local fare on the main road into the village. Seafood is the specialty throughout Padangbai, and most places offer squid, barracuda, and whatever else the fishermen have landed, served up with sauce and vegetables.

The Colonial, www.okdiversbali.com. A cut far above the bare-bones eateries elsewhere on the beach strip, the Colonial has beanbags for lounging, funky wicker furniture, and a menu featuring stylishly executed seafood and an eclectic mix of Asian and European offerings, plus cocktails. Breakfast, lunch and dinner. $$-$$$

Depot Segara, Tel: 363 41443. An old favorite looking out over the harbor, this simple restaurant catches the sea breeze in its raised dining area, and serves up a typical travelers' menu of western and Indonesian dishes. It's a particularly good place for freshly-caught fish, simply grilled and served with veggies and fries. Breakfast, lunch and dinner. $-$$

Topi Inn, www.topiinn.nl. There's always a buzz at Topi Inn, with happy diners tucking in to freshly prepared dishes at the benches and tables scattered around its garden dining area. The food is a cut well above the normal traveler fare, with some delicious curries and pastas, as well as tempting deserts and cakes from the chiller cabinet. There are newspapers and magazines, books and board games to encourage guests to linger. Breakfast, lunch and dinner. $$

DIVING

At Blue Lagoon beach, shallow waters make excellent snorkeling for all ages. For divers, the white sand beach bottom slopes gradually to 22 m (70 ft), has scattered rocks, soft and staghorn coral, and a huge array of fish life: sea horses, turtles, moray eels, rays, and octopi. There are many dive shops in town, mostly foreign-owned.

Absolute Scuba, www.absolutescubabali.com. Tailor-made diving with onsite accommodation is available at this very professional dive school on the Padangbai seafront. PADI courses are a specialty, and dive and stay packages, with accommodation in the attached Padangbai Beach Resort, are available.

Geko Dive Bali, www.gekodivebali.com. Padangbai's original dive operator is still going strong, offering a full range of PADI courses, and daily dive trips with very experienced leaders.

OK Dive Center, www.okdiversbali.com. With an excellent attached restaurant and resort, this dive operator organizes daily manta ray dives aboard one of the most modern dive boats in Padangbai, along with PADI courses with instruction available in various European languages.

MANGGIS & SENGKIDU

Manggis is a small fishing village on Teluk Amuk (Amuk Bay), west of Candidasa. Its name is the Indonesian word for mangosteen, the delicious hard-skinned purple fruit that grows nearby. (Look for the statue along the road.) The development began here with the super-exclusive Amankila and the Serai (now Alila Manggis Bali), and has blossomed from there. Sengkidu is a few kilometers east of Manggis on the same bay, followed by Candidasa further east. Clumps of trees separate the three areas, retaining their uniqueness.

ACCOMMODATIONS

Lumbung Damuh, www.damuhbali.com. Located between Manggis and Sengkidu, this delightful *lumbung* (traditional rice barn) style homestay is excellent value, right on the beach and surrounded by lovely gardens. Two of the lumbungs sleep two people each; the third is big enough for a small family. Owners live onsite and provide free breakfasts. $-$$

Alila Manggis Bali, www.alilahotels.com. There are 53 rooms here as well as two corner suites in two-story thatched Balinese pavilions with private terraces. There's a spa, and the resort has its own organic garden, which you can explore with the gardener and pick herbs to make your own tea blend. The restaurant also serves healthy menu breakfasts. $$$$

Amankila, www.amanresorts.com. Located on a seaside hill, this place provides extraordinary luxury In villas with private pools. This is where movie stars stay thanks to the ultimate in privacy and security. $$$$

CANDIDASA

Candidasa is a good place to escape the bustle of southern Bali. Accommodations are excellent, and prices for midrange and luxury properties are good value, especially in the low season. Everything is oriented along the main street which runs parallel to the coast, with most of the accommodation between the road and the sea.

GETTING THERE & GETTING AROUND

Candidasa is abour 45 km (28 miles) from Denpasar. Public buses and bemo from Denpasar, Klungkung and Gianyar to Amlapura pass through town. There are also **direct tourist shuttles** from Kuta, Ubud and other resorts, with morning departures to other tourist destinations in Bali.

Explore the area's back roads by renting a car, motorbike, or bicycle. Cars with drivers can also be arranged through your accommodation.

ACCOMMODATIONS

The Candidasa area has a range of accommodations from simple bamboo cottages to ultra-exclusive villas, and is one of the best places to seek out low season discounts, when Candidasa is particularly sleepy.

Agung Bungalows, Tel: 41535. 16 bamboo cottages are surrounded by tropical gardens here, each with a veranda. Room furnishings are basic but clean; they are fan-cooled, but come with a decent breakfast and hot water and are excellent value. $

Alam Asmara Dive Resort, www.alamasmara.com. Now transformed into a "Romantic Dive Resort" with 12 deluxe bungalows, this luxurious place is also an active PADI dive operator. Honeymoon and Romance packages are available and the attached Rendezvous Restaurant is a fine place for a romantic dinner. $$$$

Amartha Beach Inn Bungalows, Sengkidu, Tel: 41230. West of central Candidasa, the 10 bungalow-style rooms here come with fan, bathtub, and outdoor showers. Some have hot water. The restaurant serves Western and French food, and a small Bar serves cocktails. **$**

Aquaria Waterside Apartments, Jl. Puri Bagus, www.aquariabali.com. A calm oasis by the sea, the spacious, airy apartments here use feng shui principles with clean architectural lines and cool colors. There are oversized terraces, sea or pool views, an intimate restaurant, and an ionized water pool. **$$$-$$$$**

Ashyana Candidasa, www.ashyanacandidasa.com. Formerly known as Fajar Bungalows, the seafront bungalows here have been upgraded, and are fresh and airy, the traditional Balinese architecture combined with modern conveniences. There's a spa and restaurant onsite, and a pool at the ocean's edge. **$$$-$$$$**

Bali Santi Bungalows by the Beach, www.balisanti.com. There are nine individual bungalows here, all very well appointed, with open-air bathrooms, terraces, and lots of natural light. They are set in tropical gardens with an oceanfront restaurant and bar, and an infinity pool. The resort is around 10 minutes' walk from central Candidasa, but it's right by the beach. **$$$**

Bayshore Villas, www.bayshorevillascandidasa.com. Hidden from the main street, and looking directly on the beach with rice fields at the back, the six tranquil villas here feature a mix of modern and traditional architecture, some with sliding glass doors opening to the ocean, others with bamboo ceilings and ethnic art works. Excellent discount rates are available off-season. **$$$-$$$$**

Dasa Wana Resort, www.dasawana.nl. Surrounded by forest and gardens, the bungalows here are excellent value. All are simply furnished, and come with a terrace, and fridge, TV, and air-con. There's an attached restaurant, and a small swimming pool. **$$**

Kelapa Mas Homestay, Tel: 41369. A relaxing hideaway with grounds filled with coconut palms and gardens. The bamboo cottages all have terraces for lounging; some have views and the more expensive ones have hot water and air-con. The management can arrange motorbike rental, tours, and activities. **$-$$**

Lotus Bungalows, www.lotusbungalows.com. A PADI 5-star dive resort featuring 20 beautiful bungalows, each with elegant furnishings, delightful open-air bathrooms, hot water, and terraces with ocean views. Other amenities include a swimming pool, and open-air restaurant. **$$$**

Pondok Bambu Seaside Bungalows, www.pondokbambu.com. A happy, tropical resort, with bright, simple rooms, all with air-con and TV. There's a small pool and a water filtration system that makes the tap water safe. **$$-$$$**

Puri Bagus Candidasa, www.puribagus.net. The 50 rooms and suites here are decorated in traditional style, with open-air showers. There's also a dive center office, and a spa with steam room. The restaurant overlooking the ocean serves Balinese and international cuisine and great seafood; snacks are served throughout the day poolside. **$$$$**

Puri Oka Beach Bungalows, www.purioka.com. This resort offers a wide range of facilities to suit various budgets, from Spartan budget rooms to well-appointed family apartments. There are a couple of self-contained villas in the grounds, as well as a good restaurant and a pool. Friendly staff can arrange tours, boat trips, snorkeling, and diving. **$-$$$**

Rama Candidasa Resort & Spa, www.ramacandidasa-hotel.com. This large resort has 72 air-con rooms and bungalows decorated with contemporary Balinese stylings. Some rooms have secluded private balconies with ocean views. There's a swimming pool and private beach, all in a peaceful setting. A full range of activities from water sports to mountain and village experiences can be organised. **$$$-$$$$**

Temple Café & Seaside Cottages, www.balibeachfront-cottages.com. There are attractive beachfront cottages with air-con and hot water here, some with funky, semi-outdoor bathrooms, and others with striking bamboo décor. There are also budget fan-cooled cottages back from the beach, which are excellent value. The attached restaurant offers wholesome home-style Western and Indonesian food. **$-$$**

Villa Gils, Dua Gils and Rumah Kecil, www.villagils.com. Private One-, two- and three-bedroom rental villas in a small enclave surrounded by banana and coconut groves. Villa Gils and Dua Gils are located one house back from the water on opposite sides of the lane. Rumah Kecil is opposite Villa Gils, on the water's edge. The road ends at Rumah Kecil, so there's rarely any traffic. A private white sand beach is accessible by a walkway. The accommodation comes with a team of staff, and private in-house dining is possible. **$$$$**

Villa Sasoon Bali, www.villasasoon.com. The four luxury villas here are exquisitely designed and come with every conceivable luxury. Each consists of three pavilions, with private swimming pool, courtyard, entertaining area and a fully-equipped kitchen with modern appliances and an "on-call" chef. Excellent discounts can be had for walk-in guests at quiet times. **$$$$**

Watergarden Hotel & Spa, www.watergardenhotel.com. The gorgeous bungalows here are set in a network of cascading streams, pools, and elegant gardens. Mountain bikes, hiking maps, and information about local events and places of interest are available. There's a swimming pool and a spa, and the Watergarden Kafe serves innovative food in a relaxing setting, including seafood and vegetarian dishes. **$$$$**

DINING

Menus are similar in the eateries along Candidasa's main road and include various salads, Indonesian and Chinese dishes, seafood, sandwiches or pizza, and desserts. Some offer steak, curry, pasta, and cakes. Prices are very reasonable. Many restaurants on the strip doubles as bars after dark, some laying on live music or traditional Balinese dance, though Candidasa's nightlife is decidedly low-key compared to the resorts of Southern Bali.

Friends Bar & Restaurant, www.friends-bali.com. A small, cozy restaurant with a fairly priced menu. Lunch and dinner. **$$**

Lotus Sea View Restaurant, www.lotus-restaurants.com. This restaurant, part of an Ubud-based chain, does great seafood on the water's edge. **$$-$$$**

Rendezvous Restaurant, Tel: 41929. 91m (100 yds) east of Candidasa Lagoon lies this intimate dining niche with sweeping views of Nusa Penida, fresh home-made breads and lovingly prepared Indonesian dishes. Breakfast, lunch and dinner. **$$-$$$**

Toke Bar & Restaurant, www.tokebali.com. With sea views, this place offers the best combination of Balinese ambience and Western intimacy. There's excellent Indian, Balinese, and Western cuisine, and a good choice of international cocktails and wines. Lunch and dinner. **$$-$$$**

Vincent's Bar, Lounge & Garden Restaurant, www.vincentsbali.com. International and Balinese cuisine is on offer at this bar with a wide range of international cocktails, a relaxed atmosphere with modern art and frequent live Jazz. Lunch and dinner. **$$-$$$**

SHOPPING

Kiosks along the main road sell sarongs, basic beachwear, sandals, and the like. There's a German bakery on the road just past Dasa Wana Resort and a mini-market next to Watergarden Hotel & Kafé for basic necessities and snacks.

The big find is in nearby **Tenganan** village, where most of the shops are actually the front room in people's homes. Their basketry is made from a special, locally-grown reed and has decorated five-star resorts and luxury villas throughout the world. They also sell hand-woven *ikat* textiles (you might get lucky and stumble upon some of the ladies weaving). The traditional double-*ikat gerinsing*—only woven in Tenganan and two other places in the world—go for very high prices for obvious reasons. The other specialty here is stories from the Hindu epics inscribed on leaves from the *lontar* palm, and young men can usually be seen in the village courtyard honing this craft. There's a small fee to enter the village.

ACTIVITIES
Diving & Snorkeling

Bali Bubbles Dive Center, www.bali-bubbles.com. Trips to Padangbai, Tulamben and Nusa Penida can be arranged here.

Gangga Divers, Lotus Bungalows, www.lotusbungalows.com. Various packages are available including night diving excursions at various locations.

Shangrila Scuba Divers, at the Bali Shangrila Beach Club, www.divingatbalishangrila.com. Owner Graeme is a Master Scuba Diver Trainer; he offers PADI dive courses, daily fun dives, and dive packages with accommodation. New dive gear is available for sale. Safety, service, value are taken seriously here.

Snorkeling can be arranged almost anywhere. Prices for 1.5 hours of snorkeling (including roundtrip transport) at the islands just off Candidasa are around $10-$15 person in a party of up to three people, which includes the price of the fins and mask.

Cycling & Hiking

Many places rent bikes. Be sure to test the brakes before renting. Cycling tours can be arranged through many hotels. Also check out **East Bali Bike Tour,** www.eastbalibik.com, for exhilarating and memorable bike tours in Eastern Bali.

A fine three-hour, 6 km (3.7 mile), walk from Candidasa to Tenganan starts just east of Kubu Bali Bungalows. Follow the ridge-top trail and drop left into Tenganan just before the fourth major hill. Magnificent views, but start early to avoid the midday heat.

A shorter hike starts at the tip of the headland east of town: walk the hill due northeast down to a long, deserted black sand beach. Other hikes from Tenganan to Putung or to Bedabudug (Bandem) are also good.

JASRI

Luxury accommodations have started popping up in Jasri, northeast of Candidasa, where the road turns inland to Amlapura.

ACCOMMODATIONS

Turtle Bay Hideaway, www.turtlebayhideaway.com. Surf, dive, snorkel, or just soak in the soothing breeze by the pool at this secluded resort with beautiful gardens and well-appointed wooden cottages. Gourmet cuisine is prepared from the resort's own organic gardens. **$$$**

Villa Matanai, www.villamatanai.com. Just 500 m (540 yds) from the Jasri surfbreak, this place is ideal for wet season wave-riders with a decent budget. It has three levels with five bedrooms. There's a swimming pool, and a restaurant serving local and international food and cocktails. **$$-$$$**

TIRTA GANGGA, SIDEMEN, & THE EASTERN BACKROADS

Water Palaces and Bali's Most Scenic Views

Once the seat of the powerful Karangasem court, **Amlapura**, the district capital at the eastern end of Bali, is now a clean and pleasant administrative town. Formerly known simply as Karangasem, the town was given its present name after the Mt. Agung eruption in 1963 nearly wiped it out. There are several interesting palaces here, and the surrounding countryside contains superb scenery, as well as some of the most interesting traditional villages in Bali.

The Karangasem palaces

Amlapura's main attraction is its several traditional palaces or *puri*. There is a western, a northern, a southern, and an eastern *puri* as well as several others, all still occupied by members of the royal family. Of these, only **Puri Agung Karangasem** (also called **Puri Kangin**, the eastern palace) on the main road to the market in the center of Amlapura is easily visited. Built in the 19th century by

King Anak Agung Gede Jelantik, this palace is worth a look, as it gives a vivid impression of how local royals used to live. It is an eccentric blend of details borrowed from the Hindu Balinese (statues and a bas relief), Chinese (window and door styles and other ornaments), and Europeans (the style of the main building and its large veranda) set in what is essentially a traditional Balinese compound, with several pavilions and rooms surrounded by pools and connected by walkways. There are three sections in the compound. The front was where traditional art performances were held and is called Bencingah. In the middle is a garden housing two very old lychee trees and the main palace building bearing the name "Maskerdam," adapted from "Amsterdam" when the king established friendly relations with the Dutch government. Another building in the rear is the royal family's residence and is called "London," and the furniture curiously bears the crest of the British royal family.

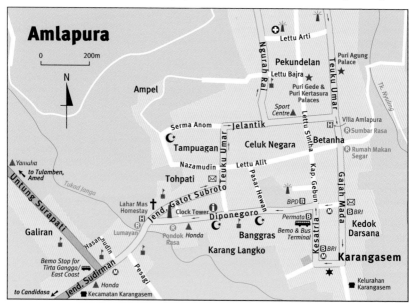

The exquisite "water palace" at Ujung is a major highlight of a visit to the Amlapura area.

The Karangasem ruling family traces its ancestry back to the 14th-century Hindu-Javanese Majapahit empire, claiming to be direct descendants of a certain Batan Jeruk who was Prime Minister of Bali during the 16th century.

There is a tale concerning the dynasty's divine origin. A woman who lived near the palace was once overheard talking to a stranger in her house. When asked who it was, she replied that it was the god of Mt. Agung. After some time, the woman became pregnant, and not long afterwards a miraculous fire descended from the mountain to the woman's house. She soon gave birth to a son atop a hill to the east of the town. This son, the "god of the eastern hill," is said to be the founder of the royal Karangasem line.

Karangasem conquered Lombok in the 17th century and in turn became a vassal of the neighboring island in the 18th and 19th centuries. As a result, there are today several Sasak settlements in and around Amlapura, and these have had a significant influence on the culture of the area. Strong family and trading relations with Lombok still exist, and intermarriages are common. When Lombok was occupied by Holland in 1894, Karangasem was transferred to Dutch control as well. Nevertheless, the ruler of Karangasem was retained as "governor" of the region, and his status was confirmed in 1938 when the Balinese kingdoms were granted partial self-rule. After independence in 1945, these princely realms vanished and were replaced by the present-day *kabupaten* or regencies. Until 1979, however, the regent, or *bupati*, of

Karangasem was a prince of the royal house and was still considered "raja" by most people in the area. Even today, members of the royal family participate in rituals held in the nearby villages.

Ujung and Mt. Seraya

In addition to being a man well-versed in letters, the last Karangasem raja, Anak Agung Anglurah Ketut (1909-1945), was an assiduous builder of opulent pleasure palaces for his frequent excursions to the countryside with his wives and children. In fact, during his lifetime he built no less than three different "water palaces"—at Ujung, Tirta Gangga, and Jungutan—which he also used for receiving dignitaries.

Ujung, 8 km (5 miles) to the south of Amlapura, is a small fishing village with distinct Islamic and Hindu-Balinese quarters. The construction of the lavish complex here—three vast pools bordered by small pavilions with a massive stained-glass and stucco bungalow in the center—began in 1901 and buildings were added until 1937. After the 1963 Mt. Agung eruption, and a 1976 earthquake, the complex was completely destroyed except for a watchtower overlooking the harbor. The ruins of this building were left untouched and still stand atop the hill as if guarding its charge.

Now officially called **Taman Soekasada Ujung**, rebuilding of the site using its original unique Balinese and European architectural styles began in 1998 funded by the World Bank, with Phase II beginning in 2001. It was dedicated in 2004. Today, the

The Ujung water palace features an elegant fusion of Balinese and European architecture.

park is a heavenly garden; on a quiet day it is almost possible to imagine how it must have been in days gone by. In the center of the largest pool is a covered building, Bale Gili—actually part of a bridge from one side of the lake to the other—decorated with ornaments and statues. Other *bales* (pavilions), one reachable by 107 steps, were used as sitting areas from which to view the park below and for banquets. In the area to the north there are statues of a rhino and a bull that recycle water into the pools. The complex is surrounded by a stone wall, part of which is original, fringed by palms and flowering plants. One of the buildings can be rented for workshops and events. It is unfortunate that villas built by members of the royal family who live in Jakarta block a dramatic backdrop view of Mt. Agung overlooking the serene gardens.

Just before Ujung there is a road to the left leading toward **Bukit Kangin** ("eastern hill") where there is a panoramic view of the area and a temple dedicated to the founder of the royal dynasty. On the full moon of the fifth month of the Balinese calendar, several villages with close ties to the ruling dynasty participate in a festival at this temple.

From the beach at Ujung, a quiet road heading east climbs up to **Seraya** village, perched on the southern flanks of Mt. Seraya, Bali's easternmost peak (1,238m or 4,062 ft). This is one of the most arid areas in Bali, and the road here hugs the hills high above the coast, offering splendid panoramas of the surrounding terrain and across the sea to distant Lombok. From Seraya, the road continues around the mountain and descends gradually on the northern side to Amed. Though a distance of only about 30 km (18 miles), the entire drive takes several hours as the road is quite steep and winding. Therefore, most travelers choose the northern road to Amed via Abang, passing the Tirta Gangga water palace en route.

Refreshing pools at Tirta Gangga

If the Ujung water palace can be described as serene, the pools at **Tirta Gangga** are best called "lush." The gardens here are more mature and are bordered by forest and rice fields, with ocean views to the east and Mt. Agung to the north. The cool, spring-fed pools at Tirta Gangga—which literally

The extensive gardens and pool complex at Tirta Gangga are a relaxing stop in the hills of eastern Bali.

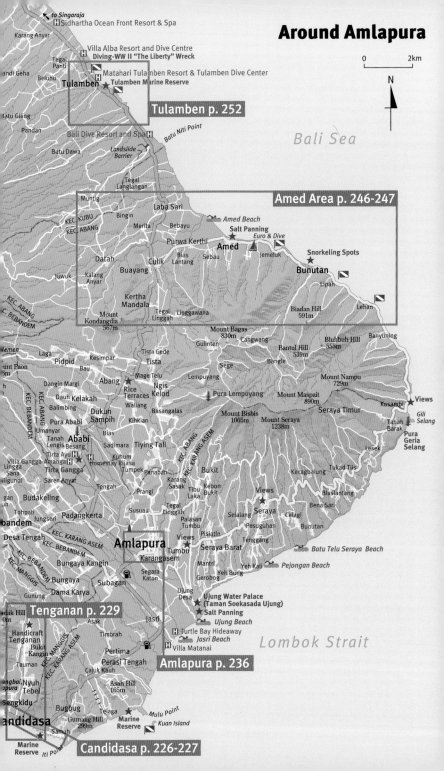

Around Amlapura

to Singaraja

H Sidhartha Ocean Front Resort & Spa

Karang Anyar

andi Geha

Tegal
Panti

Beluhu

Villa Alba Resort and Dive Centre
H Diving-WW II "The Liberty" Wreck

H Matahari Tulamben Resort & Tulamben Dive Center
★ Tulamben Marine Reserve

Tulamben

Tulamben p. 252

3atu Giling

Pandan

Batu Dawa

Bali Dive Resort and Spa H

Batu Niti Point

Bali Sea

Landslide
Barrier

Tegal
Langlangan

Muntig

KEC. KUBU
KEC. ABANG

Laba Sari

Bingin

Merita

Bebayu

Amed Beach

Salt Panning

Euro & Dive

Amed Area p. 246-247

Purwa Kerthi

Datah

Culik

Bias
Lantang

Sebau

Amed

Jemeluk

Snorkeling Spots

Buayang

Kalang
Anyar

Bunutan

Juwuk

Lipah

Kertha
Mandala

Tegal
Linggah

Linggawana

Biadan Hill
591m

Lehan

KEC. ABANG
C. BEBANDEM

Mount
Kondangdia
567m

Banyuning

Mount Bagas
830m

Cangwang

Bluhbuh Hill
555m

Gulinten

Bantul Hill
539m

emen

Laga

Pidpid

Kesimpar

Tista Gede

Tista

Sege

Bangle

unt Paon
6m

Bau

Dangin Margi

Abang

Mage Telu

Lempuyang

Mount Nampu
729m

h

Dauh Kelakah

Rice
Terraces

Ngis
Kelod

Pura Lempuyang

Mount Maspait
890m

KEC. ABANG

KEC.
BEBANDEM

Balimbing

Dukun
Sampih

Waliang

Basangalas

Kusambi

Views

Pura Ababi

Bias

Kihkian

Mount Bisbis
1065m

Mount Seraya
1238m

Seraya Timur

*Gili
Selang*

Umanyar

Tanah
Lengis

Ababi

Besang

Sadimara

Tiying Tali

KEC. ABANG KARANG ASEM

Tanah
Barak

Villa Gangga-Amanga

H

H

Tirta Ayu

Homestay Rijasa

Kuhum

Tumpek

panaban

Pura
Geria
Selang

Lingga
Sana
iligundi

Tirta Gangga

Saren Anyar

Karang
Sasak

Bukit

Tibu
Laka

Kebon
Bukit

Kecagbalung

Tukad Tiis

gan
uh

Budakeling

Tengah

Prangi

Tegal
Linggah

Palasan
Tumbu

Views

Seraya

Blastantang

Tohpati

Jungseri

Susuau

Pisiatin

Selalang

Pesuguhan

Bena Sari

bandem

Desa Tengah

Padangkerta

Tenggang

Celagi

Bunutan

KEC. KARANG ASEM

KEC. BEBANDEM

Amlapura

Views

Tumbu

Seraya Barat

Batu Telu Seraya Beach

KEC. BEBANDEM

Bungaya Kangin

Karangasem

Mantri

Yeh Bung

Yeh Kali

Pejongan Beach

KEC. MANGGIS

Bungaya

Subagan

Segara
Katon

Gerobog

Dama Karya

Ujung
Desa

Ujung Water Palace
★ (Taman Soekasada Ujung)

Gunung

Tenganan p. 229

★ Salt Panning

adak Hill
0m

Asak

Jasri

Ujung Beach

Handicraft
Tenganan

Timbrah

H Turtle Bay Hideaway

Bukit
Kangin

Jasri Beach

Lombok Strait

Tauman

Pertima

Perasi Tengah

H Villa Matanai

Amlapura p. 236

Caluk Kauh

angbai
apura

Nyuh
Tebel

Asah Hill
165m

KEC. MANGGIS KEC. KARANG ASEM

Sengkidu

Bugoug

Telaga

Mulu Point

andidasa

Gumang Hill
299m

Samuh

Marine
Reserve

Kuan Island

Marine
Reserve

Iti Point

Candidasa p. 226-227

0   2km

N

means "Ganges Water" and refers to the sacred river of the Hindus—are located some 15 km (9 miles) north of Amlapura along the road to Amed. The water originates from sacred natural springs believed by the Balinese to be a precious gift from the gods. The waters here are thought to have medicinal powers, and those who bathe in them during the full moon will be healed and blessed with everlasting youth.

Constructed by Anak Agung Anglurah Ketut Karangasem in 1948, the palace buildings no longer exist. What visitors can see is 1.2 ha or 3 ac of gardens and ponds decorated with ornate water-spouting statues, meandering stepping stones across the holy water, and an 11-tiered fountain representing lotus blossoms. Descendants of the royal family still work and live on-site, and visitors are welcome to join villagers in processions to Tirta Gangga during ceremonial occasions.

A dip in the pools is deliciously refreshing after a long drive. The village itself is small and quiet, and is a good place to pause and rest for several hours, or even several days, to take advantage of the many delightful walks in the area. There's a modest entrance fee to view the grounds, and an additional fee for the swimming pool section. A cluster of low-key eateries and accommodation options surround the parking lot.

Trekking around Tirta Gangga

There are a number of excellent treks through the surrounding countryside, and local guides can be hired at any of the guesthouses or restaurants around the water palace. One of the most spectacular begins to the north in **Tanah Aron** village on the slopes of Mt. Agung. It is reachable on foot or by car. To get there, follow the main road north from Tirta Gangga in the direction of Amed for several kilometers, then turn left at **Abang** and follow a small climbing road up to the end. From here continue on foot, enjoying the broad panoramas in all directions and the thick, tree-fern vegetation. There is no shortcut back to Tirta Gangga, and it is best not to get too far off the main path, as the ravines are quite steep and dangerous.

Another, less taxing trek begins in **Ababi**, just 2 km (1.2 miles) north of Tirta Gangga on the main road. Turn left in this village and follow the road through Tanah Lengis to

Tirta Gangga's gardens feature a menagerie of carved stone animals.

Budakling. On foot you can also reach this road by climbing the low hill behind the Tirta Gangga spring.

Ababi is an old-fashioned village, and in the fourth Balinese month a major ritual is held in the village temple, an agricultural ceremony marking the end of the dry season. In Tanah Lengis, which is closely linked to Ababi, are several unusual music clubs. One is an *angklung* orchestra, an instrument comprised of lengths of suspended bamboo that produce various tones when struck, and the other is a *cekepung* group.

Cekepung is a form of music known only in Karangasem and on Lombok, from where it originates, and is performed by a group of men. The leader begins by singing a text in Sasak (the Lombok language); this is then paraphrased by another man in Balinese. After a while the other men join in and perform a very rhythmic, interlocking song without words imitating the interplay, rhythm, and punctuation of a *gamelan* orchestra with their voices. Villagers drink palm wine during and in between the singing, making the festivities even livelier.

Budakeling village is situated on the other side of a broad river, which is almost completely dry during the dry season. This village is home to Buddhist priests, of whom there are only a dozen or so left on Bali (whereas their Sivaite colleagues number in the hundreds). It is also a renowned center for gold- and silversmithing, particularly high quality jewelry pieces that are occasionally offered for sale in Tirta Gangga. Budakeling also has several ironsmiths who produce household utensils and agriculture tools. To return to Tirta Gangga from here, turn left at the first crossroads in Budakeling and ask for directions to Padangkerta, a few miles south on the main Amlapura–Tirta Gangga road.

For a longer trip, continue westward to the important market village **Bebandem**. Entering from this direction, there are iron-smiths by the side of the road who usually work in the mornings on market days (every three days) producing cheap knives, *keris* daggers, and cock-fighting spurs. There is also a cattle market here. This is a beautiful area, with flowers grown for the offerings market. In Banjar Tilem, Bebandem, there's an unusual statue of an elephant with one foot on a human skull. Once back on the main road, you can choose to go back toward Tirta Gangga, south to Candidasa, east to Amlapura, or west to Rendang to continue on to Besakih.

A walk due east from Tirta Gangga through the rice fields brings you to **Pura Lempuyang**, one of the *Sad Kahyangan* or six main temples of the whole of Bali, perched at the summit of Mt. Lempuyang (1,065 m or 3,494 ft). Pass Kuhum and Tihingtali villages and continue on to **Basangalas**. From here it is a strenuous climb up 1,750 steps to the temple. Basangalas can also be reached by car from the south at a turn-off to the north of Tirta Gangga at Abang. If coming from the north, pass through Culik to Aang. The lower temple is usually open, but to enter the upper one (at the top of the dragon staircases), ask around and someone will lead you to the keeper, who will unlock it for you. There are magnificent sunset views from here.

A large temple festival takes place at Lempuyang every 210 days on the Thursday of the week Dungulan. Ten days later, on Sunday of the week Kuningan, there are festivals in the temples of origin (*pura puseh*) in many villages around Basangalas, including Lempuyang. These feature fine *rejang* dances by the unmarried girls of the village, accompanied by various orchestras.

Traditional villages near Amlapura

Several neighboring villages—Subagan, Jasri, Bungaya, Asak, and Timbrah—just to the west of Amlapura—are all very traditional, resembling Tenganan, the classic Bali Aga village. Asak, for instance, is a caste-less village. Bungaya, on the other hand, has groups of *brahmana*, but they do not take part in village rituals.

These villages may be reached quite easily by car or on foot. Coming from Candidasa and Bugbug in the west, turn left at Perasi village on to a picturesque back road leading to Bebandem via Timbrah, Asak, and Bungaya. Jasi and Subagan lie on the main road between Perasi and Amlapura. There is also a lovely backroad connecting Subagan with the Asak and Bungaya road.

Jasri village, close to the beach, is well known for its earthenware casks, bowls, and pots. They may be purchased locally as well as at the Amlapura and Klungkung markets. Subagan has an Islamic quarter that was completely leveled in 1963 when Mt. Agung erupted.

Timbrah, **Asak**, and **Bungaya** are villages with several interesting festivals. The biggest and best known is called *usaba sumbu*, held once a year, with certain variations in all three villages (as well as in Perasi, Bugbug, and Bebandem). This is an agricultural rite in honor of the rice goddess, Batari Sri, and the god of material wealth, Batara Rambut Sedana, as well as the deified ancestors and other village deities. It is held in Bungaya around the full moon of the 12th Balinese month, in Timbrah during the waning moon of the second month, and in Asak around the full moon of the first month. (Check a Balinese calendar for months compared to the Gregorian calendar.) Several exquisite dances are performed during the daytime. A *rejang* is performed by unmarried girls, an *abuang* by unmarried boys, and several different groups take part in mock-fight dances called *gebug*.

A blacksmith at work in Bebandem village

The dancers are beautifully dressed in costly ritual costumes, and the gold headdresses of the girls in Asak and Bungaya are justifiably renowned throughout Bali.

The dances are accompanied by some very rare and unusual music. Especially noteworthy is the sacred *selunding* orchestra, consisting of iron metallophones that are rarely played, and then only for specific ceremonies. A particular *selunding* in Bungaya, for instance, is only struck once every 10 years during a huge temple festival held there. In Asak, Timbrah, and Bugbug, the *selunding* is played once every year during the *usaba sumbu*.

Other interesting festivals are held on Galungan in Timbrah, on Kuningan in Asak and Bungaya, and during the seventh and eighth lunar months in Asak and Subagan. New Year's festivals are worth attending in any of these Villages.

The spectacular backroad to Besakih

The back road leading from Amlapura up to Rendang and thence to Besakih is one of the most scenic in Bali. From Amlapura the first villages passed are Subagan and Bebandem. Shortly after Bebandem there is an intersection, and a turn to the right goes to the small **Jungutan** village, site of the third Karangasem water palace. **Pura Tirta Telaga Tista** is much more modest than the pool complexes at Tirta Gangga and Ujung, but the quiet approach road passes through lovely countryside and little-visited villages.

Back at the intersection, the road continues west through **Sibetan**, known throughout Indonesia for its delicious *salak* (snakefruit), a crisp, tart fruit encased in a brown rind that has the look and feel of snakeskin. Several varieties are grown here, some very sweet, and many unique to Bali. The major harvest seasons are January–February, and August–September. Peel the scaly skin and enjoy the crispy pulp wrapped around a large seed. Kiosks along the road sell products made from *salak*: syrup, chips, candied *salak*, and *dodol*, a sweet, sticky candy. Thickets of the thorny palms line the road, interspersed with coffee and cacao plantations and groves of giant bamboo. This forest landscape is a refreshing contrast to the more familiar rice terraces.

Soon after the *salak* plantations, the sprawling settlement of Duda begins. A sharp left turn here at an intersection marked by a small statue leads to a truly spectacular backroad which eventually emerges at Manggis near Candidasa. There are magnificent views down to the coast along the way, particularly at Bukit Putung, marked by a small pavilion and a couple of basic shops. Back on the main road, after Duda there is another intersection. The road ahead goes west to through spectacular rice terrace scenery around Muncan on the way to Rendang, and onwards to

A ritual Usaba Sumbu dance, performed in the traditional village of Timbrah near Amlapura

Sidemen's rice terraces and mountain landscapes are the epitome of backroads Bali, making it one of the island's most appealing areas.

Besakih. The road to the left goes towards Semarapura via the glorious Sidemen Valley.

When the renowned German artist Walter Spies (1895–1942) felt the need to escape the tourist and expat bubble of his own making in Ubud in the 1930s, he fled to the supremely tranquil **Sidemen Valley**. Today, many of those visitors who find 21st-century Ubud similarly overwhelming are following his example, and Sidemen (pronounced *sid-a-men*) is home to an array of appealing accommodations, all set in a fabulous landscape of rice fields and forest. New villas and guesthouses are popping up every year, but for now Sidemen is still very much a place to get away from it all. The steep valley sides are thick with tangled greenery; temples perch on improbably precipitous ridges; and the river cuts deep gashes through the rich volcanic soil. To the north the mighty Mt. Agung looms large. At night there are only the lights of scattered homesteads amidst the velvety darkness, mirroring the stars overhead, and a soothing chorus of frog- and insect-song rises from the fields. It's easy to detect the inspiration for Walter Spies' fantastical landscape paintings here.

Entering the valley from the north, the first major settlement is **Iseh** village. It was here that Spies built his "mountain hut" in 1937. Another European artist, the Swiss painter Theo Meier (1908–1982), also made Iseh one of his subjects. The scenery here changes here from the *salak* plantations further north to terraced gardens, planted with rice in the wet season and with vegetables in the dry months. It's worth leaving the road to explore the network of paths that lead through the terraces, and to admire the intricate interlocking planting of maize, chili, onions, beans, and cassava.

Further south, Sidemen itself is the main village in the valley. There are several places here where the costly *kain songket* is woven from silk, with gold- and silver-colored threads added to create the patterns. In the center of the village a junction to the west leads downhill to the area where most of Sidemen's tourist accommodation is located, stretching several kilometers along a quiet lane. Options range from welcoming homestays to stylish villas, but virtually all places have spectacular views.

A second right turn at a small junction marked with signs for the various accommodations leads down to the valley floor, across a bridge, then up through the forest and across the ridge to meet a little-traveled backroad through picturesque rural communities, which eventually joins the Amlapura-Rendang road to the north.

Many visitors come to Sidemen simply to relax and soak up the peaceful atmosphere, but there is excellent trekking around the valley for those with a little more energy. Guides for everything from a gentle stroll through the fields to grueling assaults on the surrounding ridges can be arranged at most homestays and villas.

Continuing south on the main valley road beyond Sidemen village, there are more fine views before the ridges eventually fall back, the coastal plain opens ahead, and the outskirts of Semarapura are reached.

ACCOMMODATION PRICE CATEGORIES Prices are for a double room, including breakfast $ = under $30; $$ = $30–$70; $$$ = $70–$130; $$$$ = over $130. DINING PRICE CATEGORIES Prices are for based on a meal for one, without drinks $ = under $5; $$ = $5–$10; $$$ = over $10.

VISITING TIRTA GANGGA & SIDEMEN See map, page 239.

TIRTA GANGGA

North of Amlapura, Tirta Gangga is still a small hamlet. It gets a fair number of day trippers, but as evening falls tranquility returns; passing traffic thins to a trickle, and a chorus of insect noise rises from the surrounding fields. There's a decent selection of budget accommodation, and several new upscale places nearby, and excellent walking to be had in the surrounding countryside, all of which makes it a fine place to spend a couple of nights.

GETTING THERE

The village is on the main highway heading north from Amlapura, which makes it one of the few tourist destinations easily accessible by public transport. Buses and bemo running between Amlapura and Culik, as well as to points all along the north coast road, pass through frequently in daylight hours. Tourist shuttle operators also offer Tirta Gangga as a destination as it lies on the route to and from the larger resort at Amed, so you can get here on a direct transfer from Padangbai, Candidasa, or the southern resorts.

ACCOMMODATION & DINING

There is a clutch of simple family-run homestays on either side of the road near the water palace parking lot, and one upscale place looking out over the palace itself, as well as an increasing array of boutique hideaways within a couple of kilometers of the village. Virtually all of the accommodations have their own eateries, and there are also several simple *warung* around the parking lot and along the road back towards Amlapura.

Homestay Rijasa, Tirta Gangga, Tel: 21873. Across the road from the water palace, this friendly, family-run homestay has nine well-kept rooms in a flower-filled garden. The rooms are simple, but clean, with comfortable beds and tidy bathrooms. The more expensive ones come with hot water, and all have breezy terraces for whiling away an afternoon with a good book. The roadside café out the front has a very cheap menu of basic but tasty meals, and is the best of the basic eateries near the palace. $

Tirta Ayu Hotel & Restaurant, Tirta Gangga, Tel: 22503, www.hoteltirtagangga.com. Within the grounds of the palace, and looking right out over the pools and fountains, this delightful hotel has just three rooms and two villas, all with cool, stylish décor inspired by Balinese palace architecture. There's a small swimming pool if you don't want to take a dip in the public pool in the palace compound. The restaurant has excellent views and serves a well-delivered range of Indonesian standards and international dishes. It gets busy with day trippers, so booking is recommended. $$$$

Villa Gangga-Amanga, www.amangga.free.fr. Perched on a green hilltop, a few minutes' walk up from the water palace, this charming boutique hideaway has five exceptionally atmospheric rooms, each with its own distinct character, and each furnished with Balinese antiques, plus a pool. $$$

ACTIVITIES

Many people visit Tirta Gangga to take a dip in the healing waters of the sacred pools. (There's also a fresh-water spring by the bridge.) However, aside from the palace, there are some excellent walks here suitable for all levels of fitness. Guides can be hired on the spot in the water palace parking lot or arranged through any of the accommodations. Don't forget to bring a camera. For short strolls there's no need to take a guide; just keep to the wider, well-worn paths. Further afield, **Pura Lempuyang Luhur**, high on Mt. Lempuyang, also makes for a strenuous but rewarding hike.

SIDEMEN
(TELEPHONE CODE: 0366)

Sidemen is one of the most beautiful areas in all of Bali, a steep-sided valley with a surfeit of bucolic charms and endless opportunities for **hiking**, or simply relaxing. The accommodation scene is fast developing here, with new places opening every year. There aren't many properly cheap backpacker options, but if your budget will stretch a little further you'll find some wonderful places to stay, and significant discounts are often available at quiet times. Almost all accommodations have their own restaurants, but there are also a couple of stand-alone eateries. For cheap local eats there are a few very basic options up in Sidemen village on the main road.

GETTING THERE

Sidemen lies northeast of Semarapura (Klungkung). A few local bemo shuttle up and down the valley, but it's not a well-served route. As Sidemen grows in popularity an increasing number of tourist shuttle operators are offering it as a destination. Prices for shuttles here from Ubud, Amed, etc. are comparatively high, as demand is still modest and Sidemen isn't on the way to anywhere else., Getting here will become easier as the valley's popularity increases, but for now having your own wheels is a distinct advantage. Virtually all of the accommodation lies downhill to the west of Sidemen village, with individual places strung along several kilometers of quiet lanes.

ACCOMMODATION & DINING

Embang Homestay, Br. Tabola, Sidemen, Tel: 085-333-997-092. Towards the southern end of the lane along which most accommodations are strung, this absolutely delightful little place is easy to miss. There are just four rooms, all immaculately kept, with lovely open-air bathrooms, comfortable four-poster beds and balconies with some of the best views in the valley. The staff are extremely welcoming and the food in the attached café is simple and tasty. **$$**

Samanvaya, Br. Tabola, Sidemen, Tel: 821-4710-3884, www.samanvaya-bali.com. Nestling into the greenery of Sidemen, the rustic lodges and shaggy-roofed *lumbungs* (rice barns) at Samanvaya seem an entirely natural part of the landscape, unlike some of the other new accommodations nearby, which are following the stark modern villa-type design concept. Here natural materials reign supreme, and the place is far more atmospheric as a consequence. Not that "rustic" means "basic" in this instance: the rooms are beautifully appointed; the staff extend a very genuine Balinese welcome; and there's a pool with glorious mountain views. **$$$-$$$$**

Subak Tabola Villas, www.subaktabolavilla.com. Standing proud amidst the rice fields, the villas here have been built with redbrick Balinese temple architecture in mind. The rooms within are wonderfully airy, with four-poster beds and simple but stylish furnishings, while the bathrooms are partially open to the elements, so you can soak in the deep tubs while listening to the frogs, croaking in the dark fields beyond. **$$$$**

Warung Organic, Br. Iseh, Sidemen, Tel: 0858-5701-3416. One of the only restaurants aimed at the tourist trade on the main road through Sidemen, Warung Organic is a simple little place at the northern end of the valley (on the left, if heading north). There's a plain, open-sided terrace below a small parking lot, but the views out over forest and field make up for any deficit in the décor. The food on offer is proper Balinese home cooking, hearty and wholesome. There's no accommodation or other businesses nearby, but the place is popular with tour guides, who bring their clients here en route to and from Besakih by the back road. After lunch, it's well worth going for a walk along the maze of field paths below the restaurant. **$$**

The picturesque water palace Tirta Gangga is now a popular location for pre-wedding photo shoots.

AMED, TULAMBEN, & BEYOND

Secluded Beaches and an Underwater Paradise for Divers at Bali's Eastern Tip

Tucked away at the top of the easternmost corner of Bali, shielded from the rest of the island by the hulks of Mt. Agung and Mt. Seraya, the coastline around Amed is a world apart. The verdant rice fields give way here to drier terraces, planted with corn, cassava and tobacco, and the craggy, sun-scorched hillsides drop steeply down to black-sand beaches where fleets of bone-white outrigger fishing boats are moored. This was long one of the poorest corners of Bali, a place where local villagers eked out a hard-scrabble existence in a severe and stony landscape. These days, however, the stretch of coastline generically referred to as **Amed** is rapidly rising as one of the premier tourist destinations in Bali. The setting is stunning; the sunsets over Mt. Agung are spectacular; and just offshore there is some of the best and most accessible diving and snorkeling in Bali. Little wonder that dozens of new guesthouses, restaurants, and dive shops have sprung up in recent years. The Amed coastline is still far removed from the longer-standing resorts further south, however. Traffic is mercifully light, the nights are quiet, and traditional village life continues undisturbed in the spaces between the tourist accommodations.

Bali's newest beach resort

The area referred to as Amed actually comprises six villages, Amed itself being the first reached after leaving the main Amlapura-Singaraja road at Culik. Heading east along the coastline, after Amed the road traverses Jemeluk, Bunutan, Lipah, Lehan, and Selang. There are wonderful views all along this 10 km (6 mile) stretch of coast, and many sheltered beaches. There's a particularly beautiful view of Jemeluk bay with Gunung Agung for a backdrop from the high headland just east of the village. This spot has become something of a gathering place for international travelers who come here each evening to watch the sunset.

Until the end of the last century, lack of suitable roads into Amed virtually cut villagers off from the rest of Bali. A few foreign-owned bungalows popped up in the early 1990s, but only intrepid travelers came due to lack of public transportation into the area. All that changed in 2000 when a new road was finally installed, allowing for a rush of development.

Tourism development is gradually creeping eastwards along the coast road, but you don't have to travel too far before the last of the hotels falls behind and the unchanged world of the Balinese village returns. With your own transport it is possible to continue on along the coast all the way to Ujung and Amlapura, a journey that passes through an area as yet completely untouched by tourism.

Some villagers around Amed are involved in **salt-making**, and the process can be seen in several places along the coast. The income from this relatively new product, together with tourism, has greatly improved the lives of the local people.

The Amed area is a divers' and snorkelers' paradise, with coral reefs just off the beach. Some of the most sheltered and accessible snorkeling is in **Jemeluk Bay**, with more fine corals at **Lipah**. Amed is also a good base for underwater adventures further afield. **Tulamben** and its World War II-vintage USS Liberty wreck is only 20 minutes away, with the Kubu dive sites a bit further north. All accommodations can also arrange trekking adventure and most also rent bicycles and motorcycles for exploring back roads.

When it's time to depart, travelers can return to Amlapura and from there take the back road up to Besakih, or they can continue up the east coast road towards Singaraja.

Tulamben

Tulamben, 30 km (18 miles) northwest of Amed, has been attracting serious divers for years. The big draw here is the wreck of the US Army supply ship, the **USS Liberty**, which

What looks like a sunken temple at Jemeluk is in fact an underwater mail box, where postcards bought near the beach can be mailed.

One of the most gorgeous views of Mt. Agung is from Amed, which is increasingly popular with divers as well as visitors who wish to escape the hustle and bustle of Bali's southern beach resorts.

was torpedoed by Japanese invaders off the Lombok coast in 1942. Rendered useless, it was towed to Tulamben, unloaded, and left for salvage. When Mother Nature reared her ferocious head in 1963 in the form of the devastating Mt. Agung eruption, the *Liberty* was pushed back to sea by lava flows, where its large hull now rests in the shallows around 25 m (95 ft) from the shore, easily reached by a short swim from the beach. The amazing array of reef fish and 100 or so species of open-ocean pelagics that swarm around the wreck can be easily viewed by snorkelers, as well as divers, especially at low tide.

Apart from the *Liberty*, which draws hundreds of divers each day during high season, there are several other local dive sites worthy of exploration. **Tulamben Wall**, also known as the "Drop Off," is deeper, making it a favorite among technical divers. Seraya is a haven for muck divers who enjoy scrounging in the shallows for macro species such as tiny shrimp, beautiful crabs, and mimic octopi. Kubu is little visited and is home to several varieties of pygmy seahorse. Paradise Reef is

an artificial reef project at a depth of only 3–4 m (10–12 ft), making it excellent for night dives.

For non-divers, there's little else to see or do in Tulamben. Basically, it's a small fishing village with a golden egg that sustains it for a few months every year. The best time for diving here is October–June or July, when the sea is usually calm.

Northwest from Tulamben to Singaraja

Beyond Tulamben, 15 minutes to the northwest, is **Kubu**. Located on the opposite side of the Liberty wreck, it also caters to divers. There are a couple of dive centers and eateries here, with further development likely in future years.

The road further northwest heads towards Singaraja and northern Bali, hugging the coastline all the way. The scenery is striking. Everything in this area was completely wiped out by lava flows from the 1963 Mt. Agung eruption. Though the general vegetation has long since recovered, the scars are still plain to see. The rice fields and plantations so typical of Bali are replaced by deep gashes in the earth and enormous black boulders.

ACCOMMODATION PRICE CATEGORIES Prices are for a double room, including breakfast $ = under $30; $$ = $30–$70; $$$ = $70–$130; $$$$ = over $130. **DINING PRICE CATEGORIES** Prices are for based on a meal for one, without drinks $ = under $5; $$ = $5–$10; $$$ = over $10.

VISITING AMED, TULAMBEN & KUBU See maps, pages 246–247, 252.

With only 30 km (18 miles) separating Amed and Tulamben, deciding where to stay is a matter of personal preference. Hardcore divers interested in the USS *Liberty* wreck may choose to stay in Tulamben, but travelers looking for a wider range of activities and more choice when It comes to dining, will probably prefer the Amed area. Kubu, northwest of Tulamben, still only has low-key tourist development, but things are starting to change and there will be more options here before long.

AMED

Amed is on the easternmost tip of Bali where some of Bali's most idyllic beaches are located—though the sand is mostly black, rather than golden. Development has been moving at a significant pace here in recent years, and there are now dozens of accommodations in all price brackets, strung along several kilometers of coast from Amed village to Selang (the whole area is collectively known as "Amed"). The Amed area attracts snorkelers, casual divers, and beginners, families and folks just needing to drop out for a while. As the area's popularity has increased, more services have become available, including ATMs, money changers, and convenience stores.

GETTING THERE & GETTING AROUND

Amed's beaches are about 2 hours from the Ngurah Rai International Airport and 60 minutes north of Candidasa. Note that even though the road along the beaches has been greatly improved, Amed is still relatively remote, and **public transport** is limited. If you can make your way to Amlapura, the main town in Eastern Bali, you will find regular *bemo* running to Culik, and a few onward connections from there to central Amed, but It is far easier to reach Amed by private transport.

Thanks to its increased popularity, Amed is now well established on the tourist shuttle network. You can book door-to-door minibuses that will get you here from all the other major accommodation centers, including Ubud and Kuta. Some of these shuttles will stop in Padangbai and Candidasa along the way. There are numerous shuttle bus providers, and departures are usually early- to mid-morning, with a transfer from the southern resorts typically costing $10-$20. Perama is the best-known and most reliable shuttle operator, with departures from points all over Bali.

Helping to establish Amed's place on the backpacker circuit is the speedboat link to the Gilis, the fabled trio of islands off Lombok. There are now several competing operators, departing from Amed each morning and dropping off at each of the three Gilis. Pacha Express (www.pacha-express.com) has one of the better maintained boats, with daily 9:15 am departures from Amed for around $50 one-way. The trip takes less than an hour.

ACCOMMODATIONS

Hotels, homestays and resorts are strung all along the Amed coast, lining a road that winds in and out of sheltered coves and over exposed headlands. The pace of recent development has been swiftest at the western end of the strip, in Amed village and neighboring Jemeluk, and this is where you'll find the widest choice of budget accommodations, with some decent homestays, many right on the beach. Generally speaking, the further east you travel along the coast, the more expensive resorts and restaurants become. The six beaches that comprise "Amed" are: (from west to east) Amed, Jemeluk, Bunutan, Lipah, Lehan, and Selang.

Apa Kabar Villas, Bunutan, www.apakabarvillas.com. Right on the Bunutan beachfront, Apar Kabar has been in business since the 1990s, but the rooms have had regular upgrades, and are kept in tip-top condition. There's a small pool, a garden packed with statuary, and a choice between larger villas big enough to house whole families, and smaller cottages. The restaurant has been getting good reviews from travelers. $$-$$$

Blue Moon Villas, Selang, www.bluemoonvillas.com. With stunning ocean views and a swimming pool dramatically set on the brink of the wide blue yonder, Blue Moon has one of the best locations on the Amed coastline. The sleeping options themselves are charming, ranging from fairly simple two-person rooms, to extravagant family villas. The restaurant serves beautifully presented Indonesian and Western dishes, and some good seafood. $$$-$$$$

Geria Giri Shanti Bungalows, Jemeluk, www.geria-girishanti.com. Attached to an expat-run dive center, the spotless budget bungalows here are built in Balinese temple style, and are surrounded by a lush garden. The fan-cooled rooms are simple but very well maintained, and towels and mosquito nets are included. $-$$

Hidden Paradise Cottages, Lipah, www. hiddenparadise-bali.com. Just back from the attractive beach at Lipah, the 16 cottages here all come with hot water and air-con. The spacious interiors are light and airy, with teak furnishings, and stylish bathrooms. There's a pleasant garden with a pool, and discounts are available at quiet times. **$$$**

Jepun Bali Villas, Bunutan, www.jepunbalivillas. com. Artfully slotted onto a landscaped slope rising from the sea, the villas at this luxurious small-scale resort come beautiful teak furnishings. The main villa has its own dedicated staff, expansive living areas, and its own kitchen, while the smaller villas have outdoor terraces with daybeds for lounging. There's also an open-air spa area for treatments with sea views, and an infinity pool. **$$$-$$$$**

Kembali Beach Bungalows, Jemeluk, www.kembalibeachbungalows.com. The spacious Dutch-owned bungalows here stand in pleasant garden, right at the top of the beach. There's a pool, if you're too lazy to shuffle the few steps to the ocean's edge, and a generally relaxed and friendly atmosphere to the whole place. The rooms come with hot water, and both air-conditioning and fan, and each has a pleasant private terrace. **$$**

Life in Amed, Bunutan, www.lifebali.com. The Life in Amed management certainly make their presence felt, with conspicuous signs flagging up their presence for miles along the approach road, but the resort itself is delightfully low-key, with lots of boutique Balinese style. There are six beach cottages, two villas, and one spectacular thatched house, all surrounded by mature gardens with plenty of quiet corners. The restaurant serves decent organic fare. **$$$**

Puri Wirata Dive Resort, Villas & Spa, Bunutan, www.puriwirata.com. A modern addition to the Amed shoreline, Puri Wirata offers the full package: there's a PADI dive center onsite, along with a spa, restaurant, and fine array of accommodations. There are two swimming pools and fantastic sea views. Sleeping options range from very reasonably priced deluxe rooms, to full villas that can house whole families. Most guests come to dive, but it's a good accommodation option even for non-divers. **$$-$$$**

Vienna Beach Bungalows, Lipah, Tel: 23494. Vienna Beach gets extra marks for location: it's right on the edge of a lovely stretch of sand, with some of the most attractive and accessible snorkeling on the Amed coast just offshore. The rooms are simple, but well maintained with air-con and hot water, set in a series of two-story cottages in a pleasant garden. The restaurant offers decent food too, and there's sometimes traditional dance laid on as evening entertainment. **$$**

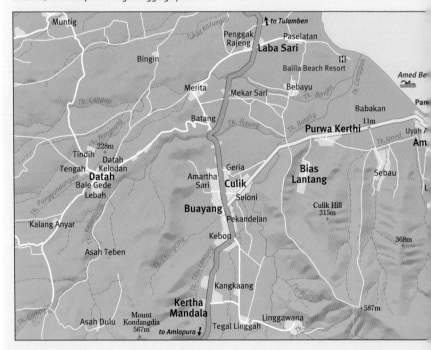

DINING

Almost all of the accommodations in Amed have their own restaurants, and there are dozens of others, lining the road that runs along the coast. The largest choice is around Amed village and Jemeluk. Further east, most of the eateries are within the resorts.

Sails Restaurant, Bunutan, Tel: 22006. A fine dining restaurant with ocean views, Sails serves excellent Indonesian, vegetarian, and Western food with a strong emphasis on local seafood. Desserts are also very good, and wine and cocktails are also available. Lunch and dinner. $$$

Warung Ole, Amed, Tel: 0819-3645-5626. This tiny café next to the Fusion freediving headquarters only has a handful of tables, and their highly prized, so you may have to queue to get in at busy times. The food is simple—a mix of burgers, fresh fish, and Indonesian standards—but it's cooked and delivered with genuine passion by the hospitable owners in a manner that keeps many guests coming back night after night. Lunch and dinner. $-$$

DIVING

There is good diving with healthy corals at Jemeluk Bay, with a gentle slope from the shore quickly dropping off a 40 m (130 ft) wall, and good drift dives with schools of barracuda, giant barrel sponges, eels, and reef fish at Bunutan for experienced

divers. Amed dive shops can also arrange dives in other areas of eastern Bali, including the *Liberty* wreck at Tulamben.

Amed Dive Center, Hotel Uyah Amed, Jl. Pantai Timur. www.ameddivecenter.com. This long-established center offers a full range of PADI dive courses, snorkeling, sailing, and sunset tours. Guides speak English, French, and German.

Ecodive Bali, Jemeluk, www.ecodivebali.com. Owned and operated by a PADI Master Instructor with over 35 years' diving experience, including 20 years in SE Asia, this professional center runs daily dive trips to the best sites in Bali, and a full range of courses from Open Water to Instructor.

Fusion Freediving & Yoga, Amed, www.fusionfreedive.com. Freediving has become a popular alternative to traditional scuba diving in recent years, and there are several places In Amed offering courses in this new frontier of underwater sport. Fusion, based in Amed village, is well established, with highly experienced staff.

SNORKELING

With a reef that follows the entire coastline, snorkeling is good everywhere; the only thing to watch is the tides. Ask at your accommodation for current tide times. Jemeluk has the most accessible corals. The waters can be rough at Lipah, but there's a small

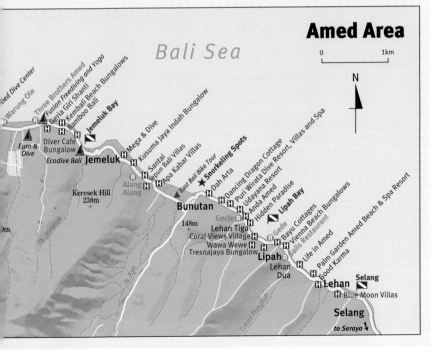

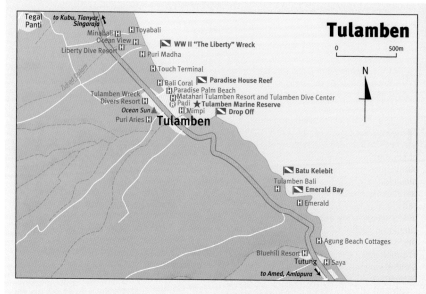

wooden shipwreck there. Snorkel equipment in good condition costs about $4/day.

TULAMBEN

With shallow fringe reefs, dramatic drop-offs, and the World War II *Liberty* wreck all attracting thousands of species of marine life at every site, Tulamben is one of Bali's most popular dive spots, and a huge draw. Underwater visibility is 2 m (6.5 ft) on average and up to 30 m (98 ft) in the dry season with the temperature a constant 28°C. Diving is relaxed and easy, suitable for all levels of experience. Almost all of the accommodations here have their own dive centers, and the vast majority of people who stay here come for the underwater attractions. That said, Tulamben also makes for a peaceful overnight stay en route between Eastern Bali and the attractions west of Singaraja. **Kubu**, which also has excellent diving, and a developing accommodation scene, is 15 minutes' along the coast from Tulamben.

GETTING THERE & AROUND

Buses and *bemo* traveling between Amlapura and Singaraja via the coastal road pass through Tulamben and Kubu, as do tourist shuttles running from Amed to Lovina. Private vehicles can be chartered for the short hop from Amed.

ACCOMMODATIONS

Matahari Tulamben Resort & Tulamben Dive Center, www.divetulamben.com. Accommodations for all budgets are available at this very

well-organized dive resort, from Spartan but spotless standard rooms, to family-sized bungalows. All are bright and airy and come with hot water and free Wif-Fi. There's a good restaurant and an excellent array of dive packages. $-$$$

Tulamben Wreck Divers Resort, www.tulambenwreckdivers.com. From simple, fan-cooled rooms for backpackers on a budget, to beachfront villas for well-heeled families, this long-running dive resort has them all. All just a short swim away from the *Liberty* wreck itself. $-$$$$

Liberty Dive Resort, www.libertydiveresort.com. Located a short way west of the *Liberty* shipwreck public car park entrance, there are 32 plain but comfortable air-con rooms at this resort. Most guests, of course, come for the diving, which is very professionally organized. $$

Toyabali, www.toyabali-resort.com. The beautiful villas here each come with their own garden, pool, and Jacuzzi, just a short distance from the Liberty wreck. Good discounts are available during quiet times. $$$

Siddhartha Dive Resort & Spa, Kubu, www.siddhartha-bali.com. A beautiful boutique hotel with ingenious architecture and interior design not usually associated with dive resorts, Siddhartha lords it over the Kubu coastline, with 30 bungalows and villas set on a large stretch of beachfront with Mt. Agung looming inland. The attached Tantris Restaurant serves high-standard Asian fusion cuisine and a good wine list. Prices are very reasonable, considering the quality. $$$

A Trio of Offshore Tropical Idylls

Three tiny islands, dark green blots on a glittering sea, each ringed with a corona of blinding white sand and a broader hem of coral. These are places where unpaved tracks meander between drooping palm trees, and traffic noise is a distant memory; where a salty breeze takes the edge off the tropical heat, and where everything moves at a deliciously languid pace. Little wonder, then, that these three small rounds of land—Gili Trawangan, Gili Meno, and Gili Air—collectively known in tourist parlance as "the Gilis" have become a fabled destination.

The Gilis actually belong to Bali's eastern neighbor, Lombok. They lie on the far side of the Wallace Line, the great ecological frontier that separates the natural worlds of Asia and Australasia, and their inhabitants are a mixture of Muslim Bugis and Sasak.

But these days, as far as many travelers are concerned, they are simply an extension of Bali, connected to Sanur, Padangbai and Amed by direct speedboat.

Desert islands

The Gilis lie just off the northwestern corner of Lombok, with **Gili** Air closest to the Lombok shore, **Gili** Meno coming next, and the largest and most popular of the three, **Gili Trawangan** furthest west. "Gili" simply means "small island" in Lombok's Sasak language. Low-lying, with very poor soil and seriously limited supplies of fresh water, for the Sasaks of Lombok—who have been Muslims since the 17th century, but who were ruled by a Balinese Hindu elite in the decades before the Dutch established control—the Gilis were long viewed as singularly inhospitable places.

There is accessible snorkeling right off the beaches of the Gilis, with clear waters and decent coral.

In the 19th century Lombok's rulers actually used Gili Trawangan as a prison.

Bugis fishermen from southern Sulawesi used the islands as a seasonal base, but until the mid-20th century there were virtually no permanent inhabitants. The first settlers to stay year-round were small-scale coconut planters. Most were Bugis who intermarried with the local Sasak population, and by the 1970s there were a few hundred residents, eking out a hardscrabble existence amongst the palms.

But then the first backpackers turned up. By the 1990s the Gilis, and particularly Gili Trawangan, were a firmly established destination on the budget travel circuit. Dozens of cheap homestays appeared, and a beachside party scene rapidly developed. A reputation for freely available drugs—in particular potent local "magic mushrooms"—and a total absence of formal law enforcement only boosted the backpacker appeal.

Offshore, meanwhile, canny dive operators had discovered some of the most accessible reefs in Indonesia, and soon a clutch of dive schools were operating from Gili Trawangan.

These days the islands are one of the most popular tourist destinations in Indonesia. While the backpackers of old had to ride the public ferry to Lombok, then negotiate a series of onward hops by public transport, today's travelers are whisked by speedboats

Open boats are the way to hop between the three islands.

straight from Bali. Gili Trawangan still has a big-time nightlife scene, with "full moon parties," and some noisy bars on the eastern coast. But the original budget lodgings have been joined by some delightful midrange villas, an increasing array of luxury resorts, and some remarkably sophisticated eateries. Gili Meno and Gili Air, while still much quieter, have also been enjoying a boom.

Inevitably, some old-timers have taken to describing the islands as a lost paradise, ruined by rampant development. But there's still no motorized transport on the Gilis; even on bustling Trawangan you can still find long stretches of empty sand on the western coast—as well as tranquil accommodations

Gili Trawangan is the largest of the three islands, with the biggest array of accommodations and services.

for those with no desire to party until dawn; village life still goes on amidst the palm groves back from the beach; the snorkeling and diving is still superlative; and the sunsets over Bali are still something to write home about. The Gilis look set to be wowing the crowds for a good while yet.

Gili Trawangan

Gili Trawangan remains by far the most popular of the three islands, home of the widest array of accommodations, and the most impressive selection of eateries. It's also the only one of the three islands that rises significantly above sea level, with a bank of low hills at its center, the highest point topped by a lighthouse, to which there are several walking trails.

As on the other Gilis, there are no motorized vehicles. Rented bicycles or rattletrap horse carts are the only forms of wheeled transport. It takes around two hours to walk around the island.

The largest concentration of accommodations, bars, restaurants and dive shops is on the east coast, where the speedboats dock. This is still the main area to hunt out cheap lodgings. The more tranquil midrange places are mostly further north, where the density of the development begins to thin out. The west coast, meanwhile, still has long stretches of deserted beach, though every year new luxury resorts are popping up here.

Many people come to Gili Trawangan for the underwater attractions, and this is one of the best—and cheapest—places to learn to dive in Indonesia. There are some long-established dive schools. Freediving has also become popular here in recent years, and several operators now run freediving courses. For those just wanting to dabble in the undersea world, there is decent snorkeling right off the main eastern beach, with equipment for rent all over the island.

Gili Meno and Gili Air

For years the two landward Gilis have existed in the shadow of their bigger, brasher western sibling. Today, both Gili Meno and Gili Air remain far quieter than Gili Trawangan, and both retain their distinctive characteristics. Nonetheless, both have recently seen much development, and are very attractive alternatives to "Gili T."

From the sea Gili Meno can still sometimes look like a genuine deserted tropical islet. The vegetation is thicker here than on

A visit to the Gilis is an unforgetable experience.

Trawangan, with banks of greenery rising at the head of the beaches. Inland, a network of sandy tracks wind through palm groves and small fields, and around a shallow, salty lake. Meno has long been regarded as a place best suited to couples seeking romantic hideaways in the midrange or luxury market, and indeed, that's still the key demographic here. There are some lovely little bungalow complexes and quirky resorts; the snorkeling is, if anything, better than that of Gili Trawangan, and the nights are dark and peaceful.

Closest to the Lombok mainland, Gili Air has always been home to the largest local community and the best supply of fresh water—and it was long overlooked by the bulk of foreign visitors. These days, however, it has come into its own as the heir to the original hippie vibe relinquished by Gili Trawangan in its headlong dash into commercialism. There are accommodations scattered across the island, but the main strip is in the southeast, where there's a definite after-dark buzz and a good selection of cheaper guesthouses. The party scene here is much less noisy than on Trawangan, however, and plenty of visitors come to chill out in the appealing midrange accommodations, to enjoy the beaches, which are some of the finest in the Gilis, and to revel in the magnificent views eastwards to Lombok's vast Mt. Rinjani—a view which might just prompt some travelers to remember that the Gilis aren't actually a part of Bali, and that there's a whole other world awaiting exploration, just a short boat ride away in Lombok and the string of wild islands beyond.

ACCOMMODATION PRICE CATEGORIES Prices are for a double room, including breakfast **$** = under $30; **$$** = $30–$70; **$$$** = $70–$130; **$$$$** = over $130. DINING PRICE CATEGORIES Prices are for based on a meal for one, without drinks **$** = under $5; **$$** = $5–$10; **$$$** = over $10

VISITING THE GILI ISLANDS See map below.

On the far side of the deep Lombok Strait and with a population of Bugis and Sasak Muslims, the trio of tiny islands collectively known as the Gilis (**gili** actually simply means "small island") are separate from Bali cultural, politically, geographically, and even ecologically (they're on the other side of the Wallace Line). But as far as many travelers are concerned, they are just an appendage of Bali, and these days the vast majority of visitors arrive aboard direct speedboats from Bali, and never see anything more of the island (Lombok) or the province (West Nusa Tenggara) to which the Gilis actually belong.

Long a waystation on the Southeast Asia backpacker trail, the Gilis are still hugely popular with the youthful gap year crowd. But there have been shifts upmarket in recent years. **Gili Trawangan** now has some seriously sophisticated accommodations and

eateries which wouldn't look out of place in Seminyak, and there are places perfect for those in need of creature comforts on the smaller **Gili Meno** and **Gili Air** too. Nonetheless, the Gilis are still islands apart, and for all the crowds there's still a sense of delightful isolation.

Many of the locals on the Gilis make their living from tourism—and with parts of the main island of Lombok amongst the poorest in Indonesia, they are profoundly aware of their good fortune and tolerant of misbehaving foreigners as a consequence. But despite good-natured local forbearance, it's important to remember that this is actually a conservative Muslim community. Topless sunbathing, public displays of affection, and conspicuous alcohol consumption, though common occurrences on the Gilis, are not really appropriate.

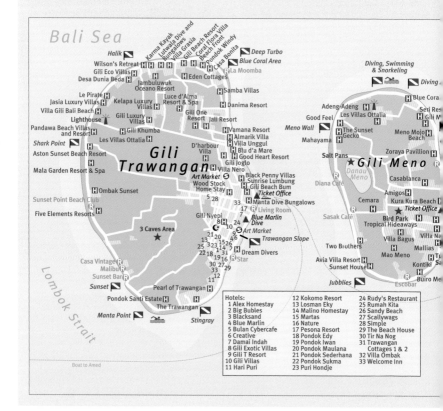

Hotels:		
1 Alex Homestay	12 Kokomo Resort	24 Rudy's Restaurant
2 Big Bubles	13 Losman Eky	25 Rumah Kita
3 Blacksand	14 Malino Homestay	26 Sandy Beach
4 Blue Marlin	15 Martas	27 Scallywags
5 Bulan Cybercafe	16 Nature	28 Simple
6 Creative	17 Pesona Resort	29 The Beach House
7 Damai Indah	18 Pondok Edy	30 Tir Na Nog
8 Gili Exotic Villas	19 Pondok Iwan	31 Trawangan
9 Gili T Resort	20 Pondok Maulana	Cottages 1 & 2
10 Gili Villas	21 Pondok Sederhana	32 Villa Ombak
11 Hari Puri	22 Pondok Sukma	33 Welcome Inn
	23 Puri Hondje	

GETTING THERE & GETTING AROUND

It's still possible to get to the Gilis the old-fashioned way, by **public ferry** and a series of onward hops by *bemo*. Public ferries depart from Padangbai to Lembar on Lombok throughout the day, for a journey that takes around four hours. From Lembar, *bemos* run onwards to Mataram, the main town in Lombok. It generally takes at least two further changes of *bemo* to cross Mataram itself from the main bus terminal, and then to travel on up the west coast past Senggigi to **Bangsal**, where small ferries run frequently to each of the three Gilis. This is the cheapest travel option, but it's time-consuming, and is best combined with some exploration of Lombok itself—a night in Senggigi at the very least.

It's also possible to fly to Lombok from Bali. There are regular, moderately priced flights with **Wings Air** and other operators. The airport is a long way from the Gilis, however, and although taxis are available for the journey to Bangsal, flights are again a sensible option only if you're planning to explore the rest of Lombok.

Most people opt instead for one of the **direct speedboat transfers**. Tickets for these trips are actually often more expensive than flights to Lombok from Bali (typically around $50 one-way), but by the time you factor in airport transfers and time spent traveling across Lombok, they are generally the best option.

With the dramatic growth of tourism in the Gilis a plethora of speedboat operators have emerged to ply the route across the strait, and boats now depart from Sanur, Serangan, Padangbai and Amed. The trip is shortest—around an hour—from Padangbai or Amed.

Travel agents all over Bali sell tickets for the Gilis, and those booked in Ubud, Kuta or one of the other southern resorts typically include a transfer to the point of embarkation (Padangbai is where most boats depart). In recent years concerns have been raised about the safety standards on some of the cheaper boats, so it's worth checking online reviews of the different operators before booking. During the rainy season, when the strait can be rough, safety standards are of particular concern.

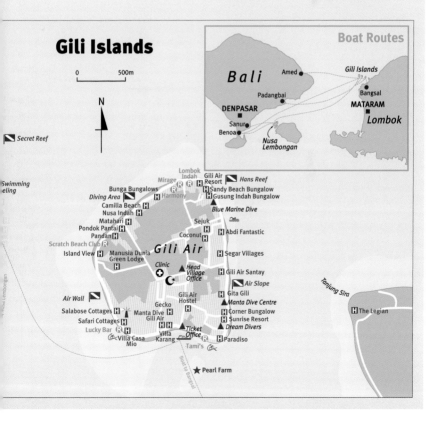

Amongst the reputable companies are **BlueWater Express** (www.bluewater-express.com), **Kuda Hitam** (www.kudahitamexpress.com), and **Gili Cat** (www.gilicat.com). Tickets can be booked online through the websites of these companies. There's also an excellent online booking service provided by **Gili Bookings** (www.gilibookings.com), which lists departures for all the major operators, and **Gili Tickets** (www.gilitickets.com). One-way tickets with the companies listed above typically cost around $50; other cheaper operators may offer seats for as little as $25. In practice hundreds of people travel with these cheaper operators every day without problems, but if you want more peace of mind, and more comfort onboard, choose one of the more reputable companies.

The small **public boats** that shuttle between each of the Gilis and the Lombok mainland cost less than $2. There are also a few small passenger ferries going between the islands, but generally you'll need to charter a boat for island-hopping.

There's no motorized transport on the islands, and rickety little horse carriages are the main means of getting around if you have heavy luggage. Drivers meet the arriving speedboats. **Bicycles** are also available to rent.

GILI TRAWANGAN

Fabled "Gili T" was the first of this island trio to embrace tourism on a large scale. The biggest and westernmost of the Gilis, it still sees by far the most visitors, and it has the biggest array of accommodations and the most sophisticated services. There's still a major backpacker party scene here, with some noisy bars, some playing host to visiting international DJs, and Thai-style "full moon parties." But away from the main strip on the east coast there is plenty of tranquil midrange accommodation. The youthful hedonists, the serious divers, the honeymooners, and the more mature tourists seeking tranquility all manage to rub along together quite happily on Gili Trawangan, without treading on each other's toes.

ACCOMMODATIONS

The greatest concentration of accommodations is still on the east coast, and this is where the main bars and dive schools are based too, but there is also accommodation right the way around the coast. The island is small enough that you can easily walk or cycle anywhere for dinner. The recent enforcement of a local bylaw meant that the pile-'em-high backpacker hostels had to redesign their dorm rooms to accommodate no more than three people, which has pushed the prices of rock-bottom sleeping options up a little.

Desa Dunia Beda, www.desaduniabeda.com. Standing in glorious isolation at the northern tip of Trawangan, this secluded eco-resort is a fine place to get away from it all. The traditional *joglo*-style bungalows are a refreshingly shady contrast to the blinding white beach just outside, with lots of rustic fabrics and bare woodwork. The boisterous party scene just down the coast feels like another world. **$$$**

Five Elements, www.fiveelementsvillas.com. One of the luxury properties that have laid a claim to the wild west coast of Gili Trawangan, Five Elements comes with epic sunset views as standard. The rooms are sleek and stylish, if a little clinical, and there's a large swimming pool for days when the nearby ocean is too rough for swimming. The rest of the Gili T scene is far away, and this is a great place to be if you want isolation. **$$$$**

Gili Beach Bum Hotel, www.gilihostel.com. For backpackers with a craving for company, this funky hostel on the main east coast strip is a sure bet. There's a dash of local style, with thatched roofs and a welcoming rooftop bar, but the Wi-Fi-fueled vibe is that of a modern hostel for the digital age. It makes the old-school bamboo bungalows where previous generations of backpackers stayed look like something from another century—which they are! **$**

Gili Nyepi, www.gilinyepi.com. The simple but spotless bungalows in this small resort offer a welcome shady respite from the scorched shorelines of Gili Trawangan. Each room comes with its own cool terrace, and the lush garden adds a sense of tropical calm. The busy main drag is just a short stroll away, but there's a sense of escape here, and the breakfasts are delicious. **$$**

Kokomo, www.kokomogilit.com. Any lingering illusions that Gili T is still the exclusive haunt of threadbare backpackers will vanish when you see this confidently stylish mini resort. The modern villas stand slightly away from the heart of the action at the southern end of the main strip. They come with private pools and expansive interiors that combine cool minimalism with classic tropical style. **$$$$**

Wood Stock Home Stay, Tel: 0821-4765-5877. The funky rice barn-style rooms at this complex in the interior of Gili Trawangan, are thoroughly atmospheric, with terraces for lounging, open-air bathrooms, and lots of stylish little touches. It's away from the beach, but it's a great setting. **$$**

DINING

Gili Trawangan is a great place for fresh seafood, and all down the east coast strip of an evening you'll find the catch of the day laid out on ice at the threshold of restaurants. There are dozens of places to eat, ranging from generic traveler cafés with all the usual pan-Asian and Western standards, to some seriously upscale eateries. If you have a hankering for authentic and cheap local cuisine, there's a night market every evening, with simple grilled meat, fish, rice and noodle dishes, just south of the speedboat jetty. **Blu d'aMare**, www.bludamare.it. The hills of Italy come to Gili Trawangan in this deceptively rustic-looking beachside café. On the menu you'll find authentic Italian home cooking, freshly baked breads, and the best pasta on the island, along with sea breezes and typically friendly Indonesian service. There are also some fine antique *joglo*-style bungalows here if you want to stay. Breakfast, lunch, and dinner. **$$$**

Kokomo, www.kokomogilit.com. In the resort of the same name, this seriously sophisticated eatery still manages to cling on to the trademark castaway style of Gili Trawangan. There is fine imported beef, creative takes on the local seafood, and the best French and Italian dessert classics this side of Sydney. Lunch and dinner. **$$$**

ACTIVITIES

There is excellent diving off the Gilis, with lots of professionally run dive shops based on Gili Trawangan. **Blue Marlin** and **Manta Dive** are two of the longest-running operators, but there are several others. Manta Point, Meno Wall, and Shark Point are amongst the most popular dive sites. Prices for a single fun dive typically start around $40, while a PADI open-water course will cost around $400. **Snorkeling equipment** is available for hire from many restaurants and accommodations. There is occasionally good surf off the southern tip of Gili Trawangan, and boards are available for hire. It is an inconsistent break, however, and if you want guaranteed waves you should head for the south coast of Lombok—or stay on Bali.

GILI MENO

Squeezed in between its busier neighbors, Gili Meno is the quietest of the three islands, with some low-key midrange and upscale bungalows hidden away amongst the trees. This is not the place to come if you are looking to party, but it is perfect if you want privacy and quiet nights.

ACCOMMODATIONS

Diana Café, Tel: 0809-3317-1943. A perfect place to soak up the rustic charms of Gili Meno, this bare-bones beachside café also has some traditional budget rooms in thatched bungalows, four alongside Meno's salt lake, and four more just by the

beach. They're basic but clean, with attached bathrooms and bamboo balconies. **$**

Villa Nautilus, www.villanautilus.com. Stylish and modern, the villas in this small complex just off the beach are surrounded by well-watered lawns. There's plenty of white upholstery inside, and a good deal of peace, and the bathrooms have fully fresh water—always a bonus on Gili Meno, where local supplies are usually rather salty. **$$$**

GILI AIR

Gili Air, long neglected as a "locals' island," has been coming into its own in recent years, picking up the backpacker slack as Gili Trawangan edges slowly upmarket. The vibe is much more mellow here, and the party scene sometimes feels like a 1970s time warp. There's also some decent midrange and upscale accommodation for those who've hung up their party shoes, and with a larger local community than the other islands, it's a nice place to be if you want to feel like you're actually still in Indonesia! The beaches are fantastic and there's some good snorkeling.

ACCOMMODATIONS

Gili Air Hostel www.giliairhostel.com The epitome of Gili Air's old-fashioned backpacker vibe, this funky, friendly hostel has small dorms and private rooms, in red-tiled *joglos*, with lots of quirky décor in the public areas, hammocks for lounging in, and a genial atmosphere. There's also a popular bar. **$**

Manusia Dunia Green Lodge, www.manusiadunia. com. Built entirely of natural materials, the six elegantly simple wooden cottages in an expansive garden here are perfect places to get back to nature. The design combo of white linen and rustic woodwork is a winner; there are hammocks and daybeds for lounging, and the owners work hard to make their guests feel at home. **$$$**

Segar Villages, www.segarvillages.blogspot.com. The bungalows here stand amidst palm trees on the edge of the sea, and have high ceilings and plenty of natural light. The bathrooms are coral-walled grottos, and the terraces are fine places for whiling away a lazy afternoon. **$$-$$$**

Villa Casa Mio, www.casamiovillas.com. Packed with quirky color, this rustic resort is one of Gili Meno's more offbeat accommodations. The rice barn-style bungalows have splashes of vivid paintwork to break up the natural earthy tones, and the open-air bathrooms are like little walled gardens. The bohemian vibe continues in the public areas, and in the welcoming beachfront restaurant. **$$**

Bali Sea

Buleleng Harbour

Singaraja p.278 – 281

Lingga Beach

Bungkulan Point

Penarukan Point

Pura Beji
Sangsit Bungkulan
Kubutambahan
Penarukan
Jagaraga
Kampung Baru
Kampung Anyar
Banjarjawa Banyuning
Sinabun
Pura Dalem
Bengkala
Jinengdelam
Menyali
Penglatan
Sawan

Seririt & Munduk p.285

Lovina Beach p.282 – 283

Tukadmungga
Singaraja
Beratan
Pohbergong
Suwug
Sudaji
Beb
Celuk Agung
Pemaron
Sukasada
Sari Mekar
Alas Angker
Panji
Lovina Beach
Enjung Buntekan
Anturan
Tegal Linggah
Pegadungan

Bedugul & Lake Bratan p.271 – 277

Celuk Buluh
Kalibukbuk
Kaliaseni
Ambengan
Silang Jana
Be
Enjung Sanglang
Gitgit Waterfall
Pegayaman
Sekumpu
Celuk Labuhanaji
Temukus
Sing Sing Waterfall
Kayu Putih
Gitgit
Lemukih

Celuk Ponjok Cukli
Enjung Pengastulan
Celuk Pengastulan
Pengastulan
Seririt
Dencarik
Tiga Wasa
Ume Anyar
Sulanyah
Kalianget
Banjar Tegeha
Patemon
Bubunan
Cempaga
Ringdikit
Hot Spring
Brahmavihara Arama
Sidetapa
Ularan
Rangdu
Banjar
Pedawa
Wanagiri
Handara Golf & Resort
Mo Pengg 215
Mayong
Views Munduk Bestala
Banyu Seri
Lake Buyan
Pancasari
Mount Mangu
Pura Pu
Unggahan
Bestala
Tirta Sari
Gobleg
Kayu Putih
Lake Tamblingan
Mount Tapak 1909m
Candikuning Bali Botanical Gardens
202
Lake Brat
Busung Biu
Gunung Sari
Munduk
Mount Lesung 1865m
Treetop Adventure Park
Pura Ul Danu B
Munduk Mengatang 884m
Titab
Kekeran
Pelapuan
Bengkel
Gesing
Pura Gubug Tamblingan
Lubang Nagaloka
Bukit Mungsu Indah
Bedu Recr Park
+ Munduk Ngandang 944m
Telaga
Kedis
Umejero
Mount Pucuk 1629m
Bedugul
Subuk
Tinggar Sari
Mount Pohen 2063m
Sepang
Bantiran
Mount Sengayang 2087m
Batuny
Pupuan
Mount Adeng 1826m
Baturiti
Puncak Sari
Pujungan
Hot Springs
Bongan Cina
Munduk Pantas 762m
Mount Batukau 2271m
Angser
Pajahan
Batungsel
Jatiluwih
Senganan
Apuan
Tista
Pura Luhur Batukaru
Rice Fields & Vista
Meka
Kebon Padangan
Sanda
Wongaya Gede
Babahan
Belatungan
Belimbing
Mengesta
Tua
Pangeragoan
Sarinbuana
Wanagiri
Tengkudak
Penebel
Biaung
Mundeh
Pitra
Yeh Ga
Payangan
Pe
Rando Hill 319m
Penatahan
Hot Spring
Pupuan Sawah
Dalang
Gunung Salak
Jegu
Burian
Marga
Lumbung
Tiying Gading
Rejasa
Margarana Memorial
Tunjuk
Sembung
Gadungan
Kesiut
Butterfly Park

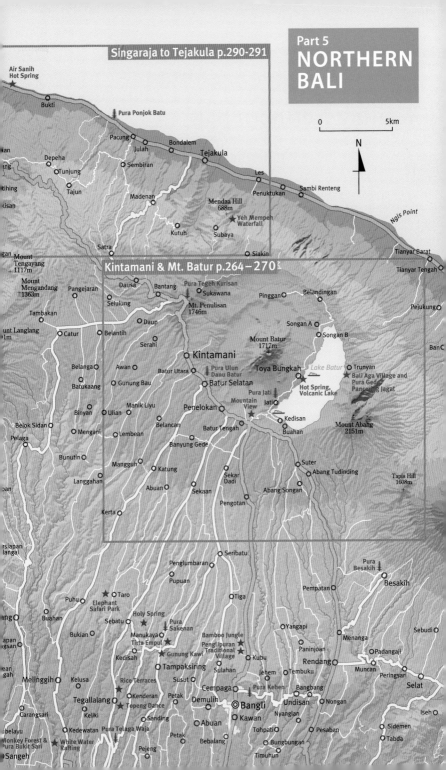

Singaraja to Tejakula p.290-291

Kintamani & Mt. Batur p.264-270

0   5km

N

Air Sanih
Hot Spring

Bukti

Pura Ponjok Batu

Pacung
Julah
Bondalem
Tejakula

Depeha
Tunjung
Sembiran
Les
Penuktukan
Sambi Renteng

Tajun
Madenan

Ngis Point

Satra
Kutuh
Subaya
Siakin

Mendaa Hill
688m
Yeh Mempeh
Waterfall

Tianyar Barat
Tianyar Tengah

Mount
Tengayang
1117m

Mount
Mengandang
1363m

Pangejaran
Dausa
Bantang
Sukawana

Pura Tegeh Kurisan

Pinggan
Belandingan

Pejukung

Selulung
Mt. Penulisan
1746m

Tambakan
Daup
Songan A
Songan B

Ban

unt Langlang
1m
Catur
Belantih
Serahi

Mount Batur
1717m

Belanga
Awan
Batur Utara
Kintamani

Batukaang
Gunung Bau
Batur Selatan

Toya Bungkah

Pura Ulun
Danu Batur

Lake Batur

Trunyan
Bali Aga Village and
Pura Gede
Pancering Jagat

Hot Spring,
Volcanic Lake

Binyan
Ulian
Manik Liyu
Penelokan

Belok Sidan
Mengani
Lembean

Belancan
Batur Tengah
Pura Jati
Mountain
View
Jati
Kedisan

Buahan

Mount Abang
2151m

Pelaga

Banyung Gede

Bunutin

Mangguh
Katung
Suter
Abang Tudinding

Tapis Hill
1608m

Langgahan
Abuan
Sekaan

Sekar
Dadi
Pengotan
Abang Songan

Kerta

rsiapan
langai

Seribatu
Pura
Besakih
Besakih

Penglumbaran
Pupuan
Pempatan

Puhu
Taro
Elephant
Safari Park
Tiga

Yangapi
Sebudi

ang
apan
gsan

Buahan
Bukian
Holy Spring
Sebatu
Pura
Sakenan

Bamboo Jungle
Penglipuran
Traditional
Village
Kubu

Paninjoan
Menanga
Rendang
Padangaji

Kedisah
Manukaya
Tirta Empul
Gunung Kawi
Tampaksiring
Sulahan
Jehem
Tembuku

Muncan
Peringsari

Melinggih
Kelusa
Rice Terraces
Kenderan
Petak
Susut
Cempaga
Pura Kehen
Bangbang

Undisan
Selat

Tegallalang
Keliki
Topeng Dance
Sanding
Demulih
Bangli
Kawan
Nongan
Nyanglan

Iseh

Carangsari
Kedewatan
Pura Telaga Waja
Pejeng
Petak
Abuan
Bebalang
Tohpati
Pesaban

Sidemen
Tabda

ubelayu
Monkey Forest &
ura Bukit Sari
Sangeh

White Water
Rafting
Bungbungan
Timuhun

INTRODUCTION

Visiting Northern Bali

For many years, Lovina Beach was Northern Bali's prime tourist destination, luring to its shores those who wanted the beach life but rejected the crowds in the south. Apart from Lovina, little else was sufficiently developed to attract large numbers of tourists. As with several other formerly unexplored areas on the island, increased investment and improved infrastructure have brought about many changes, and nearly all of them benefit travelers by giving them a wider range of climates, terrains, and activities from which to choose during their Bali holidays.

A quick look at a map will reveal that the vast expanse that is Northern Bali is dominated by two volcanoes and their accompanying cool highland climes, and a very long coastline. Thus, deciding where to stay is a relatively simple choice of sea or mountains, keeping in mind that it is completely doable to stay in both areas in one trip. For travelers who prefer to overnight where accommodations, food, and transportation are easily available, the selection can be narrowed down even more. The widest variety of accommodations for seaside life is still in and around Lovina; for the mountains it's the Bedugul Highlands. All excursions in Northern Bali can be made from either base in one day if a cursory glance is sufficient.

The north coast

The area called **Lovina** is actually a long stretch of beach passing through six villages with different names. Eateries, souvenir shops, and a complete range of accommodations line both sides of the highway. The younger crowd often chooses either budget homestays with Balinese families or the cheaper rooms in multi-storied hotels. Many of the hotels also have bungalows, which may be preferable for the more mature, although some return to foreign-owned homestays every year. Near the central beach at **Kalibubuk** village is the largest concentration of amenities; those who wish a bit of

The Brahmavihara Arama Buddhist temple near Seririt regularly hosts meditational retreats.

quiet and countryside should go east or west from the main beach. West of Lovina and south of **Seririt** is the Buddhist **Brahmavihara Arama**, and in this area there are several wellness resorts and luxury villas. There are some stunningly beautiful drives through the countryside south of Seririt.

East of Lovina is **Singaraja**, the capital of Buleleng Regency and a historic port town. Several Dutch colonial buildings on the waterfront have been restored, as has a Chinese temple dating back to 1873. Standing on stilts in the sea opposite the temple is a compound of seafood restaurants, making a nice lunch stop. Also in Singaraja is Gedong Kirtya, a library/museum/research center containing ancient *lontar* (palm leaf) texts. Continuing east from Singaraja, there are some charming old villages and unusual temples, one with baroque architecture and the other with comic reliefs. Further east from **Air Sanih hot springs** there are several spa and meditation resorts.

Bedugul Highlands—Lake Bratan

Thanks to an increased number and a variety of accommodations, it is now comfortable to stay in the **Bedugul Highlands** for a few days to enjoy the scenery and fresh mountain air, and the number of available activities makes the region worthy of more than a mere day trip. If travelling to the highlands from Singaraja, the **waterfalls** at **Gitgit** are en route. South of Gitgit are the **Twin Lakes**, surrounded by clove, coffee, and tea plantations.

At the center of the Bedugul Highlands is **Lake Bratan**, where one of Bali's most photographed temples, **Pura Ulun Danu Bratan**, sits on its western shore. The lake itself is a recreation park offering waterskiing, parasailing, canoeing, and fishing. Another popular sport is golfing, playable year round at Handara Kosaido Country Club.

The area is surrounded by plantations of cool-climate fruits, vegetables, and trees, and most hotels offer guided walks and rent out bicycles, as many paths are sufficiently well-marked for individual explorations. More exuberant trekkers might wish to climb one of the area's three mountains. South of Lake Bratan is **Bali Botanical Gardens**, an extensive complex that also includes a **Treetop Adventure Park**. If time permits, from here Mt. Batukaru is easily accessible. See the Central Bali chapter for further information.

Kintamani Highlands—Mt. Batur

An exploration of the **Kintamani Highlands** can be a quick drive-through to see the gaping hole that is an ancient crafter and fabulous panoramic views, or a longer stop to soak in the wonder of it all at leisure. Surprisingly, there is one luxury property in the caldera, but more ubiquitous are budget accommodations, usually housing climbers who require an early morning start to summit **Mt. Batur**.

The great explosion that created the giant crater is thought to have occurred around 20,000 years ago. A drive or trek through the immense caldera floor reveals house-sized boulders ejected from the volcano and except for small patches of irrigated vegetable farming and reforested sections it is barren and dry. **Lake Batur** is Bali's primary source of life-giving water. Isolated on the opposite side of the lake is **Trunyan**, a traditional village that some visitors find interesting. A regional guides association offers treks of varying durations and difficulty as well as climbs to the top of Mt. Batur.

Far above is **Penelokan** town, where several glass-fronted restaurants perched on the crater's rim have panoramic views, a particularly good choice for pausing to absorb this natural phenomenon on chilly days. There is also a museum documenting Mt. Batur's geological history.

Up the road from Penelokan is the large **Pura Ulun Danu Batur** temple complex dedicated to the lake, which was disassembled and moved here in 1927 following two devastating eruptions. Adjoining it is Pura Tuluk Biyu, relocated to this spot from active Mt. Abang.

Kintamani locals have an unfortunate reputation for being markedly less hospitable than most people elsewhere in Bali, and on cloudy, windy days the weather can be bone-chilling, so be prepared.

The Bedugul highlands are worlds away from the sweltering Balinese coast—with cool evenings, dramatic mountain sunrises and fresh air that can often be quite chilly.

KINTAMANI & MT. BATUR

An Active Volcano and a Life-giving Lake

The focal point of the mountainous Kintamani region is spectacular Mt. Batur (1,717 m or 5,633 ft) volcanic caldera with its deep crater lake, bubbling hot springs, and rugged, wild beauty. Wonderful mountain air and dizzying views in all directions, as well as several important temples, are what make Kintamani one of the most memorable stops on the Bali tourist itinerary.

Notice the architecture here. Absent are the walled family compounds with beautiful gardens seen in the south. Instead, the houses here are wooden or cement blocks with tin roofs, a primitive form of solar heating to soak up the sun's rays during the day to keep families warm in the cold mountain climate at night. The people here are different, too, being more aggressive and less gentle than the southern Balinese.

A drive-in volcano

Nearing Kintamani town, the land rises steadily toward an almost featureless horizon with only Mts. Agung and Abang in view to the east and northeast, respectively. Suddenly, the road crests a ridge, ending on the rim of a vast caldera measuring some 14 km (8 miles) across. Down in the crater sits Mt. Batur's blackened cone, surrounded on one side by the long, blue waters of Lake Batur and on the other by lava fields and cultivated vegetable patches.

The great size of the crater implies that **Mt. Batur** was once a much bigger mountain

Lake Batur as seen from the ridge at Penelokan

(as large perhaps as Mt. Agung), which blew its top around 20,000 years ago. The volcano is still active; the last serious eruptions occurred between 1965 and 1974, springing from the western flank of the mountain and leaving a vast field of black, needle-sharp lava rock. Much of the expansive crater is now being farmed and there have been reforestation efforts there for several years. Although rainfall is slight, farmers irrigate their crops with water from the lake.

Lake Batur, Bali's largest lake, is the source that feeds an underground network of springs throughout the southern-central flanks of the mountain. Homage is paid to the life-giving grace of the lake at Pura Ulun Danu Batur. The original temple is down by the lake, but during the 1920s, after two massive eruptions, what remained of the shrines was disassembled, moved piece by piece, carried uphill, and rebuilt on the western rim of the crater near Kintamani town.

There are six very old settlements around the lake, called *desa bintang danu* ("stars of the lake"): Songan, Abang, Buahan, Trunyan, Kedisan, and Batur. People will tell you that these are "Bali Aga" villages, a term often taken to mean "original" (pre-Hindu) Balinese, but which some say refers to the myth of Markandya, a legendary saint-sage who led several bands of settlers to Bali from Desa Aga on Mt. Raung in East Java. In any case, the term is in popular use, and there are a number of **Bali Aga villages** throughout the mountains around Kintamani. They are distinguished by their unusual layout and the uniformity of the houses, as if they all adhere to a single design. The traditional mountain architecture is very interesting—steep bamboo shingle roof and walls of clay, woven bamboo, or wide wooden planks—but in many places this is disappearing as houses are rebuilt using modern materials.

A paved road follows the crater's rim around its southern and western circumference. From

Lake Batur at first light is a tranquil place offering stunning views, ahead of the clouds that often roll in later in the day and shroud the lake in cool mists.

the south, the first stop is **Penelokan**, which means "lookout", and indeed the views from here are stunning. Enterprising citizens capitalize on the panorama, and there are swarms of peddlers and a string of shops, restaurants and small hotels all along the road to Kintamani town. The **Museum Gunung Api Batur (Mt. Batur Volcano Museum)**, near the junction where the road from Bangli enters Penelokan, houses historical and archaeological data focused on Mt. Batur, an audio visual room presenting general information on the geology of volcanoes, a collection of volcanic rocks, and a telescope for better viewing.

The goddess of the lake

Going north from Penelokan toward Kintamani, the many *merus* (pagodas) of **Pura Ulun Danu Batur**, an imposing complex of nine temples, appear. *Ulun danu* means the "head of the lake", and the original site of this temple was at the lake's northeastern corner, the "holiest" quarter associated with the vitality of the sun as it approaches its zenith. Violent eruptions of the volcano in 1917 buried much of the area and took the lives of nearly a thousand people. Another serious eruption in 1926 forced the decision to rebuild the temple at its present site, high up on the rim of the crater. With help from the Dutch colonial government, the shrines were dismantled and transported across the lava-strewn landscape and up the steep sides of the crater, a staggering task, especially without roads or machinery.

People from the original Batur village, at the foot of the western flank of the volcano, also moved up to the new location, Batur Kalanganyar, to tend to the temple's maintenance and ceremonies. Lava from the 1917 eruption stopped only a few meters from the village, which somehow encouraged its citizens to rebuild it, damaged by tons of residual ash. The village remains just beyond the 1965–1974 lava fields.

Ida Batari Dewi Ulun Danu is the goddess of the lake. Myriad springs on the south side of the mountain feed the rich rice-growing Bangli and Gianyar districts, and Tirta Empul in Tampaksiring is one of the springs fed by Lake Batur. The various temples in the complex thus reflect a concern with not only the invisible world, but with the world of the living as well.

Ask someone to point the following major shrines out to you. **Pura Penataran Agung Batur** is the principal temple, with five main courtyards. The dominant shrines are the *merus*, an 11-tiered one for the lake goddess and three nine-tiered ones for the gods of Mt. Batur, Mt. Agung, and Ida Batara Dalem Waturenggong, the deified king of Gelgel who is said to have ruled from 1460–1550. The Chinese-looking shrine to the northwest is for Ida Ratu Ayu Subandar, the patron saint of commerce. Another important shrine is the three-tiered *meru* to Ida Ratu Ayu Kentel Gumi, who protects crops from disease. This temple was built for the Chinese wife of the Kintamani king, and local lore has it that many of the names in

Pura Ulun Danu Batur in Kintamani, decked out for its anniversary celebration

this area, such as Pinggan village, are derivatives of her native tongue.

Penataran Pura Jati is related to the source temple on the western edge of the lake, while **Pura Tirta Bungkah** is linked to the hot springs at the water's edge. **Pura Taman Sari** and **Pura Tirta Mas Mampeh** are dedicated to agriculture. **Pura Sampian Wangi** is dedicated to crafts such as weaving, sewing, and the making of offerings and ceremonial cakes. **Pura Gunarali** is where adolescent boys and girls can invoke help to develop their natural abilities. **Pura Padang Sila** consists of 45 stone shrines for the gods and goddesses of Pura Ulun Danu Batur. The major *odalan* (anniversary) of the temple, attended by people from all over Bali, occurs sometime in March and runs for 11 days.

Pura Tuluk Biyu, just next to Pura Ulun Danu, is another relocated temple. "Tuluk Biyu" is the old name for Abang, the second highest mountain in Bali at the southern edge of the Batur crater. The original temple was at the summit of Mt. Abang, and is said to have been built by the sage, Mpu Kuturan.

Panoramic frontier town

Batur Kalanganyar village borders Kintamani town, the administrative center of Bangli Regency. This was formerly a way-station over the mountains that separate Buleleng (the old Dutch colonial headquarters) from the rest of Bali. The second hotel built in Bali was in **Kintamani**, but the place still looks like, and has the feel of, a frontier town. Notable are the delicious air and spectacular vistas: the crater to one side and all Bali extending to the sea on the other. Restaurants with panoramic views line the road and are

especially crowded with local visitors during school and public holidays.

Up the road going north through Kintamani town is a market, busy every three days on *hari paseh* of the Balinese calendar. This is interesting to visit to see the variety of produce from surrounding mountain farms: oranges and tangerines, corn and tomatoes, along with the usual vast array of scented flowers, dried fish, tools, livestock, pots, and baskets, plus a big clothing market. There are also men cuddling big furry Kintamani puppies, highly prized throughout Bali and often called into service for K-9 corps duty thanks to their outstanding intelligence.

A temple of ancient kings

Passing pine forests studded with the occasional giant poinsettia and fern tree a few kilometers past Kintamani town, on the right is the entrance to **Pura Tegeh Kuripan** temple, also called **Pura Penulisan** because of its location on Bukit Penulis (Writer's Hill) at 1,745 m (5,725 ft). Constructed around the ninth century, its location is between two mountain chains, more or less separating Northern and Southern Bali. From this point the road leads to Kubutambahan (1.5 hrs) and from there on to Singaraja.

Pura Tegeh Kuripan is a powerful place, ancient, royal, and remote. A long steep flight of stairs rises through the 11 terraces of the temple complex. The pyramidal form and the large stones that are still venerated there suggest that this place has been holy for many centuries. On the third level are Pura Panu and the temple garden; on the fourth tier is Pura Ratu Penarikan.

From **Pura Panarajon** on the uppermost terrace, the north coast of Bali and the mountains of East Java can be seen on a clear day. The proportions of the courtyard and various *balai* (pavilions) are modest, but the atmosphere is heavy with the solitude of hallowed kings. There are many sacred statues, including *lingga* (phallic symbols) and mysterious fragments housed in the open pavilions. Of particular interest is a royal couple bearing the inscriptions "Anak Wungsu" and "Bhatari Mandul", dated Saka year 999 (A.D. 1077). *Mandul* means "childless", and although it is impossible to know who this refers to, one interesting conjecture is that she was the Chinese Buddhist princess Subandar, whose shrine stands in Pura Ulun Danu, and that her barrenness was caused by a curse from a Siwaite wizard.

While Pura Tegeh Kuripan sits atop Bukit Penulis, on its eastern slope is **Pura Balingkang Dalem**. Balingkan means "king of Bali", and this temple served an 11th century royal family. The king, Sri Kesari Waradewa, had a Chinese wife who was a princess of the Chung Dynasty. Their marriage is depicted in the barong dance *ladung* that is still performed today. The Chinese influence is seen in the palace itself and also on old Balinese coins.

From **Sukawana**, just to the right of Pura Tegeh Kuripan's entrance, there is a paved road that arcs along the northern rim of the crater, offering splendid views of the lava fields below. A steep drop goes to **Pinggan**, overlooking the crater, with a road connecting it with Belandingan and Songan down by the lake.

The more usual approach to the lake is via a downward sloping road from Penelokan, descending to the water's edge at **Kedisan** and heading over to Toya Bungkah, where there is a hot spring believed to cure skin diseases. There are a number of simple hotels and restaurants here, and this is a good place from which to climb the volcano and to explore the lake area.

At Kedisan at the bottom of the road you have to turn right or left. The right turn leads to a little port with boat-taxis to **Trunyan** and points around the lake; to the left is Toya Bungkah and Songan.

Of the lake villages, Trunyan is surely the most famous, but it is also has an unfortunate—and at least partially justified—reputation for hassles. The village is virtually inaccessible except by boat, and many of the hassles reported by visitors involve demands for additional money from boatmen, after an initial transport price has been agreed. Trunyan residents have also often been criticized for aggressive begging—though it's worth keeping a certain degree of perspective and remembering that those visitors outraged by demands for money from locals are entering their community and treating it as a tourist attraction and a photo opportunity.

In recent years there have been efforts to educate locals in the delicate matter of tourism skills, and things are not quite as bad as they once were, but this is certainly one community that bucks the general Balinese trend for openness and hospitality. Trunyan is a fascinating place, however. In the **Pura**

Gede Pancering Jagat—which is not open to tourists—is a unique, 4 m (13 ft) high guardian statue, Da Tonte, or Ratu Gede Pancering Jagat, but it is stored out of view in a closed *meru*. The Trunyan people do not cremate their dead, but place them exposed under a sacred tree by the lakeshore that has the remarkable property of preventing the decomposing corpses from smelling.

Continuing on the road along the lake to Songan, at its northeastern tip the landscape is barren and strange. An eerie feeling creeps in, knowing this is the caldera of the ancient, original volcano. Enormous boulders and craggy rocks protrude from the dry earth, surrounded by tall grasses with the remnants of the old Mt. Batur looming overhead. In some areas, patches of onions and corn grow in small fields between the rocks; other parts have the advantage of irrigation and sprout cabbage and tomatoes. There are several reforestation projects here funded not only by the Indonesian Forestry Department but also by foreign countries, such as Japan.

At **Toya Bungkah** is a small office marked **Association of Mount Batur Trekking Guides**, which offers several interesting expeditions. This is one of two headquarters for area licensed guides (the other is in Pura Jati), who stress heavily that only members of the association are permitted to operate here. There's a signboard listing the tours, level of difficulty, and prices. For example, "Mt. Batur Sunrise" and trekking around the main crater—their specialty, of course—are both moderate-to-difficult hikes. Mt. Abang and Mt. Agung are both marked "difficult", but there are also easy-to-moderate excursions around both craters.

The guides can also take visitors overland to Trunyan village, arranging customized treks, and overnight camping. There are several well-marked approaches to Batur from Pura Jati and from Toya Bungkah, where the climb up and back takes about 2.5–three hours. The latter route is appreciably easier.

Near the end of the road is **Songan**, an interesting village reminiscent of an Indonesian-style San Francisco, but with tiny shops and little houses perched on the sides of the hilly main street instead of grand old houses. It's a pretty area, with irrigated vegetable farms surrounding it. The site of the original **Pura Ulun Danu Batur** is at the northern tip, or "head" (*ulun*), of the lake.

door in the sister property, Toya Devasya Resort & Spa. **$$$$**

TREKKING

If you've always wanted to walk around inside the crater of an active volcano, here's your chance. Mt. Batur is 1,717 m (5,633 ft) high, but the upper cone itself is only several hundred meters above the level of the lake and can be climbed and descended in just a few strenuous hours. At the top, there's a warm crust of ground over the cauldron. The local guides association operates as a cartel, guarding its territory jealously. Attempting to climb unguided, or with a guide from elsewhere in Bali, may lead to confrontations with the locals. It's an unfortunate situation, but local guides are generally helpful and professional—as long as you do use their services!

It's best to start while it's dark, very early in the morning, 3 am or at the latest 4 am; it's cool and you're likely to see a wonderful sunrise and avoid the mid-morning clouds. A guide will probably find you before you find him, or your homestay can recommend one.

Choose someone friendly who belongs to the **Association of Mount Batur Trekking Guides,** Tel: 52362 (ask to see proof of membership), which has one small office in Toya Bungkah and one in Pura Jati. There are signboards in both offices listing the tours, their price, and level of difficulty (around $30 per person for a standard Mt. Batur hike). Other, more expensive climbing tours include Mt. Abang, Mt. Agung on the southeastern edge of the outer caldera, and further afield to Mt. Rinjani on Lombok. They can also arrange overnight camping on Mt. Batur for an extra fee.

Take a hat and wear high-top shoes or boots: Mt. Batur's slopes are covered with fine dust in the dry season (April–September) and with mud in the rainy season (October–March). Other necessary supplies are drinking water and a snack or two. If you're fortunate, a great view stretching all the way to Lombok will reveal itself as the sun rises. On reaching the summit your guide will boil some eggs in the hot, volcanic sand and make coffee.

Going down is much easier and takes half the time than it does climbing up. It's possible to take another route down, through a shaded forest via the hot springs at Toya Bungkah. The other route crosses lava fields, which can get very hot during the day, so is best used on ascent. If you don't begin from one of the Trekking Guides Association offices, ask your guide to have his car or motorbike ready to bring you back to your original starting point once you get down. Climbing is not recommended during the rainy season.

There's a good road that circles the volcano rim from Penulisan east to Pinggan and Belandingan, where it comes to a dead end. Another route is to drive past Toya Bungkah to Songan and follow the signs west to Air Mampeh. The road leads to Penelokan through the caldera behind Batur. It is sometimes difficult to pass because of volcanic sand and stones.

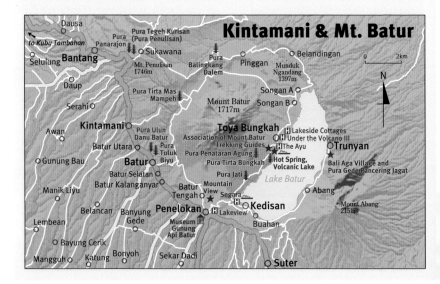

Bali's Fertile Highlands and Sacred Lakes

Heading south 30 km (18 miles) from Singaraja on the main north-south highway (Depensar-Mengwi-Singaraja) which traverses hill and dale, is the beginning of Bali's highlands in an area referred to as **Bedugul**. Southwest of long inactive Mt. Catur, it is a refreshing retreat from the beaches of the north and the overcrowded areas of the south. In the past, a lack of accommodations discouraged most tourists from spending more than just a few hours here, but as more resorts are developed highlighting delightful scenery, spectacular mountain walks and many other recreational opportunities, a new choice in experiencing all of Bali has emerged. Although crowded with tourists during local public and school holidays, it is a quiet refuge at other times.

The cool mountain retreats here are cradled in the crater of an extinct volcano and have been a popular getaway spot since Dutch times. Here lies placid Lake Bratan (also spelled Beratan), source of life-giving water for the springs, rivers and rice fields below. Verdant tropical rainforests blanket the slopes of mountains rising 2,000 m (6,560 ft) above sea level, providing temperatures several degrees lower than the plains (11-30°C), so a jacket is advised in the evenings.

Waterfalls, lakes and an upland retreat

Ten km (6.5 miles) south of Singaraja at the town of the same name is Bali's highest waterfall, **Gitgit** (Air Terjun Gitgit), looming 35 m (115 ft) above sea level. The road to Gitgit climbs steeply, offering fine views along the way. The waterfall, located about 500 m (540 yds) from the main road, is surrounded by lush, tropical vegetation. A fine, cooling mist hangs in the air, providing a refreshing welcome after the walk down. Dip your feet in the rushing river below. A rest area suitable for picnics is near the base of the falls. There are three other waterfalls in this area, the most spectacular being Gitgit Twin Waterfall.

South of Gitgit, which is surrounded by clove plantations, the road goes downhill into the crater at **Wanagiri**, on the eastern border of the **Twin Lakes, Buyan**, and **Tamblingan**, about 6 km (4 miles) northwest of Lake Bratan. There are coffee and tea shops here, overlooking stunning panoramas. A good road with breathtaking scenery follows the northern shore of the two lakes to **Munduk**, where there's a little-visited waterfall, and from there west and north back to the north coast highway at Seririt. Munduk, perched on a steep mountainside with deep valleys and spectacular rice terraces stretching out below, was originally an upland retreat for Dutch colonial officials who came to revel in the cool air at 1,200 m (4,000 ft). In recent years it has found favor afresh, and there is now an excellent array of places to stay, with a particularly good range of budget and midrange accommodations. The setting is magnificent; the nights are dark, fresh and silent; and there are infinite possibilities for wonderful walks, out into the wide green yonder.

Gitgit waterfall, one of the dramatic natural wonders found in the Bedugul Highlands.

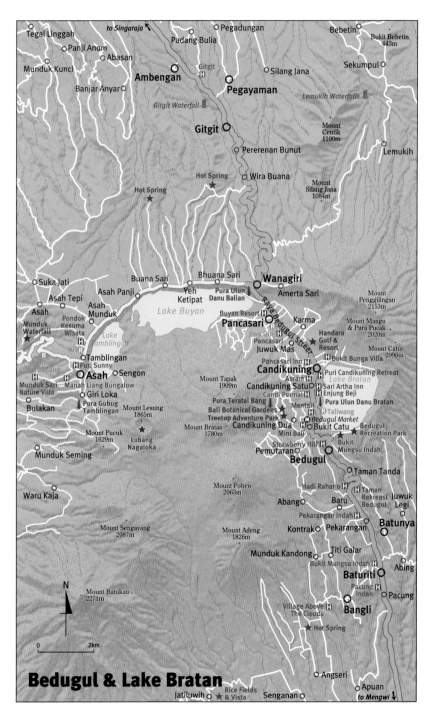

Tegal Linggah

to Singaraja

Pegadungan

Bebetin

Bukit Bebetin
443m

Panji Anom

Padang Bulia

Munduk Kunci

Abasan

Gitgit

Silang Jana

Sekumpul

Banjar Anyar

Ambengan

Pegayaman

Lemukih Waterfalls

Gitgit Waterfall

Gitgit

Mount
Centik
1100m

Lemukih

Pererenan Bunut

Hot Spring

Wira Buana

Mount
Silang Jana
1084m

Hot Spring

Suka Jati

Buana Sari

Bhuana Sari

Wanagiri

Amerta Sari

Mount
Penggilingan
2153m

Asah Tepi

Asah Panji

Yeh
Ketipat

Pura Ulun
Danu Balian

Lake Buyan

Buyan Resort

Karma

Mount Mangu
& Pura Pucak
2020m

Asah

Pondok
Kesuma
Wisata

Asah
Munduk

Pancasari

Pancasari

Juwuk Mas

Handara
Golf &
Resort

Munduk
Waterfall

*Lake
Tamblingan*

Pancasari Inn

Candikuning

Bukit Bunga Villa

Mount Catur
2096m

Tamblingan

Puri Sunny

Asah

Sengon

Asram

Puri Candikuning Retreat

Lake Bratan

Munduk Sari
Nature Villa

Manah Liang Bungalow

Giri Loka

Pura Gubug
Tamblingan

Mount Lesung
1865m

Candikuning Satu

Candi Permai

Sari Artha Inn

Enjung Beji

Mount Tapak
1909m

Pura Ulun Danu Bratan

Bulakan

Pura Teratai Bang

Mentari

Mount Pucuk
1629m

Lubang
Nagaloka

Mount Bratan
1780m

Bali Botanical Gardens

Treetop Adventure Park

Candikuning Dua

Taliwang

Bedugul Market

Bukit Catu

Bedugul
Recreation Park

Munduk Seming

Mini Bali

Strawberry Hill

Bukit
Mungsu Indah

Pemutaran

Bedugul

Taman Tanda

Waru Kaja

Mount Pohen
2063m

Hadi Raharjo

Taman
Rekreasi
Bedugul

Juwuk
Legi

Abang

Baru

Mount Sengayang
2087m

Mount Adeng
1826m

Kontrak

Pekarangan Indah

Pekarangan

Batunya

Munduk Kandong

Titi Galar

Bukit Mungsu Indah

Abing

N

Mount Batukau
2271m

Baturiti

Pacung
Indah

Pacung

Village Above
The Clouds

Bangli

0   2km

Hot Spring

Bedugul & Lake Bratan

Angseri

Apuan

Jatiluwih

*Rice Fields
& Vista*

Senganan

to Mengwi

Tropical golf

Continuing south on the Singaraja–Denpasar highway, northwest of Lake Bratan is **Pancasari** village, which is undergoing much tourist development, including new accommodations, villas, coffee plantations, jungle trekking, and fishing.

You have now crossed over into the northern reaches of Tabanan Regency. Shortly afterwards is the **Handara Golf & Resort**, at an altitude of 1,142 m (3,746 ft) above sea level, offering fresh air and cool temperatures. One of the world's most beautiful golf courses and considered one of the best in Asia, it was designed by famous golf architects Thompson, Wolveridge, and Fream. Its 18-hole masterpiece has lush, green fairways and the fastest greens found anywhere. Trees and beds of colorful flowers line the course, and there is a spacious clubhouse complete with pro shop, sauna, and fitness center, as well as a restaurant. Open to the public except on tournament days, the course is playable all year round.

Nature walks

For those who enjoy nature more without whacking a little white ball around, there are many delightful bush walks in the Bedugul vicinity. Guides are available at most hotels, and there are scheduled group departures from Bedugul Recreation Park (Taman Rekreasi Bedugul) and from the Bali Botanical Gardens.

One exhilarating hike is a six-hour walk to the summit of **Mt. Mangu**, on the northeastern side of Lake Bratan. At the peak is an ancient temple, **Pura Pucak**, built by the first raja of Mengwi, I Gusti Agung Putu. The view is spectacular. Another walk begins at the northernmost end of the botanical gardens. There is a good wide path here, so it is safe without a guide. It leads across the foothills of **Mt. Tapak** to the northern end of the valley. The 8-km (5-mile) path emerges in the midst of vegetable gardens to reach the main road at Pancasari village.

There is a further walk passing up and behind Mt. Tapak through dense jungle to a waterfall on the other side. This is a long and steep climb and should only be ventured with a local guide and good footwear. Set off early and bring food. Nature lovers will find it well worth the effort.

It's a hearty climb starting from the Bedugul Recreational Park up **Mt. Catur**, at 2,096 m (6,876 ft). Accessible from the rim is a path leading to three 25-m (82-ft) deep caves, Goa Jepang, excavated by Indonesian forced laborers for the Japanese during World War II. It is also possible to trek the 25 km (16 miles) from Bedugul to Kintamani, heading east at Gitgit.

Lake Bratan

As the road winds up Mt. Bratan there are magnificent views stretching back over the lowlands to the coast and across to the misty peaks of Bali's volcanoes—Agung, Abang, and Batur to the east. To the west, deep gorges border tiers of jungle foliage below Mt. Batukaru's hazy peak.

Near the top of the hill the road suddenly branches to the right, sloping gently down, and a striking new panorama is revealed: sparkling blue waters backed by lush, green hills. Cottages dot the hillside down to the shores of the lake, and a pier provides a mooring for boats of all shapes and sizes. This is **Bedugul Recreation Park (Taman Rekreasi Bedugul)**, a center for waterskiing, parasailing, canoeing, and fishing. Facilities include boat sheds, jumping ramps, slalom, and trick water ski equipment.

Oddly enough, on the western shore of the lake, keeping its dignity intact while all else around it indulges in fun, dramatic **Pura Ulun Danu Bratan,** one of the most photographed temples on Bali, projects into the water. Here, local farmers make offerings to Dewi Danu, the lake goddess, who is much revered as a source of fertility. Built in 1633 by I Gusti Agung Putu, the king of Mengwi, it consists of four compounds, the two outermost of which are completely surrounded by water.

Pura Ulun Danu Bratan on scenic Lake Bratan

Pura Ulun Danu Bratan is one of the most photographed temples on Bali.

When the three-tiered Siwaitic *lingga petak* was restored, the builders discovered a bubbling spring and a big white stone flanked by two red ones, a phallic lingga representing the reproductive power of Siva as the god of fertility. Towering above this, on a separate islet, is a single shrine of 11 roofs dedicated to Wisnu in his manifestation as the lake goddess Dewi Danu, who protects all living creatures.

The main temple complex on the shore, **Pura Teratai Bang**, is a *pura penataran*, or temple of origin. Its many shrines are associated with different aspects of creation and are dominated by a large seven-tiered meru dedicated to Brahma. The smaller **Pura Dalem Purwa** is dedicated to Dewi Uma Bhogawati, the goddess of food and drink.

Lush tropical gardens

In 1959, 50 ha (1245 ac) of reforested land in the foothills of Bukit Tapak in **Candikuning** was set aside by the government as the **Bali Botanical Gardens (Kebun Raya Eka Karya Bali)**, and by 2001 the area had been increased to 154.5 ha or 381.5 ac. This extensive park is a popular place for weekenders, but during the week it is a haven of peace and solitude. A research center, it also serves educational and recreational functions. Recently added with garden grounds is the **Bali Treetop Adventure Park**. Suitable for all ages, visitors can test their skills in a series of circuits as they progress from treetop to treetop using eco-friendly bridges, nets, and cables.

More than 2,000 plant species representing flora from the mountain areas of eastern Indonesia are preserved at the Bali Botanical Gardens. Specialized collections include orchids, ferns, cacti, medicinal and ceremonial plants, roses, and aquatic flora. The library and herbarium are open to visitors and knowledgeable guides are on hand at the information center.

The temperate climate, abundant rainfall, and rich volcanic soils make the surrounding crater ideal for market gardening. In the early 1970s most local farmers cut out their coffee gardens and started growing vegetables. Now Bedugul farms supply the huge Denpasar *pasars* (markets) and hotels with fresh cabbages, carrots, onions, strawberries, passion fruit, and other fresh produce. A stop at the **Candikuning pasar** (traditional market), Bukit Mungsu, will yield delicious rewards.

The Bali Botanical Gardens in Candikuning provide easy access to lush upland forests.

ACCOMMODATION PRICE CATEGORIES Prices are for a double room, including breakfast $ = under $30; $$ = $30–$70; $$$ = $70–$130; $$$$ = over $130. **DINING PRICE CATEGORIES** Prices are based on a meal for one, without drinks $ = under $5; $$ = $5–$10; $$$ = over $10.

VISITING BEDUGUL See map, page 272.

A pleasant climate, splendid views, water sports on scenic **Lake Bratan**, the botanical gardens, fresh tropical fruits, and vegetables are but a few of the things that draw travelers to the Bedugul Highlands. With its highest peaks looming 2,000 m (6,561 ft) above sea level, it gets chilly by late afternoon, so bring a sweater. Thanks to a growing number of choices in accommodations, particularly a short drive west of the Bedugul crater in charming **Munduk**, more tourists are discovering this scenic highland retreat than ever before.

ORIENTATION

Bedugul township is on the southwestern shore of Lake Bratan and houses a number of small hotels and restaurants, shops, a bank, moneychangers, and a small but colorful market, Bukit Mungsu, where local farmers sell fruit, including freshly-picked strawberries, and handicrafts. Don't forget to bargain. There's also a narrow road leading up to Bali's famed Botanical Gardens.

Beyond the village the road descends down towards the lake, turning left. The road then continues north to Candikuning. On the right side is the entrance to the **Pura Ulun Danu Bratan** and other temples. A line of souvenir shops and a big parking lot indicate the way. There's a small fee. The walk from the Bedugul market to the temples on the shore takes around 20 minutes. From the market to the entrance of the Botanical Gardens it takes about 15 minutes on foot.

GETTING THERE & GETTING AROUND

The Bedugul Highlands are situated on the main road connecting north and south Bali, 53 km (33 miles) north of Denpasar and 30 km (18 miles) south of Singaraja. It is the perfect place to stop for a night on an island tour or to use as a base to explore the mountains and north coast.

Public buses and bemo from Ubung Terminal in Denpasar travel this way via Mengwi en route for Singaraja, as do buses and bemo from Singaraja's western bus station, heading in the opposite direction. Local bemo from Bedugul town run to Munduk and around the crater.

A few tourist shuttle operators offer Bedugul as a destination, usually picking up and dropping off on the way between Lovina and the southern resorts. A few are also starting to offer Munduk as a specific destination. The shuttle operator **Perama** has a counter at the Sari Artha Inn just below the market on the main road.

Once in the Bedugul area, hire a car and driver and wander through the area at your own pace, or combine walking with local bemo. Motorbikes are also available to rent, though riding can be challenging on steep mountain roads.

SCENIC DRIVE TO BEDUGUL FROM KINTAMANI

The Bedugul Highlands are also accessible from Kintamani on a circuitous route via Singaraja and the north coast. An alternative route used by very few people leads south through the mountains with spectacular scenery and a close view of the island's vanilla, clove, and coffee-producing plantations. The road is good enough for cars or motorbikes, but it's best to allow half a day for the journey between **Kintamani** and **Luwus**, where it connects with the main road between Denpasar and Bedugul. Stop along the way, have a cup of coffee in one of the villages, and enjoy a leisurely ride.

From Kintamani, follow the main road north until just beyond Penulisan and the Tegeh Kuripan temple. Take the small road that branches off to the left towards Belantih village. Continue west past Belantih to Lampu and neighboring Catur village, where the road bends south. Lawak village marks the beginning of the vanilla-growing region, where the harvest can sometimes be seen drying in shelters.

After Belok Sidan (keep right) head for Pelaga. Just before the village there's a sharp right turn which leads to a shortcut west to Lake Bratan, but in a few stretches the road is in poor condition. Avoid the shortcut and continue south, as the best has yet to come.

Beyond Pelaga and Kiadan, the elevated area around Nungkung and Sandakan is extremely beautiful. A bit further ahead is the Muslim Angan Tiga village, with its small mosque. The next village, Kerta, has a police station and a bank. Past the bank take the right turn to Bedugul. From Kerta, the country road leads to the main highway at Luwus. Turn right for Bedugul or left for Mengwi and Denpasar.

ACCOMMODATIONS

Some hotels are in Bedugul proper overlooking Lake Bratan, while others are located on the upper slopes of Baturiti, south of Bedugual town, offering views over volcanoes, rice fields, and on a clear day, down to the sea. These days, however, there's a much nicer array of budget accommodations in nearby Munduk (see separate listings below).

Puri Candikuning Retreat, Candikuning, Tel: 2033-252, www.puricandikuning.com. At the very edge of Lake Bratan, this small villa complex is a wonderfully tranquil place for a few days in the cool of the mountains. The rooms are spacious, and there are bathrooms with sunken bathtubs open to the stars. The wooden terraces look out on a sublime vista of water and mountains. **$$$**

Sari Artha Inn, Bedugul, between the lake and the market, Tel: 21011. An old-time guesthouse with simple, but clean rooms. The more expensive ones have hot water. The Perama office is here. **$**

Strawberry Hill Hotel, Bedugul, www.strawberryhill-bali.com. Five minutes south of Bedugul town at the Km 48 marker, this is a charming mountain hotel with cozy lodges in a hillside garden. The wooden floors are much warmer under foot on chilly evenings than the tiles found elsewhere, and there are bath tubs with hot water. The restaurant serves Indonesian food plus soups, salads, chicken, burgers, and of course strawberries. There's a log-burning fireplace for cool nights. **$$**

ACTIVITIES

Handara Golf & Resort, Pancasari, Tel: 22646, www.handaragolfresort.com. A Par 72 (36 out, 36 in) natural grass championship golf course, this is one of the most challenging in Asia, at an altitude of 1,142 m (3,746 ft) above sea level, surrounded by mountains, crater lakes, and ancient forests. Pro shop, lessons, halfway houses, rentals, and carts are available, and there's also accommodation and a restaurant

Bali Botanical Gardens (Kebun Raya Eka Karya) Candikuning, Baturiti, www.kebunrayabali.com. Situated on 157.5 ha (434 ac) with temperatures of 17–25°C, there are more than 2,000 plant species here, with a particularly impressive collection of ferns, orchids, cacti, medicinal and ceremonial plants, roses and aquatics. Admission is around $1.50, and there's a small extra fee for parking. There's a library, shop, and café, and there are several accommodations available for rent within the grounds. Open 8:30 am to 6 pm.

Bali Treetop Adventure Park, www.balitreetop.com. Located inside the Bali Botanical Gardens, this giant adventure playground has 65 treetop challenges providing memorable experiences and great views. Trained Patrol Guides explain how each circuit and safety equipment works and will advise and assist. Suitable for all ages from four years up. Reservations advised.

VISITING MUNDUK See map, page 285.

Munduk village is located on a ridge along the mountain road leading from Wanagiri, just north of Pancasari to Mayong road. Overlooking coffee and clove plantations, there is pristine Lake Tamblingan with its traditional fishing community as well as forests, waterfalls, and some of the most beautiful views on the island.

Munduk is a perfect base for treks into the mountainous Balinese hinterland. Walk to Mt. Lesong (1,860 m or 6,102 ft), around Lake Tamblingan, or visit the area's five waterfalls. Munduk has long been the center for an innovative community tourism development project, with the village setting up a number of activities for visitors. There is a wide array of accommodations to suit all budgets.

GETTING THERE

Go from Bedugul to the Pancasari *bemo* terminal, then take a bemo to Munduk. Alternatively hop on a bemo at the Pempatan crossing. Each leg should cost around $1. If you hire a car or motorbike, drive cautiously on the road to Munduk; it's steep and

tortuous. A few tourist shuttle operators are starting to offer Munduk as a destination, especially in Lovina. As the area becomes more popular expect shuttle transport to become more widely available, though for now chartering a vehicle is still the easiest option.

ACCOMMODATIONS

Aditya Homestay, Jl. Pura Puseh, www.adityahomestay.com. With fabulous views from the upper floors, this family-run homestay is a well-run budget option, with tidy, hot-water rooms in a modern house. There's also a great little restaurant terrace where you have can breakfast while taking in the mountain outlook. **$-$$**

Guru Ratna Homestay, Munduk, www.guru-ratna.com. There's a dash of old-world style in the Dutch colonial cottages here, part of a traditional family complex. There are also some cheaper rooms, with good balcony views. The hosts are very welcoming, and the cheaper rooms are good value. The dining room also has good views. **$-$$**

Meme Surung Homestay, Munduk, www.
memesurung.com. The oldest of the 11 rooms here
have been around since the Dutch era, and they're
very atmospheric, with original fittings, and attached bathrooms. There's a homely feel to the
place, and fine views, off the road and up a hill in the
middle of the village. The little café serves very
decent meals. **$$**

**Munduk Moding Coffee Plantation Nature
Resort & Spa**, Banjar Dinas Asa, Gobleg, Pancasari,
www.mundakmodingplantation.com. A luxury
boutique hotel on a working coffee plantation near
the Munduk hills, the beautiful villas here are sur-
rounded by forest, coffee, and fruit trees, rice fields.
Activities include trekking, horse riding, plantation
tours. **$$$$**

Puri Lumbung Cottages, Munduk, www.
purilumbung.com. The antique traditional Balinese
lumbung (rice granaries) here have all been convert-
ed into comfortable rooms with hot water. They
stand in a fine garden, looking out over the rice
fields, and make for very atmospheric places to stay.
There are also larger family villas. Packages featuring
traditional crafts and outdoor activities are available,
and there's a good spa onsite. Cookery lessons are
also available. **$$$**

Sanak Retreat, Menagung, www.sanakbali.com.
The beautiful hardwood bungalows here stand
proud in the green mountain landscapes, with epic
rice field views, and lashings of Balinese atmosphere. The rooms are wonderfully private, yet make
the most of the natural surroundings, and come
with lots of quirky and characterful furnishings and
some interesting books left artfully for your perusal.
There's a spa, a small pool, and an excellent restaurant. **$$$$**

Village Above the Clouds, Munduk Andong
Kelod, www.desaatasawan.com. The standalone
cottages here are halfway between a Balinese rice
barn and a Swiss cottage, with lots of tropical hardwood and bamboo, and they perch on a high
ridgetop with mighty views out into the green world
below. The setting is beautiful and very serene, and
the restaurant does excellent, creative Balinese
cuisine. **$$$-$$$$**

Spectacular Munduk waterfall

Bali's Historic Northern Port City

S ituated almost in the center of Bali's northern coastline, **Singaraja** is reachable from south or central Bali via the island's major north–south Denpasar–Singaraja thoroughfare, giving travelers an opportunity to experience vast changes in topography, agriculture, scenery, and climate. An east–west coastal highway also makes it easily accessible to other parts of the island.

Although Singaraja is not a tourist destination per se, it's interesting enough for a drive through and lunch stop-over or coffee break when traveling to other parts of the island.

Singaraja tour

The sights of Singaraja reflect the city's successive historical incarnations, first as a royal court center, then in the 19th century as the headquarters for Dutch commerce and administration for all of eastern Indonesia,

Yudha Mandala Tama Independence Monument overlooks Singaraja's historic harbor, with seafood restaurants on stilts behind it.

and now as the modern capital of Buleleng Regency. Until 1953, when shipping was moved to Benoa Harbor, Singaraja remained Bali's most important port and its educational, business, and governmental center. Its population reflects its heritage as a busy trading center and includes descendants of Arab, Chinese, Buginese (from Makassar, in Sulawesi), and Javanese traders, some of whom live in areas near the harbor, which have names like Kampung Arab and Kampung Bugis. But before modern highways were built, passing through the highlands to reach Singaraja from other parts of Bali was difficult and time consuming, causing the central government to move the provincial capital to Denpasar in 1958, in the more accessible south. Today, Singaraja is an efficient and well-kept district capital with two universities, and it is Bali's second largest city after Denpasar.

Starting in the western end of the city, visit **Pantai Lingga (Lingga Beach)** just before the Banyusari bemo station. The road to Pantai Lingga ends at **Bukit Suci** ("sacred hill"), an old Chinese cemetery overlooking the sea. Now suffering from lack of care, some of the graves are most unusual. One belonging to an illustrious member of the Chinese community, is surrounded by a rail, and guarded by lions and two life-sized black guards swathed in white turbans and bearing lances. Walk through the cemetery to Pantai Lingga, a swimming spot much favored by locals.

From Pantai Lingga head east to a modern house at Jl. Dewi Sartika 42, the **Pertenunan Berdikari Handwoven Cloth Factory**. Specializing in textiles portraying traditional Buleleng motifs, it's one of the few places on Bali to see women weaving cloths. Using stand-up wooden looms, their unique designs feature characters from *wayang* puppet shows and one, called *naga candi*, depicts split-gate entrances to Balinese temples and *merus* (pagodas) bordered by two giant dragons.

East of the main crossroads of the town lies Singaraja's main **shopping district**,

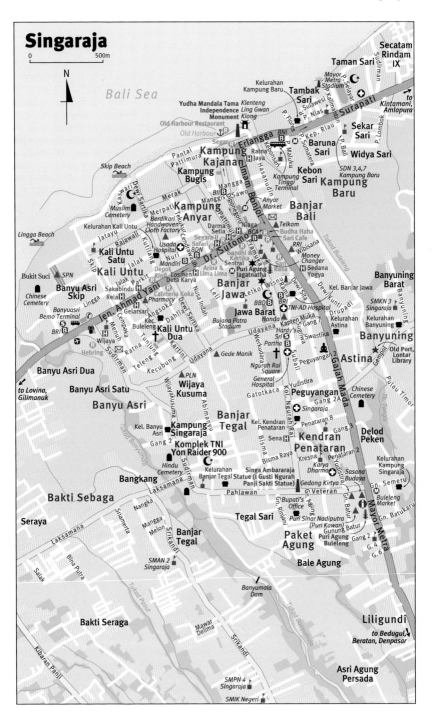

Singaraja

0   500m

N

Bali Sea

Secatam
Rindam
IX

Taman Sari

Mayor
Metra
Stadium

Tambak
Sari

Surapati

Kelurahan
Kampung Baru

Sekar
Sari

to
Kintamani,
Amlapura

Yudha Mandala Tama
Independence
Monument

Klenteng
Ling Gwan
Kiong

Old Harbour Restaurant

Old Harbour

Skip Beach

Baruna
Sari

Widya
Sari

Kampung
Kajanan

Kampung
Bugis

Kebon
Sari

SDN 3,4,7
Kampung Baru

Kampung
Baru

Lingga Beach

Muslim
Cemetery

Kelurahan Kali Untu

Berdikari
Handwoven
Cloth Factory

Kampung
Anyar

Anyar
Market

Banjar
Bali

Telkom

Budha Haha
Sari Cafe

Usada
Hospital

Kali Untu
Satu

Kali Untu

Money
Changer

Sedana
Yoga

Bukit Suci

SPN

Banyuning
Barat

Chinese
Cemetery

Banyu Asri
Skip

Banyuasri
Bemo Terminal

Banjar
Jawa

Kel. Banjar Jawa

SMKN 3
Singaraja

Kelurahan
Banyuning

Banyuning

BRI

Jen. Ahmad Yani

Jawa Barat

Honda

TNI-AD Hospital

Kelurahan
Astina

Kali Untu
Dua

Bujana Patra
Stadium

Hardy's

Swastika

Astina

Old Port,
Lontar
Library

Hebring

Wijaya

Gede Manik

Ngurah Rai
Square

General
Hospital

Peguyangan

Chinese
Cemetery

Pulau Timor

Banyu Asri Dua

to Lovina,
Gilimanuk

Banyu Asri Satu

Wijaya
Kusuma

PLN

Gatotkaca

Peguyangan

Singaraja

Banyu Asri

Banjar
Tegal

Kel. Kendran
Penataran

Kendran
Penataran

Delod
Peken

Kampung
Singaraja

Gang 2

Komplek TNI
Yon Raider 900

Sena

Bisma Raya

Kresna

Karya
Dharma

Kelurahan
Kampung
Singaraja

Hindu
Cemetery

Bangkang

Kelurahan
Banjar Tegal

Singa Ambararaja
Banjar Tegal Statue (I Gusti Ngurah
Panji Sakti Statue)

Sasana
Budaya

Gedong Kirtya

Buleleng
Market

Bakti Sebaga

Pahlawan

Bupati's
Office

Gn. Semeru

Seraya

Banjar
Tegal

Tegal Sari

Puri Sinar Nadiputra
(Puri Kawan)

Paket
Agung

Puri Agung
Buleleng

SMAN 2
Singaraja

Bale Agung

Banyumala
Dam

Bakti Seraga

Liligundi

to Bedugul,
Beratan, Denpasar

SMPN 4
Singaraja

SMIK Negeri

Asri Agung
Persada

which includes a bank, a pizza place, a few tourist souvenir kiosks, and several silver and gold shops. The heart of the city is at the intersection of Jl. Gajah Mada and Jl. Jen. Ahmad Yani, where there are banks, a post office, and several small restaurants. The Buleleng market, **Pasar Anyar**, just off Jl. Gajah Mada, is down a narrow lane that runs behind a northeast group of buildings. From sunrise throughout the morning it is packed with sellers and traders buying meat and vegetables and offering flowers, clothes and homewares. Around dusk this area turns into an animated night market. Not to be missed.

From the main shopping district it is just a short drive north to the **old harbor**, passing through streets lined with sadly deteriorating Dutch colonial buildings that are masked by large 21st-century signboards. Keep an eye out on Jl. Jen. Ahmad Yani, the main street, for an unusual **mosque** in the Dutch architectural style. Across a small bridge that was a gift from the Queen of Holland is the harbor, with a few restored buildings from the Dutch colonial period lining the now unused port, giving a glimpse into life as it must have been when spices, vanilla, and tobacco were exported, and later, before the opening of Ngurah Rai Airport in the 1970s, when cruise ships landed here and all tourists to Bali entered through this port. Standing along the shoreline is a clutch of restaurants on stilts serving tasty grilled seafood, a pleasant interlude at lunchtime cooled by sea breezes. The gigantic **Yudha Mandala Tama independence monument**, with an Indonesian freedom fighter bearing a flag, looms over the harbor and has now been surrounded by decorative brick paving blocks to form a nice terrace.

Across the street from the monument is the **Ling Gwan Kiong Chinese temple** (*klenteng*), one of the few on Bali and evidence of this community's long presence in the town. Buddhism, Confucianism, and Taoism are all practiced here. Although the building has been restored many times and looks very new, with a precisely landscaped garden, the original ceiling, constructed in 1873, is above the inner altar. A large bell in the forecourt was brought over from England, and lamps from Holland are part of the old structure. The temple is open to everyone for prayer, and the English-speaking caretaker is happy to show visitors around.

At the southern end of Singaraja, overlooking the Jl. Ngurah Rai and Jl. Veteran

junction roundabout, stands an imposing statue of Singa Ambararaja—a winged lion who gazes imperiously over the city. Another large monument on Jl. Veteran is of Ki Gusti Ngurah Panji Sakti, founder of the Buleleng dynasty. The name "Singaraja" means "Lion King."

Heading east from here along Jl. Veteran, stop in at No. 22. On the right-hand side is **Gedong Kirtya**, a library/museum/research center founded by the Dutch in 1928 for the preservation of *lontar* (palm leaf) texts collected in Bali and Lombok. Although the majority of real treasures are housed in Holland, a glass display case in the second room contains these traditional manuscripts, which are written in Balinese and Kawi (old Javanese) languages. The collection also includes books covering religion, architecture, philosophy, medicine, and black magic in Balinese, Kawi, Dutch, English, and German, as well as several *prasasti* (ancient copper plate inscriptions). You may be fortunate to see one of the employees copying an old *lontar* onto new palm leaves, or even the now rare art of making *prasati*.

Directly behind Gedong Kirtya is **Puri Kawan** (the "Western Court"), part of the former palace of the king of Singaraja. It is now the location of **Perusahaan Puri Sinar Nadiputra**, a textile mill where *sarungs* bearing Buleleng motifs were traditionally woven for the royal family and ceremonial occasions.

A few meters to the east is a major crossroads with a market on the southeast corner. To the southwest is the **Sasana Budaya** (Buleleng Cultural Center), an exhibition hall where cultural performances, art exhibitions, and festivals are held. (Check events schedules at the Tourist Information Center on arrival.) **Puri Agung Buleleng (the Royal Palace)**, also called Puri Gede, is on Jl. Mayor Metra near the Cultural Center. It was built in 1604 by Raja Ki Gusti Anglurah Pandji Sakti at the beginning of his rule of the Buleleng Kingdom, which once extended from Java to Timor, in eastern Indonesia. Renovated several times, his descendants still live here and during limited opening hours, visitors may see the old house where kings once lived, historic family photos, and the Merajan Puri royal shrine. The last Buleleng raja, Anak Agung Pandji Tisna, ruled until 1950 and established the first tourist accommodation in what is now as Lovina.

ACCOMMODATION PRICE CATEGORIES Prices are for a double room, including breakfast $ = under $30; $$ = $30–$70; $$$ = $70–$130; $$$$ = over $130. DINING PRICE CATEGORIES Prices are based on a meal for one, without drinks $ = under $5; $$ = $5–$10; $$$ = over $10.

VISITING SINGARAJA See map, page 279.

While it's possible to make a day-trip to the north coast from southern Bali, it's a very long drive and you really need to stay longer to see the entire area. It's best to base yourself either in the Lovina area, with its wide choice of hotels and restaurants catering to every budget, or in the cool climate of the Bedugul Highlands further south. From either location, the rest of northern Bali is easily accessible.

Even though Singaraja is Bali's second largest city, it hasn't quite gotten the hang of developing itself for tourism. However, it's a pleasant place to visit, with a flavor more akin to the multi-ethnic cities of northern Java than the rest of Bali. By urban Indonesian standards the traffic is manageable, and the majority of businesses are conveniently located on one main street, Jl. Jen. Ahmad Yani.

GETTING THERE & GETTING AROUND
Singaraja can easily be reached from all parts of Bali, and as a major town it's one place easily accessible by public transport. From Denpasar, it takes 2–3 hours (78 km/48 miles) by car via the Bedugul Highlands. Another road, still more breathtaking, runs through Tabanan, Pupuan, and Seririt.

There are three terminals in Singaraja: Sukasada, Banyusari, and Penarukan. *Bemos* from Denpasar's Ubung terminal and Kintamani arrive at Sukasada in the south of town, those from Gilimanuk (about $2) arrive at Banyusari to the west of town, while those from Amlapura go to Penarukan terminal in the east of town.

ACCOMMODATIONS
As the Lovina strip starts only 6 km (4 miles) to the west of Singaraja, visitors tend to head there rather than stay here. If stuck in the city, however, give these two places a try.

Sakabindu Hotel, Jl. Jen. Ahmad Yani 104, Tel: 21791. Simple accommodations in the middle of the city. $

Wijaya Hotel, Jl. Sudirman 74, Tel: 21915. There's a wide selection of relatively quiet, well-kept, if ordinary rooms here, some with air-con, conveniently located near Banyusari terminal. $-$$

DINING
Singaraja is not particularly well known for its restaurants. The best option are the seafood eateries on stilts on the waterfront in front of the Chinese temple. Good food at reasonable prices; great seaside atmosphere.

ACTIVITIES
The Buleleng government has restored some Dutch colonial buildings at the old harbor and have added a nice terrace around the independence monument and the seafood restaurants, hoping to transform the area into a tourist attraction. They are also focusing on the buildings adjacent to the Gedong Kirtya library: the handwoven fabric factory (which was once part of the palace), the Buleleng Cultural Center, the Royal Palace, and a tourist information center, all in one location.

Gedong Kirtya, Jl. Veteran, in the Sasana Budaya complex. Established by the Dutch in 1928, this museum/library/research center houses valuable *lontar* manuscripts etched on palm leaves, *prasati* transcriptions on metal plates, and books in several languages that deal with many aspects of human life. Renovated in 2008, it was transformed from a musty old library to a full museum. Open Monday–Thursday 7:30 am–3:30 pm, Friday 7 am–12:30 pm, closed on public holidays.

Puri Agung Buleleng (Royal Palace), Jl. Mayor Metra. Parts of the home of Buleleng kings since 1604 are now open to guests who want to know more about Singaraja's history. See the old house, historic family photos, and a royal shrine. Open 4–6 pm daily, closed on public holidays.

Sasana Budaya (Buleleng Cultural Center), Jl. Veteran. An exhibition hall where dance performances and art exhibitions are held. Check schedules upon arrival. Singaraja hosts two annual art festivals, with dancers, musicians, and other artists flocking to the city. The Bali Art Festival is held in May/June and the North Bali Festival in August.

MEDICAL & MONEY
Rumah Sakit Umum (General Hospital), Jl. Ngurah Rai, tel: 22046, is the largest public hospital in northern Bali. The city's **pharmacies** are concentrated along Jl. Diponegoro. The main **post office** is at Jl. Gajah Mada 156. Open Mondays–Thursdays and Saturdays 7:30 am–4 pm, Fridays 7:30–3 pm. Several banks change money and have ATMs.

WEST OF SINGARAJA: LOVINA TO SERIRIT

Tranquil Beaches on Bali's North Coast

West of Singaraja is Lovina beach resort area, which until fairly recently was the main draw of Northern Bali. Formerly thought of as Bali's best snorkeling area, it also attracted those wishing escape from the over-crowded beaches of the south. After initially emerging as a resort in the 1980s, Lovina slipped into low-level decline for a number of years. Recently, however, with fresh interest in dolphin-watching aboard local fishing boats, and a general shift away from the major southern tourist centers, there has been a renewed buzz. New resorts and spas are springing up along the shoreline, older hotels are being spruced up, and Lovina is now also a good base for exploring the fabulous scenery and outdoor activities available to its south and east. It's usually quiet, except during July and August and Indonesian school holidays.

Lovina Beach
Six kilometers (four miles) west of Singaraja is

Lovina Beach, a long stretch of black sand bordering the coastal villages Pemaron, Tukadmungga, Anturan, Kalibubuk, Kaliasem, and Temukus. Numerous eating establishments and accommodations, ranging from backpacker homestays to luxury villas, line the coast for some 12 km (8 miles). The pace of life at Lovina reflects the calmness of the sea and its rural atmosphere. With coral reefs protecting the shore and blocking the undertows prevalent on southern beaches, a shallow sea near the shore and the water warm year round, this is an excellent spot for swimming. Snorkeling is good near the reef (local colorful fishing boats—*perahu*—are available for hire), and it is a good central location from which to explore northern and central Bali. The sunsets at Lovina are particularly spectacular.

The name "Lovina" was coined by the last king of Buleleng. A convert to Christianity, he gave the name to a small tract of land that he purchased at Kaliasem, where he built the Tasik Madu ("Sea of Honey") Hotel in 1953

Lovina Beach

Restaurants
1. Poco Lounge
2. Akar
3. Zigiz Bar
4. Lumbung Bar
5. Jasmine Kitchen
6. Seyu
7. Bali Apik
8. Bali Bintang
9. Kakatua
10. Warung Kopi Bali
11. Warung Jepun Bali
12. Warung Gula
13. Kenyir Manir
14. Barcelona
15. Sea Breeze Cafe

Hotels
1. Zen Resort
2. Nirwana Seaside Cott
3. Pondok Elsa
4. Angsoka
5. Harris Homestay
6. Padang Lovina
7. Puri Manik Sari
8. Chonos
9. Rattan Resto (Amadeu

Dive Centres
1. Spice Dive
2. Malibu Dive Center
3. Sunrise Dive Center
4. Raja Dive Center
5. Permai Dive Center

Dolphin-watching is a popular pastime at Lovina Beach.

(which no longer exists). Some say the name Lovina signifies the "love" that is contained in the "heart" of all people. While the name originally applied to Kalibubuk, it has now been expanded to include four adjoining beaches, which are accessed by small lanes running perpendicular to the east–west coastal highway.

Kalibubuk village remains the center of Lovina, and north of the main road (Jl. Raya Singaraja-Seririt) is the largest concentration

of nightlife, hotels, restaurants, shops, and money changers. Those who prefer a quieter retreat might be happier at either end of the beach—in Pemaron or Temukus villages—which border farmland and traditional villages. At the end of Jl. Binaria, on **Binaria Beach** is a **Dolphin Statue**, the "mascot" of Lovina and a gathering place for both locals and visitors. Its coconut palms, simple thatch-roofed *warungs*, and volcanic black sand are an ideal backdrop for romantic sunsets.

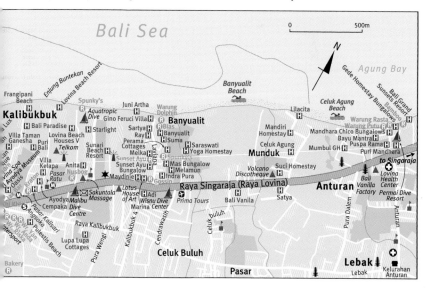

The cool upland lakes around Munduk are just a short drive from the coast at Lovina.

Dolphin-watching trips are offered at every hotel, as well as on the beaches. They depart every morning at dawn, and the hope is that there are more dolphins to see than tourist-filled *perahu*.

Further west

From Temukus at Lovina's western boundary it is 3 km (2 miles) to the twin villages **Dencarik** and **Banjar Tegeha**. Pass through Dencarik to neighboring Banjar Tegeha, home of the splendid Buddhist **Brahmavihara Arama**, which plays a central role in Buddhist religious life and education. Opened in 1970 after 10 years of construction, it replaces another founded in Banjar in 1958, which the followers merely outgrew. It combines architectural and iconographic elements found throughout the Buddhist world with a Balinese twist. Quiet, cool, and set high in the hills, it commands a view down to the ocean. The gardens and most of the compound are open to the public for meditation; however, the main building housing gold Buddhas and stupas is closed at night for security reasons. People from around the world and of all religions assemble here to practice meditation. Visitors are requested to dress in a respectful manner, to speak softly, and to remove their shoes before entering.

Banjar is also the site of the **Banjar Air Panas**, a sacred hot spring. The sulfurous spring water has been channeled into a public bathing area consisting of three pools, set in a tasteful blend of jungle and garden. The pleasant 38°C (100 °F) water, which is thought to have healing properties, pours forth from the mouths of eight *nagas* (mythical snake-dragon creatures) into an upper pool, and from there into another one below. Adjacent to these large pools is a smaller one with three upper level spouts, which do nicely for a strong massage. There are changing rooms, showers, toilets, and a restaurant. The best time to visit is early mornings, being careful to avoid weekends and public holidays when the hot springs are crowded.

Just 3 km (2 miles) west of Banjar lies **Seririt**, the former commercial center of Buleleng Regency. It was devastated by an earthquake in 1976 and was subsequently rebuilt, but some of its Dutch colonial architecture remains. There's a lively night market in the center of town. Seririt does not in itself warrant a visit. However, if you have private transport, there are two scenic drives worth taking that commence there.

A road heading south from Seririt climbs into the highlands through Bubunan, Petemon, Ringdikit, and Rangdu villages, passing some dramatic scenery along the way. This road eventually crosses the main watershed, and leads down to the Denpasar-Gilimanuk highway west of Selemadeg, A left turn at **Rangdu**, however, leads along another 13 km (8 miles) of mountain road to **Munduk**, and beyond, past the Tamblingan and Buyan lakes, to Bedugul.

A big surprise

Alternatively, continue going west to Pemuteran and the West Bali National Park. Along the beaches running parallel to the north coast highway across the border into western Bali are resorts — some of them dedicated to relaxation, meditation, and yoga — and sprawling complexes of foreign-owned luxury villas.

At Seririt the rice fields start blending in with a new crop that's more familiar to Europe than Asia: vineyards. Signs leading to resorts

and villas begin appearing here. Suddenly along the coastline near **Ume Anyar** there is new development that seems so unlikely a spot that stumbling across it is nothing short of a big surprise. Tucked off the road toward the sea are a handful of resorts on the newly developed **Ume Anyar Beach**, and next to that is a sprawling compound of luxury villas owned by foreigners, who primarily live there only a small part of the year and lease them through rental agencies for the remainder. Street after street is filled with extravagant villas, with more under construction. For travelers who desire elegant living far away from mainstream tourist areas, this may be ideal.

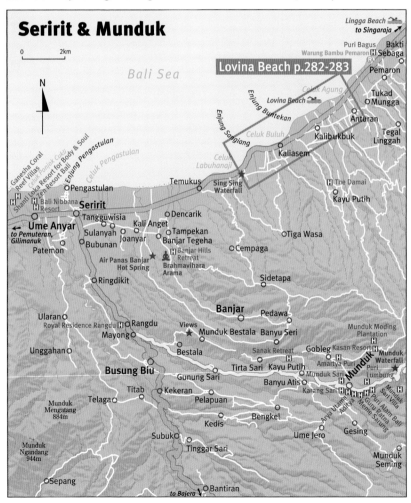

Seririt & Munduk

ACCOMMODATION PRICE CATEGORIES Prices are for a double room, including breakfast $ = under $30; $$ = $30–$70; $$$ = $70–$130; $$$$ = over $130. **DINING PRICE CATEGORIES** Prices are based on a meal for one, without drinks $ = under $5; $$ = $5–$10; $$$ = over $10.

VISITING LOVINA See map, pages 282–283.

The area known as Lovina comprises several villages along the coastal road west of Singaraja. From east to west they are: Pemaron, Tukadmungga, Anturan, Kalibukbuk (the original "Lovina"), Kaliasem, and Temukus. All offer accommodations and many other tourist services.

It is quiet and rural at either end of the beach. Central Lovina (Kalibukbuk) can be crowded during holidays. The black sand beach is beautiful at sunset and sunrise. There's no surfing, but plenty of coral areas for snorkeling. Local fishermen can also be hired for early morning trips to see dolphins offshore; arrange with the boatmen a day in advance. If you have had enough of the sea, the mountainous hinterland to the south is great for hiking.

GETTING THERE
Lovina is only ten minutes from Singaraja, which has **public transport** connections to Denpasar and other major towns. Bemos to and from Singaraja (Banyusari terminal) cost around $1. Just flag one down along the road. By private car or direct tourist shuttle from Kuta takes around 2.5 hours. Lovina is well connected to other tourist centers via shuttle buses.

There are regular direct buses to cities in Java, originating in Singaraja. Many will pick up in Lovina on the way through if booked via a travel agent there. **Perama**, Jl. Raya Lovina in Anturan, is a reliable agent. Perama also sells shuttle bus tickets.

Tours of the area, as well as snorkeling, sailing, and dolphin trips can be taken care of by all hotels. The easiest way to arrange for bicycle (note that there are a lot of steep hills away inland), motorbike, and car rentals is also through local accommodations.

ACCOMMODATIONS
After beginning to look a little faded a decade ago, Lovina recently seems to have gotten its second wind as a resort, with lots of newly established boutique hotels and villas, as well as plenty of longer-established budget and midrange options.

Binaria Beach is at the end of Jl. Binaria, where there are lots of budget guesthouses. From here there's a path through a tree-lined area to Jl. Rambutan and Rambutan Beach. And from Rambutan Beach there's a trail to Kartika Beach, at the end of Jl. Kartika. Banyualit Beach is at the end of Jl. Laviana in the easternmost part of Kalibukbuk, and is quiet and uncrowded.

Adirama Beach Hotel, Jl. Raya Singaraja-Seririt, Kaliasem, www.adiramabeachhotel.com A uniquely located, cozy hotel on a quiet, long stretch of beach with ocean view, this place has standard rooms, suites, and family rooms, all attractively furnished. The cheaper rooms are excellent value, and the breakfasts are tasty. The welcoming staff can arrange tours and transport. $$-$$$

Aneka Lovina Villas & Spa, Jl. Raya Kalibukbuk, www.anekalovinabali.com. The cottages and suites here are good value, and you'll often get an excellent discount if you walk in during quiet times. The rooms are modern and in good condition, if not particularly characterful, but the public areas including the restaurant are attractive, and the neat and tidy gardens make for a pleasant setting. $$

Bali Paradise Hotel, Jl. Kartika, Kalibukbuk, www.baliparadisehotel.com. A small hotel set in the rice fields, this is a great place to watch the daily lives of farmers, with mountain and ocean views from almost every room. The rooms come with some funky modern artwork that adds a definite dash of character. There's a swimming pool in the lush gardens, and traditional Balinese massage is available. $$

Banjar Hills Retreat, Banjar Tegehe, www.balibanjarhills.com. A small hotel overlooking the sea with twin and queen size bedrooms, all with garden bathrooms, hot water, AC, ceiling fans, and breezy terraces. There's a small swimming pool, and a restaurant. $$

The Damai, Jl. Damai, Kayu Putih, www.thedamai.com. An exquisite array of luxury villas with butler service in the hills 4 km (2.5 miles) inland from the beach, this is one of the finest accommodations in the Lovina area. The award-winning restaurant serves organic vegetables and meats from its own farm, and freshly caught fish. The spa offers therapeutic massage and body treatments using Balinese and other techniques. Most people struggle to leave the premises once they check in, so the all-inclusive packages are a good bet. $$$$

Gede Homestay, Anturan, Tel: 41526, www.gede-homestay.com. Several kilometers east of central Lovina, this is a decent budget option for those seeking peace and quiet. There are two rows of comfortable bungalows, all clean and well kept, and the more expensive ones with decent living areas and terraces. It's a friendly, family run place, in a village setting. $

Nugraha Lovina Seaview Resort & Spa, Jl. Raya Lovina, www.nugrahalovina.com. Set in a coconut grove along Lovina Beach, there's a hint of colonial style in the suites here, with their chunky four-poster beds, and vintage furnishings. The sea-view balcony rooms are a little more generic and modern, but they are also comfortable, excellent value, and the views are fabulous. **$$$**

Puri Bagus Villa Resort Lovina, Jl. Raya Seririt-Singaraja, Desa Pemaron, www.puribagus.net. There's a cozy, intimate atmosphere at this seaside hotel, with its extremely comfortable Balinese-style beachfront villas, each with private pool and dining room, terrace, and open-air shower. The beachside restaurant and bar is a great place for spectacular sunsets. The management offers water sports, land tours, and a sunrise breakfast tour on a private boat. The Java Spa is set in a "floating" building. **$$$$**

Rambutan Boutique Hotel & Spa, Jl. Mawar, Kalibukbuk, www.rambutan.org. There's a wide array of rooms at this family-run complex, all set around an attractive garden filled with fruit trees, some with unbeatable ocean views. The cheaper rooms are rather plain, but the more expensive ones are pleasantly furnished and have attractive bathrooms. There are two pools, and tours and cooking classes are available. **$$-$$$**

Rini Hotel, Jl. Ketapang, Kalibukuk, www.rinihotel.com. A good all-rounder, this popular hotel has a range of simple but well-maintained rooms in a garden setting with a swimming pool. Decent discounts are available low season. **$-$$**

Starlight Restaurant & Villas, Dusun Banyualit, Kalibukbuk, Tel: 3391-921, www.starlight-bali.com. The modern uniquely-styled cottages here come with air-con, flat-screen TVs, and comfortable furnishings. They are close the beach and set in a lovely garden with a small pool. **$$$**

Sunari Beach Resort, Jl. Raya Lovina, www.sunari.com. This large resort has decent cottages in a large, well-kept garden. The renovated villas have private plunge pools and Jacuzzis. The beach is just a few steps away, and there are good facilities onsite. Decent discounts are available low season. **$$$**

DINING

The highest concentration of food and beverage outlets are on Jl. Binaria, Jl. Pantai, and Jl. Rambutan, with a typical array of tourist offerings, from pan-Asian to Italian, plus some decent Indonesian offerings. Food stalls on Binaria beach open around 4 pm and attract both local people and visitors with their simple, cheap fare. Nearly all hotels and some of the homestays in the area have restaurants. Below are some of the most popular independent eateries.

Barcelona, Kalibukbuk, Tel: 41894. Despite the name, Indonesian cuisine, plus a few international travelers' favorites, is the name of the game here. Service is friendly, portions are generous, and prices are reasonable. Lunch and dinner. **$-$$**

Jasmine Kitchen, Jl. Binaria, Kalibukbuk, Tel: 41565. There's excellent, authentic Thai cuisine on offer in this stylish two-story building. The setting is delightful, with a fine ambiance, and the coconut ice cream for dessert is delicious. Lunch and dinner. **$$**

Buda Bakery, Jl. Damai, Kalibukbuk, Tel: 812-4691-779, Tucked away on a quiet street, and with laidback lesehan-style seating, this is a gem of a place for a stylish and delicious lunch. There are great salads and sandwiches and hot meals, including excellent fish and chips, but it's the baked goods that really take the biscuit. Breakfast, lunch, and dinner. **$$**

Lumbung Bar-Restaurant, Jl. Binaria, Kalibukbuk, Tel: 0877-6264-5167. An old-time expat hangout with terrace seating and a bamboo bar serving cold beer, cocktails, juices, and coffee. There's also an inside bar and dining area with wide screen TV and a pool table. The menu offers travelers' standards, with decent pasta, and the English-speaking staff can provide helpful tour information. Breakfast, lunch, and dinner. **$$**

Sea Breeze Café, Jl. Binaria, Kalibukbuk, Tel: 41138. This is a popular eatery west of the Dolphin Statue serving well-prepared entrees, fish, and vegetarian dinners, sandwiches, and desserts. There's live music at the weekend. **$$**

Spunky's Bar-Restaurant, Banyualit Beach, Kalibukbuk, Tel: 41134. In a quiet beachfront location, this is a fine place for a sunset cocktail, or a lazy afternoon beer. There's also some reasonably priced Indonesian and international cuisine. Lunch and dinner. **$$**

Warung Bambu Pemoran, Jl. Hotel Puri Bagus, Desa Pemaron, www.warung-bambu.mahanara.com. Between Singaraja and Lovina, this little restaurant has rustic bamboo décor, packed with an eclectic array of artworks. The menu offers some excellent Indonesian and Balinese fare, including succulent sate and traditional riijstafel spreads—a great way to sample a wide array of dishes. There is traditional Balinese dance laid on some nights, and the management also offer cooking classes. Lunch and dinner. **$$**

NIGHTLIFE

After sunset, the warungs along Jl. Binaria are popular for beer and conversation. In addition to the restaurants listed above that offer music and dance performances, there are a few other places catering to late-nighters.

Jax Bar, Jl. Raya Lovina, Kalibukuk, www.jaxbar.150m.com. Open 6 pm–midnight. Live band every night, karaoke, pool room, darts, big screen TV for sports, dance floor. Also serves Chinese food.

Pashaa Lovina Nightclub, Jl. Raya Lovina, www.pashaabalinightclub.com. Open until 3 am, this big, brash club has heavyweight DJs, laser light shows, and skimpily-clad professional dancers, plus cocktails and cold beers.

Zigiz Bar, Jl. Banaria, Kalibukuk (near the Dolphin Statue), www.zigiz-bar.com. Open until midnight, this place has live music every night, and seating across two floors. There's a large cocktail selection, plus food.

DIVING & SNORKELING

Lovina is a good base for diving and snorkeling excursions. Most hotels can arrange water sports, including snorkeling trips, not only for the Lovina area, but also for Pulau Menjangan, two hours away in West Bali National Park to the west, and Tulemben and Amed to the east. There are two major dive operators in Lovina.

Lovina Dive, Jl. Banyualit, Kalibukuk, www.lovinadive.com. Operating since 1994, this PADI dive center offers courses and fun dives to the major sites in north Bali. Dives can be tailored to individuals whether beginners, or experienced divers. Night dives are also available. Rates start at around $60 for a dive in the local area.

Spice Dive, Jl. Raya Singaraja-Seririt 225, www.spicebeachclubbali.com. Founded way back in 1989, this well-established PADI operator has been awarded many certificates of excellence, and offers day trips to all dive spots on north coast with highly trained instructor team speaking several languages. Kids welcome, and the center is now based in a beachfront lounge with a good restaurant.

VISITING SERIRIT & UME ANYAR   See map, page 285.

Until relatively recently, few travelers noticed Seririt, even when they passed through it on the way from Lovina to West Bali National Park or going to the north coast on the road from Antosari in the south. Seririt has always been not much more than a good-sized market town, and still is. A few kilometers past Seririt heading west is Ume Anyar, which can be even more easily overlooked. However, a few years ago clever real estate developers found an untouched stretch of beach in the surrounding villages and there are now hotels, wellness retreats, and an enormous complex of foreign-owned villas.

ACCOMMODATIONS

Bali Nibbana Resort, Desa Ume Anyar, www.balinibbanaresort.com. A stylish new resort located at the top of the hill in Desa Ume Anyar, this place is surrounded by fields with a view down to the sea. There are lovely tropical gardens, and the simple but attractive rooms are kept in top-notch condition. $$$$

Ganesha Coral Reef Villas, Ume Anyar, www.ganesha-bali.com. A delightful hideaway on the coast, this wellness retreat features a spa, herbal medicine, acupuncture, massage, workshops, meditation, and tai chi. the eight standalone luxury villas each come with some serious style, the netted four-poster beds standing under a high Balinese ceiling, and the bathrooms equipped with attractive stone fittings. $$$$

Royal Residence Rangdu, Jl. Muntig, Seririt, www.royalresidencerangdu.com. The luxury private villas here are set in a tranquil location, with an infinity pool and dedicated staff. The grounds have been attractively landscaped, and the mountains rise to the south, giving a fine sense of seclusion. $$$

Shanti Loka Resort for Body & Soul, Ume Anyar, www.shanti-loka.com. A wellness facility near the beach for yoga, holistic health, spa treatments, massage, cleansing, and activities, plus a yoga hall and five lovely bungalows. The restaurant serves breakfast with fruit salads, bread, and eggs, and delicious vegetarian meals for lunch and dinner. $$$$

Zen Resort Bali, Ume Anyar, www.zenresortbali.com. A luxury holistic boutique retreat to relax and rejuvenate physical, psychological, and spiritual wellness. Perched above the Bali Sea amidst rice terraces, forest, and designer gardens. $$$$

Baroque Temples and Playful Reliefs

The area east of Singaraja is noted for its ancient villages and unique temple architecture, especially those found around the coastal area from Singaraja to Kubutambahan and the region to the south. Time and again visitors have labeled this style of architecture "baroque", as the temples are so heavily adorned with reliefs that it seems no piece of stone has been spared the chisel. Another feature of this style relates to the carving of the heads and hands both of temple statues and of characters in reliefs: they protrude to such a degree that it seems as if the figures lie in wait to pounce upon unsuspecting passers-by.

Singaraja to Air Sanih (Yeh Sanih)

Not far east of Singaraja are some fine examples of charming old villages set amid lush vegetation: Sinabun, Suwug, and Sudaji, reached along a scenic road by turning right at the T-intersection prior to Sangsit.

The best example of Buleleng baroque architecture is encountered at **Pura Beji** in **Sangsit** village, 8 km (5 miles) east of

Singaraja. A small sign on the left-hand side of the road announces the location of the temple. If you subscribe to the view that once you have seen one temple you have seen them all, then cast this misapprehension aside; Pura Beji is a work of art.

Pura Beji is a *subak* temple, that is, it belongs to a rice field irrigation association. The path leading to its great, arched entrance is flanked by two serpents. The front of the arch overflows with floral motifs interspersed with demon heads. Its reverse is adorned with mask-like *garuda* heads and floral ornamentation. The main shrines have been carved just as elaborately. The beauty of this soft-pink sandstone temple is augmented by the large, gnarled frangipani trees growing in its courtyard. Note the faded paintings on two pavilions, clearly the work of master craftsmen.

Further examples of old and interesting villages are found not far to the south of Sangsit at **Jagaraga**, **Menyali**, and **Sawan**. To get there, return to the main road and take the right-hand fork at the next T-junction.

Pura Meduwe Karang in Kubutambahan is one of the many little-visited temples in northern Bali.

At Lemukih, a series of waterfalls tumble dramatically over steep cliffs.

Jagaraga, the site of fierce fighting between the Dutch and Balinese in the late 1840s, bears no obvious signs of this struggle. Visit its **Pura Dalem** dedicated to the dead and filled with statues depicting horrifying figures, the main one being of the Goddess Durga. The foreign presence in Buleleng Regency has also been captured with great humor here. See, for example, the relief of a European riding in a car held up by a knife-wielding bandit. However, such caricatures are few; this temple is dominated by the terrifying widow-witch Rangda.

From Jagaraga, drive through Menyali and follow the road as it climbs to **Sawan**, home of a well-known *gamelan* and ironsmith who can be watched at work. Head for the center of Sawan and ask for directions. His specialty is *gong kebyar*, the frenetic *gamelan* music heard throughout Bali. South of scenic **Sudaji** village at **Lemukih** are five dramatic waterfalls.

Back on the coast road, 3 km (2 miles) past the Jagaraga turn-off is old **Kubutambahan** village, best known for its **Pura Meduwe Karang** temple, which is perched high up on the left side of the road. Dedicated to the Lord of Dry Fields, although its style is more restrained than Pura Beji, it is impressive.

Three tiers of stone statues that are said to represent 34 figures from the *Ramayana* epic are positioned outside the temple. The walls are dominated by floral motifs. Renowned among the reliefs is an old one of a Dutch man riding a bicycle, its back wheel a lotus flower. It is located on the northern wall of the inner shrine.

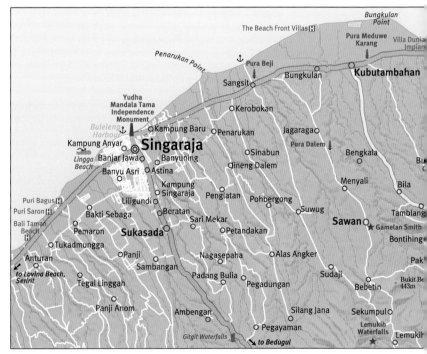

Seventeen kilometers (10 miles) east of Singaraja is the **Air Sanih (Yeh Sanih)** beach resort. Its main attraction is not its beach but rather a natural swimming pool located near the shore. Its icy water originates from a spring and is said to flow at a rate of 800 liters (211 US liquied gallons) per second. Not as popular with visitors as Lovina (and therefore less crowded), the growing number and variety of accommodations in Air Sanih make it a serene base for trekking through rice terraces and plantations, swimming along the 5 km (3 mile) coastline, snorkeling 500 m (540 yds) out, and expeditions to mounts Batur or Agung or to the waterfalls further south. On the hill above, **Pura Taman Manik Mas** offers stunning architecture.

Air Sanih to Tejakula

Situated on the coast 7 km (4.3 miles) east of Air Sanih is the important temple, **Pura Ponjok Batu**, constructed entirely of stones. Built atop a hill, it affords a fine view of the ocean and some splendid frangipani trees. Cross the road to the small fenced-in shrine that encloses a number of stones. It is said that the 16th-century priest Nirartha, drawn

to the site by its immense beauty, sat on one of these stones as he composed poetry.For a change from Hindu Bali visit the Bali Aga village **Sembiran**, 6 km (3.7 miles) east of Pura Ponjok Batu. A steep, narrow winding road brings you into Sembiran. The layout of the village differs from that of predominantly Hindu villages. However, Hindu influence is nowadays visible in the form of temples. The village appears poor with its many mud-brick dwellings roofed with zinc sheets. There are excellent views back to the coast.

Tejakula, 3 km (2 miles) past the Sembiran turn-off, is the last important port of call in eastern Buleleng Regency. Stay in a seaside villa and simply enjoy being away from the crowds while watching local fisherman in outrigger dugouts set sail every morning and evening. Otherwise, use it as a base for exploring more of off-the-beaten track Bali. Visit **Banjar Pande**, the silversmiths district, and watch them at work as they produce Balinese religious items and jewelry. Also be sure to see the **horse bath**. To get there, turn south at the T-junction. This large, elaborate structure with its graceful arches has been turned into a public bathing area.

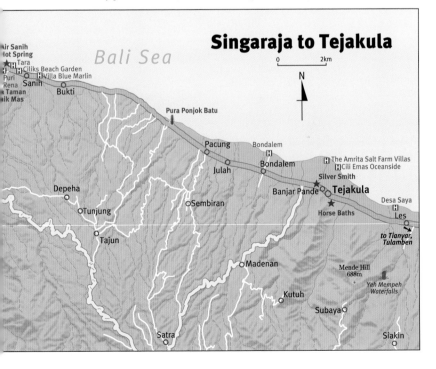

Singaraja to Tejakula

Bali Sea

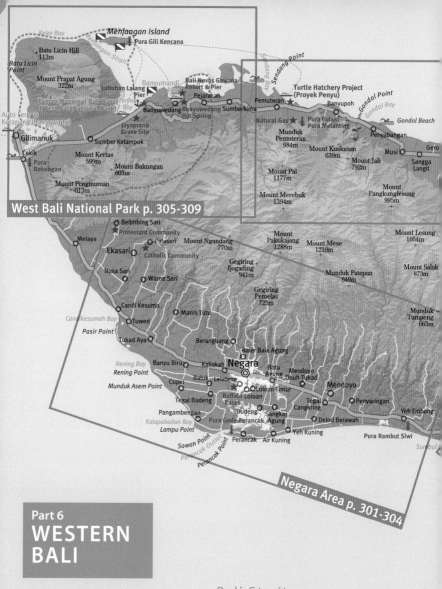

Menjangan Island
Pura Gili Kencana

Kelor Bay

Batu Licin Hill
113m

Batu Licin
Point

Mount Prapat Agung
322m

Labuhan Lalang
Pier

Taman Nasional Bali Barat (West Bali National Park)

Teluk Terima / Terima Bay

Auto Ferry to
Ketapang (Banyuwangi)

Gilimanuk

Cekik

Pura
Bakungan

Jayaprana
Grave Site

Sumber Kelampok

Mount Kertas
599m

Mount Bakungan
603m

Mount Penginuman
613m

Banyumandi

Bali Novus Gawana
Resort & Pier

Pejarakan

Banyuwedang
Banyuwedang
Hot Spring

Sumberkima

Pemuteran

Turtle Hatchery Project
(Proyek Penyu)

Banyupoh

Banyupoh

Sendang Point

Gondol Point

Gondol Bay

Gondol Beach

Natural Gas

Pura Pulaki
Pura Melanting

Munduk
Pemuteran
984m

Mount Kuskusan
639m

Mount Jali
792m

Musi

Penyabangan

Gero

Sangga
Langit

Mount Pal
1177m

Mount
Pangkunglesung
995m

Mount Merebuk
1394m

West Bali National Park p. 305-309

Belimbing Sari
Protestant Community

Melaya

Palasari

Mount Ngandang
770m

Mount
Pakukajang
1288m

Mount Mese
1210m

Mount Lesung
1054m

Ekasari

Catholic Community

Nusa Sari

Warna Sari

Gegiring
Ijogading
941m

Munduk Patepan
649m

Mount Salak
873m

Candi Kesuma

Candikesumah Bay

Tuwed

Pasir Point

Tukad Aya

Manis Tutu

Gegiring
Pemelas
723m

Munduk
Tumpeng
663m

Berangbang

Baler Bale Agung

Banyu Biru

Rening Bay

Rening Point

Kaliakah

Negara

Batu
Agung

Mendoyo
Dauh Tukad

Mendoyo

Munduk Asem Point

Cupel

Baluk

Lelateng

Tegal

Tegal Badeng

Loloan Timur

Buffalo Loloan
Races

Cangkring

Penyaringan

Pangambengan

Budeng

Sangkar
Agung

Delod Berawah

Yeh Embang

Kalapabalian Bay

Lampu Point

Pura Gede Perancak

Sowan Point

Perancak Outlet

Perancak Point

Perancak

Air Kuning

Yeh Kuning

Pura Rambut Siwi

Sumbul

Negara Area p. 301-304

Part 6
WESTERN
BALI

Bali Strait

N

0   5km

INTRODUCTION

Visiting Western Bali

Except for a handful of surfers and national park aficionados, until recently few tourists bothered to venture into Western Bali, and those who did were mostly aboard buses, hurtling along the Denpasar-Gilimanuk highway en route to or from Java. While there was always plenty of starkly beautiful scenery and rugged coastline beyond the bus windows, the absence of archetypally "Balinese" rice field landscapes and the lack of tourism infrastructure, meant that there was little impetus to stop and explore.

All that is rapidly changing, however, and the region is blossoming—not only as a water sports and nature destination, but also as a center of eco-tourism. A few years ago, small-scale investors, both foreign and local, recognized that the vast expanses of undeveloped land in Western Bali and its unique ruggedness were excellent opportunities to develop a new "green" tourism, and they set out to lure travelers away from the overcrowded south and Ubud. Reef restoration and conservation dominate the coastlines; local families invite travelers into their homes to see how they live—sharing knowledge and earning much-needed incomes in the process—and forest preservation is taken seriously. In the west, there's a whole new side of Bali awaiting exploration.

Most of Western Bali is extremely dry and less fertile than more central regions, its population is relatively small, and in the past poverty was widespread. The inhabitants here are a mixture of ethnic Javanese and Madurese—who migrated to the area to escape overcrowded conditions in eastern Java in the last century—and Balinese, many originally refugees from Karangasem Regency, who moved here after Mt. Agung's great eruption in 1963.

There are two distinctive areas where travelers set up housekeeping for their stays in Western Bali. Generally speaking, surfers and beach lovers flock to its southern coastline, while divers and trekkers cling to its north shores; there are several deluxe hideaways on both coasts.

Western Bali's southern beaches

Starting from southern Bali, the highway west goes inland north of Pura Tanah Lot, through lush rice fields near Tabanan, then turns into a coastal road south of Antosari at **Soka Beach**, where the terrain and climate begin changing to the aridness of the west.

Tranquil Pemuteran on the northwestern shore is a popular dive destination.

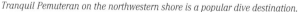

Though it lacks the steep terraces of central Bali, the Jembrana area is still important for agriculture.

Tiny Menjangan Island is part of West Bali National Park and has three high-end resorts.

Small roads lead from the highway to the sea between Tanah Lot and Soka Beach, where there are a number of budget and midrange lodgings and at least one ultra-luxurious resort catering to get-away-from-it-all guests.

West of Soka Beach, the next resort area is at Lalang Linggah's **Balian Beach**, where there are a number of villas, inns, and resorts, one of them specifically attractive to surfers, as it sits on the sea where waves crash to shore.

Moving further west, **Medewi Beach** still has its original budget surfer digs at the eastern end, but new resorts are popping up along this long stretch of beach and old ones are being renovated. Rather than attracting surfers only, these accommodations are full-service facilities suitable for families with spas, restaurants, dance performances, and innovative tour services.

Local culture

Further west is **Negara**, the only town of any size in Western Bali, and the capital of Jembrana Regency. East of Negara is **Pura Rambut Siwi**, one of several great "sea temples" constructed by the priest Danghyang Nirartha in the 16th century. Magnificently perched on a cliff overlooking the ocean is a small temple said to hold the hair that Danghyan Nirartha gave the villagers to show his appreciation for their hospitality.

Negara is known for its **buffalo races** held between July and October annually. Visitors are welcome to attend Sunday practice heats. Two unusual villages lie north of Negara, one almost entirely inhabited by Protestants and the other by Catholics, the latter with a charming church in the midst of vegetable fields.

This area is also known for its unique form of *gamelan*, called *Jegog*, the largest instrument in the ensemble being made of giant bamboo

emitting deep, resonating tones. Jegog performances can be complemented by other instruments or by dancers. Hotels on Medewi Beach either offer performances in-house or can arrange trips to village festivals, as well as tours to sites around Negara.

West Bali National Park

At the far western end of the island and encompassing a great deal of the interior is **West Bali National Park**. The primary attraction here is superb diving at **Menjangan Island** off the northwest shore. The park also offers some excellent trekking programs with trained guides, which are particularly favored by birdwatchers in search of the elusive Bali Starling. Treks range from short to long over a variety of terrains, and customized expeditions can be arranged. The only accommodations are three high-end resorts, prompting many travelers on smaller budgets to overnight in nearby Pemuteran.

Western Bali's northern coast

Pemuteran is the first town east of the park with a full range of accommodations. It still has a village feel to it even though there are several luxury resorts here, one of which has won awards for its conservation efforts and tranquility and another that was named one of the World's Best Hideaways by *Travel+Leisure* magazine and serves organic food in its restaurant. There are also plenty of budget- and midrange accommodations in Pemuteran. The diving and snorkeling are excellent here, and any one of the several dive shops can arrange packages that include Menjangan Island, macro diving, and safaris. Not to be missed is an underwater temple complex, ship graveyard, and "BioWreck" structure. There is also a turtle hatchery project protecting endangered sea turtles.

WESTERN BEACHES

Endless Beaches and Surf Breaks

Western Bali might be a new frontier for mainstream tourism, but the region has long been on the itineraries of footloose surfers. In a couple of isolated spots on the exposed southern shoreline there are first-class dry season waves to be had, and for years these places have been noted surf destinations. A few low-budget homestays and warungs sprung up to accommodate the young surfers, many of who would stay for weeks and even months on end. Some of those long-established accommodations remain, but now they have been joined by hotels, private villas, and five-star resorts, some of them owned locally and some by foreigners. This relatively new phenomenon opens up a whole new variety of choices to other travelers besides the low-budget wave-riders. Even better is that the stretch of western beaches begins only one hour away from the Denpasar airport, so those preferring to skip the crowds of the south can head straight into the wild west the moment they touch down in Bali.

Hideaway beaches

Only 20 minutes from Pura Tanah Lot, **Pantai Yeh Gangga** (Ganges River Beach) is the beginning of a long stretch of shoreline that is broken up into segments due to the absence of a coastal highway. A local driver who is knowledgeable about the area will know the small roads from Pandak Gede, north of Tanah Lot, west through Pejaten and then south through Sudimara. However, self-driving first-timers might find it more expedient to head south from Tambanan town on the road that goes directly to Sudimara. Until relatively recently, Yeh Gangga was a "secret" coastline known only to intrepid travelers. Out in the middle of nowhere, and reachable by negotiating really bad roads, is a gaggle of homestays and bungalows that have been there for a very long time, and which are still going strong—some are undergoing renovations to meet the new tourism demand after a long dry spell. There are several dirt roads along the coast to these accommodations, and clever villagers have set

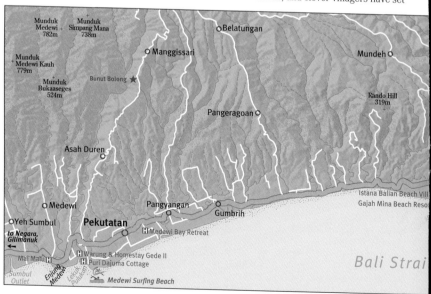

up "toll booths" on some of them to take advantage of the growing tourism. In the midst of this is a surprising complex of luxury villas built by a developer, primarily for foreigners. Down the road a bit further is a busy horse riding stable that's been there since 1994, while near Sudimara village is the WakaGangga resort, one of the award-winning Waka group of properties that specializes in blending in with the natural environment. Further development of this shore—which is already underway—will open all sorts of alternatives for Bali beach-lovers, especially if the local infrastructure is improved.

At the western end of this length of broad, black sand is **Pantai Kelating (Kelating Beach)**. To reach it, go back to the east-west road at Pejaten, and go west to the south turnoff to Kelating village. This long, once-deserted strip of paradise is now home to a super-luxe resort, Villa Soori, a hideaway for lovers of fine sand, pounding surf, and stunning views down the coast as far as the eye can see.

Bali's western beaches were first opened up for tourism by visiting surfers.

A burgeoning cottage industry

Pejaten village is worth a stop. Practically everyone here is involved in making terracotta roofing tiles, a traditional industry boosted by the area's recent construction boom. The streets of the entire village are lined with stacks of the roof tiles and of coconut husks ready to be collected and transported either to worksites or to the port at Gilimanuk for export.

At one time, Pejaten was also known for its pale green decorative pottery, and today a few artists still make it and offer it for sale along the town's main road.

Balian Beach

To get to the next beach—**Balian** (also called **Pantai Lalang Linggah**)—return to the Denpasar-Gilimanuk highway and turn west to **Selemadeg**, then south through Antosari to join the coastal road at **Soka**, where there is a **Taman Rekreasi (Recreational Park)**

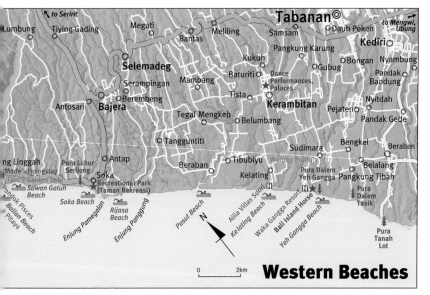

Bunut Bolong, where a country lane passes right through the middle of a sacred banyan tree.

with a large tour bus-type restaurant, accommodations, river rafting, and a large shop selling *oleh-oleh* (souvenir snacks).

Continuing west on the Java–Bali highway, about 5 km (3.2 miles) away is the beginning of Jembrana Regency. The terrain and climate begin to change here and it gets increasingly dry to the west.

To get to Balian Beach take a small road south through Lalang Linggah village, slowly sloping down to the sea. Except for a couple of older losmen (homestays), the majority of accommodations here are new. They are mostly owned by foreigners and are far more upscale than is expected from a surfing beach. One explanation is that the surfing demographic is maturing, has more expendable income, and also increasingly brings along non-surfing families on the quest for waves. Another is good business sense: in order to survive when the surfers move on, large investments must provide something else to attract guests.

The sounds, smells, and sights of Indian Ocean waves crashing up on the beach are stunning here, and the rowdy beer-drinking crowd that is usually associated with the surf scene is isolated into one area, leaving the rest of the beach a quiet, peaceful place to drop out for a while to marvel at the overwhelming natural beauty of the area.

A "Balian" is a traditional healer, and local legend has it that Balian was named for a local medicine man who lived by the river

which flows into the sea here. Even today residents of five villages come here periodically to be cleansed and blessed, a practice particularly popular for teenage girls as a rite of passage into womanhood.

Medewi Beach

An interesting side trip between Balian and Medewi beaches is the detour about 10 km (6.5 miles) north from Pekutatan to Manggissari to see Bunut Bolong ("Hole in the Banyan Tree"), a sacred tree so large that it forms a tunnel with the road passing through it. A shrine on its right side is often visited by travelers who stop to ask permission to pass through. The scenic mountain road passes clove, coffee, cacao, and rambutan plantations, and at the top overlooks a forested gorge.

Banyans are one of three tree species considered to be holy by the Balinese. They are believed to house spirits that must be appeased and treated respectfully. These trees are rarely cut, and if it becomes necessary to do so, a series of rituals is performed to ask for permission and pardon. Back on the Denpasar–Gilimanuk highway, **Medewi Beach**, beginning at Pekutatan, has a different feel to Balian. At much smaller Balian Beach, most of the resorts and homestays are on one road, whereas here several lanes leave the main road giving access to the long Medewi shoreline, which is packed with different types of accommodations, ranging from simple losmen to upmarket villas. There is a lot of renovation going on here as well as new construction.

Medewi is particularly popular with surfers for its long, left-hand point-break—one of the only such waves in Bali—which peels westwards from the rocky promontory near the river mouth. Good waves are only usually to be had here during the middle part of the year, particularly during July and August, but there's usually enough surf for beginners to have fun year-round. From here almost to Pura Rambut Siwi, the coast is rapidly developing as a resort area specializing in beachside relaxation and day trips into the countryside to experience outdoor activities and culture. Other tour programs offered by most hotels include the temple, buffalo races in Negara, treks in West Bali National Park, and snorkeling, fishing, cultural performances, and village visits.

ACCOMMODATION PRICE CATEGORIES Prices are for a double room, including breakfast
$ = under $30; $$ = $30–$70; $$$ = $70–$130; $$$$ = over $130. DINING PRICE CATEGORIES Prices
are based on a meal for one, without drinks $ = under $5; $$ = $5–$10; $$$ = over $10.

VISITING THE WESTERN BEACHES See map, page 296–297.

In the past, surfing, surfing, and more surfing was the name of the game on the Indian Ocean-facing beaches of Western Bali. These days, however, the hardy surf travelers of old have been joined by couples and families—non-wave-riders amongst them—and there's an increasing array of high-end resorts to cater to their needs.

Balian and Medewi still primarily attract surfers, though many of them now demand a greater degree of comfort on land than their threadbare predecessors, and there are some fine accommodations as a consequence. Kelating Beach and Yeh Gangga cater to a more general crowd, with some fine upscale resorts.

July and August are the prime surfing months all along this coast, and at other times it can be very sleepy, making this a good time to visit if you're seeking discounted accommodation, rather than waves. There's usually enough surf for absolute beginners to have fun year-round.

GETTING THERE & GETTING AROUND
West Bali's Denpasar–Gilimanuk south coast highway (also called the Java–Bali highway) is the main thoroughfare between Java and Bali, so traffic can be heavy at times. On a good day, though, it takes about three hours from Denpasar to Gilimanuk, passing through Tabanan, Negara, and points in between.

Local buses run from Denpasar and Tabanan to Negara and Gilimanuk, passing the turnings to the main beaches along the way. Long-haul air-conditioned coaches tend to blaze through with full loads of passengers.

The relatively recent nature of the tourist development, and the fact that the western beaches aren't on the way to anywhere else, means that this area is not well served by tourist shuttle buses (though a few operators do offer rides to Medewi). Generally you'll need to charter a car, take public transport, or bring your own vehicle. If you don't want to stay within walking distance of your accommodation, then having your own car or scooter will be a major advantage. Motorbikes can be rented around Medewi, but they're more expensive than those available in Kuta or Sanur.

KELATING & YEH GANGGA
A short way northwest of Tanah Lot, the Yeh Gangga area is surrounded by working rice fields, lush green terraces tumbling down to a beach hammered by big waves. It's not uncommon in the late afternoons to see horseback riders galloping along Yeh Gangga's stretch of glistening black sand. At night, an almost unbroken line of lights from fishing platforms stretches across the whole horizon.

At the west end of this shoreline, accessible via Kelating village, is Kelating Beach and the exclusive Villa Soori.

ACCOMMODATIONS
As well as the resorts listed here, there are a number of privately-owned villas under construction in this area.

Villa Soori, Kelating Beach, www.sooribali.com. Only 20 minutes from Tanah Lot temple, the infinity pool in the open-air lobby seems to spill into the Indian Ocean. There is elegant minimalist design throughout. The most exclusive villa here has four bedrooms, indoor and outdoor living areas with private infinity pool, and its own pathway to the beach. Less costly one- and two-bedroom villas are also available. There are several classy restaurants, a spa, and various onsite activities. $$$$

Waka Gangga, Jl. Pantai Yeh Gangga, Sudimara village, www.wakahotelsandresorts.com. The thatched bungalows here are set on a hillside, sloping down to the sea. A dining pavilion serving excellent food sits on the property's highest ground, affording a 180-degree view over the vast Indian Ocean. Facilities also include swimming pool, library, and spa. $$$$

ACTIVITIES
Villa Soori can arrange **Balinese dance lessons** in Abiantuwung village, 5 km (3.2 miles) east of the resort. Horse riding is also available.

Bali Island Horse, Yeh Gangga, www.baliislandhorse.com. The stables are located in a seaside village where rice farming, fishing, and sea salt harvesting are the main activities. Ride through gently sloping rice terraces, pause at a waterfall, visit a temple and a bat cave on a two- or one-hour morning or evening ride.

BALIAN BEACH

Ten kilometers (6.2 miles) or so west of Antosari, turning south via Lalang Linggha village, is Balian Beach, a relatively new beach resort. Between Antosari and Balian is Soka, where there are restaurants, a convenience store, and buses going east and west. From Balian, it's another 30 minute drive to Medewi Beach. A number of privately-owned villas have started to appear in this area.

ACCOMMODATIONS

Gajah Mina Beach Resort, Suraberata, Lalang Linggah, www.gajahminaresort.com. A well-established resort with a private beach, this sprawling property offers standard rooms, bungalows, and honeymoon suites with cheerful interiors, minifridge, terraces, and sea views. It's a fine place for a relaxing getaway, with attached spa and restaurant and extensive activity programs on offer. **$$$**
Istana Balian Beach Villa, Banjar Pengasahan, Lalang Linggha, www.istanabalian.com. At the top of the road within walking distance of the beach, this small, attractive compound of quiet, modern rooms is an excellent option. Rooms have aircon and flat-screen TV. Many of the local expats gather here in the evenings during the football (soccer) season to watch the games. **$$-$$$**
Made's Homestay, Balian Beach, Tel: 081-2396-3335. One of the few budget losmen on the beach, this place has simple rooms with cold-water showers and an attached warung. **$**
Pondok Pisces Bungalows, Balian Beach, www.pondokpiscesbali.com. The traditional thatched roof bungalows here are built with natural materials. There's also a beach house and ocean view rooms in lush gardens across the street from the beach. The whole place is simple, relaxed, and friendly. The attached Tom's Garden Café has an interesting Western and Indonesian menu, serving wine, beer, and cocktails. **$$-$$$**
Pondok Pitaya, Balian Beach, www. pondokpitaya.com. With classic wooden bungalows, suites, and cottages, this place has come a long way upmarket since its surf-hack beginnings. The beachfront location is great, and there are yoga classes available. **$$-$$$**

MEDEWI BEACH

Take the main highway west of Denpasar via Tabanan for about 75 km (47 miles; the Journey will take 2.5 hrs; or about an hour from Tabanan town) to the beginning of Medewi at Pekutan. At Pekutan there are surf shops, board rentals, and other services. There is no road that connects one segment of beach to the next; instead, the small roads heading south to the sea from the highway are all lined with accommodations and eateries.

The beach is rocky and not ideal for sunbathing, but the sunsets here are spectacular. The best surf is early in the mornings.

ACCOMMODATIONS

Mai Malu, Jl. Pantai Medewi, www. maimalu.co.id. Sitting high on a hill with spectacular 360-degree views of mountainous Western Bali and the sea, this place is extremely good value. The rooms are simple and small, but very well kept. Surf guides work here, and there is surfboard, motorbike, and car hire available. The restaurant is a popular hangout for surfers and other travelers. **$**
Medewi Bay Retreat, Jl. Ciwa, Br. Pekutatan, Tel: 0812-3842-252. There are nine villas with rustic charm in tropical gardens here, set back from the beach. **$$$**
Puri Dajuma Cottages, Beach Eco-Resort & Spa, Pekutatan, www.dajuma.com. Swiss-owned but locally managed with concern for the environment, this resort has 21 ocean- and garden-view rooms in a family-friendly setting. Rooms come with stylish open-air showers, and hammocks on the terraces. There's a spa, swimming pool, and two restaurants, one serving teppanyaki and Mongolian barbecue. On the resort's beach is a monument commemorating Balinese freedom fighters on the site where ammunition from Java was brought by sea and unloaded to support the struggle against the Dutch. **$$$**
Warung & Homestay Gede II, Pekutatan, Tel: 081-2397-6668. Ideal for surfers, just a short walk along the rocky beach to the north, this old-school guesthouse is funky and clean, if basic. The breezy lumbung-style, raised thatched bungalows have shared cold water baths. Ibu Ketut—the lady with the big smile—serves up delicious food in her open-air café looking out to sea. **$**

Bali's Wild West Coast

Bali's west coast has historically been the area least visited by tourists. But that is all changing. The rugged western countryside is now considered a viable nature destination with cultural attributes not seen elsewhere on the island. Thanks to new resorts, villas, and homestays being built by both local and foreign investors, improved infrastructure, and the ingenuity of those involved in tourism development, the wild West Coast is now attracting nature-loving travelers in significant numbers.

Western Bali comprises two regencies: all of Jembrana, the main population centers of which are all found along the 71 km (44 miles) of road that hug the coast, and western Buleleng on the north coast. The area is reachable from Denpasar by way of the vast rice fields and brilliant coastline of Tabanan Regency or from Singaraja via the wild, dry forests of the north. Ferries from Java berths at Gilimanuk on the island's western tip.

Temple of the sacred hair

Traveling west along the southern Java-Bali highway 18 km (11 miles) west of Medewi beach is **Pura Rambut Siwi**, near Yeh Embang village. Its entrance is marked by a small shrine at the edge of the road where Balinese travelers stop briefly to pray for safety on their journeys. Two hundred meters (210 yds) from the main road is the main temple complex, perched on a cliff at the edge of the ocean.

Pura Rambut Siwi is one of several important monuments to the priest Danghyang Nirartha, who came to Bali from Java during the decline of the Majapahit Kingdom in the hopes of fortifying Balinese Hinduism against the spread of Islam occurring elsewhere in the archipelago. Between 1546 and 1550 he traveled through the island, teaching and unifying the Hindu populace. According to legend, he stopped to pray at a village temple at Yeh Embang and made a gift of his hair to the temple. Since that time it has been known as Rambut Siwi, which means "worship of the hair."

The complex consists of three temple enclosures in a setting of great natural beauty. The first one when entering from the main road is the largest and most important, the Pura Luhur where Danghyang Nirartha's hair is kept. A majestic *candi bentar,* or split gate, on the southern wall of the inner courtyard opens on to the cliff, offering

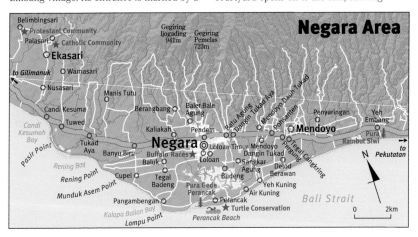

Jembrana and Negara are the only parts of Bali where fast-paced buffalo races are held.

dramatic views of the surf below. Gnarled frangipani trees litter the ground with fragrant blossoms, and incense burns at the feet of moss-covered stone statues swathed in white cloth.

From Pura Luhur it's a short walk east along the cliff to a winding stone that descends to Pura Penataran, the original temple where Danghyang Nirartha is believed to have prayed. When the Balinese worship at Rambut Siwi they first enter this temple.

Walking back westward along the beach there is a small shrine at the entrance to a cave in the cliff wall. This cave is said to be the lair of mystical animals, the *duwe*, or holy beast, of the temple. A well at the mouth of the cave is a source of holy water that is salt free despite its proximity to the ocean. Just beyond the cave, another stairway leads back up to the temple. Atop the edge of the cliff is the tiny Pura Melanting, where merchants stop to pray for prosperity.

A large open-air performance pavilion and two gazebos set amidst lily ponds to the west of Pura Luhur are excellent places to rest and enjoy a panorama of rice fields and white wave crests curling against the black sand coastline as far as the eye can see.

Continuing west along the main road, another important temple is situated along the coast southwest of Mendoyo, **Pura Gede Perancak**, where Danghyang Nirartha is believed to have first landed. A peaceful shrine of white stone sits on the banks of the placid Perancak River, which empties into the sea about 100 m (110 yds) south of the temple. To reach it, turn left off the main road in Tegal Cangkring, 8 km (5 miles) west of Rambut Siwi and follow a narrow back road 1.5 km (1 mile) to an intersection marked by a monument. Turn right and continue west about 9 km (5.6 miles). The

temple is on the right where the road turns south along the Perancak River.

At the time of Danghyang Nirartha's arrival, this area was controlled by the debauched ruler, Gusti Ngurah Rangsasa, who obliged the newcomer to pray in his temple. When the holy priest complied, the temple structures collapsed. Gusti Ngurah Rangsasa then fled, and the community rebuilt the temple in honor of Danghyang Nirartha and his teachings.

A day at the races

The Negara **buffalo races**, known locally as *mekepung*, are the most dramatic of Jembrana Regency's home-grown events. Throughout the westernmost districts, it is still common to see a team of brawny, gray, or pink buffaloes pulling wooden carts filled with cacao, coffee or bananas. *Mekepung* began when farmers playfully raced their neighbors in plowing a field or in bringing the harvest home. The races soon became an event in themselves, and the cumbersome *cikar* carts were replaced by light, two-wheeled chariots.

Today, the races are organized by the Jembrana regional government. All participants are members of a racing club (*sekehe mekepung*) and are divided into two divisions: a Western and an Eastern Group, with the Ijo Gading River that bisects Jembrana as the dividing line. These teams compete biannually, in the Regent's Cup Championship on the Sunday before Indonesian Independence Day in August and the Governor's Cup Championship each October. Hundreds of buffaloes decorated with colorful ribbons and flowers compete in these events to the delight of onlookers. There are *jegog*, music, and dance performances and traditional foods are sold by vendors.

The buffaloes in each team are ranked prior to the races, and are pitted against their counterparts on the other team. Two pairs run at a time along a circuitous 4 km (2.5 miles) route. The team with the most winners takes the cup. Apart from this, the only immediate reward for winning is prestige, but owning a prize buffalo does eventually translate into money. A good race animal can fetch almost double the normal price, if its owner is willing to part with it.

If visiting the area in July, inquire at your accommodation about rehearsals that take place every Sunday morning, beginning at 7 am, at an arena on Delod Berawan beach near **Perancak**. Area accommodations often offer tours that generally begin with breakfast at the hotel and also include a stop at the traditional market in Negara.

On the coastline near Perancak are colorful fishing boats originating from eastern Java. The best times to see them lining the beach is early mornings and late afternoons as they prepare to go out to sea. After sunset their twinkling lights, as they go further out to fish, are mesmerizing.

Turtle conservation

Perancak is also the home of a small **turtle conservation** program originated by an NGO many years ago but which is now self-run by a community group called Kurma Asih. In 1997 the first turtle in 37 years nested on this beach, and by 2005 there were 100 turtle nests here. The 10,000 eggs that were recorded in that season were taken to the hatchery and were eventually released back into the sea. Funding received through their "Adopt a Nest" program helps keep the program afloat.

Unity in diversity

Negara is the administrative center of Jembrana Regency and has little to offer tourists. However, there are a few interesting sites in the area. Indonesia's motto "Unity in Diversity" certainly applies here. About 1 km (0.65 miles) south of the city at **Loloan Timur** is a community of Bugis, originally from South Sulewesi, with distinctive traditional houses built on stilts with crossed "swords" adorning the roofs. The Bugis are mostly Muslims, as are the neighboring communities of Javanese and Madurese settlers, hence the many mosques found in Western Bali.

There's a large Protestant community at **Belimbingsari**. To get there, go west from Negara to Melaya and turn northeast. One of the largest of its kind on Bali, the community has an interesting church with Balinese elements. South of Belimbingsari at **Palasari** is a most unusual Catholic church, standing regally among landscaped gardens and agricultural fields, seemingly in the middle of nowhere. Its roof sports features similar to the meru pagoda-style seen on Balinese Hindu temples, while a *kul-kul* (warning drum) like those found in traditional Indonesian mosques calls the faithful to pray instead of a more conventional set of bells.

Both settlements were established in the 1930s by converts of Christian missionaries who were unwelcome in primarily Hindu areas of Bali.

Bamboo tones

Jembrana Regency is home to a number of art forms found nowhere else. By far the most popular and thriving of these is the fabulous *gamelan jegog*, an orchestra comprising instruments made of various sizes of bamboo which are stricken with mallets—like a xylophone or a metal *gamelan*—to achieve different tones. Travelers may see men seated on the floor in hotel lobbies playing melodic, small jegog instruments to welcome guests. There are no regularly scheduled performances. Check with your accommodation to determine if there are any local festivals with jegog players.

Jegog was created in 1912 by Kiang Geliduh, who was born in Jembrana Regency. Today, I Ketut Suwentra and his family in **Sangkar Agung** village, southeast of Negara, continue the art form and are happy to receive visitors in their home to see the instruments and learn more about them. Upon reaching the village, ask for directions (everyone knows this family). Feel free to drop in without an appointment; whoever is there will act as host.

"To understand jegog you must understand Balinese music," says Ketut Suwentra. "It's ethnic; it comes from nature." By understanding bamboo, the characteristics of the many different varieties, and its power, music can be created. The youngest of nine children, all of whom love music, Ketut feels *jegog* is his legacy from his father. His father is undoubtedly proud, as this group performs at ceremonies, wedding parties, hotels, and competitions, and has played in Japan and the United States.

One variation of *gamelan* jegog is an ensemble of 14 instruments, the largest of which are made from giant bamboo, the low-pitched tones of which are so resonant that their vibrations are felt by the body as much as the ears. With the bamboo tubes mounted on tall wooden frames, the musicians sit on elevated platforms, giving them enough leverage to strike the keys with heavy mallets. Medium sized instruments are played with the musician standing, and the smaller ones—with the players seated on the ground—spin out intricately syncopated rhythms with dazzling precision and speed. The result is a dense, multi-layered fabric of sound, above which a single bamboo flute may be added to trill sweet, sinuous melodies.

The awesome jegog *mebarung* is a competition between two or more orchestras, each playing in turn, pitting their skills against one another in a fierce musical battle; it is an unforgettable event to witness. The instruments sway back and forth, the musicians bob up and down, and the onlookers cheer enthusiastically, occasionally helping the musicians to replace a broken key. The winner is the ensemble that can make itself heard above the frenzy and produce the most resonance.

Jegog are also evaluated for their visual appearance. The wooden components of the instruments are all finely carved, and some are brightly painted, with tall ceremonial umbrellas and handsome statues affixed to the big instruments, which stand at the back of the group. A new trend is to leave the wood natural and unpainted.

Other arts

Other interesting art forms of the area include the **Jegog Dance**, as unique as the *gamelan* itself. **Pencak Silat** is a mixture of choral singing, theater, martial arts, and acrobatics, supervised by a sharp-tongued jester named Dag; and there is a daredevil knife dance called **Cabang**. All of these have roots in the performing arts of Java, Madura, and Malay culture. In recent times, I Ketut Suwentra has been instrumental in creating new music for the younger generation to help keep them connected to their culture, and traditional Balinese dances and dramas from the gamelan gong repertoire have been set to jegog music.

Kendang Mebarung, a contest of cow hide-covered drums of various sizes and shapes to create different sounds, shares the competitive spirit of jegog mebarung. The largest of the drums are 2–3 m (6–9 ft) in length and 1 m (3.2 ft) in diameter, and are sometimes accompanied by an abbreviated gamelan angklung ensemble. When they compete at cremation ceremonies, national holidays, or simply for public entertainment, the drummers play interlocking rhythms that challenge each other's resonance, volume, and rhythmic dexterity.

Another type of ensemble indigenous to Jembrana is the **Bumbung Gebyog**. Eight to 12 lengths of bamboo of varying pitches are struck on the ground in rhythmically intricate, interlocking patterns. Probably the only music in Bali that originated and has remained the preserve of women, *bumbung gebyog* derives from the pounding of newly harvested rice in hollowed trees or stone mortars (*lesung*) to remove the husks. Nowadays, it is performed on national holidays and at ceremonies related to rice agriculture, usually accompanied by narrative dances or the playful **Ngibing Dance**, where spectators may take turns joining the performer.

Gilimanuk area

At **Gilimanuk**, on the western tip of Bali, the territory becomes Buleleng Regency, which stretches across Bali's north coastline. The ferry from Java berths here. At **Secret Bay**, about 30 minutes from Gilimanuk, there is a mangrove swamp with black sand up to 9 m (30 ft) deep. The main attraction here is "muck" diving, where enthusiasts revel in exploring sand and detritus in shallow waters for tiny creatures: seahorses, frogfish, shrimps, and other tiny, strange mini-beasts. The best time to go is at high tide, when visibility is good.

At **Terima Bay** (**Teluk Terima**), east of the peninsula, visit **Makam Jayaprana**, the gravesite of Jayaprana who, according to Balinese legend, was an orphan raised by the ruler of Kalianget. As an adult he married the lovely Nyoman Layonsari from neighboring Banjar village. However, the ruler himself became enamored of Jayaprana's bride and schemed to kill Jayaprana to have her for himself. To this end, he dispatched Jayaprana with an army to contain a band of pirates who he said had arrived in northwestern Bali. On arrival at Teluk Terima the ruler's minister killed and buried Jayaprana. When the ruler asked Layonsari to marry him, however, she chose to remain faithful to her husband and committed suicide.

The temple marking Jayaprana's grave is a long, steep climb, but the views to Mt. Raung on Java, Menjangan Island, and Gilimanuk from about halfway up make the effort all worthwhile. The temple, which contains a glass case displaying statues of Jayaprana and Layonsari, is pure kitsch.

South of Gilimanuk at **Cekik** is the West Bali National Park headquarters, where information about the park is available. It was near Cekik that burial mounds were found and evidence of Bali's oldest inhabitants was unearthed, dating back to 1000 B.C.

First-hand Views of Bali's Native Wildlife

Much of Bali's natural landscape has been altered by the hand of man. Dense tropical forests that once covered the island have mostly now been cleared and the land molded into spectacular rice terraces and sprawling village settlements. But on the westernmost tip of the island, extensive forests, coastal swamps, and marine waters have to be divided into villages and farmland. Today these areas comprise the **West Bali National Park (Taman Nasional Bali Barat)**. Set aside as a nature reserve in 1941 and elevated to national park status in 1984, it consists of 19,012.89 ha (46,981.88 ac): 15,587.89 ha of land and 3,425 ha (38,518.52 ac and 8,463.36 ac respectively) of water.

Several distinct environments are within the park's protected boundaries. Forested mountains ranging up to 1,414 m (4,639 ft)

and arid savannas stand in the central and eastern sectors. The southern slopes are covered with tropical vegetation that is green year round; and the north—which is much drier than the south—hosts deciduous monsoon forests. Palm savannahs and mangrove swamps are found in the coastal areas. Four nearby islands surrounded by coral reefs are rich in sea and bird life.

The park is home to one of the world's rarest birds. The Bali Starling, also known as the Rothschild Myna (*Leucopsar rothschildi*), is indigenous to Bali, but the vast majority of the population is in the hands of bird collectors abroad. It is a small, white bird with black wingtips and a brilliant aqua-blue streak around its eyes. Only 30 or so still live in the wild, mainly on Mt. Prapat Agung on

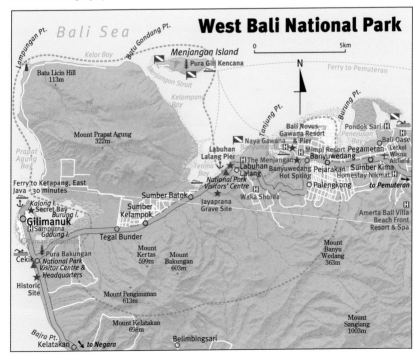

Local boats take passengers back and forth from the mainland to Menjangan Island.

the westernmost peninsula. The park has another 100 birds in its breeding center ready for release to their natural habitat; however, this program has not been a resounding success due to competition from other birds for food, predators, and poachers. Fortunately, a Bali Starling captive breeding and release program on Nusa Penida has had a higher success rate by involving local villages that still adhere to *adat* (traditional) law, requiring them to protect nature. (For more information, see www.fnpf.org.)

While the park's best known species is the Bali Starling, it also protects other rare animals: the Javan Pangolin (*Manis javanicus*), Banteng ox (*Bos javanicus*), the tiny Lesser Mousedeer (*Trangulus javanicus*), Marbled Cat (*Felis marmorata*), and Olive Ridley Turtle (*Lepidochelys olivcea*).

As with all protected government lands in Indonesia, one of the park's biggest challenges is to balance conservation with human needs on a limited budget. Additionally, patrolling its expansive boundaries to protect against illegal logging and poaching is a huge undertaking, and large areas are prone to fires during the dry season. This is where eco-tourism can help: three resorts with permits to operate within the park have their own guards, who assist park rangers in patrolling and keeping a watchful eye out for intruders and other irregularities.

Diving and snorkeling off Menjangan Island

If challenges to the West Bali National Park are the bad news, the good news is that Bali's best diving and some good snorkeling is within the park boundaries. Off the coast of **Pulau Menjangan** ("Deer Island") to the northeast of the peninsula are Bali's most beautiful reefs and best diving destinations. Less than 1 km (0.65 miles) from the mainland, Menjangan is surrounded by deep waters with steep walls comprising hundreds of species of coral, gorgonian fans, and sponges, with reefs extending 100–150 m (328–492 ft) from the shore, which then drop 40–60 m (130–195 ft) down to the ocean floor. There are eight dive sites around the island, with drop-offs and slopes with names like Underwater Cave, Anchor Wreck, and Blue Corner. Pos 1 is on the western tip of the island's southern coast and has both hard and colorful soft corals as well as small marine life on a sandy slope. Pos 2 is on the southeast corner, where there is a wall favored by divers; but its shallow reef is also good for snorkeling. Off the northeast coast is Coral Gardens, sloping 8–40 m (26–130 ft) down, with schools of fish in the shallows. Eel Garden, at the west end, is varied enough to satisfy all interests: a wall, gorgonian fans, sponges, angelfish, lionfish, eels, and a current that attracts schools of fish.

A 45-minute nature hike on Pulau Menjangan, which is uninhabited except for native deer and a few other animals, affords beautiful panoramic views of the volcanoes on the nearby mainland and the mountains of East Java in the distance. There is a temple on the island, **Pura Gili Kencana**, believed to be Bali's oldest. Annually at Kuningan, villagers flock here to pray.

To reach Pulau Menjangan, boats are available for hire at two piers: **Labuhan Lalang**, just opposite Menjangan Island on the north coast and at **Banyumandi** near Mimpi Resort. Surrounded by mangrove forest, Banyumandi has showers, changing rooms, and a warung that also sells bottled water and snacks. When leaving the Banyumandi pier, turn right to visit the **Banyuwedang hot spring**.

There are two park visitor information offices: one at Cekik, south of Gilimanuk near the intersection of the main roads from Singaraja and Denpasar; and the other at Labuan Lalang. At Cekik there is a small library with exhibits and a knowledgeable staff. Either office can organize night dives off Menjangan and can also arrange overnight stays on the island.

Trekking in West Bali National Park

There are many interesting trails within the park. Park officials stress that their guides are part of a community empowerment program, and all are from surrounding villages and have been trained and certified by the park.

The treks are designed to satisfy all types of interests and physical capabilities, and on all expeditions: short, 1-2 hrs; medium, 3 hrs; and long, 6-7 hrs. Visitors may choose between mangrove, savannah, and mountainous terrains. If a savannah hike is chosen, a boat is required, which will be an additional charge. If birdwatching is a special interest, the mangroves and savannah are better choices than the mountains, as they are the habitats of the park's more than 100 species of birds. Short and medium treks may include the mangrove and mountain forests at Labuan Lalang or south of there, the savannahs on the east side of the peninsula, or the mountains east of Gilimanuk. Long trips can consist of rainforest hiking near Mt. Kelatakan (698 m or 2,290 ft) southeast of Gilimanuk, which begins at 6:30 am. Customized hikes to meet special interests can also be arranged. All treks must be booked in advance.

There are three expensive resorts within the national park boundaries and a few more nearby, but many visitors base themselves in cheaper accommodations at Pemuteran, 15 minutes east on the north coast road, to take advantage of the diving and snorkeling there, and making day trips to the park.

The well-preserved coral reefs of Bali Barat National Park are easily accessible to divers and snorkelers.

ACCOMMODATION PRICE CATEGORIES Prices are for a double room, including breakfast $ = under $30; $$ = $30–$70; $$$ = $70–$130; $$$$ = over $130. DINING PRICE CATEGORIES Prices are based on a meal for one, without drinks $ = under $5; $$ = $5–$10; $$$ = over $10.

VISITING WEST BALI NATIONAL PARK AND MENJANGAN
See map, page 303.

Apart from the National Park and the surrounding seas, there's little to detain visitors in this area, outside of buffalo racing season.

GETTING THERE & GETTING AROUND
Ferries to Java leave Gilimanuk every half hour, 24 hours a day, and arrive at Ketapang terminal in Banyuwangi, East Java, in about 45 minutes. If you've booked a bus ticket between Denpasar and a city In Java, your ferry ticket will be included in the price. Local buses to onwards destinations are available on either side of the strait, and there are usually a few seats available on the long-haul buses heading for Javanese cities such as Surabaya and Malang—cross to Java as a foot passenger and pick one up on the far side to avoid a lengthy wait in the vehicle queue on the Bali side.

If you arrive at Gilimanuk from Java, or by public transport from elsewhere in Bali, there are *ojek* (motorbike taxis) and private drivers to take you to nearby destinations around the National Park.

ACTIVITIES
Every Sunday morning between July and October there are buffalo race practices at Delod Berawan beach near Perancak, south of Negara. On the Sunday before Indonesian Independence Day (August 17) is the Regent's Cup Championship buffalo races, and in October, the Governor's Cup Championship. Both are hugely important to the racing teams and are accompanied by vendors selling traditional foods and snacks and exuberant onlookers.

JED (Jaringan Ekowisata Desa) Village Ecotourism Network (www.jed.or.id) organizes tours to the Kurma Asih turtle conservation project at Perancak. See the Madurese-style fishing boats at Perancak Bay, try musical talents on a giant bamboo *jegog* instrument, and have lunch on the beach. All proceeds go to the turtle conservation project.

WEST BALI NATIONAL PARK
(TELEPHONE CODE: 0362)

Coming from the south, the national park office at Labuhan Lalang (where the boats to Menjangan Island depart) is about 15 minutes from Gilimanuk.

Pemuteran is 12 km (8 miles) from the park office, and it takes about 1.5 hours from the park to Lovina,

further east. Many travelers base themselves in either town to take advantage of diving, other activities, and a wider range of accommodations and food choices. Day trips to West Bali National Park are easily arranged from Pemuteran or Lovina.

ACCOMMODATIONS
The Menjangan, Jl. Raya Gilimanuk-Singaraja Km 17, Desa Pejarakan, www.menjanganresort.com. A true "jungle resort" with an environmental heart; there's a choice of rooms on the water, in the forest, or on a cliff overlooking the sea on a property so large that it's a trekking experience to reach the main lodge, housing the restaurant and overlook tower (or call reception and they will send a golf cart to pick you up). Inside national park boundaries, the resort's security guards protect the forests, and there's a tree-planting program with donations helping reforestation and nest boxes for Bali Starlings. Interesting activities include kayaking through a mangrove maze and horse riding through the forest, as well as snorkeling and diving. $$$$

Mimpi Resort Menjangan, Jl. Banyuwedang, Desa Pejarakan, www.mimpi.com. A sister to Mimpi Tulamben, East Bali, this boutique resort, dive center, and spa simulates a Balinese village with 30 terraced patio rooms and 24 walled courtyard villas. Each villa features its own hot spring water tub, and some have a private natural stone dip pools. Dive tours, PADI courses, and equipment rental are available. $$$

Naya Gawana Resort & Spa, Desa Pejarakan, www.nayagawanaresort.com. Located at the edge of the national park in monsoon forest, this is a secluded and characterful resort. The 12 Lumbung Suites overlook Menjangan Bay built using indigenous materials, decorated with native fabrics and colors. There are lush tropical gardens, sun decks, spacious living areas, and bathrooms with natural hot spring water. There are also suites with sundecks overlooking mangroves. Diving can be organised here, as can tours of the National Park. $$$$

ACTIVITIES
The National Park Visitors' Centre is at Labuhan Lalang. All activities within the national park require paying an entrance fee. Tickets are available at the park headquarters at Cekik or at Labuan Lalang. Both offices are open 7:30 am–3:30 pm

Monday–Thursday, 7:30 am–1:00 pm on Friday, and are closed Saturday, Sunday, and public holidays, but the ticket counters are open every day.

TREKKING IN WEST BALI NATIONAL PARK

All trekking with the park requires a guide, all of whom are selected from local villages and are trained and certified as part of a community empowerment program. The park guides are very knowledgeable and will help select the best location and itinerary to suit individual interests and capabilities. All treks must be booked in advance, and prices include park entrance and guide fee.

Short trek: 1–2 hrs, $24/1–2 people; $40/3–5 people
Medium trek: 3 hrs, $32/1–2 people; $50/3–5 people
Long trek: 6–7 hrs, $75/1–2 people; $85/3–5 people

Short and medium treks have a choice between the mangroves and mountain forests at Labuan Lalang or south of there, the savannahs on the east side of the peninsula, or the mountains east of Gilimanuk. Note that for savannahs, a boat must be hired for an additional charge.

Long treks can consist of rainforest trekking near Mt. Kelatakan (698 m/2,290 ft)) southeast of Gilimanuk and begin at 6:30 am. Bring your own water and snacks. Customized treks can also be arranged.

SNORKELING AND DIVING OFF MENJANGAN ISLAND

Hire boats to Menjangan Island at either Labuan Lalang (where the park office is) or Banyumandi near Mimpi Resort.

Banyumandi has showers, changing rooms, and a *warung* that also sells bottled water and snacks. Boats rent for around $40 for foreigners—look for other travelers hanging around the parking lot who want to charter a boat together and share expenses.

Both park offices can organize night dives off Menjangan, and can also arrange overnight stays on the island. Bring your own tent and sleeping bag; guides can arrange food for an additional charge.

The placid waters along the northern shore of the West Bali National Park are far removed from the more tempestuous Indian Ocean-facing shores to the south.

THE NORTHWEST COAST: PEMUTERAN TO SERIRIT

Endangered Sea Turtles, Reef Gardeners, and Commercial Pearl Farmers

A short drive east of West Bali National Park, the north coast village of **Pemuteran** is only 45 minutes west of Lovina, and about three to four hours from Denpasar airport. It has some of Bali's best beaches, and although there are rocky stretches, it has perfect sandy ones, too. Snorkeling and diving here are nothing short of divine thanks to the reef regeneration and protection projects that have been ongoing for nearly three decades, since the arrival of an Australian dive operator and a Balinese resort owner in 1991.

Pemuteran can best be described not as a tourist destination but as a friendly fishing village with a few accommodations and dive shops. It is relatively small and cozy, and definitely laid-back; an ideal spot for honing your diving and snorkeling skills or just chilling out for a little while and enjoying life. The bonus is that some of the best snorkeling and diving in Bali is a short boat hop away on Menjangan Island with in the national park.

In addition to these benefits, there are some exciting environmental and community projects here; tourism revenues help support these efforts as well as contributing to local villages, which were previously among Bali's poorest. Acutely aware that healthy reefs benefit their own livelihoods, many local communities have now become involved in protecting the marine environment.

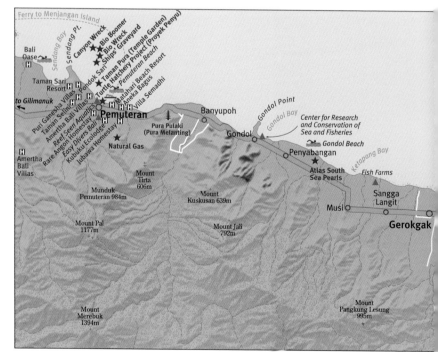

Saving endangered sea turtles

Pemuteran's Reef Seen Aquatics Dive Center has a **Turtle Hatchery Project** (**Proyek Penyu**) established to protect endangered sea turtles. Both the meat and eggs are local delicacies among the Balinese, and although it is illegal to capture and sell these creatures, the practice is still rampant and black market prices are so high that they are difficult for impoverished fishermen to pass up.

Reef Seen's turtle project began almost accidently in 1992 when its founder bought a turtle that had been caught by a fisherman, and later eggs, which he hatched and released back to the sea. The eggs at the hatchery are buried in the sand at optimum temperatures, and after emerging from their shells young turtles are kept in monitored salt water pools until they are old enough to be released when donors are found to sponsor them. The fishermen who bring them to the center receive half the donation in compensation for lost catch and repair of nets—a controversial exchange that seems to work—with the remainder going either to the hatchery project or to the fishermen's association to encourage participation.

Sea turtles are among the world's oldest living species and can live up to 200 years. Species found in Indonesian waters are Green (*Chelonia mydas*), Hawksbill (*Eretmochelys imbricate*), Olive Ridley (*Lepidochelys olivacea*), Leatherback (*Dermochhelys coriacea*), and Loggerhead (*Caretta caretta*).

Travelers are welcome to visit Proyek Penyu, and money collected from a small entry fee is used to continue their efforts as well as for marine ecology education in local villages. For an additional small donation, guests may release a turtle and become a part of the process of saving these wonderful creatures from extinction.

Local protectors of coral reefs

Reef Seen Aquatics along with The Pemuteran Foundation—supported by Atlas North Bali Pearls, Bali Diving Academy, Easy Divers, Sea Rovers Dive Centre, and Warner Lau Diving Centers—sponsor another community project, called **Reef Gardeners**. It is common throughout Indonesia for local fishermen to collect aquarium fish using cyanide and to use dynamite or "tiger nets" that strip the reefs of practically everything. In addition,

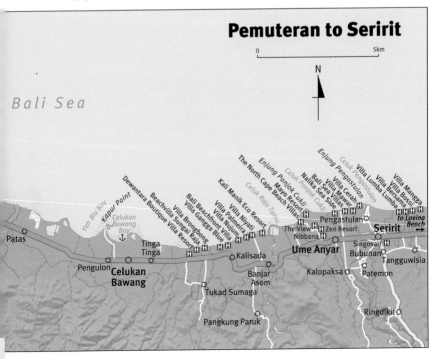

In the waters off Pemuteran, man-made structures and various sunken wrecks have been installed to encourage fresh coral growth and increase marine biodiversity.

between 1996 and 1998 a plague of coral-devastating Crown of Thorns starfish (*Acanthaster planci*) and Drupella shells (*Drupella cornus*) threatened to decimate reefs throughout the country. Since they were first established, diving centers nationwide have done their best to keep reefs clear of damaging elements and to stop illegal fishing practices, but they have had patchy results due to resistance by local fishermen, who resented their intrusion.

In 2005, AusAID sponsored the Bali Rehabilitation Fund to help create jobs for the local people following the Bali bombings. The Reef Gardeners project applied for a grant and was accepted, and it has continued—employing many villagers and spreading marine environmental awareness through innovative projects—long after the initial funds were used up, thanks to The Pemuteran Foundation.

Under the Reef Gardeners project, young village fishermen were trained as PADI-certified rescue divers. After being taught methods for protecting and repairing coral reefs damaged by careless divers, boat anchoring, nets, and natural causes, they set up patrols of the shoreline to assess and fix damage. The Reef Gardeners now work closely with villagers to protect the reefs and to educate others.

With the assistance of a Balinese resort owner, a *pecalang laut* was also established. This traditional guard comprising locals now patrols the waters with the authority to arrest fishermen who use explosives or cyanide or who otherwise damage the reefs.

Prime dive sites

The AusAID funding also provided the means for The Pemuteran Foundation to purchase locally-built wooden boats, which were sunk on an offshore reef, employing villagers to provide manpower and creating two excellent dive sites. At **Canyon Wreck**, a massive 30 m (98 ft) Bugis vessel (*pinisi*) rests at 28 m (92 ft) alongside some of Bali's best and most extensive hard coral cover at Tangked Penyu. At **Ships' Graveyard**, another 24 m (78 ft) Bugis timber vessel and nine *prahu* (fishing boats) lie at depths of 14–25 m (45–82 ft). This site also includes a 9 m (30 ft) Madurese *prahu* whose prow is only 5 m (16 ft) from the surface at low tide.

"Biorock" is a technology developed by an architect and a marine biologist to regenerate damaged reefs by charging manmade structures with low-wattage electricity to create limestone formations that quickly promote coral growth. Pemuteran's **Taman Sari Bali Resort** was one of the pioneers in constructing artificial reefs using Biorock techniques, and it worked. Today, the resort remains actively involved in marine ecology and in planning environmentally and culturally friendly tourism development in the area. Using Biorock techniques, The Pemuteran Foundation's next adventure was to create a **"BioWreck"** structure to add to its sunken ship collection. Measuring 12x3 m (40x10 ft) and made from steel shaped like a boat, it sits on the sand at depths between 7–10 m (23–32 ft). Initially electrified by a generator, solar panels have now been installed on a raft to provide a more environmentally friendly source of power. This site has the largest single species of coral (*Povaris* sp.) found in Bali.

A third manmade site, aptly called **Taman Pura (Temple Garden)**, is an undersea marvel. A recreation of a watery Balinese Hindu temple, 10 large stone statues and a 4 m (13 ft) high Balinese *candi bentar* (split gateway) rest at a depth of 29 m (95 ft). Incorporating a cleaning station with schooling batfish, it is now covered in gorgonian fans. In 2006 a second stage to the garden was constructed at 15 m (49 ft), which is ideal for less experienced divers. Taman Pura was an engineering feat; local divers carried parts of the heavy split gate one-by-one, along with 25 carved sandstone statues of mythical creatures, and anchored them to the seabed. Possibly the only undersea complex of its type in the world, it is quickly becoming a major dive attraction. In 2009, another 5x4 m (16x13 ft) steel structure called **Bio-Boomer**—named in honor of Boomer, a long-term resident turtle of Proyek Penyu—was put into place.

Eastward from Pemuteran

East of Pemuteran is a cluster of dryland temples, the most important and easily accessible of which is **Pura Pulaki**, located in unusual terrain. A rock face rises perpendicularly to the south of the road while the glimmering ocean laps the shore to the north. Pulaki, the home of many monkeys who have a reputation for snatching bags and cameras, was restored and extended about a decade ago. The temple is linked to the legendary personage of Nirartha, the Javanese priest who migrated to Bali in the 16th century and established several of Bali's impressive holy monuments. It is said that prior to his arrival, a village of 8,000 people existed here. When Nirartha visited, the village leader requested

a favor that Nirartha granted: the entire village was to be given supernatural knowledge that would enable it to attain an immaterial state. The invisible occupants of this village became known as *gamang* or *wong samar* and form the entourage of the goddess Melanting, whose abode is the nearby **Pura Melanting**.

The Balinese in these parts fervently believe in the existence of the gamangs and as a result routinely make offerings to them. For example, it is believed that the entry of gamangs into one's garden is heralded by the howling of dogs. Occasionally, sightings of gamangs are reported who have momentarily materialized. They are said to have no upper lip and carry a plaited bag over one shoulder.

Turtles, mangrove restoration and pearls

Continuing east, there are further conservation efforts funded by Japan on Turtle Island at **Banyupoh**. Along with turtle conservation, there is also reef restoration and mangrove replanting here. After that, there is a sprawling building complex. This is the Indonesian **Center for Research and Conservation of Sea and Fisheries**.

The next long beach heading east is void of resorts, which seems nothing short of amazing given that all the other beaches in Western Bali are experiencing rapid development. The reason for this dearth of tourism is that the area, called **Gondol**, is a pearl farm established by an Australian-based company that cultivates pearls here and makes them into jewelry. Operating farms across Indonesia since 1992 and on Bali since 2003, Atlas South Sea Pearls uses strict environmental and husbandry guidelines.

At Atlas' hatchery and oyster farm at **Penyabangan**, just a few kilometers east of Pemuteran, visitors can see their sea-farm from the pier that stretches into the ocean, the larva rearing room, the preparation area, and the harvest of pearls. A thoughtfully prepared brochure explains the process and the different varieties of pearls. In the showroom jewelry is for sale in a wide range of prices, the most affordable being mother-of-pearl. There's a coffee shop. This stop is definitely recommended for anyone who has the remotest interest in how pearls are formed or who loves fine jewelry.

The sheltered harbor at **Celukan Bawang** is the main port for Buleleng Regency's import and export trade to other Indonesian islands. Just past the harbor going east, northern Bali begins.

ACCOMMODATION PRICE CATEGORIES Prices are for a double room, including breakfast **$** = under $30; **$$** = $30–$70; **$$$** = $70–$130; **$$$$** = over $130 **DINING PRICE CATEGORIES** Prices are based on a meal for one, without drinks **$** = under $5; **$$** = $5–$10; **$$$** = over $10

VISITING PEMUTERAN See map, page 310–311.

In the far northwest corner of Bali, this cluster of accommodations and restaurants form an out-of-the-way resort area offering expansive corals and marine life, reef regeneration programs and marine conservation projects that don't get the attention they deserve. Nearby Pulau Menjangan (Deer Island)—15 minutes west—has 90 m (290 ft) drop-offs and undersea caves, and its shallow water tempts even beginner snorkelers to come exploring, making it Bali's top diving destinations.

GETTING THERE & GETTING AROUND
It takes 3–4 hrs to reach Pemuteran from Denpasar either traversing the scenic roads going north or looping around via the Denpansar–Gilimanuk south coast road, passing through Gilimanuk. From Lovina in the east, it's about a 45-minute drive. Regular buses and bemos service the north coast road to Gilimanuk, stopping in Pemuteran, and car hires are easily arranged from Lovina.

Day trips to West Bali National Park are available through hotels and dive shops.

Pemuteran is a small village and can easily be navigated on foot or by bicycle. Motorcycles are also available for rent. Check with your accommodation for details.

ACCOMMODATIONS
Pemuteran is popular with domestic travelers during public and school holidays and is beginning to be discovered by international tourists as well. Reservations during high seasons are recommended. Expect discounts during low seasons.

Amertha Bali Villas, Tel: 94831, www.amerthabalivillas.com. Ocean-front and ocean, mountain, and garden view rooms and suites here are set on the beach with mountains as a backdrop. Classic Bali style is the theme, and there's a fine attached restaurant and a decent pool. **$$$**
Kubuku Ecolodge, Tel: 0813-3857-5384, www.kubukuhotel.com. Away from the main road but near a white sand beach and coral project, the 14 stylish rooms here are very peaceful. Staff can arrange snorkeling, tours and transport. **$$-$$$**
Matahari Beach Resort & Spa, Tel: 92312, www.matahari-beach-resort.com. A totally surprising find in tiny Pemuteran, the Matahari has won a plethora of international awards, as well as plaudits for respecting traditional Balinese values. It's a five-star

villa resort with friendly and courteous staff, full luxury spa, and a first-class restaurant, Balinese dances are performed twice a week, and all-day dive tours to Menjangan can be arranged. **$$$$**
Pondok Sari Beach & Spa Resort, Tel: 94738, www.pondoksari.com. A wide range of rooms are available here, from standard with fan to bungalows with lush open-air showers, plus Villa Wayang, a 150-year old Javanese teak wood joglo house with three bedrooms, two bathrooms, living/dining room, and a mountain-view daybed. The resort is set in beautiful gardens winding from road to sea, and the restaurant serves excellent food. **$$-$$$**
Puri Ganesha Villas, Tel: 94766, www.puriganesha.com. Ranked one of the World's Best Beach Hideaways by *Travel+Leisure* magazine, this resort is not at all what you'd expect to find in a small fishing village. The beautifully decorated, two-story thatched-roof villas have cute names such as Senyum (smile), Sepi (quiet), Santai (relaxed) and Senang (happy). Each has air-con bedrooms, garden baths, private pool, dedicated staff, and masseur on request. The intimate seaside restaurant serves organic food whenever possible, no red meat, and a menu that changes every night. **$$$$**
Rare Angon Homestay, Tel: 94747. Near the beach, the traditional style Balinese budget bungalows here have with air-con and hot water. **$**
Taman Sari Bali Resort & Spa, Tel: 93264, www.tamansaribali.com. Together with adjacent Pondok Sari this is one of the two best moderately-priced hotels of the area. Stylish, roomy, comfortable standard rooms, suites, and bungalows are all set in spacious tropical grounds facing an almost empty black-sand beach. The good restaurant serves a wide variety of cuisines. It's very popular and always fully booked during school holidays so reservations are recommended. **$$-$$$$**
Villa Semadhi, Tel: 94831, www.villasemadibali.com. A luxury private villa on the beach with four suites, a large garden, friendly staff, a pool, and Jacuzzi. "Semadhi" means meditation, reflecting the exceptional tranquility of the setting. Reduced rates are available for weekly stays. **$$$$**

DIVING
There are several dive operators in Pemuteran. Expect to pay from $25/dive for local shore dives to $90 for those further afield in West Bali National Park.

Equipment rental runs from about $10/dive for a full set of diving gear or a full day of snorkel set use.

Easy Divers Bali, Tel: 94736, www.easy-divers.eu. A PADI dive center emphasizing personal attention, safety, experience, friendliness, and professionalism, with over two decades in the business. Supporter of Reef Gardeners.

Reef Seen Aquatics, Tel: 93001, www.reefseenbali. com. A PADI-accredited dive center with heavy emphasis on marine conservation, this company also manages the hatchery at Proyek Penyu (Turtle Project) which releases young turtles and rescues older ones. There's an Impressive program of community marine environment education— young village fishermen trained to clean and conserve reefs.

OTHER ACTIVITIES

There are some good **trekking** opportunities in the hills around Pemuteran. Ask at your accommodation for a guide or directions. Local boats can be chartered on the beach for **fishing**.

Shopping

Atlas South Sea Pearls, Jl. Nelayan, Penyabangan, Tel: 081-2387-77012, www.atlaspearlsandperfumes. com.au. Australian-owned, with headquarters in Sanur, this is the pearl oyster hatchery and pearl harvesting center of the organization, just a few kilometers east of Pemuteran. Tours take in the larva rearing room, preparation area, and harvesting section. Call first to find out tour times. The showroom sells fabulous jewelry from reasonable up to extravagant prices. There's also a coffee shop that serves sandwiches.

The man-made reef frames installed around Pemuteran have been a great success, and now support pristine corals and many fish.

INDONESIA AT A GLANCE

The Republic of Indonesia is the world's fourth most populous nation, home to more than 250 million people. The vast majority (87%) are Muslims, making Indonesia home to the largest Muslim-majority population in the world (though over half the population is to be found in Java, the most densely populated island on earth). More than 300 languages are spoken, but Bahasa Indonesia, a variant of Malay, is the national language.

The nation is a republic, headed by a president, with a 560-member legislature, the People's Representative Council or DPR, making up the elected part of a 695-member People's Consultative Assembly (MPR). There are 33 provinces and special territories. The capital is Jakarta, with a population of 9.6 million. The archipelago comprises nearly 2 million square km (772,000 square miles) of land and sea, with over 17,000 islands.

Indonesia's US$900 billion gross domestic product comes from oil, textiles, lumber, fishing, mining, agriculture, and manufacturing. Per capita income is approximately US$3,859. Much of the population still makes a living through agriculture, chiefly rice-growing. The unit of currency is the rupiah.

HISTORICAL OVERVIEW

The Buddhist Sriwijaya kingdom, based in southeastern Sumatra, controlled parts of western Indonesia from the seventh to the 13th centuries. The Hindu-Buddhist Majapahit kingdom, centered in eastern Java, had influence over an even greater area from the 13th to the 16th centuries. Beginning in the mid-13th century, local rulers began converting to Islam after several centuries of contact with Muslim traders from India, China, and the Middle East, though Bali remained Hindu and many eastern areas eventually converted to Christianity.

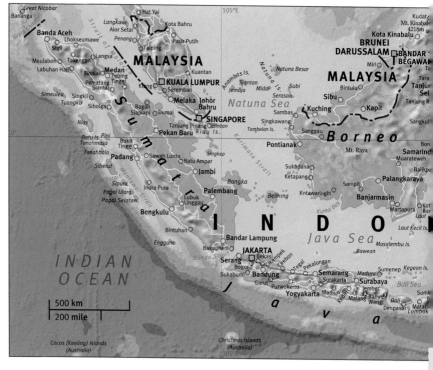

In the 17th century the Dutch East India Company (Vereenigde Oost-Indische Compagnie, or VOC) founded settlements and wrested control of the Indies spice trade from their English and Portuguese rivals. The VOC was declared bankrupt in 1799, and a Dutch colonial government was established.

Anti-colonial uprisings began in the early 20th century, as a diverse nationalist movement developed. Sukarno soon emerged as the most charismatic nationalist leader. Early in 1942, the Dutch East Indies were overrun by Japanese forces. When Japan saw its fortunes waning toward the end of the war, Indonesian nationalists were encouraged to organize. On August 17 1945, shortly after Japan surrendered to the Allies, Sukarno and his deputy Mohammad Hatta unilaterally proclaimed Indonesia's independence.

However, the returning Dutch sought to re-establish colonial rule after the war. Four years of fighting ensued before the Dutch finally recognized Indonesian independence in 1949.

During the 1960s, Indonesia lurched towards crisis, as Sukarno became increas-ingly hostile to the West, while attempting to play off various internal political forces against each other. A bungled putsch against the military top brass by left-leaning junior offi-cers on September 30, 1965, prompted a nationwide campaign of organized violence against the PKI, or Indonesian Communist Party. Hundreds of thousands of people were killed as suspected communists.

Discredited by the events of 1965, President Sukarno was edged from power by General Suharto, who became acting president in 1968. His undemocratic administration was friendly to foreign investment and the nation enjoyed three decades of economic growth. Suharto was ousted during the turmoil that followed the Asian financial crisis of 1997-98, and democracy resumed. In 2004, the first direct presidential elections took place, with Susilo Bambang Yudhoyono, known popularly as SBY, assuming the presidency. After a second term, SBY was replaced in 2014 by Joko Widodo, known as Jokowi. Today, Indonesia has the fourth largest economy in Asia, after China, India, and Japan.

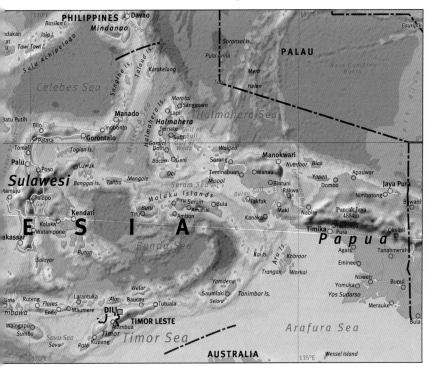

Basic Travel Information

The **Bali Tourism Board**—comprising of a group of private businessmen in the tourism industry—has a good website that might be useful: www.balitourismboard.org. It includes topics such as: how to get to Bali, geography, topography, people and lifestyle, history, flora and fauna, local transportation, economy, and climate.

POLICE

The **Tourism Police** is a specialized force that can lend a hand when trouble arises. They have stations in major resort areas, and a 24-hour helpline: 763-753 For emergencies, call 110.

VISAS

Check your passport before leaving for Indonesia, as it must be valid for at least six months after the date of arrival, and some immigration officials require at least six empty pages, one of which will be stamped upon arrival.

Currently, citizens of 45 countries require no visa to enter Indonesia via Bali's international airport, and are granted a free, non-extendable 30-day visit stamp on arrival.

Citizens of a further 30 countries can obtain a 30-day **Visa on Arrival** (VOA)(extendable once, for a further 30 days) at the airport for a fee of US$35. However, the list often changes, so check the Indonesian government's website for up-to-the online information: www.indonesia.travel/gb/en/home

Citizens of other countries need to apply for a visa to an Indonesian embassy or consulate before travelling. Sixty-day tourist visas are also available to travelers on the visa exemption and VOA lists, but these must be applied for in advance of arrival at an Indonesian embassy or consulate in your home country, or in one of the neighboring countries such as Singapore.

Beware: Visitors who overstay their visas will be fined $20 per day. Be aware that the your day of arrival counts as the first day of your visa validity. Also know that doing anything other than simply being a tourist—even volunteer work or attending a business-related seminar—can be grounds for immediate deportation. If you will be doing the above, it's best to check with your immigration department about the right visa to apply for.

Visa rules are subject to frequent change, so check the latest information online before traveling.

CUSTOMS

Firearms, weapons, explosives, and ammunition are strictly prohibited.

The standard duty-free allowance is: one liter of alcoholic beverages, 200 cigarettes, 50 cigars or 100 gm of tobacco.

Pornography is forbidden, as is "cinematographic films, pre-recorded video tapes, video laser discs, and records." Pornography in particular is a serious issue and possession can get you on the next plane out.

All narcotics, drugs and psychotropic substances are illegal in Indonesia. The use, sale, or purchase of narcotics results in long prison terms, huge fines, and the death penalty in some cases. Once caught, you are immediately placed in detention until trial, and the sentences are stiff, as demonstrated by Westerners currently serving long sentences in the Kerobokan jail for possession of small quantities of marijuana.

There is no restriction on import and export of foreign currencies in cash or travelers checks. The customs form also asks if you have bank notes in rupiah or other currency equal to 100 million rupiah or more and goods obtained overseas exceeding $250 per person or $1,000 per family.

The import of animals, fish, and plants, including their products, is also prohibited.

WHEN TO TRAVEL

The best time to visit Bali is during the dry season, April–September, when humidity is down and nights can be cool. It is still possible to visit during the rainy season, however. Downpours do occur most days between November and March, but mornings are generally dry. The busiest tourist seasons are Christmas and during May–August school holidays, as well as during the week following the end of Ramadan, when large numbers of domestic tourists arrive.

FOREIGN CONSULATES IN BALI

All the consulates and honorary consuls below, except Spain, are located in southern Bali (area code 0361).

Australia, Jl. Tantular 32, Renon, Tel: 200-0100, www.bali.indonesia.embassy.gov.au (also represents citizens of **Canada, New Zealand, Ireland**, and **Papua New Guinea**).
Brazil, Jl. Legian 186, Kuta, Tel: 757-775, brazilconsul@bytheseatropical.com
Czech Republic (Hon. Consul), Jl. Pengembak 17, Sanur, Tel: 286-465, fax: 286-408, bali@honorary.mzv.cz
Chile, Jl. Pengembak Gg. 1/3, Tel: 756-781, fax: 756-783, chilehonconsulate@bali-villa.com
Denmark and Norway, Mimpi Resort, Kawasan Bukit Permai, Jimbaran, Tel: 701-070, ext. 32, fax: 701-073, mimpi@mimpi.com
France (Consular Agency), Jl. Umalas I 80, Kerobokan, Tel: 473-0834, consul@dps.centrin.net.id
Germany, Jl. Pantai Karang 17, Sanur, Tel: 288-535, fax: 288-826, sanur@hk-diplo.de
Hungary (Hon. Consulate), Marintur, Jl. Bypass Ngurah Rai 219, Sanur, Tel: 287-701, fax: 287-456, , huconbali@telkom.net
Italy, Lotus Enterprise Building, Jl. Bypass Ngurah Rai, Jimbaran, Tel: 701-005, italconsbali@italconsbali.com
Japan, Jl. Raya Puputan 170, Renon, Tel: 227-628, fax: 265-066, denpasar@dp.mofa.go.jp
Spain, Jl. Raya Sanggingan, Br. Lungsiakan, Kedewatan, Ubud, Tel: 975-736, espana_bali@blueline.net.id
Sweden & Finland, Jl. Segara Ayu, Sanur, Tel: 282-223, sweconsul@yahoo.com
The Netherlands, Jl. Raya Kuta 127, Kuta, Tel: 761-502, dutchconsulate@kcbtours.com
United Kingdom, Jl. Tirta Nadi #20, Sanur, Tel: 270-601, consulate.bali@fco.gov.uk
United States of America, Jl. Hayam Wuruk 188, Tanjung Bungkak, Denpasar, Tel: 233-605, CABali@state.gov

WHAT TO BRING ALONG

When packing, keep in mind that you will be in the tropics, but that it can get cold in the mountains, particularly at night. Generally, you will want to dress light and wear natural fibers that absorb perspiration. Don't bring too much, as you will be tempted by the great variety of inexpensive and stylish clothes available. If you visit a government office, men should wear long trousers, shoes, and a shirt with collar. Women should dress neatly, covering knees and shoulder, with shoes. Never wear flip-flops to a government office. For those wanting to travel light, a sarong purchased upon arrival in Indonesia ($5–10) is one of the most versatile items you could hope

for. It serves as a wrap to get to the bath, a beach towel, required dress for Balinese temples, pajamas, bed sheet, and a fast-drying towel.

Tiny padlocks for use on luggage zippers are a handy deterrent to pilfering hands. Flashlights are essential for finding your way along Indonesia's poorly lit roadways and sidewalks; these can be easily purchased locally.

Bring along some pre-packaged alcohol towelettes or better yet, antiseptic hand cleaner (no litter to dispose of). Both are handy for disinfecting hands before eating or after trips to the *kamar kecil* (toilet).

The majority of Indonesian department stores and supermarkets in major towns stock Western toiletries. Contact lens supplies for hard and soft lenses are available in well-stocked supermarkets or pharmacies.

Sanitary napkins are available in convenience stores all over Bali, but tampons can be hard to find outside of the main resorts, and are often very expensive. Condoms are available at all *apotik* (pharmacies) and convenience stores. Sunscreen and insect repellent are also available locally.

PLANNING A TRIP TO BALI

These days an increasing number of visitors are avoiding the crowded tourist enclaves of southern Bali and Ubud and are heading to other areas directly from the airport—you can be in virtually any corner of the island within a couple of hours of passing through immigration. Padangbai is the launching point for boat journeys to the islands east of Bali, and ferries operate between Gilimanuk (Western Bali) and Ketapang in East Java.

When planning your trip, avoid impossibly tight schedules. Things happen slowly here, and adjusting to the local pace will make your visit more pleasant. Better to spend more time in a few places and see them in a leisurely way than to end up hot and hassled.

Also keep in mind that the tropical heat takes its toll, and the midday sun should be avoided. Get an early start before the rays become punishing (the tropical light is beautiful at dawn), retreat to a cool place after lunch, and go out again in the afternoon and early evening when it's much more pleasant.

CLIMATE

Indonesia straddles the equator and the climate is tropical, with average temperatures in Bali ranging from 28–33°C. The coasts are drier and hotter, but in the mountains temperatures can drop as low as 5°C at night. Humidity varies but is always high: between 75–100%.

In general, Indonesia has two seasons: the southeast monsoon, bringing dry weather (*musim panas*), and the northwest monsoon, bringing rain (*musim hujan*). In the transition periods between the two seasons, waves can be high (*ombak putih*) and seas rough, which is good if you're a surfer but not great if you're passing between islands by boat.

The rainy season is normally October–April, peaking around January/February, when it rains for several hours each day, usually in the afternoon. Before it rains, the air gets very sticky; afterwards it is refreshingly cool. The dry season, May–September, is a better time to visit Bali. June–August, the Balinese "winter" is particularly nice, though this is peak season for tourism.

TIME ZONES

Bali is on Central Indonesian Standard Time (Waktu Indonesia Tengah, WIT), or Greenwich mean time +8 hours. It is on the same time as Singapore but is one hour ahead of Jakarta.

MONEY

The Indonesian monetary unit is the rupiah. Notes come in denominations of 100,000, 50,000, 20,000, 10,000, 5,000, 2,000, and 1,000. Coins come in denominations of 1,000, 500, 100, and 50 rupiah. In stores small change is often replaced by candies because of a shortage of coins and their relatively low value.

Prices quoted in this book are in US dollars and are intended as a general indication.

Banking

Money changers and banks accepting foreign currency are found in most tourist areas. Exchange counters at banks are generally open from 8 am–3 pm Monday–Friday; a few open Saturdays until 11am. Bank lines can be long and slow and are less crowded at opening time. The Bank of Central Asia (BCA), one of Indonesia's oldest and largest banks, has a reliable service with branches and ATMs found virtually everywhere.

Generally, money changers give better rates than banks, are much more numerous, and keep more convenient hours, but they have a reputation for all sorts of sleight-of-hand tricks that can leave customers out of pocket, with those in Kuta being particularly notorious. Use only larger licensed money changers, and avoid those operating out of souvenir shops or travel agencies. The money changers at Bali's international airport offer rates only 5 or 10 points below elsewhere, but have a reputation for honesty.

Indonesian banks and money changers only accept foreign currency that is crisp and clean. New, uncreased, unstained US$100 bills command the highest rate of exchange.

Major **credit cards** are accepted in a wide variety of shops, restaurants and hotels in tourist areas. However, a surcharge of 2–3% is often added. All sales are transacted in rupiah, so your monthly statement will indicate interbank exchange rates. Visa and MasterCard are the most frequently accepted.

Automated Teller Machines (ATMs) are most often found in front of banks and in shopping districts in the tourist centers.

There are no exchange controls, and excess rupiah (bills only) can be freely reconverted at the airport upon departure.

Tax, service, & tipping

Most larger hotels and higher-priced restaurants add 21% tax and service to your bill, which will be itemized. Tipping is not a traditional custom here, but it is appropriate for outstanding service in tourist restaurants. In warungs and restaurants aimed at local clientele, tipping is not expected. For hotel porters, Rp 5,000–10,000 is appropriate for a regular-sized bag. For taxi drivers, you may wish to round the metered fare up to the nearest Rp 10,000.

When tipping guides, drivers, or housekeepers in a house in which you've been a guest, put the money in an envelope and present it with the right hand only. Ten percent is appropriate.

OFFICE HOURS

Government offices are officially open Monday–Thursday, 7 or 8 am until 3 or 4 pm, Fridays until 1 pm, and are usually closed on Saturday. If you want to get anything done, however, be there by at least 10 am. Always dress neatly when visiting government offices. Also note that most government offices are open at the regular time on Fridays but there may not be anyone at their desks until around 9 am because of mandatory exercises held on Fridays.

In large cities most private businesses are open 9 am–5 pm; shops often from 9 am–9 pm. In smaller towns shops close for a siesta at 1 pm and reopen at 5 pm or 6 pm.

MAIL

Indonesia's regular postal service is reliable, albeit not terribly fast. *Kilat* express service is only slightly more expensive but much faster. *Kilat khusus* (domestic special delivery) can deliver overnight to some areas. International express mail gets postcards and letters to North America or Europe in about 7–10 days from most cities.

Kantor Pos (post offices) are found in every town on Bali, open 8 am–2 pm every day except Sunday and 8 am–1 pm on Saturday. The main post office in Denpasar (Jl. Raya Puputan, Renon) remains open until 8 pm. Many smaller post offices close for lunch from noon to 1 pm.

Post offices are often busy and it can be a tedious process to line up at one window for weighing, another window for stamps, etc. Hotels normally sell stamps and will post letters for you, or you can use private postal agents to avoid hassles. Look for the orange *Agen Kantor Pos* (postal agency) signs.

TELEPHONE & FAX

Mobile phones are ubiquitous in Indonesia, and pay-as-you-go SIM cards that will work in most unlocked phones are widely available. If possible, avoid buying SIM cards in tourist resorts, where extortionate prices are often charged. They should cost no more than a couple of dollars, prices which usually include a small amount of preloaded *pulsa* (credit). SIM cards need to be registered by SMS before use; ask the vendor to do this for you. Extra phone credit can be purchased from many shops and side-of-the-road kiosks (look for signs advertising "pulsa").

There is good data and signal coverage in Bali, and overseas phones with an appropriate roaming package will work in most of the island.

To dial your own international calls, dial 007 or 008 to connect with an international (IDD, International Direct Dial) line, then country code, city code, and telephone number. The international dialing code for Indonesia is 62. Area codes for various regions on Bali are listed in Practicalities. If you do not have your own phone, most Internet cafés (*warnet*) offer international calls via web connections.

INTERNET ACCESS

Indonesia is an incredibly tech-savvy nation, and smartphones and tablets are very widely used. As a consequence, you'll find free Wi-Fi connections in virtually every hotel, tourist restaurant and coffee shop, some convenience stores, and even in some roadside local cafés. Connection speeds are not always the best if you're looking to upload or download large files, but they are usually adequate for emailing and general browsing. The rise of Wi-Fi and personal devices amongst both locals and travelers has made the once ubiquitous *warnet* (Internet cafés) something of an endangered species, but a few still survive in most resort areas (useful if you need to print out airline tickets or other online documents)). Mobile data coverage is reasonably reliable, if slow, in southern Bali and in major towns elsewhere.

NEWSPAPERS & MAGAZINES

There are various English-language publications to help keep abreast of the news or to find tourist information.

Bali & Beyond (www.baliandbeyond.co.id), and **Now! Bali** (www.nowbali.co.id), are all glossy magazines aimed at tourists.

The Bali Advertiser (www.baliadvertiser. biz) is a free paper, published twice a month and widely distributed to tourist businesses. Primarily published for expats, it consists mostly of classified ads but also has performance schedules, news, and an eclectic array of specialist columns which often make for enlightening reading. There are several similar publications, but they are generally poorly edited and with less interesting content.

The Jakarta Post (www.thejakartapost. com) is the largest English-language newspaper in Indonesia, with strong domestic coverage and commentary. It is widely available in Bali. The Post's main rival, **The Jakarta Globe**, has excellent, sharply written coverage of Indonesian happenings, but it's much harder to find in Bali. Both papers have good websites.

The Yak (www.theyakmag.com) is an up-market expat magazine published quarterly.

ELECTRICITY

220 volts at 50 cycles alternating current. Power failures are common. Voltage can fluctuate considerably so use a stabilizer for computers and similar equipment. Plugs are of the European two-pronged variety.

HEALTH

Bali is one of the most modern and developed parts of Indonesia, and many international travelers visit without taking any health precautions. However, it is sensible to check with your physician before leaving home for the latest news on recommended vaccinations. Frequently considered vaccines are: Diphtheria, Tetanus (DPT), and Typhoid; Measles, Mumps, and Rubella (MMR); and the oral Polio vaccine.

Many doctors recommend being vaccinated for Hepatitis A and B before traveling to Southeast Asia and some suggest a cholera vaccination. Vaccinations for yellow fever, smallpox, and cholera are not required, except for visitors coming from infected areas.

Find out the generic names for whatever prescription medications you are likely to need as most are available in Indonesia, but often under different brand names. Although many supposedly prescription-only medicines are readily available over the counter in Bali, it's wise to get copies of doctors' prescriptions as a precaution.

Hygiene

Hygiene cannot be taken for granted in Indonesia, and intestinal illnesses are by far the most likely health problem to befall foreign tourists. **Tap water is not drinkable.**

Indonesians avoid drinking untreated tapwater, and you should follow suit. Generally speaking, any water you are offered to drink by a local will be safe, being either boiled tapwater or UV-treated water from a dispenser, but don't be afraid to confirm this by asking, especially in remote villages (boiled or treated potable water is known as *air putih*, "white water"). Most locals and many foreign residents are happy to brush their teeth with tapwater, especially in towns where it is usually chlorinated, but it is always safer to use bottled water for this. Bottled water is available everywhere. "Aqua" is the most popular and reliable brand name.

Ice on Bali is officially made only under license in government-sanctioned factories, and even when the regulations are overlooked, it is usually made from boiled or treated water, so is generally safe.

Plates, glasses, and silverware washed in unboiled water need to be completely dry before use.

Fruits and vegetables without skins pose a higher risk of contamination. To avoid contamination, buy fruits in the market and peel them yourself.

To *mandi* (bathe) two or three times a day is a great way to stay cool and fresh. But be sure to dry yourself well and perhaps apply a medicated body powder, such as Purol or Herocyn, to avoid the unpleasantness of skin fungi and rashes caused by heat, especially during the October–April rainy season.

Exposure

Many visitors insist on instant suntans, so overexposure to the heat and sun is a frequent problem. Be especially careful on long walks and overcast days when the power of the sun is not so obvious. Wear a hat, loose-fitting, light-colored, long-sleeved cotton clothes and pants, drink plenty of water, and use a good-quality sunscreen (available in mini-markets). Do not wear clothing made of synthetic fibers that don't allow air to circulate. Tan slowly; don't spoil your trip.

Dehydration

Visitors to Indonesia are usually careful to eat clean foods and drink safe water, but they often overlook the need to keep hydrated in the equatorial climate. Don't forget to drink, drink, drink.

Diarrhea

Diarrhea is a likely traveling companion and is called "**Bali Belly**" locally. In addition to strange foods and unfamiliar micro-fauna, diarrhea is often the result of attempting to accomplish too much in one day. Taking it easy can be an effective prevention as can avoiding excessive intake of spices, chilies, and tropical fruits; and making sure the food you eat and the water you drink is hygienic. Imodium is locally available, as are medicines to help with more serious cases.

Symptoms of "Bali Belly" can include watery bowel movements and nausea, and in the worse cases vomiting, abdominal cramping, bloating, and fever. Travelers' diarrhea usually clears up within a couple of days. Relax, take it easy, and drink lots of fluids, including rehydration salts such as Servidrat (the local brands are Oralit and Parolit). Especially helpful is water from young coconuts (air *kelapa muda*) or strong, unsweetened tea. The former is an especially pure anti-toxin. Get it straight from the coconut without sugar, ice, or food coloring added. When you are ready to eat again, start with bananas, plain rice, crackers, *tempe* (fermented soybean cakes), and *bubur* (rice porridge). Avoid fried, spicy, greasy, or heavy foods and dairy products for a while. If there's no relief after three days, antibiotics may be required, so see a doctor.

Intestinal parasites

Intestinal parasites are easily passed on by infected food handlers. Prevention is difficult, short of fasting, so before leaving home, ask your physician if it is a good idea to take anti-parasite medicine. If so, brands such as Combantrin are available at all pharmacies.

If you have problems when you get home, even if only sporadically, have stool and blood tests. Left untreated, parasites can cause serious damage.

Cuts & scrapes

Your skin will probably come into contact with more dirt and bacteria than at home, so wash your face and hands more often. Cuts should be taken seriously and cleaned with an antiseptic like Betadine, available from local pharmacies, before applying an antibacterial ointment. Cover the cut during the day to keep it clean, but leave it uncovered at night so that it can dry. Constant covering will retain moisture in the wound and only encourage an infection. Repeat this ritual after every bath. Sensitivity and areas of redness around the cut indicate infection, in which case a doctor should be consulted.

Mosquito-borne diseases

Malaria, caused by night-biting mosquitoes, is occasionally reported in remote rural parts of Bali, especially in the north and east, but it is very rare, and antimalarial medication is not usually recommended for visitors. However, guidelines can change, so consult a doctor familiar with tropical diseases before leaving home. There is a more significant risk of malaria on the Gilis, and the disease is endemic in Lombok and the islands further east, so prophylaxis is recommended for journeys in these areas. Malaria symptoms can include fever, chills, and sweating, headaches and muscle aches.

The other mosquito concern is **dengue fever**, spread by the day-biting *Aedes aegypti,* which is especially active during the rainy season. The most effective prevention is to avoid being bitten (there is no prophylaxis for dengue). Symptoms can include severe headache, pain behind the eyes, high fever, back ache, muscle and joint pains, nausea and vomiting, and a rash appearing between the third and fifth days of illness. Within days, the fever subsides and recovery is seldom hampered with complications. The more serious variant, **dengue hemorrhagic fever (DHF)**, which can be fatal, may be the reaction of a secondary infection with remaining immunities following a primary attack, but tourists are highly unlikely to be afflicted by this.

Cases of **Japanese encephalitis**, a viral infection affecting the brain, have been known to occur and are an added reason to take protective measures against mosquito bites.

Preventing getting bitten is the goal. Apply mosquito repellent to your skin (the local brand, Autan, is very effective), and consider wearing long sleeves and pants, especially at sunrise and dusk when mosquitoes are particularly active. A local non-chemical solution is citronella oil (*minyak gosok, cap tawon*).

Many accomodations provide mosquito nets, and they are also available in most general stores for around $5.

Slow-burning mosquito coils (*obat nyamuk bakar*) are also widely available. They last 6–8 hours and need to be placed in a safe container to prevent fire hazards (most losmen have covered terracotta vases with decorative holes in them expressly for this purpose). Light the coil and leave it in a tightly-enclosed room before going to dinner. When ready to sleep move it outside or to another room away from the bed to avoid the noxious smell and fumes, which can cause headaches. Baygon is a good local brand and is sold most places.

Far better than coils are compact electric (smokeless) anti-mosquito devices ($2–$3, available in major towns) that simply plug into a wall outlet. Most varieties have refill pads that must be changed periodically.

AIDS & Hepatitis B

The full scale of the HIV/AIDS problem in Indonesia is not known, but health experts believe that it is far greater than official figures suggest, which makes practicing safe sex all the more imperative. Another area of concern is the Hepatitis B virus, which affects liver function and which can also be transmitted during unprotected sex. It is only sometimes curable, and can be fatal. In Indonesia, condoms are sold in pharmacies, supermarkets, and mini-markets. Select a reputable brand.

Pharmacies

The Indonesian name for pharmacy is *apotik*. The most commonly found international chains are **Guardian** and **Century**. Outside of malls the large Indonesian chain, **Apotik Kimia Farma**, is well respected. Most large apotiks have a book cross-referencing Latin and generic prescription names, which can be helpful in emergencies. They also carry first aid supplies and sundries.

Medical treatment & insurance

In Indonesian, doctor is *dokter* and hospital is *rumah sakit*. Smaller villages only have small government clinics, *puskesmas*, which are not equipped to deal with anything serious but can be handy in an emergency.

Fancier hotels often have house doctors, physicians on call, or can recommend a nearby clinic.

Many foreigners living in Bali have their favorite local clinics and doctors; however, in the absence of local recommendations there are two international clinics in Southern Bali that are generally reliable, and that are recommended by many international health insurers.

BIMC, Jl. Bypass Ngurah Rai 100X, Kuta, Tel: 761-263, www.bimcbali.com, is New Zealand-owned and operated. It is centrally located on the big roundabout opposite the Kuta Bali Galeria shopping center.

International SOS Bali, Jl. Bypass Ngurah Rai 505X, Kuta, Tel: 215-942-8226, www.internationalsos.com. American-owned, and located down the street from BIMC, this is another excellent clinic with a laboratory, X-ray, and pharmacy. Includes a 24-hr alarm center, dedicated air ambulance fleet, dental, and psychological services, in addition to clinical appointments.

For dentistry, many foreigners living in southern Bali go to **Bali 911 Dental Clinic**, Jl. Patimura No. 9, Denpasar, Tel: 222-455.

Emergency medical assistance

Outside of the big cities, general health care leaves much to be desired. Often the best course of action in the event of a life-threatening emergency or accident is to get on the first plane to Singapore. Be sure to buy **travel insurance** before leaving home with emergency evacuation coverage, as Medivac airlifts can cost as much as $30,000. The insurance policy will list emergency telephone numbers to call and describe the procedures to follow.

Both **BIMC** and **SOS** (see above) offer 24-hr emergency services and medical evacuation.

Local emergency telephone numbers:
Police 110
Fire 113
Ambulance 118
Search & Rescue 51111
Red Cross 26465.

WARNINGS

Home-brewed alcohol, *arak*, is 60–100% proof and is distilled from palm or rice wine. Although it is very popular, and is often offered in cocktail form in tourist restaurants, it is generally best avoided. Unscrupulous home-brewers sometimes add potentially toxic ingredients to give it an extra "kick." Serious illness and even death can result, and a number of tourists have died after partaking in recent years

Rabies has become a major problem on Bali in the last few years, with dozens of local deaths since 2008. The authorities have struggled to contain the outbreak amongst the local dog population. Without immediate post-bite treatment, rabies is almost invariably fatal, though the incubation period can be many months. If you are bitten by a dog, monkey, or any other mammal while in Bali it is essential that you visit one of the international clinics listed above, or the main government hospital at Sanglah in Denpasar, without delay to begin the course of post-bite injections. You may wish to consider getting vaccinated before traveling. The vaccination does not entirely negate the need for post-bite treatment, but it does allow for a shorter course of injections.

SECURITY

Bali is a relatively safe place to travel, and violent crime is very rare. However, petty crime does occur, especially in the busy urban areas of the south. Pay close attention to your belongings, especially in crowded places, such as markets. Use a small backpack or money belt for valuables. Bags can be snatched by thieves on motorbikes, so be vigilant and always hold your bag facing the sidewalk, away from the street.

Thefts from hotel rooms are generally very rare in Bali, but be sure that the door and windows of your hotel room are locked at night, and use hotel safe facilities if they are available. Make sure you have photocopies of your passport and other documents, and keep them separate from the originals.

Theft from beaches is actually remarkably rare in Bali, but it is never advisable to leave valuables unguarded on the sand while you go off swimming.

FOOD AND DRINK

Most Indonesians, including Balinese, do not feel they have eaten until they have eaten rice. This is accompanied by side dishes, often just a little piece of meat and some vegetables with a spicy sauce.

Typical dishes available in basic local restaurants all over the country include *sate* (satay; skewered grilled meat)—often *ayam* (chicken) and *kambing* (goat)—*gado-gado* or *pecel* (boiled vegetables with spicy peanut sauce), and *soto* (vegetable soup with or without meat).

Mie goreng (fried noodles) and *nasi goreng* (fried rice) are ubiquitous; *nasi goreng istimewa* (special) usually comes with an egg on top and a piece of *ayam goreng* or a few sticks of *sate*.

Indonesian fried chicken (*ayam goreng*) is common and usually very tasty, although the locally-reared chicken (*ayam kampung*) can be a bit stringy. Note that *ayam goreng* is fried in butter with no batter; for crispy fried skin, order *ayam goreng tepung* (with flour).

The main **beers** available in Indonesia are Bintang and Anker, both both light, Dutch-style pilsners. Imported spirits and wines are widely available in Bali, but they tend to be relatively expensive because of prohibitive import duties. Locally produced spirits, and even local wines, made from imported grape pulp, are generally more economical, if often less palatable.

Balinese specialties

Balinese specialties include *babi guling*, rubbed with turmeric, stuffed with spices and roasted on a spit, and *bebek betutu*, where duck is stuffed with vegetables and spices, wrapped in banana leaf, and either smoked or steamed in an earth oven. Although the Hindu prohibition on eating beef is not as widely observed in Bali as in India, many locals do avoid it, and it is not widely served outside of tourist restaurants.

Balinese brews include *tuak* (palm beer), *brem* (sweet rice wine), and *arak* (60–100 proof liquor distilled from palm or rice wine, which is best avoided because of the risk of contaminants).

Fruits

Tropical fruits are plentiful and delicious. Bali is known for its sweet *salak*, and crisp, yellowish segments within. It tastes like a cross between an apple and a walnut. *Manggis* (mangosteen), available November–March, is pure heaven hidden within a thick purple-brown cover. The juicy white segments melt away. Another favorite is rambutan. Peel away the "hairy", reddish outer skin to find delicious, sweet white flesh inside surrounding a large seed.

Vegetarianism

To indicate that you are a vegetarian, say: "*saya tidak makan daging*" (I don't eat meat), "*jangan pakai ayam*" (don't use chicken), or "*jangan pakai daging*" (don't use meat). The concept of dietary restrictions is generally well understood due to the various religions in Indonesia and spiritual practices involving food. However, finding food that truly has no animal products can be challenging, especially given the wide use of dried fish and shrimp products as seasonings. *Tempe* (soybean cakes) and *tahu* (tofu, soybean curd) are excellent sources of protein.

ADDRESSES

The Indonesian spelling of geographical features and villages varies considerably as there is no form of standardization that meets with both popular and official approval. Village names can be spelled three different ways, all on signboards in front of various government offices. In this guide, we have tried to use the most common spellings, i.e. Batujimbar instead of Batu Jimbar and Candikuning instead of Candi Kuning.

Every town has streets named after the same national heroes, so you will find Jl. (*jalan* or street) General Sudirman and Ahmad Yani in every city throughout the archipelago. When tracking down addresses you will also find that the numbers are not consecutive. For example, number 38 may be next to number 119.

Another mystery in reading addresses comes of this type: Jl Panti Silayukti 18, Br. Kecil, Padangbai, Amlapura, Bali, Indonesia. You might be asking, "So, where is this place?" Insiders tip: Jl. Pantai Silayukti 18 is the street address; Br. Kecil (found only on Bali) is the *banjar* (neighborhood within the town); Padangbai is the *desa adat* (the town, or on other islands, the *kampung* or village);

and Amlapura (which is also the name of a town) is the *kecamatan* (district). Confusing to foreigners, this system helps the post office—and the local people—find addresses more efficiently.

To **ask for directions**, it's better to have the name of a person and the name of the neighborhood or village. Thus "Ibu (Mrs.) Murni, Banjar Kalah" is a better address for asking directions even though "Jl. Hanoman 14" is the mailing address.

While traveling through the countryside, you'll generally get a more reliable response if you ask how long it takes to get someplace by whatever means of transport you are using, than if you ask the distance in kilometers (the standard Indonesian measure of distance).

THE NATIONAL CALENDAR

The Indonesian government sets national holidays every year, on both fixed and moveable dates. The fixed **national holidays** on the Gregorian calendar are the international New Year, January 1; Independence Day, August 17; and Christmas, December 25.

The Christian Good Friday, Easter Day, and Ascension Day, the Balinese New Year (Nyepi) and the Buddhist Waisak are also national holidays. These and all the Muslim holy days are based on the lunar cycle. Except for Nyepi, many restaurants, shops, and businesses remain open during public holidays.

THE BALINESE CALENDAR

Bali runs simultaneously on several different calendrical systems, including the Western calendar, a Saka lunar calendar, and a 210-day *pawukon* calendar. The important Balinese holidays include:

Nyepi. Balinese New Year, Nyepi, is a day of silence and meditation. It falls on the day after the new moon, about the time of the vernal equinox in late March. On Nyepi no physical activity occurs. This means no fire (cooking or electricity), no work, no travel, and no entertainment. Even Bali's airport is closed on this day. No touring is allowed, and visitors must stay in their hotels where special permits grant minimal use of the grounds and lights at night. Those staying in small hotels or family-owned homestays will also be required to observe the day of silence. This "silence" is taken seriously, with religiously-sanctioned guards patrolling the streets for transgressors, and should be respected by visitors. The day after Nyepi is Ngembak Nyepi and the roads are crowded

with people visiting family, friends, temples, and dance and drama performances.

On the eve of the Nyepi day, hundreds of *ogoh-ogoh* papier maché monsters are carried along the streets in all towns and villages, so be prepared to be caught in big crowds. This extraordinary cavalcade is reminiscent of a small scale South American carnival.

Galungan begins on the Wednesday of Dunggulan, the 11th week of a 30-week *pawukon* cycle. Pre-Galungan rituals involve offerings of animal sacrifices. On Galungan morning, everyone visits temples carrying colorful offerings.

Kuningan. Ten days after Galungan on the Saturday of Kuningan, the 12th week, marks the end of the celebration. It is a time for family gatherings, prayers, and still more offerings as deified ancestors return to heaven.

Saraswati Day, the last day of the *pawukon* calendar (the Saturday of Watugunung week) is when Saraswati, the Goddess of Knowledge, the Arts and Literature, is honored. All books and musical instruments are blessed and no music, reading or writing is allowed on this day. The next day is known as Sinta. This is the first day of the first *pawukon* week, when everyone goes to the beach for cleansing ceremonies.

TEMPLE CEREMONIES

In addition to holy days, Balinese Hindus hold ceremonies and perform rituals on other important days.

Odalan. Bali's temple anniversaries (*odalan*), based on the 210-day *pawukon* calendar, last alternatively one day or three days.

Temple festivals. The temple festivals based on the lunar calendar (Saka) begin on the full moon of the relevant month and last for several days.

Purnama Sasih Kasa. Full moon. Ceremonies are held in Hindu temples all across Bali and believers take offerings of food, fruit, and flowers to the temple to be blessed by a priest. The essence of these offerings will be enjoyed by the deities. The Balinese themselves are then blessed by performing various rituals using holy water, incense smoke, petals, and rice grains.

Tilem Sasih Sada. Dark moon. Celebrated by Balinese Hindus, rituals are held in major temples and family shrines. Offerings to the gods are placed on the ground at the entrance of each housing compound to beg the gods to illuminate dark thoughts.

SECULAR FESTIVALS

Bali is home to an impressive array of annual events, from traditional sporting contests to international arts festivals.

March/April

Bali Spirit Festival, Ubud. Celebrated in late March/early April to coincide with Nyepi, this six-day festival brings together music, yoga and dance. www.balispiritfestival.com

June/July

Bali Arts Festival is held from mid-June to mid-July at the Taman Werdi Budaya (Art Center) on Jl. Nusa Indah in Denpasar. A full month of dance, drama, and art and handicrafts exhibitions. Events include morning and evening performances by the winners of regency competitions from across the island. The opening ceremony is a parade beginning in downtown Denpasar worthy of international attention. www.baliartsfestival.com

Bali Triathlon. Held at Four Seasons Resort Jimbaran every June, Olympic and sprint distance events include: 1.5 km (0.9 mile) swim, 40 km (25 mile) bike, 10 km (6.2 mile) run, team relay for teams of three athletes (Olympic distance); 500 m (0.3 mile) swim, 20 km (12.4 mile) bike ride, 5 km (3 mile) run (sprint distance). Pre-race bike tour and Balinese bike blessing ceremony, live music, and beach party. www.balitriathlon.com

Omedomedan Kissing Ceremony. A June event in Banjar Sesetan Kaja, Denpasar Regency held the day after Nyepi. Participants are all single adults 17–30 years old and must be unmarried members of Banjar Kaja. (Outsiders are not allowed to participate.) After prayers, the girls and boys line up facing each other, meet and hug and kiss in this sacred ritual. As expected, things get silly and the ceremony usually ends with everyone being doused with water.

August 17

Indonesia's Independence Day. In the week or two leading up to August 17, Independence Day, games and contests are held throughout Indonesia reminiscent of the U.S. July 4th or French Bastille Day. Culminating on August 17, all celebrations include lots of food, fun, and laughter. Visitors are more than welcome to join.

Negara Buffalo Race Championships, Regent's Cup, Negara, West Bali. In celebration of Independence Day, the Regent's Cup buffalo race—with animals decorated in bright colors and jockeys bouncing and bobbing in attached carts—takes place on the Sunday before August 17 with teams hopeful of being selected to participate in the Governor's Cup Championship in October.

August/September

International Kite Festival, Sanur. Part of the Sanur Village Festival held annually. Teams from Indonesia and abroad fly enormous kites up to 10 m (33ft) long, taking as many as five men to launch compete in various divisions, including traditional Balinese and contemporary kite designs.

Sanur Village Festival. An annual celebration held August–September, drawing hundreds of locals and tourists to its many events. A four-day feast of contests (water sports and kite flying, to name two), music, dance and food, food, food; a great opportunity to mingle with the local people, hear some great music, and to eat some really good food. www.sanurvillagefestival.com

October

Negara Buffalo Race Championships, Governor's Cup, Negara, West Bali. *Jegog* music, dance performances, and traditional foods accompany an exciting event to the delight of onlookers.

Ubud Writers' and Readers' Festival, Ubud. One of the most prestigious literary events in Asia, this festival brings together authors and readers in a four-day extravaganza of workshops, readings, book launches and performances. www.ubudwritersfestival.com

BALINESE CASTES & NAMES

There are four major caste groups among the Balinese: **brahmana** (Brahman), **satria**, **wesya** and **jaba**. The brahmana are the priestly caste; the satria, the nobility; and the wesya, the former vassals of the court. Everyone else is sudra, or "commoner." Even though castes make no difference in peoples' abilities to hold certain jobs, and do not result in the oppressive social restrictions that sometimes occur in India, every Balinese keep track of them for various reasons, for example to decide what level of language to use when speaking Balinese.

Balinese names are coded to reveal caste and birth order within the family. The following are clues to interpreting names and their owner's social status:

Ida Bagus (male) and Ida Ayu (female) indicate the brahmanic caste. Gusti is normally used by members of the wesya caste, whereas Gusti Agung, Anak Agung, and Cokorda are reserved for the high-ranking members of the satria caste. Desak (female) and Dewa (male) are lower-ranking satria. I (normally male) and Ni (female) are usually used by the jaba.

Wayan, Made, Nyoman, and Ketut mean first-born, second-born, third-born, and fourth-born, respectively. Beginning with the fifth child in the family, the naming cycle is repeated. Also used similarly to indicate birth order are Putu, Kadek, Komang and Ketut. Nengah may be used by either the second- or third-born child. The birth order names are normally used only by the sudra caste, so don't call a member of the satria caste "Wayan" even if you happen to know that he/she is the oldest in the family!

ETIQUETTE

In the areas of Bali most frequented by foreigners, many are familiar with the strange ways and customs practiced outside Indonesia. But it is best to be aware of how certain aspects of your behavior will be viewed, even though Indonesians are almost always too polite to draw attention to any cultural *faux pas*. Here are some points to keep in mind:
* The left hand is considered dirty as it is used for cleaning oneself after using the toilet. It is inappropriate to use the left hand to eat or to give or receive anything with it. However, in the event that you do accidentally use your left hand, then say "*maaf, tangan kiri*" ("please excuse my left hand") or a simple "*maaf*" will do.
* The head is considered the most sacred part of the body, and the feet the least sacred. Avoid touching people on the head. Go for the elbow instead. Never step over food or expose the sole of your foot toward anyone.
* As it is impolite to keep one's head higher than others, it is appropriate to acknowledge the presence of others by stooping (extending the right arm and drooping the right shoulder while leaning forward) when passing closely by someone who is sitting or standing and engaged in a conversation.
* Pointing with the index finger is impolite. Indonesians use their thumbs (palm turned upward, fingers curled in) or open palms instead.
* Summoning people by crooking the forefinger is impolite. Rather, wave with a flat palm facing down.
* Hands on hips is a sign of superiority or anger.
* Take off your shoes when you enter someone's house. Often the host will stop you, but you should at least go through the motions until he/she does.
* Wait for a verbal offer before tucking into food and drinks that have been placed in front of you. Sip your drink and don't finish it in one gulp. Never take the last morsel from a common plate.
* You will often hear the words "*makan, makan*" ("eat, eat") if you pass somebody who is eating. This is not really an invitation, but simply means "Excuse me while I eat."
* If someone prepares a meal or drink for you it is most impolite to refuse. Even if you don't want to partake, it's polite to at least take a sip of an offered drink and a nibble of the food.

Bali may seem to have been placed here just for your personal enjoyment, but it is not a zoo. Be aware of Balinese sensibilities. Remember the Balinese are offended if the casual visitor does not **dress appropriately** when entering a temple. At major temples popular with tourists, sarongs and sashes are often provided, but if you're exploring off the beaten track it's a good idea to carry your own. Tops that expose shoulders are not really appropriate for either men or women away from the beach, and especially for visits to temples or family homes. Menstruating women are not allowed to enter temples. Never sit higher than the priest, and don't walk in front of people who are praying. Because some ceremonies last for several hours it is permissible to leave after a while, but do so inconspicuously.

Bathing suits and brief shorts and tops are acceptable on the beaches, but nowhere else. When leaving the beach areas it is more polite to wear longer shorts and shirts that cover the midriff.

Keeping your cool

If disputes or problems occur, talking loudly and forcefully doesn't make things easier and in fact can make matters worse. Patience and politeness are the order of the day and will open many doors. Good manners, proper dress, and a pleasant countenance will also work to your advantage.

TRAVELING WITH CHILDREN

Luckily for those with children, Balinese people almost always respond very warmly to children. Be sure to bring essentials: sunhats, creams, medicines, special foods, and a separate water container for babies to be sure of always having sterile water. Disposable diapers are available in big supermarkets. Nights can be cool sometimes, so bring some warm clothing for your child. Milk, eggs, fruit which you can peel, and porridges are readily available in the supermarkets. If given advanced notice, babysitters are available for a moderate charge at any hotel.

It's especially important that you have health/medical insurance for children.

ACCOMMODATIONS

Bali has an extraordinary range of accommodations, representing the best in terms of both variety and value for money anywhere in Indonesia. Even the most humble homestays here often come with at least a dash of quirky style, a decent free breakfast, and a pleasant atmosphere, and all at a price that would get you little more than a grim concrete cell elsewhere in Indonesia. In the midrange bracket, there are hundreds of delightful guesthouses and small hotels; and when it comes to the luxury market you can expect to find some of the finest properties in Asia, from large resort complexes to exclusive boutique villas.

Many of the cheaper accommodations are owned and run by local families, with guest rooms added to a traditional family compound. This is particularly the case in and around Ubud, and they are generally delightful places to stay.

The long influence of tourism means that virtually all accommodations, even the cheapest, are built to meet international tastes. It's very unusual to encounter Asian-style squat toilets these days. However, towels are usually not provided in budget lodgings, so you may want to bring your own. Also, outside of mountain areas few of the cheapest accommodations provide hot water.

Although midrange accommodations generally offer exceptionally good value in Bali, this is actually the sector where quality is most variable. Without either the personal touch of family-run budget homestays, or the rigorous requirements of luxury properties, standards can sometimes slip, especially in large, cheaply built hotels in the major resorts. Shop around and check the most recent online reviews before checking in.

The luxury market features traditional resorts, exclusive spa properties, and villas.

Of the later, many are actually resort complexes with their own restaurants, pools and other facilities, but there are also hundreds of privately owned and rented standalone villas, which can be excellent places to stay if you're looking for privacy or wanting to visit Bali for an extended period.

Advance bookings are advisable during peak tourist seasons (July–August, Christmas and New Year, the Muslim Ramadan holidays, and local public holidays). Popular resorts are always packed on weekends, and prices often double, so travel instead during the week when it's cheaper and quieter.

In many hotels, discounts of up to 40–50% off published rates are to be had for the asking during off-peak seasons, and you can often negotiate a discount at budget and midrange lodgings as a walk-in customer during quiet periods. Booking in advance through the Internet, travel agencies, or hotel association counters at airports can also result in a lower rate. Reservations are advisable throughout the year, especially July–August and December–January. Surcharges of 10–20% are often added during the peak season.

Larger hotels invariably add 21% tax and service to the bill.

See www.balispirit.com for recommended eco resorts and retreat centers.

SHOPPING

Bali is a shopper's paradise. Streets in the resort areas of the south are lined with stores, shops, and stalls selling arts, woodcarvings, handicrafts, hand-woven textiles, gifts, and souvenirs of all types. Also among Bali's best buys are ready-made clothes, stylish fashions, and gold and silver designer jewelry. Below are some shopping tips and a general picture of what to look for.

Bargaining

Outside of fixed price shops, the first price is not the last price on Bali. Try to learn the art of bargaining while you're here; it is expected that you will join in this traditional form of socialization. Items in supermarkets, department stores, and upmarket shops, as well as fees for services are generally fixed, but nearly everything else is fair game. At small hotels try asking for a discount; you'll be surprised at how often at least 10% is granted, particularly in the off-peak seasons.

There are really no meaningful rules when it comes to approaching bargaining, and oft-repeated advice about "offering half the initial asking price" is generally meaningless, as in many cases only a small discount will ever be granted, while at other times a vendor will simply chance an astronomical first price, even half of which would still be well over the odds. The only real rule is that in any extended bout of bargaining both buyer and seller will be expected to give ground. Keep on asking for the "best price" and keep on smiling. Your initial offer should be much lower than the price you really want to pay, and don't ever be afraid to make an initial offer that seems absurdly low—the vendor may very well have asked an initial price that is absurdly high!

Keep a sense of humor about the whole thing. There's no such thing as a "right price." You usually pay more than the locals, but that's the way it is. If you are planning on buying large quantities of the kind of goods on sale in Kuta and Sanur, it's worth visiting one of the large fixed-price emporiums such as Krisna on Jl. Sunset Road, where you can gauge the real market value of everything from souvenir tee shirts to budget handicrafts.

Souvenirs

For a wide selection of souvenirs, go to the hundreds of shops along Jl. Legian in Kuta, Legian, and Seminyak; the Ubud Art Market; the Sanur Art Market; and Denpasar's Kumbasari Market. The mother of all souvenir markets (*pasar seni*) is in Sukawati on the way from Denpasar up to Ubud, about 5 km (3.2 miles) south of Ubud.

Carvings

Mas and Kemenuh are the main spots for polished woodcarvings; Batuan is the place for wooden panels. Pujung, Sebatu, and Tegallalang, north of Ubud, specialize in painted carvings and giant statues. For masks, go to Mas, Singapadu, and Batuan.

Traditional Balinese stone carvings made from volcanic pumice (*paras*) are made in Batubulan. See Practicalities for these areas for specific recommendations.

Textiles

Bali is a dreamland for lovers of hand-woven textiles. Big Bali-style *ikat* workshops are concentrated in Gianyar Town, but Klungkung in eastern Bali, and Singaraja in the north also have large well-known producers. For the fancier *songket* with gold and silver threads woven into the weft, go to Sideman, Blayu (between Mengwi and Marga), and Singaraja. There are beautiful woven *selendangs* (temple sashes) in Batuan, Ubud, and Mengwi, but the exquisite *geringsing* double *ikat* cloths are made only in Tenganan, eastern Bali. Woven textiles from Sumbawa, Sumba, Tanah Toraja (Sulawesi), and Sumatra can be found in Kuta, Legian, and Denpasar.

Some of the batik worn by Balinese and found everywhere is made on Java. However, Bali has its own unique batik styles, often in brighter colors. If you want "genuine" batik be sure that you're getting hand-drawn (*tulis*) or stamped (*cap*) batik, and not the manufactured printed or silk screen batik with traditional designs on machine-processed fabric. The difference is often reflected in the price; hand-drawn batik is always more expensive.

Paintings

Ubud is the place for Balinese paintings, and the surrounding villages Pengosekan, Penestanan, Sanggingan, Peliatan, Mas, and Batuan are all lively breeding grounds for the arts. While the large galleries in Ubud display some of the best work ever produced on the island—past and present—smaller galleries and art shops in Ubud and surrounding hamlets may be your best bet for reasonably priced (but lower quality) local work. You can also visit artists in their homes and strike some good deals. Traditional Balinese calendars and *wayang*-style paintings are produced in Kamasan village near Klungkung, eastern Bali.

Antiques

Kuta, Denpasar, and all along Jl. Bypass Ngurah Rai are hunting grounds for antique dealers from abroad on the lookout for furniture, ornately carved wedding beds, palm-leaf books, fabrics, masks, Chinese ceramics, sculpture, and primitive statues from throughout Indonesia. However, be aware that the antique reproduction market is very active and very lucrative. If you like the look of old furniture but aren't fussy about authenticity, look for reproduction "antiques" in those same areas.

The best idea is to shop around until you have a good sense of quality and prices. To export anything older than 25 years old you must have a letter from the Museum Section of the Education and Culture Department.

Jewelry

Celuk, Kamasan (south of Klungkung), and Bratan in Buleleng (northern Bali) are the traditional centers for gold and silverwork. The silver is 80–90% pure; gold is 22–24 K. If you don't find anything you like ready-made, then custom order. For modern designs, go to Ubud, Kuta, and Legian. Sukawati is a traditional gold working village, or try the gold shops in Denpasar on Jl. Hasanuddin and Jl. Sulawesi. Be sure to bargain.

Beach vendors

Vendors on the beach, especially Kuta, can be rather pushy. They can be annoying, with boxes of fake name-brand watches, perfumes, statuary, and offers for massage, nail decorating, or hair-braiding. There are some good deals on *sarongs* and bikinis, but you have to bargain hard.

Shipping & freight

Shipping goods home is relatively safe and painless on Bali, though it can be expensive. Items under 1 m (3 ft) long and 10 kg (22 lbs) in weight can be sent by surface mail via most postal agents. All the packing will be done for you at reasonable cost, although it's always advisable to keep an eye on how it's done. Larger purchases are best sent by airfreight or sea cargo. Freight forwarders will handle the whole process for a price, from packing to customs. Many retailers are also prepared to send goods if purchased in quantity.

Air cargo is charged by the kilogram (minimum 10 kg/22 lbs), and can be costly. Sea cargo is cheaper, but can take several months.Don't forget to buy insurance. When shipping cargo, you are responsible for clearing customs back home and for transporting the goods from the port of entry to your destination.

PHOTOGRAPHY

Most Indonesians generally enjoy being photographed, including Balinese, are very comfortable being photographed. Indeed, since the advent of cheap digital cameras and camera phones, incessant posing for "selfies" and group shots has become a major Indonesian pastime, with even village grannies eagerly participating. All this generally makes Bali a photographer's paradise when it comes to capturing images of people, but it is still absolutely essential to be respectful and to ask permission before snapping away.

Language barriers are entirely surmountable—simply smiling, making eye-contact, miming taking a picture and asking "foto?" will get the message across. The response will usually be positive, and the personal engagement will usually result in a better photograph. Occasionally elderly people or those engaged in work or worship will make it clear that they do not wish to be photographed. With so many other willing models around, there is absolutely no excuse not to respect such wishes.

The heat and humidity of the tropics is hard on camera equipment. Be particularly careful when moving your camera from an air-conditioned room to the muggy outdoors. Moisture will condense on the inside and outside of the lens. Wait until it evaporates; don't be tempted to wipe it off. Also, always be aware of the location of your camera bag. Temperatures inside cars or on boats can be searing.

PROTECTED SPECIES

Indonesia is a signatory party to the Convention on International Trade in Endangered Species (CITES) treaty that lists protected species of plants and animals. There are more than 200 endangered species of Indonesian mammals, birds, reptiles, insects, fish, and mollusks, including orangutans, parrots, cockatoos, crocodiles, tortoises, turtles, butterflies, and corals.

There are strict laws and severe penalties for trade in endangered species, so be aware that even though you may see handicrafts for sale made of animal parts—or even the animals or birds themselves—you will not be allowed to take them out of the country. Some of the items you may see for sale that must be avoided are anything made of tortoiseshell (e.g. jewelry, combs, boxes), some clams species, Triton's trumpet shells, and pearly or chambered nautilus shells, just to name a few.

INVESTING IN BALI REAL ESTATE

An investment boom led by foreigners has taken place in Bali in recent years, with a staggering number of rental villas available as a consequence. As tempting as it might seem to own a home in this exotic land, be aware that the legalities involved—currently, foreigners cannot hold title to property in Indonesia—are incredibly complicated and are changing rapidly. Additionally, land or villas advertised as "freehold" is in reality no such thing, at least not to foreigners. If a deal seems too good to be true, then it probably is.

The experts advise that if you're thinking of investing in property in Bali, rent first for at least one year to see if it's really the right move for you. Take extensive advice from those who have made the move before you—much of which will turn out to be sobering and salutary, though happy endings are of course entirely possibly, particularly for savvy and well-informed buyers. Next, get the advice of a reputable lawyer who not only knows the changing real estate laws but can explain them in terms you can understand. Do the due diligence, including environmental, zoning, and local *adat* (traditional) restrictions, permits, tax records, and title. Finally, if you're buying with the idea of making money from other foreigners in mind, be aware that the villa market is saturated in some of the more popular areas of Bali, with many of the properties bought or built on the promise of vast rental incomes standing empty for much of the year.

WEDDINGS

Many people from throughout the world dream of a romantic wedding on Bali, and the five-star resorts have certainly risen to the occasion providing beautiful chapels by the sea, fabulous gardens, and other innovative settings for memorable events. There are also many wedding services that offer complete packages, including "legalities." Do your own research at home first to make sure a marriage officiated overseas is recognizable in your own country.

ACTIVITIES

There are so many choices of activity on Bali that the hardest decision could be how many of them can be squeezed into a holiday. Check Practicalities for each region for specifics, but here is a general overview of options.

Boating & water sports

Cruises. There are a number of vessels that sail from Benoa Harbor. Southern Bali, offering day trips for snorkeling and diving, dinner cruises, fishing, and charters.

Diving & snorkeling. Bali has several options for snorkeling and diving around Sanur and Nusa Dua, but the most exciting locations are in the island's more remote areas: Pulau Menjangan in West Bali National Park is considered the best, followed by nearby

Pemuteran, also in western Bali. Snorkeling and diving are also good at Lovina, in northern Bali; Candidasa, Padangbai, Tulamben, and Amed in the east; and Nusa Penida, Nusa Lembongan, and Nusa Ceningan Island in southern Bali.

It's advisable to use only reputable professional marine sports agencies who provide good quality equipment, current information, and adequate insurance coverage.

Fishing. Good fishing areas are Candidasa and Amed in eastern Bali, where you can go with a local fisherman early morning or late afternoon. Deep sea charter boats for game fishing are available from Benoa.

Sailing. The many local outriggers (*jukung*) that line the beaches at Sanur in the south, Padangbai, Candidasa, and Amed in the east, Lovina in the north, and other local boats in the West Bali National Park can be hired for fishing, diving, snorkeling, or sailing trips. Ask about current prices at accommodations.

Surfing. Kuta, Legian, Uluwatu, Canggu; Nusa Dua, the south and west coasts of the Bukit, some areas of Sanur and the northwest coast of Nusa Lembongan in the south; Medewi and Balian (Lalang Linggih) in western Bali; and Ketewi and Lebih, on the island's east coast have for many years been surfing areas. Generally speaking the best waves are to be had on the western coast during the dry season, and on the eastern coast during the rains. Most of the breaks listed above are reef breaks, unfurling over sharp coral, and are categorically not places to take your first steps in the world of wave-riding. Kuta, however, is a much more friendly beach break, with good conditions for beginners, and several reputable surf schools. Rip tides and undertows can still be severe here when the surf is big, however, so it's vital that you take local advice before plunging in unguided if you're not an experienced surfer.

Swimming. For the safest and most family friendly ocean swimming, go to Sanur or Nusa Dua in the south or Lovina on the north coast. The currents along the southern, western, and eastern coasts and around Nusa Penida and Lembongan are extremely strong and the undertow can be very treacherous. Swimming is at your own risk. At Kuta, there are markers to indicate no-swim areas, but no sea markers to indicate safe distance from the beach. Drownings are not uncommon.

Alternatively, the pools at most of the major hotels are open to non-guests for a small fee.

There's a water park in Tuban with pools and slides, rides, a food court, and massage.

White water rafting. Rafting has become a popular way to discover some of the hidden parts of Bali around Ubud and in Payangan, northwest of Ubud, both in central Bali. Expect the rivers to be more challenging in the rainy season.

Other water sports

There are several beachside booths at popular water sports locations (Nusa Dua, Benoa, and Sanur in the south, and Lake Bratan's Recreational Park in northern Bali) offering **banana boats**, **jet skis**, **kite surfing** (also called kiteboarding), **sea kayaking**, **parasailing**, **waterskiing**, **wakeboarding**, and **windsurfing**, with many hotels in Sanur and Benoa renting boards and giving lessons for the latter. Prices vary according to the time of year and location.

Biking & hiking

These are the best ways to get to know the hinterlands of Bali intimately. Beware of sunstroke: start off early in the morning, avoid the heat of the day, and drink plenty of bottled water, which is easily obtainable throughout the island. Sunglasses, a hat, comfortable shoes, a sarong, and sash (for entering temples) are useful, as is a map or a clear geographic notion of your destination.

Biking/cycling. The best and most conveniently accessible areas for **biking** are around Ubud and northwest of Ubud in central Bali; Kintamani and Candidasa in eastern Bali; and the Jatuluwih area and the back-country of Lovina in Northern Bali. Always check the bike before paying; brake failure half way down a volcano is no fun.

One highly professional bicycling tour organizer is **Bali Cycling Operator**, Jl. Curug Tiga No. 6B, Tuban, www.balicycling.com. While most bicycle tours offered through travel agents and booked at hotels simply take riders from point A to point B, founder I Wayan Kertayasa and his team customize tours for small groups according to their fitness and experience levels, wherever on the island they want to go.

Hiking. Trekking is good almost everywhere away from the traffic of major towns and can be tailored to physical capabilities and interests. Check out the following areas: Kintamani, Toya Bungkah (in the Mt. Batur caldera), Tirta Gangga, and Candidasa in eastern Bali; in and around Ubud and the Pupuan region northwest of Ubud in central Bali; the Bangli and Bedugul areas of northern Bali; and the West Bali National Park in western Bali.

Birdwatching tours of the Ubud area in central Bali, in West Bali National Park in western Bali, and at Nusa Penida (organized by the Friends of the National Parks Foundation) in southern Bali are available.

Climbing. Bali's many volcanoes, mountains, and hills attract climbers from amateurs to extreme. See Practicalities of the various regions for more details and check www.gunungbagging.com for route details of the major peaks.

Golf

There are several golf courses on Bali: at Nusa Dua, near Tanah Lot, in Sanur, and a new course on the Bukit in Southern Bali; and near Bedugal in northern Bali. Inquire about packages that often include accommodations or spa treatments, as these can be good bargains.

GETTING TO BALI

Bali's Ngurah Rai International Airport (also known as Denpasar Airport, though it is actually much closer to Kuta than to Denpasar itself), is one of the major international entry points for Indonesia, with many direct flights from Australia, Northeast and Southeast Asia, and a few from the Middle East which connect to onward routes into Europe and North America. The other major entry point is Jakarta's Soekarno-Hatta International Airport, which is very well connected to Bali via domestic airlines. There are more limited international routes from Lombok, and from Surabaya in East Java.

As well as the full-service airlines covering long-haul routes, Bali is very well established on the budget carrier network, with cheap, internet-booked flights available from Australia, Singapore, Kuala Lumpur and Bangkok, as well as virtually all major cities within Indonesia. Budget airlines such as Air Asia, Tiger Air and Jetstar are often exceptionally good value, particularly if you book well in advance, avoid high season, and fly midweek, even in spite of hidden costs such as additional fees for checked in baggage. However, if you're flying at peak season it's always worth checking the fares with traditional, full-service operators, as at these times they sometimes turn out to be scarcely more expensive than the budget airlines, with the added benefits of more convenient departure times.

Arriving by air

Bali's international airport has undergone a massive upgrade, and is now a sophisticated, world-class facility, far removed from the cramped and shabby airport of old.

Money changers are located inside and outside both terminals. Rates are compatible with reputable money changers in town and are better than hotel or bank rates.

The **domestic** and **international terminals** are only five minutes walk from each other. In the luggage pick-up areas of both terminals are well-staffed hotel reservations counters where English-speaking clerks can arrange free transport to a hotel of your choice. Tuban—the southernmost section of the resort strip that runs up the coast to Seminyak and beyond—begins right outside the airport gates, shading seamlessly into Kuta just a couple of miles further north, so there are no "airport hotels" to speak of. If you're arriving late and looking for convenient accommodation before traveling to more distant parts of Bali in the morning, Tuban and Kuta are the most convenient places to stay. Prepaid taxis to any destination in Bali are available outside arrivals; if you've booked ahead the driver will usually be there to greet you, holding up a sign with your name on it.

Domestic airlines

Telephone code: 0361

Air Asia, Garuda, and Lion Air all connect Bali with other cities inside and outside of Indonesia and have extensive online booking facilities.

There are also several strictly domestic carriers. Some of them don't have online booking accessible with overseas credit cards, but you can make reservations through any local travel agency. All also have ticket offices in the domestic terminal at Ngurah Rai airport, and some also have other locations.

Airport information, domestic terminal
Tel: 751-011
CityLink, www.citilink.co.id, is Garuda's commuter subsidiary, with links to Jakarta, Surabaya, Batam, Balikpapan, Banjarmasin, and Makassar.
SriWijaya Air, Jl. Teuku Umar No. 97B, Tel: 228-461, www.sriwijayaair.co.id.

Jakarta-based, links several points on Java with Sumatra, Sulawesi, Java, Bali, Timor, and Kalimantan.

Arriving overland

Traveling overland from Java to Bali requires taking a ferry. It's a pleasant one-hour trip from Ketapang (East Java) to Gilimanuk (Western Bali), with regular departures day and night. Getting on can be a hassle during the Indonesian holidays, when there are large crowds, so expect a long wait, or better yet, avoid the journey during those times.

By ferry to Lombok

You may also want to venture over to Lombok. Regular public ferries leave from Padangbai in east Bali, while fast tourist boats to the Gilis, as well as to Senggigi, also depart from Sanur and Amed.

By bus

Denpasar's main bus terminal, Ubung, is in the north of the city. It's a major hub for travel by bus within Bali, but most long-haul buses to destinations in Java now leave from a much larger terminal in Mengwi, some 12 miles (20 km) further north. It is a 7–10 hour trip from Denpasar to Surabaya in east Java. There are also direct buses to Malang and other smaller cities in East Java, as well as Yogakarta, Semarang, and even Jakarta.

Perama, Jl. Legian 39, Tel: 751-551, www.peramatour.com is a reputable private company with offices in Kuta, Sanur, and Ubud. Its well-maintained tourist buses shuttle back and forth between those areas and Kintamani, Lovina, Padangbai, and Candidasa. Perama also sells long-distance bus tickets to Lombok and beyond and east to Java. Check at their office for schedules. Also ask about pick-up and drop-off, which they provide for a small extra charge. Trips from Kuta to Lovina cost about $10.

GETTING AROUND
Taxis

Most travelers arrive on Bali through the Ngurah Rai International Airport.

A reliable **taxi cooperative** operates from the airport. Tariffs to various parts of the island are fixed (drivers don't use their meters) and are posted. There are taxi counters at both the domestic and international terminals outside on the left after exiting the baggage claim areas. Outside of the airport, taxis are metered with set government prices and are generally safe, reliable, and can be flagged down anywhere.

Highly recommended is **Bali Taxi** (Tel: 701-111, 701-621, www.bluebirdgroup.com), part of the well-respected Blue Bird group from Jakarta and the most likely company to have English-speaking drivers. **Praja Taxi** (Tel: 289-090) is also good.

Online minicab apps

Mobile phone-based minicab-hailing apps have revolutionized transport across Indonesia in recent years, and made travel much cheaper and more convenient. The local **GO-JEK** app is great for quickly hailing cheap minicab transport, and has excellent coverage in southern Bali. The Malaysia-based **Grab** app, and the international **Uber** also cover Bali, though the latter is generally more expensive. Understandably, there has been some hostility to the digital revolution amongst traditional taxi operators, and some neighborhoods, particularly in Kuta, are supposedly forbidden to the app services, though in practice you'll still be able to use them. Hailing transport with these apps is much harder in Ubud, and often impossible in more remote regions of Bali.

Car rentals

There are many rental car agencies on Bali offering self-drive or with driver, and all travel agencies have cars with English-speaking drivers for hire. Examine the car and read all contracts carefully before signing. At the airport, freelance drivers circulate among arriving passengers but they tend to overcharge.

Self-driving

Driving on Bali is not for the faint-hearted. Vehicles, people, and creatures of every size, shape, and description charge onto the road out of nowhere. The traffic is heavy and intimidating on the main highways and in Southern Bali during peak hours. Drive slowly and carefully and beware of the trucks at night and overzealous buses at all times. Road construction sites are not marked, few cyclists have reflectors, and motorcycles may have no lights. Despite all of that, having your own vehicle will give you unparalleled access to less frequently visited corners of Bali, and once you leave the busy south the roads become much more manageable, if in generally worse condition.

Gas stations are found at regular intervals along all major roads, and around all towns. Deep in the hinterlands, or if you run out of gas, small roadside fuel stands, indicated by a "*bensin*" sign, sell gasoline at a slight mark-up.

A valid **international driving license** is required for driving cars and motorbikes. If you do not have one, you can get a temporary local license at the local Polres (police headquarters) on the road between Denpasar and Kerobokan. Ask the renter to help organize this.

Insurance is not compulsory, but strongly recommended. You can get a policy from most of the rental companies and travel agents by paying about $5 extra per day on top of your rental price.

Chartering a car or minivan with a driver

Hiring a vehicle with a driver is the most relaxing way to handle a land tour: someone else worries about the traffic, hills, and dales while you watch the scenery, and you have the freedom to stop whenever things look interesting as well as the flexibility to try out some less traveled routes. This can also be an economical alternative if you are traveling in a group. A minibus can take up to seven people.

The quality of both the driver and the vehicle will determine the pleasure of your trip so don't be shy about hiring one for just a day and checking them both out before striking a deal. Your driver should be responsible and have a personality that won't grate on you over the long haul. If he knows the area you will be driving through and can speak some English, so much the better. The air-conditioning should work well enough to overcome the midday heat, and the vehicle should be clean and comfortable.

It's best just to arrange these charters on your own. For traveling around Bali count on paying about $40 a day for an AC van, including fuel but not including parking fees or entrance charges. It is understood that you will pay for the driver's meals and accommodation both while he is with you and on his journey back home. If the driver is good, a tip of about $5 per day is gratefully accepted.

Privately owned minibuses are widely available on the street. You'll be offered "transport" everywhere you go and prices are negotiated on the spot. To avoid the negotiation process, ask for assistance at your hotel or any one of the abundant travel agent

HELICOPTER SERVICES

Air Bali, Jl. Bypass Ngurah Rai No. 100X, Dewa Ruci Building, Kuta, tel: 767-466, fax: 766-581, www. airbali.com. Experience Bali by air with the region's only western-managed helicopter and light aircraft company. In addition to flying celebrities and VIPS from place to place Air Bali offers sky tours, picnic flights, excursions to Komodo and Borobudur. Also hotel and villa transfers, golf transfers, private charters, aerial photography. Note that rates are per flight, not per person.

desks. Inspect the vehicle before handing over payment and don't accept substitute vehicles that show up at the last minute.

Rental car agencies at the airport are open 9 am–10 pm. Also recommended are: **Autobagus Rent a Car**, Jl. Tukad Balian Renon, Denpasar, Tel: 722-222, www.autobagus.com. Sedans, jeeps, and limousines, long or short term rental, replacement vehicles, 24-hour call service, experienced driver service or self-drive, comprehensive insurance, and various car makes and models in excellent condition, at reasonable prices. **Golden Bird Limousine & Car Rental**, 24-hr reservations Tel: 701-111, customer serviceTel:701-621,www.bluebirdgroup.com. A member of the popular Blue Bird Group from Jakarta. Excellent service with fully-trained drivers. Bali rentals include sedans, vans, limousines and full-size buses. **Hertz**, Inna Grand Bali Beach Hotel, Tel: 768-375 or 288-511, ext. 1341, fax: 286-967; and Hotel Putri Bali, Nusa Dua, Tel: 771-020, ext. 7186. Offers the usual standard of service found with Hertz throughout the world.

Motorbike rentals

Motorcycling is one of the best ways to travel on Bali in terms of both cost and freedom. But it is undoubtedly the riskiest option, particularly on the hectic roads of the south, and journeying by bike in that part of the island can be incredibly stressful. If you're an experienced rider, a bike is certainly a viable and attractive option, but this is no place for beginners.

Motorbikes are available for rent almost everywhere, and with so much competition prices are remarkably low. A standard 125cc scooter in good condition, complete with helmets for two passengers, can be rented for around US$5 a day in Kuta or Sanur (with slightly higher asking prices elsewhere, especially in the more remote resorts further east), or even less if you pay upfront for an extended rental period. Check the bike before agreeing to any arrangement and make note of any existing damage so you don't get stuck with repair charges. Helmets and an international driver's license, or temporary local permit, are required.

Make sure you have the registration papers, in case you are stopped by the police. Also ensure you have adequate travel insurance covering bike travel. Insurance sold at time of rental normally covers damages or loss of the bike, with a minimal deductible.

Bicycle rentals

Cycling is an enjoyable way to get around and bicycles are readily available. Note, though, that city traffic can be a nightmare and in some regions the hills require good physical fitness.

The Indonesian Language

Pronunciation
Vowels
a   As in *father*
e   Three forms:
   1) Schwa, like *e* in *the*
   2) Like *é* in *touché*
   3) Short *e*; as in *bet*
i   Usually like long *e* (as in *Bali*); when
      bounded by consonants, like short *i*
      (*hit*).
o   Long *o*, like *go*
u   Long *u*, like *you*
ai Long *i*, like *crime*
au Like *ow* in *owl*

Consonants
c   Always like *ch* in *church*
g   Always hard, like *guard*
h   Usually soft, almost unpronounced.
      It is hard between similar vowels,
      e.g., *mahal* (expensive).
k   Like *k* in *kind*; at the end of word, it
      is an unvoiced stop.
kh Like *ch* in the Scottish word "*loch*"
r   Rolled, like a Spanish *r*
ng Soft, like *fling*
ngg Hard, like *tingle*
ny Like *ny* in *Sonya*

Grammar
Grammatically, Indonesian is in many
ways far simpler than English. There are
no articles (a, an, the). The verb form "to
be" is usually not used. There is no ending for plurals; sometimes the word is
doubled, but often the number is understood from the context. And Indonesian
verbs are not conjugated. Tense is com-
municated by context or with specific
words for time.

Personal Pronouns
I/me/my **saya**
We/us/our **kita** (inclusive), **kami**
(exclusive)
You/your **anda** (formal), **kamu** (for friends
and children only), **kalian** (you plural)

he/she/his/her **dia**
they/their **mereka**

Forms of address
Father/Mr **Bapak** ("**Pak**")
Mother/Mrs **Ibu** ("**Bu**")
Elder brother (appropriate for any man
younger than yourself, in an informal set-
ting) **Abang**, **Mas** (these are Sundanese and
Javanese terms, respectively, though both
are widely understood in Bali. The Balinese
equivalent is **Bli**)
Elder sister **Mbak** (Javanese, though under-
stood in Bali; appropriate for any woman
older than yourself, in an informal setting)
Elder Brother/sister **Kakak** ("**Kak**")
Younger brother/sister **Adik** ("**Dik**")

Note: These terms are used not just within the
family, but in polite speech with strangers.

Basic questions
How? **Bagaimana?**
How much/many? **Berapa?**
What? **Apa?**
What's this? **Apa ini?**
Who? **Siapa?**
Who's that? **Siapa itu?**
What is your name? **Siapa nama anda?**
(Literally: Who is your name?)
When? **Kapan?**
Where? **Di mana?**
Which? **Yang mana?**
Why? **Kenapa?**

The Basics
Welcome **Selamat datang**
Good morning (7–11 am) **Selamat pagi**
Good midday (11 am–3 pm) **Selamat siang**
Good afternoon (3 pm–nightfall) **Selamat
sore**
Good evening (after dark) **Selamat malam**
Goodbye (to one leaving) **Selamat jalan**
Goodbye (to one staying) **Selamat tinggal**
How are you? **Apa kabar?**
I am fine. **Baik baik saja.**
Thank you. **Terima kasih.**
You're welcome. **Sama sama.**
Pardon me. **Maaf.**
Excuse me. **Permisi** (when leaving a con-
versation, etc).

Numbers

1 **satu**	73 **tujuh puluh tiga**
2 **dua**	100 **seratus**
3 **tiga**	600 **enam ratus**
4 **empat**	1,000 **seribu**
5 **lima**	3,000 **tiga ribu**
6 **enam**	10,000 **sepuluh ribu**
7 **tujuh**	1,000,000 **satu juta**
8 **delapan**	2,000,000 **dua juta**
9 **sembilan**	half **setengah**
10 **sepuluh**	first **pertama**
11 **sebelas**	second **kedua**
12 **dua belas**	third **ketiga**
13 **tiga belas**	fourth **ke'empat**
20 **dua puluh**	
50 **lima puluh**	

Time

minute **menit**
hour **jam** (also clock/watch)
day **hari**
week **minggu**
month **bulan**
year **tahun**
today **hari ini**
yesterday **kemarin**
tomorrow **besok**
later **nanti**
Sunday **Hari Minggu**
Monday **Hari Senin**
Tuesday **Hari Selasa**
Wednesday **Hari Rabu**
Thursday **Hari Kamis**
Friday **Hari Jumat**
Saturday **Hari Sabtu**
What time is it? **Jam berapa?**
(It is) eight thirty. **Jam setengah sembilan**
(Literally: "half nine")
How many hours? **Berapa jam?**
When did you arrive? **Kapan datang?**
Four days ago. **Empat hari yang lalu.**
When are you leaving? **Kapan berangkat?**
In a short while. **Sebentar lagi**.

Useful words

yes **ya**	no, not **tidak, bukan**

(Note: **Tidak** is used with verbs or adverbs; **bukan** with nouns.)

and **dan**	better **lebih baik**
with **dengan**	worse **kurang baik**
for **untuk**	this/these **ini**
good **bagus**	that/those **itu**
fine **baik**	same **sama**
more **lebih**	different **lain**
less **kurang**	here **di sini**

from **dari**	there **di sana**
to be **ada**	to be able, can **bisa**
to buy **beli**	correct **betul**
to know **tahu**	wrong **salah**
to get **dapat**	big **besar**
to need **perlu**	small **kecil**
to want **mau**	pretty **cantik**
to go **pergi**	slow **pelan**
to wait **tunggu**	fast **cepat**
at **di**	stop **berhenti**
to **ke**	old **tua, lama**
if **kalau**	new **baru**
near **dekat**	then **lalu, kemudian**
far **jauh**	only **hanya, saja**
empty **kosong**	crowded **ramai**
noisy **bising; berisik**	

Making small talk

Where are you from? **Dari mana?**
I'm from the U.S. **Saya dari Amerika.**
How old are you? **Umur anda/kamu berapa?**
I'm 31 years old. **Umur saya tiga puluh satu tahun.**
Are you married? **Sudah nikah belum.**
Yes, I am. **Ya, sudah.** Not yet. **Belum.**
Do you have children? **Sudah punya anak?**
What is your religion? **Agama apa?**
Where are you going? **Mau ke mana?**
I'm just taking a walk. **Jalan-jalan saja.**
Please come in. **Silakan masuk.**
This food is delicious. **Makanan ini enak sekali.**
You are very hospitable. **Anda sangat ramah.**

At the hotel

Where's a *losmen*? **Di mana ada losmen?**
cheap *losmen* **losmen yang murah**
average *losmen* **losmen biasa**
good hotel **hotel cukup baik**
hot water **air panas**
Please take me to… **Tolong antar saya ke…**
Are there any empty rooms? **Ada kamar kosong?**
Sorry there aren't any. **Maaf, tidak ada.**
How much for one night? **Berapa untuk satu malam?**
One room for two people. **Dua orang, satu kamar.**
I'd like to stay for 3 days. **Saya mau tinggal tiga hari.**
Here's the key to your room. **Ini kunci kamar.**
Please call a taxi. **Tolong panggil taksi.**
Please wash these clothes. **Tolong cucikan pakaian ini.**

Food and eating

to eat **makan**
to drink **minum**
drinking water **air putih, air minum**
Where's a good restaurant? **Di mana ada rumah makan yang baik?**
Let's have lunch. **Mari kita makan siang.**
I want Indonesian food. **Saya mau makanan Indonesia.**
I want coffee, not tea. **Saya mau kopi, bukan teh.**
May I see the menu? **Boleh saya lihat daftar makanan?**
I want to wash my hands. **Saya mau cuci tangan.**
Where is the toilet? **Di mana kamar kecil?**
fish, squid, goat, beef, chicken **ikan, cumi, kambing, sapi, ayam**
salty, sour, sweet, spicy **asin, asam, manis, pedas**

Shopping

I don't understand. **Saya tidak mengerti.**
I can't speak Indonesian. **Saya tidak bisa bicara Bahasa Indonesia.**

Please, speak slowly. **Tolong, berbicara lebih lambat.**
(In this context, **lambat** means "slow"; it would also be understood to mean soft, as in a soft voice.)
I want to buy…? **Saya mau beli…**
Where can I buy…? **Di mana saya bisa beli…?**
How much does this cost? **Berapa harga ini?**
2,500 Rupiah. **Dua ribu, lima ratus rupiah.**
That cannot be true! **Masa!**
That's still a bit expensive. **Masih agak mahal.**

Directions

north	**utara**	left	**kiri**
west	**barat**	near	**dekat**
south	**selatan**	far	**jauh**
east	**timur**	inside	**di dalam**
right	**kanan**	outside	**di luar**

I am looking for this address. **Saya cari alamat ini.**
How far is it? **Berapa jauh dari sini?**

INDEX

Photo Credits

Notes